Peter T. Davis
Barry D. Lewis

SAMS Teach Yourself

Microsoft®

Windows 2000 Server

in 21 Days

SAMS

201 West 103rd St., Indianapolis, Indiana, 46290 USA

Sams Teach Yourself Microsoft® Windows 2000 Server in 21 Days

Copyright © 2000 by Sams Publishing

International Standard Book Number: 0-672-31703-6

Library of Congress Catalog Card Number: 99-62615

Printed in the United States of America

First Printing: October, 1999

04   03   6   5   4

Trademarks

Warning and Disclaimer

PUBLISHER
Angela Wethington

EXECUTIVE EDITOR
Chris Denny

DEVELOPMENT EDITOR
Ginny Bess

MANAGING EDITOR
Lisa Wilson

PROJECT EDITOR
Dawn Pearson

COPY EDITOR
Kate Givens

INDEXER
Erika Millen

PROOFREADERS
Megan Wade
Katherin Bidwell

TECHNICAL EDITOR
Anthony Peterson

TEAM COORDINATOR
Karen Opal

INTERIOR DESIGN
Gary Adair

COVER DESIGN
Aren Howell

COPY WRITER
Eric Borgert

PRODUCTION
Dan Harris

LAYOUT TECHNICIAN
Darin Crone

Contents at a Glance

Contents

About the Authors

PETER T. DAVIS has 24 years of experience with information systems in large-scale installations in the financial and government sectors. He is now principal of Peter Davis & Associates, a training and consulting firm specializing in the security, audit, and control of information systems.

Peter is the author or co-author of seven other books, including *Sams Teach Yourself NetWare in 14 Days, Computer Security for Dummies, Securing Client/Server Networks,* and *Sams Teach Yourself Windows NT Server 4 in 21 Days.* He is also an internationally known speaker on quality, security, audit, and control, and he frequently speaks at user and professional conferences and meetings.

He received his Bachelor of Commerce (B. Comm) degree from Carleton University. Peter also is a Certified Management Accountant (CMA), Certified Information Systems Auditor (CISA), Certified Computing Professional (CCP), Information Systems Professional (ISP), Certified Information Systems Security Professional (CISSP), Certified Novell Administrator v3.11 (CNA) and Certified Management Consultant (CMC). He is listed in the *International Who's Who of Professionals.*

Peter currently lives in Toronto, Ontario, with his wife and daughter. You can contact him via email at ptdavis@pdaconsulting.com or by visiting www.pdaconsulting.com.

BARRY D. LEWIS has 30 years of experience in data processing and more than 19 years of experience in the field of computer security. He is president of Cerberus ISC Inc. and is a Certified Information Systems Security Professional (CISSP). He has consulted with organizations in all facets of business, including government, manufacturing, finance, and technology, and has provided his clients with effective solutions using his extensive experience. He has spent many years as a volunteer on the board of directors or executive of a number of security organizations and conferences including CA-World, the Eastern Canadian CA-ACF2 Group, and the organization that is helping to set qualifications within the information security field, the International Information Systems Security Certification Consortium (ISC)2.

Barry is the co-author of four other books, including *Computer Security for Dummies, Teach Yourself Windows NT Server 4 in 14 Days,* and the newer *Teach Yourself Windows NT Server 4 in 21 Days.* He is an internationally known speaker and travels the world speaking on security, audit, and control.

Barry is a frequent speaker and seminar leader at numerous conferences and travels the world extensively. You can reach him at (416) 777-6768, or via email at lewisb@Cerberus-isc.com. You can also visit his Web page at www.cerberus-isc.com.

Barry lives in the Toronto area with his wife and son, three cats, and a dog. It remains a busy house.

Dedication

To all my friends and colleagues for their time and support through the years.

—Peter T. Davis

Life is too short for most of the things we worry about. Learn to move on. My thanks again to my long-suffering wife and son who put up with me disappearing for days at a time to write this book.

—Barry D. Lewis

Acknowledgments

Writing and publishing a book requires a great deal of dedication and hard work by many people. This book is no different. For their part, the authors would like to thank

Ginny Bess and Dawn Pearson, whose excellent editing is evident in the final product.

Anthony Peterson, because he kept us honest and gave us his valuable insight and technical advice.

Everyone at Sams who worked on this book that we didn't mention.

Everyone who contributes to Internet user forums. We found some helpful information about Windows 2000.

Everybody who encouraged us to write the book.

Barry thanks Elizabeth and Derek for putting up with him disappearing again.

Peter wants to thank Janet and Kelly for their understanding. He also would like to thank Barry for his gracious help and for his diligence on this fourth collaboration.

Tell Us What You Think!

As the reader of this book, *you* are our most important critic and commentator. We value your opinion and want to know what we're doing right, what we could do better, what areas you'd like to see us publish in, and any other words of wisdom you're willing to pass our way.

As an Executive Editor for Sams Publishing, I welcome your comments. You can email or write me directly to let me know what you did or didn't like about this book—as well as what we can do to make our books stronger.

Please note that I cannot help you with technical problems related to the topic of this book, and that due to the high volume of mail I receive, I might not be able to reply to every message.

When you write, please be sure to include this book's title and author as well as your name and phone or fax number. I will carefully review your comments and share them with the author and editors who worked on the book.

Email: `feedback@samspublishing.com`

Mail: Michael Stephens
         Executive Editor
         Sams Publishing
         201 West 103rd Street
         Indianapolis, IN 46290 USA

Introduction

If you are reading this Introduction, you obviously want to learn about Windows 2000 Server. You recognize that Microsoft has captured a very large share of the LAN market, and that knowledge of the product makes you more valuable to your present and future employers.

Regardless of your purpose for wanting to learn Windows 2000 Server, this book is for you. To provide some relief from the tedium of writing the words "Windows 2000 Server" over and over, we plan to use the shorter term, "W2K" and occasionally will drop the "Server" portion. Regardless of which we use, be assured that we are always talking about Windows 2000 Server. In those instances where we mention a separate Windows 2000 product, we will use its designated term; for example, Windows 2000 Professional.

For the next 21 days, you will find out the things that you need to know in order to operate W2K efficiently, effectively, and economically. Completing the 21-day curriculum will provide you with a solid base for embarking on the *Microsoft Certified Professional (MCP)* accreditation programs, if you desire to do so.

You will build on tasks in each lesson and progressively move to more complex tasks. At the end of the 21 days, you will have a firm grounding in Windows 2000 Server. Following is a look at how the rest of the book is organized.

Organizing the Job of Learning Windows 2000 Server

As the title of the book suggests, you can learn W2K concepts in a short period of time—three weeks. Material in this book has been organized to lead you through a logical step-by-step approach to learning W2K easily and quickly. Obviously, your speed of progression depends on your skills and background knowledge. Even though this is the case, you are encouraged to read the book in sequential day and chapter order. Days tend to build on each other; for instance, the concept of networking is introduced early in the book so that you will think about it throughout the rest of the book.

The following sections give you an idea of what you can expect to cover each day.

Day 1: Introducing Networks and Windows 2000

On Day 1, you'll explore introductory networking concepts. Included in the day's lessons are descriptions of network components and options. You also will learn basic W2K components and features.

Day 2: Installing Windows 2000 and Client Software

On this day, you'll actually install Windows 2000 on a machine and at client workstations.

You will also see how to install client software for Windows 2000 Professional, Windows 95/98, Windows for Workgroups, and DOS/Windows 3.*x* .

Day 3: Navigating and Exploring Windows 2000

Day 3 provides you with the tools to navigate your way through the files and directories in W2K.

You'll also learn to explore W2K and find out about the new tools and accessories that it offers. Finally, you'll learn about sharing and using Explorer.

Day 4: Understanding and Managing the Registry

Day 4 introduces the W2K Registry; you'll learn what this aspect of the system does and why it is so important, and you'll learn to manipulate the entries within the registry in a safe, effective manner.

Day 5: Introducing Active Directory

On this day, you'll learn all about this important new aspect of Windows 2000: what it is, what it does, how it is used to manage large numbers of W2K machines, and why it is so important to your Windows 2000 infrastructure.

Day 6: Introducing Security Services

By the end of Day 6, you will learn how security is managed in a W2K environment and how all the security components fit together. You'll also learn about some of the new security components that W2K introduces, like Kerberos and public key encryption.

Day 7: Managing User Accounts

Day 7 will give you a basic knowledge of Windows 2000 system administration. You can then log on and add users. On this day, you will learn about account management, security equivalence, restricting users, changing defaults, and detecting intruders and locking them out of your system.

Day 8: Managing Files and Using the Distributed File System

On Day 8, the beginning of Week 2, the pace quickens. First, you'll learn how to manipulate your way through the different file structures that W2K offers. You'll find out about the new file system called NTFS and learn why it is important.

You will then learn about the way in which Windows NT Server protects access to files and directories through access rights; furthermore, you'll see how trustees can be set up and you'll explore how to grant and remove these rights.

Finally, you'll learn all about using the Distributed File System, allowing you to distribute files across many systems without your users needing to know what system the files are on in order to use them.

Day 9: Managing the File Server

Day 9 demonstrates how to manage your file server and use the various server tasks that are necessary for effective server operation.

Day 10: Managing the Print Server

On Day 10, you will see how to set up and run Windows W2K print servers so that users can print output at different places on the network.

Day 11: Understanding Remote Access Services and VPBNs (RRAS)

Day 11 introduces Routing and Remote Access Services, or RRAS. You'll learn how to set up and manage an RRAS environment, which enables users to dial in and access W2K resources. Then, you'll learn all about setting up a Virtual Private Network, enabling you to fully secure your communications.

Day 12: Understanding TCP/IP and DNS

On Day 12, you will learn about important network functions and what TCP/IP is and how it works. You'll learn to implement the protocol on your server, and you'll learn how to set up a DNS server.

Day 13: Understanding DHCP and WINS

On this day, you'll discover W2K naming facilities such as the HOSTS file, LMHOSTS file, and Dynamic Host Configuration Protocol (DHCP). You'll also learn how W2K can make using WINS obsolete.

Day 14: Using Advanced Security Services

This day leads you through a number of new aspects including how the Boot process works and how to use the new disk quota facility to control the amount of disk space available to each user. You'll also learn about the new encrypting file system and IPSEC.

Day 15: File Backup and Recovery

On Day 15, the beginning of your final week, you will learn to protect your files and sensitive data from loss. Furthermore, you'll learn to set up and run an effective backup and recovery program.

Day 16: Configuring Fault-Tolerance

On this day you'll learn about ways in which to protect your W2K system against loss of data through good backup and recovery planning and procedures. There will be a discussion of ways to configure your system so that it keeps processing even when there is a hardware failure.

Day 17: Security Monitoring and Audit Trails

Day 17 shows you how to manage the auditing and tracking of important actions within your Windows 2000 system. You'll see how to set audit and security objectives and use the audit Event Viewer program.

You also will learn more details about using audit trails to detect whether someone has been trying to bypass your security measures.

Day 18: Using BackOffice and Terminal Services

On this day, you'll discover what comprises the BackOffice product, and you'll see how to set up and run the various components.

You also will learn about the Internet Information Server, Gopher, and FTP service. Configuring IIS securely is an important administrative task.

Day 19: Understanding and Using the Microsoft Option Pack

On Day 19, you will learn all about the Option Pack and what Microsoft offers in this important package. This day will lead you through many functions, and explain what they are and why you want to use them.

Day 20:Windows 2000 Performance Monitoring and Tuning

Day 20 shows you the tools that you can use to get the best performance, both from your file servers and from the network itself. You'll learn about the Performance Monitor and Network Monitor, and about tuning W2K.

Day 21: Fine-Tuning and Troubleshooting Your Network

Finally, you will find out about tools such as ARP, IPCONFIG, PING, NBTSTAT, NETSTAT, ROUTE, and TRACERT, and you'll learn how they can be used to monitor traffic on the network cable.

Appendix A: Microsoft Windows 2000 Certification Programs

Appendix A provides a useful starting point for the Microsoft Certified Professional and other programs.

Appendix B: Windows 2000 Command Reference

Appendix B lists the NET commands used by W2K in an easy-to-use format.

Appendix C: Migrating to Windows 2000

Appendix C tells you all about migrating from a Windows NT environment to your new Windows 2000 environment.

Glossary

The Glossary contains definitions of the major networking and information processing terms used throughout the book.

Conventions

The presentation of Windows 2000 is best accomplished by providing menus and screens as you will see them. You will make choices by working through these menus and screens. Because "a picture is worth a thousand words," the visual aids are supplemented with detailed descriptions of everything you need in order to use or understand the menu or screen. For that reason, as you develop new skills, you'll see screen shots of W2K to help in your understanding and to help you judge your progress.

Icons in this book will draw your attention to information considered interesting or important. The icons are used as explained here:

 Tip

The Tip icon offers advice, teaches an easier way to do something, or explains an undocumented feature.

Note | The Note icon presents interesting tidbits of information related to the surrounding discussion.

 Caution | The Caution icon helps you steer clear of disaster, alerts you to potential problems, or warns you when you should not skip a task.

NEW TERM   New terms are introduced using the New Term icon.

Furthermore, each lesson contains many different tasks. Most tasks are presented in the following format:

Description—This section provides you with the basic concepts and terminology for Windows 2000 relating to the task.

Action—This section's step-by-step instructions demonstrate the topic that you are working on. Usually, the exercises are strung together to realistically represent the working environment.

Review—This section reviews what you need to know after going through the preceding two sections. This is the reference that reminds you about the learned skill.

In addition, each lesson ends with a Workshop that includes a list of the tasks that you have learned, and questions and answers regarding the day's tasks.

In the text, terms are treated in the following manner:

- Menu names are separated from menu options by a comma (,). For example, Select File, Close indicates that you need to select the File menu and choose the Close option.
- User-typed entries appear in `computer font`.
- Information that appears onscreen also appears in `computer font`.
- Windows NT commands appear in `computer font`.
- Windows NT command placeholders appear in `italic computer font`.
- New terms introduced to the reader appear in regular *italics*.

Mark up the book. Make notes in the margin. Highlight significant sections. Tear out the commands and use them. Last of all, enjoy using this book as much as we enjoyed writing it for you.

If you have questions or comments about the book, you can send email to Barry D. Lewis at `lewisb@cerberus-isc.com` and to Peter T. Davis at `ptdavis@pdaconsulting.com`.

About This Book

This book starts where you are likely to start—at the beginning. Its design ensures that you learn concepts when you need them, as you start your exploration of Windows 2000 Server.

By following the book, with its orientation and examples, you will learn simple tasks that build on each other until you have mastered the basics of W2K. If you faithfully follow the book, you can administer a simple Windows 2000 Server and network.

Anyone with a working knowledge of DOS or Windows can learn how to back up servers, add and delete users, create logon scripts, and maintain security.

Who Should Read This Book

Anyone interested in learning to use Windows 2000 Server will find something of value in this book. The thrust of the book, however, is toward those people who will administer a W2K network and therefore must grasp the key tasks.

For both, this book covers W2K from the basics to tasks and ideas that you are sure to find interesting and useful as you progress beyond those basics.

This book is for you if one or more of the following statements applies to you:

- You are interested in becoming a Microsoft Certified Professional.
- You just found out that you'll take over administration of an existing Windows 2000 Server LAN.
- You were told that your organization will install W2K next month.
- You applied for a job at an organization that uses Windows 2000 LANs exclusively, and you want to get the job.
- You just want to learn about a widely used network operating system.

WEEK 1

At a Glance

1

2

3

4

5

6

7

DAY 1

Introducing Networks and Windows 2000

With Windows 2000 Server, Microsoft continues to carve out a market niche, known collectively as Network Operating Systems (NOS). In the not too distant past, NOS software was layered on another operating system (such as LAN Manager on DOS or LAN Server on OS/2). Now vendors are building networking into their operating systems, providing more and more functionality. These systems form the crux of today's networks.

Over the past few years, the term "network" has expanded from an arcane technological expression for big mainframe computers filling rooms in a data center to an everyday term. Do people understand the term and the technology it represents? In the olden, golden days of the mainframe, you had to be a network specialist to build and maintain the terminals and their connection to the mainframe. This specialized knowledge was necessary because mainframes are extremely complex.

These days of old changed into the networks of today and things called local area networks, or LANs. Previously, specialized technical expertise was necessary to set up a company network, but the job is a little easier today, although vastly different. Confused? Never fear; we explain it all. LANs today are far more flexible and often larger than the network you once used. Whereas once your network consisted of the terminals in your building and perhaps the adjoining building, today's networks span the country with ease.

NEW TERM The mainframe network consisted of a large computer, some wiring, and a bunch of terminals. It was *host-centric*. The Windows 2000 Server's network consists of servers, clients, wiring topologies, and protocols. It is *client-centric*, focusing on the needs of the client rather than the host.

By the time you finish today, you should understand key networking concepts, terms, acronyms, and topologies to bluff with the best of them. You will learn about servers, clients, wiring topologies, and protocols. Best of all, that understanding will help guide you through the intricacies of putting together your Windows 2000 Server network. Let's start by looking at a network.

What Is a Network?

Network is such a common term, yet it can mean so many different things. Computer users tend to think of the network as the components involved in connecting various computers that allow users to share information or resources such as printers or CD-ROM drives. After that connection exists, other sharing occurs, such as electronic mail or file transfers. Regardless of how you use the network, any connection of two or more computers qualifies as a network.

Note

> Most networks connect using some form of physical wire usually referred to as the cabling. Network staff also commonly refer to these physical cables as *bounded media*. Larger, more complex networks use *unbounded media*. This media type consists of radio frequencies, microwave transmissions, and infrared technologies. Unbounded media is typically used to transmit over great distances or in places where cables are hard to place. Although this definition sounds exacting, it's all you really need to know to set up your own server.

A typical Windows 2000 Server network consists of one or more 2000 servers, connected through coax, fiber, or twisted-pair cables to some personal computers set up to act as clients. Coax and twisted pair? Servers and clients? Aren't they all just wires and computers? Perhaps it's time to delve deeper.

Tip

If you think you know all about networks, you can skip to the section enti-
tled "What Is Windows 2000 Server?" and install your copy of 2000 Server. A
good understanding of how networks work is essential to installing and
maintaining 2000 Server, so be certain.

1

The major components of a good network include various pieces:

- Cabling
- Network interfaces
- Nodes
- Protocols

You will examine these in more detail in the following sections. You are introduced to
various other items such as the standards that help make networks more consistent by
applying a form of order to the cables, protocols, and other network devices. After you
become more comfortable with 2000 Server, I'll introduce more specific details on how
to use the various network components. Finally, remember that this book provides details
on Microsoft 2000 Server, not networks. To fully understand all the components, you
need to reference some of the available networking books, such as *Understanding Local
Area Networks* (Sams Publishing).

Network Cabling

New Term   What's a network cable and how do you use it? This section introduces you to
the physical world of cabling. What are the types of cables you can use to connect computers? Earlier, we mentioned several types, including *coax* and *twisted pair*.
Before going too far, you need to realize that *coax cable* is a shortened version of the
actual name, coaxial cable. You can use this longer name if you want, but to belong to
the secret world of network installers, you should use coax.

The objective of cabling is to connect two or more computers by plugging some type
of cable into each computer. For instance, you might use a cable and the Windows 95
software called TranXit, which provides a simple connectivity solution for connecting
your Windows 95 computers together. Although very rudimentary, this does constitute
a network.

A more typical set of cables are fiber-optic, twisted pair, and coax, so we'll review them
in a little more detail.

Coaxial Cable

Coaxial cable, or coax, is a popular means for connecting computers, and some of the earliest LANs were built using it. The cable consists of an inner wire typically made from some form of copper alloy and another wire that surrounds this main one but is separated from it by an insulating layer (or shield).

Anyone with cable television can see a typical example of coax by looking no further than the back of your television set. The cable connecting your TV to the cable provider is coax. If you look closely at one end of the connector, you can see the small piece of copper sticking out. This is the inner cable or the core. You cannot see the shield because a layer of outer insulation hides it. (You hold this layer as you peek at the small piece of copper.)

The shielded cable surrounding the common axis of copper alloy gives us the term co-axial (for common axis) cable (see Figure 1.1). Coax comes in various types, so don't rush out to use your television cable in your network! Each type relates to the way it handles the electrical impulses sent along it. A type you can use in your network is RG58/U coaxial cable.

FIGURE 1.1

A picture of coax cable.

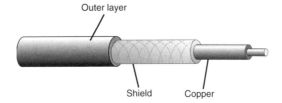

The shield shown in Figure 1.1 provides a good layer of insulation against exter-

NEW TERM nal electrical noise while also providing good bandwidth. (*Bandwidth* is a term used to denote the amount of data that can be sent across a line. For example, an Ethernet implementation typically provides a bandwidth of 10Mbps. *Mbps* is a term used in place of megabits per second.)

To connect the wires to your computer or television, you need a connector. You buy the cable in preset lengths, complete with a connector attached, such as the cable and connectors used for your television. Large companies may simply buy rolls of plain cable so they can cut each piece to a desired length. They need to manually add a connector to each end. Typical connectors are called British Naval Connectors or BNC. Coax and connectors are commonly available at most computer shops.

NEW TERM Finally, you might have heard of the terms *thin* and *thick* coax. Basically, these terms apply to the size (thickness) of the cable. The original engineering specification for thick coax consisted of cable that was about a half an inch thick in diameter. The proliferation of microcomputer networks provided a cheaper solution called thin coax (RG-58). When you purchase computer coax from your local store, it is usually thin coax and easy to use. The coax you find at the back of your television is an example of thick coax and is less pliable and therefore a little harder to install. Organizations are tending not to use coax anymore in favor of twisted pair cabling.

Twisted Pair

Twisted-pair cable consists of two wires twisted together and covered by a plastic sheath of some kind. Household telephone wiring is an example.

Twisted-pair cable comes in both shielded and unshielded varieties with differing numbers of connecting wires. The inner wires are twisted around each other to reduce radiation and electrical interference (see Figure 1.2). Electrical standards refer to these as Shielded Twisted Pair (STP) and Unshielded Twisted Pair (UTP).

FIGURE 1.2

A twisted-pair cable.

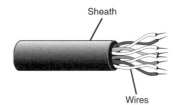

One wire sends a signal and the other wire obtains the return signal. In a small office, it probably doesn't matter which type you use because electrical interference is minimal. Larger offices have more places where the cable might rub against an electrical field (such as a large appliance), where the signal can get distorted. Using the shielded variety in these cases can minimize the interference.

Twisted pair has the advantage of being cheaper than other types of cable, such as coax. It is also easy to work with during installation and maintenance and is readily available. Many buildings remain pre-wired with this type of cable. The connectors for this cable look very similar to your telephone jack. Some, in fact, use that jack, called the RJ11, whereas most use the larger connector called the RJ45.

Some of the drawbacks to using this cable are its susceptibility to interference from electromagnetic energy and the limited distance resulting from this interference potential. Improvements in this field are legion, however, so expect these limits to be reduced over the coming years.

Twisted pair is the de facto standard for network wiring today. It has the advantage of being less expensive than other types of cable. It also is commonly available, and relatively easy to work with during installation and connection. And finally, you need to install twisted pair Category 5 should you want to use 100Mbps Fast Ethernet (100Base-VG standard using UTP and a star configuration).

Fiber-Optic Cable

Fiber-optic cable is science's latest creation and uses light to transmit its signal. You have probably seen it in use at high tech fairs because it can spread light around corners, into designs, or into small places.

Fiber-optic cable consists of a strand of material (usually plastic, but sometimes glass) inside a protective covering (see Figure 1.3). Instead of sending electrical energy down a wire, this medium uses a burst of light. It can carry huge amounts of data for tremendous distances. It is far more complex to set up and run than conventional wiring, so it is still reserved for sophisticated networks.

FIGURE **1.3**

A fiber-optic cable.

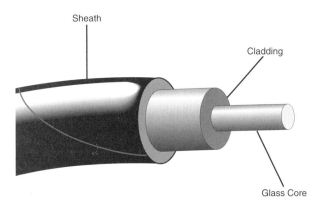

Sheath

Cladding

Glass Core

Of all the cables, fiber-optic cable is the most immune to noise and is far less susceptible to surveillance from wire-tapping techniques. As you see in the figure, connecting these cables to your network has special requirements. A special transceiver and signal amplifier turn the signal into something legible for your network, and these items are costlier than the simple connectors used in coax and twisted-pair cables.

Network Interfaces

NEW TERM Now that you understand the wiring needed to connect computers, you need to understand how they connect to each computer. Between the wire and the computer, you need a network interface card, or *NIC* as it's commonly referred to by network staff. This card provides the interface between the cable and the internal components of your computer.

1

There are many varieties of these cards. Some fit inside the computer and attach directly to the computer's internal bus, giving it fast access to the memory and computer processor. These cards typically show at the back of your computer and include a special connector or two that allow the network wires to attach.

Other types consist of small external devices that attach to the parallel port of your computer, removing any necessity to take the cover off the machine and poke around inside. The parallel port already attaches inside your computer (the port where you find your printer). Even though the external NIC isn't an actual card, it is still called a network interface card because that's easier than coming up with another name—and it does provide the same function. This card has various names:

- LAN adapter board
- Network card
- Network adapter
- Intelligent network interface card (NIC)

You can use any of these terms, although the more common terms are network card and NIC.

New Term These cards perform three major functions: They send, receive, and format data in a way that is acceptable to the network. They must obey certain rules generated by the computer and set out by the type of network in use. These rules are well defined. For example, the IEEE 802.x standards set out the different criteria for designing local area networks. (*IEEE* stands for the Institute of Electrical and Electronics Engineers, a group responsible for many OSI Layer 1 and 2 standards. OSI is a networking model developed by ISO, an international standards organization. The model defines seven communication layers and what they do.)

The card responds to directions given by software running on the computer and sends information across the network. It also responds to messages sent to it. (Each card has an address provided by the vendor and set according to another set of standards.) There is a reasonably complex method to all this sending and receiving that is described in advanced networking manuals.

Network Nodes

New Term A *network node* is the point where a cable ends and a computer begins. How these nodes connect to each other depends on the type of network you are using. We discussed types of wiring and network interface cards in the earlier section; now, we'll show how those wires and NICs form part of the network as they connect to either a server or a client computer.

NEW TERM   Computers provide two primary types of service when they are attached in a network: *server* or *client*. Each type is defined here:

- A *server computer* is one that provides services to the network. These services are typically such things as printing, storing files, or providing a connection to other computers and networks.
- A *client computer* acts as an interface to the network, allowing you to use the services provided by the servers. Simplistically, the client is a consumer of services.

In Windows 2000 Server, one computer can act as both the client and the server. Other network operating systems such as Novell need both a server and client computer before you can use the services provided. In other words, NetWare requires a dedicated server.

These terms are widely used today to describe a particular type of computing, as in client/server technology. To form an effective network, of course, you need more than just one server and one client. You will often find one server with 50 or 100 clients attached, providing a company or department with centralized services. If this sounds a lot like mainframe processing, then guess what: It is similar. The mainframe (server) connects a bunch of workstations (clients) and lets each person access various services such as printing and storing files.

Before all the purists jump all over us, note that this is merely an example to show that the underlying structure really hasn't changed all that much. What changed, of course, were the size, speed, and complexity. Client/server networks are far easier to set up, manage, and maintain than the older mainframes. In addition, the workstation changed from a passive, dumb terminal to an interactive microcomputer.

At the heart of it all, you are connecting several terminals (clients) to a central processor (server). Finally, a major difference includes the ease with which you can connect several servers across the country or across your organization, without the need for expensive cooling and the large rooms that mainframes needed. Today's organizations have more processing power in their servers and workstations than they ever had with their mainframes.

The following sections describe what the terms client and server mean in more detail.

Servers

As discussed earlier, the server consists of a computer that provides certain services to other computers—the clients. A typical server waits for a client program to request something, such as a file or printer. Servers spend a lot of time just waiting for someone to ask them for something. They must be prepared to manage any mad rush that might

1

occasionally ensue, such as when everyone signs on in the morning. The server listens for a request and performs some action.

Many organizations use a number of servers to spread the load by having each server perform a specific task. For example, one server might be set up to handle all print requests, whereas another server manages file access. In this manner, each server can be tuned to provide the most effective level of service.

Server computers can be grouped into two primary categories:

- General-purpose computers that provide a wide range of services.
- Special-purpose computers designed to provide a particular service.

In the following sections, you'll learn that each category provides some unique capabilities.

General-Purpose Servers

Most of the computers you might already know can be used in a network—from main-frame computers to your desktop microcomputer and everything in between. Attached to a network, these computers supply you with the files, processes, and features you need. Of course, the operating system also helps makes this possible. MVS, UNIX, VMS, OS/400, NetWare, and Windows 2000 Server are some of the more common operating systems. These host machines have been in use for many years, offering functions similar to the new client/server technologies.

To access these systems, you usually need to log in (or log on and sign on) and supply a special name (account) and password.

Tip

> In spite of the need to standardize how you perform tasks, the industry cannot yet agree on what to call things. For example, do you sign on, log on or log in? Are you using a userid, username, an account name, or a logon ID? Which term you hear depends mainly on the operating system the speaker is most familiar with using. For example, a person with a UNIX background refers to the personal identifier as the *account*. Windows 2000 uses the term *username* to identify the individual.

When signed on, the user can type commands and instruct the computer to perform some action such as printing a report or reading a file. What actions each person can take depend on the level of authority granted to the person by the system administrator.

Some of the more common uses for host machines include

- Sending and receiving electronic mail. The host usually acts as the central focus for all the mail entering and leaving the LAN. The mail program typically resides on the server with a small client program running on the client workstation. The mail program also might know how to communicate with the Internet or with other organizations' mail programs.

- Moving files from one computer to another. You can send files to another department in your organization with its own host computer. Perhaps you use the host as a backup for your workstation by backing up all your local files onto the host machine's hard drive. The host typically provides you with the programs and commands that let you perform these transfers.

- Allowing other computers on the network to access server files. In this instance, the host acts as a part of your computer, allowing you to see certain files as if they are just another disk drive. This can make data sharing simple for the end user, who might not even know the files she uses aren't on her machine.

The hosts mentioned can consist of large mainframe computers running MVS or VM, UNIX machines, or AS/400 minicomputers. They all support users signing on and using their services. Servers also often contain applications such as word processors and databases, enabling users to use these services without the need for a copy on their own machines.

Special-Purpose Servers

Now that you have a smattering of understanding about servers, we need to further muddy the water. There are servers and then there are servers! The client/server architecture evolves daily to provide for the needs of the user. Because microcomputers are inexpensive compared to yesterday's behemoths, diversity and specialization are welcome. Special-purpose servers have evolved to provide a specific service in the fastest, most efficient manner. This diversity helps you manage your computing needs by upgrading only those areas that need it, adding a larger hard drive on the file server or more memory on a database server.

Organizations pick and choose the specialty machines that are best suited for their present needs. Some of these might consist of the following servers:

- **Authentication server**. A specialized security server used to authenticate all users before permitting them access to the network. Usually only larger firms use this type of server, although it is starting to gain acceptance in the general business world.

- **File server**. The most common type of server on a LAN (local area network), a file server works in the same manner as the host computers mentioned previously. The remote machine establishes a network connection with the server, which allows it to view the server files it is authorized to see as though they were physically on the remote machine. The software on the client machine then evaluates each request for data and decides what request it needs to send to the server. The file server takes each request for data and, if the requester is authorized, supplies the data.

- **Database server**. A database server is an improvement over file service. Instead of providing a requester with an entire file when she might desire only a portion of the information, the database server enables her to retrieve only those specific records that are needed. (Records are just portions or pieces of a file.) Such an approach speeds up delivery of information, allowing the server to be tuned and optimized to provide this type of service. The database server acts to provide only the data you need, removing redundant network traffic, and to specialize in that task, further reducing the time needed to provide you with the information you need.

- **Mail server**. The mail server specializes in managing your electronic mail. Larger organizations with many employees use this type of server to provide the overall level of service that is necessary when communicating electronically.

- **Web server**. Many organizations have set up shop on the Internet and are offering company and marketing information, product support, Frequently Asked Questions (FAQs), and increasingly e-commerce. Some are using the same technology to build intranets and extranets.

- **Other servers**. The nature of the client/server architecture responds well to diversification, and the number and granularity of services available for specialization is almost endless. There are servers that provide gateways to other types of networks, servers that manage document printing, and communication servers that provide access between host mainframe computers and the LAN.

The diversity and classification of server types continues to expand as we witness new or improved technology such as the Internet or video communications. Look for new, fresh uses of this technology over the coming years.

Clients

When we write about client computers, we mean those machines that take advantage of a network and the services provided by the servers on those networks. There is nothing arcane or mysterious about these machines. Many consist of your typical microcomputer running DOS, Windows, or Windows 95/98/NT Workstation/2000 Professional. Others are Macintosh computers running MacOS or UNIX workstations.

In a typical Windows-based or UNIX-based machine, the microcomputer does all the things it usually does. Perhaps it runs your word-processing software or spreadsheet. It might (and should!) run specific virus-protection software to guard against viruses.

What makes these machines clients is the network connection and some special software that lets you use that network. Almost any computer can be a client, even large mainframes. Although they typically act as the hosts or servers, they can become clients to another server.

The special software knows how to talk to the network and server and manages client requests. After it receives the requested data or service, it carries on as a normal microcomputer and continues its processing.

To summarize, it's not the machine that makes a client; it is the *connection* to the network and the software that's running that defines the computer as a client machine.

LAN Wiring Topologies

NEW TERM Earlier sections in this lesson discuss wiring, interfaces, and nodes. Now we need to talk about how these things are physically connected. The physical, or geometrical, arrangement of the cables in a LAN is called the *topology*. Which particular topology you use is dictated by the standards that you plan to use in your network. For example, IBM's Token Ring standard logically uses a ring topology and must be cabled with this in mind.

There are many types of topology in use today. The more common ones include the ring, the bus, and the star. Other topologies exist, but we don't have space to discuss them all.

Ring Topology

You might think that the ring topology involves a circle or ring, and of course, you are right. The network nodes each connect in concatenation to form a circle. The path in use across these cables passes through each client machine that is attached to the ring in a circular fashion. A complete circuit involves passing through all the clients on that ring. Figure 1.4 illustrates a ring topology. As implied by its name, a token (a 24-bit piece of information) is continuously passed around the network. All data is transmitted in one direction, called a unidirectional broadcast.

To connect a new machine to the ring, you must break the ring, insert the new machine, and reconnect the ring. In a small network, you might actually manage it in this manner. Larger networks usually cannot afford to disconnect the ring every time a new client station is added, so they use a special connection device. Each machine then connects to this device. To operate, all stations must remain connected. If one is disconnected or broken, the data flow stops.

FIGURE 1.4

*A ring—specifically,
Token Ring—topology.*

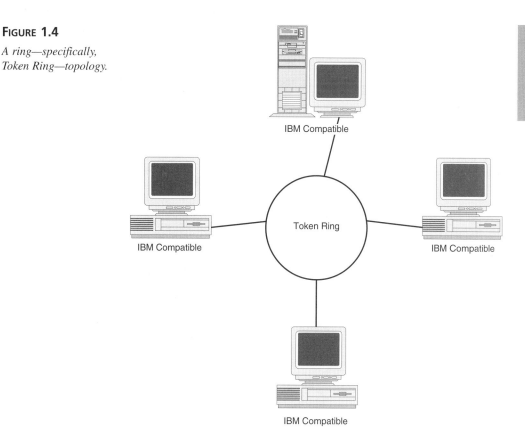

This type of network has a theoretical capacity from a low of 4Mbps to the more usual 16Mbps.

A 16Mbps network is fast enough for most types of business LANs. You can use almost any type of wiring—coax, fiber optic, or twisted pair—on a ring network, although twisted pair is the most common. IEEE standards for this type of network are set in the IEEE 802.5 specification.

Bus Topology

The bus topology runs in a straight line with each computer attaching one after the other. An advantage of this arrangement is the ease with which you can add new computers. The cable needs a special terminator at each end to tell the network where it starts and ends. In between sit all the computers that are attached in a T-shaped pattern. Signals in this network travel in both directions and every transmission is available to every attached computer. Figure 1.5 shows an example of a bus network.

FIGURE **1.5**

Bus topology.

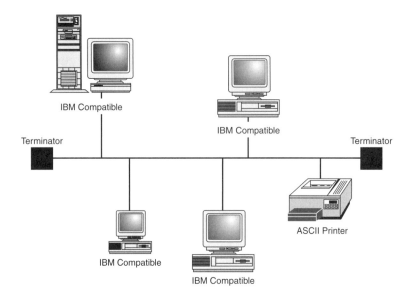

This type of network is simple and fast to configure, making it popular with small office networks. The network is fairly vulnerable, however. Should a break occur anywhere in the line, it usually disrupts the entire network. The classic example of bus technology is Ethernet using 10Base2 wiring.

Star Topology

In a star network, all communication between nodes is routed through a central device. The attached computers span out from that device, forming the star (see Figure 1.6). This type of network predominates in the mainframe arena, with the mainframe forming the device and all the terminals connecting from there. (Note that this is a greatly simplified example.)

Star also is the predominate topology for today's local area networks (LANs). A hub or concentrator is the central device in the star.

Although this type of design is prone to a single point of failure—the central device—in practice, it is extremely stable and reliable and provides for easy addition and removal of client machines. Additionally, any failure of one machine doesn't generally cause an impact to the network because the central device handles such failures. A disadvantage of the design concerns the additional cable lengths needed as each machine must be wired from the central device, even when they sit next to each other.

When you place a smart or intelligent hub in the middle of the star, you can use its security features to filter hardware addresses.

FIGURE 1.6

Star topology.

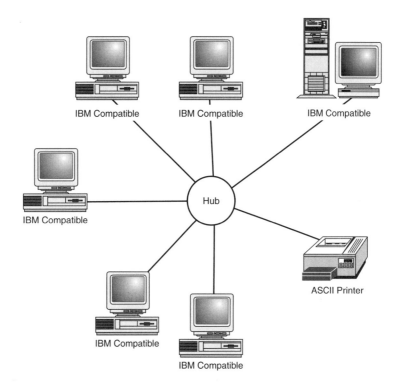

Logical Versus Physical

NEW TERM   In the examples used, the various topologies appear to be straightforward. In reality, however, things aren't so simple. *Physical* describes the manner in which the cables are connected. *Logical* refers to the way the network signal is managed, or behaves. You can touch the physical topology; you need software to manage the logical topology.

For example, Token Ring is described as a ring because the signal travels one way around the network from station to station until it returns to its starting point. Not all terminals see the signal depending on where they sit on that ring. Ethernet, or bus technology, sends the signal from the starting point in both directions and all terminals see every signal.

If you view a Token Ring network, you find that it looks suspiciously like a star topology. Confusing? It surely can be. What you need to know is that the device each machine connects to is called a MAU or media attachment unit. Although each machine connects to a port on the MAU, inside the MAU is a ring that connects all the ports! It is this technique that allows you to add or drop machines from the ring without affecting the entire network.

Today, most organizations physically wire an Ethernet network as a star using 10BaseT wiring, but Ethernet logically uses the bus topology for its internal signals. To wit, an Ethernet card sends messages to every device on the wire and still listens for its own message to see whether there was a collision.

Routers and Bridges

A major reason for the growth of LANs is the ease with which you can connect them together. After a while, however, your LAN reaches its potential in terms of the number of clients and servers attached, or you want to connect more than one LAN together. For example, your 2000 Server in the Graphics department might want a connection with the network used by Marketing to facilitate the flow of messages and files. How do you accomplish such a connection?

You need to use some type of device to provide this connection. There are three typical devices you can use:

- Routers allow you to connect different topologies together such as a Token Ring and Ethernet LAN, which are typically the most intelligent of this type of device.
- Bridges allow your LAN to connect between similar LAN technologies and also to split a busy LAN into separate segments.
- Repeaters are simple devices that allow your network to overcome some of its physical restrictions.

The following sections examine each of these devices in more detail.

Routers

The key benefit of a router is its capability to span the different cabling technologies. For example, should the Marketing department use an Ethernet LAN, a router can connect the department to the Graphics 2000 Server running on a Token Ring network.

Routers benefit us beyond connection. They offer features such as filters, which enable you to block certain protocols or IP addresses or ports to increase security and minimize network traffic. Routers, such as the CISCO 7000, also offer the capability to handle more than one protocol, such as IPX and IP. This is useful in organizations with mixed protocols.

The advantages of routers include flexibility, the capability to perform load balancing and sharing, and the capability to reduce broadcast storms. The cons of using routers include that they are difficult to set up and maintain and that some protocols aren't routable.

Bridges

A bridge is less sophisticated than a router, but it does provide some capabilities for manipulating traffic. It can also span cabling technologies. If set up with both a Token Ring card and an Ethernet card, the bridge routes traffic between these two networks. A bridge performs most of its work using the Media Access Control (MAC) header of each data packet. This address corresponds to the physical station address or hardware address of the network board.

Using these devices, you can manage the flow of data, restricting it within each LAN by setting up a bridge. This provides network traffic control (by reducing the amount of data one portion of your network sees) as well as an extra level of security. Because these devices don't have access to the routing information of the network layer of the data packets, they cannot perform the high level of routing needed in larger LANs and are more applicable in the smaller network.

The advantages of using bridges include their simplicity to install and configure and their capability to be used with protocols that cannot be routed. Cons include the lack of load-balancing capability and their inability to prevent broadcast traffic storms.

Repeaters

NEW TERM You use the repeater as a simple device to extend the physical range of your network cabling. Most cabling has a maximum length that it can be run before the signal deteriorates too much for reliable use (a phenomenon known as *attenuation*). Each network segment cannot pass this range or it might not work.

A repeater can extend the range by amplifying the signal and passing it on to the next segment of the LAN. It has no knowledge of the data passing through and it cannot be addressed itself. It follows a basic function: detect the signal, amplify it, and send it on. Repeaters are typically used only on Ethernet LANs because each station in a Token Ring acts as a repeater, so no separate device is needed.

Repeaters have an advantage in their simplicity and their capability to forward any protocol. Their disadvantage is that same simplicity and inability to route between cabling systems.

NEW TERM Previously I referred to a device known as a *hub*. A hub is really just a multiport repeater. Every signal arrives at the hub; the hub regenerates the signal, and resends it to every device attached to the hub.

Media Access Control

After a group of computers is set up to talk to each other, you need to be concerned with some code of conduct that ensures that everyone doesn't talk at the same time or interrupt each other without some form of control.

You can liken this to the CB radio. If everyone starts talking at once, all you hear are pieces of conversation with the rest of the conversation getting lost. No effective communication takes place. For a computer network, losing data is disastrous and needs to be avoided.

To avoid data loss, computer networks use two types of approaches: deterministic and contention. The following sections review these in more detail.

Deterministic Approach

The deterministic approach adds certainty to when each party can speak and how often. This is accomplished through the use of a token that is passed around the network from node to node. When a computer is in possession of the token, it can send messages. You can use this token-grabbing technique to determine the worst-case time for a computer to get access to the cable to send data.

Under a token-passing, deterministic approach, each node on the ring must wait for a token before transmitting any data. After it has the token, the node can send the data to another node on the network. The receiving node can only acknowledge that it has the data; it cannot send any data. After the sender obtains the acknowledgment, it must give up the token, even if it has more data to send. Another node then gets to pick up the token and perform its send function. In this manner, each node gets a chance to use the token.

These systems tend to be more complex than contention approaches because they must deal with the addition or deletion of nodes and lost tokens, as well as other problems. On the other hand, these methods make this approach quite reliable. Finally, the token approach gives a deterministic performance even under heavy network loads and thus can be counted on to perform in a consistent manner regardless of network load. As mentioned earlier, the IBM Token Ring (described in the IEEE 802.5 standard) uses this approach.

Contention Approach

NEW TERM The contention approach of media access control is geared toward determining whether too many stations are talking at once, or colliding. This collision approach uses the *Carrier Sense Multiple Access* (CSMA) technique to determine whether collisions are occurring. There are two types of CSMA: *collision detection* (CSMA/CD) and *collision avoidance* (CSMA/CA).

Using collision detection (CSMA/CD), a node waits until it hears no traffic on the network and then sends its data in that moment of silence. It continues to listen, however, as it sends the data and should the node hear another piece of traffic, it assumes that a collision occurred with the data it sent. The node then waits a randomly specified period of time and sends the data again. The random time period helps ensure that the two nodes don't retransmit at the same time again. After the elapsed wait time, the node tries again.

With collision avoidance (CSMA/CA), each node sends in the same fashion, waiting for silence before sending. However, the node doesn't wait to see whether others are also transmitting. Instead, it waits for an acknowledgment from the receiving node. After waiting a set period, if it has not received that acknowledgment, it assumes that something happened to the data and it is lost. It then waits for the next silence and sends the data once again.

Contention approaches are usually used on bus and star topologies, such as the Ethernet. These methods are typically referred to as *probabilistic* because you cannot precisely determine when each node gets to talk on the network. This is primarily because of the randomness that is built into each access.

Now that you have some networking background, let's move on to a discussion of Windows 2000 Server itself.

What Is Windows 2000 Server?

Windows 2000 is the latest and greatest incarnation of Microsoft networking. Early on, Bill Gates knew that networking was the key to capturing the computer business. Microsoft has been working on networking for quite a while. The company introduced MS-NET on April 15, 1985 (along with its companion operating system, DOS 3.10). IBM, which repackaged it as PC Network Support Program, and 3Com, which heavily reworked MS-NET to improve its performance, sold MS-NET. It was a DOS-based, peer-to-peer network providing print and file sharing for PCs. It was remarkably like today's Windows for Workgroups. In truth, the DOS-based NET menu system from MS-NET remains nearly unchanged in Windows for Workgroups.

LAN Manager provided a user-friendly alternative to UNIX and Novell NetWare that suited small-sized to medium-sized networks. Windows NT 3.1 and LAN Manager did not quickly saturate the market, however. Companies depend on their networks to support their business and generally don't make major changes easily.

From 1985 to 1988, Microsoft worked on the next generation of networking software. Basing the new software on its OS/2 software, it partnered with 3Com to develop LAN Manager. 3Com sold LAN Manager as 3+Open before getting out of the software business. LAN Manager's success was limited because it was tied to the Intel 286 architecture. Microsoft decided that rather than climb the processor ladder with Intel, it would develop networking software that was hardware independent.

In the mid-1980s, Digital Equipment Corporation (DEC) tried to develop an operating system to replace its popular and successful VMS operating system. Even though the DEC project failed, Microsoft recognized an opportunity and hired the designers and programmers (such as Dave Cutler, the team leader of the DEC project) to staff the new operating system project. In 1988, Microsoft earnestly started work on Windows NT. Microsoft did this at a time when it was still supporting the LAN Manager product. However, despite supporting LAN Manager into the early 1990s, Microsoft put all its eggs in the NT basket as the future of the company.

This simple story points to the fact that Microsoft carefully and thoroughly designed and developed NT. The good and bad features of MS-NET, LAN Manager, OS/2 (at one time, Microsoft partnered with IBM on OS/2), Windows, and even Novell's NetWare were evaluated when developing NT.

In August 1993, in a stroke of marketing genius, Microsoft released Windows NT Advanced Server Version 3.1. The genius of Microsoft was in assigning NT a version number that made it look like it was a release of LAN Manager, even though the two have little in common (except for the wallpaper that NT Server displays when no one is logged in is LANMANNT.BMP!). The version number of Advanced Server also coincided with the version of the desktop version of Windows. Brilliance! September 1994 brought a new version and name—Windows NT Server Version 3.5. Thirteen months later, Microsoft brought out version 3.51. Near the end of the product life cycle, Microsoft released a free add-on called Internet Information Server 1.0. This software ushered Windows NT into UNIX territory: the Internet.

In 1996, Microsoft released another version, 4.0. Windows NT Server 4.0 was an improved operating system, especially in its Internet capabilities. The TCP/IP protocol stack was greatly improved, DNS services were offered, and Internet Information Server was enhanced as version 2.0.

Microsoft had named the next incarnation as Windows NT version 5. However, marketing people figured that the Windows trademark was far more valuable than the NT trademark. After all, most people cannot even tell you what NT really means. New Technology? Not There? No Technology? Network This? Actually, the name is none of these. So, Microsoft decided to focus on the Windows trademark. Probably a good idea because NT 4 and 2000 have about as much in common as NT 3.51 and 4.

The next step in the evolution of Microsoft server software is perhaps the greatest, and the subject of this book—Windows 2000 Server.

Microsoft's Windows 2000 Server network operating system (NOS) isn't simply another program running on a PC. It is a sophisticated operating system that is purpose-built to deliver high-performance services to clients connected through a network. Its features and performance allow it to play a major role in the downsizing of information systems from traditional mainframe computers to distributed processors connected by local area networks (LANs). Windows NT Server started the mass movement to the Windows platform for networking in organizations throughout the world and Windows 2000 intends to build on it.

Getting to Know Windows 2000 Server

With every update of the Windows networking operating system, Microsoft gives you new and innovative technologies to build more useful, manageable, and scalable networks. Windows 2000 is no exception. In fact, it is the most innovative release to date. Windows 2000 comes in six flavors:

- **Windows 2000 Consumer**. Planned name of the version that will eventually replace what is currently Windows 98. Microsoft is bandying about several names for this product.

- **Windows 2000 Professional**. Formerly named Windows NT Workstation 4, Professional is Microsoft's flagship desktop operating system. Windows 2000 Professional OS will support up to two processors.

- **Windows 2000 Server**. Formerly named Windows NT Server 4, Server supports four-way symmetric multiprocessing (SMP). Upgrades from NT 4.0 Server support four-way SMP.

- **Windows 2000 Advanced Server**. Formerly named Windows NT 4.0 Server Enterprise Edition. New installations will support eight-way SMP, while upgrades from NT 4.0 Server Enterprise Edition will support eight-way SMP. Like its predecessor, Advanced Server supports large physical memory, clustering, and load balancing.

- **Windows 2000 Datacenter Server**. A new Microsoft offering that supports 32-way SMP, up to 64GB of physical memory, clustering, and load balancing.

- **Windows 2000 Embedded**. Formerly named Embedded Windows NT. You'll find this version in devices such as Storage Area Networks or thin Web servers. Each of these products includes key advancements that change how you plan, design, and deploy Microsoft networks. You can use Windows 2000 Professional in any situation where you use any other client operating system, such as Windows 95 or Windows 98. Consider Windows 2000 Professional for high-performance processing, such as CAD/CAM, graphics, or computational work. Datacenter Server, on the other hand, the most powerful of the Windows 2000 Server family of operating systems, represents Microsoft's best effort to compete in the high-end server market to date.

Windows 2000 Server, the focus of this book, runs the disks, controls memory, schedules programs to run, takes commands from the keyboard, and talks to its clients across the network.

Microsoft has found success in a very competitive market by listening to its customers and meeting their needs. Windows 2000 Server is the result of several years of working with systems engineers to determine what features their organizations need most in an operating system.

As networks grow, network operating systems need to scale upward. Modern network applications are more powerful than ever and demand more of the server. Windows 2000 is ready for these processing-intensive applications with improved support for multiple processors, huge amounts of memory, highly scaleable file systems, and clustering. Microsoft designed Windows 2000 Server to do one main function and do it well: manage resources for clients. By managing, we mean storing and retrieving client files quickly but also safely. Windows 2000 Server includes many features for high performance, as well as features to protect files against damage due to hardware problems (for example, bad disk areas). It isn't a general-purpose operating system like DOS or UNIX or OS/2. Windows NT Server was purpose-built for service.

Windows 2000 Design Goals

Microsoft had the following design goals for Windows NT:

- Compatibility
- Reliability
- Portability
- Extensibility
- Scalability
- Distributability
- Certifiability

These goals are still evident in the base product. However, with Windows 2000, Microsoft has shifted its focus to

- Internet standardization
- Ease of administration
- Scalability
- Security
- Performance
- Reliability

Internet Standardization

NEW TERM The rapid growth of the Internet is driving much of the momentum of computer networking. Windows NT Server claimed 23% of the Internet Web server market and 70% of the intranet server market during 1998. With Windows 2000 Server, Microsoft has upped the ante by increasing its support for *open standards*. Open standards are in the public domain and supported by organizations such as the ISO and IETF. Anyone can use these standards to develop products. For instance, should you develop a new operating system, you can use the TCP/IP protocol suite for communication.

Networking in Windows 2000 is vastly improved. Besides having newly polished MMC administrative interfaces, the core TCP/IP network services have been improved and updated.

Microsoft has added support for the Layer 2 Tunneling Protocol (L2TP). Although not a core network protocol, L2TP is a good replacement for the Point-to-Point Tunneling Protocol (PPTP). LT2P is an industry-standard Internet protocol used for building Virtual Private Networks (VPNs). Like PPTP, you can use L2TP to build secure tunnels across internetworks. To ensure confidentiality and data protection, L2TP can leverage public key certificates and IP Security. These tools provide you with the tools to build secure VPNs traversing public networks, such as the Internet.

In addition, Windows 2000 supports IP Security, Kerberos, and PKI (public key infrastructure). Kerberos is the preferred authentication protocol for Windows 2000. It has the following advantages:

- It's a platform-independent, widely implemented security protocol.
- It can establish sessions with other computers much faster than the NTLM mechanism could.
- Its trust relationships are all transitive.
- It supports delegation of authentication.
- It's a shared-secret, identity-based protocol that uses symmetric (or secret) cryptography.

You also have the opportunity in Windows 2000 to remove all NetBIOS traffic from your network. To make this transition, you use Dynamic DNS (DDNS)—a DNS server implementing RFC 2136 that supports dynamic update. DDNS can entirely eliminate your dependence on NetBIOS and WINS.

Caution If you are updating from Windows NT Server 4 and were using NetBIOS, you may want to review Days 12, "Understanding TCP/IP and DNS" and 13, "Understanding DHCP and WINS." You might have services dependent on NetBIOS, so plan for its eventual conversion.

The most important addition to Windows 2000 is Active Directory (AD). Active Directory is Microsoft's implementation of the ITU's X.500 directory standard. It allows any user or application to locate any available network resource. It stores more than the location of objects; it stores critical information about the objects. Windows 2000 Server's network services store information within Active Directory to take advantage of its distributed, reliable nature. A resource as critical as Active Directory must be running at all times, so you can run the service on many machines simultaneously.

Additionally, Windows 2000 supports the Lightweight Directory Access Protocol (LDAP), and Internet Engineering Task Force (IETF) standard. LDAP specifies the way clients and servers exchange directory information. AD uses both version 2 and 3 of LDAP.

Microsoft included Internet Information Services 5.0 with Windows 2000 and it features many improvements aimed specifically toward Internet Service Providers (ISPs) who offer Web hosting services. Among other advancements, it now supports HTTP compression, virtual server processor quotas, and process accounting.

Ease of Administration

To assist in administration, Windows 2000 has support for the following devices:

- PCI, AGP, PC Card, USB, and FireWire (but not ISA)
- 4,200 modems
- 2,000 printers
- 700 network devices
- 55 scanners
- 41 digital cameras

Windows 2000 has improved ease of administration through improving the management infrastructure. It does this with Microsoft Management Console, Windows Management

Instrumentation, Group Policy editor, Component Object Model, Windows Driver Model, Plug and Play, Quality of Service, and Total Cost of Ownership tools. Each of these is discussed in the following sections.

Microsoft Management Console

You should find administering a network of Windows 2000 systems easier and faster than ever because of the Microsoft Management Console (MMC). The MMC gives you control over what tools and computers you display, allowing you to create administration tools customized to your specific responsibilities. User Manager, Event View, Server Manager, Disk Administrator, and all other administrative applications have been rewritten as MMC snap-ins. Administrators should like the consistent, user-friendly interface. You will learn about MMC throughout the 21 days.

Windows Management Instrumentation

The new WMI (Windows Management Instrumentation) standards should make large, heterogeneous networks simpler to manage. WMI provides applications with an interface to monitor and manage systems, similar to the capabilities currently provided by SNMP. Where your network is entirely Windows-based, you might never have to use WMI. For most of you who administer a combination of Windows 2000 systems and UNIX systems, WMI will allow your enterprise management applications to interface with every system on your network.

Active Directory and Group Policy

Managing desktop environments will be easier than ever thanks to Group Policy and Active Directory. You can now grant and restrict user and group access to various aspects of Windows 2000, such as applications, desktop settings, network access, and the Start menu. Policies exist within Active Directory that you can quickly apply to an entire enterprise. Additionally, users and groups within the enterprise can have specialized settings that meet their specific needs. Active Directory is a key concept introduced on Day 5, "Introducing Active Directory."

Component Object Model

Generally your end users could care less about the operating system they use and are far more concerned with the applications supporting their work. The key to providing applications to users is making the product attractive to the developers. Ninety-one percent of all software developers now provide, or plan to provide soon, software for Windows 2000.

Microsoft's Component Object Model (COM) technology is responsible for attracting many developers. COM is now woven into just about every aspect of Microsoft's own software—operating systems, development tools, and applications. Ultimately, COM benefits both administrators and developers because it allows the distribution and centralized update of applications on the network.

Windows Driver Model

The introduction of the Windows Driver Model (WDM) means administrators no longer need to maintain a separate set of drivers for Windows 2000 and Microsoft Windows 98 systems. Merging the drivers for the two operating systems brings us a step closer to the next generation of Windows, when home and business operating systems merge.

Plug and Play and ACPI

Windows 2000 completely supports Plug and Play (PnP) and the advanced power management capabilities of Advanced Configuration and Power Interface (ACPI). These features will reduce the time you spend working with your server hardware. In most cases, the operating system will automatically detect and configure new hardware as soon as you add it.

Quality of Service

Quality of Service (QoS) technology benefits day-to-day administration. QoS resolves a more critical administrative problem: network bandwidth allocation and availability. With the advent of applications such as real-time audio and video, IP telephony, and conferencing comes the need for better management and prioritization of network traffic. The Windows 2000 QoS technology helps you allocate network resources differently for traffic based on priority.

Total Cost of Ownership

Windows 2000 includes improvements in enterprise management. Total Cost of Ownership (TCO) is a concern shared by many companies. In corporate networks, most TCO efforts are aimed at reducing the expense of managing desktops. Windows 2000 includes the following new enterprise management tools to help you lower desktop TCO:

- **IntelliMirror**. You can use IntelliMirror to reduce day-to-day desktop management costs. It consists of three core technologies:
    1. **User Document Management**. Provides user data mirroring and client side caching.
    2. **User Settings Management**. Helps you maintain standard desktop configurations for your networked users.
    3. **Software Installation**. Lets you assign and publish applications to Windows 2000 users using Active Directory. When users log on, Windows 2000 automatically installs the assigned applications.

1

- **Remote Installation (RI) Service**. Helps you reduce the cost of deploying operating systems.
- **Group Policy**. To configure policy in the Active Directory, you use the Group Policy editor to create a Group Policy Object (GPO) associated with sites, domains, and organizational units (OUs).

Scalability

NEW TERM   A *scalable system* is one that will run in many hardware environments. Applications should take advantage of the broad range of computers available today. Windows 2000 is adaptable to many processing environments and will take advantage of multiprocessing capabilities of a computer. You can run Windows 2000 on anything from a Pentium CISC-based system, to a RISC-based system, to a symmetrical multiprocessor (SMP).

Windows 2000 provides multiplatform support through its layered, microkernel architecture and use of the HAL (Hardware Abstraction Layer).

Windows 2000 supports two different security models—the workgroup and domain models—so you can support small networks of two or three PCs or networks with thousands of workstations.

Security

Security is an ongoing concern in computing, and it is especially vital in network systems. Windows 2000 Server includes one of the strongest security systems to date. It provides built-in support for certification authorities and smart cards, as well as the standards-based Kerberos authentication protocol.

The cornerstone of Windows 2000 security is Active Directory. Its support for granular access control, inheritance, and delegation of administrative tasks gives you the flexibility to secure resources without compromising your network's purpose.

Windows 2000 networks include several key improvements to security that are provided by the following:

- **Security Configuration Editor (SCE)**. SCE consolidates the management of Windows 2000 security settings in one easy-to-use interface. You can configure
  - Account policies
  - Local policies
  - Event logs
  - Restricted groups
  - System services
  - Registry

- File system
- Active Directory objects

- **Security Configuration Manager (SCM)**. SCM uses your template created with SCE to configure and analyze the parameters it contains. The real benefit of SCM is you can use it to compare the security parameters of any Windows 2000 computer to settings stored in a template and report the differences.
- **Windows 2000 Authentication**. Windows 2000 supports two core authentication protocols: Windows NT LAN Manager (NTLM) and Kerberos. Kerberos is now the preferred protocol for authentication. However, some clients, such as Windows for Workgroups, need to use NTLM for authentication purposes.
- **Public Key Cryptography.** Windows 2000 includes the tools to build a robust, scalable, standards-based public key infrastructure (PKI). To build your PKI, you can use Microsoft Certificate Services. Smart cards can use the Windows 2000 PKI, as they can store certificates issued by your CA to support logon. Another benefit of the Microsoft PKI is support for the Internet Engineering Task Force (ETF) IP Security standard. And finally, you also can implement a recovery policy for the Encrypting File System (EFS) with your PKI. EFS enables security-conscious organizations to use file and directory level–encryption for added privacy.

If you have ever tried to implement encryption, you know someone will ask you how it affects performance. Well, Microsoft can help you here because they have made several improvements to Windows 2000 to enhance performance.

Performance

Windows 2000 will make your file servers more reliable and efficient than ever with the new Microsoft distributed file system (Dfs). Dfs allows shares to be mirrored between file servers and enables clients to automatically choose the closest server. Ultimately, Dfs will reduce network traffic, increase uptime, and improve the load distribution between your servers.

Performance is a key issue addressed on Day 20, "Windows 2000 Performance Monitoring and Tuning."

Reliability

Windows 2000 provides reliability through the following features:

- Error and exception handling
- Component redundancy
- IntelliMirror

Each reliability feature is discussed in the following sections.

Error and Exception Handling

Generally, a system should protect itself from internal and external malfunction and tampering. It also should be robust and behave predictably in response to error conditions, even hardware errors. Under Windows 2000, a program cannot interfere with the operation of another program. Also, Windows 2000 doesn't allow a program to modify the behavior of the operating system itself. These goals are met by managing the operation of the system itself and by trapping and messaging errors.

The operating system uses structured exception handling for capturing error conditions and responding uniformly. Either the operating system or the processor issues an exception whenever an abnormal event occurs; exception handling code, which exists throughout the system, is automatically invoked in response to the condition, ensuring that no undetected error wreaks havoc on user programs or on the system itself.

Component Redundancy

NEW TERM Windows 2000 also provides reliability by providing redundant systems that protect the computer when a single component fails. This feature, *fault tolerance*, guards against failure of critical systems. For example, 2000 supports, in software, RAID (Redundant Array of Inexpensive Disks), using technologies such as disk mirroring and striping, to offer redundancy for hard drives.

Also, 2000 Server has built-in support for uninterruptible power supply (UPS) devices, which provide backup power and automatically shut down the system in the case of power problems. In addition, 2000 Server supports multiple network cards in a server, directory replication, and hot fixes for the NTFS file system. *Hot fix* is a feature in which the file system constantly monitors the disk area it is using and, when it finds a damaged area, marks the area as bad and takes it out of service.

The 2000 File System (NTFS 5) can recover from all types of disk errors, including critical disk errors. It does this through the use of redundant storage and a transaction-based scheme for storing data. The NTFS 5 file system allows for greater expandability than previous versions of Windows. New backup utilities make backup and recovery easier and more reliable.

IntelliMirror

Users will never lose access to their most critical network documents, applications, and desktop settings—thanks to IntelliMirror. Windows 2000 systems can keep duplicate copies of important information on the client and the server. When users lose access to the server, they can keep working on a network document because Windows 2000 will automatically use the locally cached copy. When you restore the server, documents are automatically synchronized. IntelliMirror also copies data from desktop systems to servers, enabling users to move from one computer to another and have the same desktop settings, applications, and documents available wherever they choose to work.

Earlier today, you saw you have options for setting up your network. The remainder of today, you will learn to plan for tomorrow's installation.

Planning Your Network

Earlier today, you saw many possibilities that open up to you when you install a network—possibilities such as sharing documents, email, and printers, as well as sharing applications such as word processors and spreadsheets. This section will help you develop a network plan so that you can take advantages of these services.

Before planning your network, gather information about how people physically move and interact to get their work done and the physical layout of your building. Talking with the people in your company about the network is a good way to get valuable feedback for your network plan.

Understanding the work flow within your company will help you decide what applications you need, determine the potential workload for the network, and identify the best layout for your network (that is, where to place printers, the topology that makes the most sense, and other layout issues). In general, you'll find that Pareto's Law applies to networking as well. (You remember Pareto; he was the philosopher who believed in the 80/20 rule. For instance, 80% of the wealth is held by 20% of the population.) Eighty percent of network traffic is usually local to a workgroup. Setting up the network involves identifying employees whom you can cluster in groups, making network administration easier. The best way to group people together for network administration purposes comes from identifying how employees fit naturally.

Knowing your building layout will help you identify potential problems that might crop up when you start putting the network in place. Although it is probably wise, in most buildings, to let the building maintenance staff or a professional install your network cable for you, it's helpful to have a few bits of information you can round up in advance. When using a professional installer, get the phone number of the maintenance person in charge of the building where you have your offices. You'll need to let him or her know that you're installing the cable for your network, and the installer will probably need permission to start or might have questions about the best way to route the cable. The maintenance person can provide access to engineering or architectural drawings of the conduits, electrical systems, or other building systems and features that might affect where the cable goes. Maintenance staff also might know about local ordinances that might come into play (although your installer should also know about them).

Get some sense of the best location for the server. You'll want to locate it in a reasonably secure area with restricted access. Most vendors state you must physically protect the server should you want to logically protect it. Also, protect it as much as possible from any potential disaster. For example, don't place it directly under a sprinkler or a washroom. You also should locate the server so that it's easy to put tapes in the tape backup system or to provide an uninterruptible power supply so your server continues to work, even during a power failure.

The key to your planning is figuring out how much of a load your network will bear. This includes the number of dial-in users and how often users will concurrently need certain types of network-related tasks such as access to a database. After you've completed these calculations, you need to buy the right hardware to accommodate that load. The primary hardware that is affected by the load includes

- Your server's CPU
- The system's random access memory (RAM)
- The hard disk
- The network adapter cards (also sometimes called network interface cards, or NICs)
- The backup devices (such as a tape drive)
- The modems

In the following sections, you'll see some key metrics to use when you start planning your network. Just keep in mind that you should over-purchase when in doubt. It's easier to grow into your hardware than the other way around.

Choosing the Right Hardware

Microsoft Windows 2000 Server can run on an abundance of hardware, as long as the processor is

- A system with Pentium-compatible chips
- Digital Alpha AXP
- Motorola or IBM PowerPC

Windows 2000 ships with MIPS, Intel, PowerPC, and Alpha code. Windows 2000 has a minimum requirement of a Pentium 166MHz CPU and 64MB of RAM. This range of hardware options means that you can find a server to meet virtually any network needs you're likely to encounter. In general, you can start with a Pentium II-based computer. After you have a Pentium II-based machine, as a general rule, buying additional RAM, such as 128MB rather than 64MB, provides more benefits than simply purchasing a faster processor.

For example, Windows 2000 Server benefits you by taking advantage of a multiprocessor architecture, such as that provided by Compaq ProLiant. There are two other ways to leverage Windows 2000's support for hardware. First, buy equipment on Microsoft's Hardware Compatibility List (HCL). Second, buy equipment that supports PCI 2.1. This standard will help you virtually eliminate hardware interrupt conflicts among network components from the various manufacturers. Make PCI 2.1 your benchmark for the server, video cards, network interface cards, and any other hardware for your server.

Do yourself a favor and make sure that the following network hardware is on the HCL and conforms to the PCI 2.1 standard:

- Server
- CD-ROM drive
- SCSI adapter
- Video
- Network adapter cards
- Uninterruptible power supply
- Tape backup system

CD-ROM Drive

Check the HCL for a CD-ROM drive. You need a CD-ROM drive to install Windows 2000 Server and third-party software and to share CD-ROM programs with users who don't have CD-ROM drives on their own computers.

SCSI Adapters

Windows 2000 supports the Small Computer System Interface, or SCSI (pronounced "scuzzy"). SCSI is an input/output parallel-type interface that can support several external devices or computer peripherals, such as hard disks, tape drives, CD-ROM drives, printers, and scanners, through a host adapter. SCSI adapters compatible with Windows 2000 Server are listed in the HCL. Check out the HCL at http://www.microsoft.com/hwtest/hcl/.

Tip

For best results, use Internet Explorer to view the Hardware Compatibility List site.

There are many reasons you might want to use SCSI devices. Here are four notable ones:

- SCSI supports multitasking to provide better performance over other technologies.
- A SCSI device has built-in controllers that free up the CPU to perform other tasks, making the server more efficient.
- You can attach SCSI devices to different types of computers because they are independent of the system bus.
- Classes of SCSI devices, such as CD-ROM, are easily upgraded because of the similarities at the interface level.

When choosing a monitor for your system, make sure you get Super VGA (SVGA) tecnology and check the monitor against the HCL.

Surprisingly, you require at least a VGA board to load 2000 Server. This runs counter to the days when you used a low-quality video display because nobody needed it for any extended period.

Network Adapter Cards

While you are planning your network adapter card selection, do yourself a huge favor: Purchase and install the same type of card in all your PCs. If you don't, you'll kick yourself the first time you must troubleshoot your network. Keep in mind that a 32-bit version of a network interface card will result in substantial performance increases over a 16-bit network adapter card.

Unfortunately, network adapter cards open up a world of arcane problems during installation. Two of the most common and most easily prevented causes of network installation problems occur with network adapter cards: hardware compatibility problems and interrupt alerts caused by duplicate usage of special hardware numbers. With patience and a little pre-installation checking, you'll avoid these issues. The most important item to remember is that the card you choose should be listed on the HCL.

If you're not running MS-DOS or Windows on your client PCs, make sure that you check with your operating system manufacturer and cross-reference its list against the HCL before you begin your installation.

Most servers now come with pre-installed Ethernet 10/100 cards.

Uninterruptible Power Supply

Uninterruptible power supplies (UPSs) come in many forms, but generally, they are battery packs that kick in when the power goes off. Trade off the expense of the more elaborate ones against the cost of having the server down when the power goes off.

Tape Backup System

There are two components to a tape backup system: the physical tape drive and tapes, and the software that controls the backup. Again, check the HCL for a tape drive.

There are a number of things you can do should you underestimate the hardware you need to keep your network running at an acceptable level, and they all hinge on how well you plan. First, make certain that the server hardware you select has the capability of accepting substantial RAM upgrades and a Single Large Expensive Disk (SLED) (or has extra slots available for attaching external disk drives or RAID packs) and has slots (or ports) available for installing additional modems and fax modems when they are required. Also, select a tape subsystem that is SCSI-based.

Choosing the Right Amount of Memory

The amount of random access memory you have in your server is a key factor in your server's performance. The law of networking is that more is better. This definitely is true for Windows 2000 Server because it holds as many active files as possible in RAM so it doesn't have to keep accessing the hard disk to get information. You can use Table 1.1 to calculate the amount of RAM that's adequate for your current needs (and make sure that you buy a server that will let you keep upgrading RAM as your network grows).

TABLE 1.1 Computing Memory Requirements

Element	Factors	Total RAM
System Memory	1. Minimum requirement	1. 64MB
Applications	2. Average size of executables run off the server	2.
	3. Number of applications run off the server	3.
	4. Multiply answer 2 by answer 3	4.
User Data	5. Average size of data files open per user	5.
	6. Number of users	6.
	7. Multiply answer 5 by answer 6	7.
	8. Total required memory (1+4+7)	8.

1

Let us offer a few points of explanation before you tackle an example using Table 1.2:

- To calculate the average size of data files open per user, go to several computers within your company and use Windows Explorer (should you have Windows 95, Windows 98, or Windows 2000 Professional), File Manager (should you have Windows 3.1x), or the MS-DOS prompt DIR command to find out the number of bytes for typical database files, spreadsheets, presentations, and word processing documents. Select templates or files that people typically share over the network. Then, average the number of bytes found in those files.

- The number of users is the number of people who would simultaneously access a file.

- To find the average size of executables run off the server, look in a couple of the directories for the applications on the desktop machines, such as the Microsoft Excel directory, and search for all the files ending with the .EXE or .DLL extension. Find out how many bytes they contain and use that number as the average number of bytes.

Sound a little confusing? Well, it's not. Perhaps a simple example would clarify things. Let's say you recently purchased Microsoft Office, so your business uses four applications regularly whose file sizes are as listed here:

Microsoft Excel	4.72MB
Microsoft PowerPoint	4.26MB
Microsoft Schedule+	.92MB
Microsoft Word for Windows	3.76MB

Add them up and average them, which gives you 3.41 for answer 2. When you multiply the number of applications (answer 3 is 4) by the average size of the executables (4*3.41), you get 13.64MB for answer 4.

Next, look at the size of the various data files created by these applications. You might see this:

Microsoft Excel	60KB
Microsoft PowerPoint	300KB
Microsoft Schedule+	60KB
Microsoft Word for Windows	150KB

Add them up and average them, which gives you 142.5 for answer 5. When you multiply this by the number of network users (suppose it's 25 for answer 6), you get 3,562.5KB.

Divide by 1024 (to convert from kilobytes to megabytes to use the same units all around), and you get 3.48MB for answer 7.

Therefore, the total system memory requirement is 64MB (answer 1) + 13.64MB (answer 4) + 3.48MB (answer 7), or 81.12MB. This means you should probably configure your system with 128MB of RAM. This amount, 128MB, most likely is the minimum for any server. Most servers should have between 192MB and 256MB of memory to load and run applications efficiently.

Choosing the Right Amount of Hard Disk Space

When you plan your hard disk requirements, consider partitioning your hard disk into three logical drives: C, D, and E. Using these partitions, you can designate certain parts of the disk for certain functions, as shown here:

- C partition, or drive C for the Windows 2000 Server operating system
- D partition, or drive D for network applications
- E partition, or drive E for user data

Again, there is a fairly simple formula to help you calculate how much hard disk space to specify when you buy your server. For drive D, you can find out the size of the applications by looking at the installation requirements for that application and the amount of hard disk space required. For drive E, in the factor "Budgeted disk space per user," you should have a corporate policy on how much space you will provide (see Table 1.2). If not, check with a representative sample of your users and see how much data (excluding the applications themselves) they have on their desktop machines. As a rough guideline for your calculations, one page of text equals approximately one kilobyte (KB).

TABLE 1.2 Computing Hard Drive Requirements

Element	Factors	Total RAM
System Disk Drive (C Drive)	1. Greater of 400MB or 300MB + server memory + 12MB	1.
Applications (D Drive)	2. Average size of installed applications	2.
	3. Number of applications run off the server	3.
	4. Multiply answer 2 by answer 3	4.
	5. Disk space per user	5.
(E Drive)	6. Number of users	6.
	7. Margin of error (10%)	7. 1.1

Element	Factors	Total RAM
	8. Multiply answer 5 by answer 6 by answer 7	8.
	9. Total hard disk space (1+4+8)	9.

As you did for system memory, you can calculate hard disk requirements. Continuing the preceding example, the sizes of the applications are as listed here:

Microsoft Excel	10.20MB
Microsoft PowerPoint	11.40MB
Microsoft Schedule+	3.18MB
Microsoft Word for Windows	7.55MB

Add them up and average them, which gives you 8.08 for answer 2. When you multiply the number of applications (answer 3 is 4) by the average size of the executables (4*8.08), you get 32.32MB for answer 4.

Next, assume you allow users 40MB of budgeted disk space (answer 5). When you multiply this by the number of network users (suppose it's 25 for answer 6), you get 1GB. Gross this number up by the 10% fudge factor (answer 7), and you get 1.1GB for answer 8.

You must also select the lesser of

- 400MB
- 300MB + 33.12MB (from the previous calculation) + 12MB, or 345.12MB

Therefore, the total hard disk space requirement is 345.12MB (answer 1) + 32.32MB (answer 4) + 1.10GB (answer 8), or 1.48GB. This means you should probably configure your system with at least 1.48GB of disk space.

Selecting a File System

Before you install Windows 2000 Server, you should decide which file systems you need. Windows 2000 Server supports the following file systems:

- Windows 2000 NT File System (NTFS)
- File Allocation Table (FAT)

Planning for NTFS

Windows 2000 Server supports NTFS. If you aren't familiar with NTFS, you can jump to Day 7, "Managing User Accounts," right now. Other operating systems, such as Windows 3.x, cannot access NTFS partitions. If you will use only Windows 2000 Server on the computer, choose NTFS. You also should choose NTFS when

- You use Services for Macintosh. (NTFS must be used where the Macintosh files are located.)
- You require file-level security.
- You will migrate directories and files from a NetWare server, and you want to save permissions.
- You want to use Windows 2000 file compression.
- You want file or directory names of up to 255 characters.
- You are going to install Active Directory on the system.

Planning for FAT

FAT is the lowest common denominator among PC file systems. The FAT file system allows access by either MS-DOS (with or without Windows) or OS/2 operating system clients. To switch or boot between Windows 2000 Server and MS-DOS, you must format one partition on the computer with the FAT file system so that MS-DOS can run.

With FAT, you cannot use the security features of Windows 2000 and you cannot support extremely large numbers of files.

Also, because FAT uses 16 bits to record the allocation status of any volume, it can support 216 or 65,536 clusters per volume. So the FAT volume is limited to 65,518 files, regardless of the size of the disk. Compare this to the 32 bits used by FAT32 and the 64 bits used by NTFS.

Other File System Considerations

In addition to the preceding considerations, you should consider the following points when selecting file systems:

- If you want to dual boot between Windows 2000 Server and MS-DOS, drive C must be FAT.
- RISC hardware specifications require that drive C be FAT.
- NTFS is the only file system that provides local security.

With any hardware you buy for your system, consult the Hardware Compatibility List (HCL) for Windows 2000 Server to ensure that the components are compatible with the operating system. Again, HCL compatible means that Microsoft tested the hardware to ensure that it works with its desktop operating systems as well as with the Windows 2000 Server operating system. Microsoft has tested thousands of machines and other peripheral devices (such as CPUs, printers, and network interface and video cards). This means you can choose from a wide range of compatible equipment. Selecting HCL-approved components helps reduce the number of problems you might encounter.

> **Tip**
>
> For more information on choosing a file system, see Day 2, "Installing Windows 2000 and Client Software."

Selecting a Network Protocol

You should decide which network protocol you will support. Protocols are part of the network operating system. For a client and server to communicate, you need the same client/server software and protocol. If networks are the information highways, protocols are the rules of the road.

When you select a protocol, some considerations will make your decision easier. If you have an existing Novell NetWare network and you want to add a Windows 2000 Server, you can use Windows 2000's IPX support.

Maybe you want to convert an existing LAN Manager network, so you'll continue to use NetBEUI.

You may select TCP/IP when you want to connect to the Internet. Because the TCP/IP protocol suite is in the public domain, it provides more flexibility, no matter how large your network.

Table 1.3 provides a simplistic view of some of the decisions involved in the selection process. Selecting an enterprise is an important decision in your organization.

TABLE 1.3   Protocol Characteristics

Application	NetBEUI	IPX/SPX	TCP/IP
Small network	X	X	X
Large network			X
Integrate with NetWare		X	
Integrate with UNIX			X
Support wide area networks (for example, a routable protocol)			X
Connect to Internet			X

As you saw earlier today, Windows 2000 is moving towards standard protocols, and provides the capability to remove NetBIOS support. Even Novell provides TCP/IP native with NetWare 5. You will learn about TCP/IP and its implementation on Day 12, "Understanding TCP/IP and DNS."

Selecting the Server's Role

You should decide the role the server will have on the network. A 2000 Server can assume one of two roles in the network:

- A primary domain controller in a new domain.
- A file or application server (member server)It is important to decide the server's role early because after you make the decision and install, you cannot change the role unless you re-install the system.

You should install a server as a primary domain controller (PDC) only when you are creating a new domain. Because no other machines are members of this domain, there are no security considerations. Remember that you can have only one PDC per domain, but you must have one.

Planning for Administration

There are a number of administrative tasks you must perform to keep your network operating efficiently and securely. These activities include creating accounts for new network users (see Day 5, "Introducing Active Directory"), giving users a password so that they can get onto the network (see Day 6, "Introducing Security Services"), and backing up the network so that your data is safe (see Day 15, "File Backup and Recovery"). Closely tied to the administration of your network is the need to think about and plan for how you want to handle network security. Understandably, you want to keep unauthorized people from gaining access to the network or to specific information, such as confidential customer data. In the following sections, you'll start thinking about administration activities, such as naming your computers, creating user accounts, and using groups.

Naming Your Computers

The best way to keep track of client PCs and other computers or printers on your network is to name them uniquely. Doing this helps you diagram and troubleshoot the system, and it also provides a point of reference for someone who might succeed you in administering the network. As part of your network plan, create a diagram that displays the location of each server and client and includes the names you choose for your computers and printers.

Naming computers is important. Should you select an inflexible naming system, you might find yourself making changes later on. Select a system that is flexible, makes

sense, and will grow with your organization. When it comes to naming network components, here are some suggestions for naming servers:

- Keep the names short. You must remember the name and enter it in systems from time to time. Therefore, select a name that is easy to remember and type. PeterDavisMacintosh isn't a good computer name. Use something like Pdavis instead.

- Choose a name that people can remember and pronounce.

- Don't use locations to name computers because locations often change. ComputerOnNorthSide is also a bad computer name.

- Don't use spaces in computer names. Marketing System is a bad name, whereas MarkSys is a good name.

- Choose a name that represents how the client uses the server or the name of the group that uses it; for example, Sales1 is a good name for the first server in the Sales department.

- Use a consistent scheme; for example, you can use mythological characters, such as Kerberos, or Greek letters, such as Alpha.

- Use names that allow you to use the Internet, connect to the server, and use applications such as SQL Server.

For workstations, consider the previous suggestions, as well as the following ones:

- Choose a name associated with the person who uses the system.

- Use the owner's first name and the first initial of his or her last name; for example, PeterD is a good name.

- Use the owner's first initial and last name; for example, Blewis is also a good name.

- If you use email, use the owner's email name.

Creating a good naming scheme can save you time in the future. Make sure your naming scheme can carry you into the future. After you create an account-naming scheme, you can create some accounts.

Creating Accounts

Clients of the network must have an account set up. The system uses the account to identify clients. After the owner of the client account enters a valid password to authenticate himself, the system gives that user certain rights and privileges—that is, authorities. A user account gives that customer certain privileges, such as changing the configuration of the machine, adding new devices, and accessing data.

As part of your plan, write down the rights and privileges that you want to give your clients. You'll use this information later when you actually set up the server. Table 1.5 offers a brief description of accounts and the circumstances where you might assign the rights.

TABLE 1.4 Windows 2000 Accounts

Account	Description and When to Use
Administrator	Manages the overall computer configuration. A most powerful account because as an administrator, you can perform almost all tasks, including setting security, defining accounts, adding devices, and troubleshooting. One trusted person in the organization should have the privilege associated with this account. This may be the person in your office who will administer the server.
Guests	Allows occasional or one-time users to log on and provides limited privileges on the server. The system disables this account by default and should remain so because of the challenges of using it securely.

Using Groups

Usually, the user rights for access to data such as sales contract templates, current pricing lists, and customer information is the same for a number of clients of your network. Groups let you grant privileges to a set of users so that your clients with the same job function have the correct privileges to do their jobs. You also can group users to ensure that people who perform a variety of functions or who are part of several groups can easily be assigned the correct privileges. As a member of two groups, an individual can have the rights and privileges of both. Start planning how you will group your users. After you know the various groups you need to create, you can develop templates to save you time, instead of creating a new, individual account profile for each person in a group.

For your expedience, Windows 2000 Server has built in the following local groups:

- Account Operators
- Administrators
- Backup Operators
- Guests
- Print Operators
- Replicators
- Server Operators
- Users

In addition, Windows 2000 Server offers the following built-in global groups:

- Domain Admins
- Domain Guests
- Domain Users
- Enterprise Admins

By default, each of these groups is granted a particular set of tasks or user rights. For example, the administrative group has the user rights of an administrative account, but rather than set up each person you want to be an administrator with a unique set of rights, you can simply add their accounts to the administrative group, and they will obtain all the rights and privileges of that group.

NEW TERM *User rights* allow individual users or groups to perform specific tasks on a computer running Windows 2000 Server. User rights provide the capability both to log in locally to a network based on Windows 2000 Server and to access a server across the network.

As mentioned, using groups is an easier method of granting or restricting access to resources than trying to control access on a user-by-user basis. Depending on your needs, you might also want to create customized groups with special rights and privileges. Groups you create usually depend on the structure of your organization and the needs of your users.

For example, an administrator might create groups containing users with the same job, access requirements and restrictions, or location. Again, start planning how to group people in your organization according to the groups to which they naturally belong so that later during setup, it will be easy to create the accounts you'll need.

> **Tip**
>
> You will learn about the Security Reference Model in greater detail starting with Day 4, "Understanding and Managing the Registry."

Planning for Security

Windows 2000 Server includes full security for both the network and the resources stored on the server. As an administrator, you can control server resources your clients can access. Following are some of the major features that make Windows 2000 Server a secure system:

- Mandatory logon to access resources on the server
- Controlled access (and the method of access) to shared resources (for example, files and directories)

- Customized user account security
- Capability to define whom can perform specific tasks
- Tracked access to resources and tasks
- Security on network resources such as CD-ROM drives, printers, directories, and files

All these features represent areas where you have control and areas where you need to plan how you will exercise that control. As you plan and install your network, you should think about using these features to control your system.

A key to Windows 2000 Server security is the requirement that users log on to the server with a password each time. In planning, you should decide on an account policy for your network, including the maximum password age, the minimum and maximum password length, and the password composition.

Using Active Directory

Active Directory is hierarchical, storing each of your company's resources logically, forming a Tree structure that mirrors your enterprise. Every resource in even the largest networks is easy to find and manage.

Planning for Active Directory is one of the most important tasks in your company's transition to or implementation of Windows 2000. When your Active Directory design is good, you can leverage all its benefits. The building blocks of networks built with Active Directory include the following:

- Domains
- Organizational units (OUs)
- Trees
- Forests
- Sites
- The global catalog

Domains

NEW TERM In Windows 2000 Server, a *domain* is a linked set of workstations and servers sharing an Active Directory database that you can administer as a group. Users with an account in a network domain can log on to and access their accounts from any system in the domain. The server that authenticates domain logins and maintains the security policy and the master database for a domain is called the domain controller. A domain name simply is the name of a domain within the network. With a single server, there is usually a single domain. Obviously, creating domains and selecting adequate names is key to a successful Windows 2000 implementation.

Note

Domains built using Active Directory can store millions of objects. The types of objects that can be stored in Active Directory domains are those considered interesting to the networked community. For example, an interesting object can be a user, a group, a printer, and so on.

The types of objects that can be stored in Active Directory domains are defined in the schema. The Active Directory schema is extensible. You can extend it to support objects and properties that are unique to your company. This flexibility gives you the option to store additional types of data in Active Directory to make it more useful, such as an employee hire date.

Each new object and property that you add to the schema requires a unique object identifier (OID). You can obtain a root OID for your organization from your National Registration Authority or NRA. You can find a list of NRAs at http://www.iso.ch. In the United States, the NRA is the American National Institute (ANSI) at http://www.ansi.org.

You can dynamically update the schema in Active Directory. For example, an application can extend the schema and start using the new attributes.

Organizational Units (OUs)

New Term Domains are the smallest units you can use to group resources in NT networks. In Windows 2000, an *Organizational Unit* (OU) is the smallest division. OUs are created to further delineate the domain namespace. This lets you group users, groups, file shares, and other information into a usable hierarchy.

The most significant benefit of configuring OUs in your domains is gained when delegating administrative tasks.

Trees

New Term Like OUs, you can use Trees to further define the Active Directory namespace. A *Tree* is a hierarchy of Windows 2000 domains; each represented by a partition in Active Directory. Your first Windows 2000 domain forms the root of this Tree. Every domain created after it becomes its child. The child domains in turn may have child domains of their own, which creates a parent-child relationship.

An advantage of this parent-child relationship is that children inherit some of the attributes of their parents. For example, when a new domain joins the Tree, it is automatically configured with its parent's common configuration, global catalog, and schema. This information binds the new domain to your Tree. After joining the Tree, your domain maintains its own security. Just as with NT, domains in Windows 2000 are still a security boundary. Parent domain administrators aren't given authority over child domains. However, this doesn't mean that you can't implement a Tree that is centrally administered—you can configure Trees for decentralized or centralized administrative needs.

By leveraging granular access control, you can delegate administrative tasks to sub-administrators for objects in a portion of your domain while retaining control of others. You don't need a resource domain in Windows 2000 for every sub-administrator.

Forests

New Term
If you decide to create your Windows 2000 network with more than one Tree, you can form a Forest. A *Forest is* a collection of two or more Trees, each with its own distinct namespace. When you create a Forest of Trees, a transitive trust relationship is established between the root domains in each Tree. Because this trust is transitive, every domain in the Forest can automatically share resources. Each Tree in a Forest has a common configuration, schema, and global catalog.

Sites

Sites give domain controllers and other computers in a Tree or Forest information to identify areas of good network connectivity. When a site is configured in Active Directory, you assign it one or more TCP/IP subnets. Among other capabilities, sites let you define replication schedules for the partitions in Active Directory. This lets you throttle intrasite and intersite replication traffic.

The Global Catalog

Each domain exists in a separate partition in Active Directory. A domain's partition stores every object in the domain and in each of its properties. The objects contained in one domain aren't replicated to another domain. This is where the global catalog fits in.

The global catalog is built automatically by Active Directory. It has an entry for every object and property existing in a Tree or Forest. The global catalog isn't simply a merged version of every domain partition—every value for each property in a Tree or Forest isn't stored in the global catalog. Instead, it contains the values for a subset of object properties useful to the global community, such as the Logon Name property for a user or the Members property in a universal group.

The global catalog has two main functions:

- Allows network logon by providing Universal group membership information to a domain controller.
- Facilitates directory information lookup regardless of the domain in the forest containing the data.

You have learned quite a lot today. However, one issue still needs to be discussed before you start your installation—licensing.

Managing Your Licenses

To access a Windows 2000 Server network and to meet licensing requirements, you need licenses for the server and for each client connected to the network. This section reviews your licensing options so you can pick the one that best suits your needs.

When you have only one server in your environment, license planning is simple. Just count the number of client workstations that will access the server and purchase client access licenses equal to that number.

When you have more than one server, a better understanding of how your users will access those servers is important because Windows 2000 Server has two licensing options—Per Server and Per Seat. With the Per Server option, you assign each client access license you buy to a particular server, which lets you make one connection to that server. You need as many client access licenses for the server as the maximum number of dedicated clients that will connect to it. This is the most economical option for networks where clients tend to connect to only one server, connect infrequently, or connect to special purpose servers.

With the Per Seat option, a client access license is given to a client. The license gives that client the right to access any Windows 2000 Server in the network. This option is the most economical in a network where clients tend to connect to more than one server.

When you are unsure of which option is optimal for your organization, select the Per Server option because as part of that option you get a one-time, no-charge opportunity to convert your licensing option to Per Seat.

Licensing is complex and causes problems, so Microsoft came up with a tool called the License Manager. Using it is simple.

Task 1.1: Using the Licensing Tool.

Step 1: Description

This task describes how to use the License Manager to see purchase history and product information.

Step 2: Action

1. Log on to the Windows 2000 Server as Administrator.

2. From the Start menu, select Programs, Administrative Tools, Licensing. This opens the dialog box shown in Figure 1.7.

3. Click the Purchase History tab to see a record of all the software licenses you've purchased and entered into the database. The database knows only what you tell it.

FIGURE 1.7

The License Manager dialog box.

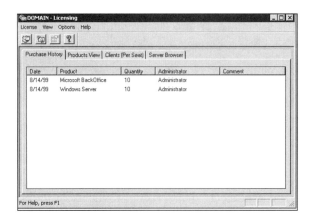

4. Click the Products View tab to see product information for either the entire network or a selected domain. Double-clicking the product name shows a dialog box similar to the one shown in Figure 1.8. Click OK to return.

FIGURE 1.8

The Properties of Microsoft BackOffice dialog box.

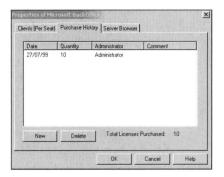

5. Click the Clients (Per Seat) tab to see information about clients who have accessed a particular product throughout the network or for a selected domain.

6. Click the Server Browser tab to see information for other domains. You also can add and delete Per Server client licenses for servers and products and add new Per Seat licenses for the entire enterprise.

Step 3: Review

Use the License Manager to help you ensure that you are in compliance with your licensing agreements.

We have covered a lot on the first day. Take some time to review the following summary information.

Summary

This day discussed many of the elements involved in building a network. However, the information provided is only a guide to assist in the installation and management of your Windows 2000 Server operating system and therefore is far from detailed. Understanding and building a network is an involved and technical task, so we recommend additional study beyond that supplied in this lesson.

In this lesson, you discovered the following points:

- LANs consist of several items, including cables, network cards, and nodes such as servers and clients.
- Servers manage the requests of client machines, allowing specialization and optimization.
- Network standards allow some consistency in how each system operates. Standards such as Token Ring and Ethernet allow you to use standardized hardware and software.
- Devices such as routers and bridges allow several networks to connect and exchange data.
- The sophistication of the Windows 2000 Server network operating system.
- The differences and advantages of Windows 2000–supported file systems.
- The differences and advantages of Windows 2000–supported protocols.
- The planning activities necessary for setting up Windows 2000 Server.

Workshop

To wrap up the day, you can review tasks from the lesson, and see the answers to some commonly asked questions.

Task List

In this lesson, you learned how to perform the following task:

- Use the Licensing Tool

Q&A

Q What wiring topology should be used with Microsoft 2000 Server?

A You can use the wiring that best suits your purpose. Generally, organizations tend to standardize on one type of topology for ease of use. One of the more common configurations in a large office consists of the star-wired configuration. As you might recall, both Token Ring and Ethernet use this configuration.

Windows 2000 Server runs whether you use Token Ring or Ethernet. Ethernet tends to be less expensive.

Q When the 2000 Server fails, does access to the network become unavailable?

A On a Microsoft Windows 2000 Server network, access to the server is necessary for most of the things you might do in your day-to-day work. Access to files, programs, and mail, for example, might become unavailable. If your network consists of only one server, you will be unable to log in. However, many networks contain more than one server, and Windows 2000 allows you to set these up in such a way that if one fails, another takes over, minimizing your loss. You can read more about this in Day 16, "Configuring Fault-Tolerance."

Q Can I connect Windows 2000 Server LANs together?

A You can connect multiple Windows 2000 servers to one LAN. You also might use a Windows 2000 Server as a router between two LANs using different topologies. For example, you might set up a Windows 2000 machine with both a Token Ring card and an Ethernet card and use it to manage traffic between a Novell Ethernet LAN and a Windows 2000 LAN.

Q I want to purchase some hardware and need to know whether my hardware is compatible with Windows 2000 Server. Where can I get a copy of the Hardware Compatibility List?

A The Hardware Compatibility List or HCL ships with every package of Windows 2000 Server software. You also can obtain it from Microsoft Sales Fax Services at 800-727-3551. The order numbers for the Hardware Compatibility List can be found in the Windows 2000 Server section of the catalog. In addition, you can find the HCL online at `ftp://ftp.microsoft.com/services/whql/win2000hcl.txt` or `http://www.microsoft.com/windows/server/default.asp`.

Q What workstation operating systems work with Windows 2000 Server?

A Windows 2000 Server can support workstation computers running MacOS System 7 or greater, MS-DOS, OS/2, Windows 3.1x, Windows for Workgroups 3.11, Windows 95/98, Windows NT Workstation, and Windows 2000 Professional.

DAY 2

Installing Windows 2000 and Client Software

The first benefit gained from purchasing Windows 2000 Server is a greatly improved installation process. Although the older Windows 2000 was not hard to install, Microsoft has added plug and play to this version, and that makes it a much simpler process. Like everything in life, however, there remain plenty of caveats. Windows 2000 is a big, complex piece of software, but handled properly, it is almost simple to install.

Now you might still ask, "If it's so easy to install, does that mean I don't need a Microsoft Certified Professional to help?" Well, as always, the answer depends on you. If you follow the instructions outlined during this day with particular zeal, you might never need additional assistance. Miss a step or two, however, and get out the checkbook.

> **Note**   Throughout this book, we will refer to Windows 2000 Server using the
> shorter term, Windows 2000, as we find the longer term, well, too long! To
> avoid confusion, we will always refer to any other version, such as Windows
> 2000 Professional, using its official, complete name.

In this day, you learn the following points:

- How to use the Hardware Compatibility List prior to installing Windows 2000
- What preparation is necessary before the installation of Windows 2000
- How to license your software using a Per Server or Per Seat method
- Which type of hard disk format you should use during install
- How to configure Windows 95 and 98, Windows 2000 Professional, and MacOS
  clients
- How to log on to Windows 2000 Server from the various clients
- How to join a computer to a domain

First Things First

Windows 2000 Server remains very, very particular about the hardware base it resides
on. Before you begin, therefore, you must ensure that the hardware you use is fully
prepared and compatible with Windows 2000 Server.

To load Windows 2000, ensure that you have these requirements:

- Machine and devices from the Hardware Compatibility List
- Appropriate Intel or Alpha version of Windows 2000
- Pentium 166 or greater with 64MB of memory
- At least 650MB of hard drive space

Microsoft offers a number of ways for you to check your hardware configuration before
you load Windows 2000. First, your machine might already be designed for it and will
have the "Designed for Windows 2000" logo on it, similar to the older "Designed for
Microsoft Windows 2000" logo. In addition, Microsoft still publishes a Hardware
Compatibility List (HCL) that contains every device that manufacturers have paid
Microsoft to test and add to the list. If you don't find particular vendors on the list, don't
despair! Call them and ask if they are Windows 2000–compatible. They might not have
paid the Microsoft fee, or their software might still be in the test phase. You can find the

HCL on the Internet, complete with a search engine that will make your search easier, at the Microsoft address:

`http://www.microsoft.com`

Windows 2000 runs on a number of different platforms, including Intel and Alpha. Make sure you have the correct version of Windows 2000 for your platform. Microsoft now recommends at least a 166MHz Pentium class processor to run Windows 2000. A Pentium III is probably desirable.

Windows 2000 4.0 ran using 12MB of memory, although if you actually wanted to do something, you needed at least 16MB. That is no longer the case. (My, how times change!) You now need a minimum of 64MB of memory and at least 650MB of hard drive free space before Windows 2000 will let you complete the install! Once installed, however, the actual hard drive space used will likely be less. Microsoft recommends using at least 128MB of RAM. To calculate how much disk space you need, Microsoft makes a number of recommendations.

Microsoft suggests starting with 850MB and adding 2MB for each MB of memory on your computer. Next, you'll need to consider whether additional components are being installed; the more components, the more space needed. In addition, if you insist on using a FAT-based file system, it will require 100MB–200MB of additional free disk space.

Finally, space depends on the method used for installation: For installing across the network, you need to allow for 100MB–200MB of additional space because additional driver files need to be available during installation across the network, as compared to installing from the CD.

Caution	Don't install Windows 2000 or upgrade to Windows 2000 on a compressed drive unless the drive was compressed with the NTFS compression utility. Uncompress a DriveSpace or DoubleSpace volume before running Windows 2000 Setup on it.

As with any version of NT, oops, I mean Windows 2000, the more memory you feed it, the faster it goes. I run Windows 2000 Server on my Dell laptop with 128MB of RAM, and it runs very well, but I don't really make any true use of it. (I use it mostly for writing this book and doing seminars.) It would not even load on my older Toshiba, because that machine has only 40MB of memory. To run additional services such as IIS or SQL Server, you are going to need even more memory, and you are likely to find 128MB or more becoming the norm.

Many of the hardware limitations in the older version are removed, and Windows 2000 offers enhanced capabilities. Microsoft strongly recommended using a VGA video card on the server. Windows 2000 now supports a huge number of video cards and, if you want to use your ATI Technologies XPERT@Work (3D Rage Pro PCI) or other high-end video card, go right ahead. Just be sure that the card you choose is on the HCL. The Windows 2000 VGA driver remains a default option, however, and is just fine for the average server. After all, it is your workstations that really need high-end graphics, not the average server.

Windows 2000 supports most types of hard drives, although its SCSI host adapter support is very good and worth considering for several reasons. First, SCSI is faster than EIDE and, second, disk mirroring and RAID need SCSI to work well.

NEW TERM Before starting to install Windows 2000, check the hard disk for errors. Windows 2000 loads data to disk heavily in a process it calls *paging*. This allows Windows 2000 to use disk space as additional memory. When Windows 2000 recovers that paged data, it doesn't check to see if what it saved is what it gets in return. It expects the data to be reliable and safe. Make sure that your disk drive is fully tested for errors before you begin to load Windows 2000.

A good CD-ROM drive is a must when installing Windows 2000 Server. Microsoft recommends using at least a 12x CD-ROM, although I have installed it with older 4x drives. No one uses floppy disks anymore and, in fact, you cannot get Windows 2000 that way, so you must use a CD-ROM or network drive to install it. Almost all machines come with a CD-ROM drive these days, so this generally isn't a problem. If you are using an older machine, don't. It isn't likely to be fast enough, might not be supported, and will only cause you pain. Support the local economy and buy a new machine. You'll never regret it.

The type of network interface card (NIC) you use is entirely up to you—as long as it is listed in the HCL, that is. Whether you plan to use an ethernet or token ring network, make sure that you write down any settings you use when installing the card. You might need them later when things go bump in the night. Test the card before continuing with the Windows 2000 installation.

You test NICs in a couple of ways. Perform the onboard diagnostic. Perform a loopback test. If you have a network already set up, you might also try a live test. These tests are usually found on the diagnostics disk that ships with your network card. The first test verifies the card settings, such as the IRQ and I/O address. The loopback test sends a piece of data out and back to the card, verifying basic functioning. You need a specific connector for this that you purchase at your local network dealer. The network test does the same thing as the loopback, except that it passes the data through the network using another machine.

Windows 2000 now includes the Plug and Play technology you are familiar with from Windows 95 and 98. Devices (for example, video and network "cards" or adapters) are automatically recognized by the operating system, configuration conflicts are avoided, and you no longer have to specify each device's settings by hand. You need to be aware, though, that Microsoft has not included the number of devices you might be accustomed to with Windows 98. It's still best to be sure that you are using compatible equipment or you might need to manually verify and add components. Worse, you might find that there is no support for that device.

After you've verified all your hardware, you are ready to install Windows 2000. One last message: Check the Hardware Compatibility List. I cannot stress this enough. Although the installation process is greatly improved in Windows 2000, it still pays to minimize your potential problems. If all your equipment is listed, your install has a great chance of going so smoothly that you'll be amazed. Also, if it isn't on the list, you might receive only limited technical support from Microsoft until that device is replaced or updated with one that is on the HCL.

Preparing for the Install

Now that you have all the hardware verified, you can move to the next step. If you are moving to Windows 2000 from another server, now is the time to back up your data. If you are setting up a brand new server, there really isn't anything to do in the way of data backup. The following sections guide you through the backup process. These steps will ensure that your data is safe if you should have problems installing Windows 2000.

Use Another Machine for Backup

If you have the luxury of more than one server on your network, you might use one of the other servers to do your backup, provided it has sufficient disk storage. Do an XCOPY /S command from the server you are upgrading to the other machine. After you have Windows 2000 set up and running, do an XCOPY to get the data back.

Use a Tape Drive to Back Up

You can use a tape drive to back up all your data. Use third-party software such as Cheyenne ARCserve to back up the data and later restore it. There are some problems with this approach, however. If you move from a DOS *File Allocation Table* (*FAT*) file system server such as Windows for Workgroups to the *New Technology File System* (*NTFS*), the files that you previously backed up become unavailable.

The reason for losing access to your data comes from the manner in which tape backup devices work. When recovering files, most tape drives depend on the operating system that was used to back up the files, and many of the tape backup programs use proprietary formats to write data back onto the hard drive. Using a DOS-based backup program and running it under NT to recover the files just won't work. In the book *Mastering Windows 2000 Server 4* (Network Press, 1996), the authors suggest that one sound method consists of backing up to a FAT volume and initially setting up Windows 2000 Server 4 with a FAT volume. After it's set up, restore the backups and then convert the new NT volume to NTFS. This is a tried-and-true method of ensuring that your data remains available to you after the conversion.

 Note

> Earlier, we discussed the problems associated with backup if you used a FAT-based system prior to installing the newer NTFS. Although this still applies, we believe most readers will be migrating from an NT system using NTFS, so this should not be as much of a problem in Windows 2000.
>
> Although Windows 2000 offers the option of installing on a FAT-based hard drive, doing so will not support Active Directory. This advanced feature is a major part of the new operating system, and not using it eliminates the ability to set up domains. In addition, to obtain the file and directory security features of Windows 2000 Server, you must use NTFS.

Be sure that any software you use to back up your data onto tape will run on the new Windows 2000 system or you might experience difficulties trying to restore the data.

Final Thoughts Before Installation

Now you are almost ready to insert the CD-ROM. Before you do, think of these questions and provide the answers:

- Do you know how you want to partition the hard drive?
- Are you going to install or upgrade?
- Do you have all the hardware settings documented?
- If you plan to use TCP/IP, what are all the protocol settings? What type of server do you want?
- What kind of product license do you want to use?

Thinking about these questions and providing the answers before inserting that CD-ROM will make your install perform as smoothly as a NASA space shuttle launch. (Not that you need to be a rocket scientist or anything—oh, heck. You know what I mean.)

Partitioning the Hard Drive

As you remember from earlier versions of NT, using NTFS has its strengths; it allows file-level security. It also has its weakness; you cannot use DOS-based, low-level utilities to read or manipulate the drive. Unless this is the first NT system you've ever installed, you will already know this. Unlike older versions, Windows 2000 also supports the newer FAT32 file system. However, unless absolutely necessary, stick to NTFS. Note that you must use NTFS on all domain controllers.

Install or Upgrade?

Deciding whether to install or to upgrade is dependent on you. An upgrade usually means installing on top of your existing system, eliminating it and replacing it with the new version. A new install allows you to choose between two different systems if one already exists on your machine. Do you have one machine running Windows 2000 or Windows 95 on it and want that system in addition to Windows 2000? Do you have a new machine that you are planning to use only for this exercise?

You can upgrade to Windows 2000 from

- Windows 95 or 98
- Windows 2000 Workstation
- Windows 2000 version 3.51 Server
- Windows 2000 version 4.0 Server or Windows 2000 version 4.0 Terminal Server

Since it is hard to know which upgrade each reader might choose, for the purpose of this book, I provide directions for a new installation.

Documenting Hardware Setup

Since you go through your new machine setup, you will find that there is little need for documenting all the settings for the NIC, modem, sound card, and so on like there used to be. Windows 2000 Plug and Play will manage most of these installations automatically, ensuring that hardware conflicts and setting IRQs and the like are a thing of the past. It's similar to Windows 95 or 98 in this manner. You might want to preempt any difficulties and document all these settings before you begin. Sometimes a little work performed early is worth its weight in gold later on.

TCP/IP Settings and Server Selection

Setting up TCP/IP still requires a copious number of addresses: IP addresses, subnet masks, default gateways, and DNS servers as they are distinct to your organization. Make sure you know them all before beginning. That way, you will not get stuck in the middle of an install, trying to guess.

The type of server you want is a little more complicated. The Windows 2000 install program wants to know if you plan on creating a standalone server or are adding to an existing domain. It doesn't use the terms *primary domain server* or *backup domain server* as NT 4.0 did during its install process.

The decision to make your machine standalone or part of the network is less critical than it was. One reason is that the new version doesn't insist on setting up one particular type of machine like NT 4/0 did. As you might recall, that version wanted to know whether your machine was going to be a domain controller or a standalone server. Windows 2000 doesn't insist anymore that you decide at install time and lets you decide at a later date. Now Windows 2000 only needs to know whether you are adding the machine to a network you already have installed or want to start a new one. You'll learn more about this on Day 5, "Introducing Active Directory."

NEW TERM   What's this *domain* thing? The word is used in many ways but, within the Microsoft Windows 2000 Server world, it means groups of Windows 2000 machines that delegate security tasks to one or more of their machines. They call these machines *domain controllers*.

The older NT 4.0 system operated on a master/slave basis, with one machine designated as the boss—the primary domain controller. This machine then managed all user accounts, passwords, and other security features. Windows 2000 uses all controllers in a multiple master domain relationship, with each machine providing that function using a thing called Active Directory.

NEW TERM   To understand what Active Directory is, you need to know that a *directory* is an information source used to store information about objects. A *directory service*, such as Active Directory, includes the directory itself and all the services that are used to make the information available.

With Active Directory, users can access resources anywhere on the network, using a single network logon. Similarly, administrators have a single point of administration for all objects on the network, which can be organized into a hierarchical structure.

Windows 2000 domains provide a number of benefits:

- Grouping objects into domains allows you to implement Windows 2000 and have it reflect your company's organization.
- Each domain is a piece of the network, storing only the information about the objects located in that domain. By splitting it this way, Active Directory lets you scale up to as many objects as you need. NT 4.0 limited the size of your domain.

- Each domain remains a *security boundary*, meaning that security policies and settings (such as administrative rights, security policies, and access lists) don't cross from one domain to another. The administrator of a domain has rights to set policies only within that domain.

In Windows 2000, a domain contains objects such as organizational units (OUs), users, computers, printers, and files. If you understand how NetWare 4.x is managed, you will find it very easy to understand the new Windows 2000 objects. Microsoft states that the directory of each domain can contain as many as 10 million objects, so the size of domain is no longer much of an issue. You'll learn more about this on Day 5.

Windows 2000 Server administrative rights are granted at the domain level by default, but you can also grant administrative rights using a finer granularity. One welcome new change allows you to give users rights to perform specific administrative tasks on specific portions of the domain, thus eliminating the need for all your administrators to have sweeping authority over an entire domain.

With Windows 2000, servers can have one of three roles:

- Domain controllers
- Member servers
- Standalone servers

Domain controllers contain matching copies of the user accounts and other security data for a given domain. Member servers belong to a domain and are administered as part of that domain but don't contain a copy of the Active Directory data. Standalone servers don't belong to a domain at all but instead belong to a workgroup. Obviously, a domain must have at least one domain controller and should generally have multiple domain controllers, providing backup and logon support to users.

I recommend that you plan the roles that each server will occupy within your domain before running Setup, but if adjustments are necessary to these roles, unlike NT 4.0, they can still be made after Setup.

When you install Windows 2000, you are asked whether the machine you are installing is part of a network or a standalone machine.

I will assume you are setting up your first Windows 2000 machine and aren't planning to join an existing domain. You could join your company's NT domain; however, if you are reading this book, you are likely testing or learning about Windows 2000. That means your test machine should not be part of your company network. Create a new network, use an existing testing network, or create a standalone machine and learn. It's safer.

2

After you create your first machine, you tell Windows 2000 to make it a controller and install Active Directory, hence creating a Windows 2000 domain. You then add other servers and designate each one a task, ensuring that at least one is another controller for backup. As backups, they contain the security information necessary to allow them to share the workload by verifying user authentication (login) requests.

Finally, you add member-servers as needed to complete your network. These might be machines that provide services or applications to clients but require login and authentication before allowing any access.

In a domain, Microsoft decided that users might not want to log on to each and every server they encounter before getting access to files and services—hence, the approach of a domain controller using Active Directory. These machines control all user logins and authentication. The difference with Windows 2000 machines is that all controllers act in this role. There is no primary machine as there was with NT 4.0. With this approach, a user needs to log on to the network only once and, each time he needs the services of a different server, Windows 2000 manages the login—a single sign-on with one user account name and one password. Neat! The closest controller authenticates the user, reducing wait times on a busy network and spreading the login load across many machines. To maintain itself, Windows 2000 ensures that it replicates any changes made on one controller to all the other controllers at regular intervals. It is no longer critical to decide the order in which you create your servers. Before, if you were creating a new domain, you made the first server you added the primary domain controller. Additional servers became backup domain controllers as needed. Now, Windows 2000 lets you change the type of machine after installation.

Finally, during this phase of the install, Windows 2000 creates an Administrator account for you. This account has authority over all servers in the domain, so don't forget the password! If you do, you must re-install the server or learn a few specialist tricks.

| Tip | Day 5 discusses domain management in more depth. |

Server Licensing

Finally, the type of server license you use is determined by a complex, arcane algorithm created by Microsoft to make life as difficult as possible. I would have thought that Bill Gates might have considered changing this aspect to make life easier for all those Windows 2000 support folks, but oh no! That would be too easy. So you're stuck with the same old process.

Microsoft allows two types of client licenses for its Windows 2000 Server software, Per Seat and Per Server. What's a client license? After buying the server software, you need to license each person who uses that server. This license is figurative. It doesn't actually do anything; it merely allows you to use the server legally.

It is easier to understand if you consider the Per Seat as a Per Person approach. You must decide which approach you'll use before you install the product, because the installation asks for your decision and doesn't continue until you enter your choice. After you decide, it allows you to change your mind only once without re-installing the server.

A Per Seat approach to licensing means you need to buy a license from Microsoft for each user. If you have 100 users who will log in and use the domain, you need 100 licenses. Each of these users can access all your Windows 2000 servers using this license. It becomes a complicated decision, depending on how many users will access the domain at any one time. For example, if your organization employs temporary workers, how many licenses do you buy? In a fluid employee situation, you can easily have licenses but no people to use them.

The Per Server license works differently. It suggests that one person access the server at a time. Buy 100 Per Server licenses, and you can have 100 people on the domain at any one time. In a shift worker situation, you could buy enough licenses for one shift because another shift never (theoretically) signs on at the same time. In the Per Seat approach, you need enough licenses for all the workers, regardless of shift. You buy additional licenses for each server you add. Generally, if you have two or more servers, the Per Server option is the way to go.

Outfitted with this information, you are ready to continue and start installing Windows 2000 Server.

Tip

For more information on licensing, see the Licensing Manager task in Day 1, "Introducing Networks and Windows 2000."

Installing the Windows 2000 Server Program

You have two ways to start the installation program. Either way works just fine. Microsoft recommends a fast CD-ROM drive, but I have installed it using an old 4x drive. The two ways to start the installation program are

1. Use the WINNT or WINNT32 program on your CD-ROM.
2. Insert the CD-ROM and the first startup floppy and reboot.

The following sections discuss these methods.

Tip

> Before you begin, consider running an up-to-date virus protection program. The Windows 2000 install process gets really annoyed if it finds a virus, and it doesn't allow the install to conclude properly. Be sure to remove the virus program before the Windows 2000 install, however, and make sure it doesn't get started automatically when the machine restarts. A Windows 2000 installation requires a reboot and becomes ugly if it finds a virus scanner running. In addition, unplug any UPS devices you might be using, because the installation process might have trouble detecting them.

Using the WINNT or WINNT32 Program

The beta CD-ROM that Microsoft supplies with Windows 2000 Server arrived with only one version of the product and didn't offer Alpha or other platforms. This might change by the time it reaches general release. Intel users will still choose the folder called I386, whereas Alpha-based machines will use a different directory.

You install Windows 2000 from the CD-ROM, from a network drive, or from a hard disk on the local machine. To do either of the latter, copy the appropriate directory, such as I386, onto the desired location and run the WINNT or WINNT32 command from there. You use the WINNT command if you're installing from DOS or Windows, and you use the WINNT32 command if you are upgrading from an older version of Windows 2000. On Windows 2000, 95, or 98 machines, the installation CD-ROM automatically starts after you insert the CD-ROM. Finally, use the /b and /s switches following the WINNT or WINNT32 command to install solely from the CD-ROM.

 Tip

> Before installing Windows 2000, you can see what options are available by inserting the CD (hold the Shift key so the install doesn't start) and typing **Winnt /?** at a command line. This opens a window showing you a number of options you can use when installing the product.

Using the Floppies and CD-ROM

Using the floppies and CD-ROM is only slightly different in execution. Insert the floppy called "Setup Boot Disk" into drive A and reboot your machine. Not all the Windows 2000 software is on these floppies, only the bare minimum needed to start up the install program. The first thing Windows 2000 install does is run a machine configuration program called NTDETECT.COM that determines what kind of hardware and software you have on the system. A message from the program tells you that it is inspecting your hardware configuration. Finally, if you're performing a new installation and your machine will boot from the CD, place the Windows 2000 CD in the drive, and then power-on the machine. The install will start automatically.

> **Tip**
>
> If NTDETECT.COM hangs and doesn't appear to want to continue with the setup, reboot the machine under DOS and run the debug version. This version tells you everything it does (in painful detail, so don't use it indiscriminately) and allows you to see where the problem lies. Follow these steps:
>
> 1. Rename the existing NTDETECT.COM or copy it to a safe location.
> 2. Copy the file called NTDETECT.CHK from the CD-ROM. (It's located in a directory called support/debug/i386/ntdetect.chk.)
> 3. Rename this file NTDETECT.COM and execute the program.
> 4. Remember to replace everything at the finish so you don't run the debug version later inadvertently.

If you started the install and already have a Windows system on the machine, you'll see a message asking if you want to upgrade that system to Windows 2000.

Next, you see a blue screen and the words "Windows 2000 Setup" as the install continues. The next thing you see is the End User Licensing Agreement. If you are in the habit of ignoring these, don't. You cannot continue without clicking Yes. After Windows 2000 asks for the second floppy, a few messages appear that indicate that Windows 2000 configuration data, fonts, PCMCIA (or PC card as it's becoming known), and other items are being loaded. Finally, the Windows 2000 kernel loads and tells you the version and build number and sets up the Welcome to Setup message with options to continue, repair, or exit. Because this is a fresh install, ignore the repair option. You use that option to fix Windows 2000 when things go wrong. That option is discussed more in the section called "Creating the Emergency Repair Disk," later in this lesson.

Choosing not to upgrade a machine with Windows 2000 already on it and using the original install directory removes all prior security information, forcing you to start all over and add all your users and other information. (I'll tell you all about this on Day 5, when I discuss Active Directory.) This might be okay if you decide that the old version needs rebuilding anyway. If your previous version was well used and you don't want to re-enter all your users, choose the upgrade option. The upgrade option keeps the existing security information, preserving all your user account data. (This doesn't prevent you from installing more than one copy of NT on your machine. In fact, many sites place a backup copy on the server for recovery purposes by selecting the latter option above and specifying a new root directory for the second install.)

To gain up-to-date information and details concerning special considerations, such as upgrading from beta versions or older versions of NT, read the setup.txt file in your specific installation directory.

Replying to the prompt by pressing Enter (to continue) and loading disk 3 and disk 4 continues the setup.

Windows 2000 Setup

Now that Setup is underway, Windows 2000 continues finding out what hardware is on your system. If you followed the earlier instructions when setting up the machine for this installation, this phase will pleasantly surprise you as it continues with few, if any, problems.

When you pass this step, Windows 2000 Setup tells you what it believes you have on the system. This includes the following components:

- The type of PC
- Video card
- Keyboard
- Mouse

By now, you should be getting accurate information. The only interesting part here concerns the video driver. You notice that the Windows 2000 Setup program sets your video card to VGA mode. This might be disconcerting if you know that you have super VGA capabilities on your card.

Windows 2000 does this for a very good reason. The good people at Microsoft figured that if they let administrators pick a video card, they might mess it up and pick the wrong one, making the install unable to boot. Knowing that current VGA drivers work on almost every card available today, they decided that using this mode helps ensure a smooth install. You change the mode later after Windows 2000 is set up. Finally, to make sure you can always boot Windows 2000 regardless of whether you mess up a video card change, the Windows 2000 Setup program includes an option in the OS Picker called [VGA Mode]. No matter what you do, you can always use this command to load Windows 2000, because changes you make to video card drivers modify the other command line, the default startup command, always leaving you with the [VGA Mode] command to fall back on.

Disk Partitions

Now that you have progressed smoothly, Windows 2000 Setup wants to know what disk partition you want to install Windows 2000 on. It starts by showing you the available partitions. If you have only one, choose that partition and press Enter. If you have multiple disk partitions, select the specific partition Windows 2000 will reside on and press Enter.

The Setup program gives you a number of options concerning this partition, and it is at this stage of the setup that you decide whether to use a FAT-based file system or move to NT's NTFS.

If you are dual-booting Windows 2000, make sure you don't choose to format or convert the existing partition to NTFS, or your Windows, NT, or other operating system will be gone if you are using the same partition for both operating systems.

FAT or NTFS?

Which system should you use? It depends. Take a look at some of the considerations. First, unless there is a compelling reason why you shouldn't use NTFS, you should use it. Why? Windows 2000 file and directory security is dependent on the newer NTFS. Secondly, Windows 2000 insists on this for domain controllers. Using a FAT-based partition leaves your server vulnerable to unauthorized access and provides no user controls over access to the files and directories on your system.

If you maintain old DOS-based programs or files, this is a reason to stay with the FAT-based file system. Perhaps you might maintain a small FAT-based partition for this reason. It is unlikely that you need the entire system to be FAT based. Having a separate FAT-based partition does allow some of the DOS-based utilities available for use in case you have server problems. This will leave the FAT-based partition vulnerable but ensures that your server files and programs are protected with available NTFS security options. You will find though, that most DOS applications work just fine under NT on NTFS volumes.

Tip

Moving to NTFS doesn't prevent you from booting from a DOS floppy and reading the hard disk. You need third-party software to do it, but this has been available on the Internet for some time, allowing anyone to read an NTFS file after booting from a DOS floppy. Try this site for further information:

http://www.sysinternals.com

Using NTFS offers the ultimate protection for your server. Among these benefits are sorted directories, access permissions for each file and directory, faster access, filenames of up to 254 characters, and improved space utilization.

After you decide on which file system to use, the Setup program asks you to tell it what directory it should use to install the files. Use the default of \winnt or create your own if you have a corporate naming standard. After checking your hard disks for corruption, Windows 2000 Setup copies more files and finally (after about 10–15 minutes using the CD-ROM) asks you to reboot the system.

Continuing Setup

After your computer reboots and finishes running the NTDETECT program (I told you to replace the debug version), you get a short message indicating that you can return to the "Last Known Good Menu." NTDETECT and this message appear each time you boot Windows 2000. You cannot make use of the message at this time because there isn't a previous menu but, in the future, it allows you to recover from some of your boo-boos, such as making a mistake when editing the Registry.

Windows 2000 next asks you to personalize your copy by entering your name and company name. I suggest leaving your name blank, unless you really want the recognition in perpetuity. Use the correct product number because if you leave it blank or create a random number, you cannot communicate with any other server using the identical number. Click Continue when you are finished and again to verify.

Now you need to enter what type of licensing option you are using, Per Seat or Per Server. The Per Seat option is considered Per User, whereas Per Server means each person must have a license for each server they connect and log on to. Specify the proper number of licenses you own in the box provided, or printer and file services, among others, will not start.

| **Caution** | You use the Licensing icon in the Control Panel to change from Per Server to Per Seat only once before needing to re-install. You cannot legally change from Per Seat at all without re-installing. |

Now you need to specify what type of server you are creating. Remember that I discussed the pros and cons of each type earlier. (Before specifying the server type, you have to assign a computer name to your server.) Remember that, unlike NT 4.0, you get to change your mind later if necessary. The install asks if you are connecting to an existing network. For our purposes, don't connect to an existing network, because I don't want to confuse things at this stage by having your machine interface with existing NT machines. When you finish this book, you can choose to convert existing machines and add Windows 2000 to your network.

Remember to carefully account for any Administrator passwords you create. Not only must you guard against unauthorized persons discovering the password, but you also must guard against losing or forgetting the password. It cannot be easily re-created without re-installing Windows 2000. A good idea for this password is to make sure it is at least seven characters long and contains a few special characters, such as &, %, and $.

Creating the Emergency Repair Disk

What is an emergency repair disk and why do you need one? One of the options available when installing Windows 2000 is to perform an emergency repair. If you prepare a disk at this stage, the disk will provide Windows 2000 with just enough information to bring up your system (during an emergency) based on the last time you updated the disk.

When something goes wrong, you first attempt to recover using the Last Known Good option provided when Windows 2000 first loads. This option supplies you with the last time Windows 2000 started successfully and at least one user signed on. If this fails to recover the system, use the emergency repair disk.

The emergency repair disk stores the critical system configuration files needed to recover Windows 2000. The first time you run the disk, it creates the system with Guest and Administrator accounts only. All your user data is lost. (I'll tell you how to update the disk a little later in this chapter.) To repair a system, boot your machine and insert the disk when requested, replying **R** for repair when asked. It then asks for your setup disks; follow the instructions to finalize the repair and reboot the system. This is somewhat analogous to Windows 95/98 startup disks, offering a way to fix startup problems.

Tip

> If you cannot find your repair disk or didn't create one despite our warning, Windows 2000 helps by keeping a version of it in your main Windows 2000 directory in a subdirectory called repair. You can just copy this to a floppy or point the repair process to that directory.

Because it is unlikely that you'll want to restore your Windows 2000 system to the original setup parameters (after you use Windows 2000 for a while), you need to update this repair disk regularly.

To do this, run the program called Backup; on the Welcome screen you'll see an option called Emergency Repair Disk. Follow the instructions until it finishes. You find the program in Start + Programs +Accessories +Backup.

A new feature of this program is its capability to also back up the system state information. Figure 2.2 shows the Backup program open at the Welcome screen.

FIGURE 2.1

Running the Backup program.

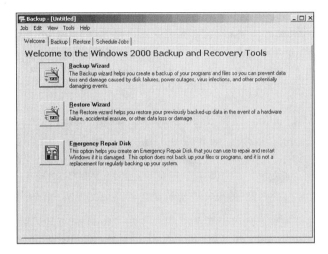

Within the options available is one called System State. This option backs up your Registry and Active Directory, among other things. It provides the ability to recover the system if you should lose or corrupt system files. Backup updates the directory called \winnt\repair (assuming you installed Windows 2000 in the winnt directory) as well as providing a repair floppy disk.

Following this process helps ensure that the final option, re-installing Windows 2000, is rarely needed. You find more detailed information on backup and recovery techniques on Day 15, "File Backup and Recovery," and Day 16, "Configuring Fault-Tolerance."

How often do you run the Backup Repair disk option? I recommend that you run it each time you make major changes to your system, such as adding a multitude of users or programs. You can also run it at least on a monthly or weekly basis, depending on the amount of change to your system. This way, the next time you need to repair Windows 2000, your Registry and SAM will be up to date, and you will not need to re-enter too much information.

Naturally, if you are using commercial software such as Cheyenne's ARCserve program, it might be unnecessary to run Backup, because these commercial programs are far better at providing for both system and data backup and recovery.

As you continue the Setup program, you encounter the section that requires you to tell Windows 2000 what software components to install. These include items such as Microsoft Messaging and Remote Access Services. Include those you need and follow the instructions as presented. Don't worry about it if you are unsure of what you want to use. You can add them later.

The Windows 2000 installation then moves to the next phase, installing networking components.

Network Setup

During the network setup of Windows 2000, you will need to address the following issues:

• Connecting to the network

• Installing network cards

• Installing the protocols you have selected to use

• Service installation

• Security needs of setup

• Time zone and rebooting

Connecting to the Network

First, the Windows 2000 installation moves into the network phase by asking you how you will connect. If you are setting up Windows 2000 as part of an existing network, you need to be physically connected to that network.

The install process informs you that Windows 2000 needs to know how this computer should participate in a network.

The install process shows you the following messages and asks for your input:

```
Do not connect this computer to a network at this time.

This computer will participate on a network.

Wired to the network.

Remote access to the network.
```

Reply by selecting This Computer Will Participate on a Network or Wired to the Network to cause the Windows 2000 installation to continue. After you reply, you are asked if you want to install Microsoft Internet Server (IIS). To simplify the install, reply No at this time. You will review the install and setup of IIS in several days when you review Day 18, "Using BackOffice and Terminal Services."

Installing Network Cards

Setup now asks you to select and install your network card. Windows 2000 does a very good job of finding and auto-detecting your card, especially if you use only approved hardware. If not, you might find out now why it is a good idea to use compatible components—when Windows 2000 cannot automatically find and configure your network card.

If your card isn't automatically detected, you might find it by manually reviewing the choices provided. You do this by selecting the option No, I Want to Select Hardware from a List. Windows 2000 then shows you a list of hardware. Select Network Adapters from the list and then select the vendor of your device. If it isn't there, click the Have Disk button and use the Windows 2000 driver software supplied with your card. You see an example of this in Figure 2.2.

FIGURE 2.2

Selecting a network card.

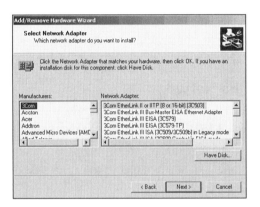

 Tip

Software? With the card? Now, you are really in deep. Take our advice. If you cannot find a Windows 2000 driver for your card, save yourself oodles of trouble and go buy a new card that is on the approved list. You won't regret it!

Now that your card is set up, you need to tell the install the IRQ, I/O, and RAM addresses your card uses. Because you wrote those down when you installed the card, just insert them now.

Installing Protocols

Next, you need to tell the install process what protocols you are using. The install automatically assumes you want NetBEUI, TCP/IP, and IPX/SPX. Unless you plan to use Novell's NetWare with this server, deselect IPX/SPX. NetBEUI, on the other hand, is necessary, so continue the install using that option.

> **Tip**
>
> For more information on what type of protocols to select for your network, refer back to Table 1.4 in Day 1.

Service Installation

Setup then asks if you want to install services. It installs the RPC configuration and NetBIOS interface by default. You can install a whole pile of other services, but we suggest you bring up a fairly light version first to become used to Windows 2000. Add services later as you become more accustomed to the product.

Some of the services you can add include

- Internet Information Server
- Gateway Services for Novell
- DNS and DHCP Servers
- Remote Access Service (RAS)
- TCP/IP and SNMP

Windows 2000 Setup continues and installs those services selected. This might take a while, depending on how many services you select. Remember, though, for the purposes of this book, don't go hog wild and add everything; it will just get confusing for you later.

Security

If you chose to install into an existing domain, Setup wants some more information about the role of security on your machine. Recall that in NT 4.0 you decided what type of machine to install—domain, backup, or standalone server. You need to tell Windows 2000 whether this machine is joining a workgroup or domain. This is because all Windows 2000 servers and workstations must be granted access to join a domain; they cannot just add themselves.

Windows 2000 Server is a very secure system and needs to validate all other machines in the network, with one caveat: They are validated only if they are Windows 2000 servers or Windows 2000 workstations or earlier versions of NT. A DOS, Windows, or OS/2 machine isn't validated. As long as you have a valid account and password, you can use these machines on the network, but only the Windows 2000 and NT machines will be centrally managed by the administrator. If you are adding a new Windows 2000 machine to an existing domain, you need to use Server Manager and tell the existing machine to expect to hear from a new one.

Setting the Time Zone and Rebooting

Finally, initial setup is nearly complete. Setup will want you to tell it the time zone you are in. Follow the prompts to select the appropriate zone. The Windows 2000 Setup program will reboot (possibly more than once, depending on the options selected earlier, such as using the NTFS conversion program), and you have the basic operating system up and running. Before you can do anything, you will need to press Ctrl+Alt+Del. Although this might seem strange, it remains Windows 2000's way of ensuring that you sign in before doing anything. You'll learn more about this is Day 6, "Introducing Security Services." You now see that the initial Windows desktop has changed from the blue clouds of NT 4.0 to one that looks as shown in Figure 2.3.

FIGURE 2.3

The Windows 2000 Server main screen.

Does this mean you're finished? Well, yes and no. Use the present system for the next couple of days and get a feel for what Windows 2000 looks like and see how similar it is to the Windows 95 and NT 4.0 interface. You might decide later to add additional printers or some application programs to see how they run.

Migrating from Other Systems

If you are currently using another product such as Windows, NetWare, or Windows 95 and 98, there a few issues you want to review prior to your install of Windows 2000. These include

- Dual booting
- Migrating applications from Windows
- Migrating applications from Windows 2000 3.51

Dual Boot

NEW TERM   *Dual boot* means retaining an existing operating system such as Windows 95 or Windows 98 and choosing which system to use at boot time. Most people don't use this system because Windows 2000 Server is rather expensive for occasional users. However, there are times when you might choose such an option. For example, I installed Windows 2000 Server in dual boot mode on my laptop. This allows me the option of using my existing system for consulting work while retaining the capability to boot Windows 2000 Server for client seminars and, of course, for writing this book.

The good news with Windows 2000 is that it automatically installs itself in dual boot mode if it finds another system on the install drive and you tell it not to convert that system. This applies to DOS, Windows 95, Windows 98, and older versions of Windows NT.

When you boot your system after installing Windows 2000 in addition to another operating system, you see messages such as these:

1. `Windows 2000 Server`

2. `Windows 2000 Server [VGA Mode]`

3. `Microsoft Windows`

4. `Using default version in 30 seconds`

The boot process will automatically bring up Windows 2000 after a default time period of 30 seconds if you do nothing. Otherwise, select the system you plan to use and continue with the boot process.

The only major caveat to dual booting concerns the hard drive and security. Some of you might be under the illusion that Windows 2000 security is so strong, physical control over the server is unnecessary. Get this straight right now: If anyone has physical access to your server, you don't have any security! The chapters on security discuss this in more detail, but it's important enough to mention here. Regardless of whether you use a FAT-based or an NTFS-based file system, if someone gains access to the server, he can break any level of file security used by the operating system and access your data. The only way you change this is by using an encryption tool to fully encrypt your data files.

> **Caution**
>
> Windows 2000 can use Microsoft's newer FAT32 file system. Unlike NT 4.0, which cannot be booted from a FAT32 partition, you can choose any of the Windows partition types. Trying to dual-boot using FAT32 for Windows 2000 and a Windows 4.0 system will cause the NT 4.0 version to fail.

For the hard drive, the caveat concerns the space and type of file system you use in a dual boot scenario. For DOS or Windows, you need to remain FAT based, leaving you without the advantages of NTFS unless you set up multiple partitions. NTFS provides greater speed and more effective use of the space than FAT-based file systems. Unless there is a real business need, you might want to remove the older system from your server and fully convert to Windows 2000 instead.

Migrating Applications from Windows

The good news is that moving from a DOS-based or Windows 95 and 98 system to Windows 2000 Server poses no real problems. You no longer have to reinstall all your applications. Windows 2000 provides an install that recognizes and converts the existing applications you might already have loaded so they can be used in your new system.

A number of programs still won't work or will damage the system, including most system-level utilities such as data recovery programs like Undelete and fax programs that aren't specifically designed for Windows 95 or Windows 2000. Other programs such as Norton Utilities or Rescue Data Recovery Software will not operate unless you purchase a specific Windows 2000 or NT version.

Some software will operate under Windows 2000 if you choose the executable and double-click it under Explorer. I tried this on some shareware packages that are made for Windows 95, and they ran just fine. After determining that the program runs, add the icon to the desktop or to the Start menu under Programs.

Migrating from Windows 2000 3.51

Microsoft does a good job handling a migration from Windows 2000 3.51. During install, the Windows 2000 Setup program detects the older version and allows you to choose between updating it to the new version (effectively removing 3.51 from your system) and adding the new version in a separate directory and setting up a dual boot mode automatically. Windows 2000 doesn't recognize versions earlier than 3.51, however.

If you are upgrading a server that is widely used and has been extensively modified to include numerous user accounts, choose the upgrade option. Windows 2000 keeps all the data from your SAM and includes it in the new version, enabling your users to access the system without needing to be re-created. Be aware that migrating an existing domain is rather complicated and beyond the scope of this book. You need to manage that process carefully to ensure you select the right options and are able to recover if the upgrade fails.

If you are updating a test system or a system you'd rather start from scratch, choosing the refresh option wipes out all prior information from the SAM and leaves you with a disabled Guest account and one Administrator account. You then add all your users and their access levels as needed by your organization.

Licensing Those Users

You've installed a few services and added a number of clients. Everyone seems happy getting used to the new Windows 95 look and feel and using the services. Did you license all those users? You don't want to do anything illegal, do you?

Microsoft provides a tool called License Manager to manage adding and removing users and services. If you performed the task on Day 1, you are already familiar with how to view purchase history and product information in License Manager. You find License Manager in the Administrative Tools group (see Figure 2.4).

FIGURE 2.4

License Manager.

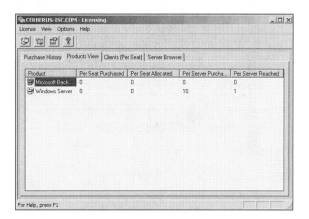

This tool provides a number of neat methods and processes for managing your licenses. It includes an area that allows you to update a small database with all the software licenses you've purchased. You need to manually add this information, but using it will save you time and hassle later as you find a need for the information.

As you learned on Day 1, License Manager shows you the products for your domain or network, depending on your selection. This section shows you which products are licensed and which are not and whether each product is at its license limit. You can also add and delete Per Seat licenses using this section of License Manager.

A server browser gives you access to the license information of other servers that are available to you. In this section, you add or delete Per Seat and Per Server licenses, allowing you to perform all your license maintenance from a central location.

Task 2.1: Modifying the Number of Licenses in Use on Windows 2000 Server.

▼ Step 1: Description

This task enables you to modify the number of licenses in use on Windows 2000 Server. You should perform this each time you add or remove licensed users or software.

Step 2: Action

1. Log in using the Administrator account.

2. Under the Start menu, find the License Manager submenu. Your screen looks like the one shown in Figure 2.5.

FIGURE 2.5

Finding License Manager.

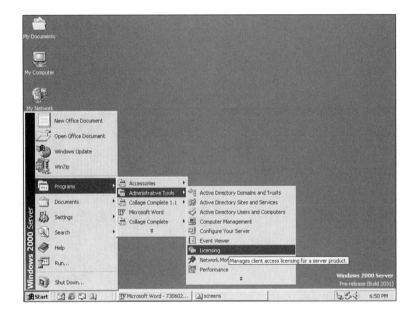

3. Click License Manager to start the program. You see a screen like the one shown earlier in Figure 2.4.

4. Click the Purchase History tab, and you see a list of all the products you entered into the database. It is empty at this time because you have not entered any information. As you install products, it's a good idea to update this section, because it makes managing all the product licenses a lot easier.

5. Click Clients (Per Seat) to see your license information. If you used the Per Server option during the install, click that instead. You see the number of licenses you are allowed on the server. Keep this up to date according to your license agreement with Microsoft.

▼

▼   6. Click the Help file to obtain detailed information on how to use License Manager.
      This Help file is extensive and answers most of your questions. When you are
▲   finished, click License, Exit to leave the program.

Step 3: Review

In this task you learned to manage your software licenses by using Microsoft's License
Manager tool. By updating this information regularly, you can enhance your ability to
quickly ascertain what products you have and how they are licensed.

Installation Problems

As you have progressed through this day, you might have encountered various problems
and difficulties during installation. Here are some of the more common ones:

- **System freeze-ups**   When encountering a system freeze while installing Windows
  2000, remember that this chapter warns you to stick to regulation equipment.
  Verify that all the hardware in use is on the Microsoft Hardware Compatibility List
  (HCL). Remember that although Windows 2000 is less fanatical about proper IRQ
  and I/O settings, it will still occasionally have a huge hissy fit if these settings are
  incorrect. Don't forget to run an antivirus program before starting because virus
  infections often result in system freeze-ups, and don't forget to discontinue using
  the virus program while installing Windows 2000.

- **Boot cannot find NTLDR**   Please insert another disk. Windows 2000 won't load
  without the loader program NTLDR, and it must find it in the root directory. On
  some larger systems with FAT-based hard drives, the root directory can fill, causing
  Windows 2000 to be unable to find the loader program. This is because FAT-based
  file systems can have only 512 files in the root directory. Remove some files and
  start the install again, or better yet take our earlier advice and use NTFS.

- **Cannot read drive a**   During the install, you cannot read one of the floppy disks.
  This error can result from many causes such as spilling your drink all over it first
  or accidentally setting it on the magnet in your office. Seriously, sometimes the
  disk is unreadable, so what do you do? Insert the CD-ROM and run the WINNT32
  program. Other causes include a hardware error or problem with the actual drive.
  If you followed the earlier install criteria and checked all your hardware before
  starting, you might be able to eliminate this as a cause. Otherwise, correct the
  problem and begin the install again. Don't forget that you can add the /b and /s
  switches after the WINNT or WINNT32 command to eliminate the need for a floppy
  and run solely from the CD-ROM.

Though the installation process is relatively simple, don't forget to use the Hardware Compatibility List. Prepare for installation through careful planning and documentation, and don't forget to back up your system before starting. Prevention is key to success when troubleshooting installation problems. In the next section we'll show you how to install client machines. When you are finished, you will have a complete Windows 2000 network running if you follow all the steps carefully.

Installing Primary Clients

As a Windows 2000 Server administrator, you will spend a great deal of your time dealing with your Windows 2000 machines. Naturally, the file server is one focus of your attention because it provides the resources your users need.

Having resources isn't much use, however, when clients cannot get to them. You must spend some of your time setting up your client's computers—adding new workstations, changing network interface cards, and updating client software versions.

In this section, you'll get details about installing the proper software and configuring it so that your clients can get to your servers. You'll see how Windows 2000 Server works with MS-DOS, Windows 3.x, Windows for Workgroups, Windows 95 or 98, Windows 2000 Workstation, and MacOS.

Compared to the complexities of Windows 2000 Server, adding and running a few files on a client computer must be a snap, right? Well, like many other areas of computers, installing and configuring workstations can go very smoothly. It also can be one of your worst nightmares. With that admonition, take a look at configuring the various clients that Windows 2000 Server supports.

What Is Client Software?

Client software lets desktop computers connect to your network. The software is designed to interact with a specific operating system on the client PC. Table 2.1 shows you what resources are available to the various clients. If you want to use the available resources, you need different client software for each operating system where you want to connect. Windows 95 and 98, Windows 2000 Workstation, and MacOS have this software built in. The rest is available on the Windows 2000 Server installation CD; you just have to install it on your various clients.

TABLE 2.1   Client Sharing Resources

Operating System Clients	Resources
MacOS	Can share with MacOS or Windows 2000 network clients. Macs can use Windows 2000 resources directly while also using MacOS-based network resources.
Windows for Workgroups	Can share and use resources.
Windows 95/98	Can share and use resources.
Windows 2000	Can share and use resources.

Before starting your installation, you should make sure that you have all the required information.

Pre-Installation Checklist

When you are ready to install software on a client, you need to gather the following information:

- Software: The Windows 2000 Server installation CD, this book, and the Microsoft documentation.

- Hardware: A client workstation, which is listed in the Windows 2000 Hardware Compatibility List (HCL).

- CD-ROM drive: You need a CD-ROM drive for your Windows 2000 Server to copy the software for all the clients you want to support. You also need the manual for your CD-ROM drive (just in case). Make sure that Windows 2000 will recognize and support your drive if it is a DVD-ROM. (These of course, are the new drives that let you play movies on your computer.)

- Floppy disks: During the installation process, you might need to create client installation disks for MS-DOS/Windows, and Windows 95 or 98 clients.

- Network configuration information: You need the hardware interrupt (IRQ) number and the base Input/Output (I/O) address (300h, 320h, 340h, 360h, and so on) for the network interface card.

Tip

> You can run WINMSD, the Windows 2000 diagnostics tool, to see and print the IRQ and base I/O addresses.

Installing the Client's Network

Other than the workstation itself, the only other hardware you need to access the network is a network interface card (NIC) or network adapter board. As you learned on Day 1, there are several popular types of networks—for example, ethernet, token ring, and ARCnet. (Developed by Datapoint Corporation, ARCnet, or Attached Resource Computer Network, is a token-passing bus architecture with 2.5Mbps capacity. ARCnetplus has 20Mbps capacity.) Even within these types of networks, different types of media exist. For example, one ethernet variety, known as 10Base2, uses coaxial cable, whereas another, known as 10BaseT, uses unshielded twisted-pair cable.

Physically installing the card is relatively straightforward. Just follow the manufacturer's instructions. Getting the card to work, on the other hand, might not be as easy, even with good instructions. Task 2.2 should help you install your card.

▼ TASK

Task 2.2: Installing a Network Interface Card.

Step 1: Description

This task describes how to install a network interface card (NIC) in a workstation.

Step 2: Action

1. Install the network interface card in an open slot in your workstation. Due to the varied cards and options, follow the recommendations from your card manufacturer.

2. If necessary, use your manuals and set the card to an IRQ number and a base I/O address that don't conflict with other workstation devices (such as the CD-ROM, video card, fax card, and so on). This is usually only necessary on software other than Windows 95 or 98, which will try to set them for you and avoids conflicts based on what is already in use on the machine.

Tip	Regardless of the settings you select for your card, write down the IRQ and I/O address.

▲   3. Connect the NIC to the network cable.

Step 3: Review

Use your manufacturer's manual to learn how to install your client's NIC. You might want to simplify things by trying to use the same type of NIC for every machine. You'll gain experience with the product and its various configurations as you install and configure subsequent cards.

Tip

Don't close the workstation's cover yet because you might have to adjust the card and its settings. Fortunately, most network adapters come with configuration programs that can help determine the correct settings or at least diagnose conflicts. In addition, later versions of DOS and Windows come with the Microsoft Diagnostics program (MSD.EXE and WINMSD.EXE). This program and others like it examine the hardware and software on your system and report details such as the in-use hardware interrupts. These programs are very valuable in helping you determine conflicts.

Software Installation Overview

In this section, you will learn to configure Windows 2000 Professional and Windows 98 or Windows 95 clients and communicate with a Windows 2000 Server.

When installing a client of any ilk, you need:

- Software: An operating system, such as Windows 98, preinstalled.

- Hardware: A workstation with an NIC.

- Protocol: You must know whether you're going to connect using NetBEUI, IPX/SPX, or TCP/IP.

- Username and password: You should set up a valid account for your new users, so you can test the connection after installation.

Ensure that you know the information in the list above before beginning; this will prevent you from searching for it in the middle of your configuration. The following task will help you learn how to configure a Windows 2000 Professional to use Windows 2000 Server and how to add a workstation client to the domain.

Task 2.3: Configuring Windows 2000 Professional.

Step 1: Description

This task describes how to install and configure a Windows 2000 Professional client. You might find that the original Windows install process already configured these options. Whether they are set correctly will be the issue you need to resolve by following these instructions.

Step 2: Action

1. Double-click the Control Panel icon and then double-click the Network and Dial-up Connections icon and select Local Area Connection, Properties. If you don't have one of these icons, select Make New Connection instead. You will see a dialog box that should look like the one shown in Figure 2.6 for an existing network connection.

FIGURE 2.6

Network settings panel.

2. Select the Internet Protocol tab and double-click it or select Properties. This opens the network properties for your network card, as shown in Figure 2.7. On our card you see that I have set specific settings to enable us to connect to our network.

FIGURE 2.7

The Network Protocol setting.

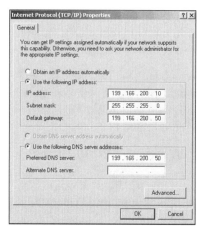

> **Tip**
>
> Windows 98 and 2000 both will default to use a special IP address range feature using Automatic IP Addressing, so you might be able to ignore this section and still connect to a Windows 2000 server. The addresses 169.254.0.0 to 169.254.255.255 are reserved for this so they don't conflict with any routable addresses. You must ensure that both the server you are connecting to and your workstation are configured to use a dynamically assigned IP address.

▼   3. Choose the settings you need and then click OK. You might find that you only
        need to set the option Obtain IP Address Automatically. You need to know whether
        you are running dynamic or static IP addresses on your server. You can verify this
        by performing these same steps on your server and selecting similar settings.

     4. Complete your network configuration information and click OK. The system will
        then allow you to see the network. Windows 2000 doesn't require you to restart the
        machine after changing network settings. This is a real blessing if you connect to
        multiple networks all the time like I do and need to reset these each time.

▲   5. You should be able to connect to the network. Try to see if other machines are
        there by clicking the My Network Places icon on the main screen.

Step 3: Review

After you install and configure a Windows 2000 Professional client, you must configure
your workstation so that it knows about your network settings you need for your
network.

Task 2.4: Adding a Workstation Client to the Domain.

Step 1: Description

This task describes how to add a Windows 2000 Professional to a Windows 2000 domain.
Merely creating a Windows 2000 Workstation doesn't allow it to participate in a domain.
You have to tell the domain and have it authorize the addition of your workstation. This
can be done two ways. In this task, you tell the domain about the workstation before
installing it. You perform this step and then install Windows 2000 Workstation. (During
the install, your Workstation should be connected to the network so it can complete the
installation by communicating with the domain.) Note that only Windows 2000 machines
need to be added in this manner, Windows 98 or Windows for Workgroups machines
aren't considered part of the domain although, as you will see, they can still access
Windows 2000 resources.

Step 2: Action

   1. Log in to your Windows 2000 domain as Administrator.

   2. From the Start menu, select Programs, Administrative Tools, Active Directory
      Users and Computers.

   3. Select Action, New, Computer from the menu. This opens the dialog shown in
      Figure 2.8.

   4. Enter the computer name of the workstation (not the user's login ID) you want to
      add to the domain and click OK. You need to decide what to call the workstation,
      although you will not have installed it yet.

FIGURE 2.8

In this dialog box you can add a computer to the domain.

5. Repeat step 4 and add all the Windows 2000 workstations you are setting up. When you install each workstation, it will be allowed to participate in the domain.

Step 3: Review

Configuring the workstation is half the battle—you still need to add the workstation to a Windows 2000 domain. Remember that you are defining the workstation, not the individual who might use the workstation.

Task 2.5: Joining the Domain as a Workstation Client.

Step 1: Description

This task describes how to join a Windows 2000 Server domain as a Windows 2000 workstation. You need not have done the prior step, but you will need a domain Administrator's account and password to complete a workstation's participation in the domain. You can choose to add the workstation using either this task or the prior one or even during the actual workstation install process.

Step 2: Action

1. Press Ctrl+Alt+Del, and log in to the Windows 2000 Professional machine as Administrator. Click OK.
2. From the Start menu, select Settings, Control Panel and double-click System.
3. From the System panel, click the Network identification tab and then click Change to display the Identification Changes panel.
4. Click Domain and enter the name of your Windows 2000 domain.
5. Click OK to lock in the settings and enter the Domain Administrator's account and password when asked. Ensure that the workstation's Computer Name field is unique and that a workstation with the same name doesn't already exist.

6. Restart your workstation and log in to the workstation again.

Step 3: Review

After logging into your workstation, you joined a Windows 2000 Server domain by selecting Network from Settings, Control Panel under the Start menu.

Configuring a Windows 95 or 98 Workstation

If you already have Windows 95 or 98 installed, connecting to a Windows 2000 Server is relatively easy. If the PC already connects to a peer-to-peer network, you just have to select the domain. If the PC is currently a standalone workstation, you need to install an NIC (see Task 2.2) and select a network adapter and protocol for the workstation.

Task 2.6: Configuring Windows 95.

Step 1: Description

This task describes how to install and configure a Windows 95 client.

Step 2: Action

1. From the Start menu, select Settings, Control Panel and double-click the Network icon.

2. On the Configuration tab, click Add to open the Select Network Component Type dialog box, shown in Figure 2.9.

FIGURE 2.9

The Select Network Component Type dialog box.

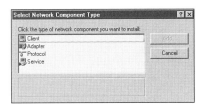

3. Highlight Adapter and click Add to open the Select Network Adapters list, shown in Figure 2.10.

FIGURE 2.10

The Select Network Adapters dialog box.

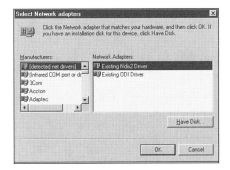

4. Choose the appropriate network adapter card manufacturer from the Manufacturers list. Select the appropriate card in the Network Adapters list. Click OK to return to the Select Network Component Type panel. (You can also just run the Add New Hardware Wizard to detect the adapter card.)

> **Note**
>
> If your card isn't on the list, it probably isn't on the HCL. You have to click the Have Disk button on the Select Network Adapter panel. You need a Windows 95 or 98 driver from your card manufacturer.

5. From the Configuration tab, double-click your network adapter card in the installed network component list to open the Properties dialog box for your card. You should see a screen that looks as shown in Figure 2.11.

FIGURE 2.11

The Adapter Properties dialog box.

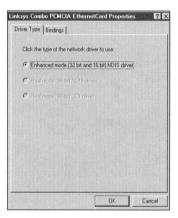

6. On the Driver Type tab, select Enhanced Mode (32-Mit and 16-Mit) NDIS Driver.

7. On the Resources tab, make any corrections you need to make for your particular network adapter.

8. At this point, you need to select a protocol to bind to the network adapter. (If you already connect to a network, double-click the Network icon after selecting Settings, Control Panel from the Start menu.) Select the Bindings tab and select the protocol you want to install. Click OK to return to the Network dialog box.

9. On the Configuration tab, click Add to open the Select Network Component Type screen, shown previously in Figure 2.9.

10. Highlight Protocol and click Add to open the Select Network Protocol list shown in Figure 2.12.

FIGURE 2.12

The Select Network Protocol dialog box.

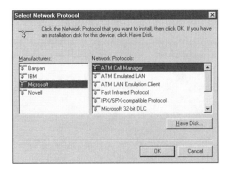

11. Choose Microsoft from the Manufacturers list. Select NetBEUI in the Network Protocols list. Click OK to return to the Select Network Component Type panel.

12. Click OK to approve all your changes.

Step 3: Review

You learned how to configure the network adapter card and protocol for a Windows 95 or 98 client. After you get this far, you can connect the Windows workstation to the server.

Task 2.7: Connecting the Windows 95 or 98 Workstation.

Step 1: Description

This task describes how to connect a Windows 95 or 98 client to the network.

Step 2: Action

1. From the Start menu, select Settings, Control Panel and double-click the Network icon.

2. On the Configuration tab, click Add to open the Select Network Component Type panel, previously shown in Figure 2.9.

3. Highlight Client for Microsoft Networks and click Properties to open the Client for Microsoft Networks Properties dialog box, shown in Figure 2.13.

4. In the Logon Validation box, select Log on to Windows 2000 Domain. Enter the name of your Windows 2000 domain and click OK, which returns you to the Network dialog box.

5. On the Identification tab, you should see information you provided during setup. Change this information when it is incorrect. In either case, click OK once, and click OK twice to lock in your choices.

6. Restart your computer when prompted.

FIGURE 2.13

*The Client for
Microsoft Networks
Properties dialog box.*

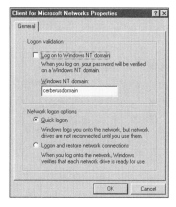

Step 3: Review

In this task, you learned how to connect a Windows 95 or 98 client. Select Client for
Microsoft Networks and make sure that you have selected Log on to Windows 2000
Domain. Now, you can test your network connection.

Task 2.8: Testing Your Network Connection for a Windows 95 or 98 Workstation.

Step 1: Description

This task describes how to verify that you have successfully connected a Windows 95
client to the network.

Step 2: Action

1. From the desktop, double-click the Network Neighborhood icon. You see a display
   of the network devices your workstation can see.

2. Double-click the icon for your Windows 2000 server to display the shares available
   for this workstation. If you see share resources, you are connected and viewing
   files on the hard disk.

Step 3: Review

This simple task described how to test your Windows 95 connection. Select the Network
Neighborhood icon to see what you can access. Now, you have configured a Windows 95
workstation as a client running on your Windows 2000 server.

Activating Services for a Macintosh Workstation

In addition to Microsoft clients, you might have Macintosh clients. Installing services
for MacOS clients is fairly complicated; you should read pages 1–5 of the Services for

Macintosh Help file on your Windows 2000 installation CD under the support/docs subdirectory. (Our beta CD is missing this file, but I believe it will be added as it was in place on the NT 4.0 production CD.) Macintosh clients must have version 6.07 or higher of the operating system, must support LocalTalk, Ethernet, Token Ring, or Fiber Distribution Data Interface (FDDI), must support AppleTalk Phase 2, and must be capable of using AppleShare.

Task 2.9: Configuring the AppleTalk Macintosh Client.

Step 1: Description

This task describes how to configure Macintosh (MacOS) clients.

Step 2: Action

1. Under the Apple menu, select Control Panels.
2. Double-click the Network icon.
3. In the Network Control Panel, highlight either LocalTalk or EtherTalk and close the panel.
4. Under the Apple menu, select Chooser.
5. Click the AppleShare icon. In the right-hand scroll window, select Windows 2000 Server and click OK.
6. When prompted, select Microsoft Authentication and click OK.
7. When prompted, connect to the server in the zone you want.
8. Click Registered User, enter your login name and password, and click OK.
9. When prompted, select Microsoft UAM Volume and click OK. The Microsoft UAM Volume icon pops up on the desktop.
10. Close Chooser.
11. Double-click the Microsoft UAM Volume icon.
12. Inside the window, double-click the AppleShare folder. Click the left arrow symbol on the menu bar and then select the System folder.
13. When you have the AppleShare and System folders open on the screen, drag the Microsoft UAM Volume icon from the AppleShare folder to the System folder.
14. Restart the client and perform Steps 5 through 11 to remount the Microsoft UAM volume.

Step 3: Review

You used the Control Panels to configure network information and the Chooser to select the Windows 2000 server. Acquiring a Windows 2000 server volume is equivalent to acquiring a shared volume on an AppleTalk network.

Summary

Today, you learned the following points:

* Avoid installation problems by carefully following the Hardware Compatibility List.

* The best protection is being proactive. Making backups of important data before beginning is essential to your well-being and peace of mind.

* Licensing your software on a Per Server or Per Seat method is critical to understand because you are offered only one chance to change before needing to re-install Windows 2000.

* You choose which type of hard disk format to use during install, either FAT-based or NTFS. Using a FAT-based system allows you to dual boot your machine with a variety of operating systems but is less efficient than NTFS. You must use NTFS if you plan to use file- and directory- level security.

* How to configure Windows 95, Windows 2000 Professional, and MacOS clients.

* How to log on to Windows 2000 Server from various clients.

Workshop

To wrap up the day, you can review tasks from the lesson and see the answers to some commonly asked questions.

Task List

With the information provided in this chapter, you installed Windows 2000 Server and a number of clients and learned the pitfalls to avoid during installation. You also learned how to carry out the following tasks:

* Modifying the number of licenses in use on Windows 2000 Server

* Installing a network interface card or adapter

* Installing and configuring Windows 2000 Workstation, Windows 95, and AppleTalk Macintosh clients

* Adding a workstation client to the domain

* Joining the domain as a workstation client

* Testing a Windows network connection

Q&A

Q What do I need before starting the install?

A You can use any equipment you like to run Windows 2000, but if you don't want a million headaches, start by using the HCL and buying equipment that is on the list. Clones might save you money initially but, if they don't work with Windows 2000, you have a major problem. In addition, getting up-to-date Windows 2000 drivers can be next to impossible.

Q How can I find out what NTDETECT is actually doing?

A NTDETECT determines the hardware in use on your machine. If a conflict occurs, the program might just stop running, leaving you puzzled. You find out all the steps that this program is taking by using the debug version. I outline exactly how to do this in the section earlier today titled "Using the Floppies and CD-ROM."

Q What can I do to help ensure an easy install?

A Use approved equipment. Test all components before trying to install Windows 2000 Server. In this manner, you can be more assured that a problem lies with the install and not with some hardware malfunction. Write down all relevant information, such as all I/O and IRQ settings of PC cards (formerly known as PCMCIA), sound cards, and so on.

Think carefully about the following queries and decide on the answers. Make sure you decide how you intend to license your software. Will you use a Per Server or Per Seat approach? Is the machine being added to an existing domain? If so, will it be a backup controller or an ordinary server? Doing some homework prior to laying your hands on the software helps ensure that your install is relatively painless.

Q Should I use a FAT-based or NTFS file system?

A If you plan on using Windows 2000 as your primary server with no other operating system, using NTFS provides sound, effective security and more efficient use of disk space. Use a FAT-based system if you need to boot different operating systems or have application needs that depend on FAT-based files.

Q Do I have to activate services for Macintosh clients or can they use resources directly?

A Yes, you must activate services for your Macintosh clients. Read pages 1–5 of the Services for Macintosh Help file included on the Windows 2000 Server CD in the support/docs subdirectory.

Q Can I make my workstation C drive available to other users?

A Not through Windows 2000 Server, but you can provide file service to your
local drives through a peer-to-peer network operating system, such as AppleTalk,
Windows 95, or Windows for Workgroups. Suppose you have Windows 2000
Server client programs and Windows for Workgroups client and server programs.
You make your C drive available to the other users and provide them with any
passwords they need. They then use Windows for Workgroups client programs
to access your drive.

Q Can I use protocols other than NetBEUI?

A Yes, you can use IPX/SPX and TCP/IP. In fact, you might want to use one of these
protocols because NetBEUI isn't a routable protocol. You will learn about TCP/IP
on Day 12, "Understanding TCP/IP and DNS."

DAY 3

Navigating and Exploring Windows 2000

Now that you have learned about networks and installed a basic Windows 2000 Server environment, you can begin to explore and navigate through your Windows 2000 network. The easiest method of learning something is to actually try it, so in this chapter, you'll learn how to log on and log off, manipulate your way through the Windows menu system, and use various Windows 2000 tools.

Note

> Yesterday, Windows 2000 indicated Windows 2000 Server. Well, the repetitive stress is getting worse, so today W2K will denote Windows 2000.

Logging on to Windows 2000 Server

You can log on to W2K from a client workstation only after you complete a number of steps. You learned how to set up the various client workstations in

Day 2, "Installing Windows 2000 and Client Software." Now that you have installed Windows 2000 Server, you can log on. A Windows 2000 Server installation automatically sets up a Guest account and an Administrator account. No other accounts exist.

> **Note**
>
> If you're upgrading to W2K from a prior version of Windows NT, you can choose to upgrade or install. If you choose to upgrade, your old user accounts are available to you and you can use them at this time. During Day 5, "Introducing Active Directory," you'll learn that this is where Windows 2000 maintains all security information, such as your username, password, and resource access.

> **Note**
>
> If you opted to install other services such as Internet Information Services, Microsoft Certificate Services, and Microsoft Terminal Services, you might notice other accounts such as IUSR_computername, IWAM_computername, krbtgt, and TsInternetUser as well.

The Guest Account

NEW TERM W2K automatically sets up an account called Guest, but leaves it disabled so that it cannot be used. The *Guest* account is typically used by staff or visitors to your business who want to perform some simple tasks such as typing letters or printing documents. Many organizations leave this account disabled because of the potential security risks involved.

A Guest account often is the first used by interlopers to gain access to your system. So what, you might ask? If it cannot do anything and is limited in its capability to see and modify data, what kind of risk does the Guest account pose? First, anyone can try to access your system by typing Guest at the account prompt and then typing a blank password. If the Guest account is active, the user has access to a number of objects, including any rights to objects that have been provided to the Everyone group. Many organizations put information and resource access into this group because doing so is easy and the information applies to everyone in the organization. The organization might get sloppy over time and include items that aren't for public or non-staff access. Additionally, NTFS gives the Everyone group default access rights to all files and folders on your disks. Now when someone uses the Guest account, who knows what data and resources that person can gain?

Second, should you enable the Guest account, W2K thinks that you want people to access the resources available to this account and therefore allows such access even without their using the account. How does this work? When you use your workstation, no sign-on is needed for a DOS-based or Mac machine. If you have a local account on your Windows 2000 Workstation, you can use that machine's resources. As you work away at your workstation, you forget that you're not signed on to the network and request a domain resource. If the domain resource is one that is permitted to the Guest account, Windows 2000 allows access even though you have not logged onto the server.

Finally, you cannot delete this account, but you can rename it. I recommend that you rename the account to something less obvious and leave it disabled.

The Administrator Account

NEW TERM The *Administrator Account* is the Big Cheese, the numero uno, the whole enchilada on Windows 2000 Server. It is all-seeing, all-knowing, and all-powerful, which makes it a huge target for external, unauthorized access. Naturally, the account is enabled and ready for use at completion of the installation. (Not having it enabled would be kind of silly—no one could sign on!) Remember that you should have secured the password you used to create the account during the installation process. You need that password now. If you have forgotten what it is and where you placed the written backup, you are in deep trouble and need to go back to Day 2. (Ugh. I really don't like suggesting that you write down passwords, but people are prone to error and forgetfulness, so what can I do? Make sure that you keep the copy somewhere really safe, however.)

The account is always available from the time you complete the installation; it is for this reason that you need to think of ways to protect it. Windows 2000 doesn't let you delete the account, so that's not an option. Deleting it would be pretty silly at this stage anyway—you wouldn't have any other accounts to use and you'd end up with the most secure W2K system in the world, as nobody would have access. Windows 2000 protects you from yourself, however, by making this option unavailable. So now that you know the account is always available, how can you protect it from unauthorized access attempts?

One good way to protect the Administrator account is by creating and using an effective password. Consider using a long password composed of a couple of words strung together with a number or two interposed throughout. You must use some common sense, so avoid the rather vulgar, common terms, and use terms similar to these:

Its2lovelyaday2day

Byethe9byehesaid

Where2goeththou

3

Silly, but effective. Stringing words together is one of the most effective ways of creating long passwords that remain reasonably undetectable. So how long a password can you use? Windows 2000 allows a maximum length of 14 characters. You determine the minimum and maximum length of a password in the Security Policies. You'll learn how to adjust this setting in Day 6, "Introducing Security Services." You should select at least six characters as the minimum length for any password. You increase the protection of any given password by remembering that this field is case-sensitive, so you can mix upper- and lowercase letters.

As you do with the Guest account, rename the Administrator account to something less obvious. It remains a target for hackers, so make it as hard as possible to crack by using an account name that doesn't stick out like a sore thumb. I recall hearing of one administrator who called his account God, because it was so powerful. This type of name makes the account an easy target. Also, avoid using Admin1, Admin2, and so on. Using a name similar to one of your users however, makes it much harder to find and increases the level of knowledge required to detect it.

Log On Using the Administrator Account

Now Windows 2000 Server is set up and ready for use. The installation process is finished, and you are eager to check out the system. If you haven't installed any workstations yet, can you log on at this time? On a Novell NetWare system, you cannot log on at the server as you do at a workstation—you must connect from another machine. Windows 2000 enables you to log on at the server and use the machine as a workstation. Although with this type of logon ability, your server can act as a workstation, I recommend against it. You will slow the machine down and you can potentially cause it to "hang" and prevent anyone from using it. (You know the drill where you have to perform the three-finger salute—Ctrl+Alt+Del.)

I installed W2K on my laptops, for example, and used those machines to log on, run programs, and create the screen shots for this book. No workstation was attached or needed. I understand that you probably will make better use of the machine than this example, but being able to use Windows 2000 in this manner is handy. For example, for security's sake you might want to force the Administrator to log in only at the console (or server).

New Term Your first task is to log on to W2K and see what happens. When Windows 2000 Server boots, you see a screen that indicates someone can log on. As part of Windows 2000's security, you must press the Ctrl, Alt, and Del (Delete) keys simultaneously to begin the logon process. This security helps ensure that a Trojan Horse doesn't capture your logon keystrokes. A *Trojan Horse* is a term used to describe a program that pretends to be one thing while actually performing a different function. For example, it would pretend to be a login window, capture your credentials for later unauthorized use by the programmer, and then pass control back to the real login sequence. Although the

Windows 2000 process isn't entirely secure, it certainly helps because using Ctrl+Alt+Del flushes any processes that are running and calls the W2K login program. After you press this key sequence, W2K loads its logo screen.

The logon screen asks for your username and, when required, your password. Remember that W2K, like most systems, allows the use of blank password fields. I don't recommend setting up an account with no password because it doesn't provide any user accountability and presents a security exposure. Also, when you're using a workstation, W2K needs to know what domain you want to use. On Day 5, you'll learn about this field in detail. For now, use the default you created when you first set up W2K Server.

The username you use is Administrator or whatever username you've assigned to that account. As you create and set up new users, they sign on with the names assigned to them. A username in W2K Server can be 20 characters long and consist of upper- or lowercase characters. It cannot include special characters such as " / [ ] ; : !. Ideally, you should set up usernames with a consistent standard across your organization, regardless of platform. Many organizations use an individual's last name and initial to create accounts. In this manner, you can track the person across the organization and multiple platforms, and you help give the person a sense of ownership. As a result, he or she might take better care of protecting his or her account and password.

After you enter the username and password, W2K Server authenticates that information using the SAM database it created during the installation. If the information is correct, W2K logs you on. If you made it this far, you should see a screen that looks like a Windows 98 desktop.

Figure 3.1 shows your Windows 2000 Server desktop with its new look. Whether you love it or hate it, you're stuck with it, so you might as well enjoy it.

Caution

After you sign on, remember that the username you're presently using has total control over this system. Don't leave it logged on and wander off to lunch or coffee. You might not have access when you return because someone has changed the password, or others might have provided themselves with all kinds of privileges while you were away. Always log off before leaving your workstation. If you don't want to log off, consider pressing Ctrl+Alt+Del and clicking on Lock Workstation to lock the machine. This way, your programs continue to run and other people cannot gain access to your machine. You need to enter your password to regain machine access (see Figure 3.2).

FIGURE **3.1**

*A sample Windows
2000 Server desktop.*

FIGURE **3.2**

*Computer Locked
message box.*

Task 3.1: Logging On to Windows 2000 Server.

Step 1: Description

This task enables you to log on to W2K Server. You perform this task each time you
want to use the server.

Step 2: Action

1. Boot your workstation or server. Be aware that most times you use a workstation to
   log on, an administrator boots the server first. Here, you use the server you just
   installed rather than a workstation.

2. When prompted, press Ctrl+Alt+Del to start the logon process.

3. Type in your username in the User Name field.

▼   4. Press the Tab key or use the mouse to move to the Password field and enter your assigned password.

▲   5. Click OK to continue the logon process.

Step 3: Review

By using the Ctrl+Alt+Del key sequence, you executed your first command on the W2K network in this task. You included your username to identify yourself to the network and included your password (where required) to verify you're accountable for the use of that username.

Typically, you log on using your workstation rather than the server console. The process does differ depending on the operating system in use on your workstation but will appear as shown for any W2K machine. You need to install the proper client software before W2K will allow the access. You learned how to set up workstations and log on using those workstations yesterday. Only the administrator should have access to the server console as this poses a certain risk. You'll learn about these risks three days from now when you begin working on Day 6.

If you need to log off from a session to go to lunch, leave for the day, or for any other reason, go to the "Logging Off from Windows 2000 Server" section later in this lesson.

Using Windows 2000 Server Utilities

Several utilities are available in W2K. These tools are typically divided into the following groups:

- Command prompt utilities
- Administrator Graphical User Interface tools

Command prompt utilities such as NET START and NET SEND operate from the Run command or from a Command Prompt window. These commands are often ignored, yet they serve a quick and useful function. They work on W2K workstations and W2K Server; however, some commands run only from the server. Workstation and server NET commands are listed in Appendix B, "Windows 2000 Command Reference."

NEW TERM   Administrator *Graphical User Interface* (GUI) tools are specifically designed for a supervisor's use. They are extremely powerful and must be used judiciously. Examples of these utilities include Active Manager Users and Computers, DHCP Manager, and Terminal Services Manager.

Using the Command Prompt Utilities

Some of the command prompt commands are available only to administrators; however, the remaining commands are available to users. See Appendix B for details as to what commands can be used by each type of account.

To begin using these utilities, you open a window that allows connectivity from the command prompt. You can find it by choosing Start, Programs, Accessories, as you can see in Figure 3.3. You also can run the commands from the Run line in the Start menu; however, this way the commands execute by opening and then promptly closing the window, leaving no trace of what happened. This method might be all right for a quick command that you're sure will produce the desired result, but most of the time you want to see what happens and the ensuing results of your command. If this is the case, stick with the command prompt window.

FIGURE 3.3

Opening the Command Prompt window.

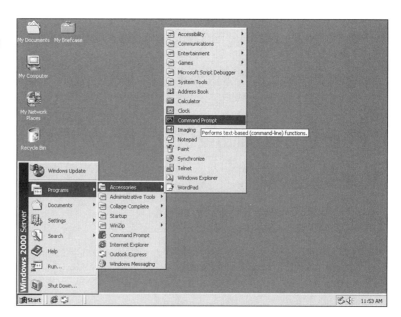

The commands you use in the Command Prompt window include being able to start and stop services, manipulate user accounts, view and change domain members, and send and receive messages. You can get Help from W2K Server if you need to explore the commands in more detail.

Using NET HELP

If you're new to Windows networking, you will probably use the NET HELP command the most until you become familiar with each NET command. This command shows you all the variables available in the help database and the syntax for obtaining the appropriate help information. Figure 3.4 shows an example of the NET HELP command in use. Note that the reply shows a list of available commands but not the specific options each command has available to it. That information comes later.

FIGURE 3.4

Using the NET HELP *command.*

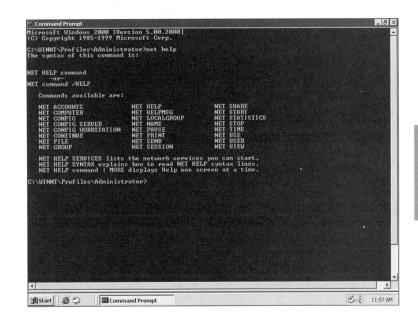

As you begin to learn the available commands, you might need specific help on a particular command. You find it by adding the command name to the end of your NET HELP command. To get help on the VIEW command, for example, type **NET HELP VIEW** in the Command Prompt window.

Don't forget to use the ¦more switch for commands that offer more than one screen of information. For example,

NET HELP USER ¦ MORE

Using this command provides you with the information shown in Figure 3.5.

As you saw in Figure 3.4, the help command doesn't provide any assistance for a number of services available in W2K. As you come across these services and require additional understanding, you need to reference the W2K documentation or some of the excellent books currently available. For example, consider acquiring an older but still excellent book: *Windows NT Server 4 Unleashed,* Sams Publishing, by Jason Garms, et al, 1996.

FIGURE 3.5

Using the ¦more switch to view command information.

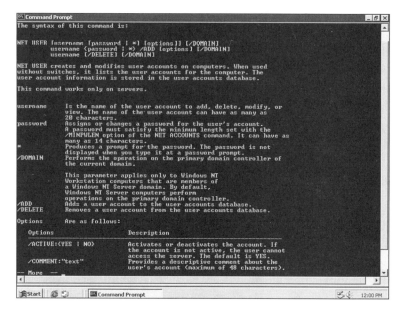

If you use the NET HELP SERVICES command, you find that help is available for most services. You might have to use other books and information sources when manipulating W2K.

If you're unsure of some of the conventions used in the help area of W2K, use the command NET HELP SYNTAX, as shown in Figure 3.6, to familiarize yourself with the particulars.

Task 3.2: Using the NET HELP Command.

Step 1: Description

This task shows you how to obtain help within W2K Server. You perform this task each time you need additional information on a particular command.

Step 2: Action

1. Make sure that you are signed on with an Administrator account.

2. Choose Start, Programs, Accessories, Command Prompt. The Command Prompt window then opens.

3. At the prompt, type **NET HELP SYNTAX** and press the Enter key. (Remember to add ¦more after the word SYNTAX when too much information is available to fit on one screen.)

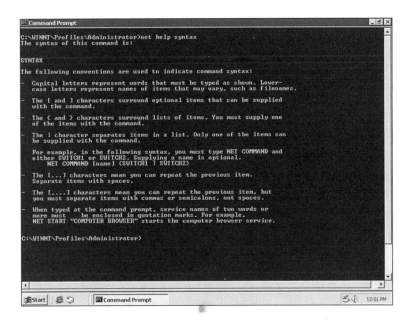

FIGURE 3.6

Help command syntax.

4. After reviewing any command syntax you might need, type **CLS** and press Enter to clear the screen. (Remember that the case of the letters doesn't matter.) Although clearing the screen isn't entirely necessary, doing so makes it easier for you to read the information presented from each command.

5. Type in the help command you need. For this example, to get more information on how to use the SEND command, type **NET HELP SEND**. You can enter any valid command after the word HELP to get specific help on that topic.

6. After you're finished, type **EXIT** to close the Command Prompt window.

Step 3: Review

By using the command prompt and various help commands in this task, you obtained the information necessary for you to understand how the W2K commands work. You'll use this task repeatedly as you learn to manage Windows 2000 Server.

Using Other NET Commands

A number of commands are available from the command prompt. They are handy when you prefer keying commands to using the GUI interface. In the following sections, you'll read about some of the more useful commands. If you remain unconvinced of the benefits, use the GUI interface. After all, my intent is to introduce you to W2K, not change your particular keying preference.

NET STATISTICS

The NET STATISTICS command provides statistics for the computer on which you run it. The list includes all the services you're running that provide statistics. You can run this command for either the server or the workstation. The command doesn't travel the network, though; it applies only to the machine on which you execute it. As you can see in Figures 3.7 and 3.8, the command provides you with the number of password and permission violations as well as the number of files accessed and other information. To run the command, select either workstation or server, and append whatever you select to show either NET STATISTICS WORKSTATION or NET STATISTICS SERVER.

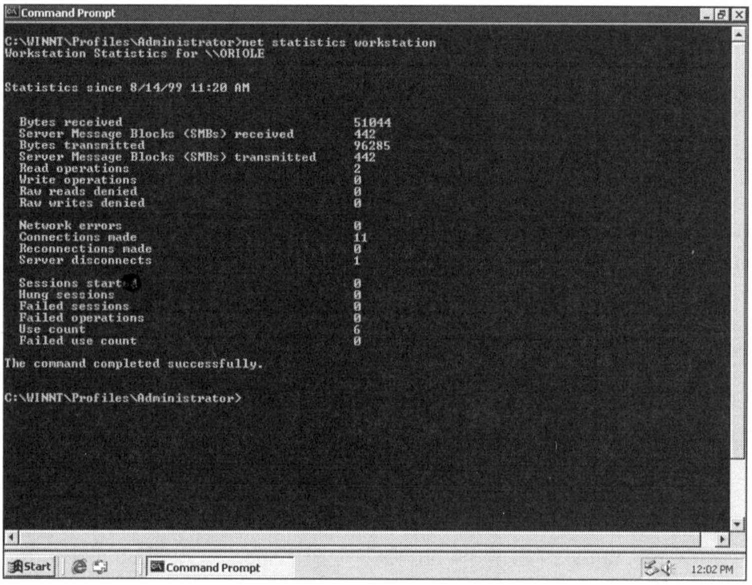

FIGURE 3.7

Running the NET STATISTICS WORKSTATION *command.*

NET SEND

The NET SEND command helps you send messages to the servers and workstations on your network. You use it to send a message to an individual user, the users within your domain, or all the users connected to the server.

This command works only when you add parameters that tell it who and what to send. This command is a useful alternative to electronic mail, but if your organization is already functioning well with an electronic mail package, you likely will use the send message infrequently. Typically, you use the send command to tell everyone that the network will be unavailable at a certain time and to log off. The major advantage to using this command is its prominence on the user's screen. When a person on a W2K workstation receives a send message, the message pops up on the screen immediately and doesn't disappear until he or she clicks OK. Electronic mail messages are easily buried within a user's mailbox, never to reappear until it's too late.

In versions of Windows NT, you could use this command to send files across the network. This capability is no longer supported in W2K.

The typical parameters you use at the command prompt look like

NET SEND *name message*

In this example, *name* is the field used to identify the person or persons you want to receive the message, and *message* is the text you want to tell everyone. You don't need to use quotation marks, and you can send fairly long messages. A typical message can be as long as a dozen lines or so, more than enough for day-to-day messaging needs.

FIGURE 3.8

Running the NET STATISTICS SERVER *command.*

You can get help on this command using the NET HELP SEND command, as shown in Figure 3.9.

FIGURE 3.9

Getting help with the SEND *command.*

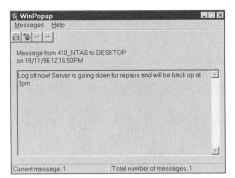

```
C:\WINNT\Profiles\Administrator>net help send
The syntax of this command is:

NET SEND {name ! * ! /DOMAIN[:name] ! /USERS} message

Sends messages to other users, computers, or messaging names
on the network. The Messenger service must be running to receive messages.

You can send a message only to an name that is active on the network.
If the message is sent to a username, that user must be logged on
and running the Messenger service to receive the message.

name                       Is the username, computername, or messaging name
                           to send the message to. If the name is a
                           computername that contains blank characters,
                           enclose the alias in quotation marks (" ").
*                          Sends the message to all the names in your group.
/DOMAIN[:name]             Sends the message to all the names in the
                           workstation domain. If name is specified, the
                           message is sent to all the names in the specified
                           domain or workgroup.
/USERS                     Sends the message to all users connected to
                           the server.
message                    Is text to be sent as a message.

NET HELP command ! MORE displays Help one screen at a time.

C:\WINNT\Profiles\Administrator>_
```

The NET SEND command provides you with a relatively simple method of reaching your user community. As long as each user is logged on and running a messenger service on his or her machine, he or she gets any message sent. W2K machines, specifically, need to run the messenger service. Windows and Windows 95/98 machines should run the WinPopup program, as shown in Figure 3.10. WinPopup can be run minimized but must be running all the time for the user to receive messages. Place this program in the user's startup box so that it runs each time the user starts Windows.

FIGURE 3.10

Receiving a message with WinPopup.

Message from 410_NTAS to DESKTOP
on 19/11/96 12:16:50PM

Log off now! Server is going down for repairs and will be back up at 3pm

Current message. 1   Total number of messages: 1

After receiving the message, the user might want to reply to the sender. Figure 3.11 shows a message being returned using the WinPopup Send command and specifying the server as the receiver. Figure 3.12 shows how the message appears on the server.

FIGURE 3.11

Replying to a message.

FIGURE 3.12

The reply on the server.

3

You can use the following sample commands over the next few days to send surprise messages to any users you might have installed in your W2K system.

To send a simple message telling everyone on the domain to log off, type this

```
net send * Log off now, please
```

To send a message to a computer named Desktop on your system, type this

```
net send desktop Hi machine user, How are you?
```

To send a message to Bill who is part of another domain, such as Accounting, type this

```
net send bill \accounting This is a test of the send command
```

Experiment with other commands until you're familiar with the send message and know some of its quirks.

NET CONFIG

The NET CONFIG command enables you to see the current configuration information for any W2K server or workstation. Although you also can change some of the information, I discuss viewing data only. It's better for new users to use the GUI interface when changing data until you fully understand the ramifications.

Remember that your server can also act as a workstation (mine does), and this capability is one advantage over a Novell system in which you would need a second machine to get to this part of your three-week journey. Remember though that you don't want to use a production server as a workstation. Using the NET CONFIG command, you can specify either server or workstation as a variable. The command gives you the following information:

- The computer's name
- The software version in use (Note that it doesn't differentiate between Windows 2000 Server and Windows 2000 Professional)
- The network card and its address
- Whether the server is visible to the network, how many users can log on, and how many files each user can open
- The current idle time

Using this command, you can quickly determine some basic configuration information. Figure 3.13 shows an example of a workstation command.

FIGURE **3.13**

Using the NET
CONFIG WORKSTATION
command.

NET VIEW

The NET VIEW command provides a quick overview of the resources being shared on a computer. When used without any other options, it displays a list of computers in the current domain or network.

To see what resources are available to the computer you're using, type

`net view`

Figure 3.14 shows the output from this command on a server with one connected desktop workstation.

FIGURE 3.14

Using the NET VIEW *command.*

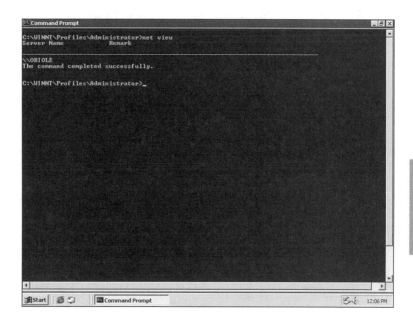

To see what resources the server is sharing with the network, type

`net view \\servername`

Here, *servername* is the server you want to select. Figure 3.15 shows the output from this command on a server called \\ORIOLE.

A number of other commands are available within W2K. The commands listed in this chapter are primarily information-gathering commands and as such can be relatively harmless. Other commands enable you to set up new users, change domain memberships, and set the time across the network. You'll see some of these other commands demonstrated in the following sections using the GUI interface that W2K provides.

Using Administrator GUI Tools

As an administrator on a Windows 2000 server, you have a lot of powerful tools available to you for managing the server accounts and restricting access in an appropriate manner. You'll learn more details about security in Day 6. In that chapter, you'll be taken on a tour of the tools and shown around the city, so to speak.

FIGURE 3.15

Using the NET VIEW
\\servername *com-
mand.*

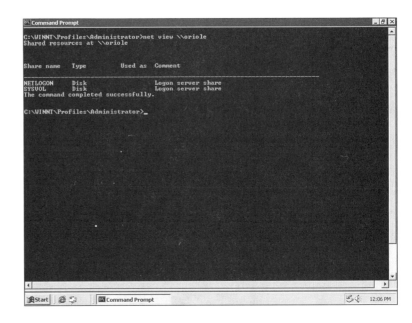

You can find the Administrator GUI tools by choosing Start, Programs, Administrative
Tools on your desktop machine, as shown in Figure 3.16. These tools are available on
both Windows 2000 Professional and Server, although they are slightly different in each
machine.

FIGURE 3.16

*Finding the Windows
2000 Server
Administrative tools.*

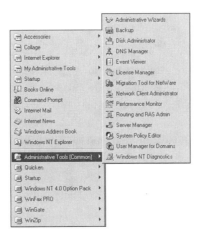

Windows 2000 Server provides a number of tools for the administrator, as you can see in Figure 3.16. You will find administering a Windows 2000 network easier and faster than ever because of the Microsoft Management Console (MMC). The MMC gives you control over what tools and computers you display, allowing you to create custom administration tools catered to your specific responsibilities. If you are converting from an older version of Windows NT, you will need to get up to speed on MMC. Microsoft has rewritten User Manager, Event View, Server Manager, Disk Administrator, and all other administrative applications as MMC snap-ins. These snap-ins each have a valid use, but as the administrator, you'll use some more than others in the day-to-day operation of your network. Experienced administrators should quickly adapt to the new tools, while new administrators will learn faster thanks to the consistent, user-friendly interface.

During the rest of the 21 days of working through this book, you'll use these tools as you perform the tasks assigned to each day. Here, you get an overview so that you understand what is available and gain an understanding of the purpose of each tool. This way, you are prepared should problems occur and you need to resolve them using the tools available to you.

Active Directory Sites and Services

When a user logs on, W2K authenticates the credentials, providing access to network resources. Because Active Directory uses multimaster replication, any Windows 2000 domain controller on the network can service all requests including modifications to the Directory by users in their domain controller's domain. This might work when you have a small network of well-connected computers, but not very efficient when you have a global network. You might not want users attempting to authenticate in London, using the directory in New York. Active Directory Sites and Services can improve the efficiency of directory services for most networks through the use of sites. Sites facilitate authentication, replication, and Active Directory enabled services.

You can access Active Directory Sites and Services by selecting Start, Programs, Administrative Tools. You will see a screen similar to the one in Figure 3.17.

Note

> You might have noticed that you can access many of these tools another way. Try Start, Settings, Control Panel and double-click on Administrative Tools.

FIGURE 3.17

Active Directory Sites and Services tool.

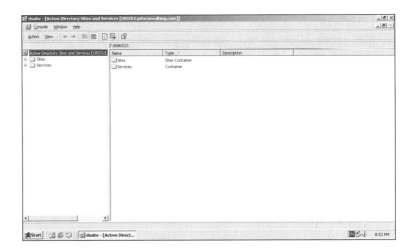

Active Directory Users and Computers

You can use Active Directory Users and Computers to add, modify, delete, and organize Windows 2000 user accounts, computer accounts, security and distribution groups, and published resources in your organization's directory. Active Directory Users and Computers is a directory administration tool installed on domain controllers.

Note

Normally, you use the Administrative Tools from the domain controller, but there is an optional Administration Tools package that lets you do it from other locations. You can install this package on Windows 2000 Professional computers so you can manage user and computer accounts and groups from a computer that isn't a domain controller.

Microsoft designed Active Directory Users and Computers for your daily administration. Daily tasks might include adding, deleting, and modifying users and computer accounts within the domains, organizational units, and groups you have established in your directory. You also can use Active Directory Users and Computers to modify the properties of user, computer, group, organizational unit, and shared resource objects in your directory. You will learn more about this tool on Day 7, "Managing User Accounts."

Component Services

With Component Services, administrators can deploy and administer COM+ applications, or automate administrative tasks using a scripting or programming language. Software developers can use Component Services to visually configure routine component and application behavior, such as security and participation in transactions, and to integrate components into COM+ applications.

To open Component Services, select Start, Settings, Control Panel. If you double-click Administrative Tools, and then double-click Component Services, you should see a screen such as the one in Figure 3.18.

Tip

For information about using Component Services, click Action, and then click Help.

FIGURE 3.18

Active Directory Sites and Services tool.

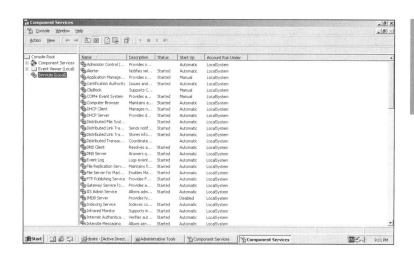

3

Event Viewer

NEW TERM You use the Event Viewer tool to monitor events occurring within W2K. *Events* consist of any significant occurrence in the operating system, such as an interrupted power supply or a server hard drive that has run out of free space.

These are the three main event logs:

- Application
- Security
- System

The Application log records events logged by your applications. You can record database errors and other application-related problems in this file.

The Security log provides details about attempted logons and file and object accesses. The events shown in the Security log are a result of using the Group Policy Editor.

The System log records all events logged by the W2K system components such as the failure of tape and modem drivers or other components during startup.

Task 3.3: Setting the Group Policy.

Step 1: Description

This task shows you how to set a Group Policy from the Active Directory Sites and Services snap-in. You perform this task each time you want to change the Group Policy.

Step 2: Action

1. Make sure that you are signed on with an Administrator account.

2. Choose Start, Programs, Administrative Tools. Select Active Directory Users and Computers.

3. From the right panel, right-click the domain for which you want to create a policy.

4. Select Properties from the menu.

5. Select the Group Policy panel from the Properties window.

6. Select Default Domain Policy and click Properties.

7. Select the Security panel.

8. Select System, and click Advanced.

9. From the screen shown in Figure 3.19, click View/Edit.

FIGURE 3.19

Access Control Settings.

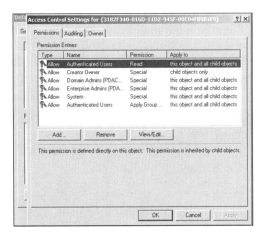

▼   10. Select and deselect the permission you want.

▲   11. Click OK four times.

Step 3: Review

You just learned how to use Group Policy to set permissions.

Event logging starts automatically when you run W2K. You examine this audit process further on Day 17, "Security Monitoring and Audit Trails."

Licensing

You learned about the License Manager tool in Day 2. You'll learn how to set up licenses and track them across the domain using this tool in Day 17. Note that Licensing doesn't enforce licensing requirements. Compliance must still come from within each organization. Remember to observe all legal requirements to save your organization from the embarrassment and cost of a lawsuit.

Network Monitor

You or your network administrator can use Network Monitor to detect and troubleshoot networking problems on the local computer. You might use Network Monitor to diagnose hardware and software problems when the server computer cannot communicate with other computers.

Microsoft's Systems Management Server (SMS) includes a full version of Network Monitor. SMS Network Monitor can capture frames sent to and from all computers in a network segment, as well as edit and transmit frames. Frames captured by Network Monitor can be saved to a file and then sent to professional network analysts or support organizations.

On Day 20, "Windows 2000 Performance Monitoring and Tuning," you'll learn how to use this tool effectively.

Performance

Performance is a graphical tool that measures the performance of your computers. It provides detailed information on the behavior of processors, memory, cache, threads, and processes. This tool gives you valuable information about queue lengths, delays, and throughput or congestion information.

Performance, shown in Figure 3.20, provides a number of different options that enable you to tell it to provide ongoing charting, alerts, or logging. You can select these activities for different computers on your network. Use this tool regularly on your network to ensure that no bottlenecks or problems have an impact on the user community.

FIGURE 3.20

Performance Monitor.

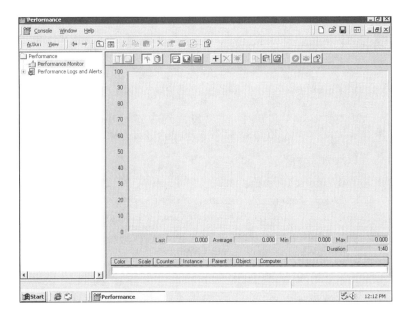

You'll also learn how to use this tool effectively when you reach Day 20.

Routing and Remote Access

Version 3.5*x* of W2K offered a service called Remote Access Service (RAS). In Windows NT 4, Microsoft tried to rename this facility Dial-up Networking (DUN), just as in Windows 95. (See, I told you that the plan is to eliminate Windows 95/98 eventually and have W2K take over the world.) Basically, DUN sets up your dial-in modem access to run and look just as though you were on the local area network. However, throughout W2K documentation you find both terms used, so a complete name change remains in limbo and RAS remains more common in the W2K world. I stick to RAS in this chapter because this term is currently the one best known by those using W2K.

This service enables a user to connect to another machine and gain LAN access. W2K makes your modem act like a network card, connecting you to the network just as though you were physically connected via a NIC, rather than dialing in from some remote location.

An advantage of using this tool over third-party tools is cost. RAS comes with W2K and is therefore essentially free. The other tools get expensive as you increase the number of users who need remote access.

Dial-up Networking enables you to use your computer as an Internet gateway, an Internet service provider, and for remote dial-in to W2K or other servers. This tool is really flexible and reasonably robust. You'll learn how to set up and use RAS in Day 11, "Understanding Remote Access Services (RRAS) and VPNs."

System Tools

Microsoft has moved some tools from the Administrative Tools menu to Start, Programs, Accessories, System Tools. So if you previously used an older version of Windows NT, these tools have not disappeared, but have been moved. Figure 3.21 shows you how to locate System Tools.

FIGURE 3.21

Opening System Tools.

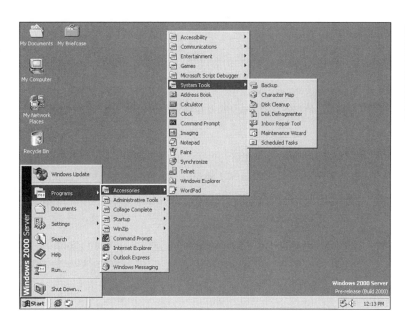

Backup

The Backup tool provides you with a method for performing backup and recovery of server data. The first time you start the program, it runs for awhile collecting all the relevant data on your file structure and discovering what tape backup device you're using. Sometimes W2K doesn't find your tape device even though it exists on the HCL, or it tries to install the wrong one. In these cases, you need to install the device manually.

Most organizations use more robust products to back up their systems, such as Seagate's Desktop Management Suite with the Backup Exec program for both NetWare and W2K. If you have a smaller site and don't need these more expensive tools, the Backup tool performs reasonably well. Figure 3.22 shows the Backup Wizard.

FIGURE 3.22

The Windows 2000 Backup Wizard.

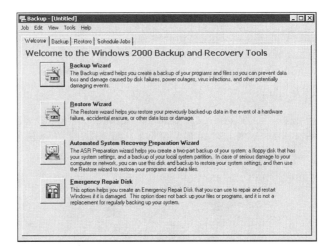

Using the Backup Wizard, you can back up, restore your data, and manage your backup tapes. You can find more detailed information on using Backup in the extensive Help menus.

Maintenance Wizard

The Maintenance Wizard helps you schedule regular maintenance tasks, such as scanning drives for errors and cleaning up disk space.

Scheduled Tasks

Using Scheduled Tasks from System Tools, you can schedule tasks and times to automatically execute. You can schedule a time for Windows to clean up the hard drive by deleting unnecessary files.

Understanding and Using Windows 2000 Books Online

In the W2K Start menu, Microsoft provides Windows Update. Using Windows Update, you can access the latest W2K manuals online and update outdated system files automatically. You access Books Online using Windows Update from the Start menu. Windows Update is an online extension of Windows 2000 help. Alternatively, you can get the same information using Internet Explorer to view `http://www.microsoft.com/windows/server/`.

From the Web page shown in Figure 3.23, you can select Product Help.

FIGURE 3.23

Windows Update Web page.

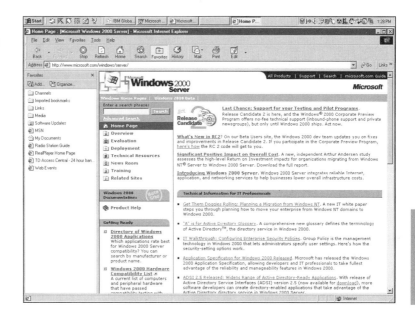

You will find the following books:

- Welcome
- Getting Started with Windows 2000 Server
- Active Directory
- Security
- Users and Computers
- Files and Printers
- Connections
- Networking
- Network Interoperability
- Client Services
- IntelliMirror
- Storing Data
- Disaster Protection
- Monitoring and Diagnostics Tools
- Internet Tools and Services

- Automating Administrative Tasks
- Application and Programming Tools
- Troubleshooting and Other Resources

These books can be placed on the server or left on the W2K CD-ROM. If space is an option, leave them on the CD-ROM and make them available when needed. To use the books, follow the steps outlined in Task 3.4.

Task 3.4: Using the Microsoft Windows 2000 Server Online Books.

Step 1: Description

This task shows you how to obtain additional help within W2K Server using the Online Books. This task demonstrates using the books from a W2K workstation.

Step 2: Action

1. Sign on to your workstation in the normal fashion. You don't need Administrative privileges to view the books.

2. Choose Start, Windows Update. Click on Product Help from the web page shown previously in Figure 3.23. You should see a window listing the available books.

3. Select the main topic shown in the window under Contents. Then press Enter or double-click. You see the books under the main entry.

4. Select one of the books. For this example, select Networking. Then press Enter or double-click your selection. You then are shown a series of chapters.

5. Choose a chapter that interests you, and take a look at it. At any time, you can exit by clicking the close button.

Step 3: Review

By using the Books Online function in this task, you obtained the information necessary to understand how to manage W2K networks. You'll use this task as needed while you learn all about Windows W2K Server.

Logging Off from Windows 2000 Server

You have now finished exploring the wonders of W2K Server. It's time to log off from the network. Logging off disconnects you from the network properly. Never disconnect from the network by turning off your computer or rebooting your workstation because these methods can cause problems with the files and programs you're using. In a similar vein, as mentioned previously, never walk away and leave your workstation logged on because an unauthorized person could gain access to the network and your files and programs. As mentioned earlier, you might use the Lock Machine option or consider setting up a password-protected screen saver instead of logging off.

Logging Off Windows 2000 Workstations

To log off a Windows 2000 workstation, choose Start, Shut Down and then select the appropriate option. If you're finished for the day, for example, choose Shut Down the Computer? Then click the Yes icon. If you're rebooting the machine, choose Restart the Computer. If you want to log on as a different user, choose Close All Programs and Log On as a Different User. If you have installed IE 5 with the Active Desktop component, a Logoff <username> option appears on the Start menu and you can use this to log off.

Logging Off Windows 95/98 Client

To log off from a Windows 95/98 client, follow the steps in the preceding section. You choose Start, Shut Down and then select the appropriate option. If you're finished for the day, for example, choose Shut Down the Computer? Then click the Yes icon. If you're rebooting the machine, choose Restart the Computer. If you want to log on as a different user, choose Close All Programs and Log On as a Different User. If you have installed IE 5 with the Active Desktop component, a Logoff <username> option appears on the Start menu and you can use this to log off.

Logging Off Windows and DOS Workstations

To log off from a Windows or DOS workstation, get to a DOS prompt and type **net logoff**. Then press Enter.

You now know that you can log off using various commands depending on the workstation you use to attach to the network.

Exploring Windows 2000 Server

Earlier, you spent time learning how to navigate Windows 2000 Server. In this section, you expand on that knowledge and gain a more in-depth understanding of the nuances involved in exploring all the facets of W2K. You start with the simple task of finding out who you are when connected to the server. This task is easier than finding out who you are in the metaphysical sense.

Discovering Who You Are

Discovering who you are is such a common challenge. You go through life attempting to refine this process. Or perhaps you're comfortable in the knowledge of who you are and you're no longer searching. In W2K, the process is a little different.

Typically, you know how you signed on and what username you're using, but you might be unsure. You can find this information while logged into a workstation by submitting the NET CONFIG command in a command prompt window. Figure 3.24 shows a Windows 95 client example of this type of window.

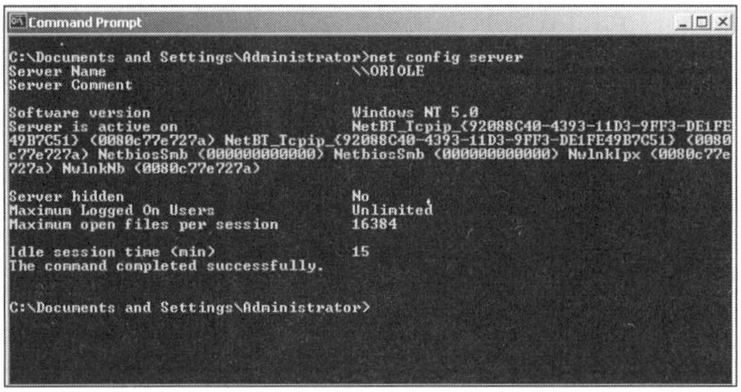

FIGURE 3.24

Using the command
NET CONFIG.

In this figure, you can find various pieces of information. This information includes the name of the computer and the username you're using. The workgroup you are part of is also shown. (You'll learn about workgroups in more detail in the chapters about domains and security within W2K.) Finally, you'll see information concerning the version numbers of the software in use.

When you use a Windows 2000 Workstation, the command looks a little different, as you saw earlier today.

Manipulating the Command Prompt Window

You probably use the command prompt a lot, but perhaps by now you want to change how the window appears on the desktop. When I first used the command prompt, the box was too small, so I made it appear larger and then made that size the default.

How do you manipulate the window? You see in W2K that this window cannot be enlarged using the standard drag-and-drop windows formatting. You can make the window smaller, but not any larger. That's strange, don't you think? By playing with the fonts however, the window will automatically size itself larger or smaller depending on what font size you use.

How do you manage this chore in W2K? One method is to begin by opening a command prompt window. Next, place the mouse cursor somewhere on the blue top section of the open dialog box (the title bar), right-click, and select Properties. (Should you place the mouse cursor actually in the open box, the left button doesn't work.) A Properties dialog box similar to the example shown in Figure 3.25 then appears.

FIGURE 3.25

The Command Prompt Properties dialog box.

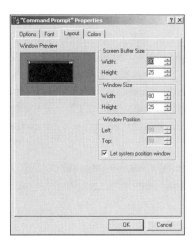

Within this properties dialog box are four main tabs:

- Options
- Font
- Layout
- Colors

You explore each of these tabs in the following paragraphs. Because you use the command prompt so often, you might as well ensure that the open window suits your personal preferences.

On the Options tab, you can perform various changes. The first change is modifying the size of the cursor. If you're like me, and small items are getting a little harder to see, select the large cursor option. Instead of seeing a small blinking box, you then see one about three times larger. A medium selection gives you a cursor about twice as large as the standard one. When you select the different size, W2K asks whether you want the selection to apply to the current window or whether you want it to become the one used each time you open the command prompt. W2K doesn't make this decision awfully clear, however, as the prompt asks the following two questions:

- Apply Properties to Current Window Only
- Modify Shortcut Which Started This Window

The second option makes your changes more permanent by telling the system to add this change each time it opens the command prompt window. The first (and default) option applies the changes to the open window but doesn't save the changes, so you need to add them each time you open the window.

In the Display Options field, you can select whether the window opens in Full Screen or Window mode. The typical setting is Window mode, which is the default on an x86-based machine. With this option, you can use the command prompt and still see other parts of the desktop. Full Screen does just that—it makes the open window fit across the entire screen, hiding all other parts of the desktop. Choose the option you want to use. Press Alt+Enter to toggle between the two settings while a command prompt window is open.

Command history works in a similar fashion to the old Doskey command that enabled you to reuse previously keyed commands.

Tip

> You don't need to add Doskey anywhere in a Windows 2000 Server or workstation. Command reuse is always available in the command prompt window.

How many commands are available for scrolling depends on the Buffer Size you use. W2K defaults to save commands automatically using four buffers, each with a size of 50. This number affords many keystrokes—more than you'll probably need. You can discard duplicate entries by selecting the Discard Old Duplicates check box.

If you like using the mouse to select text, select the QuickEdit Mode check box. Insert mode allows text to be inserted at the cursor instead of being replaced.

On the Font tab, you can modify how the text appears in the window. You select the size and particular font you want to see by clicking in the appropriate Size and Font option boxes.

On the Layout tab, you modify how and where the screen appears on the desktop. You select the Screen Buffer size, which sets the amount of data the buffers hold, and you select a Window Size by increasing or decreasing the Width and Height as needed. Finally, you either let the system place the window on the screen or set specific placement options.

You can play with the colors of the command prompt window on the Colors tab until the cows come home. W2K enables you to set a color for the text and the background.

> **Tip**
> You need to restart the command prompt window to see the changes made using the Font, Layout, and Colors options. Changes made in the Options component take effect in the current window.

Task 3.5: Resizing the Command Prompt.

Step 1: Description

This task enables you to change the default size of the command prompt window. You perform this task any time you want to use a different size window.

Step 2: Action

1. Log on to W2K. You learned this process earlier in this lesson.

2. Open a command prompt window. Choose Start, Programs, Command Prompt.

3. Place your cursor on the line where you see the words Command Prompt and right-click. Then select Properties.

4. In the Properties dialog box, click the Layout tab. You then see three selection boxes called Screen Buffer Size, Window Size, and Window Position.

5. Move the cursor to the area called Window Size and change the settings. You see the effects of your change in the small preview window on the left. Try different settings until you're comfortable with what you see.

6. Click OK when you're ready to continue. W2K asks whether you want the change to apply to the current window only or to all future command prompt windows. The message isn't very clear. When it asks whether you want to modify the short-cut that started this window, W2K really is asking whether you want to make the change permanent.

7. Select the Apply properties to current window button and click OK. You then see the new window size.

8. Repeat these steps as needed. If you like a certain size, choose the option to make those changes permanent. You can change other options at the same time such as the background and text colors or font type and size.

Step 3: Review

By using the Properties dialog box, you manipulated the command prompt window to suit your particular idiosyncrasies. I changed mine, for example, to appear with a blue background and black text.

Understanding and Using UNCs

NEW TERM *UNC* is the acronym given to the *Universal Naming Convention* in Microsoft products. When you want to access a machine or a share on another drive, you need some way to tell W2K where that machine or library is contained. To understand this convention properly, you need to review the system for sharing data in W2K. (This sharing might be familiar to you should you use other Microsoft products such as Windows 95.)

To allow access to a particular directory on a Windows 95/98 machine, you can set up a share name and allow people to have access as long as they know the password. On a W2K machine, you do the same but tell the system what users are allowed to access the share. This common method helps you understand the UNC standard. You can use command-line tools or Explorer to set up shares. In your W2K system, sharing is enabled by default.

How do you set up a share? First, you decide what directory to share and then you need to tell W2K to allow access to the directory and call it by a particular share name. To allow access to my Desktop directory called Data, for example, I need to tell the network software that I want to allow access to C:\Data and reference it by the share name called PeterData. PeterData, then, is the share name for the Data directory and the name that people on the network will use to access that directory. You can call this share name anything, as shown in the example. It doesn't have to equal the actual directory name being shared.

You can name machines using up to 15 characters; you can set up share names using up to 12 characters. Finally, the desktop needs to be told to allow the share. You do so using the following command:

```
NET SHARE Peter_Data=c:\data command
```

A more common method is to use W2K Explorer. Right-click on the folder you want to share, select Sharing, and then Shared As and then modify the remaining fields as desired to provide access. In Windows 95, you need to use the Control Panel options to perform the same function. You can find sharing under the Network, Access Control settings in the Control Panel. By choosing an option here, you set up the machine to allow sharing to occur. Figure 3.26 shows an example.

FIGURE 3.26

Setting up sharing in Windows 95/98.

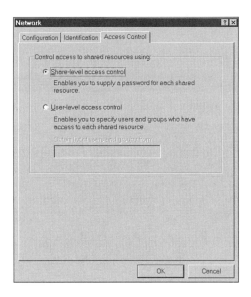

After you're set up to allow sharing, you can just left-click in Explorer, go to Sharing, and permit it as mentioned previously.

Now that you have a shared directory, you need to tell other people it is available and give them the name they should use to access it. To access the example, another user needs to use the following command:

```
NET USE d: \\desktop\Barry_Data
```

NEW TERM At this point, the Universal Naming Convention, or UNC, is needed. You can break down the command in the following manner. First, the two backslashes tell the network that what follows is a *machine name,* and the backslash that follows is the *share name* Peter_Data, not an actual directory name. The command isn't case sensitive. The network software on the other user's machine now understands that it has a drive letter of D with a directory called Barry_Data available to it. Naturally, you might just use Network Neighborhood and double-click on the share that shows up.

Task 3.6: Creating and Removing Shares with W2K's GUI Interface.

▼ **Step 1: Description**

This task enables you to create new shares in W2K.

▼ **Step 2: Action**

1. Log on to your server. You must be an Administrator, a Server Operator, or a Power User to manage shares.

2. Double-click the My Computer icon on the desktop. You then see the list of drives available on your computer.

3. Double-click on the drive you want shared to display a list of file folders. Select the folder you want to share, and right-click to display the context-sensitive menu. Select Sharing.

4. Select the Sharing tab to display the available options. By default, the folder is shown as Not Shared. Click the Share This Folder button to activate the remaining controls in the dialog box.

5. Type a descriptive name for your share in the Share Name box. This is the name your users see when looking for available shares on the network. There is an optional Comment box.

6. When desired, specify the User Limit information. By default, any number of users can use the share at the same time. Use the Allow button to select a limited number of users, and then fill in the specific number of users in the space provided.

7. Decide what level of access users should have to the Share by clicking on the Permissions button and setting the rights as needed. You see that by default W2K allows everyone to access the share.

8. You can remove shares by following the first four steps of this task, and selecting the Not Shared option and clicking the Apply button.

9. You can modify the share name by following these steps and changing the name in the Share Name box. This changes the name your users see when looking for available shares on the network.

▲

Step 3: Review

By using the W2K GUI interface, you created and managed shares on your W2K Server. You use this technique any time you add or change a file folder and want to let other users access the folder.

The negative side to this operation concerns not knowing what the machine and share names are unless you are told by someone. In a small office, this situation is fine because you can call across the room and ask for the information. This situation isn't as simple in larger businesses where you might be separated from other people by offices, floors, or even buildings. So how do you find out what machines and shares are available?

The solution used by Microsoft is called *Browse Services.* What other networks call *name servers,* Microsoft decided to call *browse masters* or *master browsers.* (Either name is correct.) In a Microsoft network, each machine broadcasts a request for a browse master until it finds one. Yoo hoo! Is there a browse master in the network?

NEW TERM   The first browse master to hear the request returns a call telling the machine to direct all future name service requests to it. After a server finds a browse master, it tells the browse master to add its shares to the list the browse master is maintaining. You see this list, called a *browse list,* when you open Windows 95 Network Neighborhood or Windows 2000 My Network Places. You can see an example in Figure 3.27.

FIGURE 3.27

A sample browse list in Windows 95/98.

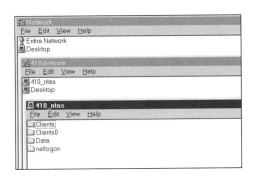

3

By clicking the particular machine icon in the browse list, you can see the actual list of shares that machine has to offer. In DOS, you type the **NET VIEW** command to get the list of servers and then add the machine name of the server you want by using the UNC as described earlier.

For the example, you use net view \\desktop. This command provides the same general information as clicking Network Neighborhood does in Windows W2K.

This method works fine in small networks, as I mentioned earlier. But what about using this browser when you have hundreds or thousands of servers? Scrolling through long lists to find the particular server you need becomes awfully hard. At this point, Microsoft workgroups come into play.

Task 3.7: Opening a Browse List in Windows 2000.

Step 1: Description

This task enables you to see what resources are available to you on the network.

▼ **Step 2: Action**

1. Log on to the workstation.

2. Double-click the My Network Places icon on the desktop. You then see a list of servers you might be able to access.

3. Select a server and double-click that server's name.

4. Select the data folder you need, and double-click again to see what files are available. You can also see any printers available for you to use after you have selected a server.

▲   5. After you're finished, choose File, Close to return to the desktop.

Step 3: Review

By using the My Network Places icon, you executed a command to list what resources are available to you on the network. Remember that the list can change from time to time as servers are added or removed from the network.

You can use some of the shortcuts available to both Windows 95 and W2K machines when browsing. To browse a server quickly, for example, use the Start, Run, *servername* command. Using the Run option in the Start menu, you can type in a server name and go directly to the shared directory of that server, as shown in Figure 3.28.

FIGURE 3.28

A sample run command to access a server.

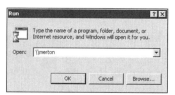

Using this command can be a fast way to go directly to servers you commonly use without waiting for W2K to search through the entire network and build a complete list of available resources. You can create shortcuts for these server shares by dragging the particular data folder from the open window onto the desktop. Then you can access the data on that server by merely clicking the desktop icon you just created.

Workgroups

All a workgroup really consists of is a subdivided browse list. Using it is like using a DOS directory structure. Should you place all the files in the C: root directory (as some new users do), when you list the root directory, the listing scrolls forever. Hard to see what's in the machine and find anything of value, isn't it? In large networks, the browse list can look just like the DOS root directory. A mess. Hard to read. Even harder to find anything.

Workgroups come to the rescue by placing all the servers into useful groupings so that a particular machine sees only the servers it needs to see. Workgroups are often set up in a manner similar to a corporate structure, with Accounting, Finance, Executive, Sales, and Manufacturing. Now when a user browses for available resources, he or she sees only the resources in his or her workgroup.

Note

> Workgroups should consist of a group of people who mostly share data among themselves and rarely share that data outside the workgroup. Workgroup names in W2K can be 15 characters long, like machine names.

You join a workgroup in Windows 98 by updating the Control Panel, Network, Identification options. You have little security or control over adding a machine to a workgroup. On a DOS machine, you set the workgroup using the network Client Setup program or by manually updating the [*network*]|*workgroup*= parameter in the SYSTEM.INI file.

Although I said that no real security is involved with workgroups, Microsoft does enable you to hide the share. Hiding the share in Windows 2000 is as easy as naming it with a $ at the end. If you want to hide Peter_Data, for example, you add the $, making the share name equal Peter_Data$. W2K, however, still shows you these hidden shares when you use the command `net shares`.

You add a password to control access on a Windows 95/98 machine. In Windows 95, a password applies to all users of that share. It's a generic password that applies to the resource, not the person. Not bad, but could be better. The problem with this approach is that after you give out the password you have no idea who is using it. Worse, should you want to remove access from one person, you must implement a new password and tell everyone else what it is except that person. Cumbersome process, isn't it?

W2K goes one step further, enabling you to set a restriction for each person who wants to use the share. On a W2K workstation, you don't put passwords on the share; you create user accounts for all the people using the machine and then tell W2K which people can access which shares. Before access is granted, you need to identify yourself to W2K, whether you're signing on from a DOS machine or a W2K workstation.

When you get to Days 5 and 6, you examine security and domains, so some of this information will begin to make more sense to you.

3

New Programs and Accessories in Windows 2000

For those of you not aware of Windows 95 or the newer Windows 98, Microsoft added a new look to the way you manipulate through the W2K file system. First, on W2K and Windows 95/98 machines you no longer see the familiar Program Manager and File Manager you were used to in Windows 3.x. You start programs by choosing Start, Programs, *program name*. All the programs are placed within the Programs menu in groups, similar to earlier versions of Windows, or in W2K 3.51.

W2K sets up some basic groups, shortcuts, and applications as you install products on the server. The basic list includes:

- Accessories
- Startup
- Windows Update
- Internet Explorer
- Outlook Express

A couple of these groups are dependent on the options you replied to during W2K installation. The Accessories folder continues to provide groups that include Accessibility, Communications, Entertainment, Games, Microsoft Script Debugger, and System Tools, as well as objects such as the Address Book, CalculatorCa, Command Prompt, Imaging, Notepad, Paint, Synchronize, Windows Explorer, WordPad, and Fax.

Startup menu allows you to select programs you want to start every time you start Windows 2000. Just create a shortcut and drag it into the folder and the program will start when you restart your system.

You use Windows Update to scan your system looking for outdated system files and automatically replace them with the most current version.

Internet Explorer (IE) is a free World Wide Web browser shipped with Windows platforms. Use IE to access HTML pages, FTP and GOPHER sites, access newsgroups and even send messages.

Outlook Express is a free and licensed e-mail and news client.

Using Explorer

The old Windows 3.x File Manager is replaced with Windows Explorer, which offers the added benefit of displaying all the drive connections you have available to you in one window. If you're looking for the familiar MS-DOS prompt, it is now called *command prompt* and is found under the Accessories group as you learned earlier.

The process of copying files becomes a little different in this new Explorer. You essentially copy and paste just like you've always done for text, except now the procedure applies to files also.

First, open Windows Explorer and select a file. From the Edit menu, choose Copy. Open the folder where you want to place the file; then choose Edit, Paste. Presto, file copied.

The Explorer looks different, as you can see in Figure 3.29, but still provides the basic functions you have in the Windows NT 3.51 and Windows systems.

FIGURE 3.29

The new Windows Explorer.

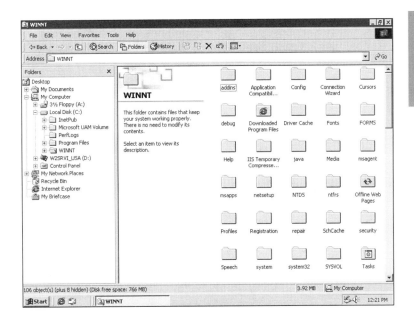

You can accomplish several tasks in Explorer by dragging files. You can do all of the following:

- You can print a file by dragging the file from an Explorer window onto a printer icon.
- You also can drag and drop files to new locations. Make sure that you can see the place where you want to drop a file before starting to drag it. If you drag a file to another location on the same disk, it is moved. If you drag the file to a folder on another disk, the file is copied. Also, for .exe files, holding the Shift key while

dragging the file moves it, and holding the Ctrl key copies it. Dragging an .exe file to anywhere other than a floppy disk drive creates a shortcut.

- Finally, you can drag files using the right mouse button and get a context menu that allows you to select whether you want to Copy, Move, or Create a Shortcut.

Learning to manipulate files this way takes a little additional effort until you're comfortable with the process. After you become comfortable, however, the process becomes an essential part of your day-to-day work. You'll use Explorer frequently in the coming days, so take some time now and practice until you're familiar with the process.

Using Active Desktop

You might find your computer looking slightly different than that which you had in older Windows systems. This is because of the new Active Desktop from Microsoft. This facility allows you to display your desktop as though it were a Web page, providing single click access to those tasks available to you.

Active Desktop allows you to configure the desktop to suit your preferences. You can customize your desktop by right-clicking on the Desktop and selecting Customize My Desktop.

This option is already available on Windows 98 and is the default on Windows 2000 machines.

Using Scraps

If you write a lot of policies and procedures or other material on a W2K machine, one handy hint makes life a great deal easier. You might be familiar with the cut and paste operations of Windows. This feature goes one step further by letting you throw scraps onto the desktop, making them readily available for pasting into documents. It's faster than cut and paste, and it enables you to store a bunch of separate items rather than the one item that Clipboard allows. This feature works only for applications such as MS Word or WordPerfect that support the drag-and-drop features of OLE. It doesn't work for WordPad, unfortunately.

To use the feature, select the text or graphic you want to copy and drag it onto the desktop. W2K creates an item called a *scrap* that you can then drag and drop into another program or use later in a document. After you finish with the item, delete it from the desktop.

Internet Information Server for Windows 2000 Server

An accessory bundled with Windows 2000 is the Internet Information Server (IIS) program. Web server programs enable you to publish home pages and documents on the Internet using your own machine rather than an external Internet service provider, or ISP.

IIS, which is Microsoft's answer to Netscape, is being given away free to generate market share. (At least, that's what I think; Bill Gates might disagree.) This extremely powerful new program is far too detailed to go into here although I talk more about it on Day 19, "Understanding and Using the Microsoft Option Pack."

Setting Up and Managing Printers in Windows 2000 Server

Back in 1988, one of this book's authors, Barry, wrote an article on the paperless office and the expected decrease in the use of paper. In the article, he postulated that computers were increasing rather than decreasing the amount of paper. He certainly doesn't think he's wrong today! An office without a printer is cast adrift, lost forever in the need to put screen to paper.

Printers, however, cost money. They can cost big money—especially when everyone needs one and needs it close by or even on his or her desk. The client/server revolution provided the answer to the need for printers. Place printers strategically around the organization, and network everyone so that they can reach a printer close to their workspaces.

The W2K printer sharing services seem easier to use than most other systems, and therefore the process is fairly straightforward. You do need to understand the following buzzwords, however, before you get started:

- **Printing device**—The actual printer. It typically is the big machine that spews out paper when you least expect it.
- **Printer**—Nope. You might like to think that this word represents the physical device, but as you see, it doesn't. It is the logical printer—what W2K Server sees. You typically use this printer in combination with the printing device, as you'll learn later in this section.
- **Network-interface printers**—Most printers in use on the server connect to the network using a print server that is the device actually connected to the network. Network-interface printers have built-in network cards that allow them to connect directly to the network just like a workstation.
- **Print server**—The machine that stores the printer drivers and allows printers to connect directly to it. You can consider a normal desktop with a printer attached to the Lpt1 port to be a print server when you allow that computer to let other machines use the printer.
- **Queue**—A place you spend way too much time, lining up for just about everything. Actually, on W2K Server, the queue represents the group of documents that are sent to a printer and are waiting to print.

3

These terms provide you with an understanding of how W2K considers the facets of printing. Understanding them is important because they differ somewhat from other operating system terms.

Almost any system on the network can become a print server. It doesn't have to be W2K Server or workstation machines. In addition to W2K, you can use Windows for Workgroups, Windows 95, and even good old MS-DOS with Windows, although this machine needs a special package called MS Workgroup DOS Add-On. So the advantage of using a print server appears obvious. Rather than purchase a printer for each person, you can purchase one printer for each group of persons, with proximity to each other being the criteria for the group.

Windows 2000 Printer Features

I mentioned earlier that adding and using printers in W2K is simpler than what you might be used to. Why? Because W2K usually doesn't require you to obtain special printer drivers. Connecting the workstation to a new printer is therefore as easy as starting the Add New Printer Wizard and following the prompts. These prompts guide you to what printers are available on the network, so all you need to do then is double-click to connect. When W2K cannot find a suitable driver on the machine that the printer is connected to, or when you are connecting to a network interface printer, W2K requests the install CD so that it can load the necessary driver.

W2K provides support for printers with an internal network interface card. This card enables you to connect the printer directly to the network just like connecting a workstation. These printers don't have to be attached to a print server. You find an appropriate connector on the network card at the back of the printer and plug in the network cable. They work with both Token Ring and Ethernet topologies. Using these special types of printers enables you to place them anywhere you have a network connection instead of limiting the connection to a serial or parallel port on a server. This capability provides you more flexibility.

One downside to a directly connected printer that is attached to the network without using a print server is the single data path. Because it is a connected device with only one network card, when the printer receives a print job, it must make all other print jobs wait until that job finishes because no queue is available. For this reason, connecting these printers to a print server is best. To do so, you need to load the Data Link Control protocol on the server.

Then the printer can queue jobs because they are sent through the multiple data paths of the print server. You learn all about this in Day 10, "Managing the Print Server."

Adding a Printer

Adding a printer is quite simple. You don't need Print Manager as you did with LAN Manager and older versions of Windows NT. Just use the Control Panel, Printers window for all your print needs. (You can also use Start, Settings, Printers.)

To add a printer, go to the Printers window in the Control Panel and click the Add Printer icon. As I mentioned earlier, an Add Printer Wizard guides you through all the necessary steps of adding the printer to the network. You see this dialog box in Figure 3.30.

FIGURE 3.30

Add Printer Wizard's opening dialog box.

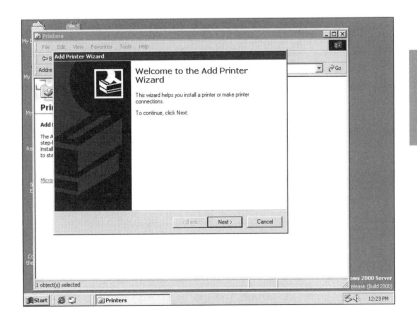

3

Select Local Printer to set up a printer for the server to manage, or select Network printer to connect the machine to an existing printer on another server somewhere in the network. As a user, you would most likely choose the Network Printer option because you want to connect to existing printers. You use the Local Computer option when you're physically adding a new printer either directly onto the network or onto the computer.

Because you just installed W2K yesterday, I'll show you how to add a printer to this server now. Click Local Computer and then click Next. The Plug and Play option makes this relatively easy when your printer is on the HCL.

W2K asks whether this printer is going to be shared with other users. If you're planning to share it, you need to assign a share name first.

If you plan to share the printer, create a name that makes sense to others on the network, and then select all the operating systems that will be using the printer. You need to have the drivers for the systems you select. Finally, click Next and the last wizard window asks whether you want to print a test sheet. After you select Yes or No, click the Finish button and you're done. Now everyone can use the printer.

Now you know all there is to adding a printer in W2K. Pretty straightforward process, isn't it?

Task 3.8: Adding an Existing Printer.

Step 1: Description

This task enables you to add an existing printer to the W2K workstation. You then can print jobs across the network onto that printer. You perform this task each time you want to use a new printer.

Step 2: Action

1. Make sure that you are logged into the workstation.
2. Click the Printer window in the Control Panel.
3. Double-click the Add Printer icon.
4. Select the Network Printer Server option on the opening screen of the Add Printer Wizard.
5. You can either select Find a Printer in the Directory, type in a printer name, or enter a URL for a printer on the Internet or on an intranet. If you need to browse for a printer click on Next after selecting Type the Printer Name.
6. Select the printer. You see the Printer field with a machine name and the printer name. For example, mine looks like \\DESKTOP\HP4. Click OK. Windows 2000 workstations use the printer drivers stored on the printer server, so you don't need to add any.
7. Click Finish. The printer is added and available. You can try it by sending a small print job and watching for the output to show.

Step 3: Review

By using the Add Printer icon, you added your first network printer. You perform this task each time a printer is added or changed on the network and you want to use it.

Changing Printer Properties

After a printer is set up, you might want to change the setup and specify additional information such as the printer's location and when it is available for printing. You can set up printers to print only at certain hours of the day, print separator pages between jobs, or manage who can use the printer.

You change properties for a printer by choosing Start, Settings, Printers. After the Printers window opens, select the printer you want to change, and right-click the icon to go to the Properties dialog box like the one shown in Figure 3.31.

FIGURE 3.31

Printer properties.

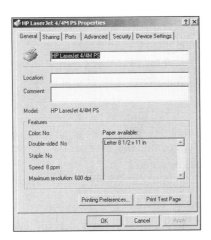

In the Properties dialog box, you can select and change various items. In a large office, for example, the Location text box is useful for guiding staff to where the printer actually resides in the building. You should use this text box unless you work in a small office with only one printer.

You can set up the printer to print special separator pages between each job. Using separators is a good practice because it clearly identifies each job and provides a useful way of separating the various stacks of output. By selecting the Separator Page option, you can designate a particular page as your job separator. Create a unique page by manipulating the sample pages provided by Microsoft as \winnt\system32*.sep files.

NEW TERM In a large organization, you might want to create a printer area and have all output routed to this print department, which then handles all distribution. To do so, you need to use *Printer Pooling*. Using a number of identical printers, you set up the ports where each printer is located. W2K then automatically spools output to the printers on a predetermined priority basis.

In addition to these options, W2K enables you to set up the hours when a printer can produce output. This way, printers cannot produce paper when they are unattended.

You also can set the permissions to decide who is allowed to control these options and who can use the printer. By default, W2K allows Administrators, Print Operators, and Server Operators to modify settings and allows the Everyone group to use the printer.

I have touched on some of the available functions in the printer properties. On Day 10 you go through these tasks in detail in the chapter on managing the print server.

Task 3.9: Changing a Printer to Print Only During the Day.

Step 1: Description

This task enables you to ensure that the printer prints only when staff is on hand to manage the paper trays or clear sensitive documents quickly before unauthorized people see them.

Step 2: Action

1. Make sure that you are logged into the workstation with an Administrator, Print Operator, or Server Operator account.

2. Click the Printer window in the Control Panel.

3. Left-click the Printer icon you want. Then select Properties.

4. Click the Scheduling tab. In the From list box, select the hours you want to have the printer available. The printer still queues jobs regardless of this setting. It doesn't physically print anything outside the hours you select.

5. Change the From time to show 8:00AM. Change the To time to show 7:00PM. You change the hours by using the scroll keys. To show PM, however, you need to select AM and then type PM. You'd think Microsoft would know how to change the time, wouldn't you?

▲ 6. Click OK to finish. The printer then prints only during the specified hours.

Step 3: Review

By using the Printer properties, you made the printer more secure. Now output is printed only during the times staff is on hand to pick up the output.

Summary

In this chapter, you learned the following points:

- How to log on to W2K Server using an Administrator account or a User account
- All about the Help function available in W2K and how to migrate through the various panels

- How to use the command prompt and access the NET utilities available to you as an administrator
- What the various Administrator tools are and how they assist you in the day-to-day administration of W2K networks
- How to access and use the Microsoft Books Online to get help in understanding Windows W2K
- How to properly log off the network
- That the NET CONFIG command provides information about you and the machine you're using
- What the command prompt window is used for and how to change how it looks to suit your personal preferences
- That UNC is an acronym for Universal Naming Convention
- That Microsoft calls its name server either browse master or master browser
- What a workgroup consists of and how it is used
- What's new in programs and utilities in Windows 2000
- How to set up and modify printers

Workshop

To wrap up the day, you can review tasks from the lesson, and see the answers to some commonly asked questions.

Task List

With the information gained in this chapter, you can begin to explore the facets of W2K Server. You now know how to log on and use Help and how to get additional detailed information using the Microsoft Books available online. You learned to do the following tasks:

- Log on to Windows 2000 Server
- Use a number of NET commands to get information about the network
- Set the Group Policy
- Obtain additional information using Microsoft Books
- Resize the command prompt window and change other facets of the window such as color and font type
- Create and remove shares with Windows 2000's GUI interface

- Open a browse list to discover what machines and printers are on the network
- Add a printer to the network and make it available for use
- Change printer options, control when the printer produces output, and control who can change the printer properties

Q&A

Q Is a Help menu still available?

A As you learned in this chapter, you can get help from a number of locations. Each window usually offers a Help menu specific to that particular function. Additional help is available in both the Microsoft Books and when you use the NET command through a Command Prompt window.

Q Should I use the command prompt or GUI interface?

A W2K provides both options for a number of tasks. If you're more comfortable issuing command-line options, then by all means use this tool. For beginners and those more familiar with pointing and clicking, use the GUI interface. There is no right or wrong way here; your choice is primarily a personal preference.

Q Can I use my server machine as a workstation?

A One of the major differences between Windows 2000 and NetWare is the capability to run a one-machine network. In most cases, running such a network is hardly a valid reason for having a server because it defeats the purpose of building a network. Being able to use the server in this manner occasionally is handy, especially in small organizations, so that you don't have to buy a dedicated server machine. I find it useful for doing training seminars because I don't always have to bring a second machine to demonstrate W2K server facilities. There are a number of downsides to using a production server as a workstation. For example, loading user applications on a machine can sometimes cause the machine to lockup and suffer other problems. When this machine is your network server it doesn't cause just one person trouble, but everyone.

Q I don't like the type of text used in the command prompt because it's too small for me to see clearly. Can I change the size?

A Yes, you can modify most of the parameters used by the command prompt window. You can change the size of the text and also change the background colors to create a combination that is more pleasing to your eye.

Q **I have a printer that is used by our executives. They don't want anyone using the printer or having a reason to approach the area because they often print sensitive documents. Can I restrict who can use that printer?**

A You can set a number of variables to manage printers. You learned how to change these properties in a task in this chapter. You can select Start, Settings, Printers and left-click to select properties. In the Properties dialog box, choose the Security tab and change the options as needed. Another possible solution is to hide the printer share by adding the $ sign to the end of the share name. This doesn't stop anyone accessing it when they know it exists, but does stop it appearing on the network.

Q **I often use the same text numerous times when creating procedure manuals. Clipboard allows only one selection, but I need to reuse more than that.**

Is there a better way than constantly moving back and forth, cutting and pasting?

A Windows 2000 provides a technique called scraps to help with just this problem. You can select the text you want and drag it onto the desktop. Do so for each of the pieces you need to reuse. Then just drag a copy into the document as needed. When you're finished, delete the scraps from the desktop.

3

DAY 4

Understanding and Managing the Registry

To this juncture, you have been creating, looking at, or talking to Registry objects. Before you learn how to create Registry objects, you need to learn about the Registry. What is a Registry? Why a Registry? To support the services on a W2K network, including accounting and security, the system must have a place to define and maintain objects. The Registry is that place, and it is critical to the operation of W2K because it is the place where you define all system objects, such as users, groups, and computers. When an object is requested, the system can retrieve and use information about the object before carrying out the request. The Registry, therefore, is the heart and soul of the Windows system.

As you learned in the latter part of Day 1, in the section titled "What Is Windows 2000 Server?" Windows 2000 was designed as an extensible and scalable operating system—one that could evolve in a consistent, modular way over time. The configuration manager, for example, represents the demise of the AUTOEXEC.BAT file, the CONFIG.SYS file, and all the INI files you are most likely accustomed to seeing, fiddling with, and sometimes breaking. The configuration manager consists of several components, the most important being the Registry. The Registry is a repository for all information about the computer hardware where the operating system is running, the software installed on the system, and the person or persons using the system.

The purpose of the Registry and its associated software is, first and foremost, to make the system easier for you to manage. It does so by examining the hardware and learning what it can at boot time, by configuring automatically as much of the system as possible, by asking you a minimum number of questions when the operating system is installed, and by storing all the information it gleans in the Registry so that you never have to be bothered twice for the same information. Device drivers, applications, and users also can place information in the Registry, and they can query the Registry to retrieve the information they need. You can view, update, or modify configuration information by using the graphical Registry Editor. Information in the configuration Registry is stored in key objects, which are subject to the security mechanisms and other semantics applied to W2K executive objects. This design allows W2K to maintain a unified storage facility for this seemingly random information and, at the same time, to make it available in a distributed but secure manner on networked systems.

As a system administrator, you face an enormous challenge in managing hardware, operating systems, and applications. In W2K, the Registry helps simplify the burden by providing a secure, unified database that stores configuration data in a hierarchical form, enabling you to use the administrative tools in W2K to provide local or remote support easily. This chapter covers the inner workings of the Registry and its use. The Registry is integral to using W2K, and it is so complex that you will spend a whole day focusing on it. In this chapter, you'll learn the fundamentals of the Registry and you'll start using the Registry Editor.

Registry Overview

Does anybody remember Windows 3.1? If you're familiar with earlier versions of Windows, you probably remember all those INI, SYS, and BAT configuration files. But where did Windows keep its color settings? Let's see, they could be in SYSTEM.INI or WIN.INI. But wait, that kind of stuff is set by the Control Panel, and you also have a CONTROL.INI. Or maybe these settings are in AUTOEXEC.BAT? And this is just the color setting. What about all the other components and software? Obviously, something needed to change.

W2K tries to improve on this configuration mess with the Registry. The Registry works in conjunction with these INI files and even makes the old MS-DOS stalwarts (AUTOEXEC.BAT and CONFIG.SYS) more or less unnecessary. The Registry is remarkable in that it's one big, central, secure database containing all the configuration information about the server, its applications, and its users. Everything's here, from color settings to users' passwords. (In case you're wondering, you can't directly access the part containing the passwords.) The Windows 2000 Registry describes the hardware configuration, installed system and application software, user and group account security, desktop settings and profiles, file associations, and applications supporting Object Linking and Embedding (OLE). When you make a configuration change on the server, the system usually records it in the Registry database. Even better, the Registry uses a fault-tolerant approach to writing data to ensure that the Registry remains intact even when a failure occurs in the middle of a Registry update.

Starting at boot time, the Registry is populated by a variety of W2K system modules and is added to or modified by the configuration tools in Control Panel, the Windows 2000 Setup applet, Active Directory Users and Computers, third-party configuration tools, and software installation procedures.

Some Windows 2000 Server configuration information isn't available in menu format. Instead, you must manually edit the Registry to make changes. Editing can be extremely dangerous when you don't know what you're doing—you can render the system inoperable with the wrong changes. Don't edit the Registry unless you absolutely have to and have investigated the changes thoroughly. Furthermore, make a backup of the Registry when you plan to make changes so that you can get back to where you started if anything goes wrong. Later today you'll learn about Registry backup.

4

Every server maintains its own Registry containing the information for that server. The Registry is a database containing configuration data for applications, hardware, and device drivers, as well as data on network protocols and adapter card settings. Each record in the database represents an object. (If you want to add a new user before you learn about the Registry, skip to Day 7, "Managing User Accounts.") It is an object-oriented database containing definitions for users, groups, and other objects on the network.

Changes to the Registry can be made through applications in the Administrative Tools directory, applications within Control Panel, or by opening up Registry Editor and manually changing field values. To edit the Registry, you must run the Registry Editor utility. You can launch the Registry Editor by choosing Start, Run and then typing `regedt32`. Doing so pulls up a window with five embedded windows called subtrees. You'll learn about these and other important Registry components next.

| Caution | Because the Registry has no cautionary messages for entering incorrect values in fields, you should refrain from directly changing field values. |

In summary, the Registry provides several benefits to an administrator:

- It collects all configuration information while accommodating the data and storage needs of system components. The Registry replaces the complex and fragmented collection of batch, initialization, and configuration files used in Windows 3.1x and provides all the data required for describing and operating a specific workstation or server.

- It allows discretionary access control to local and remote configuration data. Each key in the Registry can be protected by an Access Control List (ACL), which allows some users to modify Registry contents and grants other users read-only access to the same data.

- It records and preserves security and desktop information on an individual basis. Although W2K currently supports only one interactive user, it is common for workstations and servers to have multiple concurrent network connections. In the Registry, you can find a permanent record of per-user, per-application, and per-machine configuration information.

- You can use the Registry to determine all the hardware components installed on a local or remote system, the BIOS revision levels for motherboards and video adapters, the numbers and types of SCSI adapters, the devices installed on each adapter, and IRQ and base address and DMA channel assignments for specific components. On the software side, you can see installed applications and system configuration data set by various Windows 2000 applets.

So you've just got to like Windows 2000's Registry—except, of course, for the annoying things about the Registry, including its cryptic organization and excessively complex structure. But read on, and it will become clearer.

What Is the Registry?

As just mentioned, the Registry is a hierarchical database of settings, much like INI files, that describe your user account, the server's hardware, and your applications. Knowing how to work with the Registry is an important key to tuning and controlling servers and workstations. You might be relieved or saddened to know that it is not, by the way, the same as the Registry that is part of Windows 95, although it is similar. Windows 95 experts will know, for example, that you can do some very powerful things under Windows 95 by exporting a Registry to an external file, modifying that file, and re-importing it to a Windows 95 Registry. In W2K, you can only save the Registry to an external file and restore it later.

Simply, the Registry is a database you view and manipulate through a program called the Registry Editor. The Registry Editor uses a hierarchical structure to display subtrees that allow access to the contents of the database. At first glance, the hierarchical structure displayed in the Registry Editor looks similar to Explorer's hierarchical directory structures. The difference lies in the kinds of information contained in the Registry and the impact that manipulating the Registry has on the system.

Under Windows 3.1x, whenever you started the system, connected to a network, or ran an application, the system hunted for and read several configuration files to set up its operating environment. In contrast, W2K stores and checks the configuration information in only one location—the Registry. The Registry contains the following types of configuration information:

- AUTOEXEC.BAT, CONFIG.SYS, WIN.INI, SYSTEM.INI, CONTROL.INI, LANMAN.INI, PROTOCOL.INI, and miscellaneous INI files
- Device driver data
- Network protocols and network adapter settings

The following W2K components and applications use the Registry:

- **Setup**. Whenever you run the Windows 2000 Setup program or other setup programs for applications or hardware, the Setup program adds new configuration data to the Registry.
- **Hardware Detector**. Each time you boot a W2K machine, the Hardware Detector places hardware configuration data in the Registry. This information includes a list of hardware detected in the system at startup.
- **Windows 2000 Kernel**. During system startup, the Windows 2000 Kernel extracts information from the Registry, such as the device drivers to load and the order in which to load them. The NTOSKRNL.EXE program also passes information about itself to the Registry, such as its version number.
- **Device drivers**. Device drivers send and receive load parameters and configuration data from the Registry. This data is similar to what you might find on the DEVICE= lines in the CONFIG.SYS file under MS-DOS. A device driver must report system resources it uses, such as hardware interrupts and DMA channels, so that the system can add this information to the Registry. Applications and device drivers can read this Registry information to provide users with smart installation and configuration programs.

4

- **Administrative tools**. The administrative tools in W2K, such as those provided in the Control Panel and in the Administrative Tools program group, can be used to modify configuration data. The Registry Editor is helpful for viewing and occasionally making detailed changes to the system configuration. You also can use the Windows 2000 Diagnostics program (WINMSD.EXE) to view configuration information stored in the Registry.

Now, editing the Registry is likely the part you won't like about W2K. The Registry isn't documented very well in the pile of manuals you get from Microsoft.

Understanding the Registry will make you a better administrator, should you take the time to study it. The goal for this chapter, then, is to give you a feel for the Registry, how to edit it, and when to leave it alone.

Understanding Registry Terminology

To get a first insight into the Registry, look at the Registry Editor. You can see it by running the program REGEDT32.EXE (it's in the C:\SystemRoot\SYSTEM32 directory, where SystemRoot is typically winnt). The simplest method is to type **REGEDT32** on the RUN command line offered on your Start menu. Run it and click the HKEY_CURRENT_USER window. You should see a screen like the one in Figure 4.1.

FIGURE 4.1

The Registry Editor.

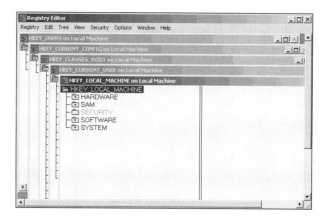

The terms to know so that you understand the Registry are subtree, key, value, data type, and hive. The following text covers these terms.

> **Caution**
>
> Accidentally blowing away important data is easy with the Registry Editor. You might be wise at this point to put the Editor in read-only mode by choosing Options, Read Only Mode.
>
> You always can reverse the read-only state whenever necessary in the same way. You simply can render a server completely unusable with a few accidental Registry edits, so be careful.

NEW TERM The first step in mastering the Registry is understanding the design and layout of the database. Learning how to interpret the database, relate keys and values to specific hardware or software components, and modify and add keys and values is an essential survival skill for system and network administrators. A key contains data items called value entries and may also contain additional subkeys and can be considered to be analogous to directories with the values being equal to files.

Because the Registry contains data critical to system operation, such as data accessed by loaded device drivers and client or server processes, be careful when performing modifications.

The Registry is composed of thousands of individual data items that describe every aspect of a specific operating system installation, from the hardware to valid users to customized logon messages and performance monitoring profiles. These data items are organized into keys and optional values. Keys are grouped so that related information can be accessed and cross-referenced.

Each area of the Registry has a standard set of keys that are common across all Windows W2K installations. Within these keys, system-specific values describe hardware components, operating system components, and bootable configurations. Then the variations begin. If a network card is installed, for example, several entries describe the hardware type (such as NE2000 and EtherExpress), the IRQ and base address, loaded driver, and related network services. Additional entries indicate the protocols that have been bound to the network driver for the card. Another common variation is the type of graphics adapter installed or the type and mode of a sound card or SCSI adapter.

Standard Keys

If you compare one key with another, you find standard keys with a significant variation in value entries. Each hardware component causes multiple subkeys to be placed in the hardware, software, and ControlSet keys. When one system has several applications and another has only a couple, the system with many understandably has more keys in the software section. Similarly, when one system is a domain server, many entries appear in the users' area, as compared to only one or two entries for a standalone workstation with a single dedicated user and only two network connections.

NEW TERM The Registry is one database, structured like a hierarchical file system. If you ever supported Windows 3.1x, you know that it had two essential INI files, WIN.INI and SYSTEM.INI. Generally, WIN.INI contained user-specific settings and SYSTEM.INI contained machine-specific settings. Windows 2000's Registry is divided up as well. It is presented in five major views called *subtrees*. Each Registry subtree contains keys holding configuration data about a specific computer and each of its users. These subtrees describe hardware and software configuration, security data, all connected-user operating environments (profiles), the currently logged on user, and file associations used for Object Linking and Embedding. Each view has a name that begins with HKEY, which stands for Handle to a Key. A *handle* is a programming construct used to access W2K objects. These are the subtrees shown in Figure 4.1:

HKEY_LOCAL_MACHINE

HKEY_CLASSES_ROOT

HKEY_USERS

HKEY_CURRENT_USER

HKEY_CURRENT_CONFIG

HKEY_LOCAL_MACHINE

The most important subtree is HKEY_LOCAL_MACHINE because in it the system stores hardware, software, and security information. It contains information about the local computer system, including hardware and operating system data such as bus type, system memory, device drivers, and startup control data. In this subtree, you most often make changes to the Registry. It contains five main keys—HARDWARE, SAM, SECURITY, SOFTWARE, and SYSTEM—described in detail in the following subsections.

The HKEY_LOCAL_MACHINE\HARDWARE Subtree

This HKEY_LOCAL_MACHINE\HARDWARE database describes the physical hardware in the computer, the way that device drivers use the hardware, and mappings and related data that link kernel mode drivers with various user mode code. All data in this subtree is volatile and is re-created whenever the system is started. The Description key describes the actual computer hardware—the make of the motherboard, type of video adapter, SCSI adapters, serial ports, parallel ports, sound cards, network adapters, and so on. The DeviceMap key contains miscellaneous data in formats specific to particular classes of drivers. The ResourceMap key describes which device drivers claim specific hardware resources. The Windows 2000 Diagnostics program (WINMSD.EXE) can report on this database's contents in an easy-to-read form.

All information in HKEY_LOCAL_MACHINE\HARDWARE is disposable (or more correctly, volatile), meaning that the settings are recomputed each time the system is started and then discarded when the system is shut down—they aren't saved. Hardware configuration changes are reflected in the HARDWARE key at the next boot. Applications and device drivers use this subtree to read information about the system components.

The Registry contains both volatile and non-volatile keys. This means that the data in some keys gets changed by the system, for instance when new hardware is added (volatile), while the data in the other keys remains the same (non-volatile) unless manually updated by an administrator or program.

Do	Don't
Do, instead, use Windows 2000 WIN-MSD.EXE to view hardware data in an easy-to-read format for troubleshooting.	**Do not** try to view or edit the data in HKEY_LOCAL_MACHINE\HARDWARE because much of the information appears in binary format, making it difficult to decipher.

4

The HKEY_LOCAL_MACHINE\SAM and HKEY_LOCAL_MACHINE\SECURITY Subtrees

The Security Account Manager (SAM) and SECURITY keys have no visible information, as they point to site security policies such as specific user rights, as well as information for user and group accounts and for the domains in Windows 2000 Server. This information is in Active Directory Users and Computers, and it also appears in the lists of users and groups when you use the Security menu commands in Explorer. You create, modify, and remove keys and values in these two keys with Active Directory Users and Computers.

Caution

The information in the SAM database is in binary format. You should not use Registry Editor to change it. Errors in this database might prevent users from logging on to the computer—another reason that system administrators should not allow users to log on as members of the Administrator group.

The HKEY_LOCAL_MACHINE\SOFTWARE Subtree

HKEY_LOCAL_MACHINE\SOFTWARE is the per computer software database. Remember that you learned about this database in Day 1, "Introducing Networks and Windows 2000." This key contains data about software installed on the local computer, along with miscellaneous configuration data. The entries under this handle, which apply for anyone using this particular computer, show what software is installed on the computer and also define file associations and OLE information.

The HKEY_LOCAL_MACHINE\SYSTEM Subtree

The HKEY_LOCAL_MACHINE\SYSTEM database controls system startup, device driver loading, W2K services, and operating system behavior. The SYSTEM key describes bootable and nonbootable configurations in a group of ControlSets, where each ControlSet represents a unique configuration. Within each ControlSet, two keys describe operating system components and service data for that configuration. This key also records the configuration used to boot the running system (CurrentControlSet), along with failed configurations and the LastKnownGood configuration.

HKEY_CLASSES_ROOT

The HKEY_CLASSES_ROOT subtree contains information on file associations (equivalent to the Registry in Windows 95) and data required to support Microsoft's Object Linking and Embedding technology. This subtree is a clone of data contained in the HKEY_LOCAL_MACHINE view and is separated primarily for usability reasons because the machine subtree is so large and complex.

The Classes subkey provides information on filename-extension associations and OLE that can be used by Windows shell applications and OLE applications.

The OLE information must be created by the specific application, so you should not use Registry Editor to change this information. When you want to change filename-extension associations, use Explorer. Under View, Options, use the File Types tab and associate extensions.

HKEY_USERS

A third subtree, HKEY_USERS, describes a default operating environment and contains one top-level key for each user logged on either interactively or via a network connection. It contains all actively loaded user profiles, including HKEY_CURRENT_USER, which always refers to a child of HKEY_USERS, and the default profile. Users who are accessing a server remotely don't have profiles under this key on the server; their profiles are loaded into the Registry on their own computers.

HKEY_CURRENT_USER

The HKEY_CURRENT_USER subtree contains the user profile for the user who is currently logged on, including environment variables, personal program groups, desktop settings, network connections, printers, and application preferences.

HKEY_CURRENT_CONFIG

The last subtree, HKEY_CURRENT_CONFIG, contains the volatile information for the present hardware configuration. Because the HKEY_LOCAL_MACHINE subtree is so large, the system duplicates some information in this subtree.

To summarize, the Registry stores all information about a computer and its users, as shown in Table 4.1.

TABLE 4.1 Current Subtrees

Subtree	Description
HKEY_LOCAL_MACHINE	Contains information about the hardware currently installed in the machine and about programs and systems running on the machine. You do most of your work in this subtree. The information includes, but isn't limited to, startup control, data, memory, and devices and drivers. Applications, device drivers, and the Windows 2000 system also use the information in this database to establish configuration data for the local computer, regardless of who's logged on and what software is in use.
HKEY_CLASSES_ROOT	Holds the file associations, information that tells the system, for example, "whenever the user double-clicks a file with the extension .BMP in the File Manager, start up PBRUSH.EXE to view this file." It also contains the OLE registration database, the old REG.DAT from Windows 3.1x. This subtree contains information about the file-class associations and Object Linking and Embedding (OLE). This subtree is actually redundant, as you can find all its information in the HKEY_LOCAL_MACHINE subtree.
HKEY_USERS	This subtree contains information about active users. It also includes profiles on any user who has local access to the system. It contains two user profiles: a DEFAULT profile used for someone logging in who hasn't logged in before, and a profile with a name like S-227362152... (the Security ID of the user), which is the profile of a user already known to the system.

continues

TABLE 4.1 continued

Subtree	Description
HKEY_CURRENT_USER	This subtree contains the user profile for the person currently logged onto the Windows 2000 machine. This information includes the user's profile groups, desktop settings, printers, application preferences, and network connections.
HKEY_CURRENT_CONFIG	This subtree contains configuration information for the particular hardware configuration you booted with.

Sometimes these subtrees contain conflicting information. Data in HKEY_CURRENT_USER, for example, might include some of the same parameters as HKEY_LOCAL_MACHINE; in this case, HKEY_CURRENT_USER takes precedence. Users might change their desktop settings for example and this will cause the HKEY_CURRENT_USER key to be updated making it different from what is stored in the HKEY_LOCAL_MACHINE parameters.

Where the Registry Lives: Hives

NEW TERM Mostly, the Registry is contained in a set of files called the *hives*. Some of the Registry is built automatically every time you boot up the system. The system doesn't know devices on a SCSI chain, for example, until you boot. Hives are binary files, so you can't look at them without a special editor of some kind, like the Registry Editor. Using hives is, however, an easy way to load or back up a sizable part of the Registry.

Most, although not all, of the Registry is stored in hive files. They're not hidden, system, or read-only but are always open, so you're somewhat limited in what you can do with them.

Below each subtree is a collection of hives and files. You're probably wondering why Microsoft picked the name hives; it did so because the structure resembles a beehive. Below the HKEY_LOCAL_MACHINE subtree, for example, you typically find the following important hives:

- **HARDWARE**: Contains information about the system's hardware and configuration.
- **SAM**: Contains information about the Security Account Manager (SAM) that houses domain, user, and group security information.
- **SECURITY**: Contains information about the local security information that this machine's security subsystem uses.

- **SOFTWARE**: Contains information about the local software and its configuration.
- **SYSTEM**: Contains information about the operating system and related information.

By default, all hives are stored in the \SystemRoot\SYSTEM32\CONFIG subdirectory, which also includes SYSTEM.ALT and the .LOG files, which are backup hive files. Whenever a new user logs onto a computer, the system creates a new hive for that user. Because each user profile is a separate hive, each profile is also a separate file. (If you prefer, you can store profile hives in other directories.) You can copy a user profile as a file and view, repair, or copy entries using Registry Editor on another computer.

A Look at the Hive Files

The hive files are in the \SystemRoot\SYSTEM32\CONFIG directory. As they're listed in Table 4.2, you can see the hive files corresponding to parts of the subtree.

Table 4.2 needs a few explanatory notes. First, about the HKEY_CLASSES_ROOT subtree: It is copied from HKEY_LOCAL_MACHINE\SOFTWARE\Classes at boot time. The file exists for use by 16-bit Windows applications. While you're logged on to the server however, the two keys are linked; if you make a change to one, the change is reflected in the other.

4

TABLE 4.2 Subtrees and Hives

Subtree/Key	Filename
HKEY_LOCAL_MACHINE\SAM	SAM (primary) and SAM.LOG (backup)
HKEY_LOCAL_MACHINE\SECURITY	SECURITY (primary) and SECURITY.LOG (backup)
HKEY_LOCAL_MACHINE\SOFTWARE	SOFTWARE (primary) and SOFTWARE.LOG (backup)
HKEY_LOCAL_MACHINE\SYSTEM	SYSTEM (primary) and SYSTEM.ALT (backup)
HKEY_USERS\DEFAULT	DEFAULT (primary) and DEFAULT.LOG (backup)
HKEY_USERS\Security ID	xxxxxnnn, xxxxxnnn.LOG
HKEY_CURRENT_USER	USE### or ADMIN###(primary); USER###.LOG or ADMIN###.LOG (backups); ###=system ID for user
HKEY_CLASSES_ROOT	(Created from current control set at boot time)

The user profiles typically live in \SystemRoot\Documents and Settings\username, where each user gets a directory named username. I've got a user account named "lewisb," for example, so I have a directory named d:\winnt\Documents and Settings\lewisb on my computer. If I look in it, I find the files ntuser.dat and ntuser.dat.log.

One question remains about the user profiles, however. Why do all the files have a paired file with the extension .LOG? You'll learn about these LOG files later in the chapter.

Values

Progressing down the Registry tree, below the hives you'll find Registry keys, which contain items called value entries. This is typically the place where you edit, add, or delete values. Be sure you know what you're doing (and have a backup)!

Registry Keys

Figure 4.1 shows the Registry Editor displaying five cascaded windows, one for each subtree. HKEY_LOCAL_MACHINE is on top; you can see the other four subtrees' windows, too. The HKEY_CURRENT_USER window has right and left panes. The pane on the left looks like a screen from the Explorer or the old Windows 3.1 File Manager.

In the File Manager, the folders represented subdirectories. Here, however, they separate information into sections, in the same way that old Windows INI files had sections whose names were surrounded by square brackets, names like [386enh], [network], [boot], and the like. Compare the HKEY_LOCAL_MACHINE window in Figure 4.1 to an INI file. If it were an INI file, the name of its sections would be [hardware], [sam], [security], [software], and [system]. Each of these folders or sections is actually called a key in the Registry.

But at this point the analogy to INI files fails: you can have keys within keys, called subkeys (and sub-subkeys, and sub-sub-subkeys, and so on). Opening the SYSTEM key, you find that it contains subkeys named Clone ControlSetO01, ControlSetO02, CurrentControlSet, Select, and Setup; and CurrentControlSet is further subkeyed into Control, Enum, Hardware Profiles and Services.

Notice, by the way, the key called CurrentControlSet. It's very important. Almost every time you modify the system's configuration, you do so with a subkey within the CurrentControlSet subkey.

Key-Naming Conventions

The tree of keys gets pretty big as you drill down through the many layers. CurrentControlSet, for example, has dozens of subkeys, each of which can have subkeys. Identifying a given subkey is important, so Microsoft has adopted a naming convention that looks just like directory trees. CurrentControlSet's fully specified name would be, then, HKEY_LOCAL_MACHINE\SYSTEM\CurrentControlSet. In this book, however, you'll see it just called CurrentControlSet for space and simplicity's sake.

Value Entries, Names, Values, and Data Types

If you drill down through CurrentControlSet, you can find the subkey Services, and within Services are many subkeys. In Figure 4.2, you can see some of the subkeys of CurrentControlSet\Services.

FIGURE 4.2

Subkeys of CurrentControlSet\ Services.

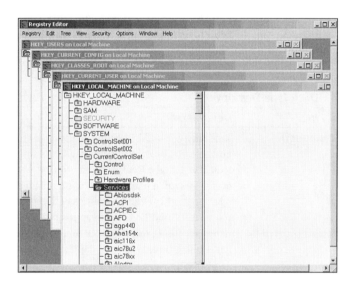

One of these keys, Browser, contains subkeys named Enum, Parameters, and Security. After you get to Parameters, however, you can see that it's the end of the line—no subkeys from there. Just to review Registry navigation quickly, the key you're looking at now is in HKEY_LOCAL_MACHINE\SYSTEM\CurrentControlSet\Services\ Browser\Parameters.

In the right-hand pane, you see two lines:

```
IsDomainMasterBrowser:REG_SZ:False
MaintainServerList:REG_SZ:Yes
```

In this way, the Registry says what would be, in the old INI-type files, something like this:

```
IsDomainMasterBrowser=Yes
MaintainServerList=Yes
```

Each line like IsDomainMasterBrowser:REG_SZ:False is called a value entry. The three parts are called name, data type, and value, respectively. In this example, IsDomainMasterBrowser is the name, REG_SZ is the data type, and False is the value.

Most of this explanation is fairly straightforward, but what is REG_SZ? It's an identifier to the Registry of the kind of data to expect: numbers, messages, yes/no values, and the like. The Registry Editor currently contains five data types (although others could be defined later). A value entry has three components, which always appear in the following order: the name of the value; the data type of the value; and the value itself, which can be data of any length. Microsoft notes that each value entry cannot exceed about lMB in size. Imagining one that size is difficult, but it's worth mentioning.

Table 4.3 lists the data types currently defined and used by the system.

TABLE 4.3 Data Type Descriptions

Data Type	Description
REG_BINARY	Raw binary data. Most hardware component information is stored as binary data. Data of this type usually doesn't make sense when you look at it with the Registry Editor (unless you're a robot). Binary data shows up in hardware setup information. It can be displayed with the Registry Editor in hexadecimal format or via the Diagnostics program (WINMSD.EXE) in an easy-to-read format. The data is usually represented in hexadecimal for simplicity's sake. Editing binary data can get you in trouble when you don't know what you're doing.
REG_DWORD	More binary data represented by a number that is 4 bytes long. Many parameters for device drivers and services are this data type and can be displayed by the Registry Editor in binary, hexadecimal, or decimal format. For example, entries for service error control: ErrorControl:REG_DWORD:0xl.
REG_EXPAND_SZ	An expandable data string, which is text that contains a variable to be replaced when called by an application. It's often information understandable by humans, like path statements or messages. It is "expandable" in that it might contain information that will change at runtime, like %username%—a system batch variable that is of different sizes for different people's names. For the following value, for example, the string %SystemRoot% is replaced by the actual location of the directory containing the Windows 2000 system files: File:REG_EXPAND_SZ:%SystemRoot%\file.exe.

Data Type	Description
REG_MULTI_SZ	Another string type (a multiple string) that enables you to enter a number of parameters on this one value entry. The parameters are separated by binary zeros (nulls). Values that contain lists or multiple values in human-readable text are usually this type. The following value entry, for example, specifies the binding rules for a network transport: bindable:REG_MULTI_SZ:dlcDriver dlcDriver non non 50.
REG_SZ	A simple string of characters representing human-readable text. For example, a component's description: DisplayName:REG-SZ:Messenger.

If you first met a Registry with Windows 95, you might notice a few differences here. Windows 95 has six subtrees but only three data types: string, which is like REG_SZ, REG_MULTI_SZ, and REG_EXPAND_SZ; dword, which is like REG_DWORD; and binary, which is like REG_BINARY.

And should you be wondering how on earth you'll figure out what data type to assign to a new Registry value, don't worry about it; if you read somewhere to use a particular new value entry, you'll be told what data type to use.

Working with the Registry: An Example

Now, probably you want to get in the Registry and try it out despite the numerous warnings, so here's an innocuous example. Remember: It's innocuous only when you follow the example to the letter; otherwise, it will soon be time to get out your installation disks.

We're not just whistling Dixie. Don't get mad should you blow away the server because you didn't pay attention to the warnings. Actually, you can avoid a reinstallation if the thing you modified was in the CurrentControlSet key; W2K knows that you often mess around in there, so it keeps a spare. In that case, you can reboot the server and wait for the message that says Press Spacebar now to restore Last Known Good menu. Again, pressing the Spacebar doesn't restore the entire Registry; it just restores the control set. Fortunately, the current control set is a lot of the Registry.

Now that you know what the Registry is, how it works, and what it contains, you might want to know how to manipulate its entries. In any case, you can try out something relatively harmless. For this example, change the name of the organization that you gave W2K when you installed it. The Registry Editor enables you to change organization names without reinstalling.

4

Task 4.1: Changing the Registry.

Step 1: Description

This task enables the Administrator to change the Registry.

Step 2: Action

1. Ensure you are logged on as Administrator.

2. To open the Registry Editor, choose Start, Run.

3. In the command line, type **REGEDT32** and press Enter.

4. Click Window and choose HKEY_LOCAL_MACHINE. Maximize that window, and you see a screen somewhat like the one in Figure 4.3.

FIGURE 4.3

The Registry Editor local machine box.

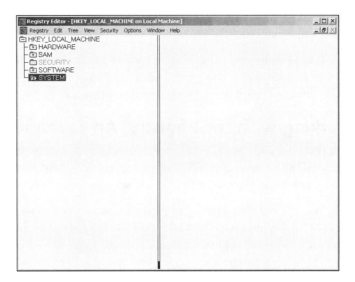

5. Modify the value entry in HKEY_LOCAL_MACHINE\Software\Microsoft\ Windows NT\CurrentVersion. To do so, double-click the Software key and then double-click the Microsoft key. Next, double-click the Windows NT key, and finally, double-click the CurrentVersion key. You see a screen like the one in Figure 4.4. On the left pane, you still see the Registry structure including the subkeys for CurrentVersion. On the right, you see a number of values such as CurrentBuild and InstallDate.

FIGURE 4.4

The CurrentVersion window.

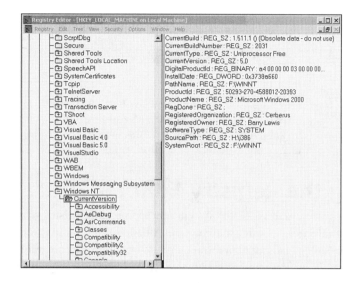

6. Double-click RegisteredOrganization, and you see a screen like the one in Figure 4.5.

FIGURE 4.5

Updating the CurrentVersion window.

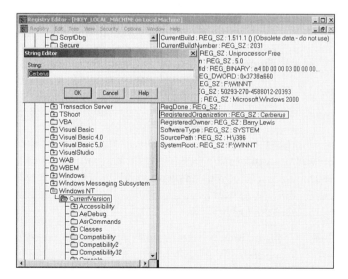

7. Highlight the old value and replace it with Cerberus ISC. Click OK and then close the Registry Editor.

8. Click Help and About for any program (even the Registry Editor will do), and you'll see that your organization is now Cerberus ISC.

Step 3: Review

In this task, you learned how to use the Registry to change the name of your organization. To rename it to your own company again, follow all the steps above replacing Cerberus ISC with the name of your company.

 Caution | Click all you like, but you won't find a Save button or an Undo button. When you edit the Registry, it's real-time and it's forever. So, again, be careful when you mess with the Registry.

Using the Registry Editor

When you install W2K, the system sets appropriate Registry values for the local hardware and software configuration. Although the standard tools do a good job of maintaining configuration information, for many entries no graphical user interface exists. In this case, to make adjustments to system configuration or operation, you must directly edit the configuration database.

 Caution | The full pathname for the Registry Editor is SystemRoot\system32\ regedt32.exe, where SystemRoot normally is the directory where you installed W2K (most probably, winnt). The system doesn't load the Registry Editor as an icon at installation. Note that another file in the SystemRoot directory, called REGEDIT.EXE, exists for compatibility with Windows applications. Don't use the older version to access the Registry—it might trash the system.

With the Registry Editor, you can load either the local or a remote Registry, when you have a valid username and necessary rights and permissions on the target system. When the database is in place, you can display, add, modify, and delete keys and values in the database, protect keys with an ACL, modify user profiles, and audit the success or failure of access to selected keys.

If all you need is to examine information stored in the Registry, use the Windows 2000 Diagnostics tool, called WINMSD.EXE. The fastest way to access the program is typing that name on your Run line. It's a handy tool and a whole lot safer than mucking about with the Registry Editor. You can also use Start, Programs, Administrative Tools, Computer Management and navigate to the System Information area.

With Windows 2000 Diagnostics, you can display specific data from the Registry in an easily readable format. You cannot edit value entries using Windows 2000 Diagnostics, so the Registry contents are protected while you browse for information. You can, however, select and copy any value if you want to paste information in a Registry Editor edit box or text editor. You need to be careful of course to ensure that you only copy the values you need.

Before going on to perform what could very well amount to open-heart surgery on the system, you should acquaint yourself with two very important tools used for Registry management:

- Backup: Backs up Registry hives as part of a tape backup routine.
- Emergency repair disk: Restores default hives to the system.

The processes of backing up and restoring the Registry are covered later in this chapter. As a precautionary measure, back up the Registry and critical system files. Also, make sure that you have an emergency repair disk on hand to rescue the system from any Registry-tweaking mishaps. If you have a good set of backup files, you can restore damaged or missing Registry hives.

Running the Registry Editor Program

The Registry Editor program doesn't appear on the Start menu after you install W2K, but it is installed automatically.

Run the REGEDT32.EXE file from the Explorer or by using Run on the Start menu. Or type **start regedt32** at a command prompt and press Enter. You should see a Registry Editor window similar to the one in Figure 4.1. The four local windows appear, each of which bears the name of a predefined key:

- HKEY_CURRENT_USER. The HKEY_CURRENT_USER window is the root of the configuration information for the user who is currently logged on. Information such as the user's program groups, screen colors, and Control Panel settings are stored here. This information is referred to as a user's profile.
- HKEY_USERS. The HKEY_USERS window is the root of all user profiles on the computer. HKEY_CURRENT_USER is a subkey of HKEY_USERS.
- HKEY_LOCAL_MACHINE. The HKEY_LOCAL_MACHINE window contains configuration information particular to the computer (for any user).
- HKEY_CLASSES_ROOT. The HKEY_CLASSES_ROOT window is a subkey of HKEY_LOCAL_MACHINE\SOFTWARE. The information stored here is used to perform operations such as opening the right application when a file is opened from File Manager (file association) and for Object Linking and Embedding (OLE).

- HKEY_CURRENT_CONFIG. The HKEY_CURRENT_CONFIG contains information similar to HKEY_LOCAL_MACHINE; that is, information about the local computer.

Each subtree contains multiple keys, and each key contains a plus sign if it can be expanded with a double-click of the mouse. The display is normally divided into two; keys appear on the left, and values, if any, appear on the right. You can display keys (tree) only, values only (data), or both (tree and data) by making the appropriate selection from the View menu.

If the currently highlighted key has a value or series of values, they appear to the right of the key in the data portion of the window. Some keys have a single value; others have 20 or more, depending on how the Registry entry is used. A value consists of three parts separated by colons: a field name, data type, and the actual data. There are six standard data types: REG_BINARY, REG_DWORD, REG_EXPAND_SZ, REG_MULTI_SZ, and REG_SZ. Many Registry entries are written in one of the three string formats— REG_SZ, REG_EXPAND, REG_MULTI_SZ—which represent a single string, a string that contains variables such as SystemRoot as well as text, and a string consisting of multiple strings, respectively.

Note

Your ability to make changes to the Registry using Registry Editor depends on your access privileges. In general, you can make the same kinds of changes in Registry Editor as your privileges allow for Control Panel or other administrative tools. Choose Options, Read Only Mode to protect the Registry contents while you explore its structure and become familiar with the entries.

Managing the Registry

So far in this lesson, you changed the organization name in the Registry. When you want to change that value, how do you know to go to HKEY_LOCAL_MACHINE\ Software\Microsoft\Windows 2000\CurrentVersion? Well, you can find it by poking around in the Registry. But, at this point, you still might feel nervous around the Registry. This nervousness is understandable considering the ramifications of a false move. So, in this section, you'll learn how to perform the following tasks:

- Use the Registry Editor and Windows 2000 Diagnostics
- Manage the Registry for a remote computer
- Edit Registry value entries
- Maintain the Registry

Now, you can start managing the Registry.

Altering Registry Data

Poking around isn't a desirable action or a time-saver, and this points out a glaring weakness of the Registry Editor: it has no effective search routine. Suppose you know that you have something called RegisteredOrganization, but you have no idea where it lives in the Registry. You're just out of luck. REGEDT32 includes a View/Find Key, but you can use it to search only the names of keys, not value entries. Because RegisteredOrganization is a value name within the key CurrentVersion, you can search for it only when you know that the key's name is CurrentVersion, which isn't very likely.

> **Tip**
>
> You can use REGEDIT.EXE to search both key names and values. But weren't you told earlier not to use this program because it might damage the Registry? Well, yes, you were. You can use REGEDIT to view, but not edit, the Registry. This application displays the Registry as one tree and makes finding particular values easy, because it searches for partial matches.

Within the Registry, you can alter the value entries for a selected key or assign new value entries to keys. This section covers how to find keys and edit, add, or delete keys and value entries.

> **Note**
>
> When possible, use the graphical administrative tools such as Control Panel to make configuration changes, instead of using the Registry Editor. Using the administrative tools is safer because these applications know how to store values properly in the Registry. Should you make errors while changing values with the Registry Editor, you get no warning because the Registry Editor doesn't understand or recognize errors in syntax or other semantics.

The location of a Registry key in the tree structure might be different from what is described here, depending on whether a computer is running W2K as a workstation or as a server, and other factors (such as your version). You can search for a specific key name in the Registry tree. Key names appear in the left pane of the Registry Editor windows. The search begins from the currently selected key and includes all its descendant keys.

Each search is local to the tree where the search begins; that is, when you're searching in the windows for HKEY_LOCAL_MACHINE, the search doesn't include keys under HKEY_CURRENT_USER.

4

Task 4.2: Searching for a Key in the Registry Editor.

Step 1: Description

This task enables the Administrator to find a key in the Registry.

Step 2: Action

1. Log on to the Windows 2000 Server as Administrator.

2. Choose Start, Run and type **regedt32**. You should see a Registry Editor similar to the one shown in Figure 4.6.

FIGURE 4.6

Registry Editor windows.

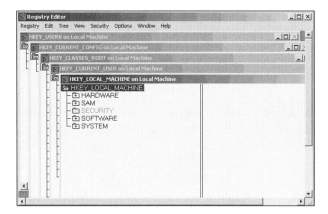

3. Choose View, Find Key.

4. In the Find box of the Find Key dialog box, type the name of the key you want to find.

   If you want to restrict the scope of the search or define the search direction, select the Match Whole Word Only box, the Match Case option, or Up or Down in the Direction box.

   To see the next occurrence of the key name you specified, click Find Next.

5. Click Find. Because key names aren't unique, searching for additional occurrences of a specific key name is a good idea, to ensure that you find the key you want.

> **Tip**
>
> Some key names include spaces (such as Session Manager); others use underscores (such as Ntfs_rec) or a continuous string (such as EventLog). To ensure that you find the key you want, search for a portion of the name, and make sure that the Match Whole Word Only check box is unchecked in the Find dialog box.

Step 3: Review

Working with the Registry is a key system administration responsibility. Before you can alter any entry, you need to find the entry. This task showed you how to find a key.

Now that you have found the key, you can edit the value using the Registry Editor.

More Cautions About Editing the Registry

If you're just learning about the Registry, you're probably eager to wade right in and modify a value entry. Before you do, however, let me just talk about using caution when manipulating the Registry.

The vast majority of Registry items correspond to some setting in the Control Panel, Computer Management, Active Directory Users and Computers, or the like. For example, you saw earlier today that you could change the value of RegisteredOrganization directly via the Registry Editor. That example, however, is fairly illustrative and simple to understand. In general, don't use the Registry to modify a value that can be modified otherwise.

Suppose, for example, you choose to set a background color on the screen to medium gray. That color is represented as a number triplet: 128 128 128. How do you know what these color values mean? Because they're the same as Windows 3.1x color values. Color values in Windows are expressed as number triplets. Each number is an integer between 0 and 255. When you input a value greater than 255, the Registry Editor neither knows nor cares that you're putting in an illegal color value. Now, in the case of colors, that probably wouldn't crash the system. In the case of other items, however, the system could easily be rendered unusable. Suppose you're running Windows 2000 Server on a system with a single Pentium processor; the Registry would reflect that, noting in one of the Hardware keys that W2K is running in "uniprocessor" mode. Altering that to a multiprocessor mode wouldn't be a very good idea.

Why, then, learn about the Registry Editor? Here are three reasons:

- Some settings—important ones—can be altered only with the Registry Editor, so there's no getting around the fact that an administrator has to be proficient with the Registry Editor.

- You can use the Registry Editor to change system value entries on remote computers. Here's a simple example: You're in New York, and you want to change the background color on a server in Atlanta. One way to do so would be to get on a plane and travel to Atlanta to run the Control Panel on the W2K machine at that location. A better way, however, would be to start up the Registry Editor, choose Registry, Select Computer, and edit the Registry of the remote computer. (This way assumes that you're running Windows 2000 or NT, and you have the security

4

access to change the Registry of the remote computer; that is, you're a member of the Administrators group on that computer.)

- A program called REGINI.EXE that comes with the Resource Kit enables you to write scripts to modify the Registry. Such a tool is quite powerful. You could write a REGINI script, for example, to reconfigure a Windows 2000 setup completely. Again, however, before you start messing with that program, be sure that you have become proficient with the Registry. As explained earlier, you can get into all kinds of trouble when working with the Registry Editor. Imagine what kinds of automated disasters you could start at 300MHz with a bad REGINI script!

Editing Keys with Registry Editor

The following task shows you how to edit a key with the Registry Editor. Don't forget that once you edit the key, you have changed it forever. You can't undo an edit without reperforming the same task.

Task 4.3: Editing a Key with the Registry Editor.

Step 1: Description

This task enables the Administrator to edit a key in the Registry.

Step 2: Action

1. Open the Registry Editor by typing **REGEDT32** on the Start/Run command line. Be sure to save a copy of the hive you are modifying so you can recover if needed. Use the option under Registry, Save Subtree As.

2. In the right pane of the Registry Editor window, double-click the value entry, or from the Edit menu, choose the String, Binary, Dword, or Multi String command as appropriate for the selected value.

3. Edit the value that appears in the related Editor dialog box and then click OK.

> **Tip**
>
> To view numbers in decimal format, double-click the value entry and select the Decimal format option. Cancel the dialog box when you finish checking the value.

Step 3: Review

Working with the Registry is a key system administration responsibility. This task showed you how to edit a value.

The Binary and Dword editors give you the flexibility to select the base of a number system in which you want to edit the data. In the Binary editor, you can edit the data as binary (base 2) or hexadecimal (base 16) format. In the Dword editor, you can edit the data in binary, hexadecimal, or decimal (base 10) format. Hex is the default base for both editors. The Registry Editor always displays these types of data in hex format in the right pane.

Information stored in a nonvolatile key remains in the Registry until you delete it. Information stored in a volatile key is discarded when you shut down the system. Everything under a volatile key also is volatile. Everything stored under the HKEY_LOCAL_MACHINE\HARDWARE key, for example, is volatile.

Adding Keys to the Registry

You can add a key to store data in the Registry. You might, for example, add a subkey under CurrentControlSet\Services to start a service process you have written or to install a device driver that doesn't have an installation program.

Task 4.4: Adding a Key to the Registry Editor.

Step 1: Description

This task enables the Administrator to add a key to the Registry.

Step 2: Action

1. Select the key or subkey under which you want the new key to appear. Then choose Edit, Add Key, or press the Ins key.

2. In the Key Name box of the Add Key dialog box, type the name you want to assign your key. The key name cannot contain a backslash (\). It must be unique in relation to other subkeys at the same level in the hierarchy; that is, Key1 and Key2 can each have a subkey named Key3, but Key1 cannot have two subkeys named Key3.

3. Leave the Class box blank, as this entry is reserved for future use.

4. Click OK to display the new key in the Registry Editor window.

Step 3: Review

This task showed you how to add a key to the Registry using the Registry Editor.

Saving Registry Data

Using the Save Key command, you can save the information in a key and all its subkeys in a hive file. Then you can use this hive file with the Restore and Load Key commands.

Changes in the Registry are saved automatically, whether you make changes by using Registry Editor or by changing settings in applications. The Save Key command specifically is used to save portions of the Registry as a file on disk. To use the Save Key command, you need Backup privileges, which you have when you're logged on as a member of the Administrators group.

You can use the Save Key command on any key. This command, however, doesn't save volatile keys, which are destroyed when you shut down the system. For example, the HKEY_LOCAL_MACHINE\HARDWARE key is volatile, so it isn't saved as a hive file.

 Tip

If you want to view the Hardware hive for debugging, you can save it in a text file by choosing Registry, Save Subtree As.

 TASK

Task 4.5: Saving a Registry Key.

Step 1: Description

This task enables the Administrator to save a Registry key.

Step 2: Action

1. Select the key you want to save as a hive file on a disk.

2. Choose Registry, Save Key and then complete the filename information in the Save Key dialog box. Under the FAT file system, this filename cannot have an extension. When the key you're saving is in the Registry of a remote computer, the drive and path you specify for the filename are relative to the remote computer.

Step 3: Review

This task showed you how to save a Registry key using the Registry Editor.

The selected key is now saved as a file. When you use the Load Hive command, you can select the filenames for any files saved using the Save Key command. As part of system maintenance, for example, you might use the Save Key command to save a key as a file. When the key you saved is ready to be returned to the system, you use the Restore command.

Using the Restore Command

You can use the Restore command to make a hive file a part of the system configuration. The Restore command enables you to copy information in a hive file over a specified key. This copied information overwrites the contents of the specified key, except for the key name.

To use the Restore command, you need Restore privileges, which you have when you're logged on as a member of the Administrators group.

Task 4.6: Restoring a Registry Key.

Step 1: Description

This task enables the Administrator to restore a Registry key.

Step 2: Action

1. Select the key where you want to restore the hive.

2. Choose Registry, Restore and then complete the filename information in the Restore Key dialog box to specify the hive you want to restore. If you're running the FAT file system, this filename cannot have an extension. Also, when you're restoring a key on a remote computer, the drive and path of the filename are relative to the remote computer.

Step 3: Review

This task showed you how to restore a Registry. You cannot restore keys or subkeys that have open handles. For this reason, you cannot restore the SAM or SECURITY subtrees (Windows 2000 always has handles open in these keys). You use the Restore command only for special conditions, such as restoration of user profiles on a damaged system. You should generally have little need to use this command to restore a Registry.

Compacting Registry Data

The memory the system uses for the Registry approximately equals the size of a hive when loaded into memory. Hives vary in size on disk from 20KB to over 500KB. The space used depends primarily on how many local user profiles you keep and how much information is stored with each user profile.

You should remove unused or out-of-date user profiles from a computer by choosing the Delete User Profiles command in Windows 2000 Setup. (Use the Setup program because it protects you from deleting the profile for a currently logged-on user.)

You can use the Save Key command to save a user hive and then use the Restore command so that you can use this smaller hive. Using Save Key after deleting unused entries compacts the key. How much space you gain depends on how much was stored in various user profiles. You will want to repeat this procedure whenever you have many unused or out-of-date user profiles. Set up a procedure to monitor routinely used profiles with the aim of compacting the key. This procedure is useful only for user profiles, not for the SAM, SECURITY, SOFTWARE, or SYSTEM hives.

You might want to examine the contents of a Registry key as text for troubleshooting. You can save a key as a text file, and you can print data from the Registry Editor, including a key, its subkeys, and all the value entries of all its subkeys.

4

The Save Subtree As command also works for the HKEY_LOCAL_MACHINE\ HARDWARE subtree, which you cannot otherwise save as a hive file.

To save a Registry key as a text file, in a Registry window, select the key you want to save as a text file. Then choose Registry, Save Subtree As and specify a filename.

To print a Registry key in a Registry window, select the key you want and then choose Registry, Print Subtree.

Limiting Registry Size

The total amount of Registry space that the Registry data (the hives) can consume is restricted by the Registry size limit, which prevents an application from filling the paged pool with Registry data. Registry size limits affect both the amount of paged pool that the Registry can use and the amount of available disk space.

By default, the Registry size limit is 25 percent of the size of the paged pool, and depends upon the size of your hard drive, so the default Registry size limit is a variable. You can see a default value in Figure 4.7.

FIGURE **4.7**

The default paging and Registry size settings.

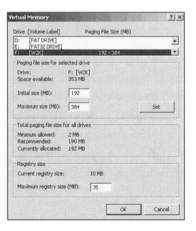

Setting the PagedPoolSize value under the CurrentControlSet\Control\Session Manager\Memory Management subkey also affects the Registry size limit. The system ensures that the value for Registry size limit is at least 2MB and no greater than about 80 percent of the size of PagedPoolSize.

The Registry size limitations are approximate. You can set the PagedPoolSize to a maximum of 128MB, so RegistrySizeLimit can be no larger than about 102MB, which supports about 80,000 users (although other limits prevent a Registry this large from being very useful). Also, RegistrySizeLimit sets a maximum, not an allocation (unlike some similar limits in the system). Setting a large value doesn't cause the system to use that much space, unless it is actually needed by the Registry. A large value also doesn't guarantee that the maximum space actually is available for use by the Registry.

Tip

> Incidentally, you also can adjust the PagedPoolSize and the Registry size by using the System icon within the Start, Settings, Control Panel. Select the Advanced tab and then the Performance tab and click Change under the Virtual Memory section. Highlight the volume, change the page size values and the Registry values, and then click OK. You will need to click OK again to exit the System applet.

The space controlled by RegistrySizeLimit includes the hive space, as well as some of the Registry's runtime structures. Other Registry runtime structures are protected by their own size limits or other means.

To ensure that you always can at least start the system and edit the Registry when the size is set wrong, quota checking isn't turned on until after the first successful loading of a hive (that is, the loading of a user profile).

As you learned earlier today, by convention, when similar data exists under both HKEY_CURRENT_USER and HKEY_LOCAL_MACHINE, the data in HKEY_CURRENT_USER takes precedence. Values in this key, however, also might extend (rather than replace) data in HKEY_LOCAL_MACHINE. Also, some items (such as device driver loading entries) are meaningless when they occur outside HKEY_LOCAL_MACHINE.

Fault Tolerance in the Registry

As you learned previously, every hive file has another file named the same but with the extension .LOG. This convention is really useful because Windows 2000 Server and Windows 2000 Professional for that matter use it to protect the Registry during updates.

Whenever you or the system changes a hive file, the change is first written into its LOG file. The LOG file isn't actually a backup file; it's more a journal of changes to the primary file. After the description of the change to the hive file is complete, the journal file is written to disk. Often, a disk write ends up hanging around in the disk cache for a while, but this write is flushed to disk. Then the system makes the changes to the hive file based on the information in the journal file. If the system crashes during the hive write operation, enough information is present in the journal file to roll back the hive to its previous position.

4

The exception to this procedure comes with the SYSTEM hive. The SYSTEM hive is really important because it contains the CurrentControlSet. For that reason, the backup file for SYSTEM, SYSTEM.ALT, is a complete backup of SYSTEM. When one file is damaged, the system can use the other to boot.

Notice that HKEY_LOCAL_MACHINE\HARDWARE doesn't have a hive. That's because the key is rebuilt each time you boot, so W2K can adapt itself to changes in computer hardware. The program NTDETECT.COM, which runs at boot time, gathers the information that W2K needs to create HKEY_LOCAL_MACHINE\HARDWARE.

Confused about where all the keys come from? You can find a recap in Table 4.4. It's similar to Table 4.2, but it's more specific about how the keys are built at boot time.

TABLE 4.4   Key Construction

Key	How Constructed at Boot Time
HKEY_LOCAL_MACHINE:	
HARDWARE	NTDETECT.COM
SAM	SAM hive file
SECURITY	SECURITY hive file
SOFTWARE	SOFTWARE hive file
SYSTEM	SYSTEM hive file
HKEY_CLASSES_ROOT	SYSTEM hive file, Classes subkey
HKEY_USERS_DEFAULT	DEFAULT hive file
HKEY_USERS\Sxxx	usernameOOO hive file
HKEY_CURRENT_USER	usernameOOO hive file

Remote Registry Modification

As you just learned, you can modify another computer's Registry, perhaps to repair it or to do some simple kind of remote maintenance, by loading that computer's hive. You do so with the Registry Editor by using the Load Hive or Unload Hive command.

You can load or unload the hives only for HKEY_USERS and HKEY_LOCAL_MACHINE. The Load Hive option appears only after you select one of these two subtrees. Unload Hive is available only after you select a subkey of one of those two subtrees.

Why might you load a hive or a remote Registry? First, you might load a hive to get to a client's profile. Suppose that a user has set up all the colors as black or navy blue on black and made reading the screen impossible. (Believe it or not, this happens! At least one consultant has made money troubleshooting this one!) You could load the hive corresponding to that user, modify it, and then unload it.

Second, you can use the remote feature to view basically anything on a remote system. Suppose you want to do something as simple as changing screen colors. You would do so on a local system by running the Control Panel, but the Control Panel doesn't work for remote systems. Answer: Load the Registry remotely.

You could load and save hive files to a floppy disk, walk the floppy over to a malfunctioning machine, and load the hive onto the machine's hard disk, potentially repairing a system problem. This solution isn't possible when you're using NTFS, unless you have multiple copies of W2K on the system—something most people don't have. But if you have a W2K machine running a FAT file system, you can always boot from DOS, replace the hive files under DOS, and then reboot under W2K.

When you boot under W2K, you see the reference to a "known good menu." That's because W2K keeps track not only of the current control set, but also the previous control set. This way, when you mess up the system, you always can roll back to the previous good configuration. These control sets are kept in the same key as the CurrentControlSet. Within HKEY_LOCAL_MACHINE\SYSTEM\Select\Current, \Default, \Failed, and \LastKnownGood are numbers indicating which of the two kept control sets are current, good, failed, and so on.

In the same way that you can use Event Viewer or Active Directory users and computers to view details on another computer, you can use the Registry Editor to view and change the contents of another computer's Registry when the server services on the remote computer are running. This capacity to view a computer's configuration remotely enables you, as a system administrator, to examine a user's startup parameters, desktop configuration, and other parameters. You therefore can provide troubleshooting or other support assistance over the telephone while you view settings on the other computer from your workstation.

Note

> Auto Refresh isn't available when you're viewing the Registry from a remote computer. When Auto Refresh is turned on, manual refresh is disabled. Therefore, when you open a remote Registry, Registry Editor checks to see whether Auto Refresh mode is on. When it is, the Registry Editor displays the following message: Auto Refresh isn't available for remote registries; Registry Editor disables Auto Refresh mode.

To view the Registry from a remote computer, do either of the following procedures:

- Choose Registry, Select Computer and then select or type the name of the computer whose Registry you want to access.
- Double-click the name of a computer in the Select Computer list. Under Windows 2000 Server, the first name in this list represents the name of a domain. When no computer name appears after this domain name, double-click the domain name to view a list of the computers in that domain. You can see an example in Figure 4.8.

FIGURE 4.8

Accessing a remote computer's Registry.

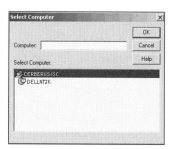

Two Registry windows appear for the remote computer: one for HKEY_USERS and one for HKEY_LOCAL_MACHINE. You can view or modify the information on keys for the remote computer when the access controls defined for the keys allow you to perform such operations. If you are logged on as a member of the Administrators group, you can perform actions on all keys.

You can use the Load Hive and Unload Hive commands in the Registry Editor to display and maintain another computer's Registry without viewing it remotely. As mentioned previously, you can load and save files to a floppy and walk them over to a machine that isn't working, so you can do the reverse. You can load and save the hive files from a malfunctioning machine, and then look at them on your machine. You might want to use this method to view specific values or to repair certain entries for a computer that isn't configured properly or cannot connect to the network.

The hives that make up the computer's Registry are loaded automatically when you start the computer, and you can view the contents of these hives in the Registry Editor. Should you want to view or change the contents of other hive files, you must use the Load Hive command to display their contents in the Registry Editor.

The Load Hive and Unload Hive commands affect only the Registry windows that display HKEY_USERS and HKEY_LOCAL_MACHINE. To use these commands, you must have Restore and Backup privileges, which you have when you are logged on as a member of the Administrators group. The Load Hive command is available only

when you select HKEY_USERS or HKEY_LOCAL_MACHINE. The Unload Hive
command is available only when a subkey of one of these handles is selected.

Task 4.7: Loading a Hive into the Registry Editor.

Step 1: Description

This task enables the Administrator to load a hive in the Registry Editor so that you can
view or change the contents of a hive.

Step 2: Action

1. Select the HKEY_LOCAL_MACHINE or HKEY_USERS root.

2. Choose Registry, Load Hive.

3. Use the File Name, Drives, and Directories boxes and the Network button of the
   Load Hive dialog box to select the file containing the hive you want to load, and
   then click OK. (If you're loading a hive on a remote computer, the drive and path
   in the filename are relative to the remote computer.)

> **Tip**
> You can find the directory location and names of hives on a computer in
> HKEY_LOCAL_MACHINE\SYSTEM\CurrentControlSet\Control\Hive list.

4

This file must have been created with the Save Key command (as described earlier
in this chapter), or it must be one of the default hives. Under the Windows 2000
file system, the filename cannot have an extension.

If you're unable to connect to another computer over the network, you can load
a hive file that you copied to a floppy disk.

4. In the second Load Hive dialog box, type the name you want to use for the key
   where the hive is loaded, and then click OK. This name creates a new subkey
   in the Registry. You can specify any name using any characters including blank
   spaces. You cannot load an existing key. Data from the loaded hive appears as a
   new subkey under HKEY_USERS or HKEY_LOCAL_MACHINE (whichever
   handle you selected before loading the hive). A loaded hive remains in the system
   until it is unloaded.

Step 3: Review

The Load Hive command creates a new hive in the memory space of the Registry and
uses the specified file as the backup hive file (filename.LOG) for the hive. The specified
file is held open, but nothing is copied to the file unless the information in a key or value

entry is changed. Likewise, the Unload Hive command doesn't copy or create anything; it merely unloads the loaded hive.

To unload a hive from the Registry Editor, select the key that represents a hive you previously loaded, and then choose Registry, Unload Hive. The selected key is removed from the window and is no longer actively available to the system or for editing in the Registry Editor. You cannot unload a hive that was loaded by the system. Also, you cannot unload a hive that contains an open key.

Backing up and Restoring a Registry

Mark this section, because you'll no doubt want to come back to it when you need to perform maintenance on the Registry. You might need to restore backed-up versions of Registry hives, for example, when you replace your current W2K computer, when a disk controller or hard disk goes bad, or when an electrical failure zaps large parts of a disk.

By now, you should understand that the Registry is important and should be protected. As stated before, it protects itself pretty well with its LOG files, but how can you back it up?

Unfortunately, the fact that Registry hive files are always open makes it tough for you to back up the Registry because open files stymie most backup utilities. However, the NTBackup program that comes with W2K works well, allowing you to back up to a variety of devices, from tape to recordable CD-ROMs. Nevertheless, if you use NTBackup—which is pretty good, particularly for its price—then you should tell it to back up the Registry every night.

The Ntbackup program offers a simple backup wizard when you run it, making the process even simpler. It provides you an option to backup the System State, which includes a number of critical operating system files, as well as the Registry. These system files include Active Directory, ntldr and ntdetect and a number of other libraries, allowing you to restore your system.

Outside of NTBackup are a couple of other protection possibilities. A program named RDISK creates emergency repair disks. And the Resource Kit includes two useful utilities: the REGBACK.EXE program enables you to back up a Registry file, and the REGREST.EXE restores it.

Backing Up Registry Hives

You can back up Registry hives using one of four methods:

- Using an external device such as a tape drive and the Windows 2000 backup program (NTBackup), select the Backup System State option in the Backup Wizard dialog box to include automatically a copy of the local Registry files in the backup set. In addition, you can select the System State after starting the backup program by selecting it in the list of drives under the Backup tab. You can see an example of this in Figure 4.9.

FIGURE 4.9

The NTBackup program.

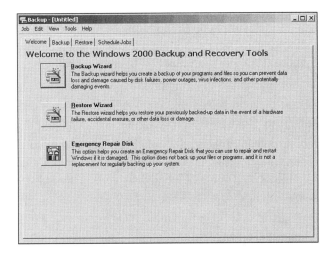

- If you don't have a tape drive, run the REGBACK.EXE or REPAIR.EXE program from the Windows 2000 Resource Tool Kit, or use another tool that uses the same techniques to back up Registry files.
- Start the computer under a different operating system. Then copy all files in the SystemRoot\SYSTEM32\CONFIG directory to a safe backup location.
- Use the Save Key command in the Registry Editor. This command essentially performs the RegBack procedure manually.

For each direct subkey of HKEY_LOCAL_MACHINE and HKEY_USERS, you must choose Registry, Save Key and then specify filenames that match the key names. For example, save the SYSTEM key to \BACKDIR\SYSTEM. On the FAT file system, the filename should not have an extension.

Don't use Save Key with the HARDWARE hive, which contains volatile data. You won't get any data because Save Key cannot save volatile keys to disk.

Restoring Hives from Backup Files

To restore a damaged Windows 2000 system, you must first restore the basic operating system installation. You have two options for restoring the operating system:

- You can use the Emergency Repair disk to restore the system to the same state it was in just after installation.

- You can run Windows 2000 Setup again. You end up with a system that starts the computer but lacks changes made since you first set it up. You can recover most of those changes by copying files from backups by using the Windows 2000 backup program for tape backups or by copying from disk backups.

Restoring the basic operating system is only half the battle. Registry hive files are protected while W2K is running, so you cannot simply copy these files back onto the system. So, after the system and all the additional files such as device drivers are restored, you must restore the Registry. Just how you restore the Registry depends on which backup mechanism you used:

- For tape backups, you can use the Windows 2000 Restore program to restore the Registry. Then restart the computer.

- Start the computer using an alternate instance of the operating system (or using MS-DOS when the system files are on a FAT partition). Copy back the files to the SystemRoot\SYSTEM32\CONFIG directory. Then restart the computer using the regular operating system.

- Use the REPAIR.EXE program from the Windows 2000 Resource Tool Kit.

- Use the REGREST.EXE program from the Windows 2000 Resource Tool Kit. The RegRest program performs a ReplaceKey operation, which swaps backup files for the default files that the Emergency Repair or Windows 2000 Setup programs installed, and saves the default files under other filenames. Restart the computer after running the RegRest program to see the restored Registry.

Securing the Registry

You have seen the importance of the Registry in this chapter and the preceding chapter. Obviously, you need to protect the Registry. One way to restrict access to the Registry Editor and its subtree is to place the Registry files on an NTFS system partition and restrict access to the directory through the file directory permissions. This method is easier to administer than changing the default security permissions for each of the subtrees.

The Registry contains data that should not be accessed by all users. Even when the Registry resides on a FAT system partition, security permissions and auditing can be implemented through the Registry Editor. The default security permissions for files within the Registry Editor vary by subtree.

By now, you understand how the Registry affects the Windows 2000 system and how important it is to keep the Registry intact. As you begin to set up more W2K installations in your enterprise, you need to plan strategies for protecting the Registry for each of the new installations. Following are some suggestions for protecting Registry files under most conditions:

- Don't allow anyone to log on as a member of the Administrators group unless that individual has administrative duties.

- Because you can administer any workstation from a remote computer, you can remove REGEDT32.EXE from workstations. If, for some reason, you need the ability to administer each workstation locally, you can place access controls using Explorer on REGEDT32.EXE, thereby limiting the rights of users to start this program. Day 8, "Managing Files and Using the Distributed File System," introduces you to file access rights.

Note

> Windows 2000 enforces access control on Registry files, so it is difficult for users accidentally or intentionally to damage or delete hives on a running system. While the system is running, it keeps hive files open for exclusive access on all file systems. If the Windows 2000 SystemRoot isn't on an NTFS volume, the Registry files can be tampered with; specifically, users can remove hives for user profiles that currently aren't loaded. With NTFS, you can prevent such tampering.

One of the most common Registry mistakes occurs when a user inadvertently deletes the Registry. You can protect the Registry from accidental deletions in one of two ways:

- **Read-only mode**. Choose Options, Read Only. When this command is checked, Registry Editor doesn't save any changes. Use this all the time until you are comfortable and know what you are doing.

- **Confirmation**. Choose Options, Confirm On Delete. When this command is checked, the Registry Editor asks you to confirm deletion of any key or value.

Protecting Registry Files for User Profiles

You can protect the Registry hive files for user profiles in the same way that you protect other files in Windows 2000—by restricting access through File Manager. If the files are stored on an NTFS volume, you can use Explorer to assign permissions. You should change permissions only for user profile hives. The permissions for other hives are maintained automatically by the system and should not be changed.

Assigning Access Rights to Registry Keys

You can assign access rights to Registry keys regardless of the type of file system on the partition where the W2K files are stored. To determine the users and groups with access to specific Registry data, set permissions on the Registry keys. This process is sometimes called changing ACLs, in reference to the Access Control Lists governing who has access to data. You also can add or remove names from the list of users or groups authorized to access the Registry keys.

 Caution | Changing the permissions to limit access to a Registry key can have severe consequences. Be careful not to set No Access permissions on a key that the Network Control Panel application needs for configuration; doing so causes the application to fail.

At a minimum, ensure that administrators and the System account have full access to the key so that the system starts and an administrator can repair the Registry key.

Because assigning permissions on specific keys can have drastic consequences, you should reserve this action for keys you add to accommodate custom applications or other custom settings. After you change permissions on a Registry key, be sure to turn on auditing in Active Directory Users and Computers, and then test the system extensively through a variety of activities while logged on under different user and administrative accounts. You also should audit the key for failed access attempts.

Task 4.8: Assigning Permission to a Key.

Step 1: Description

This task enables the administrator to assign permissions on a key. In the Registry Editor, the commands on the Security menu for assigning permission and ownership of keys work the same as similar commands in File Manager for assigning access rights for files and directories.

Step 2: Action

1. Make a backup copy of the Registry key before making changes.

2. Select the key for which you want to assign access permission. Choose Security, Permissions.

3. In the Registry Key Permissions dialog box, assign an access level to the selected key by selecting an option in the Type of Access box as described in Table 4.5, and then click OK.

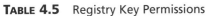

TABLE 4.5   Registry Key Permissions

Type of Access	Meaning
Read	Allows users on the Permissions list to read the key's contents but prevents changes from being saved
Full Control	Allows users on the Permissions list to access, edit, or take ownership of the selected key
Special Access	Allows users on the Permissions list some custom combination of access and edit rights for the selected key

  4. Turn on auditing and then test the system extensively to ensure that the new access control doesn't interfere with system or application operations.

Step 3: Review

Changing the permissions to limit access to a Registry key can have severe consequences, so be careful how you use this task to set permissions.

As a system administrator, you might need to take ownership of a key to protect access to it. You take ownership of a Registry key by choosing Security, Owner in the Registry Editor and then completing the Ownership dialog box. You also can add users or groups to the Permissions list by following the procedure for managing lists of users and groups that appear throughout W2K.

You (or any user) can take ownership of any Registry key by logging onto the system as a member of the Administrator group. When an administrator takes ownership of a key without being assigned full control by its owner, however, the key cannot be given back to its original owner, and the event is audited.

Learning More About Managing the Registry

In addition to the Registry Editor, W2K includes the program called Policy Editor that you are familiar with from NT 4.0. You should only use this tool with Windows 95, 98, and NT 4.0 clients. To open it, type **Poledit** on the Start, Run command line. After the program starts, choose Files, Open Registry to see some of the icons that W2K provides. This utility enables you to change Registry settings on a limited basis for only HKEY_CURRENT_USER and HKEY_LOCAL_MACHINE. (Windows 2000 changed the icon names to confuse you a little.)

In W2K, you perform the same type of function with the tool called Group Policy Editor in the Start, Programs, Administrative Tools, Active Directory Users and Computers. Right-click the Organizational Unit, select Properties and click on Group. Next, click the Group Policy object in the Group policy window, and then click Edit to start the Group.

If you want to stay on the safe side and only view information, use the Windows 2000 Diagnostics program, WINMSD.EXE (choose Programs, Administrative Tools, Windows 2000 Diagnostics). Think of this program as a way to inspect the Registry's configuration information in read-only mode.

You've learned only the basic concepts of the Windows 2000 Registry. Before you make any changes manually, read Microsoft's in-depth discussion of the Registry in Appendix A of its Concepts and Planning Guide.

If you have the Windows 2000 Resource Kit from Microsoft—and if you don't, then get it—you'll find approximately 150 pages detailing each and every key. Additionally, the Registry keys are documented in an online help file. Unfortunately, some keys aren't documented anywhere except in bits and pieces on Microsoft TechNet or another support group. The Microsoft Technet Web site is located at: `http://www.microsoft.com/technet/default.asp`.

If you don't have the Resource Kit, you can download the Registry key help file from the WINNT forum on CompuServe. You also can find some tools that make it easier to search for things in the Registry.

Summary

The Registry is a convenient and powerful component of the Windows 2000 Server operating system. As stressed throughout this chapter, you should exercise caution when working with the Registry. In this chapter, you learned about the following topics:

- The Registry
- Subtrees, hives, and values
- Using the Registry Editor to change the Registry
- Remote management of the Registry
- Saving and compacting Registry data
- Backing up the Registry
- Protecting the Registry

The Registry is an important database. You will use it on Day 7 to create users. The system stores a lot of this information in the Windows 2000 Registry. Now, however, you can review what you learned today.

Workshop

To wrap up the day, you can review tasks from the lesson, and see the answers to some commonly asked questions.

Task List

With the information provided in this chapter, you now can begin your understanding of Windows 2000 objects. You learned how to carry out the following tasks:

- View the Registry
- Change the Registry
- Search for a Registry key
- Edit a Registry key
- Add a key to the Registry
- Save a Registry key
- Restore a Registry key
- Back up and restore the Registry
- Load a hive
- Secure the Registry

Q&A

Q How do I look at the Registry?

A You can view the Registry through applications in the Administrative Tools directory, applications within the Control Panel, or using the Registry Editor.

Q What happens when the Registry isn't available?

A Well, for one thing, users can't log in because system software consults the Registry to determine whether the username is a valid account and then matches the password supplied to the one stored in the Registry. You can't create new objects, such as new users. Also, you can't use any Windows 2000 process or device. So, the short answer is, not very much.

DAY 5

Introducing Active Directory

In the preceding days, you learned about installing and exploring Windows 2000 and managing the Registry. In the next two days, you'll learn all about Active Directory Services (ADS) and security. First, you'll review, update, and manage domains, trees, and forests and tomorrow, you'll learn the nuances of security within 2000 Server.

Managing your network resources is a key administration task that previously consumed a lot of time. Without some kind of network directory, networks are difficult to manage. Also, your users have difficulty finding network resources without a directory.

Previous versions of Microsoft Windows included services to help users and administrators find network resources. Users found Network Neighborhood useful in some cases, but often complained about the interface. An administrator could use WINS Manager and Server Manager to list systems on the network. As an administrator, you might have used User Manager to add and delete users. With these applications and tools, you and your clients could do the job, but it was difficult especially with larger networks. This was due in part to the architecture used in downlevel versions of Windows NT.

With Windows NT, all network objects resided in a common container: the Microsoft Windows NT domain. Windows NT domains worked best in small and medium networks. Administrators in large networks had a very difficult time. For these reasons, Microsoft introduced Active Directory to replace domain functionality. You will find parts of Domain Name Service, Windows Internet Naming Service, and even other directory services, such as NetWare Directory Services, in ADS.

Active Directory will improve your life considerably. Microsoft built Active Directory from the ground up to support Internet-standard technology with an emphasis on security, distribution, partitioning, and replication. The designers wanted Active Directory to work with networks of all sizes—from a single server with a few hundred objects up to thousands of servers with millions of objects. Also, Active Directory is a consolidation point, so you can isolate, migrate, centrally manage, and reduce the directories you maintain.

NEW TERM At the heart of Active Directory is a directory. A *directory*, in the most generic sense, is a comprehensive listing of objects. Active Directory will store information about organizations, sites, systems, users, shares, and just about any other network object that you can imagine.

In this lesson, you will learn about

- Objects, schema, object classes, attributes, and other Active Directory components
- Planning for Active Directory
- Installing Active Directory
- Adding new directory objects
- Changing the schema

Active Directory is key to Windows 2000, so please take your time today and study the concepts and tasks. Tomorrow and the next day, you will get a chance to use the Active Directory for security and managing your users. Let's get started today with the components of ADS.

Active Directory Components

Before working with ADS, you need to understand the basics of the following:

- Objects and attributes
- Containers
- Domains

- Trees
- Forests
- Sites
- Schema
- Global catalog
- Namespace
- Naming conventions

The following sections describe each of these.

Objects and Attributes

NEW TERM Everything in Active Directory is an *object*. An object is any user, group, computer, printer, resource, or service within Active Directory. The generic term *object* is used because Active Directory can track a variety of items, and many objects can share common *attributes*.

Attributes describe objects in Active Directory. For example, all User objects share attributes to store a username, full name, and description. Systems also are objects, but they have a separate set of attributes including a host name, an IP address, and a location.

The relationship between object classes, attributes, and the objects causes confusion with many people. Objects are created based on an object class. Attributes describe an object class. When you create an object, it inherits all the attributes of its object class. Here's where it gets confusing: Object classes and attributes also are objects in Active Directory.

An object can either refer to something concrete or the actual useful information itself. For example, Windows 2000 stores every bit of information about a user account within Active Directory. However, Active Directory only stores a reference or pointer to a disk volume. Although the pointer isn't useful in and of itself, you can use it to locate the volume on the file server. When creating new object classes, carefully consider whether the object will store a reference to something external or whether all necessary information will be contained in the object's attributes. Although Active Directory is extremely convenient, you should not use it to store large amounts of information, constantly changing information, or rarely used information. This will affect AD performance.

NEW TERM Anytime you add a user or a computer to Active Directory, you create an object. You can refer to the creation of an object as *publishing* because it starts a process that replicates the new information across all Active Directory servers in the domain. You will learn how to publish an OU later today.

5

Standard Object Classes

Windows 2000 Server relies on Active Directory to store a great deal of useful information about users, groups, and computers, which is of particular interest to administrators because they will be the most commonly accessed parts of Active Directory. The MMC user interface might not seem intuitive at first, but after you spend some time with it, you will begin to appreciate it.

Users

You will no longer manage user accounts using the specialized User Manager tool. Instead, administrators use the Active Directory Users and Computers MMC snap-in. You will learn how to use this tool on Day 7, "Managing User Accounts."

If you're familiar with previous versions of NT, you will find that the user accounts themselves have changed significantly. Windows NT 4.0 simply kept the username, full name, description, password, and a handful of other attributes for each user. Windows 2000 Server takes advantage of Active Directory to extend these attributes. You now can use Active Directory to keep the personal information you need about people, including phone number, address, employee number, and manager name. This personal information is entirely optional.

Groups

Active Directory groups are similar to user groups in previous versions of Windows NT. However, there are several new features. The newest version of Microsoft Exchange allows you to use groups as email distribution lists. To make this more useful, you can add email accounts to the groups to allow distribution to users who aren't members of the same Active Directory tree. To assist in administration, you also can nest groups within each other. This should greatly reduce the amount of time you spend managing users and groups.

With Windows 2000, there are now three types of user groups. *Universal Groups* is the most commonly used type, and can contain users and other groups from anywhere in the forest. They are replicated outside of the domain and appear in the global catalog. *Global Groups* can only contain users and groups from the same domain. Global Groups are listed in the global catalog, but their membership list doesn't leave the domain. *Domain Local Groups* can only be applied to ACLs (access control lists) within the same domain but can contain users and groups from other domains. They are neither replicated outside of the domain nor listed in the global catalog. Any of these types of groups can participate in domain security or merely function as a distribution list.

 Windows 2000 Server provides many groups by default. These groups are called the *built-in groups*. Administrators can use these default groups for most purposes, and can add their own groups as needed. You will find out about these built-in groups on Day 7.

Machine Accounts

Windows 2000 automatically gives systems that join a domain a computer account in Active Directory. This is similar to adding a system to a Windows NT 4.0 domain. However, an administrator can add systems to the domain even when they don't participate in domain security. For example, you can create a computer object for a UNIX system to help the administrators track that system.

Containers

NEW TERM   A *container* is a special type of object used to organize Active Directory. It doesn't represent anything physical, such as a user or a system. Instead, you use it to group other objects. Container objects can be nested within other containers. In the same way that a file folder contains files and documents, a directory container is a container for directory objects.

Organizational Units

Organizational units (OUs) are another type of directory object contained within each domain—an extremely important one at that. Your company can use OUs to organize its resources in a more meaningful hierarchy. OUs are container objects. Organizational units can contain the following types of objects:

- Users
- Groups
- Computers
- Printers
- Applications
- Security policies
- File shares
- Other OUs

Note   As you will find out later today, the ADS schema is extensible, so you can change your schema.

OUs are most useful when you use them to delegate administrative tasks. For example, you can delegate a user the ability to manage all the objects in a particular OU. You have quite a bit of flexibility in Windows 2000 when delegating administrative tasks. You can let someone reset passwords and maintain special rights for a particular container. An administrator might find it efficient to grant a user administrative rights for only a sub-tree of OUs, or even for a single OU.

Domains

Domains are merely groups of 2000 machines that are either Windows 2000 workstations or servers. No other client operating systems such as Windows 95, Windows 98, or Windows for Workgroups can join the domain, although all these machines can access resources and login.

If you already use Windows NT, try to forget what you've learned about domains and trusts. You'll still use the term *trusts*, but trusts work very differently. In Windows 2000, there is no distinction between one-way and two-way trusts because all Active Directory trusts are bidirectional. Further, all trusts are transitive. So, should Domain A trust Domain B, and Domain B trust Domain C, then there is an automatic implicit trust between Domain A and Domain C. This is a powerful feature that you need to keep in mind.

Trees

NEW TERM   The term *tree* is used to describe a set of objects within Active Directory—a hierarchy of objects. When containers and objects are combined hierarchically, they tend to form branches; hence, the term tree. A related term is *contiguous subtree,* which refers to an unbroken branch of the tree, including all members of any container in the path.

NEW TERM   In a tree, the endpoints are *leaf nodes*. Leaf nodes are *noncontainer objects* because they cannot contain other objects.

Nodes are where the tree branches are *nonleaf nodes* or simply containers.

The tree is the prevalent way to connect several domains. The connections are done to form a hierarchical structure.

Forests

NEW TERM   Continuing the tree metaphor, the term forest describes trees that aren't part of the same namespace but that share a common schema, configuration, and global catalog. Or, in other words, a forest is a set of one or more domain trees that doesn't form a contiguous namespace. This means the trees in a forest don't share a common root. A forest allows administrators to join two domain trees that have no common parts.

For example, the cerberus-isc.com and pdaconsulting.com domains have no obvious relationship to each other. These domains are an example of *disjointed naming*, where the domains aren't part of the same domain tree, but can be joined as a forest.

Each tree in a forest shares a common schema, configuration, and global catalog. In addition, trees in a forest all trust each other, so objects in these trees are available to all users where the security allows it. Organizations that are divided into multiple domains should group the trees into a single forest to ease administration. The only real difference between a tree and a forest is that each tree has its own namespace. The other names for a forest—noncontiguous or disjoint namespace—bring this point to mind.

Sites

NEW TERM   As defined in Active Directory, a *site* is a geographical location. Sites correspond to logical IP subnets, and as such, applications can use sites to locate the closest server on a network. Typically, a site has a physical boundary similar to a LAN.

At logon, the Active Directory client finds the AD server in the same site as the user. A workstation finds its site by presenting its subnet (IP address with subnet mask) to the first AD server contacted. The first AD server uses the presented subnet to locate the site object for the site where the workstation is located. When the current server isn't in that site, the server notifies the workstation of a better site to use. Using site information from Active Directory can profoundly reduce the traffic on wide area networks.

Schema

NEW TERM   The set of attributes available for any particular object type is called a *schema*. The schema makes object classes different from each other. Basically, the schema defines the objects that you can create in the directory and the attributes that you can assign to those objects.

Schema information is actually stored within Active Directory, which allows administrators to add attributes to object classes and have them distributed across the network to all corners of the domain, without restarting any domain controllers.

Global Catalog

NEW TERM   Active Directory provides a *global catalog* (GC). This doesn't mean that you can find any object on the planet, but you might use GC to find them on your network. Active Directory provides a single source to locate any object within an organization's network.

The global catalog holds all objects from all domains in the Windows 2000 directory, along with a subset of each object's properties. Internally, the global catalog implements

5

the same hierarchy as the domain tree. LDAP queries, however, usually return results in a flat record set or list. This allows the global catalog to be used as a repository that functions like a global address book (comparable to the Microsoft Exchange Global Address book). You can use global catalogs for tree-wide searches. When you can find all information on a global catalog, Windows 2000 need not create LDAP referrals to other domain controllers.

The global catalog is a service within Windows 2000 Server that allows users to find any objects from any domain where they have been granted access. This functionality far surpasses that of the Find Computer application included in previous versions of Windows because users can search for any object within Active Directory—servers, printers, users, and applications. You will see how to use this command later today.

This feature is especially important because of the complexity of LDAP names. Older versions of Windows relied on 15-character NetBIOS computer names, which users could often remember. Few people would be able to recall LDAP names, such as the following:

```
/O=Internet/DC=COM/DC=Pdaconsulting/DC=Consulting/CN=Computers/CN=Oriole.
```

Because users can easily search the GC for objects, remembering names is much less important.

The GC is an index stored on Active Directory servers. It contains the names of all objects in the Active Directory server, regardless of how the server has been partitioned. The GC also contains a handful of searchable attributes for each object. For example, the GC would store the distinguished names, first names, and last names of all users—allowing someone to search for anyone named Peter and find the distinguished name of the user. (You'll learn all about names and naming in the next section.) The global catalog is a subset of Active Directory, and only stores those attributes that users tend to search on. Microsoft provides useful defaults, and administrators can specify other search attributes by using the Active Directory Schema, described later in this day. It is a good idea to have at least one global catalog in each site. By doing so, clients always have a local repository for search operations. This should improve performance and make for happy clients.

Note

Should you attempt to log on when the global catalog server isn't available, you'll only have access to the local machine, that is, unless you're a member of the Domain Admins group. In that case, you'll still have access to the network.

Namespace

NEW TERM Microsoft designed ADS to overcome the weaknesses of domain-based networks. Active Directory stores information about network components. It allows your clients to find objects within its *namespace*. The term *namespace* (also known as *console tree*) refers to the area where you can locate the network component. For example, the table of contents for this book forms a namespace where you can resolve chapters to page numbers. Similarly, the index at the back helps you resolve terms to page numbers. The Domain Name Service namespace resolves host names to IP addresses. Your telephone book is a namespace for resolving names to telephone numbers. And Active Directory is a namespace for resolving the names of network objects to the objects themselves. Active Directory can resolve a wide range of objects, including users, systems, and services on a network.

Naming Conventions

NEW TERM Each object in an Active Directory has a *name*. These aren't the names that you are accustomed to, like "Peter" or "Barry," or even those 15-character NetBIOS computer names. They are LDAP *distinguished names*. LDAP distinguished names are complicated, but they allow you to uniquely identify any object within a directory regardless of its type.

Active Directory supports the following name types:

- Distinguished Name (DN)
- Relative Distinguished Name (RDN)
- User Principal Name (UPN)
- Globally Unique Identifier (GUID)

Distinguished Name

Understanding the structure of distinguished names is important, as you will refer to them often in the course of your job. My distinguished name on the PDACONSULTING network is /O=Internet/DC=COM/DC=Pdaconsulting/DC=Consulting/CN=Users/ CN=Peter Davis. Consider Figure 5.1, which shows how the name fits into an Active Directory tree. The distinguished name starts to make some sense—it identifies each container from the very top down to the bottom object. A slash and an identifier separate each container. For example, COM, Pdaconsulting, and Consulting are preceded by /DC=. The DC stands for Domain Component, which identifies a DNS domain. CN stands for Component Name.

5

FIGURE 5.1

Distinguished names.

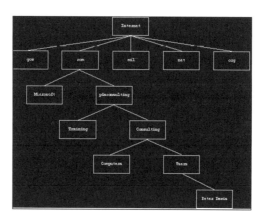

Relative Distinguished Name

To simplify distinguished names, you also can use relative distinguished names. The relative distinguished name of the previous example is CN=Peter Davis, identifying the username but not the context where it resides. The context must be known already for the relative distinguished name to be an effective identifier.

User Principal Name

Distinguished names are great for computers but difficult for people to remember. People have grown accustomed to email addresses, so Active Directory provides these addresses as a shortcut to the full object name. In Figure 5.1, Peter Davis is a user of the consulting.pdaconsulting.com domain. An administrator could create a user principal name within the pdaconsulting.com domain to allow simpler access to my user account and hold a place for the email address, such as ptdavis@pdaconsulting.com.

Users will rely on their UPN (user principal name) to log on to their Windows 2000 systems. In other words, user principal names will replace the usernames used in older Windows networks. Obviously, this helps the users by saving them the trouble of typing their distinguished names. However, it also benefits users because the user principal name will stay the same even when administrators move or rename the underlying user account.

Globally Unique Identifier

As Active Directory creates new objects, it assigns a unique 128-bit number called a GUID (globally unique identifier). The GUID is useful because it stays the same for any given object, regardless of where you might move the object. The GUID won't change even when you rename the object. Applications that reference objects in Active Directory can record the GUIDs for objects and use the global catalog to find them even after they've moved.

 Note When you move or rename an object, the GUID won't change. These actions would force a change to the DN and possibly the UPN and RDN.

Active Directory Naming Support

To use the names listed previously, you need to adopt a naming convention in your organization. Fortunately, Active Directory supports several common name formats for directories as enumerated in Table 5.1. This support for diverse name formats allows you to adopt a naming convention that fits your organization and not the other way around.

TABLE 5.1 Naming Support

Name	Description
RFC 822 Names	Supports the Internet email address format. Active Directory provides the UPN in RFC 822 format. For example, `ptdavis@pdaconsulting.com`.
HTTP URL Names	Supports access from Web browsers using the HTTP protocol and Microsoft Internet Information Server (IIS). For example, `http://www.pdaconsulting.com/directory/default.htm`.
LDAP URL Names	Supports access using any LDAP-enabled client. For example, `LDAP://balliol.pdaconsulting.com/CN=Peter Davis,OU=Consulting,O=pdaconsulting,C=CA`.
UNC Names	Supports the UNC used in Windows 2000 Server-based networks for shared volumes, printers, and files. For example, `\\pdaconsulting.com\consulting\clients\budget.xls`.

Now that you have an understanding of Active Directory and its components, turn your attention to planning for its implementation.

Planning for Active Directory Services

Right about now you might be extremely confused. Don't be, Active Directory isn't that difficult. If you grew up using DOS and Windows, the directory structure is quite familiar. Think of how you structured the directory tree in DOS. Use an OU the same way you would use a subdirectory. Generally, you created a subdirectory to ease access or aid management. Well, the same holds true when designing the structure of your ADS tree.

5

Some General Design Considerations

Clients rely on site information to identify the closest Active Directory server. Because sites correspond to IP subnets, you should place Active Directory servers on each subnet. You should also make sure that all systems on the same logical subnet are connected via LAN hardware. Some routing technologies, such as Proxy Address Resolution Protocol (ARP), can allow systems to use the same logical subnet but different physical network segments. This setup will trick clients into thinking systems are closer than they really are.

Make sure you have planned your Active Directory structure before you start migrating your network. You'll be given the option of creating a new tree or joining an existing tree. Obviously, when you're the first domain in the network to be migrated, you'll want to create a new tree. However, when you are merging multiple domains into a single Active Directory domain, you will want to join as a child of the existing tree.

New Term   Microsoft wants it to be as easy as possible to migrate to Active Directory. Always migrate the Windows NT 3.51 or 4.0 PDC (Primary Domain Controller) to Windows 2000 Server Active Directory first. This way, Windows 2000 will automatically transfer users and groups from your current domain into Active Directory, and existing clients will interface with the new domain controller exactly as if it were still a PDC. As long as you have both Active Directory servers and legacy BDCs (backup domain controllers) in operation simultaneously, your domain will function as a *mixed mode domain*. Mixed mode domains cannot take full advantage of the new Active Directory features because Active Directory must ensure backward compatibility. For example, you cannot use nested groups in mixed mode domains.

New Term   You should migrate the BDCs after you are sure the mixed mode domain is functioning correctly. When you have migrated all domain controllers, you can switch the domain to *native mode,* reboot the domain controllers, and take full advantage of the new features. Member servers and workstations are completely supported and require no changes to interact with Active Directory servers. You will realize more benefits by upgrading the member servers as well, but always start by upgrading domain controllers.

Windows NT Workstation clients should be upgraded to Windows 2000 Professional to take advantage of the new features of Active Directory. A service pack will be made available for Microsoft Windows 95 and Windows 98 clients that will make them Active Directory-aware and allow them to participate in Kerberos security.

The addition of Active Directory to Windows 2000 Server is the most significant reason to upgrade your network. Active Directory combines Windows NT domains with Internet domains and makes them scalable to enterprise proportions. Although the most significant benefit will be the reduced cost of ownership, users will directly benefit from the advanced search capabilities of the global catalog.

Wizards are provided to transfer DNS responsibilities to Microsoft DNS dynamic update protocol servers. Users and groups from legacy Windows NT domains are automatically imported. Finally, every aspect of Active Directory setup is intuitive and GUI-oriented, and handles most complexities automatically. Later today, you will set up your Active Directory using the Installation Wizard.

Now that you understand some of the logic behind the various types of domains and the trust relationship process, you might want to consider what happens when you bring Windows 2000 into your organization. Although there are significant things to consider, here are some of the basics.

Designing the Active Directory

You should consider your company's physical and operational structure, as well as the requirements of your network administrators. To form a design strategy for your Windows 2000 domain, you must take the following actions:

1. Assess your current environment.

2. Determine when to create a Windows 2000 domain.

3. Organize your domain into trees or forests.

Assessing Your Current Environment

To evaluate guidelines for creating Windows 2000 domains with any effectiveness, you must first assess your current environment. You can establish your domain design strategy by first understanding how your company is organized—operationally, physically, and administratively. An appraisal of your company's operational environment will give you a better understanding of how it conducts its day-to-day business. You also must understand the characteristics of your company's physical environment. The way that your company is physically organized will help you define your technical requirements for your design. Your company's administrative needs must also be considered. How your company plans to manage its resources will influence your design as well.

Determining When to Create a Domain

You should build a solid foundation for Windows 2000 by examining your company's operational, physical, and administrative characteristics. To put Windows 2000 into service, your company will require a minimum of one domain. You might need more than one Windows 2000 domain under the following conditions:

- To support decentralized administration: Regional offices might want complete and total control over their local resources.

- To isolate domain replication traffic: To prevent domain controllers from periodically replicating changes with domain controllers in the same domain, create a new domain to isolate it from the existing domain replication traffic.

- To balance domain replication traffic: If a domain contains more than one million objects, you should create multiple domains to balance the load.

- To support multiple domain policies: When you need to support several different domain policies, you have no option but to create multiple domains.

- To address international differences: If your company operates abroad, you should create domains to reflect its geographical differences—in language, currency, and day-to-day business practices.

- To comply with internal political pressures: Executives or other personnel might ask you to create additional domains for a level of privacy or autonomy.

Organizing Domains in Trees and Forests

After you establish the number of domains that is appropriate for your company, you must consider how to organize them into a useful hierarchy. As one of your essential Windows 2000 design tasks, you need to decide whether to arrange your company's domains into a tree or a forest.

Comparing Trees and Forests

Some companies need a single tree to support their enterprises, whereas others need a forest of trees. Trees and forests both form a structure where every domain shares the same configuration, global catalog, and schema. When you join one of your domains to this hierarchy, it establishes a two-way transitive Kerberos trust relationship with its immediate parent. Therefore, all domains forming a tree or forest can share their resources globally.

There are more differences than similarities between trees and forests, however. To decide whether to organize your company's Windows 2000 domains into a tree or forest, consider the differences listed in Table 5.2.

TABLE 5.2 Distinctions Between Trees and Forests

Trees	Forests
Form a single contiguous namespace.	Formed of several disjointed namespaces.
For companies operating as a single legal entity.	For companies operating as several entities, such as partnerships, holding companies, conglomerates, pooling and joint ventures.

Trees	Forests
Easier for users and administrators to navigate and understand.	More difficult for users and administrators to navigate and understand.
LDAP searches in a tree are always resolved by LDAP referrals.	LDAP searches in a forest are not always resolved—limited to replicated attributes in the GC and objects in the tree where the search came from.

To summarize, a domain tree is one or more domains with

- A common schema, configuration, and Global Catalog
- Transitive trust
- A contiguous namespace

And, a forest is one or more domain trees with

- A common schema, configuration, and Global Catalog
- Transitive trust
- A noncontiguous namespace

Determining When to Create an OU

There are very different reasons for creating OUs and creating domains. The various domains in your organization represent large groups of resources that are often managed by a team of administrators. You can use OUs to logically organize and manage these resources with more granularity.

Tip

It is recommended that you limit your company to a maximum of 10 OU levels. LDAP search performance will begin to degrade noticeably at around 5 OU levels.

Microsoft suggests seven different models for OU structures:

- Geographic
- Object-based
- Cost center
- Project-based
- Division or business unit

- Administration
- Hybrid or mixed

The following sections look at each of these OU models.

Geographic Model

Companies that use single domains to group different physical offices can organize their OUs by location.

When you open a new office in one of your regions, you can add an OU for that office beneath an existing top-level OU. As you can see from Table 5.3, there are advantages and disadvantages to this model.

TABLE 5.3 Geographic Model—Advantages and Disadvantages

Advantages	Disadvantages
OUs fairly stable.	Locations or offices don't change frequently. Doesn't mirror the business practices of your organization.
Supports centralized policy setting.	Entire structure is one large partition or single domain. This means that you must replicate any change to all objects across all geographic locations.
Easy to determine where resources are physically located.	
Easy for users and administrators to understand.	

Object-Based

You can base your OU structure on object types. An administrator would create a first-level container for each class of object in the tree.

Note   Below the first level, you might find that a geographical layout is easier to administer.

Table 5.4 enumerates the advantages and disadvantages of the object-based model.

TABLE 5.4   Object-Based Model—Advantages and Disadvantages

Advantages	Disadvantages
Resource administration is easier because each OU represents a specific class of object.	Harder to define OU-based policies because all users are in the same containers.
Permission based on OUs so it is easier to create OU-wide permissions, such as All Users Can Use All Printers.	Structure will have to be created in each domain.
Administration easily delegated by resource type.	Too many top-level OUs.
Company reorganization should have little effect on design.	If schema is extended to accept new object types, new OUs will need to be created.
DNs consistent for all objects in a class.	

Cost Center

You might decide that the OUs should reflect your company's cost centers. The cost center model doesn't really take advantage of Active Directory as shown in Table 5.5.

TABLE 5.5   Cost Center Model—Advantages and Disadvantages

Advantages	Disadvantages
Each cost center can manage its own resources.	Users might not be grouped in a way that reflects the way resources are used.
	Delegation of administrative privileges is difficult.

Project-Based

Your company might prefer to organize an OU structure around project teams. This is an effective strategy when you want to create an OU for each resource group. Of course there are advantages and disadvantages as shown in Table 5.6.

5

TABLE 5.6 Project-Based Model—Advantages and Disadvantages

Advantages	Disadvantages
Good for environments where you need to track resources and costs.	OUs will need to be deleted and resources redistributed when a project ends.
Because each project is a separate OU, security between projects is easier to maintain.	When projects change frequently, the structure requires a lot of work.

Division or Business Unit

Companies that rely on single domains to organize separate divisions, practices, or business units can arrange their OUs by function. The first level of OUs in the company's domain represents how it functionally operates. Check out Table 5.7 for the advantages and disadvantages of the division or business unit model.

TABLE 5.7 Division Model—Advantages and Disadvantages

Advantages	Disadvantages
Structure is "user-friendly" because it is based upon a pre-existing structure.	Business units might change causing a redesign of the OU structure.
Easier to locate resources because it is based on a pre-existing structure.	

Administration

Many organizations choose a structure based upon common administrative groupings within the company. As you can see from Table 5.8, this model works well because it is based upon the actual business structure of the company.

TABLE 5.8 Administration Model—Advantages and Disadvantages

Advantages	Disadvantages
Designed from the perspective of the network or system administrator and makes their job easier.	All resources from a single division or department are grouped under a single OU causing confusion for users.
Because most companies are departmental, this model fits from a logical and physical perspective.	When many resources shared between departments, model might not reflect business model of the company.
It is the way most organizations implemented Windows NT.	

Tip   The Administration model is one of the more commonly implemented OU models. It works well because it matches the organizational chart. In other words, you already designed your structure, now all you have to do is implement it.

Hybrid or Mixed

When single domains are used to organize resources by both function and location, companies can build a hybrid OU structure. You might decide to base your top-level OUs on location. Because your company has offices in the United States, Europe, and Asia, it created three OUs at the first level: UNITED STATES, EUROPE, and ASIA. Then, you will use the second-level OUs to represent the functional divisions within your company. Table 5.9 lists the advantages and disadvantages of the hybrid or mixed model.

TABLE 5.9 Mixed Model—Advantages and Disadvantages

Advantages	Disadvantages
Uses the model to customize the way you do business in your company.	Requires a greater understanding of the company and the way it does business.
Reflects the way users work.	

5

Before you decide how to organize OUs in your individual domains, take the time to explore your company's distinctive traits and requirements. All your up-front design work will help you avoid rebuilding OUs at a later date. Use OUs effectively to delegate administrative tasks.

In this section, you examined the valid reasons for creating OUs, how to organize OUs into a meaningful hierarchy, and some of the common ways to use OUs to delegate administrative tasks. In the section that follows, you will learn how to plan a site structure in Active Directory.

Planning a Site Structure

The logical structure of an NT 3.x-4.0 network almost always mirrored its physical structure. In Windows 2000, however, the logical and physical structure of your network doesn't have to match. The tree or forest forming your company's domain namespace represents your network's logical structure. To define the physical structure of your network, you must configure one or more site objects in Active Directory.

Use your company's site objects to define areas of good network connectivity. To configure a site object in Active Directory, you associate it with one or more TCP/IP subnets. Each TCP/IP subnet that you define for a site should share a high bandwidth link (512Kbps or greater). In general, you will create a site object for each area of your network that is separated by low bandwidth. The site objects you create for your company can be used for any of the following reasons:

- To throttle replication traffic
- To isolate workstation logon traffic
- To identify resources by proximity

Installing Active Directory

Designing the structure of your ADS is an extremely important task that you should do before starting implementation. At this point, you now are ready to install Active Directory.

Task 5.1: Installing Active Directory.

Step 1: Description

This task will walk you through the use of the Active Directory Installation Wizard to install your Active Directory. The wizard will install Active Directory on your computer, promote your computer to domain controller, and create a domain.

▼ Step 2: Action

1. Log on to the Windows 2000 Server as Administrator.

2. From the Start menu, select Programs, Administrative Tools, Windows 2000 Configure Server. Alternatively, select Start, Run, type `dcpromo.exe`, and click OK. This opens the Active Directory Installation Wizard shown in Figure 5.2.

FIGURE 5.2

Active Installation Wizard.

3. Click Next. The Create Tree or Child Domain panel in Figure 5.3 appears. You have two choices:

   - New domain tree: When you create a new tree, the new domain isn't part of another domain. You can create a new tree in an existing forest, or you can create a new forest.

   - New child domain: When you create a new child domain, the new domain is a child domain in an existing domain.

FIGURE 5.3

Create Tree or Child Domain panel.

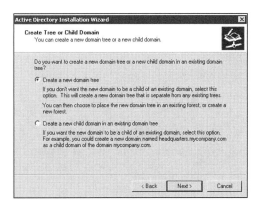

▼   4. Select Create a New Domain Tree, and then click Next. You should see the panel shown in Figure 5.4.

FIGURE 5.4

Create or Join Forest panel.

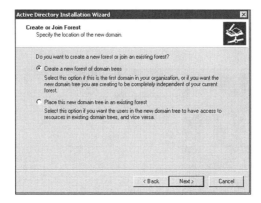

5. Select Create a New Forest of Domain Trees, and then click Next.

6. Because you have not at this point installed a Domain Naming Server, you will see the panel in Figure 5.5. Select No, Just Install and Configure DNS on This Computer, and then click Next. You will configure DNS on Day 12, "Understanding TCP/IP and DNS."

FIGURE 5.5

Install or Configure DNS panel.

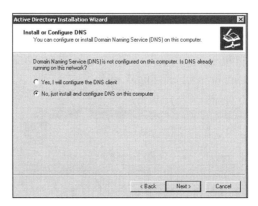

▼   7. The New Domain Name panel in Figure 5.6 appears. In the Full DNS Name For New Domain box, type a domain name such as **pdaconsulting.com**, and click Next.

FIGURE 5.6

New Domain Name panel.

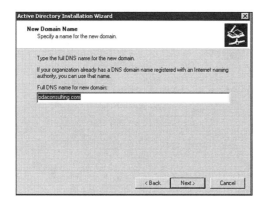

> **Note**
>
> During installation, if you decide to use NetBIOS you will see another panel. On the NetBIOS Domain Name panel, type **PDACONSULTING** (or a short form of the DNS name you selected) in the Domain NetBIOS Name box, and click Next. If you didn't, you'll see the panel in Figure 5.7.

8. On the Database and Log Locations panel, ensure that C:\WINNT\NTDS is the location of the database and the log as shown in Figure 5.7. Click Next.

FIGURE 5.7

Database and Log Locations panel.

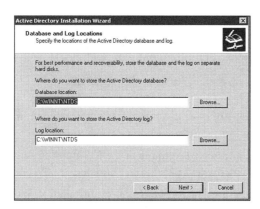

5

9. On the Shared System Volume panel shown in Figure 5.8, ensure that the sysvol location is C:\WINNT\SYSVOL, and then click Next.

FIGURE 5.8

Shared System Volume panel.

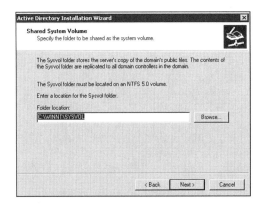

10. In the Windows NT 4.0 RAS Servers panel shown in Figure 5.9, select No, Do Not Change the Permissions, and then click Next.

FIGURE 5.9

Windows NT 4.0 RAS Servers panel.

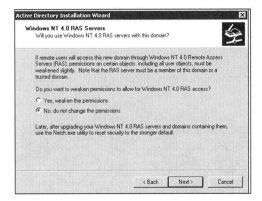

11. Review the summary page that appears (such as the one in Figure 5.10), and click Next.

12. In Figure 5.11, you see an example of the Configuring Active Directory progress indicator. The process will take several minutes.

13. Then the Completing The Active Directory Installation Wizard panel appears. A sample panel is shown in Figure 5.12.

14. Click Finish, and then click the Restart Now button.

▼

FIGURE 5.10

Active Directory Summary panel.

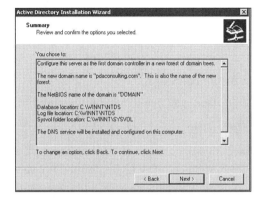

FIGURE 5.11

Configuring Active Directory progress panel.

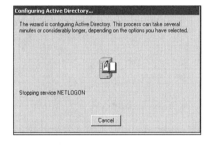

FIGURE 5.12

Completing the Active Directory Installation Wizard panel.

5

▲

Step 3: Review

In this task, you installed Active Directory. As you already learned today, AD is a key component of Windows 2000.

Confirming Installation

In subsequent tasks, you will learn to modify parts of the Active Directory. Before you do, you should ensure that ADS installed correctly. The most important thing is to ensure that DNS added service records or *SRV records* to its database. To do this, you need to confirm two things:

1. Check the DNS file for the SRV record.
2. Check the DNS database, and make sure it is working correctly.

Check for SRV Records

To check to ensure the installation created an SRV record, look at the file in \%SystemRoot%\system32\config named Netlogon.dns. You can use WordPad to view the file. Your LDAP record should look something like the one in Figure 5.13. On this system, it is the second record.

FIGURE 5.13

Checking the Service Record.

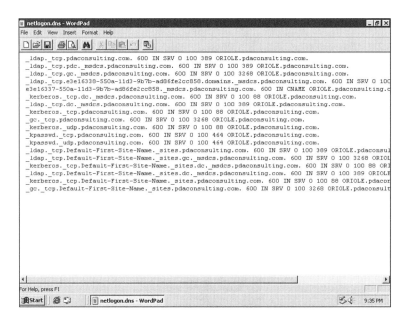

Checking the DNS Database

To verify that the DNS database is working correctly, you will use NSLOOKUP. To confirm this, perform the following steps:

1. Select Start, Programs, Accessories, Command Prompt.

2. At the command prompt, type **NSLOOKUP**.

3. Type **SET TYPE=SRV**, press Enter.

4. Type **ldap.tcp.<Active_directory_domain_name>**, where
   <Active_directory_domain_name> is the name you chose for your domain name.
   Press Enter.

5. If you see the server name and IP address, then the SRV records are working
   correctly. Type **Exit**.

Now, let's ensure you can see your domain.

Task 5.2: Viewing Your Domain.

Step 1: Description

With this task, you learn how to use the Directory management snap-in to view your
domain.

Step 2: Action

1. Log on to the Windows 2000 Server as Administrator.

2. From the Start menu, select Programs, Administrative Tools, Active Directory
   Users and Computers.

3. In the console tree, double-click the name of your domain.

4. In the console tree, click Domain Controllers. You should see the name of your
   server.

5. Close Directory Management.

Tip

> You can view your domains another way. Log on as Administrator and
> double-click My Network Places. From the My Network Places window,
> double-click Entire Network, click the entire contents, and then double-click
> Microsoft Windows Network. Double-click the Domain icon. You should see
> the domain you created. (If you double-click that icon, you should see a
> window like the one in Figure 5.14.) To exit, close the Microsoft Windows
> Network window.

5

FIGURE 5.14

*Oriole Domain
components.*

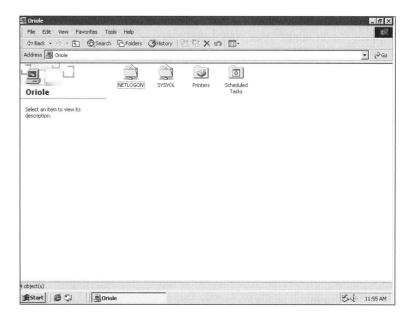

Step 3: Review

In this task, you saw how to view your domain using My Network Places and the
Directory Management MMC snap-in.

You need to do one more thing, which is to switch from mixed to native mode. Mixed
mode allows the domain controller to interact with any domain controllers in domains
running previous versions of Windows NT (sometimes called downlevel servers). When
you have decided that you no longer need downlevel support or when the computer just
installed is the only one, you'll want to switch from mixed to native mode.

Task 5.3: Switching Your Domain Mode.

Step 1: Description

With this task, you learn how to switch the mode from mixed to native. Switching to
native means you have no downlevel domain controllers in your network.

Step 2: Action

1. Log on to the Windows 2000 Server as Administrator.
2. From the Start menu, select Programs, Administrative Tools, Directory Tree
   Management.

▼ 3. Right-click the name of your domain, and then click Properties.

4. From the General tab, click Change to Native Mode.

5. In the Warning dialog box, click Yes, and then click OK.

6. Restart your system.

Caution	The change from mixed mode to native mode is one-way—you cannot go back.

▲

Step 3: Review

When you have upgraded all your domain controllers, you can move from mixed to native mode. This facility is a transitional device. Use the Directory Tree Management MMC snap-in to change modes.

Managing Active Directory

The Active Directory Users and Computers MMC snap-in is the most useful tool for administering your Active Directory. After you install Active Directory, it is directly accessible from the Administrative Tools program group on the Start menu. It replaces and improves upon Server Manager and User Manager from Windows NT 4.0. Take a few minutes to familiarize yourself with this tool. It is very intuitive—just be sure not to make any modifications until you understand how Active Directory works.

Creating Active Directory Objects

When you want to add new user accounts, groups, or printers, you create new Active Directory objects representing these resources. Assuming you have the authority, you can add the objects in Table 5.10.

TABLE 5.10 Common Objects and Their Contents

Object	Contents
User Account	Required information to allow users to log on, such as username.
Group	Collection of user accounts, groups, or computers that you can create and use for administration.

continues

TABLE 5.10 continued

Object	Contents
Shared Folder	A pointer to the shared folder on a computer. When you publish a shared folder or a printer in AD, you are creating an object that contains a pointer to the shared folder.
Printer	A pointer to the printer folder on a computer. When you publish a shared folder or a printer in AD, you are creating an object that contains a pointer to the printer.
Computer	Information about a computer that is a member of the domain.
Domain controllers	Information about a domain controller including description, DNS name, and location.
Organizational unit	Can contain other objects and used to organize Active Directory objects.

Adding a new resource creates one of the objects above. The next task teaches you how to create an organizational unit.

Task 5.4: Creating an Organizational Unit.

Step 1: Description

You create part of the organizational structure of a domain by creating an organizational unit (OU). Again, you use the Directory Management snap-in to do this.

Step 2: Action

1. Log on to the Windows 2000 Server as Administrator.

2. From the Start menu, select Programs, Administrative Tools, Directory Management.

3. In the console tree, click the domain where you want to create the organizational unit (OU).

4. On the Action menu, point to New, and then click Organizational Unit. You should see the Create New Object – (Organizational Unit) dialog box.

5. In the Name box, type **Training**, and then click Next. You should see the new OU as well as the default OUs in your domain.

6. Under the domain, create a second OU called Training.

 7. Exit.

Step 3: Review

In this task, you learned how to create an OU to support your organizational structure. Just use the Directory Management snap-in and select the domain where you want to add the OU. On Day 9, "Managing the File Server," you will learn to create user accounts—another type of directory object.

Having created a new object, you might want to locate that directory object or others. To do so, follow the task in the next section.

Task 5.5: Locating an Object.

Step 1: Description

To locate Active Directory objects, you will use the Directory Management snap-in.

Step 2: Action

1. Log on to the Windows 2000 Server as Administrator.
2. From the Start menu, select Programs, Administrative Tools, Active Directory Users and Computers.

> **Note**
>
> If you don't see any Active Directory tools under Administrative Tools, don't despair. Instead, do the following:
>
> 1. Select Start, Run, type `mmc /a`, and click OK.
> 2. From the Console menu, select Add/Remove Snap-in or use Ctrl+M.
> 3. Click Add.
> 4. Select Active Directory Domains and Trusts, and click Add.
> 5. Select Active Directory Sites and Services, and click Add.
> 6. Select Active Directory Users and Computers, and click Add.
> 7. Click Close, click OK.

5

3. Right-click the OU you just created in the console tree.
4. Click Find. You should see a User Directory Management dialog box.
5. The Find Users, Contacts, and Groups dialog box lets you find user accounts, groups, and printers.
6. Pull down the Find list and select Directory Folders. Windows 2000 places each OU in its own folder. Your options are Users, Contacts and Groups; Computers; Printers; Shared Folders; Directory Folders; Custom Search; and Routers.
7. Pull down the In list and select your domain, for example, pdaconsulting.com.
8. Select the Advanced tab.
9. Select Field.

▼ 10. Enter the search criteria.

11. Click Add.

12. Click Find Now.

▲ 13. To exit, click the X on the upper-right corner of the dialog box.

Step 3: Review

In this task, you used the global catalog to find information regardless of the domain it resides in. Active Directory automatically generates the contents of the GC.

Schema: Attributes and Object Classes

As previously mentioned, a schema is a set of attributes used to describe a particular object class in Active Directory. Different types of information need to be tracked for different object classes, and that's why the schema is so important. For example, the Users object class needs attributes for a first name, last name, phone number, email address, and mailing address. The Printer object class must have many different attributes—users will want to know how fast a printer is and whether it can duplex or print in color. These attributes can be viewed and edited using the Active Directory Schema MMC snap-in. The Active Directory Schema doesn't have an icon within the Start menu; you must launch the MMC interface and add the snap-in named Active Directory Schema.

By default, object classes come with a logical set of attributes that will fit most organization's needs. However, many organizations will need to track additional information about particular object classes. For example, if employees are assigned a badge number, it is useful to track that information in the object class. The first step is to create an attribute called BadgeID. The second step is to make the new attribute optional for the Users class. Attributes can be added with the Active Directory Schema snap-in.

The schema is stored within Active Directory just like other objects. Therefore, the schema inherits the capability to be automatically replicated throughout a domain. It also benefits from the security features of Active Directory, and allows administrators to delegate authority over the schema to different users and groups. By changing the ACLs on a schema object, an administrator can allow any user to add or modify attributes for an object class.

 Caution

By default, Active Directory servers don't allow you to edit the schema. Before you can, you must edit Schema Update Allowed, and add a REG_DWORD value and set it to 1. You will add this value to the following Registry key:

    \HKLM\SYSTEM\CurrentControlSet\Services\NTDS\Parameters

Yesterday you learned about Registry editing, but let me remind you today to back up the Registry before making any changes.

New attributes have several properties that must be set. The user creating a new attribute must define a name for the attribute (such as Badge ID #), the type of data to be stored (such as a string or a number), and the range limits (such as string length). A unique Object Identifier (OID) must also be provided. New attributes can be indexed, which adds the attributes to the global catalog. Indexes should be created for attributes that users will search with. In this example, if security needs to look up user accounts by the Badge ID number, this attribute should be indexed. For a search to occur on a non-indexed attribute, a slow and processor-intensive walk of the directory tree must be done.

You cannot delete a class or an attribute with the Active Directory Schema or any other tool. After you create them, they will exist forever within your Active Directory. The only option you have is to deactivate a class, which stops it from being used in the future. You cannot deactivate a class or an attribute that has dependencies within Active Directory. For example, if an attribute is still used by an active class, that attribute must remain active.

Active Directory servers cache the schema for performance. Therefore, it could take up to five minutes for the ADS to update the cache after your change. So, wait several minutes before you try to create objects based on your new object classes and attributes. Should you need to reload the cache immediately, add the attribute schemaUpdateNow to the root object (that is, the one without a distinguished name) and set the value to 1.

Extending the schema of Active Directory is a powerful capability. However, most administrators will never need to use anything but the default classes and attributes from Microsoft. To install the Active Directory Schema Manager, use the MMC procedure described above.

5

Active Directory plays an important role in the future of Windows networking. You need to protect your directory from attackers and users, while delegating tasks to other administrators where necessary. This is all possible using the Active Directory security model, which associates an access control list (ACL) with each container, object, and object attribute within the directory. Tomorrow, you will find out about security services in Windows 2000. Surely you agree that this is enough for today.

Summary

You learned many of the surrounding infrastructure issues and design considerations when looking at Active Directory in this lesson. In addition, you learned the various AD components and how to plan, implement, and manage ADS.

Today, you learned the following points:

- Objects, schema, object classes, attributes, and other Active Directory components
- Planning for Active Directory
- Installing Active Directory
- Adding new directory objects
- Changing the schema

Workshop

To wrap up the day, you can review tasks from the lesson, and see the answers to commonly asked questions.

Task List

The information provided in this chapter shows you how to manage the various domains that Windows 2000 makes available. You learned to perform the following tasks:

- Install Active Directory
- View your domain
- Switch your domain mode
- Create an organizational unit
- Locate an object

Q&A

Q Are OUs part of the DNS namespace?

A Even though this is jumping ahead a bit, the question deserves an answer here. No, OU names aren't part of the DNS namespace. Your users don't use DNS to find an OU. They use it to find an IP address.

Q Can I delegate the administration of OUs?

A By all means. You might allow other administrators to do the following:

- Change container properties
- Create, delete, and change child objects

- Update attributes for a specific class of object
- Create new users and groups
- Manage a small subgroup of objects within the tree

Q Can I demote a domain controller to a member server?

A You sure can. Run dcpromo.exe and click Remove. This will remove Active Directory from the domain controller and demote it to a standalone server. Remember that if you remove AD from all domain controllers in the domain, you also delete the directory database for the domain, and the domain no longer exists.

Q What is the shared system volume?

A The shared system volume is a folder structure that AD creates during installation and that exists on all Windows 2000 domain controllers. The system uses it to store scripts and some of the group policy objects for the current domain and the enterprise. As you saw, the default location for the shared system volume is \%SystemRoot%\sysvol.

Q I think something went wrong when I installed my AD. Does the Active Directory Installation Wizard keep a log?

A To see a log of the results of each step in the installation process, look in \%SystemRoot%\debug.

Q I have a lot of objects in my organization. How big is the Active Directory database?

A Active Directory uses the Extensible Storage Engine (ESE) used with Exchange 4.0/5.0, Access, and WINS. With ESE, you can create a database of up to 17 terabytes. This gives the database the theoretical capacity of over 10 million objects.

5

DAY 6

Introducing Security Services

From the beginning, you have probably noticed a major difference between W2K and other operating systems such as Windows 2000, 3.1*x*, MS-DOS, or OS/2. As you learned on Day 1 (in the section "What Is Windows 2000 Server?"), Microsoft included security in W2K as part of the initial design specifications. Security is pervasive throughout the entire operating system. Figure 6.1 shows how the Windows 2000 security subsystem fits into the overall Windows 2000 architecture.

The W2K security subsystem is an integral subsystem rather than an environmental subsystem because it affects the entire W2K operating system. Security is an important part of any network operation; it is necessary for protecting one user's data from being accessed by other users, an organization's records from being tampered with by outsiders, and so on. Security, however, has some administration associated with it.

FIGURE 6.1

The Windows 2000 architecture.

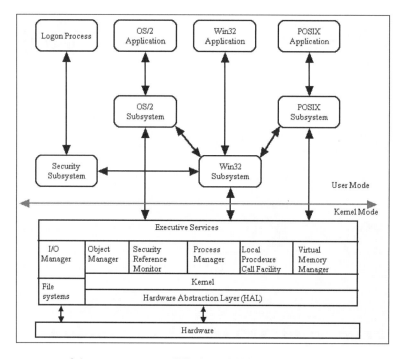

Before you can access any of the resources on a Windows 2000 system, you must first log on and be authenticated by the Windows 2000 system. Authentication is required on any W2K machine, whether workstation or server; that is, the system authenticates you even when you access a standalone Windows 2000 computer not connected to a file server or another host computer.

Today, you learn about the following topics:

- The logon process
- Windows 2000 security architecture and how it performs its role
- Kerberos and how it provides user authentication
- Public Key cryptography
- Discretionary access

A connection to a Windows 2000 server isn't required to achieve initial resource protection. W2K can provide this local security because all machines have a full security subsystem with a security database that may or may not be coupled to a Windows 2000 server. The security model includes components that control who accesses objects (such as files and shared printers), what actions a user can take on an object, and what *events* a user can audit.

NEW TERM When a user logs on to W2K, the system creates a special data structure called a *token object* or *ticket* to represent that user. W2K associates this token—or a copy of it—with every process that the user runs. This process-token combination is called a *subject*. Subjects operate on Windows 2000 objects by calling system services. When the system accesses protected objects such as files and directories, it compares the contents of the subject's token with the Access Control List (ACL) using a standard *access validation* routine. The access validation routine determines whether to grant the subject the right to perform the requested operation. The access authentication routine can also generate audit messages as a result of a security mismatch.

The Windows NT Security Subsystem

As mentioned earlier, the Windows NT security subsystem affects the entire Windows NT operating system. It provides a single system in which all access to objects— including files on disk, processes in memory, or ports to external devices—is checked so that no application or user obtains access without the proper authorization.

The security subsystem components described here are shown in Figure 6.2. Seeing all the major security data structures at work is useful because it helps you understand how Windows NT protects objects. The security subsystem consists of the following components:

FIGURE 6.2

Security subsystems.

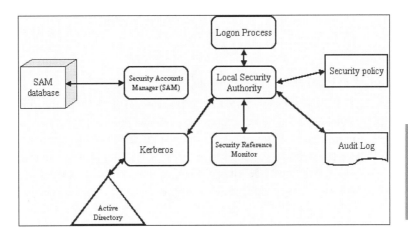

- **Local Security Authority (LSA)**—Ensures that the user has permission to access the system.
- **Security Account Manager (SAM)**—Maintains the local machine's user and groups accounts database and validates users for LSA.

- **Active Directory**—Maintains the user and groups accounts database for the domain and validates users for LSA.
- **Security Reference Monitor (SRM)**—The kernel-level process that checks access permissions and enforces access validations and audit policies defined by LSA.
- **Logon processes**—Provide the initial interactive logon and display the Logon dialog box.

The User Interface (UI) utilities, which are a part of the operating system, also play an important role in the security model of W2K. The UI is the only hint to most users of the underlying security mechanisms. As the system administrator, you typically use the UI to perform administrative functions such as adding or removing users from the system and looking at the audit logs.

In addition to the preceding list, W2K offers the following security components:

- Discretionary access controls
- Kerberos tickets
- Access tokens
- Access Control Lists
- Event auditing

These elements, combined with the logon process, Security Account Manager, Active Directory, Local Security Authority, and Security Reference Monitor, provide a number of integrated features that form the backbone of security in W2K.

Local Security Authority

The *Local Security Authority* (*LSA*), also called the security subsystem, is the heart of the Windows 2000 Server security system and provides many services. LSA ensures that the user has permission to access the system. It generates local access tokens, interfaces with Kerberos, manages the local security policy, and provides interactive user validation services. The Local Security Authority also controls the Audit policy and logs the audit messages generated by the Security Reference Monitor. Specifically, it performs the following tasks:

- Creates access tokens during the logon process
- Allows Windows 2000 Server to connect with third-party validation packages
- Manages the security policy
- Controls the Audit policy
- Logs audit messages to the Event Log

Security Account Manager and Active Directory

As mentioned earlier, the W2K security subsystem affects the entire W2K operating system. It provides a single system in which all access to objects—including files on disk, processes in memory, or ports to external devices—is checked so that no application or user obtains access without the proper authorization.

The *Security Account Manager* (*SAM*) maintains the security account database in NT 4.0, called the SAM database. In Windows 2000 domains the *Active Directory* replaces this database. You learned all about Active Directory on Day 5, "Introducing Active Directory." This database contains information for all user and group accounts. It provides user validation services, which by default uses Kerberos v5 authentication. The concept of a *security identifier* (*SID*) for each user and each group or machine on the network remains. You'll recall that SIDs are created and used by Active Directory to identify a user, group, or machine.

SIDs are retired when an account is deleted. They are never re-used. Gone. Lost. Zapped. After you delete a user account, you cannot re-create it because the SID for that account no longer exists. You can create a new account with the same name, but the system assigns a different SID. Fortunately, the new account doesn't retain previous privileges. This prevents you from accidentally assigning rights to a new employee with the same name as a previous employee.

Depending on the configuration of the network, each different machine contains a SAM database or Active Directory. (In actual fact the SAM database remains even on machines set up for Active Directory, it just isn't used.) Which database is accessed at logon depends on a number of things including

- Whether the user is logging on to a workstation.
- Whether the user is logging in to a network using a domain controller.

The Active Directory database is interesting because in a network environment it will exist on a number of machines called controllers. When a user logs on to a local machine, the SAM on that machine retrieves user IDs from its database pretty much in the same fashion as it did in NT 4.0. In a Windows 2000 domain network environment, user account information is stored in an Active Directory database on one or more servers called domain controllers, which share and update account information. This shared database enables users to log on once to access resources throughout the network.

6

Security Reference Monitor

The *Security Reference Monitor* (*SRM*) is a kernel mode Windows 2000 Server component that is responsible for enforcing the access validation and audit generation policy
held by the Local Security Authority subsystem. SRM isn't visible to the user. It protects
resources or objects from unauthorized access or modification by preventing direct
access to objects by any user or process. The SRM provides services for validating
access to objects (files, directories, and so on), testing subjects (user accounts) for privileges, and generating the necessary audit messages. The Security Reference Monitor contains the only copy of the access validation code in the system. This component ensures
that object protection is provided uniformly throughout W2K, regardless of the type of
object accessed.

NEW TERM — W2K prevents direct access to objects; instead, the Security Reference Monitor
must first validate requests by users for access to objects. When a user opens a
file to edit, for example, W2K first compares the security descriptor for the file with the
security information that is stored in a user's token. Then, a decision is made whether to
enable the user to edit the file. The security descriptor for the file includes all the *access
control entries* (*ACE*s) that make up the file's ACL. A file without an ACL indicates that
any user can access the file for any type of access.

A file with an ACL indicates that the Security Reference Monitor must check each ACE
in the ACL and determine whether the user can access the file for the requested type of
access. After the Security Reference Monitor grants access to the file, no further access
validation check is necessary to access the file. Further attempts to access the file are
made through a handle that was created to refer to the file.

New Security Protocols

The W2K security infrastructure supports a number of primary security protocols. Each
are used to support different aspects of security depending upon the operating system and
network activity. The current protocols are as follows:

- Kerberos becomes the primary authentication mechanism for Windows 2000. The
  Kerberos Version 5 authentication protocol replaces NTLM for access to resources
  within or across Windows 2000 domains. It is a mature industry standard that has
  been in use for some time and offers several advantages for Windows network

authentication. These include mutual authentication of both client and server, reduced server load during connection establishment, and support for delegation of authorization from clients to servers through the use of proxy mechanisms.

- Windows NT LAN Manager (NTLM) authentication protocol remains the protocol used by Windows NT 4.0 and previous versions of Windows NT. It continues to be supported and used for network authentication, remote file access, and connections to earlier versions of Windows NT.

- Public key protocols provide for privacy and reliability over the Internet. SSL is the current standard for connections between Internet browsers and Internet information servers. (A new IETF standard protocol definition based on SSL3 is currently known as the Transport Layer Security Protocol, or TLS.) These protocols, which use public-key certificates to authenticate clients and servers, depend on a public-key infrastructure. Windows NT 4.0 provides secure channel security services that implement the SSL/PCT protocols.

- Distributed Password Authentication (DPA) is a shared secret protocol used by organizations such as MSN and CompuServe. This authentication protocol is part of Microsoft Commercial Internet System (MCIS) services and is specifically designed for users to use the same Internet membership password to connect to any number of Internet sites that are part of the same membership organization. The Internet content servers use the MCIS authentication service as a back-end Internet service, and users can connect to multiple sites without reentering their passwords.

Each protocol interacts with different authentication services and account information stores. NTLM security provider uses the W2K NetLogon and MSV1_0 authentication service on a domain controller to authenticate the client. The Kerberos security provider connects to a Key Distribution Center (KDC) and interacts with Active Directory to generate session tickets. The DPA uses the MCIS security services for membership authentication and server-specific access information. DPA is part of MCIS services and is specifically designed to enable users to use the same Internet membership password to connect to any number of Internet sites that are part of the same membership organization without reentering their passwords.

Finally, secure channel services are based on public-key certificates that are issued by trusted Certificate Authorities. In the next few sections I tell you all about these protocols and the general logon process.

6

The Logon Process

> For the most part, this section describes logon procedures for Windows 2000 Server and Windows 2000 Professional computers. You might find some variation in the background procedure when you log on to a Windows 2000 network from Windows 95/98 and Windows for Workgroups computers.

NEW TERM You should beware that two types of logon exist: interactive and remote. An *interactive logon* occurs when you first log on to a computer and confirm your identity to that local machine. A process verifies that you are who you say you are based on the credentials (that is, username and password) that you typed in the Logon dialog box. After they are validated, your credentials are kept because the system might require them again for a remote logon authentication.

The interactive logon process is Windows 2000's first line of defense against unauthorized access. The process begins with a Welcome box that asks a user to press the Ctrl+Alt+Del keys simultaneously. (To enhance security in your organization, precede this dialog box with a legal notice.) Pressing Ctrl+Alt+Del offers a strong defense against any application running in the background, such as a Trojan horse, that attempts to capture a user's logon information.

> Windows 95 computers and other non-Windows 2000 computers don't have the Ctrl+Alt+Del logon protection feature. Thus, they are susceptible to a Trojan horse acting as the logon process. A Trojan horse is a program in which malicious or harmful code is contained inside apparently harmless programming or data. In this way it can get control and do its chosen form of damage, such as pretending to be the legitimate logon authority while actually keeping an unauthorized copy of your logon credentials.

The Ctrl+Alt+Del key sequence assures you that a valid Windows 2000 logon sequence will initiate. This key sequence always needs to be pressed when logging on to a machine that is already running.

Regardless of which method you use for logging on, the logon process also enables you to have your own personal desktop configurations on your desktop systems. When you log on, the settings you had in a previous session are fetched from a profile and restored.

You can either log on to a local computer using an account on that computer, or you can log on by being validated by another computer. In domains, a domain controller holds a copy of the directory database that is used to validate you. The outcome depends on what you select in the Domain field of the Logon dialog box. The options are as follows:

- When you select the local computer name in the Domain field, the local computer logs you on to the local system.
- When you type a domain name in the Domain field, a Remote logon takes place. The logon request is sent to a domain controller for verification. When the specified domain isn't the local domain, the domain controller forwards the request to the authorized domain controller in the domain you specified.

Note

You learned about domain controllers in Day 5.

Domain controllers authenticate your account name and password by comparing them to entries in the Active Directory database. If the entries are valid, account identification information is sent back to the logon computer through the domain controller that originally tried to verify the user account. When a normal logon fails, you might get logged in to the Guest account, but only when the Guest account is enabled and passwords aren't required.

New Term Assume that you are already logged on and attempt to access resources on other computers. In this case, the credentials that were used to verify the original logon are passed through to the new server and used to authenticate you for access to those resources. This process, called *passthrough authentication*, frees users from having to log on to every new resource they access. I discuss this in more detail in the Kerberos section a little later on.

Note

In the next paragraph, the local computer is the computer on which you're working (that is, the one you logged on to); the remote computer is a computer in the local domain or a trusted domain with a shared resource—such as a folder or printer—that you want to access.

6

New Term A *remote logon* occurs when you attempt to access some shared resources, such as a folder or printer, after you logged on using the interactive logon process. Remote logon really is the process of reverifying that you are an authentic user. When the remote computer is satisfied that you are authentic, it returns a special token that you can use for any future requests for service.

Now, assume that you attempt to access a computer in another domain that cannot authenticate you because you don't have an account in that domain. The remote computer must send your credentials to a domain controller in its domain, and that domain controller asks a domain controller in your domain to authenticate you. This process is similar to getting cash from an ATM of a foreign bank: The issuing bank checks with your bank to verify that you are a customer and that you have adequate funds.

Local and Domain Logon

You need to understand where the user account database that enables users to log on to a computer or network is stored. The database is stored either on a local computer (that is, the computer at which you are physically sitting when you log on) or on a domain controller. Once again, the following discussion assumes that you're logging on at a W2K computer rather than a Windows 95 computer, and that you're using domain networking rather than workgroup networking.

When you log on, you can choose to log on to an account on the local computer, log on to an account on the local domain, or log on to an account on some remote domain (usually called logging on to a trusted domain.) Ideally, all these accounts are the same, but that often isn't the case when different networks have been joined together.

When you log on to the local computer, your credentials are verified against a user account database stored on that computer. A problem occurs when you try to access a resource on the network because you might need to log on again and have your credentials verified against the user account database on a domain controller.

Assume that you log on to the workstation, and then try to open a shared resource on a server. Also assume that you have an account on the local computer, and an account in the domain with the same name but a different password. In this case, your original username and password are passed through to the server, but an `Access is denied` message appears because the passwords are different. Although the passwords can be synchronized, it is better to only have one account on the domain controller and always log on to the domain rather than have separate accounts on different machines.

The same principle also applies when your network consists of multiple domains. Assume that you need to access resources in other domains. One way to do so is to have a separate user account in each domain; then you can log on to each account when you need to access the domain. However, having separate accounts can cause confusion and problems. It is better to have one account in one domain, and then set up a special relationship that allows your account to access resources in a trusting domain. Then, you can log on once with one password.

Logon Sequence Details

When you press Ctrl+Alt+Del at a W2K computer, the Logon dialog box appears with the Username, Password, and Domain text entry fields.

What you put in the Domain field makes a big difference to what happens during the logon process, as it determines where W2K should look for your user account and password.

Note If you originally set up the user's machine as a member of a workgroup and not a domain, you don't see the Domain field in the Logon dialog box.

The user's logon information can be authenticated in a user account database on the local computer, on the home domain controller, or on a domain controller in a trusted domain. To reiterate:

- If you type a local Windows 2000 Workstation name to log on locally, the local security account database (SAM) is used to validate you.
- If you type a home domain name, the Active Directory service on a home domain controller validates you.
- If you type a remote domain name to log on to another trusted domain, the logon request is passed through to a domain controller on the trusted domain, where you can be authenticated. This domain will use either Active Directory (a Windows 2000 domain) or the SAM database on a Primary or Backup Domain Controller (NT 4.0 domain).

The steps in the initial logon process are as follows: The credentials (username, password, and domain name) that you typed in the Logon dialog box are taken, and you are authenticated. For an NT 4.0 logon, the security system on the computer (called the Local Security Authority) then calls up an authentication package (technically, the MSV1_0). For W2K, the security system called the Local Security Authority then calls up a different authentication package called Kerberos. The authentication package then checks your credentials in the user account database, using either the SAM or Active Directory database primarily depending upon whether it is a workstation logon or domain logon. If you specify a domain logon, this last step takes place over the network at a domain controller.

6

NEW TERM If your credentials are authentic, they are cached for later use and an *access token or ticket* is created to identify you for all subsequent requests for resources. The access token contains your security identifier, group IDs, and user rights.

The security system determines the access to a resource by matching the user's requested access with the access permissions stored in the ACL for the resource. The user ID determines which access token is compared against the ACL for the resource. If a match is found and you (or the group) have not been specifically denied access, the requested access is granted.

An Overview of Kerberos

Kerberos has been around the block, so to speak. Far more common in the UNIX world, it began to make inroads in other platforms many years ago. But until now, this protocol has arguably languished. It remains to be seen whether Windows 2000's integration of this protocol will raise it from relative obscurity and bring it into the forefront of the security world. Now, I know that those statements might inflame all those who have worked with Kerberos for years, but in most business environments it just isn't widely used. I'll have to see how this changes with the acceptance of Windows 2000. There are a huge number of books devoted to Kerberos. In this book, we can only provide small coverage due to space restrictions, so we'd recommend you consider additional reading to fully understand this complex protocol.

 Tip
> To obtain additional information on Kerberos, go to **www.microsoft.com/ ntserver** and enter "Kerberos" in the search box. This will yield a couple of dozen results for different articles and white papers on NT security including Kerberos. Also, simply entering Kerberos in any Internet search engine, such as www.excite.com, will provide you with additional reference sources like MIT (which created Kerberos) and Stanford.

The name Kerberos is derived from Greek mythology. (Cerberus is the English version of the same word.) In the Greek underworld, a three-headed dog called Kerberos watched over Hades and guarded the gates, so to speak. Six eyes and a large number of teeth. Just what a good security program should contain. In the software world however, Kerberos was created in the 1980s as part of Project Athena, a development project that examined how to design and implement distributed environments. It wasn't until the fourth iteration that Kerberos began to become popular outside of MIT. Most major implementations of Kerberos are based on Kerberos version 5. This version supports multiple encryption algorithms making it far more secure than the older DES-based versions.

Note

The Kerberos authentication protocol uses a thing called a *Key Distribution Center* (KDC). W2K implements a KDC as the authentication service on each domain controller by default. While Kerberos uses the term realm to denote groups of machines, Windows 2000 domain can be considered the equivalent so Microsoft continues to use the term domain. Microsoft implemented the Windows 2000 Kerberos based on the Internet Request For Comment (RFC) number 1510. (You can do a search on your browser for RFC1510 if you want to read the gory details.) Windows 2000 integrated initial Kerberos authentication with the WinLogon single-sign-on architecture. The Kerberos server (KDC) uses Active Directory as the account database for users and groups.

NEW TERM The Kerberos authentication protocol is implemented as a *security support provider* (SSP), which is a dynamic-link library supplied with the operating system. W2K also includes an SSP for NTLM authentication. By default, both of these are loaded by the LSA on a W2K computer when the system boots. Either SSP may be used to authenticate network logons and client/server connections, depending upon the capabilities of the computer on the other side of the connection. The Kerberos SSP is always the first choice because Kerberos provides far better security than the older authentication protocols in Windows NT 4.0.

Kerberos is called a shared-secret authentication protocol because both the user and the KDC share a secret. The basic concept is fairly simple in that as long as the secret is known to only two people, then either person can verify the identity of the other by confirming that the other person knows that secret. Like the mythological Kerberos, the Kerberos protocol has three parts (or heads): a client, a server, and a trusted third party to mediate between them. The trusted third party is known as a Key Distribution Center (KDC).

NEW TERM Kerberos uses a series of exchanges between the client, the KDC, and servers to obtain and use things called *tickets*. When a user initiates a logon to Windows, Kerberos obtains an initial ticket (TGT) based on an encrypted hash of the user's password. W2K stores this TGT in a ticket cache for later use. Once signed on, each program that the user runs that attempts to access a network service is intercepted by the Kerberos runtime program that checks the ticket cache for a valid session ticket to the server. If a ticket isn't available, the TGT is sent in a request to the KDC for a session ticket that allows access to the server. Confusing? The next section takes you through it step by step so it should get easier to understand.

Once obtained, this session ticket is added to the ticket cache and may be reused for additional connections to the same server until it expires. This ticket expiration period is defined by domain security policy and is typically set to last about eight hours. If it

6

expires during the middle of an active session, Kerberos tells the client and server to refresh the ticket, generate a new session key, and resume the connection.

NEW TERM   Kerberos also offers a thing called *mutual authentication*, allowing machines to authenticate each other across the network. The NTLM protocol allows a server to verify the identity of a client, but it doesn't allow clients to verify a server's identity, or one server to verify the identity of another server. It was designed for a network environment in which servers were assumed to be trusted. Kerberos allows W2K to ensure that a server is who it says it is and helps ensure that it has not been compromised.

Finally, Kerberos policy, like most policies in Windows 2000, is defined at the domain level and implemented by the domain's KDC. It is stored in Active Directory as a subset of domain security policy. By default, the policy options can be set only by Domain Administrators.

Kerberos policy includes these settings:

- **Maximum User Ticket Lifetime**. A "user ticket" is the TGT. Settings are inactivated in hours. The default is 10 hours.
- **Maximum Lifetime that a User Ticket Can Be Renewed**. These settings are in days. The default is seven days.
- **Maximum Service Ticket Lifetime**. A "service ticket" is a session ticket. They are set in minutes. The setting must be greater than ten minutes and less than the setting for Maximum user ticket lifetime. The default is ten hours.
- **Maximum Tolerance for Synchronization of Computer Clocks**. Again, these settings are in minutes, with a default of five minutes.
- **Enforce User Logon Restrictions**. When this option is enabled, the KDC validates every request for a session ticket by examining user rights policy to verify that the user has the right either to Log on Locally or to Access This Computer from Network. Verification is optional because the extra step takes time and may slow network access to services. The default is enabled.

You can see an example of these settings in Figure 6.3.

Kerberos offers enhanced authentication security over the old NT 4.0 methods but is more complex and perhaps harder to understand. It is used for all W2K authentication by default, but other authentication methods can be used instead if desired as I showed earlier in the chapter. In the next section, I show you how the logon process works using a Kerberos session.

FIGURE 6.3

Kerberos policy settings.

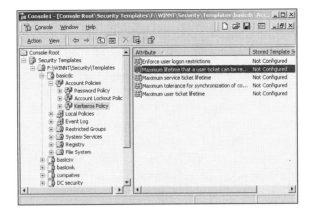

The Kerberos Logon Process

So how does the system log you on? The logon process can be seen in Figure 6.4.

FIGURE 6.4

The Kerberos logon process.

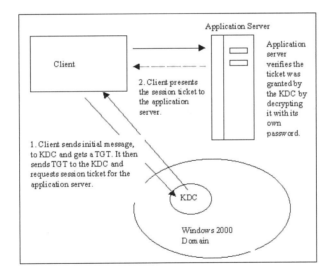

The Kerberos domain logon process is outlined as follows:

1. The user presses Ctrl+Alt+Del and the WinLogon process presents a logon screen. When the logon screen appears, you enter your username and password and the name of the computer or domain where you want to log on. The username is used for identification, and the password is used for validation.

2. A plain-text message is sent to the KDC, requesting a ticket. The message contains the user's name, the name of the KDC server (the domain), and a time stamp.

3. The KDC returns an encrypted message to the client. It is encrypted with the user's password and contains a time-stamped session key and a general ticket granting ticket (TGT). This session key will be used for later authentication within the realm or domain of the KDC.

4. The client then sends an encrypted message to the KDC requesting the right to communicate with a given service or server. The client uses the session key provided earlier to encrypt the request. The message contains the name of the server or service, a time stamp, and the TGT received earlier. When the KDC gets this message it knows it came from the right client because it is encrypted with that clients session key.

5. The KDC then produces a shared session key for use by both the client and the server. It also produces a specific ticket for the server containing the session key, name of the client, address of the client's network card, ticket's validity period, and a time stamp. Whew! It's sort of difficult to follow, isn't it?

6. The KDC next sends a message to the client containing the encrypted, shared session key and the encrypted ticket. The shared key is encrypted with the client's session key and the ticket is encrypted with the server's session key.

7. The client now sends a message to the server informing it that the client has the right to communicate with the server. Access controls will then determine what files and directories that client might access. This message contains the encrypted ticket that the client received from the KDC and a time stamp. It is encrypted with the shared session key. The server can now use its own password to decrypt the ticket and get the shared session key. The server uses this to decrypt the time stamp so it can check the ticket's validity. If all is well, the server accepts communication.

8. After the server approves the client, the server sends an encrypted message telling the client it accepts and communication between the two finally begins.

At this point, you are identified to the requested system and can begin accessing objects based on the discretionary access controls on those objects. If you return to that server later to access another service or program, steps 2 and 3 aren't needed as the same TGT can be used until it expires.

In a Windows 2000 domain, Kerberos Key Distribution Centers are located within each domain controller, so any controller can authenticate each client. Kerberos integrates with Active Directory and uses Active Directory for its user account repository.

Caution

All these logon procedures go a long way to ensure that the user is valid, but after the user is logged on, information is sent in clear text between clients and servers. You must use encryption to protect data transmissions. W2K offers a number of options including the new IPSEC protocol and a Virtual Private Network (VPN) solution.

Using Kerberos to Log On Across Domains

When you log on to access a resource in another domain, that domain must authenticate you—or have some other computer do the work. Kerberos typically performs this function in Windows 2000 domains. The Kerberos logon process for accessing multiple domains is outlined as follows.

In this type of authentication I assume that you are already logged on in your home domain. In that case of course, you already have a Ticket Granting Ticket. The steps follow this logical flow:

1. The client sends an encrypted message to be KDC. This message contains a request for a session key, which makes communication with the KDC in the other domain possible.

2. The KDC sends the client an encrypted message, which contains a ticket to the KDC server in the other domain. Now, the client can contact the other KDC directly and ask for a ticket to access the server or service it wants to use. These two steps only apply, of course, if the two domains have a trust relationship.

3. The client now sends an encrypted message to the KDC requesting the right to communicate with a given service or server. The client uses the session key provided in step 2 to encrypt the request. The message contains the name of the server or service, a time stamp, and the TGT received earlier. When the KDC gets this message it knows it came from the right client because it is encrypted with that client's session key.

4. The KDC then produces a shared session key for use by both the client and the server. It also produces a specific ticket for the server containing the session key, name of the client, address of the client's network card, ticket's validity period, and a time stamp.

5. The KDC next sends a message to the client containing the encrypted, shared session key and the encrypted ticket. The shared key is encrypted with the client's session key and the ticket is encrypted with the server's session key.

6. The client now sends a message to the server informing it that the client has the right to communicate with the server. As with a local domain, access controls will determine what files and directories the client might access. This message contains the encrypted ticket that the client received from the KDC and a time stamp. It is encrypted with the shared session key. The server can now use its own password to decrypt the ticket and get the shared session key. The server uses this to decrypt the time stamp so it can check the validity of the ticket. If all is well, the server accepts communication.

After the server approves the client, the server sends an encrypted message telling the client it accepts and you begin to access that server.

Remember that Kerberos serves as the authentication method for clients that know how to deal with this protocol and currently that only means W2K machines. W2K still uses the old NTLM authentication for all the downstream clients like Windows 3.1 and Windows 98 or even Windows NT 4.0.

Logging on Using Smart Cards

NEW TERM One of the neat new advances Windows 2000 offers is support for smart cards. The term *smart card* is typically used to describe credit card–sized devices with varying capabilities to store information. They differ from the more familiar magnetic-stripe cards used by your credit or debit cards in that they offer a larger, more intelligent data storage capability.

A smart card is essentially a miniature computer, embedded in plastic that looks like a credit card, with data storage and processing capability. The circuitry in a smart card gets its power from a smart card reader. Smart card readers can typically be connected to a computer using RS-232, PCMCIA, or USB interfaces.

You can set a user account policy in W2K to enforce the use of smart cards for logons, called "smartcard required for interactive logon," that tells Windows to require a smart card for that user to log on. What this means is that once the policy is set on an account, the user cannot use a password to log on to the account, interactively or from a command-line. You see an example of this in Figure 6.5.

FIGURE 6.5

The smart card policy.

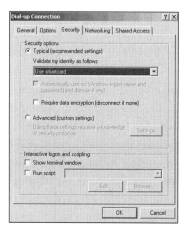

How does this provide better security, you ask? Well, because it eliminates the need for a user to think up and use a password. As you may already know, ensuring that users are creating and using good passwords is the bane of security folks everywhere. A smart card eliminates this weakness because the "password" is stored on the card. If someone wants to log on using your account, they will need to know your account name and will have to steal the card, as well as know what the PIN number is for that card.

NEW TERM With W2K and smart cards, you can set an *on smart card removal* policy on a per machine basis that would automatically disable the machine when the user takes the card out of the card reader. This can help enhance security by locking the machine when the card is removed.

Of course, an additional consideration is what happens when an employee forgets his or her card. Users typically don't have to remember to bring something with them to work so they can logon because they are generally using a password. If smart cards are used to enhance security, you'll also have to set up options to handle forgetful users. One option is to issue a temporary smart card with a certificate that has a short expiration such as one day. A second option is to change the user's logon policy and allow them to temporarily use a long password that is subsequently reset the next day.

It is an extension in the Kerberos version 5 protocol that allows for the use of a public key certificate, and hence a smart card, instead of a password when you logon. This extension is used to provide smart card logon support in W2K. A user's private key is stored on the smart card and used for authentication. To really understand the use of smart cards, you must have some idea of how public key encryption works. If you already use encryption, perhaps for securing your email, you might already know how it works and you can skip the next few paragraphs.

Public Key Encryption

NEW TERM It is the concept of public key encryption that allows us to use smart cards in W2K. Basically, encryption is the science of protecting data or messages. It uses mathematical algorithms that combine input containing plaintext data and an encryption key to generate encrypted data that is usually referred to as *ciphertext*. In order to decrypt this ciphertext you need additional data, called a decryption key, to perform the transformation back into something understandable.

The word *encryption* originates from the Greek words kryptos (to hide) and logos (word) and is far from new. In fact the ancient Egyptians used encryption 4000 years ago. Encryption has really become important in modern society with the advent of the computer.

In traditional secret (or symmetric) key cryptography, the encryption and decryption keys are identical and must be shared by multiple parties. People who want to communicate with secret-key cryptography must find a way to securely exchange this key before they can exchange encrypted data. Any person who knows the key can both encrypt and decrypt the message.

6

Public-key (PK) cryptography, however, uses different encryption and decryption keys and is properly called *asymmetric*. Encryption with a public key is a one-way function; the plaintext turns into ciphertext, but the encryption key is unrelated to the decryption process. In order to decrypt the message you need the private key that is related, but not identical, to the encryption key. This is where the term *two-key encryption* is derived. So every public key user has a pair of keys consisting of a public key and a private key. By making the public key available to anyone, it is possible to let anyone send you encrypted data that can only be decrypted by using your private key. Think of the secret key as the password that unlocks a message sent to you by another person who uses your public key to encrypt a message. After they encrypt that message with your public key, even they won't be able to see what the message contains, only you can. You can see how this works in Figure 6.6.

FIGURE 6.6

Two-key cryptography.

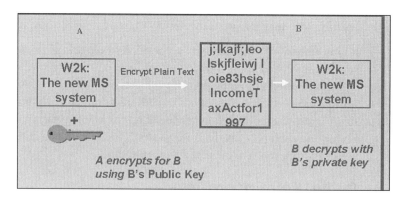

Authentication typically requires some type of challenge-response between authenticating parties. Public key cryptography provides a means by which a challenge-response can be accomplished between two parties who have never met because the public key and private key are distinct and separate. Separation of the private and public key enables distributed authentication because it doesn't require that the parties share a key. Likewise, public key cryptography can also be used to generate a shared key without the parties having to meet in secret to pass that information around.

In order to use asymmetric (public key) encryption though, there has to be a way for users to find out each other's public keys. In a small environment you can merely give everyone a copy of your public key manually by walking up to them with the key on a disk. This isn't practical though for people you have never met or organizations that you don't know. So the typical technique is the use of *digital certificates*, or certificates for short. A certificate is merely a package of information that identifies a user or a server, contains things like the organization name, the organization that issued the certificate, the user's email address, and of course their public key.

When you want to have a secure encrypted communication with someone, you send a query over the network to the other party, who sends back a copy of their certificate. The other party's public key is extracted from the certificate and used for communicating with them from then on. Certificates, however, can do more than this because they can also be used to uniquely identify the holder.

NEW TERM A number of trusted organizations, called *Certificate Authorities (CAs)*, issue certificates to individuals and corporations. VeriSign is one such organization. These certificates contain not only details about the person and their public key, but they also contain the public key of the Certificate Authority. Reputable CAs apply rigorous checks to ensure that applicants actually are who they claim to be by requiring the applicant to send them tax and business information, and so on. By doing so, you can trust that the information (name, public key, and so on) in any certificates they issue is going to be accurate. Before providing users with their own personal certificate, the CA digitally 'signs' it using a *private* key. So if you can decrypt this signature using their *public* key, you know that it can only have come from that CA.

Most browsers come with the popular CA root certificates already installed. In Microsoft Explorer 5.0 you can see these by going to Tools, Internet Options, Content, Certificates, Trusted Root Certification Authorities. The list contains those companies deemed trusted by Microsoft and others.

Businesses may not wish to use these trusted organizations, however, as they are a commercial enterprise and it costs for each certificate they register. In a large company this can add up to big money (the last I heard, VeriSign wanted about $100 for each certificate). So many organizations are using products like Microsoft's Certificate Server that comes with Windows 2000 Server to do the same thing, establish certificates for their staff. Note however, that in these cases the organization is implementing encryption within their company; most don't offer certificate services for other people.

It is primarily because of this concept of public key cryptography that smart cards can be used to authenticate you to W2K. They can contain your key pair.

Your public key is used to authenticate you to Windows 2000. How is this used? Let's go through the process step by step.

1. When you log on using a smart card the process begins when you insert the smart card into its reader.

2. This signals W2K to prompt you for a Personal Identification Number (PIN) instead of a username, domain name, and password. (Inserting the card is equivalent to the familiar Ctrl+Alt+Del secure attention sequence used to initiate a password-based logon.)

3. The logon request goes to the LSA who forwards it to the Kerberos authentication package running on the workstation. This Kerberos package sends a request to the

6

KDC service running on the domain controller requesting authentication and a Ticket Granting Ticket (TGT).

4. Your public key certificate that is stored on the smart card is retrieved from the card and included in the request to the KDC. An *authenticator* is included as well, digitally signed by your private key so that the KDC can verify the request originated from the owner of the public key certificate.

5. The KDC performs some complex checking to ensure that your certificate can be trusted. It then verifies the digital signature that was included using your public key. Because the certificate was retrieved from the smart card and was signed using the private key stored in the smart card, the digital signature must be legitimate because you had to authenticate to the smart card (enter your PIN) in order for the private key to sign the authenticator. After verifying the signature, the KDC service must then validate the timestamp to ensure it hasn't expired.

6. The KDC service then queries the domain's Active Directory to obtain your account information. A TGT is created that includes your SID and the SIDs of any groups you might belong to and encrypts the ticket using a random key. This key is encrypted with your public key so you can retrieve it.

7. After you have the TGT, the standard Kerberos version 5 protocol is used to request tickets for other domain resources.

You can see that this method of logon can be very simple for the user while increasing security (you need the PIN and the smart card) and hiding a great deal of information and processes.

It will remain to be seen whether this helps increase the use of smart cards. Most security professionals already understand the higher level of security possible but are grappling with the associated costs involved in adding this type of technology. In addition to the cost of the device, which might be perhaps $100 per user, there is the additional cost and complexity involved with implementing and maintaining the cards. A cost of $100 per user may seem a small sum but, when it is multiplied by thousands of users, it quickly adds up to significant amounts of money. In addition, you have to set up a public key infrastructure to handle all the keys, set up an organization to distribute and manage the cards, and set up procedures for lost, stolen, or broken cards. It is a lot of work.

You can learn a lot about public key encryption through the many books available and through the many Web sites devoted to this topic. I only touch on the subject here to help describe how smart card technology can be used.

Secure Channel Security

Secure channel technology is one way in which Microsoft provides privacy, integrity, and authentication during network communications between such things as your Web browser and a Web page on a server. Microsoft provides Secure Sockets Layer (SSL) 2.0 and 3.0 and Private Communications Technology (PCT) to enable secure channel communication. This feature is used as part of Internet Information Server 4.0.

You see Internet Web pages using SSL support in their applications all the time. You can recognize it by looking for the little padlock that appears on your browser whenever you connect to a secure page. (If you use Netscape Navigator, you'll see a small Key instead.) You can see the padlock in Figure 6.7.

FIGURE 6.7

Using secure sockets padlock.

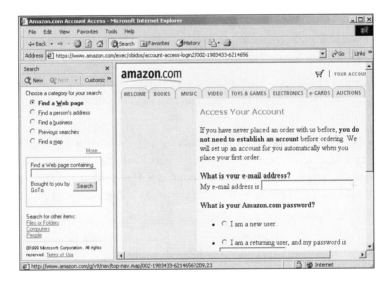

You want confidentiality of your Web page information any time you send personal data or credit card information across the Internet and SSL provides that for you by preventing the content of your communication from being seen by unauthorized parties. These mechanisms are used by the financial industry to ensure that your banking and other sensitive transactions are secure as they travel over the Internet.

SSL implements a symmetric (single key) encryption algorithm through a complex series of interactions with your browser and the secure Web server. The process basically uses your public key pair and the public key pair on the server to encrypt a new, one-time-only single key that exists only between you and the server and changes each time you access the Web page. It is a very safe process and is widely used across the Internet by stores, banks and other sites requiring secure encryption of Web pages.

6

The PCT protocol is a Microsoft implementation of SSL and isn't widely used.

The Internet Engineering Taskforce (IETF) is creating a new protocol called the Transport Security Layer (TLS) to unify a number of these existing protocols (SSL, PCT, and Secure Shell Rlogin). So as usual, by the time you figure out how it all works, it'll have changed.

Using the Security Configuration and Analysis Tool

This tool brings together two important aspects of security in W2K, analysis and configuration. The older version of NT provided little opportunity to analyze the current state of security (unless you downloaded and installed this tool along with Service Pack 4). Regular analysis enables an administrator to track and ensure an adequate level of security on each computer in their domain.

Security Configuration and Analysis enables a quick review of your current analysis results. The tools present recommendations for improving security next to the current system settings.

This tool can also be used to directly configure a system. Using its personal databases, you can import security templates created with the Security Templates snap-in, and apply these templates to local computer policy. This will immediately update that system to a specific set of practices that you specify in the template.

In NT 4.0, if you installed this tool it radically changed the way permissions were presented to you and once installed, you could not easily remove the tool. W2K provides this by default, so if you tried it but didn't like it with NT 4.0, you better get used to it as there is no choice in W2K.

Discretionary Access Controls

NEW TERM   *Discretionary access controls* enable resource owners to specify who can access their resources, and what they can do. Access controls specified through ACLs identify resource access permissions granted to users and groups. System resources include the system itself, files and directories, printers, network shares, and other objects.

Windows 2000 Server provides tools for controlling access entry to resources. Table 6.1 lists some of these tools.

TABLE 6.1 Tools for Controlling Access

Tool	Enables You To
Explorer	Share files and directories on the network.
Printers in Control Panel	Share printers on the network.
Active Directory Users and Computers	Manage user accounts and group member rights; define security policies.
Computer Management	Define limits for sharing a computer's resources with other users on the network.
	Start and stop network services.

The following examples describe the use of these tools to set discretionary access controls:

- Example of discretionary access control through User Manager for Domains for a user account—Peter is the administrator of a Windows 2000 server. Peter specifies through Active Directory Users and Computers that user Janet's account is to be disabled. When Janet attempts to log on to the domain, access is denied.

- Example of discretionary access control through File Manager for a file—User Peter is the owner of Pfile. Peter specifies through permissions and special access in File Manager or Explorer that user Janet can read Pfile.doc, and that user Barry can both read and write Pfile.doc. If Janet attempts to write to the file, her request is denied. The permission settings for files and directories include No Access, List, Read, Add, Add & Read, Change, Full Control, Execute, Delete, Change Permissions, and Take Ownership.

- Example of discretionary access controls using Print Manager for a printer—The administrator is the owner of printer1. The administrator specifies through Print Manager that user Janet can print to printer1, but that user Barry cannot. When Barry tries to print to printer1, his request is denied. Permission settings for printers include No Access, Print, Manage Documents, and Full Control.

Discretionary access controls over resources can be applied to specific users, multiple users, groups of users, no one, or everyone who can connect to the Windows 2000 network. A resource owner, the user who has access to the Administrator account, or any user who is granted authorization to control resources on the system can set discretionary access controls.

As was mentioned previously, objects in W2K include everything from files to communication ports to threads of execution. Every object can be secured individually or as a group. Objects have different types of permissions that are used to grant or deny access to them. Directory and file objects, for example, can have Read, Write, and Execute permissions, whereas print queues have permissions such as Manage Documents and Print. Also, note that directories are container objects that hold files, so permissions granted to the container are inherited by the file objects in it.

Keep in mind that access controls and user account rights are two different aspects of the W2K security system. User account security identifies and validates users, whereas access controls restrict what users can do with objects.

All objects have a security descriptor describing their security attributes. The security descriptor includes the following components:

- The security ID of the user who owns the object, usually the one who created the object
- The Access Control List, which holds information about which users and groups can access the object
- A system ACL, which is related to the auditing system
- A globally unique identifier (GUID), which is assigned by Active Directory to computers
- A group security ID that is used by the POSIX subsystem (a UNIX-like environment)

An ACL is basically a list of users and groups with permissions to access an object. Every object has its own ACL. Owners of objects can make entries in the ACL using tools such as the File Manager or by setting properties for files and folders (in Windows 2000). Other utilities for setting permissions include the Network and Services utilities in the Control Panel.

Users might have multiple entries in an object's ACL that provide them with different levels of access. A user might have Read permission to a file based on the user account, for example, and Read/Write permission based on a group membership. Each of these permissions is listed in a separate entry in the Access Control List. You'll find them all explained in the chapters dealing with file security in Day 8 and 9.

When you attempt to access an object, you usually have a certain desired access such as Read or Read/Write. To grant—or deny—access, the Security Reference Monitor compares information in the user's access token with entries in the ACL. Remember that the access token contains security IDs and the list of groups that the user belongs to. The SRM compares this information with one or more entries in the ACL until it finds sufficient permissions to grant the desired access. If it doesn't find sufficient permissions, access is denied.

When the SRM finds several entries for the user, it looks at each entry to see whether that entry, or a combination of the entries, can grant the user the desired permission to use the object.

Access Tokens

As you learned in the section "The Logon Process," security access tokens are objects that contain information about a particular user. When the user initiates a process, a copy of the access token is permanently attached to the process.

During the logon process, the creation and use of the access token are critical. When a user—or a process associated with the user—attempts to access an object, the SID and the list of groups to which the user belongs that is stored in the user's access token are compared to the ACL for the object. If the object's ACL includes permissions for the user or for one of the groups to which the user belongs, the user can access the object.

Table 6.2 describes the objects common to all access tokens.

TABLE 6.2   Access Tokens

Token Object	Description
User Security ID (SID)	Uniquely identifies the authenticated user on whose behalf the token was created.
Group Security ID	Group SID in which the user is a member.
Privileges	Privileges assigned to the user.
Owner	SID that is assigned as the owner of any objects created on behalf of the user who is represented by the token. This SID must be one of the user or group SIDs already in the token.
Primary Group	SID that is assigned as the primary group of any object created on behalf of the user who is represented by the token. It is specific to the POSIX subsystem.
Default ACL	ACL that is assigned by default to any objects created by the user SID.

Access Control Lists

Access Control Lists (ACLs) allow flexibility in controlling access to objects, and are a form of discretionary access control. They work in conjunction with the file system to protect files from unauthorized access. They enable users to specify and control the sharing of objects or the denial of access to objects. Each object's ACL contains access control entries (ACE), which define access permissions to the object. ACEs contain security identifications and specific access permissions, and are inserted into an ACL when the owner sets discretionary access controls for the object. If the object owner doesn't set discretionary access controls for the object, a default ACL is created. Table 6.3 lists the ways in which ACLs for several types of resources can be administered.

TABLE 6.3 Administration of ACLs

Resources	Source of ACL
Files	Explorer
Printers	Printers in Control Panel
Users	Computer Manager (Windows 2000 Professional)
	Active Directory Users and Computers (Windows 2000 Server)

When users attempt to access an object, their personal security IDs—or the security ID of one of the groups to which they belong—are matched to the list of ACEs, and their desired activities are compared to the access permission defined in the ACE. If a user's security ID and access request match an ACE's security ID and permission, the user ID is granted access.

ACEs are prioritized by access type: deny access and grant access. W2K first checks ACEs with a deny access, and then it checks ACEs with a grant access. Deny access always overrides a grant access.

If any group to which a user belongs is denied access, that user is denied access regardless of any access rights he or she is granted in either a personal user account or the accounts of other groups to which that user belongs. Therefore, when the No Access permission is given to the Everyone group, all users are denied access, including the owner. No Access, however, doesn't prevent the owner from changing permissions on the file and restoring access.

Using Domains

For each W2K computer in your organization, you can choose whether to have it participate in a domain or a workgroup. In most cases, you want each W2K computer to participate in a domain. This way, you have more control over what a user can and cannot do at a computer in the configuration.

A Windows 2000 workstation participating in a domain receives all the benefits of the domain's user and group database. It is easier to manage and control from a central location and it can be updated with new software using remote software like System Management Services (SMS).

A W2K computer participating in a workgroup has its own database of users; it processes logon requests by itself. Computers in a workgroup don't share account information. On a workgroup computer, W2K logs on or gives rights only to those user accounts created at that computer.

In a Windows 2000 Server environment, a domain is the basic unit of security and centralized administration. A domain consists of one or more servers running Windows 2000 Server; all the servers function as a single system using Active Directory. You learned all about domains in the chapter on Active Directory.

Using the Windows 2000 Auditing System

Remember that the Windows 2000 security subsystem performs two primary tasks: It restricts access to objects and it provides an auditing service that keeps track of operations on objects. The auditing system collects information about how objects are used, stores the information in log files, and enables you to monitor events to identify security breaches. If you discover a security breach, the audit logs help you determine the extent of the damage so that you can restore your system and lock out future intrusions.

You can control the extent to which the auditing system tracks events on your systems. Too much auditing can slow a system down and use tremendous amounts of disk space. You need to evaluate carefully how much auditing you need. When you suspect unauthorized activities, the best approach is to audit the following events:

- All changes to security settings
- Failed logon attempts
- Attempts to access sensitive data
- All System startup and shutdown events

You can use the Event Viewer to view the following security events:

- User and group management events, such as creating a new user or changing the membership of a group
- Subject tracking tracks the activities of users, such as when they start a program or access objects
- Logon and logoff events on the local system or for the network
- Object access, both successful and unsuccessful

6

- Changes to security policies, such as changes to privileges and logon policies
- Attempts to use privileges
- System events that affect the security of the entire system or audit log
- On a domain controller you can also audit Directory Services
- Events occurring on your DNS server
- Events occurring in your File Replication Service

Task 6.1: Using the Event Viewer to View the Audit Log.

Step 1: Description

In this task, you'll use the Event Viewer to view the audit log.

Step 2: Action

1. Log on to the Windows 2000 Server as Administrator. You must have administrative privileges to view the security log.

2. Choose Start, Programs, Administrative Tools, Event Viewer. You see an Event Viewer.

> **Note**
> You can use the setting outlined in step 2 on a domain controller. You can also select Start, Programs, Administrative Tools, Computer Management, System Tools, Event Viewer.

3. Choose the Security Log and click on the icon.

4. By double-clicking any event in the log, you can get detailed information about that event.

Step 3: Review

In this example, you opened the Event Viewer to view the security log. You can imagine that tracking these types of events requires quite of bit of the system's time and disk space when many clients are using your system. Of course, you can also view all the other logs available to you from this same tool, such as Application Log, Directory Service, File Replication, and other logs. You can see an example in Figure 6.8.

FIGURE 6.8

Using Event Viewer.

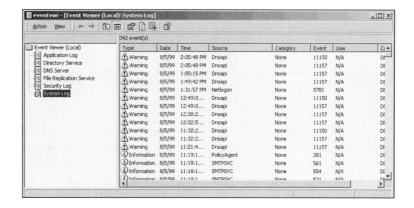

The auditing system tracks security events by two IDs: the user ID and the impersonation ID. This setup helps identify users who might otherwise be impersonated by certain processes in the system. A process-tracking mechanism is also used to track new processes as they are created and to provide information about both the user account that is performing an action and the program that was used to perform the action.

Tip

You probably want to know how to use the auditing system right now, but this is enough for today. Look forward to Day 17, "Security Monitoring and Audit Trails."

Security Configuration and Analysis

The Security Configuration and Analysis tool enables you to review, set up, and analyze your security settings in W2K. It offers a powerful method of configuring and then monitoring your systems.

In large organizations and small, your operating system and applications are always changing. Perhaps you have a temporary need to modify security on a server to resolve an application conflict or maybe a new administrator makes an inappropriate change to a security setting. In most companies, these changes are often forgotten and not reversed, meaning that security isn't the same across all your machines. This new tool offers you the ability to not only make those changes, but ensure that they return to an appropriate setting after the change is no longer necessary.

6

Security settings that you can modify include:

- User account policies, such as password length, expiration, and history
- Access control to files, the Registry, or services
- Kerberos
- Event log settings

In order to use Security Configuration and Analysis however, you need to know a little about the new tool for Windows 2000 that is called Microsoft Management Console or MMC. You can use MMC to create, save, and open a collection of the administrative tools (called MMC consoles) you are used to using. These are similar to the old tools you might have been familiar with in Windows NT such as User Manager and Server Manager but they are no longer provided as stand-alone tools, instead you use them through a single interface, the Microsoft Management Console. MMC is a feature of the Windows 2000 operating system, but you can also run it on Windows NT, Windows 95, and Windows 98.

MMC doesn't perform any administrative functions by itself; it just hosts the tools that do the work. This allows you to create MMCs that are very specialized in function. For example, you might create an MMC for security administrators and a different one for the LAN operators. Each would contain just the functions that they need to do their work. Microsoft calls the main type of tool that you can add, a snap-in. You can also add ActiveX controls, links to Web pages, folders, console taskpads, and tasks.

You can use MMC in either of two modes:

- **User mode**—use existing MMC consoles to administer a system
- **Author mode**—create consoles or modify existing ones

As an administrator you will open and use MMCs in author mode as this allows you to add or change the console to suit your needs. You might set up special user mode consoles for decentralized security officers perhaps because you might not want them changing the console and affecting your security procedures manual.

NEW TERM Each MMC console consists of a window divided into two panes. It looks similar to Microsoft Explorer in that manner. The left side is called the *console tree* and the right side is called the *details pane*. The console tree shows you all the items that are available to you. The details pane contains information and functions pertaining to these items. As you click on the different items in the console tree, the information in the details pane changes. The details pane can display a number of different types of information including Web pages, graphics, and tables. Finally, each console has its own menus and toolbar, separate from those of the main MMC window, to help you perform each task.

In a new console (Start, Run, MMC), the only item on the console tree is a folder called Console Root. From here you can create the tools that you want to have by adding items to the console.

After you create and save a new MMC console, you can use it on your local computer, send it to other users via email, or copy it to a floppy disk and install it on other computers.

To use a console, you must have access to the services and administrative tools included in the console; they must reside on your local computer or be available on your network. Naturally you must also have whatever administrative permissions are necessary for each of the components on the system you are administering. You learned about this in Day 3, "Navigating and Exploring Windows 2000."

To configure or analyze system security you need to follow a few steps. These are as follows:

- Start the Security Configuration and Analysis tool.
- Specify a security database for analysis.
- Import security templates containing the security values you want to use for configuration purposes into the database.
- Configure or analyze the system.

To use the Security Configuration and Analysis tool you first need to add it to a console.

The following task shows you how to start up and use the Security Configuration and Analysis tool by adding it to a new MMC. You can then configure or analyze the system after you have created the new console. I recommend that you only analyze the system at this stage. I will show you later how to configure your system.

Task 6.2: Setting Up the Security Configuration and Analysis Tool in MMC.

Step 1: Description

In this task, you'll add the Security Configuration and Analysis Tool to a new MMC window.

Step 2: Action

1. Log on to the Windows 2000 Server as Administrator. You must have administrative privileges on the server to modify security settings and update MMC.

2. Choose Start, Run, and type MMC on the command line shown. This will start a new MMC like the one shown in Figure 6.9.

FIGURE 6.9

A New Microsoft Management Console (MMC).

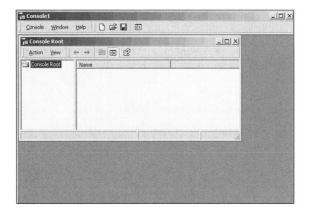

3. Click on Console, Add/Remove Snapin. This will open a window like the one shown in Figure 6.10.

FIGURE 6.10

Adding a snap-in.

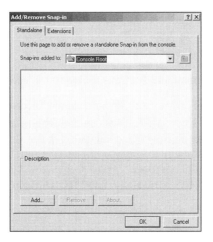

4. Click on the Add button. This brings up a screen similar to the one shown in Figure 6.11. It lists the components you can add to the console.

5. Scroll down the list until you see the Security Configuration and Analysis Tool and click on it. Now click on the Add button. Click on Close. This returns you to the MCC you are setting up. You should see a console that looks like that shown in Figure 6.12.

FIGURE 6.11

Available Snap-in modules.

FIGURE 6.12

Microsoft Management Console with Security Configuration and Analysis added.

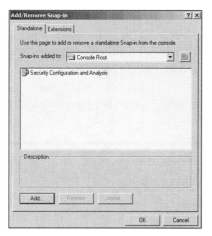

6. Click OK and you are returned to your MMC console. It now shows the new tool as an option. Double-click on the new option and it opens a Help window showing how to open an existing database or start a new one.

7. Now you need to create a new database. Right-click on the Security Configuration and Analysis item and select Open Database. Type in a new filename in the area titled File name: and click Open.

8. You should see a window similar to the one shown in Figure 6.13. It shows a number of existing templates that you can use as a base to work from when configuring your system. You see that the tool offers you helpful hints as you go along. Use these to learn more as you progress through each step.

6

FIGURE 6.13

Opening a new Configuration database.

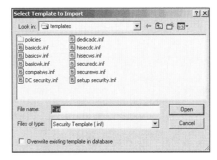

9. For this exercise, choose DC Security template from the list shown. You are shown a list of settings such as Account and Group Policies, Event Log, Restricted Groups, and so on.

10. Right-click on Security Configuration and Analysis and you see a number of options like those shown in Figure 6.14. The example shows those that occur on a controller. If you have only installed a member server, the DC templates will not show. When you first use this tool or when you create a new database, you need to select Analyze Computer Now before the options show. Do this now if you do not see any options.

FIGURE 6.14

Configuration options.

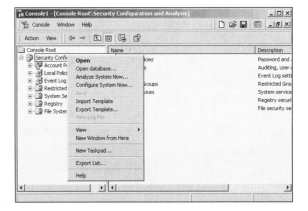

11. Don't choose the Configure System Now option as it will make changes to your machine. For the purposes of this step I want to know that from here you can analyze the system, import templates from other machines, and update the security on your existing machine.

12. Choose the Analyze System Now option if you like. It will compare your current settings (which will contain default settings if you are following the book carefully) against the template you just imported. When the program finishes,

▼   double-click on the Account Policies item then on Password Policies and you will
    see a comparison of the settings on your machine compared to those in the policy
    you added in step 9. It should look similar to that shown in Figure 6.15.

FIGURE 6.15

*An analysis of account
policy.*

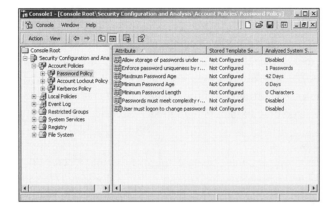

Your stored template shows that most options aren't configured. That is because on
all Windows 2000 systems you must take the necessary steps to configure your
system according to your needs. This section provides you with some of the methods for doing that.

13. Click on Console and select Save as. Choose a name for your console or leave it as
    the default called Console1.msc. Now click on Console, Exit to close the MMC
    window.

14. The MMC console you save is stored in your My Documents folder by default if
    you did not choose a different folder. You can see it by opening your My
▲   Documents folder by using Explorer.

Step 3: Review

In this example, you opened a new MMC console and added a component called
Security Configuration Editor. You then added a security template and analyzed the existing system against that template.

You can also use the command line to open existing consoles that you create. The complete command-line syntax for MMC is:

```
mmc path\filename [/a /s]
path\filename
```

This starts MMC and opens the saved console specified by filename. You need to specify
the complete path and filename for the saved console file. If you don't specify a console

6

file and leave this option blank, MMC will open a new console. When you stored the earlier example, by default it placed it in F:\Documents and Settings\Administrator\ My Documents. (F: will be the hard drive that W2K resides on in your machine. My machine has many different partitions.)

/a

This option opens a console in author mode. It is used to make changes to existing consoles or to create new consoles. When MMC is started with this option, all the console files are opened in author mode, even when the default is user mode. This doesn't change the default mode setting for a file though. When you omit this option, MMC opens console files according to their default mode settings.

/s

Using this prevents the annoying display of the splash screen that you see each time MMC starts. The splash screen doesn't display for saved console files.

Over time, I think this tool will become a welcome and trusted ally for security administrators. Managing large or even small domains and ensuring they are all configured according to your security standards has always been a chore. This should make it easier.

Security Templates

So now that you can see how to analyze existing security configurations, what can you do to set up and ensure that all your machines follow the same configuration? As you probably can guess, you can use templates and the Security Configuration and Analysis Tool. In the previous task, you added a template called DC Security (Domain Controller Security). So how do you know what is in this template and how would you create one that fits your organization's security needs?

A template is merely a one-stop storage place for all your security settings. It merely provides you with a centralized method of defining security with the Security Template snap-in tool that you can add to a MMC. It is a single point of entry where the full range of system security can be viewed, adjusted, and then applied to a local computer or imported to a group policy object. They don't introduce new parameters; they merely organize existing attributes into one place for ease of use. As you saw in Task 6.2, they can also be used as a basis for analyzing security when used with the Security Configuration and Analysis snap-in.

This eases overall security administration by allowing you to configure more than one machine at a time. By importing a template into a Group Policy, any computer or user accounts in the site, domain, or organizational unit that the Group Policy is applied to will receive those settings. Local group policy cannot override domain based policy however.

Each template is saved as a text-based .INF file. This lets you copy, paste, import, or export some or the entire template attributes. You can of course, also work with the actual .INF files in a word processor; however, this isn't recommended for beginners. You can see an example of a security template .INF file that is opened using a text editor in Figure 6.16.

FIGURE 6.16

An open .INF template file.

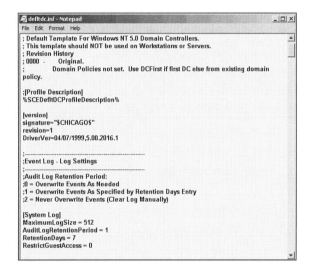

For experts, using a text editor is faster than using the Security Template Editor.

The initial template that is applied to a W2K computer is called the Local Computer Policy. This Policy can be exported to a security template *file*, in order to save the initial system settings. This lets you restore those settings later if you change your mind or need to return to them for some other reason.

You can define and then apply these setting to either a Group Policy affecting a number of machines or to the local machine. To use them you need to

- Start the Security Template program
- Define a template
- Apply the template

First you need to look to the Security Template tool. The following task will take you through the process of adding the tool to a new MMC console. You can add it to your earlier console that you saved if you like by starting at step 4.

Task 6.3: Adding the Security Template Tool in MMC.

Step 1: Description

In this task, you'll add the Security Template Tool to a new MMC window for later use.

Step 2: Action

1. Log on to the Windows 2000 Server as Administrator. You must have administrative privileges on the server to modify security settings and update MMC.

2. Choose Start, Run, and type MMC /s on the command line shown. This will start a new MMC like the one shown earlier in Figure 6.9. (The /s eliminates the splash screen.)

3. Click on Console, Add/Remove Snapin.

4. Click on the Add button. This brings up a screen similar to the one shown earlier in Figure 6.11. It lists the components you can add to the console.

5. Scroll down the list until you see the Security Templates and click on it. Now click on the Add button. Click on Close. This returns you to the MCC you are setting up.

6. Click OK and you are returned to your MMC console. It now shows the new tool as an option. You see an example of this in Figure 6.17.

FIGURE 6.17

MMC with Security Template.

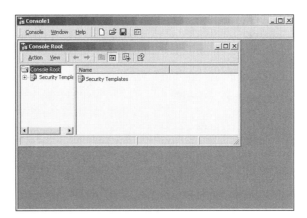

7. Click on Console and then Save As. Enter a name for your new console in the File Name area and click on Save.

8. You have created a new MMC console with the Security Templates as an option. Click on Console and then Exit to close the MMC.

Step 3: Review

In this example, you opened a new MMC console and added another component called Security Templates. In a later exercise you will re-open the console and edit a template to modify your machine's security settings.

Now that you know how to access the Security Templates for your machine, you need to set up and change a policy. There are a number of predefined policy files that Microsoft provides with W2K.

These predefined templates can be assigned directly to a computer as is, or can be modified to suit your unique security needs. You should not apply any templates to production systems without thoroughly testing them to ensure that the right level of application functionality is maintained and that you don't cause problems with your implementation.

The predefined security templates provided with your Windows 2000 system include:

- Default workstation (BASICWK.INF)
- Default server (BASICSV.INF)
- Default domain controller (BASICDC.INF)
- Compatible workstation or server (COMPATWS.INF)
- Secure workstation or server (SECUREWS.INF)
- High Secure workstation or server (HISECWS.INF)
- Dedicated domain controller (DEDICADC.INF)
- Secure domain controller (SECUREDC.INF)
- High Secure domain controller (HISECDC.INF)
- Setup (setup security.INF)

Remember that DC templates only show if you have a domain controller. By default, all of these templates are stored in `\%systemroot%\security\templates`.

Microsoft designed the templates to cover five common types of security. You can generally see which level the template belongs to by the first part of the template name. For example, all templates providing basic security coverage begin with the word basic (like BASICDC.INF). The five general types are seen in Table 6.4.

6

TABLE 6.4   The Default Security Templates

Type	Description
Basic (BASIC*.INF)	The basic configuration templates are provided to allow you to reverse something you might have done earlier. They apply the Windows 2000 default security settings to all security areas except those pertaining to user rights. User rights aren't modified in the basic templates because application setup programs commonly modify user rights, to enable the application to run successfully. These templates won't undo such modifications.
Compatible (COMPAT*.INF)	This template is provided to ease the transition from NT 4.0 to Windows 2000. In Windows 2000 users are members of the Power Users group as this provides them the ability to do more on their workstation. Windows 2000 security is configured to provide members of the local users group with ideal security settings while members of the local Power Users group have security settings more similar to Windows NT 4.0 users. This default configuration enables for development of new applications in a secure Windows environment using the local security settings, while still allowing existing applications to run successfully under the less secure, Power User configuration.
	This might be too unsecure for some companies, where they expect users to only be members of the Users group, and still have applications run successfully. The compatible templates are designed to set this straight. By lowering the security levels on specific files, folders, and Registry keys that are typically used by applications, the templates allow most applications to run successfully. In addition, all members of the Power Users group are removed.
Secure (SECURE*.INF)	The secure templates implement a recommended set of security settings everywhere except on files, folders, and Registry keys. These items aren't

Type	Description
	modified because the standard settings are considered to be secure by default.
Highly Secure (HISEC*.INF)	Highly secure templates are used to define a level of security settings that are considered appropriate for W2K network communications. They are set to require maximum protection for network traffic and protocols used between computers running W2K. Because of this, computers that have been configured with a highly secure template can only communicate with other Windows 2000 machines. You won't be able to communicate with computers running Windows NT 4.0 or Windows 98.
Dedicated Domain Controller (DEDICA*.INF)	User security on domain controllers running W2K isn't set up to be secure by default. This allows Administrators to run applications on domain controllers that aren't recommended. By not running server based applications on your domain controllers the default file system and Registry permissions for the local users group can be secured in a better fashion, which is what this template accomplishes.

Each of these templates offers a standard method of securing the various machines found in a Windows 2000 domain. You can use them as provided, remembering to test them before using them on a production machine, but you will probably want to modify them to suit your own needs. The setup template offers you a method for returning to the default W2K values should you make a mistake using other templates or just choose to return to the defaults after an exercise.

Ideally, you want to set up a template that works for your company and is based upon your companies' security policies and standards. This may or may not be the same as one of the default templates Microsoft provides. You should decide what level of control you need, whether you need different levels for different machines and how you are going to test each template. Then, you can begin to design your templates and implement them.

I don't have space in this book to go into all the different security settings and what might be appropriate, so you will have some homework to do. In the next task, I show you how to set up a new template based upon one of the existing default ones.

6

Task 6.4: Creating a Custom Security Template Based on a Default Template.

Step 1: Description

In this task, you'll open the MMC with the Security Template Tool in it and customize an existing template to meet your own needs.

Step 2: Action

1. Log on to the Windows 2000 Server as Administrator. You must have administrative privileges on the server to modify security settings and update MMC.

2. Choose Start, Run, and type `MMC filename` on the command line shown. (You can also just use Explorer to browse your My Documents folder and double-click on the template you created in Task 6.4. This is shown in Figure 6.18.)

FIGURE 6.18

Opening an MMC Console with Explorer.

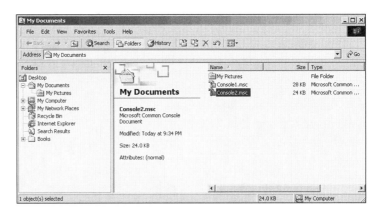

3. Click on the icon to maximize the inner box so it fills the window and lets you see more.

4. Double-click on Security Templates in the left frame window to expand it. Next, double-click on the path below to expand that also. You should now see all the templates Microsoft offers. You can see this in Figure 6.19.

5. Right-click on the BASICDC.INF file and choose Save As. Specify a new name for your template and click on Save.

6. Double-click on the new template to expand it and display the security settings. It should look like Figure 6.20.

FIGURE 6.19

The available security templates.

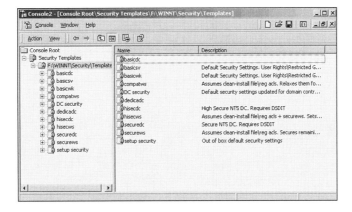

FIGURE 6.20

Expanded security template.

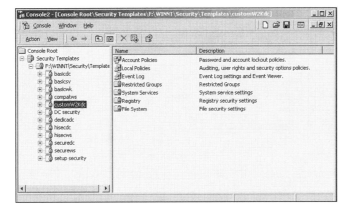

7. Expand the node you want to modify. For this task, choose Local Policies and then Audit Policy by double-clicking on each one. If the Exclude This Setting in Analysis check box is selected, click on it to allow configuration. You find that by right-clicking on the item and selecting Security.

8. Double-click on the setting called Audit Account Logon Events. (You can also select Action, Security to do the same thing.) You see a window similar to that shown in Figure 6.21.

9. Click on Audit Failed Attempts and then click on OK. You have set the policy to include audits for all failed logon attempts.

10. Click on Console, Save, and then Exit to conclude the task. You will be prompted to Save the template you just created. Click OK to save your work.

6

FIGURE 6.21

*The Audit Account
Logon property.*

Step 3: Review

In this example, you opened your Security Templates MMC console and selected an existing template. Then you used that template to create a new custom template in which you modified the Audit settings.

Now that you have a template of your own you might want to implement it on your machine. To do that you need to do the following:

- Open Security Configuration and Analysis.
- Import the template you created.
- Right-click the Security Analysis and Configuration node.
- Click Configure System Now.

This will update your system with the settings you made earlier in Task 6.4. Be careful with what you do as you don't want to impact your system this early in the book. Be aware that you can recover your system settings by choosing the Setup Security template that returns all security settings to those out of the box.

Using the Command Line to Update and Manage Security Templates

Now you have some idea of how to use a template and create one of your own. In addition, you know how to use the configuration and analysis tool to check your templates and update your machine's security. You might be feeling pretty sure of yourself or you may just be one of those "command-line weenies" that lurk in I.T. organizations around the world. (Just kidding now. There is nothing wrong with being a lover of the command line in this GUI-based world.)

So how can you do some of the things in the previous tasks, using a more automated approach? The good news is, you can do it. The great news is, it isn't that hard to accomplish. Microsoft offers a command-line program called SECEDIT.EXE that you can use in batch programs or on a Windows 2000 command-line interface. This program allows you to fully automate the use of templates.

The program allows you to create, apply, or analyze system security. It is great for performing these functions in off-hours (without you needing to be in at two in the morning when it runs). The use of this tool does imply that you are updating and creating templates using a text editor to make those changes. After you have a template you are comfortable with you then use SECEDIT.EXE to use that template to configure a system, or analyze security of a system based upon the assigned template.

I show you how to configure a system and analyze a system in the following paragraphs. There are more options available to this tool, as there are to the GUI-based Security Configuration and Analysis Tool, but space limits me to acknowledging the most common uses. For example, you can also import and export templates, and you can check the syntax of a template. Use the Help system to learn about additional aspects of each tool as you become more familiar with them.

Configure System Security

This syntax allows you to configure a system's security using a stored template.

```
Secedit /configure [/DB filename] [/CFG filename] [/overwrite]
➥[/areas areas] [/log logpath] [/verbose] [/quiet]
```

All the fields that are surrounded by [ ] are somewhat optional. You need to choose which you want to use and apply them according to the specific information provided below next to each command. The brackets of course, don't form part of the actual command; they merely inform you that this field is optional depending upon your needs. For example, you might use the command:

```
Secedit /configure /DB f:\secedit.sdf /CFG f:\newtemplate.inf /verbose
```

This command tells the program to update the SECEDIT.SDB database using the NEWTEMPLATE.INF file and to provide detailed progress information.

The details of each component of the program are outlined in Table 6.5.

TABLE 6.5 Configure System Security Using The SECEDIT Program

Type	Description
/DB *filename*	The path to the database containing the template that should be applied. This is required.
/CFG *filename*	You only use this argument with the one above. It provides the path to the template that is to be imported into the security database. If you don't supply this parameter, the template currently stored in the database will be used.

continues

TABLE 6.5   continued

Type	Description
/overwrite	You only use this parameter when the /CFG parameter is used. It specifies whether the template identified in the /CFG parameter should overwrite and not append the template already in the security database.
/area *areas*	Specifies what security areas you want to apply. If you don't use the parameter, it defaults to all areas. Otherwise you can apply just part of a template. The areas are shown in Table 6.6.

TABLE 6.6   Configuring Security Areas within the SECEDIT Program

Type	Description
Securitypolicy	Account, audit policies, and so on.
group_mgmt	Restricted group settings.
user_rights	User logon rights and privileges.
Regkeys	Security for local Registry keys.
Filestore	Security on local files.
Services	Security on all defined services.
/log *logpath*	The path for your log file. If not specified, a default will be used.
/verbose	Provides detailed progress information.
/quiet	Provides no screen or log output.

As you can see with the command structure, you can configure a system with existing, new, or partial template information and obtain a lot of information or no information about the program's progress.

Analyze System Security

Using the following syntax allows you to analyze a system's security.

```
Secedit /analyze [/DB filename] [/CFG filename] [/log logpath] [/verbose]
➥[/quiet]
```

All the fields that are surrounded by [ ] are somewhat optional. You need to choose which you want to use and apply them according to the specific information provided below next to each command. The brackets, of course, don't form part of the actual command; they merely inform you that this field is optional depending upon your needs. For example, you might use the command:

```
Secedit /analyze /DB f:\secedit.sdf /CFG f:\newtemplate.inf /verbose
```

This command tells the program to analyze the security parameters in the
SECEDIT.SDB database using the NEWTEMPLATE.INF file and to provide detailed
progress information.

The details of each component of the program are outlined in Table 6.7.

TABLE 6.7   Analyze System Security Using the SECEDIT Program

Type	Description
/DB *filename*	The path to the database containing the configuration to be analyzed. This is required. If you specify a new database, you must use the next parameter also.
/CFG *filename*	You only use this argument with the one above. It provides the path to the template that is to be imported into the security database for analysis. If you don't supply this parameter, the analysis will be performed against the configuration already stored in the database.
/log *logpath*	The path for your log file. If not specified, a default will be used.
/verbose	Provides detailed progress information.
/quiet	Provides no screen or log output.

Finally, you might want to validate a template that you created with a text editor before
trying to use it in any way and there is a command-line structure that allows you to do
that.

The command is fairly simple and verifies that the template syntax is correct. It doesn't,
of course, validate that you are doing the right things. You can increase or decrease security over your system to a fault if you are not careful. As with all things administrative,
whether command line- or GUI-based, what you do to your security is up to you.

The command syntax is secedit /validate *filename*

You change the filename to the name of your template that you want validated.
Naturally, the full path must be specified. An example might be

```
secedit /validate f:\newtemplate.inf
```

There are far more things that you can do with templates. Too many for this book to deal
with in one chapter. I recommend that you do some additional reading of the Help files
in W2K to further familiarize yourself with all the available options.

6

Summary

Windows 2000 has several security options that you can apply to software and physical security. This chapter covered many of these security options. Today, you learned about the following topics:

- The Local Security Authority
- The Security Account Manager
- The Security Reference Monitor
- The logon processes
- Smart cards and Secure Channel communications
- Viewing Audit logs

You will learn more about security administration in subsequent days. Now, however, you can review what you learned today.

Workshop

To wrap up the day, you can review tasks from the chapter and see the answers to some commonly asked questions.

Task List

With the information provided in this chapter, you can now begin your understanding of Windows 2000 security. You learned how to carry out the following tasks:

- View the Event Log.
- Set up the Security Configuration and Analysis Tool in MMC.
- Add the Security Template Tool in MMC.
- Create a Custom Security Template Based on a Default Template.

Q&A

Q How can I evaluate the security of my server?

A W2K offers a new tool called Security Configuration and Analysis that brings together two important aspects of security in W2K, analysis and configuration. The tool enables an administrator to perform a quick review of the current level of system security and compare it to previous analyses. It also enables administrators to implement enterprise-wide security in a consistent manner.

Q How do I know which authentication is being used for my users?

A This answer could get fairly complicated but suffice it to say that if your users are connecting with Windows 2000 client machines, they are being authenticated using Kerberos. If they are using Windows 95 or older workstation systems they will be using NTLM. Finally, it is unlikely they are using smart card authentication unless you have specifically activated it and provided them with smart cards and readers.

6

DAY 7

Managing User Accounts

At this time, you have a good grounding in Windows 2000 Server basics. You have studied network topologies, cabling, filing systems, domains, the desktop, the Start menu, the toolbar, the Registry, Active Directory, and security. Today, you look at managing your clients. In this chapter, you take your first look at W2K commands for managing users and groups.

Today you will learn about the following topics:

- User accounts
- Security, distribution, universal, local, and global groups
- Setting an account policy
- Changing a user's account restrictions
- Changing a user's time restrictions
- Changing a user's station restrictions
- Setting intruder lockout
- Unlocking a user's account
- Requiring and restricting passwords for users

Introduction to Accounts

NEW TERM User accounts are the foundation of Windows 2000 Server's security. In any system, *identification* and *authentication* of the people using the system are of primary importance; this is the role of user accounts. In Windows NT, Microsoft referred to this account as the username instead of user account. Username simply was a method for referring to user accounts. With Windows 2000, Microsoft uses new terminology—*user logon name*—instead of user account *or* username. You will see the terms user account, username, and user logon name used interchangeably throughout the book, except where a W2K screen that uses the actual word *User name*—such as the login screen—is being shown.

You assign usernames and passwords for each domain (hundreds of thousands of users for very large enterprises). In addition, you can specify the times that a user can log on, and control where the user can log on. You also can set a minimum character limit for the password length and a limit to the amount of time that the password can be kept. These controls reduce the chances that an unauthorized user can guess the password. Usernames and passwords are the basis for logon security. User account information, such as the username and password, resides in the Active Directory database of the machine that is managing security. As in the previous domain discussion, this is the Domain Controller's *SystemRoot*\system32\config directory. If you aren't using a domain, it is the same directory on the machine that you log onto and use.

As you learned in Day 6, "Introducing Security Services," logon security is an important layer of the NTS security model. Following are the other security layers that you'll learn about in this book:

- Rights security (Day 8, "Managing Files and Using the Distributed File System")
- File and print server security (Day 9, "Managing the File Server," and Day 10, "Managing the Print Server")

NEW TERM Logon security controls *access* at the *portal*—the entrance to the network. Logon security is effective because it requires an authorized username for identification and a valid password for verification. The username and password must match exactly the information kept by the system. Because you enter your account's username first, this chapter looks at accounts and usernames first.

Understanding User Accounts

User accounts provide the first point of access. They identify the user of an account; the username is the identification. Usernames can be anywhere from 1 to 20 characters in length. You can use any upper- or lowercase characters, except the space and tab (DOS command-line delimiters), the 32 control characters, and the characters shown in Table 7.1.

TABLE 7.1 Invalid Characters for Usernames

Character	Description
=	Equal sign
>	Greater-than sign
<	Less-than sign
|	Vertical bar or pipe
+	Plus sign
[	Left square bracket
]	Right square bracket
\	Backslash
/	Slash
*	Asterisk
;	Semicolon
:	Colon
.	Period
,	Comma
?	Question mark
"	Quotation mark

NEW TERM As you learned on Day 4, "Understanding and Managing the Registry," user accounts are automatically assigned a *security identifier* (*SID*) when they are first created. A SID is a unique number for identifying an account in the Windows 2000 Server security system. The system never reuses SIDs; when an account is deleted, its SID is deleted with it. SIDs look like the following:

S-1-5-99-D1-D2-D3-RID

In this example, S-1-5-99 is a standard prefix; S identifies that this is a SID; 1 is a version number, which hasn't changed since NT 3.1; 5 signifies that the SID was assigned by NT; 99 contains a number that corresponds to the type of object (such as 4 for the interactive group); and D1, D2, and D3 are 32-bit numbers specific to a domain. When you create a domain, NT sets D1 through D3, and all SIDs in that domain henceforth have the same three values. The RID stands for *relative ID*. The RID is the unique part of any given SID on the domain.

7

Every new account always has a unique RID number, even when the username and other information are the same as an old account. So, if you think you can just re-create a deleted user account, think again; it will look the same to you, but it will have a brand new SID because the RID portion will have changed. Therefore, it won't acquire any of the rights and permissions of the old account. Four billion RIDs are possible, so you aren't likely to run out of them for a while.

When you create a new Windows 2000 domain, the system creates the following two user accounts:

- Administrator
- Guest

To view the built-in user accounts, select Start, Programs, Administrative Tools, Active Directory Users and Computers. If you don't see this tool, you created your own console on Day 5, "Introducing Active Directory." In Figure 7.1 you see the MMC snap-in I created called Console1. In the right-hand panel of the window, you see the built-in accounts. The following sections look at two of these accounts.

FIGURE 7.1

The Active Directory Users and Computers window.

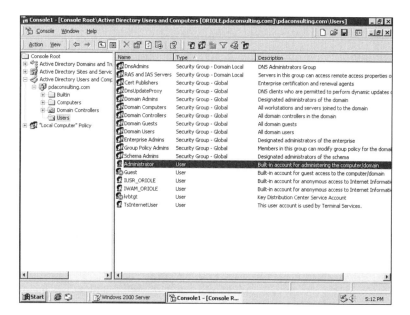

Administrator Account

 When you create a Windows 2000 Server Domain Controller, or any other 2000 machine, the *Administrator* account is created automatically. The purpose of the

Administrator account is to manage accounts on the file server. Generally, the Administrator can do the following:

- Access any file or directory
- Create and delete users and groups
- Establish trust relationships
- Manage printers and print sharing
- Assign operators
- Create and modify logon scripts
- Set default account policies
- Set and change passwords
- Manage auditing and security logs
- Not be deleted

The Administrator is a member of the following groups by default:

- Administrators
- Domain Admins
- Domain Users
- Enterprise Admins
- Group Policy Admins
- Schema Admins

The Administrator account is omnipotent—with complete power over the machine. You need to control its use tightly.

You might want to create some accounts—Account Operators—with responsibility for a group or groups of users. Distributing responsibility to a few people is a good control—separation of duties—and gives the Administrator time to concentrate on system-management functions as opposed to user-management functions. Logging on as a member of the Account Operators group prevents you from using some of the system's capabilities, but you can manage most user accounts.

Guest Account

Guest is another account that is created automatically on your file server when you create a Windows 2000 Server domain. A Guest is anyone that the domain doesn't recognize. By default, the Guest account is disabled and needs to remain that way. With most other operating systems, you can access the operating system by logging on with the username Guest and a blank password. In other operating systems, such as NetWare, the Guest account has a simple *raison d'être*: A Guest account enables users to access the server's print queues when they don't have accounts on the server. With NetWare, they can use NPRINT and CAPTURE to do so. Usually, the Guest account is restricted in what it can do. That's true with W2K, as well, although you need to remember that the Everyone, Domain Guests, and Guests groups include the guests.

The Guest account in Windows 2000 does work differently. Suppose someone tries to log on to a W2K network with the Guest account enabled. She logs on as KELLY with the password grade4. If this domain doesn't have a KELLY account, it rejects the logon. On a DOS, Windows for Workgroups, Windows 95 or Windows 98 workstation, KELLY can still do work because these operating systems don't require users to log on to a domain to access the local workstation. On a W2K workstation, KELLY might log on to an account on the local machine. Now she's working at a computer and tries to access a domain resource—and KELLY gets in!

Even though an explicit domain logon requires that you use the username Guest, you needn't explicitly log on to a domain to use Guest privileges. If your network is attached to my network and you enable the Guest account, I can browse through your network and attach to any resources that the Guest can access. I needn't log on as Guest because enabling the Guest account leaves the back door open. Therefore, don't enable the Guest account.

Note

> If you have a low security environment and you insist upon using the Guest account, assign it a password. Also, you can rename the Guest account—but, you cannot delete it.

Now look at how to create some user accounts of your own by using different tools.

Creating User Accounts

You can divide user account administration into two phases: creating user accounts and maintaining user accounts. You can create user accounts in several ways. The most popular way is to use the Active Directory Manager program because it is easy to work with. You will become very familiar with its use. You can use Active Directory Manager when you need to create one or two user accounts. In addition, you can use the NET commands.

First look at User Manager because you might select it as your tool of choice.

Using Active Directory Manager

The Administrator uses Active Directory Manager to perform the following tasks:

- Create, modify, and delete user accounts
- Assign logon scripts to user accounts
- Create and manage groups
- Manage the domain's security policies
- Establish trust relationships

Existing accounts always need managing, whether it's modifying account properties, disabling accounts, or deleting accounts. Here you'll learn about creating, copying, and deleting user accounts.

Task 7.1: Creating User Accounts Using Active Directory Users and Computers.

Step 1: Description

In this task, you'll use the Active Directory Users and Computers program to create new users.

Step 2: Action

1. Log on to the Windows 2000 Server as Administrator.

   Choose Start, Programs, Administrative Tools, Active Directory Users and Computers. You see a window similar to the one in Figure 7.1.

3. Click the domain, right-click Users. Choose New, User. The Create New Object— (User) dialog box appears, as shown in Figure 7.2.

FIGURE 7.2

The Creating a user dialog box.

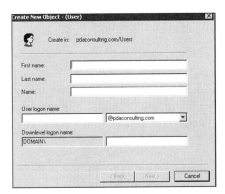

▼   4. Type the new user's first name KELLY in the First name box. Press Tab to move to the next field.

5. Type the user's last name, such as Davis, in the Last name box. The full name you just entered should show in the Name box.

Note
The name you select that shows in the Name box must be unique for the OU. This is what W2K displays in OU where the user account resides.

6. Press Tab twice to move to the next field.

7. Enter the user's unique logon name in the User logon name box.

8. Enter the user's downlevel name in the Downlevel logon name box. The downlevel name is sometimes referred to as the *SAM account name* or *Downlevel Domain name*. You use this account to log on from Windows NT 4.0 or 3.51 clients. This is required and must be unique. You can leave the one the system created, which is the same as the user logon name. Click Next. You should see the window shown in Figure 7.3.

FIGURE 7.3

Password and password options dialog box.

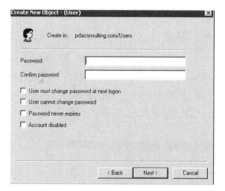

9. Enter a password of 1 to 14 characters in length for the user. A strong password of 6 to 8 characters improves computer and network security. If you need help with creating a good password, jump ahead to the section "Creating Strong Passwords." Press Tab to move to the next field.

Note
Windows 2000 Server displays the password as asterisks to protect its confidentiality as you enter it.

▼

▼   10. Confirm the password by retyping the password that you entered in step 9.

      11. Select the appropriate options for the additional user properties (listed in Table 7.2).

TABLE 7.2   New User Options

Option	Default	Description
User must change password at next logon	OFF	Selecting this option forces users to change the password when they log on the first time. Selecting this option is a good idea so that the administrator doesn't continue to know the users' passwords (because they are forced to change them).
User cannot change password	OFF	Selecting this option prevents users from changing the password. Selecting it isn't a good idea, especially when the users have access to confidential or critical data.
Password never expires	OFF	Selecting this option bypasses the Maximum Password Age account policy. Again, selecting it isn't a good idea because the password does not change and becomes easier to guess with time.
Account disabled	OFF	Selecting this option creates an inactive account. You can use this feature when you're creating accounts for future use, or when you think that system intruders are using the account.

Tip

You can also select Account Disabled to suspend an account before you delete it. If you immediately delete the account, you might create orphan files. The administrator needs to take ownership of orphaned files to ensure that ownership remains appropriate. (You will look at ownership on Day 8.)

      12. Click Next. You should see the acknowledgement window shown in Figure 7.4

      13. Click Finish.

      14. To add another user account, repeat steps 3 through 13.

▼   15. From the Console menu, select Exit when you are finished creating new accounts.

7

FIGURE 7.4

Acknowledging creation of user object with characteristics selected.

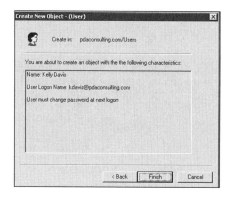

Step 3: Review

With this task, you created your first user account. You'll place some restrictions on this account later in this chapter.

To delete a user's account, you perform basically the same steps as you do for copying a user account. First, select the user's name by choosing Start, Programs, Administrative Tools, Active Directory Users and Computers, then choose the domain, Users, and then right-click the username and click Delete. You will need to confirm your intention to delete this account.

If you like command lines, you can manage user accounts another way. If you don't want to use the Active Directory Manager, you can use the NET USER command-line option. With this command, you can add, change, or delete a user account from the domain database.

> **Note**
>
> In Day 3, "Navigating and Exploring Windows 2000," you learned about the NET commands, but should you have forgotten—select Start, Programs, Accessories, Command Prompt, and then type NET HELP USER ¦ MORE.

The command works with the parameters shown in Table 7.3 as shown here:

To add a new user account, enter the following:

```
NET USER username [Password *] [/ADD] [Options] [/DOMAIN]
```

To modify an existing account, enter the following:

```
NET USER username [Password *] [Options] [/DOMAIN]
```

To delete an existing account, enter the following:

```
NET USER username [Password *] [/DELETE] [/DOMAIN]
```

TABLE 7.3 The NET USER Parameters

Parameter	Description
Username	Specifies the name of the account that you want to create, change, or delete.
Password	Specifies the password for the username. Alternatively, you can use *; the system prompts you for the password and masks the characters that you enter.
/DOMAIN	Specifies that the action applies to the Primary Domain Controller. This parameter applies only to Windows NT Workstation computers that belong to a Windows NT Server domain.
/ADD	Adds a username to the user accounts database.
/DELETE	Removes a username from the user accounts database.
Options	Specifies one or more options as shown in Table 7.4. You must separate your options with at least one space.

TABLE 7.4 The NET USER Command Options

Option	Description
/ACTIVE:{NO ¦ YES}	Enables or disables the account. The default is to enable the account.
/COMMENT:"User Description"	Provides a maximum length 48 character descriptive account about the user.
/COUNTRYCODE:NNN	Specifies the user account country code. A value of 0 specifies the default system country code.
/EXPIRES:{Date ¦ NEVER}	Specifies that the account expires on the date shown, or never. The date is either MM/DD/YY or DD/MM/YY depending on the country code.
/FULLNAME:"Username"	Specifies the user's full name.
/HOMEDIR:"pathname"	Specifies the path for the user's home directory. The specified path must exist; otherwise, you get an error message.
/PASSWORDCHG:{YES ¦ NO}	Specifies whether the user can change the password.
/PASSWORDREQ:{YES NO}	Specifies whether the account requires a password. The default is to require a password.

continues

7

TABLE 7.4 continued

Option	Description
/PROFILEPATH:"*Pathname*"	Specifies the pathname for the user profile.
/SCRIPTPATH:"*Pathname*"	Specifies the pathname for the user's logon script. The pathname is relative to the logon server's logon script path.
/TIMES:{*Times* ¦ ALL}	Specifies the valid logon times for the user in the format *Day* [-*Day*], *Time* [-*Time*], where the day can be spelled out or abbreviated and the time can be in either 12- or 24-hour notation. For example, M-F, 0600-1800 specifies 6:00 a.m. to 6:00 p.m. Monday through Friday.
/USERCOMMENT: "*User Description*"	Changes the user comment field.
/WORKSTATIONS: {*Computername* *}	Specifies up to eight workstations (separated by commas) where the user can log on. The * specifies that there are no restrictions.

Figure 7.5 shows a sample usage of the command line in practice. By using the command line, you learned a second way to create, modify, or delete user accounts. Later, you'll learn about account restrictions.

FIGURE 7.5

Using NET USER *to create and delete an account.*

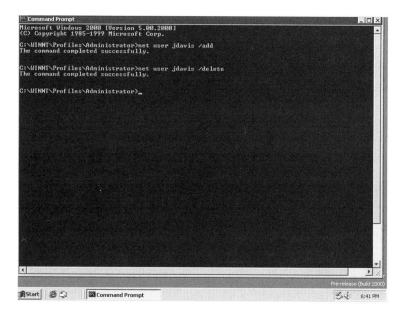

Creating Groups

 After creating user accounts, you might want to create some groups and add users to them. Groups simplify administration because you can assign rights at the group level. To simplify administration of user accounts that have similar resource needs, you can categorize the user accounts into groups. A *group* is a name, similar to the username of a user account, which can be used to refer to one or more users. Using groups provides a convenient way to give and control access to users who perform similar tasks. Without groups, you have to modify each user's account so that it has the same capabilities or restrictions as another user's account. By placing users within a group, you give all the users in that group the same capabilities or restrictions in a single action. If you need to change the permissions or rights assigned to the users within the group, you have to modify only one account—the group account.

> **Tip**
>
> To find out which user accounts belong to a group, open the Active Directory Manager and double-click the name of the group. Select the Members tab from the properties window. You see a list of its current members.

As you briefly learned on Day 5, "Introducing Active Directory," three types of groups exist in the Windows 2000 environment: *local groups, global groups,* and *universal groups.* The terms local group, global group, and universal group don't refer to the contents of the group, but to the scope of the group's accessibility. Local groups are local to the security system where they were created. Domain local groups have rights and permissions in a single domain. Member servers (Windows 2000 Servers that aren't domain controllers) and Windows 2000 Professional computers have their local groups with rights and permissions on those computers only. With a Windows 2000 Workgroup workstation, the operating system uses the group only on the workstation itself. Think of local groups in terms of tasks that need to be done or resources that users need to access.

With a server domain group, the operating system uses the group only on the servers in the domain. A local group is available only on the domain controllers within the domain where you create the group, whereas a global group is available within its own domain and in any trusting domain. Thus, global groups extend the network without increasing the administrative burden. A trusting domain can use a global group to control rights and permissions given to members of some other trusted domain.

Think of global groups as a logical grouping of people. You can add a global group (and therefore its members) to a local group to give the former the rights and permissions of

7

the latter. Windows 2000 has default local and global groups, as you'll learn in the following sections.

Often Windows 2000 users are confused by global groups because the name seems to imply a group that contains accounts from all over the network, or possibly a group of users who can be assigned rights for the entire network rather than just a computer or domain. In fact, a global group contains only members from a single domain, and you can add the group to a local group or to a local group in another domain. Microsoft likes to call global groups *export* groupsand local groups *import* groups. Global groups are imported into local groups.

The procedure for setting up global groups is to add a user's account to a global group in the user's domain and then add the global group to a local group, either in the same domain or in another domain where a trust relationship has been established. Global groups already might belong to local groups when you add a new user to the group. The new user then receives all the rights and permissions already assigned to the global group.

For the simplest of groups, you will use universal groups to assign permissions to related resources in multiple domains. ACLs for universal groups can appear anywhere in the forest, and can include other universal groups, global groups and users from anywhere in the forest. If you have a small installation, do away with global and local groups, and only use universal groups. You will find a universal group and its membership in the Global Catalog.

| Caution | You can only use universal mode when you are using native mode: not mixed mode. |

Table 7.5 summarizes the three types of groups in Windows 2000.

TABLE 7.5 Group Types

Group	Description
Domain Local Group	Open membership: members can come from any domain
	Members can access resources only in the local domain
Global Group	Limited membership: members only come from local domain
	Members can access resources in any domain
Universal Group	Open membership: members can come from any domain
	Members can access resources in any domain

Following are some other points to keep in mind:

- Local groups on domain controllers have rights only on the domain where they were created.
- Local groups on Windows 2000 Workstation computers and member servers (non-Domain Controllers) have rights on the computer where they were created.
- Local groups cannot contain other local groups; they can contain only user accounts or global groups from the same domain or other domains.
- Global groups contain user accounts from only one domain. They cannot contain local groups or other global groups.
- Universal groups contain user accounts from any domain. They can contain universal accounts, global groups, local groups, and user accounts.

Sometimes you want to create groups for security purposes, such as the granting of permissions. Other times, you want to group users for other purposes, such as the sending of mail. To help you with this, Microsoft has added new classes of groups. New to Windows 2000 are two new types of group objects: Security and Distribution groups.

Security Groups

Windows 2000 only uses security groups. You can list *security groups* in ACLs to define permissions on resources and objects. You can make computers, users, and other groups members of a security group. Also, you can use security groups as an email group. Because W2K only uses security groups, you will focus on them today.

Distribution Groups

Applications can use distribution groups as lists for non-security-related reasons. You cannot list distribution groups in ACLs, and distribution groups have no assigned permissions or rights.

 Tip

Security groups have a superset of functionality of distribution groups. So, should you wish, you can use a security group as a distribution group.

How do you take advantage of these groups and use them to promote security? You can start by creating precise global groups for users with specific job titles and tasks. Then you can easily set rights and permissions.

For security reasons, the members of universal and global groups must be reviewed on a regular basis. Because you can add global groups to local groups, and because the global

7

groups thereby obtain the rights and privileges of the local groups, some members of those global groups might obtain inappropriate access rights. Suppose a former member of your team, for example, moves to another department in another domain. If that person is a member of a global group that is added to your local Administrators group, that person gains administrative rights that might be inappropriate in the new job because the person knows a lot about your department.

You might not consider some users in other domains trustworthy. One approach is to remove the user from the global group in the other domain where you have permissions to do so. You can also create a new global group with only appropriate users, or you can remove the global group from the local group and add only the accounts of users who have access to the local group.

Tip

> Keeping on top of the global groups that are available on the network—and the members of those global groups—is a good idea. Fully document the rights and permissions available to both local and global groups.

Using Local Groups

NEW TERM Local groups define permissions to resources only within the domain where the local group exists. Hence, the term *local* defines the scope of the resource permissions granted to users within the group.

Using local groups isn't only an effective way of collectively assigning user rights and permissions for a set of users within the home domain; you also can use them to gather together numerous global groups and users from other domains. Therefore, you can change access to domain resources globally with a single modification to the local group permissions.

Using a local group is a good way to import a group of users and global groups from other domains into a single unit for use in the local domain. Remember that a local group can contain user accounts or global groups from one or more domains, and that you can assign the group privileges and rights only within its own domain. Local groups created on a Windows 2000 Workstation computer or a Windows 2000 Server computer in a workgroup are available only on that computer.

Local groups can contain users and global groups from the local domain (but not from other local groups), as well as users and global groups from trusted domains. However, you can assign a local group permissions and rights only in its home domain. Table 7.6 summarizes the possible contents of local and global groups.

TABLE 7.6   Local and Global Groups

Local Groups	Global Groups
Can contain local users, global groups, and other domain accounts (trusted)	Can contain local users
Cannot contain other local groups	Cannot contain local groups

Predefined Local Groups

Windows 2000 automatically creates several default local and global groups during installation.

Table 7.7 lists the predefined local groups on both Windows 2000 Server computers and Windows 2000 Workstation computers.

TABLE 7.7   Predefined Local Groups

Name	Description
Administrators	Members can fully administer the local computer and any domain resources. This group is the most powerful. Within the Administrators group is a built-in account that you cannot delete.
Account Operators	Members can use User Manager for Domains to manage domain user and group accounts. An Account Operator cannot change or delete the Domain Admins, Account Operators, Backup Operators, Print Operators, or Server Operators groups. Also, an Account Operator cannot change or delete administrator user accounts or administer security policies.
Backup Operators	Members can perform backups and restores, and can bypass the security restrictions on directories and files to back them up.
Guests	Members can access the server from the network but cannot log on locally. In other words, Guests have limited access to the domain. In effect, these users can log on if they know the Guest account and password, but they cannot change any settings on the local computer. This group is for the occasional or one-time user to log on. The built-in Guest account is automatically a member of the Guests group.
Power Users	Members can do everything that members of the Users group can do. In addition, these members can create user accounts, modify the user accounts that they created, put any user accounts on the computer into the Power Users, Users, and Guests built-in groups, share and stop sharing files and directories and printers located at the computer, and set the computer's internal clock.

continues

TABLE 7.7 continued

Name	Description
Print Operators	Members can administer the domain printers. They can create, manage, and delete printer shares for an NTS server.
Replicators	Members can manage replication services. They are granted the appropriate privileges to replicate files in the domain. Use this group only to support the Directory Replication service.
Server Operators	Members can manage the servers in the domain. Tasks include logging on locally, restarting the server, and shutting down the server.
Users	Members can access the server from the network but cannot log on locally. They are normal users of the domain and have limited access to the domain and their computers. They can make some configuration changes to their environment but have limited functionality. They cannot create new shared directories, for example, or stop and start services.

Tip Because you cannot disable the Administrator account, you might want to create a backup Administrator account for emergencies.

Note Account Operators, Print Operators, and Server Operators local groups are available only on Windows 2000 Server computers acting as a Domain Controller. The Power Users group is available only on Windows 2000 Professional computers or on Windows 2000 Server computers not acting as domain controllers.

Using Global Groups

A global group, available only on Windows 2000 Server domains, contains only individual user accounts (no groups) from the domain where it was created. After you create a global group, you can assign it permissions and rights, either in its own domain or in any trusting domain. In fact, because they have no user rights associated with them, global groups are powerless until you assign them to a local group or to a user right.

NEW TERM Using a global group is a good way to export a group of users as a single unit to another domain. In a trusting domain, for example, you can *grant* identical permissions for a particular file to a global group; these permissions then pertain to all individual members of that group. Also, global groups defined in a domain can be exported to Windows 2000 workstations because domain Windows 2000 workstations support local groups; they can, therefore, make use of global groups defined in either the workstation's own domain or other domains. In fact, this is how W2K sets up control so that the Administrator can control all the 2000 servers and workstations in a domain. By placing the Domain Administrator group into the machine's Local Administrator group, the Domain Administrators can own that machine.

By using trust relationships, users within a global group can access resources outside their locally defined domain. Global groups are, therefore, quite suitable for large, multidomain networks. Global groups can provide an inclusive list of all user accounts within a domain that require a particular type of access to resources that exist within another domain.

A local group and a global group sharing the same name are two separate entities, each with its own distinct security identifier. Permissions assigned to one group don't apply to the other group that shares the same name.

Tip

> It probably is not a good idea to create local and global groups with the same name. As you can appreciate, this can get rather confusing. Should you need the same name, use a qualifier to show one is local and the other is global.

When Windows 2000 Server is installed on a computer, it is configured with three predefined global groups (as shown in Table 7.8).

TABLE 7.8 Default Global Groups on Windows 2000 Server

Group	Description
Domain Admins	Members can fully administer the home domain, the workstations of the domain, and any other trusted domains that added this group to the local Administrators group. These members are added automatically to the Local Administrators group.
Domain Guests	Members can access the Guest account, and can potentially access resources across domains. Members are added automatically to the Guests group.
Domain Users	Members have normal access to the domain and to any W2K workstation in the domain. The group contains all domain users, and its members are added automatically to the local Users group.

7

Using Universal Groups

When planning to use universal groups, keep these thoughts in mind:

- Use universal groups to give users access to resources located in more then one domain. Unlike domain local groups, you can assign permissions to universal groups for resources in any domain in your network.

- Use universal groups only when their membership is static. In a domain tree, universal groups can cause excessive network traffic between domain controllers whenever you change membership for the universal group. This is because the system may replicate changes to the membership of universal groups to other domain controllers.

- Add global groups from several domains to a universal group, and then assign permissions for access to a resource to the universal group. This allows you to use a universal group like a domain local group.

Special Built-in Groups

Besides the predefined local, global, and universal groups, Windows 2000 has a few special groups with no members. The name special groups doesn't refer to the privilege level of users, but rather to access to computer resources. These groups have no members because they apply to any account using the computer in a specified way. You don't see these groups listed in Active Directory Manager; however, they might appear when you're assigning permissions to directories, files, shared directories, or printers.

Windows 2000 uses special groups to organize users according to how they access different resources. You cannot assign users as members of a special group; users are either members of these groups by default or they become members by virtue of their network activity.

Table 7.9 lists the special groups created under Windows 2000 Server.

TABLE 7.9 Special Groups

Group	Description
Anonymous Users	Any unauthenticated user on the computer.
Authenticated Users	This group consists of users who provided a valid username and password at some point.
Batch	Any batch process accessing a resource on the computer.

Group	Description
Creator Owner	A user who creates or takes ownership of a resource, such as subdirectories, files, and print jobs.
Dialup	Any user who has access to resources on the computer using dial-up networking.
Everyone	All users who access a computer, whether locally or remotely. This group includes both interactive and network users.
Interactive	Users who log on to the local computer. Interactive users access resources on the machine at which they are sitting.
Network	Users who log on to a network or remote computer using their account or an enabled Guest account.
Service	Any service.
System	The operating system.

Note

The System account and the Administrator account (Administrators group) have the same file privileges, but they have different functions under Windows 2000. The operating system uses the System account. Services running under Windows 2000 use the Service account. Many services and processes within Windows 2000 need to log on internally (for example, during a Windows 2000 installation). System and Service are internal accounts, don't show up in Active Directory Manager, cannot be added to any groups, and cannot have user rights assigned to them. The System account, however, does show up on an NTFS volume in the Windows 2000 Explorer in the Security tab of the Properties window. By default, the System account is granted full control of all files on an NTFS volume (as does the Administrator account).

It is important to understand the difference between the Network and Interactive groups because it affects permissions. Consider the following example: User KELLY logs on to machine BALLIOL and accesses only the resources physically attached to machine BALLIOL. That user is a local or interactive user, and Windows 2000 assigns the user KELLY to the Interactive group. If user KELLY moves to another machine, for example MERTON, and uses the network to access the same resources on BALLIOL, user KELLY then works with permissions assigned to the Network group and becomes a member of that group. The permissions assigned to the Interactive group are no longer valid for user KELLY.

7

Now that you know about the various types of groups, you can learn how to create group accounts.

Task 7.2: Creating Groups Using Active Directory Manager.

Step 1: Description

In this task, you'll use the Active Directory Manager program to create new groups.

Step 2: Action

1. Log on to the Windows 2000 Server as Administrator.

2. Choose Start, Programs, Administrative Tools, Active Directory Users and Computers.

3. Click the domain, right-click Users. Choose New, Group. The Create New Object—(Group) dialog box appears, as shown in Figure 7.6.

FIGURE 7.6

The create new group panel.

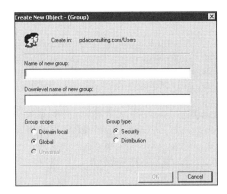

4. Type the new group name WRITERS in the Name of new group box. Press Tab to move to the next field.

5. Type the downlevel name in the Downlevel name of new group box. The system fills this in automatically for you when you enter the name in box above.

6. Select the Group scope: Domain Local, Global, or Universal.

7. Select the Group type: Security or Distribution.

8. Click OK to close the window.

9. Double-click the group you just created.

10. In the Writers properties window shown in Figure 7.7 select the Members tab.

FIGURE 7.7

The Writers Properties panel.

11. Click the Add button.

12. From a window similar to the one shown in Figure 7.8, highlight the user you created, and then click the Add button.

FIGURE 7.8

The Select Users, Contacts, or Computers window.

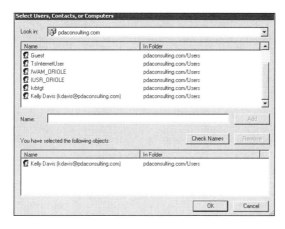

13. After you add all the members of the group, click OK. Click OK again.

Step 3: Review

In this task, you created your first local group by choosing Start, Administrative Tools, Active Directory Manager.

7

To delete a group, choose Start, Programs, Administrative Tools, Active Directory
Manager, double-click the domain and then select User. Highlight the group's name from
the right pane, and then right-click and select Delete or press the Delete key. You'll have
to confirm that you really mean to delete the group.

If you like using command lines, you can manage groups another way. If you don't want
to use the User Manager for Domains or the Administrative Wizards, you can use the NET
GROUP and NET LOCALGROUP command-line options. With these commands, you can add,
change, or delete a global (GROUP) or local (LOCALGROUP) group.

To add a new global group, enter the following:

```
NET GROUP "groupname" /ADD
```

To add a user to an existing global group, enter the following:

```
NET GROUP "groupname" username /ADD
```

To add a new local group, enter the following:

```
NET LOCALGROUP "groupname" /ADD
```

To add a user to an existing local group, enter the following:

```
NET LOCALGROUP "groupname" username /ADD
```

To delete a user from an existing local or global group, enter the following:

```
NET [LOCAL]GROUP "groupname" username /DELETE
```

If you want to add the account PETER to the WRITERS local group, for example, type the
following command at the DOS prompt:

```
NET LOCALGROUP "WRITERS" PETER /ADD
```

If you just want to list all the groups on a machine, you can use the same commands
with no options at the DOS prompt:

```
NET GROUP
```

```
NET LOCALGROUP
```

To list the users within a group, add the actual groupname after the command. For example, to list users in the Administrators group, type the following:

```
NET LOCALGROUP Administrators
```

Managing User Access

On Day 6 you learned that logon security is an important part of the Windows 2000
Server security model. You also learned that usernames and passwords are integral parts

of logon security. Earlier in this chapter, you learned all about users and different types of groups. At this point, you're ready to learn about another key part of logon security. By looking closely at passwords, you gain knowledge about the W2K verification system; today, you also learn about the authentication portion of the NTS security.

What does all this mean? First, look at the generic security process. When you make a request for data, you need to go through the steps illustrated in Figure 7.9.

FIGURE 7.9

The security process.

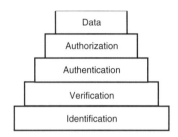

At the first step, you provide a username to the system for identification. The username identifies you as the administrator (or whomever). A password is associated with a username—you supply the password to prove you are the administrator. The system verifies that you are the administrator by matching the password that you supplied with the stored password. If the password match is successful, the system makes assumptions about you.

Next, the system authenticates you by checking restrictions, such as workstation access, time of day, and day of week. If this check is successful, you can request data. When you request data, the system checks whether you are authorized to access the data according to the file and directory attributes and your access rights. If you qualify, the system sends the data back over the network to you.

NEW TERM This chapter introduces you to the authentication step of this process. On Day 8, you will look at attributes and rights, and you will get your first glimpse of the *authorization* step. Start by quickly looking at passwords and their use.

Managing Passwords

Earlier, you looked at creating and controlling accounts. This section covers passwords and the parameters associated with them. You probably have direct experience with passwords; indeed, you might think that passwords are something that you know plenty about, but take the time to study this section. Because of the nature of NTS, passwords are the major control mechanism on your system. One poorly administered or derived password can put all your valuable data at risk. Many users consider using passwords a

7

waste of time. The problem is that when one unauthorized individual has access to one account, that individual can compromise the whole network.

The stories about systems being broken into because of poor passwords are too numerous to name in this book. At this time, you probably have an appreciation for the need for passwords. Consequently, in the following sections you'll learn how to manage passwords and ensure that other users understand the need for good passwords.

Understanding User Account Passwords

In Windows 2000 Server, passwords are optional—but highly recommended. They provide an effective strategy for filtering out unwanted users. W2K provides a number of restrictions for passwords. Password protection can be enhanced by making passwords mandatory, by setting minimum lengths, or by expiring them after a set period of time.

NEW TERM   Assigning a password immediately on completion of the creation of a user account is a good idea. Users can then choose and change the passwords that you created. This way, you aren't aware of the users' passwords. This process enhances the users' *accountability*. The following lesson on how the system uses the password might help your understanding.

Creating Strong Passwords

As you have learned, passwords are an integral part of logon security, so you want to create strong passwords. A W2K password can consist of any ASCII character except the 32 control characters. Passwords are case-sensitive.

A Windows 2000 password can have from 1 to 14 characters. Thinking of a good password isn't easy. A good password is something that the user can remember, but that others won't guess. Some passwords are too obvious or easily guessed. The following are passwords to avoid:

- Words in the dictionary
- First and last names
- Street and city names
- Valid license plate numbers
- Room numbers, Social Security numbers, Social Insurance numbers, and telephone numbers
- Beer and liquor brands
- Athletic teams
- Days of the week and months of the year

- Repeated characters
- Software default passwords

The temptation for users to create weak passwords is overpowering. You want to enable users to change their passwords, yet you want strong passwords. Fortunately, Windows 2000 Server provides several password controls that you can set. When setting the security policy, you make decisions about password options and parameters for the system and individual users. You learn about the account policy later in this chapter. There is a lot of debate about what constitutes a good password; at a minimum you need to create one that is alphanumeric (contains numbers and letters), but that doesn't violate the items in the preceding list. For example, Peter1 is alphanumeric; however, it is also my name, so it's a bad password.

Changing passwords is simple. While you're logged on, press Ctrl+Alt+Del. You see a Windows 2000 Security dialog box in which you select Change Password. To prevent people from trying to change a password at a workstation where someone has walked away, enter your old password. Then, in the appropriate boxes, type in your new password and retype it to confirm the new password.

In addition to passwords, you can set other authentication parameters for restricting user access.

Managing User Account Properties

You can modify or customize the properties associated with a user account by right-clicking a username in Active Directory Manager. Figure 7.10 shows you the Properties window. You can set these parameters when creating a new account, or you can modify these parameters for an existing account. Table 7.10 lists and describes the tabs in the Properties window.

TABLE 7.10 The New User Dialog Box Buttons

Tab	Description
General	This tab captures tombstone data for the user, for example, name, description, office, telephone numbers, email address, home page URL, and other Web pages.
Address	Use this tab to document street address, P.O. Box, city, state or province, zip or postal code, and country or region.
Account	This tab documents the user's account options. These options are described in Table 7.11.

continues

7

TABLE 7.10   continued

Tab	Description
Profile	Use this tab to set a profile path, login script, home directory, and shared document folder. See the next section, "Assigning Profiles."
Telephones/Notes	Use this tab to document home, pager, mobile, fax, and IP phone numbers and any comments you might have regarding these numbers.
Organization	This tab documents the user's title, department, company, manager, and any direct reports.
Member Of	Use this tab to document the groups where the user belongs.
Dial-in	Use this tab to document the dial-in properties for the user.

FIGURE 7.10

The Properties window.

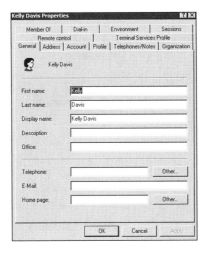

If you added other services, such as Terminal Services, you could see other tabs. For example, install Terminal Services and you should see the Remote Control, Terminal Services Profile, Environment, and Sessions tabs. Also, because AD is an extensible directory service, you can add more attributes to the user account class.

Now let's turn our attention back to the Account tab. Figure 7.11 shows the Account tab. Use the Account tab to manage your users. Table 7.11 describes each of the buttons on the Account tab.

FIGURE 7.11

The Account tab.

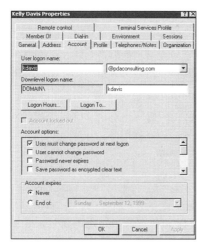

TABLE 7.11   The New User Dialog Box Buttons

Button	Description
User logon name	Specifies the user logon name, which you selected at account creation.
Downlevel logon name	Entered when account was created.
Logon Hours	Restricts the days and hours during which a user can connect to a server.
Logon To	Restricts the computers at which users can log on to domain accounts.
Account options	Defines account options as shown in Table 7.12.
Account expires	Select Never should you never want the account to expire. For others, select End of and then enter a date in the adjoining box. Notice the default (grayed out until you select it) is one month in advance.

When creating or managing a user account, you can set the account to expire after a certain amount of time. If you have a consultant or other temporary personnel, you don't want them to log on to the network beyond the time for which they are authorized (or after the contract expires). An expiration date is a useful tool for temporary employees or students in an academic institution. It enables you to lock an account after a specific date. A locked account cannot be used without being reset. The account therefore expires at midnight on the expiration date. By default, the expiration date is set to Never. Setting an account to expire helps you avoid the problem of temporary employees logging on when they're not supposed to.

7

An account with an expiration date becomes disabled (not deleted) on the day specified in the Account Expires section of the dialog box. If the user happens to be logged on when the account expires, the system doesn't terminate the session, but the user can't make any new connections. After the user logs off, she can't log back on.

Table 7.12 describes the account options you can select from the Account tab.

TABLE 7.12   Account Options

Option	Default	Description
User Must Change Password at Next Logon	OFF	Selected when you created the account, but you can change it here.
User Cannot Change Password	OFF	Selected when you created the account, but you can change it here.
Password Never Expires	OFF	Selected when you created the account, but you can change it here.
Save Password as Encrypted Clear Text	OFF	Selecting this option allows your Macintosh clients to log on, which is the only password the Macintosh computers can send.
Account Disabled	OFF	Selected when you created the account, but you can change it here.
User Must Log On Using a Smart Card	OFF	Selecting this option forces your users to use smart cards, which require additional hardware. You learned about this option yesterday.
Account Is Trusted for Delegation	OFF	Selecting this option allows administration of this account to be delegated to, for instance, a departmental manager.
Account Is Sensitive and Can Not Be Delegated	OFF	See above.
Use DES Encryption Types For This Account	OFF	Sets the encryption algorithm for use with, say, Kerberos.
Don't Require Kerberos Authentication	OFF	Selecting this means the user doesn't use Kerberos for authentication.

The following sections look at account restrictions in more detail.

Assigning Profiles

NEW TERM One of the most powerful methods available to administrators for managing user environments is through user profiles on Windows 2000 computers. A *profile* defines the application settings, Control Panel settings, printer connections, window size and positioning, and screen colors. Setting up and managing profiles are jobs that require extensive knowledge and can cause problems if inappropriately developed. Although this brief task is provided to tell you how to implement a profile, it is suggested that you do extra reading and studying that is beyond the scope of this book prior to making significant changes.

Task 7.3: Creating a User's Environment by Assigning Profiles.

Step 1: Description

In this task, you'll learn to create a user's environment.

Step 2: Action

1. Click the Profile tab on the Username Properties dialog box. The Profile panel appears, as shown in Figure 7.12.

FIGURE 7.12

The Profile panel.

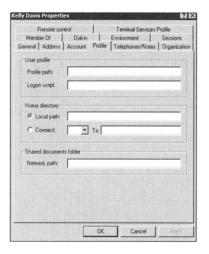

2. To assign a user profile, type its full pathname in the Profile path box. The path needs to be a network path. The filename can be that of a personal user profile (with a .DAT filename extension) or a mandatory user profile (with a .MAN filename extension). You might type, for example, \\winnt\profiles\profile.man.

7

▼   3. To assign a logon script, type the filename in the Logon script box. If the logon
        script is stored in a subdirectory of the logon script path, precede the filename with
        the relative path.

     4. To specify a home directory, select the Connect box, specify a drive letter, select
        the To box, and then type a network path. Or select the Local path box and type a
        local path (including the drive letter). You might specify drive F, for example, and
        type a network path of \\winnt\users\writer. You also might type a local path of
        c:\users\writer. When you're administering domain user accounts, specify a net-
        work path. Optionally, substitute %username% for the last subdirectory in the path.
        You might specify drive Z:, for example, and then type a network path of
        \\winnt\users\%username%. When no home directory is assigned, the system
        assigns the user account the default local home directory (\USERS\DEFAULT on
        the user's local drive where Windows 2000 is installed).

▲   5. Click OK.

Step 3: Review

This task showed you how to create a user profile and a home directory. Giving users a
home directory is important so that they have somewhere to store their data. Otherwise,
they might look for somewhere to store data—and that place might not be where you
want it.

Restricting User Access

The primary authentication mechanism for user access is logon restrictions. Logon
restrictions include the following types of restrictions:

- Time restrictions
- Workstation restrictions
- Account restrictions
- Dial-in restrictions

Each of these restrictions is studied in turn, in the following sections.

Permissible Logon Hours

You can restrict user access to a Windows 2000 server based on the time of day and the
day of the week. Time restrictions are useful because you can control when users can
access the system. You can apply these restrictions as a system default for all users, or
you can apply them for individual users.

After carefully studying the requirements of your network, you might decide to set
default time restrictions. If you have only one work shift each day, for example, it is

unlikely that anyone logs on at 3:00 a.m. You also might want to set time restrictions to prevent workers from logging on during off-hours if they are contractor staff, or when backups are being run.

You might argue that some users need to log on at any time. You are right. For that reason, you can change time restrictions on a user-by-user basis. You can set default time restrictions in the same way that you set account restrictions.

Note

When you apply time restrictions with a plan or according to a company policy, they provide extra protection. On the flip side, improperly conceived parameters hamper the work of your users.

Time restrictions are dynamic; that is, after you come across a blank time period, the system clears your connection. You do, however, have approximately eight minutes to log out. After several minutes in a disallowed period, you receive a message telling you to log out. If you choose to ignore this first message, you receive a second message. If you ignore the NTS message, Windows 2000 Server clears your connection after another minute.

So how do you use this facility? Suppose you have clients on your system who you know use the system only from 9:00 a.m. to 5:00 p.m., Monday through Friday. If this is the case, for no reason do these clients need to have access to the system outside these hours. NTS enables you to set permissible hours for all clients.

By choosing the Hours button in the New User dialog box, you can specify the days and hours during which a particular user of your system can access the network. Click the Logon Hours button on the Account tab of the Properties panel for any user, and you see a dialog box similar to the one in Figure 7.13.

FIGURE 7.13

The default Logon Hours dialog box.

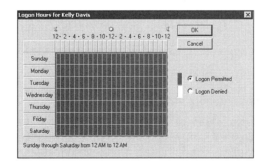

7

By default, a user can connect to the network all hours of all days of the week. As you can see in Figure 7.13, all times of all days are allowed for this new user. If, for some reason, you don't want a user to have access to the network all the time, you can use this dialog box to restrict them.

To administer the hours that you want to allow the user account to access the network, select the hours by dragging the cursor over a particular block of hours, and click the Logon Denied radial button. Conversely, you can select all the hours of a certain day by clicking that day's button, or you can choose certain hours across all seven days by clicking the button at the top of an hour's column. Then click either the Logon Permitted or Logon Denied button to grant or deny access to the network at the selected hours. Filled boxes indicate the hours when the user is authorized to connect to the network; empty ones indicate the times at which access is denied. After you finish setting logon times, click OK. In Figure 7.14, you can see that the user no longer has access on Sundays.

FIGURE 7.14

A modified Logon Hours dialog box.

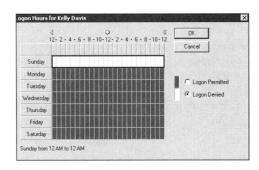

As its title implies, you must understand that the Logon Hours dialog box controls logon hours. Suppose that you've restricted your client to log on between 9:00 a.m. and 5:00 p.m., and the client tries to log on at 8:59 a.m. In this case, your client cannot get on, and sees the following message (if you have a Windows 2000 workstation):

```
Your account has time restrictions that prevent you from logging on at
this time. Please try again later.
```

If the client has a Windows 95 workstation, the client sees the following message:

```
You are not allowed to log on at this time.
```

DOS clients see a more verbose message:

```
Error 2241: You do not have the necessary access rights to log
on at this time. To change access rights, contact your network
administrator about changing the logon hours listed in your account.
```

Of course, when your client tries to log on a few minutes later, after 9 a.m., he gets in without a problem. But what happens when your client is still logged on at the end of the logon hours? What happens, for example, when 5:01 p.m. rolls around? Does the system dump the client?

No, not by default. Later in this chapter, you will see the Security Templates dialog box. (If you want to look ahead to it, turn to Figure 7.17 or go to the Active Directory Manager and choose Security Templates, basicdc, Local Policies, Security Options.) Security Templates is a big dialog box, and it is easy to miss the attribute labeled Forcibly Logoff When Logon Hours Expire. By default, the attribute isn't configured. If you select it, the client in the example receives the following message five minutes before the end of the logon hours:

```
Your logon time at ORIOLE ends at 5:00 PM. Please clean up and log off.
```

Three minutes later, the message becomes more ominous:

```
WARNING: You have until 5:00 PM to log off. If you have not logged off
at this time, your session will be disconnected, and any open files or
devices you have open may lose data.
```

Finally, at the appointed hour, the client is history:

```
Your logon time at ORIOLE has ended.
```

To receive these messages, your client must start a message receiver such as Winpopup (for Windows for Workgroups or Windows 95 clients) or the Alerter service on a Windows 2000 workstation. The client is logged off even when he isn't running a message receiver—he just doesn't know that it's going to happen.

After the system boots your client, whatever network resources the client was using just seem to vanish. A network drive named F:, for example, likely generates the following error message (or one similar to it):

```
No files found on directory F:.
```

Trying to browse in a domain server might lead to an error message similar to the following:

```
ORIOLE is not accessible. You are not allowed to log on at this time.
```

Caution

> The system tells you twice to log out when a disallowed time period arises. After the system warns you of an impending time restriction violation, log out immediately. If you don't log out, the system clears the connection, which means that the file you're working on doesn't get saved.

7

Remember that changes to a user's account don't take effect until the next time the user logs on, so changing someone's logon hours today probably won't have any effect until tomorrow.

Controlling logon locations is similar to controlling logon hours. By choosing the Logon To button, you can limit the workstations from which a user can log on.

Controlling Where Users Can Log On

Restricting the physical workstations where users log on is another way to control user access. When you choose the Logon To button in the Username Properties dialog box, the Logon Workstations dialog box appears, as shown in Figure 7.15. In this dialog box, you can restrict the workstations from which the user can log on. As with the logon times, the default is no restrictions. A user can, therefore, log on at any workstation on the network.

FIGURE 7.15

The Logon Workstations dialog box.

If you want to restrict the user's choice of workstations for logging on to the network, click the User May Log On To These Workstations button and type in the computer names (without preceding backslashes) of the allowed workstations. You can specify as many workstations as you want. If the machines that your client regularly logs on to are WS_1000 and WS_1001, for example, you can just type those names with no preceding backslashes. This feature works for all workstation types.

Note   You need the NetBIOS protocol to use the Login Workstations feature.

Workstation restrictions, like other authentication mechanisms, can enhance access security. When you apply workstation restrictions with a plan or according to a company policy, they provide extra protection. Like time restrictions, however, improperly conceived restrictions hamper the work of your users. When a user's workstation is broken, perhaps the user cannot log on to the network. You can handle these contingencies when you create your users' list and ensure that there are at least two terminals that they can use.

> **Tip**
>
> Earlier today, you learned about the Account Operators group. Now is a good time to make use of this group. Because you have users who can administer accounts, you can restrict the use of the Administrator account to a workstation in a physically secure location.

Dial-in Restrictions

The last tab for today is the Dial-in in the Properties dialog box. Choose this tab when you want to grant the user permission to dial in to the network from a remote location; that is, to use Dial-Up networking to connect to the network. The service called RAS needs to be running for this dialog box to be useful. For information about RAS, refer to Day 11, "Understanding Remote Access Services (RRAS) and VPNs." Click the Dial-in tab in the Properties dialog box to display the Dial-in dialog box shown in Figure 7.16.

FIGURE 7.16

The Dial-in dialog box.

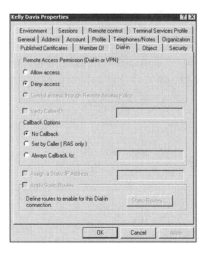

If you want to enable the user to dial in, select the Allow Access radio button. You can then configure the callback options.

Callback Options deal with calling a user back at a predefined number and preventing intruders who have obtained valid logon information from dialing in at an unauthorized location. The options also provide an additional bonus for remote and mobile users by reversing the charges on calls—which is probably the more typical reason for using this facility. When a client calls in, the server authenticates the user; it then hangs up the call and calls back. This way, the call is charged to the server.

Following are the three callback options:

- **No Callback**—This option disables callback options.
- **Set by Caller (RAS Only)**—This option reverses toll charges for users. When a user calls in, the server authenticates him and a dialog box appears asking for the callback telephone number. The server then disconnects the call and calls the client back. Note that this option provides no additional security.
- **Always Callback to**—This callback option does provide some security because you specify in advance the telephone number where the user can be called back.

In the following sections and tasks, you practice setting up a Security Template.

Managing Security Templates

Every network operating system, whether Novell NetWare or Banyan Vines, has certain rules for user accounts that can be used to provide additional security for the network. Windows 2000 Server is no exception. To establish these rules, choose Security Templates from the MMC window. Then double-click C:\SystemRoot\Security\Templates, and double-click basicdc. You can set policies for passwords, account lockout and security policies. Select Account Policies and then Password Policy, as shown in Figure 7.17. In this window, you can set the options listed in Table 7.13.

TABLE 7.13   The Password Policy Options

Option	Description
Allow Storage of Passwords Under Reversible Encryption	Password doesn't use a one-way encryption option. Not a good selection for a secure environment.
Enforce Password Uniqueness by Remembering Last	The number entered in the Passwords field specifies the number of passwords that the system records in the history list. The history list is a record of old passwords. Any password in this record can be used by the user when it is time to choose a new password. Do Not Keep Password History is the default.

Option	Description
Maximum Password Age	You can require a user to change the password every so often by specifying a number in the Days field. Changing the password frequently helps reduce the possibility that someone might guess it. Depending on the type of data on your system, a good value for maximum password age is between 30 and 45 days.
Minimum Password Age	By specifying a number in the Days field, you can establish a minimum length of time before the user can change the password. This feature provides two benefits. Use this field when you enable the Password Uniqueness option; it prevents a user from setting the password back to the password used immediately before the one that just expired. Allow changes immediately is the default.
Minimum Password Length	To specify the minimum length of a password, enter a number in the Characters field. When you set this parameter, remember that the shorter the password, the easier it is for the user to remember. Having a short password, however, also makes it easier for someone to gain access by guessing. Long passwords are harder for users to remember. A good minimum password length is six characters. Permit Blank Password is the default.
Passwords Must Meet Complexity Requirements	Allows you to require alphanumeric and special characters in the password, plus upper and lowercase. Default is disabled.
User Must Logon to Change Password	Forces user to log on to change password. Default is disabled.

You can also set Account Lockout Policy. Select Account Policies and then Account Lockout Policy, as shown in Figure 7.18. In this window, you can set the options listed in Table 7.14.

7

FIGURE 7.17

*The Password Policy
Attributes.*

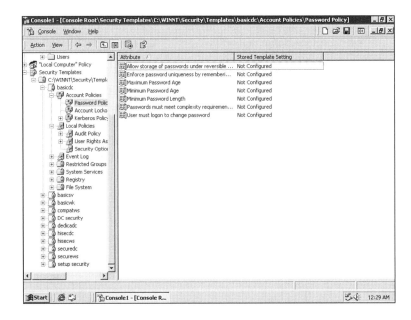

FIGURE 7.18

*The Account Lockout
Policy attributes.*

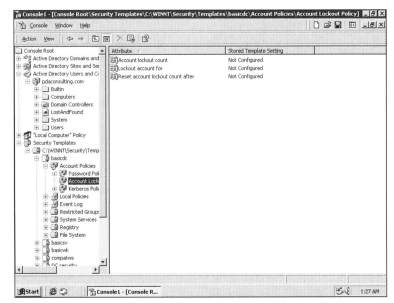

TABLE 7.14 The Account Lockout Policy Options

Option	Description
Account Lockout Count	This option is your best defense against system intruders because it limits the number of times that a user account can be used with the wrong password before the account is disabled. On the downside, it can also lock out users who forget their passwords during a logon sequence. Specify the number of logon attempts before an account lockout occurs in the Invalid logon attempts field. No account lockout is the default.
Lockout Account For	In the Lockout Account For, you can specify whether the account is locked out for a specific period of time by entering a number in the Minutes field.
Reset Account Lockout Count After	This number is based on the Minutes field, which specifies the time frame for determining the number of bad logon attempts. If the number of attempts occurs within the time frame that you specify here, the account is locked out.

Note

Default account restrictions work for all accounts after the parameters are set. New default parameters, therefore, have an effect on existing accounts. Consequently, you need to look at setting the default parameters before you start adding all your users—and don't change these settings without giving it a lot of thought.

NEW TERM Before moving on, here are a few words about intruder detection and lockout. In your travels or reading, you might have heard of intruder detection and lockout. Your first question is probably "What do you mean by intruder?" An *intruder* is someone who attempts to gain unauthorized access to someone else's account. Generally, intruders get this access by guessing passwords. Intruders might be internal to an organization (for example, disgruntled employees) or external (for example, *hackers* or *crackers*). If an intruder succeeds in guessing—or otherwise deriving—a password, the intruder has all the rights and privileges of the account. Unfortunately, the Administrator and Guest accounts often become the targets of intruders.

NEW TERM Because an intruder normally doesn't know the passwords, the intruder might try a *brute-force attack*; that is, the intruder manually or automatically tries random passwords until finding a match. In such a case, the Account Lockout feature kicks in.

Account Lockout isn't so much a restriction as it is a security feature. This feature tracks invalid logon attempts; that is, users who try to log on with incorrect passwords. It keeps

7

track of invalid password attempts and locks a user account when the user reaches the threshold number of password attempts. Users activate Account Lockout as soon as they enter an invalid password. The system increments the bad logon attempts count for invalid passwords. The `Reset account lockout count after` is a complementary parameter describing the period during which you track bad logons. After you reach the threshold within that period—you guessed it—you can lock out the user account.

An example might be appropriate at this juncture. Assume that you set `Account lockout count` to three and `Reset account lockout count for` to 30 minutes. The system tracks all invalid logon attempts and locks the user account when the number of invalid logon attempts exceeds three in a 30-minute period.

You don't have to lock out an account that has passed the threshold; however, you can. You arm Account Lockout by setting the lockout duration. Normally, you want to activate lockout upon detection of an intruder. You need to decide the appropriate time to lock the account. Then you specify the amount of time that must pass before the account automatically unlocks. If you set this number to a day or two, users need to come to the administrator to have it reset. In real life, whether you set the lockout time to 30 minutes or use the Forever option, your users end up calling the administrator or Help desk regardless. So don't spend a lot of time agonizing over which time period is best.

In the following task, you set up a default security policy for your organization.

Task 7.4: Setting a Default Security Policy Using the Security Templates.

Step 1: Description

In this task, you'll use the MMC program to set default user account restrictions that apply to all your users.

Step 2: Action

1. Log on to the Windows 2000 Server as Administrator.
2. Choose Start, Programs, Administrative Tools, Console1. Remember to substitute the name of the MMC console you created for Console1.
3. Choose Security Templates, C:\SystemRoot\Security Templates, basicdc, Account Policies, Password. The Account Policy attributes window then appears (refer to Figure 7.9).
4. Double-click Maximum Password Age. Uncheck Exclude This Setting From Configuration. Type **30** in the box. Click OK. Thirty days is a safe amount of time to keep a password. If you have users who always deal with confidential or critical data, you might want to set this number to fewer than 30 days. Don't use anything more than 90 days. The maximum value is 999 days (actually Forever).

▼ 5. Double-click Minimum Password Age. Immediately, a 30 pops up in the Days field (or whatever you entered in step 4). Select 1 as the value; it ensures that your users cannot change their password more than once per day, thus preventing them from looping through passwords and returning to their original password. If you don't enter a value here, users can enter a number of passwords to get around the password uniqueness feature and use the original password. The maximum value is 999 days.

6. Double-click Minimum Password Length. Uncheck Exclude This Setting from Configuration. Immediately, a 0 pops up. This value is inadequate; because it permits blank passwords. Choosing seven or more characters is even better. Click OK. Using combinations of seven letters and numbers (exactly 78,364,164,096), you can come up with enough combinations for more than 300 passwords for every person in the United States. The maximum value is 14.

7. Double-click Enforce Password Uniqueness By Remembering. Uncheck Exclude This Setting from Configuration. Immediately, a 0 pops up, which is Do Not Keep Password History. If you force periodic password changes, you might prevent users from repeating passwords. If you don't require unique passwords, users can change the password from alpha to beta and back to alpha; this option was created for exactly that reason. Normally, you want users to change their passwords because you're worried whether the password is still confidential. You don't require a change to improve typing skills; allowing users to use the original passwords defeats the purpose of forcing password changes. If you decide a user needs unique passwords, W2K maintains a table of the old passwords. A good value is 10, which is similar to what other systems provide. The maximum value is 24.

▲ 8. From the Console menu, select Exit.

Step 3: Review

In this task, you practiced using Security Templates MMC snap-in to set default user account restrictions that apply to all new users.

Configuring Account Policies from the Command Line

Earlier, you learned that you can create user accounts and groups from the command line. Just as you can create user accounts and local or global groups from the command line with the NET command, you can also specify the domain account policies. Following is the NET syntax using options listed in Table 7.15:

```
NET ACCOUNTS [/FORCELOGOFF{Minutes NO}] [/MINPWLEN:Length]
[/MAXPWAGE:{Days UNLIMITED}] [/MINPWAGE:Days] [/UNIQUEPW:Number][/DOMAIN]
```

7

TABLE 7.15 The NET ACCOUNTS Command Options

Option	Description
/SYNC	Updates the user accounts database.
/FORCELOGOFF	Specifies that the system issues a warning message minutes before a user is forcibly logged off. When No is specified, users aren't forced off the system.
/MINPWLEN	Specifies the minimum password length. The default is 6; valid password lengths are 0–14.
/MAXPWAGE	Specifies the maximum time that a user's password is valid. The default is 90 days; the valid range is from 1 to 999.
/MINPWAGE	Specifies the minimum amount of time before a user can change a password. The default is 0; the valid range is 0–999.
/UNIQUEPW	Specifies that a user cannot reuse the same password for the number of changes defined. The valid range is from 0–24.
/DOMAIN	Specifies that the operation needs to be performed on the Primary Domain Controller when the command is executed on a Windows NT Server operating in server mode or from a Windows NT Workstation.

Summary

Today, you learned about user accounts in general, and about Local, Global, Universal, and Special groups. You learned that Windows 2000 allows for different types of users. Review the different types and how you can use them in your particular case. You are now thoroughly familiar with the Active Directory Manager and MMC snap-ins. Although you use it again in subsequent chapters, you are probably comfortable with it now. Finally, you learned about the Administrator account. You must treat this account with respect. This account's rights and privileges make it powerful. With privileges comes responsibility. You must learn to use the Administrator account responsibly—and only when necessary.

Take time to practice using Active Directory Manager to create and delete users and groups. Practice, as they say, makes perfect.

You learned all about managing user accounts. First, you learned about user profiles and home directories, time restrictions, workstation restrictions, expiration dates, and dial-in restrictions. You saw how to set an account policy for your server, and you mastered the procedure for changing the account restrictions for individual users. This chapter emphasized controlling users and demonstrated one of Windows 2000 Server's primary security mechanisms. Study these account restrictions and use them where they are applicable to improve the security of your network.

Workshop

To wrap up the day, you can review terms and tasks from the chapter, and see the answers to some commonly asked questions.

Terminology Review

access—The capability and the means necessary to approach, store, or retrieve data, and to communicate with and make use of any resource of a computer system.

access period—A segment of time, generally expressed on a daily or weekly basis, when access rights prevail.

accountability—The quality or state that enables violations or attempted violations of a security system to be traced to individuals who can then be held responsible.

administrator—The person responsible for the operation of the network. The administrator maintains the network, reconfiguring and updating it as the need arises.

authentication—The act of identifying or verifying the eligibility of a station, originator, or individual to access specific categories of information.

authorization—The process that grants the necessary and sufficient permissions for the intended purpose.

brute-force attack—A computerized trial-and-error attempt to decode a cipher or password by trying every possible combination. Also known as exhaustive attack.

cracker—One who seeks to gain unauthorized access to computer systems.

grant—To authorize.

group—A name, similar to the username of a user account, that can be used to refer to one or more users.

hacker—A computer enthusiast.

identification—The process that enables recognition of an entity by a system, generally by the use of unique machine-readable usernames.

intruder—A user or other agent attempting to gain unauthorized access to the file server.

portal—The entrance to the network.

7

Task List

The emphasis of this chapter has been to introduce you to accounts and their management. As a system administrator, you repeatedly use these commands in your daily work. The emphasis of this session has been to set up proper password controls. Following are the tasks that you need to understand from this chapter:

- Using Active Directory Manager
- Using NET USER, NET ACCOUNT, NET GROUP, and NET LOCALGROUP
- Creating user accounts
- Creating groups
- Setting a security policy
- Changing a user's account restrictions
- Changing a user's time restrictions
- Changing a user's station restrictions
- Setting intruder lockout
- Requiring and restricting passwords for users

Q&A

Q Should I keep the Guest account?

A The Guest needs to remain disabled unless you have a specific, well-researched need for the account. When your organization's policy is to require users to have unique accounts to provide accountability, you can remove the Guest account.

Q Should users share accounts?

A No. The whole reason for having account names is to provide accountability for the actions of the owner of the account. When users share an account, how do you tie the actions of the account to one user? You cannot. As soon as you have problems with a shared account, everybody does a lot of finger pointing.

Q When do I use the Administrator account?

A Use the Administrator account only for problem resolution and for setting up security restrictions and managers and operators. Don't use the Administrator account for sending electronic mail, accessing network services, or composing documents.

Q What should my usernames look like?

A Your organization needs to have a standard for the composition of usernames and passwords to which all Windows 2000 Server usernames adhere. If you're developing a standard for usernames you might want to use the user's last name and first initial. Remember that usernames aren't meant to be security mechanisms, and you might use them as electronic mail addresses; therefore, they need to be meaningful.

Q How do I make sure that users aren't members of a particular group in a domain?

A To make sure, carry out the following steps:

1. Highlight the users in the Active Directory Manager window.

2. Choose Users.

3. Double-click the group you want to check in the right pane. A box pops up. Select the Members tab to show the users in the group. Then, you can select all the users you don't want in the group and click Remove.

4. Click OK to save the change.

Q How can I boot everyone off the server at 2 a.m. so that a scheduled backup can occur?

A That's simple. Just write a batch file with the following commands:

```
Net pause server
Net send * The server is shutting down in 15 minutes for routine
➥maintenance.
Sleep 900
Net stop server
```

The `pause` command keeps anyone new from logging on. The `send` command sends a message to everyone running the messenger service and a network pop-up. The `sleep` command tells W2K to wait for 900 seconds—15 minutes. (SLEEP.EXE isn't shipped with 2000, but it does come with the *Resource Kit.* Install the SLEEP program for instances such as this one.) The `stop` command shuts down the server, disconnecting everyone. A separate batch file can then be run to start the service back up again when you are ready.

Q If I use Account Lockout, to what do I set my thresholds?

A Normally, you set bad logon attempts to three. Any more than three attempts is probably something other than pilot error.

Q When and where do I use workstation restrictions?

A Using workstation restrictions is an excellent control for enforcing program pathing. By using program pathing, you can force specific users to execute programs from specific locations. You might want to ensure, for example, that payroll transactions come from workstations only in the human resources area. Also, tie the use of the Administrator account to a specific workstation used by the system administrator. Doing so obviates the exposure of an unattended workstation in session to the administrator. You also might want to tie the Guest account to a specific workstation. Any jobs or processes without passwords also need to be associated to a workstation.

7

Q What is a good password length?

A The length of a password determines the potential security of your system.

A password length of one reduces the potential password space to the number of characters in the composition set—for example, 0–9 for numeric and A–Z for alphabetic. Increasing the length of a random password can make it drastically more difficult to discover. With each additional character, both the number of possible combinations and the average time required to find the password increase exponentially. A length of two characters squares the number, a length of three cubes this number, and so on.

Having said this, the consultant's answer is that the length needs to be such that it cannot be easily guessed during the lifetime of the password. The practical answer is that your passwords need to be at least six characters long to thwart a brute-force attack.

But this probably doesn't help; so what is a good password length? In this chapter, you learned that the minimum password length is 0 (you can have a blank password), but there is also a maximum password length. Practically, the maximum password length is 14 characters. Practically, because Active Directory Manager enables you to create a maximum 14-character password. The password field itself, however, is 52 characters—but most of us cannot remember a 52-character password. The practical answer is that your passwords need to be at least six characters long, and no more than 14, to thwart a brute-force attack.

WEEK 2

At a Glance

DAY 8

Managing Files and Using the Distributed File System

In preceding days, you have learned about installing and exploring Windows 2000 and managing the Registry. You have also learned all about Active Directory and delved deeply into the security that Windows 2000 offers.

In today's session, you'll learn all about how Windows 2000 manages files and you will learn how to use the Distributed File System.

NEW TERM Today, you'll learn that Windows 2000 offers choices for setting up and managing files. You'll discover that in addition to the *File Allocation Table* (*FAT*) file system, Windows 2000 uses a new version of the file system called *New Technology File System* (*NTFS*). You'll also discover that file and directory-level security depends on the use of NTFS and that using the older DOS FAT format limits the amount of security available to you. Later today, you'll learn all about setting access controls over files and directories to control who can access what within Windows 2000.

Reviewing the Basics

First, let's take a few minutes to review the basics of files and directories. In particular, this information concerns the hardware and how it is set up within the machine and the operating system.

NEW TERM In all systems, you begin with a *physical drive* that is mounted in the server and attached with screws; it is the actual hard drive. You cannot change the size of the drive without physically removing it and replacing it with a new drive. Someone performs a *low-level format*, or *physical format*, so that you can begin using the drive. The vendor usually does this long before the machine arrives in your office. This formatting cannot be done from Windows 2000; it is done with tools that usually exist within the hard drive controller. Because each drive is different, you need to review the manuals that come with your particular drive for details on how to format it. Rarely does an administrator need to perform this function.

You might have worked on systems that cannot recognize large hard drives. If you have, you will be pleased to know that W2K recognizes hard drives that are larger than any in use today.

NEW TERM Windows 2000 also uses, just as other operating systems do, *logical partitions*. Such a partition is the opposite of the physical drive; it's a drive created by using software. When you run the DOS FDISK command on a hard drive, for example, it asks whether you want to set up one or more partitions. Be careful using this command, however, because it can destroy all information that already exists on the hard drive.

To run the FDISK command, you must first ensure that all your data is backed up safely onto tape or another disk. FDISK, in its zeal to create the partition, destroys any information that already exists. You can see FDISK in action in Figure 8.1. Remember that because this process destroys all the data on the disk, you shouldn't play with FDISK carelessly.

You can create only four partitions on any one physical hard drive. A primary partition is the only partition that is bootable, meaning that an operating system uses that partition for starting up. Why would you need more than one primary drive? In most cases, you might not, but if you plan to share your machine with more than one operating system, you do so by formatting more than one primary drive. To run both Windows 2000 Server and Windows 95, as I do on my laptop, for example, you might create one drive for running Windows 2000 Server and another for running Windows 95.

You can run both Windows 2000 and Windows 98 using only one drive, but doing so limits you to using only the FAT type of drive. Windows 2000 runs better and more securely when it uses its own file system, NTFS. Therefore, you need to create additional drives to handle this inconsistency. If you use Disk Administrator, you see the primary partition indicated through a dark purple stripe across the top of the screen. Windows 2000 shows you a different color for each type of partition, enabling you to quickly see the different partitions. These colors change according to the capabilities of your video card, however, so yours might look slightly different.

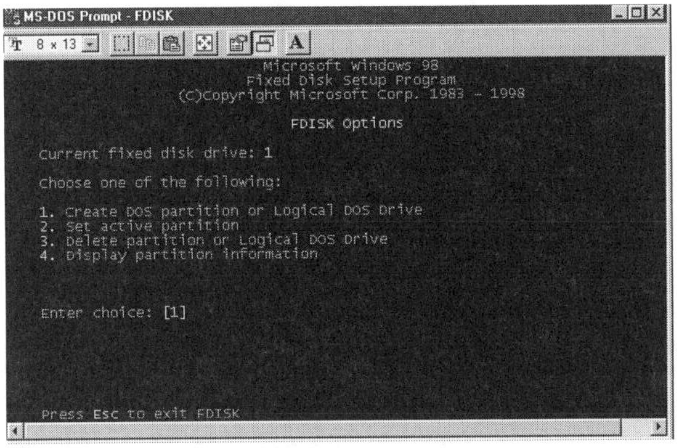

FIGURE 8.1

Using FDISK *to format a hard drive.*

Note

You must define and use the NTFS format with Windows 2000 Server to be able to utilize file- and directory-level security and control. There are other reasons to use NTFS. For instance, NTFS is more efficient, supports better recovery processes, and ultimately offers improved operating efficiencies over the other file systems. The FAT system works just fine in your Windows 2000 Server, but it doesn't allow you the granularity of protection and efficiency that you get with NTFS.

NEW TERM The other type of partition is an *extended partition*, which is created by using the free space available on a given drive. Extended partitions can be further subdivided into smaller units called *logical drives.*

The logical drives that an extended partition provides act as though they are physical drives for the user. You can use as many logical drives as you need, with these exceptions:

- You have only 25 fixed-disk drive letters (assuming one floppy).
- Each logical drive must be at least 2MB in size.
- A logical drive can extend across only one physical drive.

Royal blue stripes indicate logical disk drives in the Disk Administrator.

> **Tip**
>
> Here's some sound advice: You should back up all your data before messing around with partitions. You always need to back up data, regardless of the type of activity you're performing, because sooner or later you're going to lose data and regret not taking a more aggressive approach to data safety and backup. As any security guru will tell you, the three most important rules are: back up, back up, back up.

One other way of dealing with partitions is to use special software that helps automate management of multiple partitions. As I began this book, I had laptops with a couple of partitions for Windows 98 on them. Prior to setting up the network, I installed Windows 2000 on the laptops alongside of Windows 98. Windows 2000 easily installed on the machine to coexist with Windows 98. An additional benefit of *dual-booting*, as this process is called, is that Windows 2000 co-exists easily with Windows, more so than NT 4.0 did. It can use FAT, FAT32, or NTFS drives, as I explained earlier.

Rather than go through backups, partition creation, and restores, I use a tool called Partition Magic from Power Quest. This tool manages FAT-based, NTFS, and other file systems and enables you to create, modify, and maintain partitions without all the steps outlined earlier. Note that I always backed up the machine first, regardless. I mean, would you trust any software to protect all your data? After regular backups, I used Partition Magic and created a new partition for Windows 2000 to use. This way, I managed to keep our FAT-based Windows 98 systems while changing Windows 2000 to use its NTFS system. The newest version of Partition Magic works with NTFS as well as with Windows 95 or 98 and DOS-based file systems. After NTFS is installed, you can use NT's Disk management program to manage changes if you prefer. In the following task, you learn how to use Disk management to view your present disk structure.

Task 8.1: Using Disk Management to View Your Current Disk Drives.

Step 1: Description

This task enables you to see all the colors I keep talking about and to find out what types of disk drives are available on your system. The available drives change as you add new disks, with Disk management automatically finding the new drives.

Step 2: Action

1. Log on to your system by using an Administrator account.
2. Choose Start, Programs, Administrative Tools, Computer Management.
3. Click Storage and then double-click on Disk Management to open the dialog box. You then see the current disk setup for your server, as shown in Figure 8.2.

FIGURE 8.2

Using Disk Administrator.

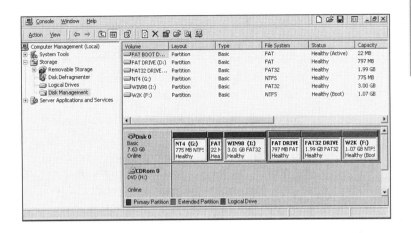

In the example, Windows 2000 is using an NTFS-based hard drive, and there are a number of other partitions. (I am running three systems on this laptop including Windows 2000, NT 4.0, and Windows 98.)

4. Choose Console, Exit or click the Close button on the upper-right corner of the window to close Disk management.

Step 3: Review

By using Disk management, you see how your drives are partitioned and can modify the existing setup. Be careful playing with this tool because serious damage can occur should you execute a command you later regret. You'll examine the use of this tool in more detail later today in the section, "Managing Disk Volumes and Partitions."

Reviewing Windows 2000 Specifics

You reviewed the basics of Windows 2000 earlier in this day, but now you can delve deeper and discover some of the additional file and directory capabilities in Windows 2000.

NEW TERM   Along with partitions, extended partitions, and logical drives, Windows 2000 uses volume sets. A *volume set* is a drive that is combined with other physical drives to make one large volume. (Disk Management displays yet another color—yellow—to indicate a volume set.) As you might recall, logical drives apply to only one physical drive. What happens if you need a huge database that cannot fit on one drive? With volume sets, you can create a volume that uses the space available across a number of physical hard drives. A volume set can combine raw, unformatted free space on one or more physical drives or partitions into one large logical drive. The free space used to create a volume set can be of different sizes and can come from 1 to 32 different physical disks. A volume set can also combine areas on SCSI, ESDI, and IDE drives. This way, you can use your free disk space more efficiently by assigning the needed increments to a volume set. You can enlarge a volume set after it is created, but you can reduce that size only by deleting it and creating a new set.

You might believe that with your data spread over a number of volumes, it is safer. You might think that when one drive fails, the others are still operating. However, this isn't the case with volume sets. Extending volume sets increases your risk because you then have the potential for more drives to fail and affect one set of data. Failure of any one of the drives within a volume set destroys the volume set, leaving you with no data. Follow the earlier advice: back up, back up, back up.

NEW TERM Another concept to learn is mirroring. *Mirroring* is a fairly simple, effective way to provide protection for your data while speeding recovery of any lost data. With mirroring, you have one controller and two drives. Disk mirroring copies all your data onto another identically sized area on another disk drive. The original and copied data combined are called a *mirror set*. If anything happens to your original files, you can use the copies stored on the other drive.

Each drive must use the same data size for mirroring to work. This process isn't very efficient because you need to duplicate all your data exactly, meaning that you need twice the space. It does provide a backup solution with little or no loss of time because each disk drive can perform its own writing. Disk management shows these drives with yet another color—magenta. It's a shame that this book isn't in color so that you could see all the colors rather than shades of gray.

NEW TERM Another similar method of backing up files and data is called *disk duplexing*. This process is essentially identical to mirroring, except that in duplexing, the data is written to drives that run on their own disk controllers. This means you have two controllers and two drives. In this way, the possibility of failures is minimized because each drive has its own controller. In mirroring, each drive runs off the same disk controller, which means this solution is more vulnerable than others. Windows 2000 doesn't differentiate between terms, so the term *mirroring* is used to refer to either duplexing or mirroring.

NEW TERM Now you need to learn about stripe sets. You use stripe sets to increase security of your data and possibly increase your disk's read time, speeding things up. A *stripe set* consists of two or three selected areas of free space on your disks that are combined to store data. Data in a stripe set is stored in certain sizes, called *stripes*. After you

8

format a new stripe set, the system assigns a drive letter and the stripe set acts just like a disk drive. It is, of course, only a logical partitioning of data across a number of different drives to provide additional security and speed.

Each time you write to a stripe drive, Windows 2000 writes your data in chunks across all members of the set. Striping isn't unique to Windows 2000. It is a familiar tool in NetWare and other operating systems. Because the data is written to several drives with the same performance and storage characteristics, operating efficiencies are gained. In other words, your file is spread across the drives and can be combined and manipulated faster because, as one drive is busy, the system uses the other drives. Typically, you use three drives, two to hold the chunks of data and the third to manage disk parity and re-create lost data. Although you can use striping with only two drives, without the parity portion, all parts of the stripe must be working; otherwise, all the data is lost. Parity allows recovery where one drive is lost, hence the more common use of three-drive stripe sets.

The use of disk drives to provide data redundancy is typically referred to as Redundant Array of Inexpensive Disks (RAID). We cover this topic in more detail in Day 16, "Configuring Fault-Tolerance."

Managing Disk Volumes and Partitions

As an administrator, you need to manage the machines in your domain. Your job includes setting up, removing, and maintaining partitions and logical drives. Using the concepts you have learned so far today, look at the steps needed to perform some of these critical tasks.

Task 8.2: Using Disk Management to Create an Extended Partition.

Step 1: Description

This task shows you how to set up an extended partition as a first step to creating logical partitions on your system. Windows 2000 uses the logical drives as if they were disk drives, enabling you to manage your resources more effectively. You use this procedure when you install a new drive or implement an application that you want to segregate onto its own partition.

Step 2: Action

1. Log on to your system by using an Administrator account.
2. Choose Start, Programs, Administrative Tools, Computer Management.
3. Click Storage and then double-click on Disk management to open the dialog box. You then see the current disk setup for your server.

▼   4. Choose the drive you want to use, and right-click the free space indicated for that drive.

      5. Choose Next, and then choose Extended Partition. The resulting dialog box tells you the amount of space available.

      6. Select the size you want for the new drive by using the arrows and follow the wiz-
▲   ard prompts to complete the task.

Step 3: Review

Using the Disk management, you set up new drives easily and quickly. Be careful when using this powerful tool, however. After changes are committed, it's too late to back out.

After creating the extended partition, you need to format it into the logical drives you want. This second step is necessary to finish the task of setting up new partitions for data use.

In the following task, you'll set up a new logical drive using the space provided by the extended partition you just set up.

Task 8.3: Using Disk Administrator to Create Logical Drives.

Step 1: Description

After you set up extended partitions, you can continue by setting up the logical drives. This task enables you to set up a logical drive, picking up where you left off in Task 8.2.

Step 2: Action

      1. Log on to your system by using an Administrator account.

      2. Choose Start, Programs, Administrative Tools, Computer Management.

      3. Click Storage and then double-click on Disk management to open the dialog box. You then see the current disk setup for your server.

      4. Click the area of the newly created extended drive to select it.

      5. Right-click while that area is selected and choose Create Logical Drive.

      6. Select the size you want for the new logical drive and follow the prompts to finish the task.

      7. When you leave Disk management, you see a dialog box, asking you to confirm that you want to save the changes you just made. Click Yes to save. The program then shows you another dialog box, indicating that the changes were successfully
▲   made and suggesting that you update your emergency repair disk.

Step 3: Review

Using Disk Management, you set up your logical drives and make them ready for use. You must format the drives before you can actually store any data on them. You merely right-click on the volume and choose Format.

You need to decide whether to use the NTFS or FAT file system for your new drive as part of the format task. Using NTFS is best unless you have a compelling reason to do otherwise because this system provides faster data access and better security options.

Examining NTFS

You've learned about using NTFS in the preceding lessons and in today's lesson. What is this new system, and how might it have an impact on your decision whether to use NTFS or continue with a FAT-based server?

NTFS is the file system that was designed to be part of the Windows 2000 operating system. Presently, only Windows 2000 Server and Professional and older versions of NT (with Service Pack 4 or later installed) use this file system. Note the following major differences between this system and the FAT-based system (non-Windows 95 or 98) you might be used to working with:

- NTFS uses a file-naming standard of 256 characters. This standard is 248 characters longer than the old DOS system is capable of using. As a result, you can use names that mean something to you when creating a file instead of needing to create cryptic eight-character names.

- With NTFS, you see the filenames in glorious uppercase and lowercase. Having mixed case means only that the filenames look pretty, though, because Windows 2000 doesn't enable you to search by case. This system sure seems more civilized, though.

- NTFS maintains a log of activities so that you can restore the disk in the event of a power failure or other type of interruption.

- NTFS is designed for security and allows access restrictions at the file level. No such facility exists within the DOS FAT system. Both systems allow restrictions at the directory level.

- Within NTFS, you can create and use mirror sets, stripe sets, and volume sets, providing a greater degree of efficiency and availability.

- NTFS enables you to handle huge hard drives. Windows 2000 enables you to use hard drives to a size in the terabyte range. Nice when you have 'em.

- The version of NTFS that comes with Windows 2000 is an updated version of the older NT 4.0 file system. This newer version supports Active Directory and file-level encryption.

Within the NTFS file-naming structure, you can include spaces and separating periods. Additionally, you can use uppercase or lowercase but cannot use certain special characters that are reserved for other functions. Windows 2000 doesn't allow the following characters within filenames: | : < > / \ " or ?.

W2K supports these long filenames and also allows compatibility with the older DOS format by converting any long name into the 8.3 DOS format. It accomplishes this by taking the first six characters of the NTFS filename and adding a tilde (~) and a sequence number.

In addition, during the conversion, W2K ensures that no illegal DOS characters remain, removes all spaces and periods (except the last one because Windows 2000 assumes that it marks the beginning of an extension), and truncates any extension present to three characters. Therefore, a file called `Recipes for Holidays.doc` becomes `recipe~1.doc`. If you start several files with `Recipes for` and use the next characters to differentiate them, W2K leaves you with a list that looks like the following:

recipe~1.doc

recipe~2.doc

recipe~3.doc

recipe~4.doc

As you can see, these filenames aren't descriptive enough to read in a DOS program, so you have to spend time trying to figure out which file contains what data. Consider putting the descriptive identifier in the first six characters if you use many DOS-based programs. You can see how using a naming convention is important so that you can readily understand what is in a particular file as DOS strips away your nice long filename and replaces it with something that leaves you guessing about what is in the file.

You'll discover additional advantages of using NTFS as you move through this day. Directories in NTFS, for example, are automatically sorted and can consist of uppercase and lowercase characters, making them easier to read. Access to files larger than 0.5MB is faster, as is all access to Windows 2000 disk files. Finally, for all Macintosh users, NTFS allows compatibility between Windows 2000 and Mac. Mac users cannot share volumes with Windows 2000 unless it uses NTFS.

One last important feature that NTFS provides is the capability to constantly monitor the disk area for errors. If the file system finds any damaged sectors, it automatically removes the data to a safe place while taking the affected area out of service.

8

Windows 2000 and Floppy Drives

Just when you thought it was safe to go in the water again, Microsoft muddies it up a bit. You cannot format a floppy with NTFS; it just doesn't work. Windows 2000 doesn't offer the option to you if you try and format using Explorer. This is primarily because a floppy doesn't have the room to support the NTFS file system.

Windows 2000 formats floppy disks using the FAT-based file system. I'm not saying that Windows 2000 doesn't work on floppy drives or that you cannot use long filenames. The system places two names on a floppy for each file—the long name that Windows 2000 knows about and a DOS-based 8.3 name. This way, both DOS and you get to see and work with files from floppies.

The process isn't entirely perfect, however. If you use Windows 2000 to update and save changes to these files, the names are maintained. If you use a DOS-based program and change one of these files, good old DOS obliterates the NTFS long name, leaving you with only the 8.3 name. The file itself is fine; only the NTFS name disappears. As long as you have some sensible naming convention, you can quickly ascertain what the file contains and reuse it in W2K.

File Forks

NEW TERM   Mac users are already familiar with the term *file forking*. This capability provides a lot of the ease of use and simplicity Macs are known for. A fork tells Windows 2000 to do something when the file is opened. For example, Microsoft uses the .doc extension for its word processor, Microsoft Word. When a user opens Explorer and double-clicks a filename with this extension, W2K sees the fork and knows to also start up a copy of the word processor. Bingo, bango—the application you need is automatically started merely because you select the file.

W2K uses a form of forking by providing an area that keeps track of file extensions and associates a program with each extension. True file forking would place a pointer with each file regardless of the extension used. Windows 2000 should, in effect, just know that Word creates a particular file even when you save the file without the extension .doc.

Using Windows 2000 Explorer

If you used Windows or Windows NT 4, you surely remember using File Manager to manipulate files and directories. You're used to the click-and-select type of action that File Manager provides and the options and idiosyncrasies of the tool.

In Windows 2000, you still use Windows Explorer. If you already use Windows 95 or 98, little of this section will be new to you, so you might feel comfortable skipping it and moving on to the next section.

You find Windows 2000 Explorer by choosing Start, Programs, Accessories, Windows Explorer. I think Microsoft changed the location just to confuse things. Choosing this menu item opens a new window for you, like the one shown in Figure 8.3. As with other programs, you can open as many Explorer windows as your system resources allow.

FIGURE 8.3

The Explorer window.

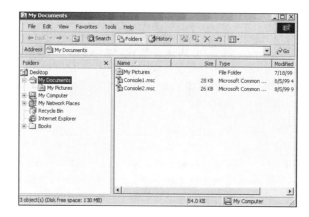

Explorer opens, showing a list of your hard drives and floppies, and includes any network components you have.

Actually, I already mentioned one of Windows 2000 Explorer's main benefits. It shows all the drive connections. In a networked world, seeing these connections is nice. Rather than merely being content to show you your C: and D: drives, Windows 2000 Explorer shows you all of them, right up to its limit of 24.

Explorer is Windows 98's File Manager. Take a quick tour around the menus. Windows 2000 Explorer starts with a File menu. No surprise here. Inside the File drop-down menu are a number of options, including Open With, New, Send To, Delete, and Properties. If you don't see these options, your cursor is selecting a folder name from the left side of the window. Explorer offers fewer options there. (Move the cursor to the right-hand selection box and select any folder.) If you choose File, New, you see a submenu providing several additional options.

In Windows 2000, directories are called *folders*, just as in Windows 95/98. Note that Folder is the first option on this submenu. If you choose Folder, a new entry is placed in the currently selected folder. That entry, called New File Folder, appears with a blue color over it and the cursor blinking there as if it expects you to do something. Of course, you do exactly that—something. If you press the Enter key (Don't! Oh, too late. Read until the end of the paragraph before attempting all these commands, okay?), Explorer creates the file folder called New Folder, unless one already exists. If one does already exist, Windows 2000 Explorer creates another folder called New Folder(2). You can go on for some time until you understand that perhaps you can find another way of managing these folders so that you don't end up with hundreds of folders named New Folder(x).

Before pressing Enter (go back to the start and try again if you pressed Enter earlier), press the Backspace key to remove the words New Folder. Now you can type the name you want to use. Just enter the characters you want, and when you're ready, press Enter. Remember that these names can be really long, so enter the name you want here to make the folder easily identifiable. You might call the folder My First Test of Explorer Folder Creation. Notice that Windows 2000 maintains all the capital letters exactly as you type them.

Explorer doesn't show you the entire name you just typed. What's wrong? Did you miss something? Well, not really. The default setup allows a certain size and uses icons to represent folders. You can modify this size. First, you can size all the sections (Name, Size, Type, Modified, and Attributes) by moving the cursor directly over the connecting lines and dragging the boxes until they are the sizes you want. When you're in the correct place, Windows 2000 places an X-like cursor between the Name and Size separators. You can also place your cursor between the separators and double-click. This action sets the size to the largest name currently onscreen.

Another aspect of Explorer is the Send To option on the File drop-down menu. If you choose Send To, you see the following three options:

- 3 1/2 Floppy (A)
- Desktop (create shortcut)
- Mail Recipient
- My Documents

This is shown in Figure 8.4.

The first option is easily understood. Choosing it sends the file or folder you selected earlier directly to the floppy drive. This feature is one of the quick and easy tools Explorer offers.

The second option will place a pointer on your desktop that allows you to double-click on it to take you directly to the document.

If you install a mail program on Windows 2000, you see the icon called Mail Recipient in the menu. (Don't worry if it's not there; this just means you don't use a recognized mail program.) This icon enables you to send the file to a mail program such as Microsoft Outlook.

FIGURE 8.4

The Explorer Send To window.

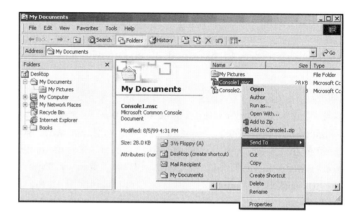

Using My Documents will place the document you are selecting into that folder. It's a quick method of moving files from one location to your main library.

Additional options in the File menu offer you the chance to set up sharing and to delete and rename files. You can also create a shortcut to a file and place it on your desktop. Because Windows 2000 uses forks, when you double-click the desktop shortcut your file opens, along with the application that created the file. Using shortcuts is a nice method of quickly accessing something you're working on. Place a shortcut to the policy and standard document you're creating, for example, and you can get to it each day by simply double-clicking.

Task 8.4: Using Explorer to Create a New Folder.

Step 1: Description

Explorer enables you to add directories (called *folders*) in your system quickly and easily. After adding a new folder, you can use Explorer to copy or move files into this folder. In this manner, you can organize your desktop and make it more efficient.

Step 2: Action

1. Log on to your system by using your user account.

2. Choose Start, Programs, Accessories, Windows Explorer.

3. To see all your drives, double-click on the folder called My Computer. Choose your main drive icon, and click once to highlight the drive, typically the C: drive. Look for the little icon that indicates a disk drive and has C: beside it.

4. Choose File, New, Folder. A new folder named New Folder is highlighted under the main drive icon on the right side of the window. The cursor is already in place for you to type in a folder name.

8

5. Type the words **My New Folder for Windows 2000 Testing** and press Enter. You don't need to erase the initial string called New Folder because it is already highlighted and therefore is overtyped. Explorer now shows a folder called My New Folder for Windows 2000 Testing, complete with upper- and lowercase letters. You have created a new folder.

6. After you complete step 5, double-click the folder to open it. Naturally, the folder is empty because it is new. Now move and copy some files from other parts of the system into this folder.

7. Use your cursor to move the scrollbar until you see the folder called winnt. (If you installed Windows 2000 in another directory, use that name instead.) This time, place the cursor on the small box with a plus sign next to the folder called winnt. Don't click elsewhere in the window. Click once on that small box, and you see the Windows 2000 folder open, but you remain with the right window open to the new folder you created in step 5.

    The winnt folder contains a number of subdirectories or folders within it. Double-click the winnt folder now to see all the files that are in the folder.

8. Find and select a file by right-clicking on it once.

9. Move the cursor to the window called All Folders on the left and, using the scrollbar, find your new folder. It's the one called My New Folder for Windows 2000 Testing. Don't select the folder. Move the cursor back over the file you selected. Without letting go of the mouse button, hold the Ctrl key, click on the selected file, and drag it over to the new folder. By using the Ctrl key, you copy the file instead of moving it. Alternatively, you can right-click and drag to copy and move files to new folders.

10. Click the new folder, and you see a copy of the file inside.

11. Now that you are finished creating and copying files in Explorer, remove the new folder (no sense leaving test material lying around the server is there?) by clicking once on the My New Folder for Windows 2000 Testing folder. Then press the Delete key. Windows 2000 asks you to verify that you want to remove this folder. Reply Yes to complete the task.

Note

Don't forget that Windows 2000 moves deleted items to the Recycle Bin, and you need to empty the bin occasionally if you want to free up additional space on your hard drive. By default, Windows 2000 provides for 10% of the space on your drive, and this amount becomes significant on larger drives.

Note

> Note that if you perform a step and want to undo it, click on Edit and right beneath that will be a command that allows you to undo the last transaction you took. For example, if you delete a file, the Edit menu will have an Undo Delete line beneath it.

▲

Step 3: Review

Using Explorer, you have created a file folder, manipulated data by using drag and drop, and performed general file and directory tasks. Explorer is easy to use after you're used to the concept.

Explorer Hints and Tricks

You now know how to manipulate your files by using Explorer. But a number of neat tricks provide you with even more ease of use and speed.

- When you're in a folder, use the Backspace key to move up the hierarchy. Explorer moves you up to the next higher folder. If you're in the winnt\forms\Configs folder, for example, using the Backspace key takes you back to winnt\forms. Use it again, and you're placed in the \winnt directory. Use it one more place and you're back up at the C: drive icon.

- You can obtain a quick view of a file by selecting the file, right-clicking it, and choosing Quick View from the menu. This method works only with certain files that are registered to the program, and it doesn't always view the file correctly. For other files, you must use the Open option.

- You can set options to either hide or show filename extensions. To do so, choose View, Options, and then select the Hide File Extensions for Known File Types check box to either hide the extensions or show them. In this same dialog box, you can set other options such as displaying the full path or using colors to differentiate compressed files.

- You can check the disk volume for errors by using Explorer. Right-click the volume you want to check, and choose Properties, Tools. Select Check Now to start the error checking. You can also back up files from this dialog box by selecting the Backup Now option and following the directions.

- Sort the files within an Explorer window when you're in Detail view by clicking the column heading. To sort in reverse order, click once more. You can sort files by size and by type by using this method and selecting either the Size or Type heading.

8

- Quickly copy files to the Briefcase or drive A: by selecting the file, right-clicking, and then selecting the Send To option.
- To copy a file when using drag and drop, also use the Ctrl key. Press Ctrl+Shift while dragging a file to create a shortcut. Again, you can right-click and drag to copy and move a file.
- You can bypass the automatic starting of CD-ROMs by pressing the Shift key as you insert the CD-ROM in your machine. This capability is handy when you want to reference your Windows 2000 installations CD-ROM without having the automatic installation program start.
- Windows 2000, like Windows 98, places deleted files into the Recycle Bin in case you change your mind and want to recover them. If you're sure that a file can be deleted and don't want to have it take up disk space, press Shift+Del while selecting the file. Windows 2000 deletes the file completely and doesn't keep a copy in the Recycle Bin.
- To move quickly between frames in Explorer, press the F6 key. Press the F5 key to refresh Explorer after manipulating a bunch of files.
- Use the right and left arrows when selecting folders to expand or collapse the folders quickly.

Explorer offers a multitude of shortcuts, hints, and techniques. I offer these more common ones to help speed up your manipulation of files and directories.

Managing Windows 2000 Server File and Directory Access Rights

So far in this day, you have learned about the file systems that Windows 2000 uses, and about using Disk Administrator and other Windows 2000 tools. You have also learned all about different types of file mechanisms to provide for duplicate copies of your important data and how to use the new Explorer program rather than the old File Manager program.

In the following sections, you'll learn about setting access controls over files and directories to control who can access what within W2K.

As you have learned, Windows 2000 Server allows use of FAT and NTFS. You get security with NTFS, but not with FAT. Security is one really sound reason to use NTFS, unless some extenuating circumstances make this impossible. For example, one of our clients runs a mission-critical application that relies on a FAT-based file system. It's a legacy system the client has not had time to convert, so this restricts the client's use of NTFS on the Windows 2000 Server network.

Note

Windows 2000 supports two primary files systems: the older FAT file system, and its own file system, NTFS. You need to be aware that in Windows 2000 Server, native support for the OS/2 file system called *HPFS* (*High Performance File System*) was dropped. If you are upgrading from NT 3.51 to Windows 2000, support continues to be available with the 3.51 drivers.

To control access to files in Windows 2000, you use the concept of either *shares* or *file and directory permissions*. You can use both concepts, although this method can be a little confusing. They are actually three separate levels of control. Share-level permissions provide network-level access control over directories. Directory-level controls using NTFS provide a different type of control, and file-level controls are the most granular level of the three types of control. To help separate fact from fiction, I'll start with the controls available to FAT file systems and move on to NTFS controls.

Windows 2000 Share-Level Control Using FAT-Based Files

Let's review the earlier comments about FAT system file security. You read that file and directory permissions are available only with NTFS. Does this mean that there is no control over who accesses files on a FAT-based server? For all intents and purposes, that is exactly what I mean. The level of control available to you is minimal and not nearly as extensive as the control available to NTFS users.

One of the missions of W2K is to secure desktop files as effectively as the server files. You can set up Windows 2000 Professional to allow multiple people to sign on and use the desktop machine (at different times, of course) but not allow access to any data belonging to one of the other authorized users. But this setup is for NTFS. What do you do for FAT-based controls?

Access to files on a server typically happens only when those directories are *shared*. This designation tells the server that users from the network might need to use or manipulate the shared directories. Note that I say *directories* and not *files*. This is because sharing is performed only at a directory level, not at the file level. When a directory is shared, users have access to all the files in that directory.

By default, only those user accounts in the Administrator and Server Operators group can set up shares in Windows 2000 Server. You can set up sharing in Windows 2000 Server in various ways:

- By using the command prompt
- Through the My Computer icon
- By using Microsoft Explorer

The command prompt provides access for the "command-line geeks," the old DOS and UNIX types who just love that command line and typically eschew GUI interfaces as a matter of principle. Finally, the more common method is to use Explorer or My Computer. Windows 2000 has taken sharing a step further with its Offline access option.

Note   Windows 2000 introduces a new concept to sharing called Offline that places a copy of the share into a cache on the user's machine so they are available even when the server is offline.

This Offline concept allows an administrator to set up caching options in addition to directory level security for each share the administrator creates. You can see this in Figure 8.5.

FIGURE 8.5

The New Offline Sharing option.

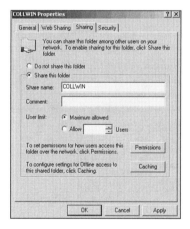

To make Shared files available offline, the option called Offline Files stores a version of them on your computer in a place called a cache. Your computer can access this cache regardless of whether it is connected to the network. An administrator has three caching options to choose from when setting up a share:

- Manual Caching for Documents
- Automatic Caching for Documents
- Automatic Caching for Programs

Manual Caching for Documents provides offline access to only those files that the person who is using the share specifically (or manually) identifies. This option is ideal for a share that contains files being accessed and modified by a number of different people. This is therefore the default option when you set up a share for offline use.

Automatic Caching for Documents makes every file a person opens in your share available to them offline. Note that this doesn't make every file available to them offline, only those files they open. If the person doesn't open a file, it won't be available to them offline.

Automatic Caching for Programs provides offline access to shares containing files that aren't changed by the user. This option is ideal for making files available offline that are only read, referenced, or run, but that aren't changed or modified by the user. This option helps reduce network traffic because the offline files are opened on the person's machine once they are cached, and as such don't generate any further network activity. You must be sure to restrict permissions on the files contained in these shares to *read-only* access.

It remains to be seen how widely this new option will be used as it does appear to offer a significant amount of network traffic savings; however, each workstation will need to monitor the amount of caching space provided. The default cache size is set to 10% of the available space on the disk drive. This can be altered using the Offline Files tab of Folder Options. The option is found by opening Explorer, selecting Tools and then Folder Options. You see this in Figure 8.6.

FIGURE 8.6

Setting the New Offline Sharing option.

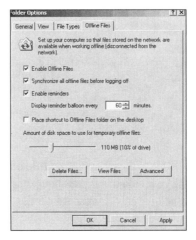

By clicking on Enable Offline Files on your machine, you set it up to begin caching. The option is cleared on Windows 2000 Server but is automatically set on Windows 2000 Professional. After the option is set, you then have to choose the shares you want synchronized. This enables the other options shown in Figure 8.6. They allow you to automatically perform a full synchronization of the folders when you log off, obtain a warning notice that you are using offline folders, and enable you to place a shortcut to the offline files on your desktop. You are also able to specify the amount of hard drive space used by the offline files.

The Delete Files option allows you to delete the offline files in your computer as well as those that are in the share. To do this of course, you must have the necessary access rights. Be careful using the command; it doesn't offer an "are you sure" warning. To view all your offline files, click on the View Files button.

Finally, the Advanced option allows you to specify what you want to happen if your network connection is lost. You can begin working offline or you can specify that you never use the offline files without the network share being available.

By clicking on the Add button, you can set up individual computers to respond differently from the default. For example, you want to continue working offline as a general default on most computers but you don't want to work offline whenever you are using files from one particular computer. By adding this computer's name to the exception list and selecting the Never Allow My Computer to Go Offline option, you will always need to access that machine to work on your files as they will never be available offline.

You can also see how much space the cache is currently using by going to the Explorer, Tools, Folder Options, Offline Files, View Files and clicking Properties on the File menu. (You can also just open the folder by clicking on it on the main folder menu when you open Explorer as you see in Figure 8.7.)

FIGURE 8.7

To view Offline Folders, click on the Offline Files Folder.

This is a new and fairly exciting option for Windows 2000 networks. It will remain to be seen how it is used in organizations. Offline sharing is really neat, but you typically set up shares first so this next task shows you how to do that on your system.

In the following task I show you how to create a share using Microsoft Explorer.

Task 8.5: Using Explorer to Set Up Shares.

Step 1: Description

This task enables you to set up share permissions by using Microsoft Explorer. Because you often use Explorer to manage the files within Windows 2000 Server, this is the fastest way to set up shares.

Step 2: Action

1. Log on to your system by using an Administrator account.

2. Go to Start, Programs, Accessories, Windows Explorer.

3. Select the folder you want to share and then right-click on the folder to see the drop-down menu.

4. Select the Sharing option. Windows 2000 Server shows you the Properties window with Sharing options. The window defaults to Not Shared. (You can get here by clicking on the Properties page also if you like and then selecting Sharing.)

5. Click the Shared As button and fill in the details as needed to set up a share. For example, type the new share name you want users to see, and type a description of the files in the share. Set up the maximum number of users as needed. Windows defaults to a share name that is the same as the directory you are setting up to share, but you can change this to anything you like.

6. Click the Permissions button. You then see the Permissions dialog box. Add and remove access as needed by using the Add and Remove buttons. These allow you to select users and the type of access you want them to have. Double-click on the groups you want, and select the type of access. Click OK. Return to this screen a few times as needed to add any number of groups and access levels.

7. Click OK to complete the sharing task.

Step 3: Review

By using Explorer to set up shares, you managed the task quickly, easily, and without the need to open a special program. You can set up shares for any directory by using this technique.

Hidden Shares

W2K allows you to set up shares and hide them so that casual browsers cannot find them. You do this by adding a $ character to the end of the share name. These shares are then not displayed. The purpose of this facility is to allow administrators to hide certain shares to minimize the clutter when users browse the server.

Some people on the Internet NTSEC newsgroup appear to think this is a security solution—that you hide sensitive shares (and user accounts) so that attackers cannot find them. There are two problems with this idea:

- The shares are easily seen through the Net program.
- You can still access the shares when you know their names.

It is still a good idea to hide shares to avoid clutter, but don't depend on security through obscurity. It's a false sense of security.

Microsoft uses the hidden share concept for some shares during the installation process. These automatically created shares in Windows 2000 Server include

- **ADMIN$**—The directory that contains the Windows 2000 programs.
- **IPC$**—A resource that is essential for communication between programs. It is used during remote administration of a computer and when viewing a computer's shared resources.
- **NETLOGON$**—Microsoft's administrative shares or logon script shares that are hidden on domain controllers.
- **C$ D$**—All hard drive partitions and CD-ROM drives are automatically shared at the root.

Microsoft allows only administrators to access these shares; if you remove or modify them, Windows 2000 automatically rebuilds them the next time you load the system.

Figure 8.8 shows an example of using the NET SHARE command.

FIGURE 8.8

Showing hidden shares by using NET SHARE.

How Sharing Works with File and Directory Permissions

In the preceding section, I discussed shares and how you use and hide them. You need to also understand how these shares interact with file and directory permissions.

You'll learn all about the file and directory permissions later in the lesson, but for now you need to understand how the two types of controls interact. By default, sharing sets up the Everyone group for full control over the selected directory. Does this mean that you obtain this access when using an NTFS partition?

Maybe. Good answer, isn't it? It's just like a consultant to never be specific. Seriously, however, the answer lies in which set of controls overrides the other. These are the basic rules:

- Sharing never allows more than file and directory permissions permit.
- Sharing can reduce the level of access provided by file and directory permissions.

Remember that shares apply only to user accounts signing on over the network. So they are somewhat limited. If you allow the default share access on a directory (full control) and set file and directory permissions that are less restrictive (read-only), the user has read access and can do no more. If you attempt to reduce a user's access by setting up a share with read-only access and then try to provide a new user with full control through file and directory permissions, the user has only read access.

 Caution   Share restrictions apply even to members of the Administrator group. If you restrict access to a directory to read-only, you won't be able to add or remove any files, even when you are an administrator.

Finally, Windows 2000 domain controllers create the NETLOGON share with the default access. You should change this share to remove the Everyone group and apply share permissions to Domain Users with read-only access. Next, implement NTFS file restrictions to each user's logon script so that users only see their scripts.

Setting Up Shares Remotely

The previously described technique works fine when you are attached to the domain that has the folders you want to share. But what if you are in California and the domain on which you want to set up a share is in Florida? When you aren't physically attached, you cannot use Explorer or My Computer to set up shares.

In this case, you need to use Active Directory users and Computers. This program allows you to set up shares in the same manner as with Explorer. To use Active Directory users and Computers, you need to be sitting at a controller.

Task 8.6: Using Active Directory Users and Computers to Set Up Sharing.

TASK

▼ **Step 1: Description**

This task allows you to set up shares remotely. It is handy for administrators who manage large networks that cross buildings, cities, or states. Explorer and Computer Management are available only for local access, so Active Directory Users and Computers is necessary when you don't want to physically visit each place where you have domains running. Of course, don't tell the boss that you can manage the domains remotely when one of your sites is Hawaii! It would be a shame to miss out on a trip.

Step 2: Action

1. Log on to your system by using an Administrator account.

2. Choose Start, Programs, Administrative Tools, Active Directory Users and Computers.

3. Select the root object and select Computers. You can see this in Figure 8.9.

FIGURE 8.9

Accessing a remote computer.

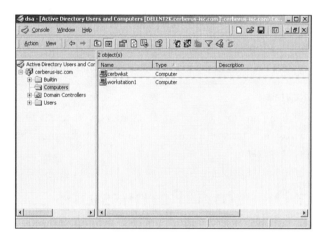

4. Click on the machine that you want to add shares to and right-click to see a menu. Select Manage. A Computer Management dialog box will appear. Click on the field called System Tools to see a number of options including Shared Folders on that machine. You see this in Figure 8.10.

5. Right-click on the Shares menu. In the dialog box that opens select New Share. This opens the Create Shared Folder Wizard. Select a folder from the list and click on Next.

▼

Figure 8.10

*Viewing Shared
Folders on a remote
machine.*

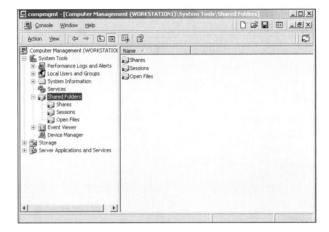

6. Follow the prompts to complete sharing of a selected directory. Choose a share name, add a comment where appropriate, and set the number of users in the Limit Users box. After you fill in the share information, the Permissions button is enabled, letting you set up the specific permissions you want.

7. Complete the task in the manner you need, and then click OK to finish.

Step 3: Review

By using Active Directory Users and Computers, you saw how easy it is to manage domains across the street or across the country. Use this program whenever you can't use the Explorer program.

File and Directory Permissions

If you aren't running a server with an NTFS partition, this section is of little use to you. Feel free to skip it and return to it later, after you have set up an NTFS partition.

One of the main strengths of NTFS is its capability to provide access-level restrictions down to the file level. What does this mean? Will you set up all your users to have individual file-level access so that they are tightly controlled and the security and audit folks are happy?

Not really, although it is good to have this level of control. It's important to remember that you need to administer access daily, and restrictive levels of control can cause a lot of work. So how do you mitigate this seeming difference? You need to use the concept of job-function or group-level control.

Job-function control suggests that you decide the needs of a particular group of users and then set up file and directory access for them by using the group function of Windows 2000 Server. In this manner, when you add a user to the specific group, the user automatically obtains all the file access that is appropriate for that user's job.

File- and directory-level access control applies to both Windows 2000 Server and Windows 2000 Workstation, providing a level of control over data previously unavailable.

 Note   This has been said before, but it's important enough to reiterate. File- and directory-level controls are available only on NTFS partitions.

Calculating Permissions

Windows 2000 changes how files and directories are protected. There are several rules for determining what access rights someone has to an object, whether a file or a directory. These rules include

- Moved or copied files and directories
- The number of individual permissions
- Deny and allow permissions
- Inheritance of permissions
- Shared or standard folder permissions

I talked about moving and copying files and directories earlier and what effect that has on assigned permissions. When a user has more than one access entry for a file or directory, Windows will calculate the actual access based upon the total accesses provided. For example, if you assign a user Read access to her user account and also provide Write access to a group the user belongs to, Windows will give the user both Read and Write access.

The rule above applies as long as there is no specific rule given that denies access. When you specify that a user is denied access to a file or directory, then regardless of what other rules the user has, she won't be given access. No Access overrides all other rules. For example, give a user account Full Control to a directory. Now give a group that that user account* belongs to No Access to that same directory. The user will no longer have any access. In addition, rules given at the file level override those provided at the directory level. You don't need directory level access to have access to a file, although the user will need to specify the location exactly when accessing it.

Finally, inheritance has changed in Windows 2000. By default, permissions that are assigned to a directory are inherited by the files below it. (Although you can override this by specifying file permissions directly, remember what I told you earlier about using directory level access controls for better efficiency.) You can block inheritance by setting these more specific controls on files or subdirectories. You can also use the options provided when assigning access to remove or allow inheritance. When you assign access to a directory you see the field called Allow Inheritable Permissions From Parent to Propagate to This Object. You can choose to allow or deny this by clicking on the check box shown.

Finally, when you use Sharing, the most restrictive permissions apply. For example, if you only assign Read access to a Share and allow Modify on the directory it points to, users accessing the directory through the share will only have Read access.

The Encrypting File System

This is a new option that Windows 2000 offers and it provides an additional degree of security over your machine's hard drive if it is ever lost or stolen.

The Encrypting File System (EFS) is new to Windows 2000. It offers the ability to implement encryption on all the files on your NTFS drive. That's the good news. The bad news is that it represents a fairly significant investment in time and resources to implement as it relies on some form of Public Key Infrastructure (PKI) and that is still a new area for most companies.

When in use, EFS works in the background, hidden from the view of the user. Thank goodness. Can you imagine having to explain encryption to the average user? I.T. staff tend to forget that users often could care less about all this technical stuff; they just use the machine to do their job, whether that is accounting or sales.

When you implement encryption the user sees no difference between an encrypted file and a non-encrypted file. Windows manages all files for them, opening, decrypting, or encrypting as needed.

When used, EFS automatically generates a public-key pair for file encryption for a user, if one doesn't exist. File encryption and decryption is supported on a per-file or directory basis. All files (and subdirectories) created in a directory marked for encryption are automatically encrypted. Each file has a unique encryption key that makes it safe to rename it without losing the encryption. If you rename a file from an encrypted directory to an unencrypted directory on the same volume, it remains encrypted.

The user uses encryption and decryption services from within Windows Explorer. In addition, command line tools and administrative interfaces are also provided for advanced users. Because the file is actually encrypted twice, once by the user and another time by the system, an administrator can access an encrypted file using a recovery agent should a user leave the firm or accidentally destroy his encryption key.

Once implemented, a user can decide what action to take by accessing a File and Folder Encryption menu in Explorer. This provides them the ability to use the following options:

- **Encryption**—Encrypts the currently selected file. If the current selection is a directory, the user can encrypt all files (and subdirectories) in the directory and mark the directory as encrypted.
- **Decryption**—This option is the reverse of encryption. It allows the user to decrypt the currently selected file. If the selection is a directory, it lets users decrypt all files in the directory and resets the directory as unencrypted.
- **Configuration**—Users can generate, export, import, and manage public keys used for EFS-based file encryption. Configuration is integrated with the rest of the user security settings. This feature is intended for advanced users who want to manage their own keys. Typically, users don't have to do any configuration. EFS automatically generates keys for the user who doesn't have one configured for file encryption use.

Users can also use a command line interface to manipulate their files as well using the command called `cipher`. Open a command prompt window and type **cipher /?** to see a list of available commands.

One important thing to note is that EFS isn't designed for sharing encrypted files between different people. It is designed to protect your files against unauthorized access. To open an encrypted file you must be the person who encrypted it or be an administrator with recovery rights. You also cannot encrypt a file that is Read Only, is compressed, or is a system file.

Using encryption sounds like a great idea but it is likely too much for us to delve into any deeper in this book. You can find out some additional aspects on Day 9, "Managing the File Server."

File Ownership

Adding to the complexity of setting permissions and using shares to control access, Windows 2000 also assigns ownership of a file to the account that creates the file. By default, ownership is granted to the creator of the file, and it cannot be given away. It can be taken away, however, and there is a distinction between the two terms.

Why do I care so much about file ownership? Because the act of creating a file provides the creator with the ability to do anything to the file; even delete it. The creator has full control. In an NTFS system, full control means the ability to read, modify, and delete the file, as well as change the access to grant someone else full control rights. If this file is a production, mission-critical file, ensuring that these rights are properly handled is crucial. You don't want the owner assigning an unauthorized person access to the file.

What the owner (or anyone else for that matter, even the administrator) cannot do is give away ownership of the file to someone. All the owner can do is allow another person full control and let her take ownership by using the permissions she has been granted. This process can quickly reduce the level of control within a Windows 2000 environment.

Let's recap. If you create a new file, you own it and gain full control access to the file. If you copy a file, you become the owner of the copy, with the same rights. As the file owner, you can remove everyone's ability—even administrators—to access the file. Needless to say, it would be pretty easy to create havoc when you are the owner of critical files. Ensuring that files are appropriately owned and managed is one of the keys to effective security with Windows 2000 Server.

How do you bypass someone trying to cause difficulty in this manner? The administrator can grant someone full control access to the file, and then that person can take ownership.

Task 8.7: Taking Ownership of a File.

Step 1: Description

In this task, you'll learn how to take ownership of a file. Note that the current owner or an administrator must grant you full control access in order for you to take ownership. You might do this when a file is created for testing purposes, and then when it becomes a production file, ownership will be changed to reflect that status.

Step 2: Action

1. Log on to your system by using an Administrator account.
2. Choose Start, Programs, Accessories, Windows Explorer. Open the directory the file resides in.
3. Select the file you want to reassign by left-clicking once on the filename.
4. Right-click on the file to see the drop-down menu.
5. Select Properties.
6. Select the Security frame and then Advanced to see three options:
    - Permissions
    - Auditing
    - Owners

7. Select Permissions. Grant the user account that needs ownership full control over the file by using the Add button. Click OK when finished.

8. Log off, and then log back on with the user account that needs to take over the file ownership.

9. Open Explorer and find the file. Select it, and then left-click and select Properties. Select Security and then Advanced. Remember that this tab only shows when you are accessing a file on an NTFS partition.

10. Select the Owners tab.

11. You see a dialog box with your user account listed. Select your account to take ownership.

12. Log off. This user account now owns the file.

Step 3: Review

By using a simple process, you can take control and change ownership of a file. Use this process any time ownership of a file is in question or needs to be changed.

Having ownership of a file doesn't mean that you have access to the data within the file. Ownership implies the ability to change the permissions on the file, not to access it. Of course, as owner, you can set up permissions so that you do have access, but the reverse is also true—you can set up permissions that deny your account access.

Permissions

You set file or directory permissions by selecting either a file or a directory in Windows Explorer and then selecting Properties, Security. You see a dialog similar to the one shown in Figure 8.11. You'll notice it isn't the same as the dialog box you used to get in Windows NT 4.0.

FIGURE 8.11

The Permissions dialog box.

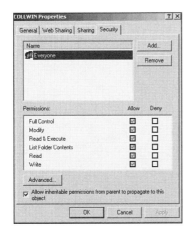

What are the permissions you can use within an NTFS partition? You can see a larger list by selecting Properties, Security, Add, Advanced, View/Edit. You'll see a table listing the options available similar to that shown in Figure 8.12.

FIGURE 8.12

The Directory Permissions dialog box.

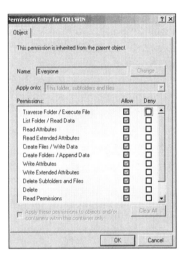

Table 8.1 sets out the various types of security available on each file or directory. Note that when you set permissions on a directory, you are asked whether those permissions should also apply to the files within the directory. I'll talk more about this topic later. You can select multiple files when setting permissions and multiple group and user accounts. The permissions you select are then applied to the collection of groups, users, and files.

You can set permissions on files and directories using default groups of permissions. For example, by telling Windows that you want someone to have Modify access, you actually provide the person with Read, Write, Execute, and Delete. For files, these are the main groupings:

- Full Control
- Modify
- Read & Execute
- Read
- Write

In a directory the groups consist of

- Full Control
- Modify

- Read & Execute
- Read
- Write
- List Folder Contents

These groups derive from a number of special permissions that you can assign individually if you like. Table 8.1 shows the types of permissions available for use within Windows 2000 Server.

TABLE 8.1 Windows 2000 Directory Permissions*

Permissions	Grouping					
	Full Control	Modify	Read & Execute	Read	List Folder	Write
Change Permission	A					
Create Files/Write	A	A				A
Create Folders/ Append Data	A	A				A
List Folder/Display Data	A	A	A	A	A	
Delete	A	A				
Delete Subfolders/ and Files	A					
Read Attributes	A	A	A	A	A	
Read Extended Attributes	A	A	A	A	A	
Read Permissions	A	A	A	A	A	A
Take Ownership	A					
Traverse Folder/ Execute Files	A	A	A		A	
Write Attributes	A	A				A
Write Extended Attributes	A	A				A

*Actions indicated apply to regular permissions, not special, where both are available.
A = Allowed
blank = Not applicable

One last thing. For POSIX compliance, there is a hidden permission called DELETE_ CHILD that allows someone with full control of a directory to also delete any file in the directory, regardless of file settings. This often confuses new administrators who think they have secured file deletion from those with directory access. This permission is added only with full control and can be eliminated by applying RWXDPO directory permissions instead.

During your foray into Windows 2000, you'll come across some abbreviations. The following list shows the current abbreviations in use for each of the permissions used:

No access

Execute (X)

Read (R) *

Write (W)

Delete (D)

Change (RWXD) *

Change permissions (P)

Take ownership (O)

Full control (All) *

You can select and use each of these permissions on your files as needed for excellent security and control. There are some things you should remember when granting access using these permissions. When you grant a user read access from the primary list, the user automatically obtains execute access. You need to use special access—read when you don't want the user to execute a program that might be contained in the folder you are granting this access to. Additionally, by granting the user execute only in the program, you can allow a user to run a program but not see what is in it. Be sure to test the access first to ensure that the program will run normally with only this permission set; some programs require additional permissions.

Read access allows you to see the files displayed in the directory, display the directory's attributes, and display the directory's owner and permissions. Write allows you to add files and subdirectories, as well as change the attributes and display them.

Table 8.2 shows how each permission applies to some typical actions on files.

TABLE 8.2 Actions of Permissions on Files*

Permissions	Grouping				
	Full Control	Modify	Read & Execute	Read	Write
Change Permission	A				
Create Files/Write	A	A			A
Create Folders/ Append Data	A	A			A
List Folder/Display Data	A	A	A	A	
Delete	A	A			
Delete Subfolders/ and Files	A				
Read Attributes	A	A	A	A	
Read Extended Attributes	A	A	A	A	
Read Permissions	A	A	A	A	A
Take Ownership	A				
Traverse Folder/ Execute Files	A	A	A		
Write Attributes	A	A			A
Write Extended Attributes	A	A			A

Actions indicated apply to regular permissions, not special, where both are available.
A = Allowed
blank = Not applicable

You need to consider a few additional items when dealing with directories in Windows 2000. You select and update permissions just as you do for files, except that instead of selecting the file and its properties, you select a directory (folder) and its properties.

There are a couple of differences between files and directories. When you select a directory, two additional dialog options are shown near the bottom of the main window. The first option allows rights from the parent directory to flow down into the directory you are viewing. By default in Windows 2000, access rights are inherited down the tree structure. Turning this off by clicking on it allows you to set a different level of control over this directory. To replace permissions on the files and subdirectories in the directory you are viewing, choose Replace Permissions on All Child Folders and Enable Propagation of Inheritable Permissions. You can see this in Figure 8.13.

FIGURE 8.13

The Inherit Access fields.

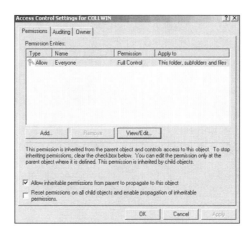

As you can see, W2K offers a wealth of options, and you can quickly get into trouble when you randomly assign permissions without using some forethought. With Windows 2000 file and directory security, you can gain a level of fine detail in security and control that was previously unavailable. Now you can create the environment that best suits your organization's needs for integrity and control.

Windows 2000 file and directory security works on the principle of no permission, no access. In other words, it isn't necessary to set permissions to deny access for user accounts because Windows 2000 treats any access that isn't defined as equivalent to no access.

You do need to look at default permissions, however, when organizing the security of your machine. The Everyone group is especially important because it offers the opportunity for ease of use yet can become a security risk. For example, when creating a new partition and formatting it for NTFS, W2K issues a default permission of Everyone–full control for file access. This might not be appropriate, and you should change the default to something more appropriate for your needs. You might decide to do this and modify the permissions for directories as they are created; but on the other hand, you might be setting up a drive for production use, and letting everyone have access isn't necessary.

Some administrators put the general access that they believe all users should have into the Everyone group. This makes life easy yet becomes a problem when inappropriately used because it becomes cluttered with access permissions. Over time, these permissions tend to become inappropriate, as access needs change. Set up a well-defined architecture that spells out what and where access should be applied, and put a reporting and auditing mechanism in place to verify that architecture. I'll talk more about auditing on Day 17, "Security Monitoring and Audit Trails."

Task 8.8: Assigning Directory Permissions.

Step 1: Description

In this task, you'll see how to restrict access to a directory. You can use this task to manage file-level control within your organization by changing the necessary parameters of user accounts, permissions, and files as needed. You should generally always set controls at the directory level and not the file level as this is far more efficient.

Step 2: Action

1. Log on to your system by using an Administrator account.

2. Go to Start, Programs, Accessories, Windows Explorer.

3. Select the directory you want to reassign by left-clicking once on the directory name. If you hold the Shift key while dragging the cursor over a list of directories, you can select a group of them.

4. Right-click to see the drop-down menu.

5. Select Properties.

6. Select the Security frame.

7. If some groups are already showing (the Everyone group is probably showing), select those groups first and click the Remove button. This action clears all unneeded users from the list. Be careful not to leave the list blank or no one will have access. Click the Add button to add new groups or user accounts for which you want to provide access from the list provided, and double-click to select the one(s) you want. Click OK. Now set the desired access by clicking on Read, Write, and so on.

8. Click OK to complete the task.

Step 3: Review

By using Explorer, you set up permissions over directories, as you need them. You'll use this task often in administering user access. You can change the access as needed, as long as you are an administrator.

Task 8.9: Assigning File and Directory Permissions as a User.

Step 1: Description

It isn't necessary to be an administrator to set up file permissions. Of course, you must have full control over any file you want to change. In this task, you will see how to determine whether you have the necessary access and then perform the changes. You can use this task to give others within your organization access to your files by changing the necessary parameters of user accounts, permissions, and files as needed.

Step 2: Action

1. Log on to your system by using your user account.

2. Go to Start, Programs, Accessories, Windows Explorer. Open the directory containing the file(s) you want to provide access to.

3. Select the file or files you want to reassign by left-clicking once on the filename. If you hold the Shift key while dragging the cursor over a list of files, you can select a group of files.

4. Right-click on the file(s) to see the drop-down menu.

5. Select Properties.

6. Select the Security frame.

7. Select Permissions. Verify that you are allowed access by clicking the permissions. Windows 2000 shows an error message, indicating that access is denied or that you have permission only to view security information if you don't have full control, ownership, or the special permission called change ownership.

8. After you get to the Permissions window, when groups that you want to remove are already showing, select those groups and click the Remove button. This action clears all unneeded users from the list. Be careful not to leave the list blank or no one will have access. Click the Add button to add new groups or user accounts for which you want to provide access from the list provided, and right-click each to select them.

▲   9. Click OK to complete the task.

Step 3: Review

Even user accounts can change file and directory permissions if they are authorized to do so. By using Explorer, you can allow or refuse access to files, as you desire. You'll use this task often in administering user access to files. You can change the access as long as you are authorized.

Task 8.10: Using the Command Line to Process Permissions.

Step 1: Description

Regardless of how easy it is to use the supplied GUI interfaces, I always run across people who are adamant about using the command line. Sometimes there is good reason, such as wanting to run a bunch of changes at the same time. GUI interfaces are typically ill-equipped to handle multiple requests. (Are you listening, Microsoft?) So you need to be able to set up *batch* jobs using command-line operatives. In this task, you'll learn how to restrict access to files by using the command-line interface.

Step 2: Action

1. Log on to your system by using an Administrator account.

2. Go to Start, Programs, Accessories, Command Prompt. Relax—this is as GUI as it gets.

3. Now you need to understand the command syntax for adding and removing permissions. Select the file or files you want to assign, and remember the names because you'll need them later.

4. The command you use is CACLS. You can get assistance by typing the command at the prompt and pressing Enter. Windows 2000 lists the syntax of the command for you. A picture of the command is shown in Figure 8.14.

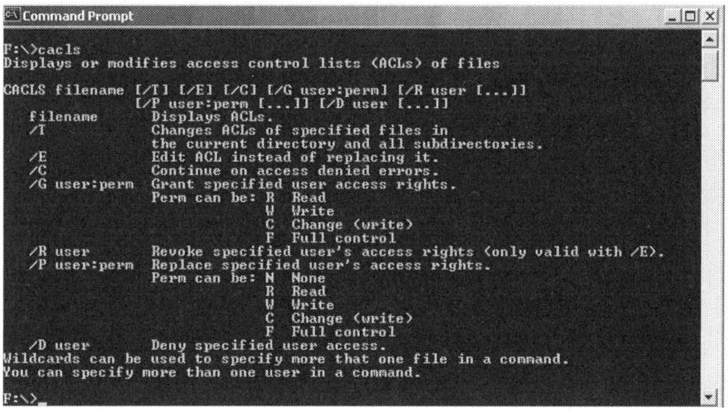

FIGURE 8.14

The CACLS *command.*

```
F:\>cacls
Displays or modifies access control lists (ACLs) of files

CACLS filename [/T] [/E] [/C] [/G user:perm] [/R user [...]]
               [/P user:perm [...]] [/D user [...]]
   filename      Displays ACLs.
   /T            Changes ACLs of specified files in
                 the current directory and all subdirectories.
   /E            Edit ACL instead of replacing it.
   /C            Continue on access denied errors.
   /G user:perm  Grant specified user access rights.
                 Perm can be: R  Read
                              W  Write
                              C  Change (write)
                              F  Full control
   /R user       Revoke specified user's access rights (only valid with /E).
   /P user:perm  Replace specified user's access rights.
                 Perm can be: N  None
                              R  Read
                              W  Write
                              C  Change (write)
                              F  Full control
   /D user       Deny specified user access.
Wildcards can be used to specify more that one file in a command.
You can specify more than one user in a command.

F:\>
```

5. Type **CACLS** and press Enter.

6. Select the file you want to change. Our example uses a file called test.txt.
   I'll add the user called Barry and grant the user read access in this example.

7. Type the following command to add the read permission for file test.txt to user Barry and retain the existing permissions:

   `cacls d:\test.txt /e /g barry:r`

▼   The /e ensures that existing commands are left in the permissions group. If you
        exclude that, the new command completely replaces existing permissions.

▲   8. Type **exit** to close the command-prompt window.

Step 3: Review

By using the command line, you can set up multiple access and manage large permission
changes more readily. This method is also faster than the GUI interface after you get to
know the commands really well. Still, it's just not Windows 2000 to continue using this
rather arcane method over the glory of Windows.

Let's explain a few of the options you can use with the CACLS command. You can also
specify the filename only to get a list of current permissions:

The /T option applies the change you are performing to all the files and subdirectories
below the directory specified.

Using the /E option is your most common default because it tells Windows 2000 to
add the change you are making to the set of existing permissions. Without this, your
changes become the only permissions in the *access control list* (*ACL*). Any other permissions that might have been present are removed.

If you are processing a lot of changes in a batch job, use the /C option because it
allows the processing to continue if an error is encountered. This way, most of your
changes are completed and you only need to fix the one or two that might fail.
Without the option, your processing stops at the error.

/G *user:perm* grants users specific permissions. You use this to add rights to your
user accounts or groups. The syntax consists of *user*, which is the user account you
want to change, and *perm*, which are the rights you want to assign the user. Remember
to add the /E to add these changes rather than make them the only ones that apply.

/R *user* revokes a user's permissions and works only in conjunction with the /E
option. For example, to revoke the rights of user Barry, type the following command:

```
cacls d:\test.txt /e /r barry
```

The command replies with a rather cryptic message: processed file: d:\Test.txt.
What it is saying is that it removed the rights from Barry to the file.

/P *user:perm* also adds permissions for a user. You use this to add rights to your user
accounts or groups. The syntax consists of *user*, which is the user account you want
to change, and *perm*, which are the rights you want to assign the user. Remember to
add the /E option to add these changes rather than make them the only ones that
apply. The difference between this and the /G option is that this option only modifies
permissions of existing users in the ACL, whereas /G adds a new user to the list.

The /D option denies a user access.

There you have it—a complete list of the CACLS command to use in batch jobs or if you really, truly love carrying out command-line commands at a DOS prompt.

Moving and Copying Files

In Windows 2000, when you copy a file, the security permissions for the file are inherited from the destination directory. This means that security over the file might change. As an administrator or a security officer, you need to be aware and manage these copies to ensure that a file with a high level of security isn't copied to a directory that has a lower level of security.

When a file is moved, however, it keeps the specific file permissions and doesn't get any others, regardless of where it is placed within the Windows 2000 partition it resides on. Moving a file onto a separate disk partition will mean the security might change as it will inherit the rules of the directory it is placed into.

After any file copy operation, verify that the level of control remains and isn't changed.

Understanding and Using the Distributed File System

The Distributed File System (Dfs) is a single hierarchical file system whose contents might be distributed across any number of servers. Dfs provides a logical method for accessing those files while not requiring the user to know what machine they reside upon.

One Dfs shared folder can point users to a number of other shared folders across the enterprise. One primary reason for Dfs is the ability to mask the location of the files while allowing the user to gain access in a fast, efficient manner. What Dfs does is use a tree structure containing a root and child nodes, very similar to a normal hard drive directory structure. The big difference is that this one can be on any number of different machines while a normal directory or even a share, is contained to one drive.

To access and use Dfs you must be running a Dfs client on your workstation. Windows 2000 Professional, Windows 98, and Windows NT provide this client. You need to download the client for Windows 95.

You can see how Dfs works in Figure 8.15.

Dfs starts with the root of the Dfs tree. Child nodes are the logical representations of shared network directories. A leaf node is a single entity with no child nodes, while a

branch node has child nodes under it. You can use single or multiple Dfs trees to distribute all your shared resources. You might set it up so that each child node on your Dfs tree

Figure 8.15

*The Distributed File
System architecture.*

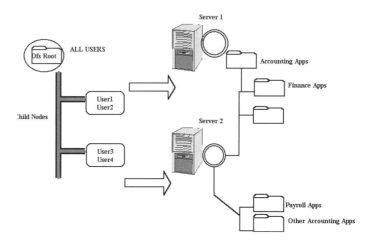

belongs to a department or division or is just a collection of individual files. You use
standard Windows 2000 security controls to permit access to Dfs shares.

In Figure 8.15 you see that there is a root called All Users. Under that are several child
nodes, one for each department. Finally, under that child are a number of additional child
nodes, one for each user in the department. Using Dfs, I can place the data directories for
each department onto different servers and the users in that department would not need
to know which server their data resides on.

Using Dfs allows for

- Organization of resources into a tree structure
- Facilitation of network navigation
- Facilitation of network administration
- Preservation of network permissions

As I explained earlier, using a Dfs share provides a tree structure containing a root and
child nodes. You create the root first and then add nodes as needed. Each child node represents directory shares across your network.

Dfs makes navigating the network a lot easier for users as they no longer need to know
what machine to go to see where their data resides. After locating the root, they can
migrate up and down the tree as needed.

If a server on your network fails, you can move a child node to another server without
having to inform the users. Users continue to use the same root tree to find their data.

A user gains access to shared folders only if appropriate permissions are in place that allow that access.

If you ensure that the distributed file system root is put on a domain member computer, the Dfs tree topology is automatically published to Active Directory. This allows a measure of fault tolerance for the Dfs root and lets you use replication as well to increase the availability of Dfs shares.

NEW TERM When creating a Dfs root, you have the option of establishing it in either a *fault-tolerant* or *standalone* mode. In standalone mode the root doesn't use Active Directory and cannot have root-level replicas. It also has a limited hierarchy and can only have a single level of child nodes. In a fault-tolerant mode it must be hosted on a domain member computer and the tree topology is automatically published to Active Directory. A fault-tolerant node can have root-level replicas and doesn't have a limited hierarchy.

You manage Dfs using the Distributed File Service. You start it by going to Start, Programs, Administrative Options, Distributed File System. The first time you start it you will see a message telling you there are no root Dfs structures. It will tell you to click Action and then Connect To Existing Root. You can see this in Figure 8.16

FIGURE 8.16

The Start-up Dfs message.

In Task 8.11 I show you how to create a new Dfs root directory and add a child node.

Task 8.11: Creating a Dfs Root and Adding Child Nodes.

Step 1: Description

In this step I show you how to set up your first Dfs file system and provide users with an easy way of accessing files without their needing to know where those files actually reside. This step shows you how to create a fault-tolerant root using your Active Directory. If you did not set this up as shown in Day 5, "Introducing Active Directory," you can read these for future use. Before starting this task, make sure you have a shared directory available. Refer to Task 8.5 on how to create shares and create a share called Accounting Apps using a new directory called Accounting. (You specify Accounting Apps in the Share Name field.)

Step 2: Action

1. Log on to your domain controller using an Administrator account.
2. Go to Start, Programs, Administrative Tools, Distributed File Manager. Click OK when you see the message indicated by Figure 8.16 that you saw earlier.

▼   3. A picture of the Dfs manager is shown in Figure 8.17.

FIGURE 8.17

The Dfs Manager.

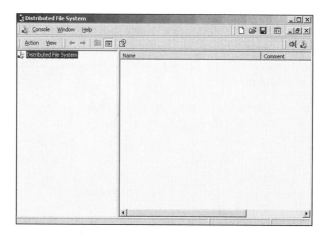

4. Click on Action, New Dfs Root Volume. Windows starts the Dfs Help Wizard. Click Next.

5. The Wizard asks you to select the type of Root you want, either Stand-Alone or Fault-Tolerant. If you are using a domain controller, choose the Fault-Tolerant option.

6. Now choose the domain where your Dfs root should reside. If you are just implementing Windows 2000, you probably only have one entry, so choose that. It should look something like that shown in Figure 8.18.

FIGURE 8.18

Choosing the root domain.

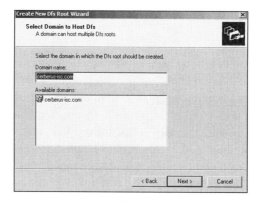

7. Next, enter the name of the Server. You will likely only have one option so choose that machine.

▼

▼ 8. Dfs manager will show you a list of existing shares. Choose the Accounting Apps share that you created for this exercise. You can use the drop-down bar at the right of the screen to see all the shares. Figure 8.19 shows this screen.

FIGURE 8.19

Choosing the root share.

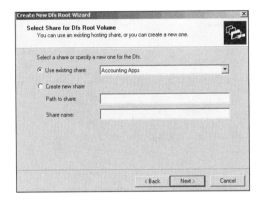

9. As you can see if you want to choose a different share or even create a new share, you do it using this window. Now click on Next. The window that now appears allows you to use yet a different name for the root directory. To keep things simple, leave it as is and click Next again.

10. You should now see a Completing Wizard screen that offers a recap of the options you selected.

11. Click on Finish to end the task. You should see a message telling you the Dfs root has been successfully set up. Click OK to return to the Dfs Manager screen.

You have successfully set up a Fault-Tolerant Dfs Root called Accounting Apps. Now you could create child nodes that send specific users to their particular applications. For example, you could add a Finance and a Payroll child node where users of those departments would find applications specific to their job. You can quit this task now, or you can take the next couple of steps and create a child node called Finance. If you choose to continue, take the time to create a share called Finance Apps on your machine or even on another Windows 2000 machine on your network if you have one available.

12. Let's now create a child node called Finance Apps beneath our Root of Accounting Apps. Although the Dfs Manager is still open, right-click on the node you just created called Accounting Apps. You see a list of options like those shown in Figure 8.20.

13. Select the option called New Dfs Child Node and click on it. You see a window
▼ with a number of fields in it. Type in the words **Finance Apps** in the field called Child Node.

FIGURE 8.20

*Adding a Dfs
child node.*

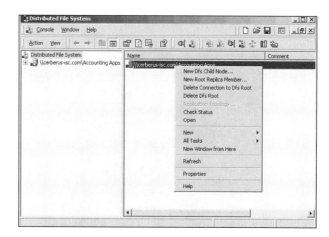

14. Now click on the field below called Send the User to This Network Path. You need
to tell the Dfs Manager where the new child node resides. If you have a second
machine available you could specify this share on that machine and you would end
up with a truly distributed file system. For this task though, I assume you only have
one machine.

15. Use the Browse button to locate your machine and the Finance Apps share or just
type in the name of the machine and share if you know it. (You must use Universal
Naming Conventions (UNC) to do this. So you would type something like
\\server1\finance apps.) You see an example in Figure 8.21. In that picture I
have used server1 as our server name. You would use your actual server name here.

FIGURE 8.21

*The Add to Dfs
box.*

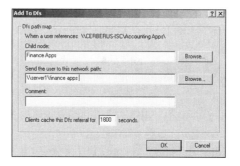

16. You can add a comment about the share in the Comment area if you like to further
explain to your users what the share contains. The client cache time specifies how
long clients will cache this referral before querying the server again to locate it.
Click OK to continue.

▼

▲

17. You are returned to the Dfs Manager main screen where you can see you now have a Root and a new child node. Add more nodes as needed using this task to set up a full Dfs environment for your users. Click Action, Exit to end the task.

8

Step 3: Review

By using the Dfs Manager program you created a new Root directory and then added a child node to it. Using Dfs allows your users to find the finance files across your network regardless of what machines you store the data on. Remember that each folder should be secured by appropriate access rules to ensure that only authorized users can access the files.

Now when a user browses the network, she will see your Dfs root share and from there will be directed down that tree to all the other shares you might have placed in there like the Finance Apps share I created in Task 8.11.

The Distributed File System offers a great way to extend normal file sharing and provide simplified network access to your user community.

Summary

You've learned how NTFS is superior to the FAT system, and you've learned some of the reasons to use NTFS instead of a FAT-based file system. Using files and folders and manipulating them is fairly easy with W2K's Explorer. In addition, you have discovered a lot about using FAT- and NTFS-based servers. In Day 9, "Managing the File Server," you will learn about other important features including Disk Quotas, Removable Storage Manager, and Graphical Disk Management.

Today you learned the following:

- The FAT file system has a use within Windows 2000.
- The advantages that the new NTFS file system offers over other file systems.
- The different types of partitions and why you use each type.
- How to format a drive and ensure that data is backed up before starting the format.
- What forking is and the benefits that it provides.
- The differences between disk duplexing and disk mirroring.
- How to use Explorer efficiently and effectively to manage your files and folders.
- File- and directory-level security is possible only on NTFS-based systems.
- This version of Windows 2000 doesn't include HPFS support.
- File and directory control extends to Windows 2000 workstations, providing a great degree of security over a Windows 2000-based client/server solution.
- You can perform file and directory security via three methods: My Computer, Explorer, and the DOS command line.

- Share names can be 12 characters long, but you might want to use only eight characters if you have DOS clients.
- You can hide shares and user accounts by appending a $ to the end of the name, but because there are simple ways to find these, this should not be used as a security tool.
- Windows 2000 offers an extensive list of file access options, allowing you to provide a degree of control that was previously unavailable.
- Windows 2000 offers the Distributed File System that allows you to manage shares more effectively.

Today you have learned some of the fundamental exercises that are performed in administering files and directories with an NTFS-based Windows 2000 machine. You have learned how to set up and manage shares for those volumes that are FAT- or HPFS-based and then learned both GUI and command-line options for maintaining security over your files and directories.

You also learned all about Dfs and how it allows you to set up shares across a network and allow users to access them without their needing to know what machine the share resides on.

When you combine this knowledge with the information you'll learn on Day 15, "File Backup and Recovery," Day 16, and Day 17, you should become quite proficient in managing security within Windows 2000 Server.

Workshop

To wrap up the day, you can review tasks from the day, and see the answers to some commonly asked questions.

Task List

The information provided today shows you how to manage the files and folders within a Windows 2000 server. You have learned to do the following:

- Use Disk Administrator to view drives and create partitions
- Format a new drive to enable the operating system to use the drive
- Use Explorer to create new folders
- Use Explorer to set up sharing
- Use Active Directory to set up shares
- Take ownership of a file
- Assign directory permissions
- Assign file and directory permissions as a user
- Use the command line for processing permissions

Q&A

8

Q Is NTFS really superior to FAT-based file systems?

A Yes. The NTFS system allows faster data access than do FAT-based systems. It also provides greater data recovery options and doesn't waste as much space when creating files and folders. It also allows for long filenames and enables you to use file-level security controls.

Q Can I run Windows 2000 Server with only a FAT-based file system?

A Yes, on a member-server or standalone server but not if you are implementing a controller. However, you don't gain any of the advantages that NTFS offers, in particular file-level security. On some occasions, however, such as with a recalcitrant mission-critical application, you are forced to use the FAT-based system.

Q I cannot find File Manager in my Windows 2000 system. What happened to it?

A File Manager has been replaced in Windows 2000 Server with Windows Explorer. Although each of these tools works differently, Explorer offers more functionality and time-saving techniques, such as right-clicking to open menus. For example, you can quickly copy a file to the floppy drive by right-clicking while selecting the file to be copied.

Q Can shares be used with NTFS permissions?

A Yes. The NTFS system allows far more detailed levels of security than do shares, however, and they apply no matter how you access the system. Sharing applies only to users who sign on remotely and applies to all users rather than to individuals.

Q As a new administrator, is there an easy way for me to set up accounts and permissions without having to spend a lot of time learning?

A Yes, although I recommend that you take some courses to become truly proficient in managing your server. The Administrative Wizard guides a new user through the steps for adding new users and setting up permissions. It is designed to be very easy to follow, and you can use this wizard until you are comfortable with the other methods explained in this day.

Q I really don't like GUI-based processes, and I like to know exactly what is happening when I manage a server. Is there a command-line interface for setting up permissions?

A You don't have to use the GUI interface in W2K. As this day explains, the command-line program CACLS allows you to set up and remove permissions from users and groups. CACLS is also handy when you have a lot of changes to make and want to set them all up in a batch job instead of performing them one at a time.

DAY 9

Managing the File Server

Last week, you learned about exploring and managing files and directories. Today, in this chapter, you'll learn to set up and control your Windows 2000 Server as a file server, and in tomorrow's chapter, you'll learn to manage a print server. This chapter introduces some simple file server commands and utilities to enable you to provide effective use of the server and ensure that those in your user community can obtain the files they need.

You'll learn about setting the time and date across all your servers and how to start and stop the myriad services that your server might run. Later in the chapter, you'll learn about a tool that provides you with desktop shortcuts and domain synchronization.

Let's begin by seeing how to start and stop services within W2K.

Starting and Stopping Windows 2000 Services

What is a service? Services are applications that can be selected to run automatically at startup or that can be run manually. Examples of services include the Alerter program, SQL Server, and Microsoft Exchange.

Finding out what services you have is easy in Windows 2000 Server. You use Server
Manager for this and other tasks. One of the duties you perform as an administrator is
stopping and starting services. You'll learn how in this task.

Task 9.1: Starting and Stopping Services in Windows 2000.

Step 1: Description

In this task, you'll learn to start Server Manager and find out about the services that
W2K is running. You start and stop services using this window. Services are all those
programs that make up your server, including Browser, Eventlog, Messenger, and Net
Logon, as well as the server itself.

Step 2: Action

1. Begin by signing on to your server as Administrator.

2. Select Start, Programs, Administrative Tools, Computer Management. This
   selection starts the Computer Management program as shown in Figure 9.1.

FIGURE 9.1

*The Computer
Management program.*

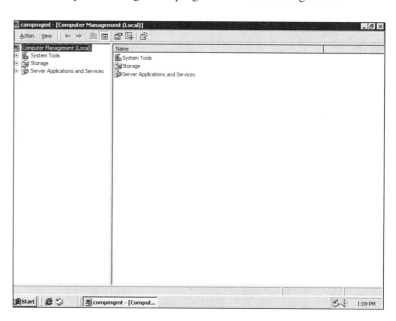

3. Double-click System Tools and then double-click Services. This allows you to
   see which services are running and which are stopped. You see an example in
   Figure 9.2.

9

FIGURE 9.2

*Viewing services in
Windows 2000.*

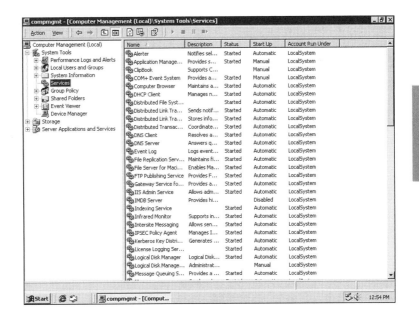

By scrolling through the list of services, you see what is currently active and what
is available but not started.

The viewing box provides the following information:

- Service Name and Description, which tells you the name of each available
  service.

- Status, which indicates whether the service is active, paused, stopped, or
  disabled.

- Startup, which tells you whether the service starts automatically as part
  of W2K's startup or whether it is a manual process that requires your
  intervention.

- Account Run Under, which tells you the authority of the program; that is, the
  account that the program is running under.

Tip

If you prefer, you can open Services through the Control Panel. Select Start,
Settings, Control Panel. Double-click Administrative Tools and then open
Component Services. Under the Console Root (shown in Figure 9.3), open
Services (Local). Again, in the right pane you see all installed services.

FIGURE 9.3

Viewing services using
the Control Panel.

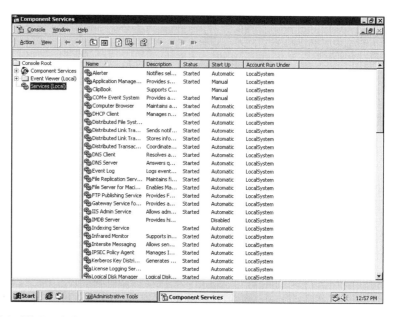

4. Double-click ClipBook Server using the mouse. (If this service is running, choose another service that is set to Manual.) A window like the one in Figure 9.4 should appear.

FIGURE 9.4

ClipBook Properties
window.

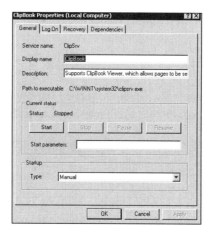

5. On the General tab, under Current status, you see a Start button (all the others are grayed out). Enter any start parameter the service requires. Click the Start button to start the service. Windows 2000 goes into some disk shuffling, and you then see that the Status is changed to Started. That's all there is to starting a service.

▼   6. At the bottom of the General tab, you see a section titled Startup. This allows you
       to decide whether a service should automatically start when the server is booted or
       whether an administrator needs to take action or whether to disable the service
       itself.

    7. You can also decide what account a service should use to sign on to the system.
       You do this from the Log On tab shown in Figure 9.5. Services typically sign on
       when they start and use the System account. You change this if you modify how or
       what privileges your service needs and have set up special accounts for it to use.

FIGURE 9.5

Properties Log On tab.

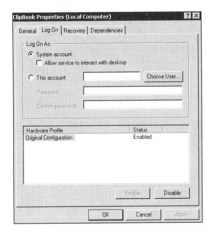

    8. The Hardware Profiles is used to modify the services that run at startup when you
       boot the system using specific hardware profiles. The System tool in the Control
       Panel creates hardware profiles. You enable or disable configurations using the but-
       tons provided.

    9. There are two more tabs for the service. Select the Recovery tab and you see a
       window like that in Figure 9.6.

   10. First, decide the Action to take when the service fails. You need to set these for:
       First Attempt; Second Attempts; and Subsequent Attempts. Your choices are:

       • Take No Action

       • Restart the Service

       • Run a File

       • Reboot the Computer

   11. The Dependencies tab (shown in Figure 9.7) lists the services that must be running
       for a service to work correctly. It also shows those services that require this service
▼   to run.

FIGURE 9.6

*Properties
Recovery tab.*

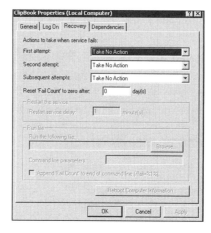

FIGURE 9.7

*Properties
Dependencies tab.*

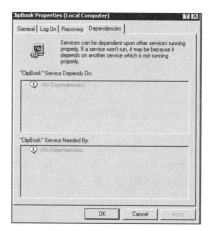

12. Click OK when you have finished setting up all the properties for the service.

13. To stop the service, select the service using your mouse (continue using the same example) and click the Stop button. Windows 2000 doesn't provide a warning message asking whether you are sure that you want to stop the service—so make sure you want to stop the service. Note that the dialog doesn't provide a Stopped indicator. You know that a service isn't running when you see a blank in the Status field. Click OK.

14. To pause a running service, select a service (such as Infrared monitor) from the list and right-click it. From the menu shown in Figure 9.8, select Pause. Windows 2000 shows you the progress message indicating that it is about to pause the service.

▼		Click the Yes button to continue. Now you see the word Paused in the Status
		column next to the service you paused.

FIGURE 9.8

Selecting to pause a service.

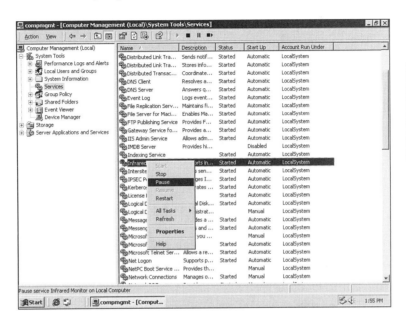

15. To continue the service you paused, right-click it and select Resume from the menu. After a brief delay, your service resumes, and you will see Started for Status.

16. When finished, press Alt+F4 (or from the computer icon menu, select Close to exit
▲		the Computer Management program).

Step 3: Review

Starting and stopping services is part of the administration of Windows 2000 Server. You saw how easy it is to do, and you realized that it is equally easy to pause or stop a service for some reason and then forget to reset the service. You must take care to ensure that you don't affect your clients.

As you see, services are those programs W2K uses to manage items such as the Event Log and the server itself. You start and stop these services as needed for performing maintenance, introducing new releases, and troubleshooting problems. In some cases, services must be stopped and restarted before any configuration changes can take effect.

This tool allows you to start and stop services across the network, managing all the W2K machines in your organization. You do this by selecting the computer you want to manage in the main Computer Management window and then opening Services. This allows for extensive flexibility and operability and lets you centralize this important task.

Adding Computers to Your Domain

As administrator, you will need to add and remove computers from your domain. Before any computer can be a domain member and participate in the domain security, it must be a W2K machine and specifically added to the domain.

Windows 2000 offers three ways to add machines to the domain. First, you add a machine during its installation, whether a workstation or server. To add a machine during installation, you must be an administrator of the domain and the machine must be connected to the network. Next, an administrator adds machines by using the Network and Dial-up Connections tool in the workstation's Control Panel. Finally, you add machines by using Active Directory Manager if you are an administrator or Account Operator. First, you add the machine by specifying a computer account name in the domain database, and then you let the user add the computer using that name in her Network and Dial-up Connections tool. With this method, a user machine might give away the user's domain name to another machine, creating a security exposure. Although this method allows you to manage machine names across the network, it also poses this potential exposure.

The computer name, as you'll remember from Day 2, "Installing Windows 2000 and Client Software," is a 15-character unique name that identifies a machine across the network. This begins the process of establishing a Domain Trust Relationship between machines in your network. You may recall that you covered domains and trust relationships on Day 5, "Introducing Active Directory."

Task 9.2: Adding Computers to Your Domain.

Step 1: Description

In this task, you'll learn to start Active Directory Manager and add a new computer name.

Step 2: Action

1. Begin by signing on to your server as Administrator.

2. Select Start, Programs, Administrative Tools, Active Directory Users and Computer. This starts the Active Directory Users and Computers MMC snap-in.

3. Right-click Computers under the domain where you want to add the computer. Select New, Computer. This starts a dialog box for specifying the computer.

4. Type your new computer name in the Computer name field. For our example, type the name TESTMACHINE. You need to select the computer role. Two options are available: Computer Is a Workstation or Member Server, or Computer Is a Domain Controller. Note that there is no option for any other type of machine. The initial

▼   selection is to add a workstation or server; this is obviously the most often used
     option. Click OK when you are ready. You'll set parameters for this computer shortly.

5. Right-click the TESTMACHINE computer you just added, and select Properties.
   You should see a Properties window like the one in Figure 9.9. Table 9.1 describes
   the tabs in the window.

FIGURE 9.9

*Computer Properties
window.*

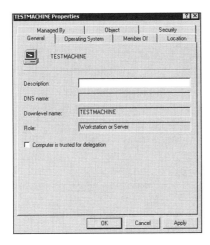

TABLE 9.1   The New Computer Panels

Tab	Description
General	This tab shows the information you supplied during creation—device, name, and role.
Operating System	Use this tab to document the name and version of the operating system running on the machine, as well as any service packs that you might have applied to the system.
Member Of	Use this tab to document the ADS security group where this computer is a member.
Location	This tab documents the location of the computer.
Managed By	Use this tab to describe who has responsibility for managing this computer.
Object	This tab shows the computer's pathname, object class, creation date, modification date, Update Sequence Number (USN) creation date, and USN modification date.
Security	This panel documents the users and groups and their permissions on this object. Clicking the Advanced button shows you Figure 9.10. Table 9.2 describes the three tabs on the Access Control Settings window.

▼

FIGURE 9.10

*Access Control
Settings window.*

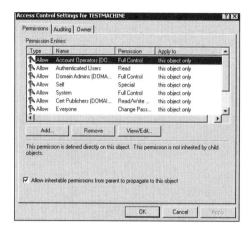

TABLE 9.2   Access Control Settings Panels

Tab	Description
Permissions	This tab shows the access type—allow or deny, the name of the object with permissions, the permissions themselves, and the object to apply the permissions. From this tab you can add, remove, or view/edit the permissions. Finally, you see that the default is that you allow inheritable permissions from the parent to propagate to this object.
Auditing	Use this tab to view the auditing entries for the object. Again, you can add, remove, or view/edit auditing on the object.
Owner	This tab shows the owner of this object (the creator) and those you can give ownership. You do this by highlighting a name in the list box and clicking the Apply button.

6. If you made any changes, click the Apply button to apply changes. Then click OK to close the window.

7. Right-click the computer you just created.

8. Select Manage from the menu. The Computer Management snap-in for the computer will start for the selected computer.

 9. If you are finished, close any active MMC snap-ins currently running.

Step 3: Review

Adding computer names provides a degree of security because no one except a privileged domain user can add computers. This means that no Windows 2000 computers can be added without your knowledge. As you saw, the process for adding a computer isn't onerous.

Deleting a machine if you make a mistake or merely want to remove a machine is simple. Open Active Directory Users and Computers snap-in, select the OU and then the machine name you are deleting, and press the Delete key. Windows 2000 provides a warning message to ensure that you want to perform the delete operation, as shown in Figure 9.11.

FIGURE 9.11

Removing a computer from the domain.

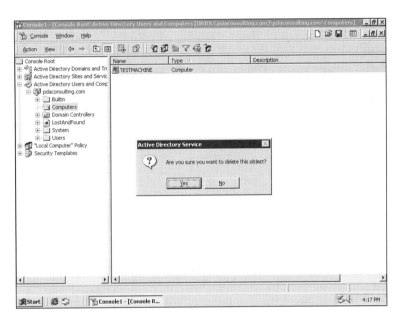

Click the Yes button to remove the computer. Windows 2000 shows you a message indicating that the action was successful.

> **Tip**
>
> Alternatively, you can right-click the computer name, and then select Delete. Just as before, ADS will ask you to confirm the deletion.

Using Active Directory Manager allows you to create and manage the machines in your network without needing to provide sensitive privileges to users. As domain Administrator, you add the name that provides control over which names are used, and the user adds her machine by using that name in her Identification section.

When the computer is added to the domain, the Domain Admins group is added to the new computer's local Administrators group, allowing you to administer this machine either locally or remotely.

Adding a computer name creates a unique Security Identifier Number (SID). If you accidentally delete an account as Administrator, that machine must rejoin the domain to access the new SID. You cannot just use Active Directory Manager and re-create the computer name. Although this technique will appear to work, Windows 2000 creates a new SID that doesn't match the one on the client workstation or server. The client must rejoin the network to establish the new identification.

Managing the Time and Date in Windows 2000 Server

Setting the time and date used to be so easy. On your DOS machine or Windows client, you just enter the DATE command in a command prompt and set the new date and time. Presto, it's done. It can still be done via the command prompt in Windows 2000 Server.

Just like Windows 95 and 98, however, Windows 2000 offers a GUI-based time and date dialog box. You find it by opening the Control Panel and double-clicking the Date/Time icon. You also can select it by double-clicking the clock in the system tray on the task bar. Windows 2000 shows you a dialog box (see Figure 9.12).

FIGURE 9.12

Date/Time Properties.

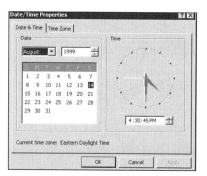

You adjust the date by using the drop-down arrows and selecting the month and year you want the computer to use. You change the day by clicking on it in the month's calendar. You modify the time by selecting the up or down arrows and increasing or decreasing the time as needed.

In the Time Zone tab, Windows 2000 allows you to set the machine for a particular time zone and choose to allow the time to automatically adjust for daylight savings.

Keeping the time accurate is a difficult task in any computer system, and it is no different for Windows 2000. How fast or slow your clock keeps time depends on your particular hardware, and after time, the battery managing the clock does wear down.

One method of managing to keep the time accurate is by using a third-party program that dials out and obtains the time from one of the many atomic clock timekeepers around the world. One such company, Somarsoft, offers a demo version of its product that you can obtain from the company's Web site. The program is called Somar ACTS.

Somar ACTS is a program for Windows 2000 and Windows 95 that allows you to set your computer clock with an accuracy of around one second, using either the National Institute of Standards and Technology (NIST) or United States Naval Observatory (USNO) time source. The program dials the service you choose, receives the current time, and uses it to set your computer's time. This shareware costs a minimal amount. You'll find the Web site at http://www.somarsoft.com; look under the older products section. You also can find an extensive list of free and shareware time synchronization utilities at the following site:

http://www.enet.it/mirror/WWW/winsock/win95/time.htm

Setting and maintaining the time on a server is a thankless job, but accurate time minimizes problems. Using an automated program frees you from having to worry about this task.

 Tip

> After you set the right time on the server, you can synchronize each of your clients' time/date with the server by using the NET TIME command in the login script.

Replicating and Synchronizing the Domain Database

In your network, the AD database that contains all your user account names and machine accounts resides physically on the domain controller. One Active Directory server updates its database to another domain controller. (If you have only one domain controller, you will learn how to back up your system on Day 15, "File Backup and Recovery.") This process is known as replication. Replication requires a homogeneous environment; that is, all domain controllers involved in the replication are Windows 2000 servers with identical schemas. This method provides your network with redundancy and safety. If you lose one DC, another DC can take over, allowing minimal interruption to your clients as they use the file server and other servers in the domain.

NEW TERM Microsoft also defines the term synchronization for the update of a domain controller. Directory synchronization involves dissimilar implementations of a directory service, such as NetWare Directory Service (NDS). Why would you do this? Well, you might want to create users in NDS, but manage them from ADS. In such a case, a *security principal*—an agent—would perform the synchronization, importing or exporting objects from one directory to another. Microsoft is developing a snap-in called MS DirSync. MS DirSync will provide the following:

- Directory one-way synchronization from AD to the target directory
- Less dependence on other tools to complete repetitive administration of the other directory
- A single point of administration in the form of an MMC snap-in to simplify daily, user-related tasks

We talked about server failure in the preceding paragraphs, and this is an important aspect of server management. Ensuring that you are able to manage regardless of machine loss is the result of many things, including data backup, fault tolerance, and domain management. In the meantime, let's look at customizing your desktop.

Creating Desktop Shortcuts and Start Menu Updates

Modifying your desktop is essential to most people because everyone likes to set up their system using their own ideas of efficiency. In this section, you'll learn how to modify the Start menu using the Microsoft Management Console as an example.

As you have learned, MMC is a key tool available to the administrator for user, group, and computer maintenance. It creates, saves, and opens administrative tools, which are called MMC consoles. MMC doesn't provide management functions, but instead hosts applications called snap-ins for your Windows 2000 Server.

You can easily launch MMC from the Run dialog box, but you might want it close at hand so that you can customize your environment. This quick little task shows you how to add the program to your Start menu.

Task 9.3: Adding MMC to the Start Menu.

Step 1: Description

In this task, you'll learn to add a program to the Start menu. You can use this information to add any item to the menu.

▼ Step 2: Action

1. Begin by signing on to your server.

2. Move the cursor to the Start menu and right-click once. You are presented with a small menu. Choose Open All Users and click once. Windows 2000 opens a small window. You see an example in Figure 9.13.

FIGURE 9.13

The All Users folder.

3. Select File, New. Choose Shortcut from the resulting menu list. Type MMC in the command line that next appears, as shown in Figure 9.14. You will need to type the fully qualified path to the file, or click Browse to find it, if it isn't in a directory that is part of the path environment variable.

FIGURE 9.14

The Create Shortcut dialog box.

4. Click the Next button to continue. The program asks you to select a name for the shortcut. Enter MMC in the field provided.

▼ 5. Click the Finish button to complete the task.

▼   6. Close any windows that remain open. As you see in Figure 9.15, MMC is now a part of your Start menu.

FIGURE 9.15

*MMC as part of the
Start menu.*

▲   Now the MMC program is available to you whenever you use the Start menu.

Step 3: Review

Adding an item to the menu gives you control over how your system looks and feels, and offers some degree of efficiency as you devise the setup that feels most comfortable.

You can use this skill to add any program to your menu by changing the various aspects, such as program and location. You can place the same shortcut directly onto the desktop by selecting it in Explorer and just dragging it onto your desktop. Windows 2000 automatically places an icon prefaced with Shortcut To on your desktop. To start the program at any time, you double-click on the new shortcut.

Note

Windows 2000 creates a shortcut during a drag and drop only for an EXE file. To create a shortcut for any other type of file during a drag and drop, hold down Ctrl+Shift during the operation. You also can drag and drop using the right mouse button instead of the left. This gives you a context menu that allows you to choose the type of drag and drop operation.

Scheduling Tasks in Windows 2000 Server

As an administrator of the server, you often need to run a task at odd hours of the day or night. Coming in at 2 a.m. to run a task so that there is little user impact isn't always enjoyable.

Windows 2000 Server provides the AT command for scheduling jobs and automating this task. If you purchase the Resource Kit, you'll find a newer GUI-based product called WinAT that is a lot easier to use.

To use the AT command effectively, you create a new user and place it in the group that provides sufficient authority to run the jobs you plan to automate. This is because by default, the Task Scheduler uses the System account, and this might not provide the access you require. For our example, we created an account called Job Scheduler, provided a password that never expires, and placed it in the Administrators group. You see this account in the list shown in Figure 9.16.

FIGURE 9.16

A new Job Scheduler user account.

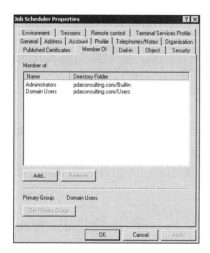

Now you need to configure the Schedule Service to use this account rather than the default user account. You can choose any account you think is appropriate for the exercise as long as it is authorized to do the work that's set out in any jobs you run. Be careful not to expose the service to unauthorized use, because with an Administrator account, it can perform many sensitive tasks.

Task 9.4: Changing a Service to Log in Using a New Account.

Step 1: Description

In this task, you'll learn to modify a service, such as Task Scheduler, to log on to W2K with a more powerful user account. You might use this task to add or remove privileges from a service by providing an account that has more or less authority than the current account in use.

Step 2: Action

1. Sign on to your server as Administrator.

2. Select Start, Programs, Administrative Tools, Computer Management. Double-click System Tools, and then Services. This starts the Services snap-in. (Or, you can open it through the Control Panel.)

3. Locate the Task Scheduler service, and select it by double-clicking on the item. You see a Task Scheduler Properties window with a Log On tab.

4. Click the button next to This Account to select a new user account. Next, click the Choose User button to select a new user account.

5. Windows 2000 shows you a list of all current accounts. You see a dialog box like the one shown in Figure 9.17. From the Select User scrolling window, choose the new account—in our example, Job Scheduler—and click the Add button. Click OK to complete the selection.

FIGURE 9.17

Selecting a new user account for the Task Scheduler.

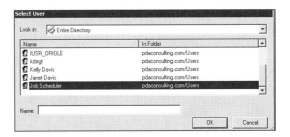

6. Enter the user account password in both the Password and Confirm password fields. If you forget, W2K doesn't tell you. It merely indicates that you need to enter a valid password.

7. Click Apply, and you should see the window shown in Figure 9.18.

FIGURE 9.18

The confirmation window when granting Log On.

▲ 8. Click OK to conclude.

Step 3: Review

Adding a new user account to a service provides you with a method for managing these services and permitting or restricting access.

Now that the AT command can be scheduled and is able to perform the necessary tasks, you need to see how to set up jobs that use this command.

Be sure to start the Task Scheduler service before setting up all your jobs and thinking you are done. Using the AT command consists of typing the command using the following general syntax at a command prompt:

```
at ¦ computer ¦ time ¦ interactive ¦ how often ¦ later ¦ command
```

Note that the sample syntax shows the general approach and doesn't constitute the actual commands. You don't use the separator lines at all; these are shown only to break up the different parameters. These parameters are shown in the following list, followed by some actual commands to clarify their use.

- `computer`: Use the syntax \\computername to tell Scheduler on which computer the job needs to run. For example, on our network, you might use \\TOSHIBA_7020 as the computer name. Leaving out this parameter makes the command run on the computer on which it is entered.

- `time`: Use a 24-hour clock and enter the time with a colon between the hours and minutes; for example, 11:00 or 17:30.

- `interactive`: Allows the command to interact with the desktop.

- `how often`: You use a particular syntax to make the job run every day or on certain days of every week: /every:day, where day is the day of the week spelled out or abbreviated to M,T,W,Th,F,S,Su. For example, /every:M,W,F makes the job run every Monday, Wednesday, and Friday.

- `later`: You use a particular syntax to make the job run next week or on the next specified day of the week: /next:day, where day is the day of the week spelled out or abbreviated to M,T,W,Th,F,S,Su. For example, /next:M,F tells Scheduler to run next Monday and Friday. You also use the days of the month to specify a date each month.

- `command`: Run any legitimate command, program, or batch file. Here you specify what you want done on the schedule created using the earlier parameters. Enter the command in quotation marks for it to be recognized.

Let's look at a series of commands to give you a good idea of how this all works and enable you to get comfortable with using the at command. Use the following examples to practice on your server until you are sure how the commands work and can set your own:

1. `at 10:30 /interactive dir`

   Runs the directory list command at 10:30 a.m. on the local machine.

2. `at 10:45 /interactive rdisk`

   Starts RDISK at 10:45 a.m. on the local machine.

3. `at \\toshiba_7020 16:00 /every:M,W,F "backup.bat"`

   Runs a batch job called backup.bat every Monday, Wednesday, and Friday at 4 p.m. on the computer toshiba_7020.

4. `at \\toshiba_7020 01:30 /every:28 "monthbup"`

   Runs a job called monthbup every 28th of the month at 1:30 a.m. on the computer toshiba_7020.

5. `at 21:30 /next:M "copy d:\test.bat D:\tested.bat"`

   Runs a copy of one file to another next Monday at 9:30 p.m.

Each time you enter a command, the schedule numbers it, incrementing the number using the last one it recognized. To see which jobs are still waiting in the system, type the **at** command.

To see which jobs are running on any other machine, add the computername to the at command: `at \\toshiba_7020`.

If you want to remove a command before its execution, you can delete it with the following syntax. You need to know what number the command is, so list it first using the previous commands:

`at \\toshiba_7020 3 /delete`

This example deletes command number 3 on Toshiba_7020.

As you see, using this command can be tedious, but it does offer an opportunity for you to avoid that 2 a.m. onsite visit.

There is an easier way to schedule a task to start automatically. You can use the Scheduled Task Wizard, as shown in Task 9.5.

Task 9.5: Using the Scheduler Task Wizard.

Step 1: Description

In this task, you'll learn to use the Scheduler Task wizard to schedule the launching of the Address Book.

Step 2: Action

1. Sign on to your server as Administrator.

2. Double-click My Computer, double-click Control Panel, and then double-click Scheduled Tasks.

3. Double-click the Add Scheduled Task icon. The Scheduled Task Wizard appears, as shown in Figure 9.19. Click Next.

4. Windows 2000 shows a list of currently installed programs (see Figure 9.20). To schedule a program not listed, click Browse to locate the program. The Select Program to Schedule window appears.

5. Select Address Book and click Next.

6. In the Name box, type **Launch Address Book** as shown in Figure 9.20.

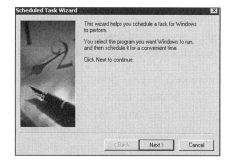

FIGURE 9.19

The Scheduled Task Wizard panel.

9

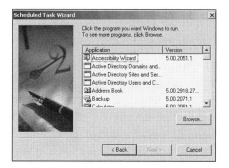

FIGURE 9.20

The Scheduled Task— Launch Address Book.

7. Click One time only, and then click Next.

8. In the Start Time box, enter a time 5 minutes after the current system time. You can confirm the current time by looking at the taskbar.

9. Click Next.

10. Complete the Enter the Password and Confirm Password boxes and click Next.

11. Click Finish.

12. To confirm that you scheduled the task successfully, wait until the time you selected for the Address Book to launch.

13. Close the Address Book.

Step 3: Review

Scheduling an application is as easy as using the Scheduled Task Wizard. The Scheduler will launch the application at the time you select. In the task, you launched the Address Book. You might want to open the Address Book every morning so you can send your mail.

Configuring UPS for Your Server

A file server or any mission-critical machine can use an uninterruptible power supply (UPS). You'll learn a little more about these devices on Day 16, "Configuring Fault-Tolerance," but you might need to set up and administer such a device before then.

You should consider this one of your more important tasks because without it, your machine is very vulnerable, and customer service is easily affected by brownouts, power loss, or power spikes. The year 2000 promises an increase in sunspot activity. So as you are learning all about W2K, you might face brownouts and blackouts. Not to mention the possible impacts of the year 2000 problems themselves. It's better to be able to slowly bring the server down and preserve user data than to lose it instantly due to a power loss.

Windows 2000 provides software for supporting these devices. As usual, check the HCL to see whether Windows 2000 supports your UPS and save yourself a lot of headaches.

Be sure to properly follow the manufacturer's directions concerning a new UPS device, and fully charge the battery before using it. Being impatient can cost you a battery and make the device ineffective. Test the device using a monitor or some other device before using it on your server. This way, you are sure it works before you need it for production use. One quick test is to plug in a monitor and then unplug the UPS from the wall and see what happens. If you have the time and resources, you might do a load test and ensure that the device suits your needs before installing it. Finally, a word of caution. UPS devices generally cannot handle the electrical load of a laser printer; therefore, it's not a good idea to plug one into your UPS.

Task 9.6: Installing a UPS Device.

Step 1: Description

In this task, you'll learn to set up Windows 2000 to handle a UPS device and set the options you want to apply in case the device is needed.

Step 2: Action

1. Test and install the device. Then sign on to your server as Administrator.

2. Open the Control Panel and select UPS.

 Tip

As you already saw in this lesson, you can open the Control Panel by double-clicking My Computer on the desktop.

▼   3. Double-click the UPS icon. You are shown a dialog box.

4. Select the serial port your UPS is connected to using the drop-down menu shown on the first line of the dialog box. This lights up a number of options.

Keep your UPS documentation handy because you'll likely need it to select some of the options you're offered. These are the various options in the UPS dialog box:

- *Power Failure Signal:* Select this box if your device is capable of sending a signal to Windows 2000 when a power failure is detected. Read your device documentation to see what your device sends, and select either Negative or Positive in the UPS Interface Voltages.

- *Low Battery Signal at Least 2 Minutes Before Shutdown:* This field is used if your device sends a signal to Windows 2000 when it detects a low battery and plans to shut down. Again, choose either Positive or Negative signal.

- *Remote UPS Shutdown:* Some devices are intelligent enough to act based on a remote command sent to them across the network. If yours is, select this option and specify Positive or Negative.

- *Execute Command File:* Windows 2000 allows you to run a job or command before shutting down by keying it in this field.

- *Expected Battery Life:* Select an appropriate number based on your device documentation. Be sure to consider all the devices using the UPS and their power load when determining the number. You can select between 2 and 720 minutes.

- *Battery Recharge Time Per Minute of Run Time:* This field is used to determine how long the UPS needs to recharge for each minute of use. For example, if the UPS is used for 5 minutes for a small power loss and then power is recovered, it takes 500 minutes (using the default 100) to recharge the battery. You'll find this drain calculation in your UPS documentation. An incorrect setting provides you with an incorrect calculation of present battery capacity.

- *Time Between Power Failure and Initial Warning Message:* This value determines how long Windows 2000 waits after a power failure to send an administrative alert letting you know that it is on UPS power. The default of 5 seconds is typical, but you can specify between 0 and 120 seconds.

- *Delay Between Warning Messages:* After sending its first message to you, Windows 2000 continues to let you know that it is on UPS power. This option determines how often these additional warnings occur. Windows 2000 will send messages regardless; all you can do is determine the time delay between them. You don't want the messages sent too often or they clutter up

▼

▼

the console, yet not often enough might let the situation slip someone's mind
in a busy environment. The default of 120 seconds would appear to be adequate. You might set it to 60 seconds if you have full-time administrators
monitoring the servers, because they can react quickly.

5. Consider each value carefully and enter it into the appropriate place. Click OK to
   finish.

▲ 6. Close the Control Panel to complete the task.

Step 3: Review

You set up the UPS by reading the documentation and placing the desired values in
the appropriate box. After you finish this task, Windows 2000 takes over and manages
UPS use.

After you finish the UPS setup, Windows 2000 automatically starts the UPS service and
sets it so that it starts all the time when the server is started. Although you performed an
equipment test earlier, it is useful to know that all is still working, and you can test it
again now to verify that Windows 2000 is sending the proper signals and that all functions work.

One way to test the equipment is to ensure that all users are logged off and unplug the
UPS from the wall. See whether Windows 2000 sends you the proper message telling
you that it is using UPS power. Plug it back into the wall outlet. Does W2K properly
send the message in the number of seconds specified after UPS power was detected?
Does W2K re-send the message in the expected interval?

Finally, it might be prudent to see that W2K properly shuts down before UPS battery
power fails. Pick a time when no activity is being performed, and unplug the device. See
that W2K performs properly and shuts down in an orderly fashion. You really don't want
to find out there is a problem at some future time because you chose not to conduct this
test.

One last thing on power. After all this testing, be sure to let the UPS have sufficient time
to recover before it is needed again.

File Server Security

Yesterday, in the lesson "Managing Files and Using the Distributed File System,"
you learned about securing files and directories using the new NTFS file system. You
also learned that use of a FAT-based partition offers no security and that even an NTFS
partition can be read when someone gets hold of the hard drive.

Physical security is a necessity for any server, but especially for your file server, where all your important data is stored. We often enter a client's organization and observe servers sitting under desks or behind doors that are never locked.

There is a saying in the security field that if you get access to the server, you get access to the system. Physical security must be a component of your overall operation, or you run the risk of exposure and data loss.

If you provide this level of control and couple it with the use of NTFS, a sound security policy, and user awareness, your security is vastly improved over what it is if you don't follow all these tasks.

Limit the number of security administrators on your system. Many organizations have far too many staff who have this extensive level of authority, and it typically is unnecessary. If you aren't part of day-to-day administration, you should not have administration access.

Tip

> Another good idea is for the network administrator to use a separate user account for administrative tasks and his or her normal computing tasks. This avoids the possibility of accidental errors. It also minimizes the possibility that a computer will be left unattended and logged in as an administrative user.

Keep strict control over all the system logs, and ensure that they are appropriately backed up and placed offsite for safekeeping. These are your guides to what happened, and you might need them some time to retrace the events of a particular day.

Note

> Previously, on Day 6, "Introducing Security Services," you were introduced to security. On Day 14, "Using Advanced Security Services," you'll learn more about the powerful tools you can use to protect your data. In addition, Day 17, "Security Monitoring and Audit Trails," delves into audit trails and their use.

Virus Protection

There is a lot of confusion and misunderstanding concerning viruses. You'll find some discussion groups even focusing on whether the plural is viruses or some other term. We choose not to get into those discussions. Whatever the spelling, the basic premise of a virus is a program that can infect other programs by modifying them to include a copy of itself and become self-replicating.

Most virus programs cost organizations in cleanup and system maintenance rather than in data recovery because the viruses usually don't delete files. Although some virus programs certainly can and do delete data and erase hard drives, most create a different kind of havoc. When a virus strikes a firm, the staff is left without workstations until cleanup is performed, and staff is needed to perform a time-consuming, rather tedious cleanup job. This is the true cost of these programs.

What can you do to minimize the chance of virus infection? Start with a sound management policy on bringing data from outside the firm into the workstations. You might allow staff to use home machines but require all disks to be reviewed by a virus-check program before being used onsite.

Implement a virus-checking program on the server, and ensure that it always runs. We often see organizations that indicate that they are safe because they use this or that program, yet upon further questioning, we learn that the program is run sporadically. Anti-virus software is only effective when it continuously scans diskettes and downloaded files and binaries. The following companies provide anti-virus products:

- Cybersoft's Vfind
- Data Fellows's F-PROT
- Dr. Solomon's Anti-Virus
- Eliashim's eSafe
- IBM's Anti-Virus
- Integralis's MIMEsweeper
- McAfee's VirusScan Security Suite
- Sophos's Anti-Virus/D-Fence
- Symantec's Norton Anti-Virus

Ensure that users are aware of the risks and the possibility of infection. Also, prepare a response team to quickly discover where an infection occurred and eradicate it both on the machine showing symptoms and any other machines that might possibly have been affected before the virus was noticed.

Finally, ensure that you check all the floppy disks that might have been used during the time frame indicated. Although this is an arduous task, doing it right the first time saves you from returning again and again. Also, be sure to update your virus program definition files continually to ensure that your programs are always aware of the most recent viruses. Contact your vendor to determine how often the vendor makes these updates available.

Summary

Today, you learned about many of the components involved in managing a file server. You learned to manage a file server and control the various components.

You learned to use the Computer Management program to start and stop system services. You learned to set up and run scheduled jobs and, thus, manage your backups or other programs without needing to be onsite.

People will not use your server and network when they perceive it is not secure. So security is a primary responsibility for all system administrators. Day 6 introduced you to Security Services. On Days 14 and 17, you'll learn more about security and the audit tools you can use to protect your data.

The last thing covered in the lesson was virus protection. Computer viruses are a fact of life. They lead to lost or corrupted data, lost productivity, and system unreliability. You need to evaluate and install anti-virus software on the server as well as all workstations.

In this lesson, you discovered a lot about running the server. You learned the following points:

- How to start and stop Windows 2000 services
- How to add computers to your domain
- How computers are removed from the domain
- How to set the time and date using either the old DOS method or the newer GUI-based settings and using even newer software that automatically dials a time clock and sets the time for you
- How to create desktop shortcuts to improve your ease of use
- How to replicate and synchronize the domain controller
- How to set up the UPS for your server

Workshop

To wrap up the day, you can review tasks from the lesson, and see the answers to some commonly asked questions.

Task List

The information provided in this lesson showed you how to manage the File Server and operate it effectively. You learned to do the following tasks:

- Start and stop services
- Add computers to your domain

- Add MMC to your Start menu
- Change a service to log in using a new user account
- Add a UPS device and configure it

Q&A

Q Why would I change a service to use a different login user account?

A As you saw earlier in the day, at times you might decide to improve control over a particular service. For example, suppose that you want to allow the Backup Operators to run scheduled backups each night using the Task Scheduler. The default user account it uses doesn't allow access to all the files you will back up, so another method is needed. You might create a backup user account and grant it a permanent password and then use this to perform scheduled backups.

Q How important is the virus concern to my Windows 2000 Server network?

A The answer to this question really depends on how important your network is to your business. It appears that many organizations today are affected by viruses as users scan the Internet, download files from friends, and pass information between home and work. Using a virus program on a regular, ongoing basis isn't only prudent business practice, but necessary.

DAY 10

Managing the Print Server

Ask any system administrator and he will tell you that printing is a very difficult resource to share effectively on a network. At the same time, network printing is an extremely useful function of your network while being a pain in the neck. Printers are essential in any office where employees use computers. Everybody wants to print reports, memos, letters, graphs, and so on. These needs quickly turn into user demands, and they can take over all of your time. So it is extremely important that you understand printing concepts. This is why this day deals exclusively with the subject of printing.

On your first day, in "Introducing Networks and Windows 2000," you learned that Microsoft heeded the experience of other software vendors when developing this platform. Printing is an excellent example of this diligence. Microsoft took a clue from the most oft-heard complaint about the older versions of Novell NetWare: Network printing is difficult to configure and maintain.

To fully understand printing, you must fully understand printing components and their configuration. In this day, you'll learn about these topics:

- Printer devices, print queues, and print servers
- Creating and fine-tuning network printer queues
- Optimizing the printing process
- Controlling access to the printer

This day looks at these components in depth, including their use and function.

Understanding Printing Basics

Before setting up printers and servers, it is important that you grasp the meaning of printing terminology. So begins your journey.

NT Server uses some special vocabulary when discussing printing:

- **Network-interface printers**—Whereas other printers connect to the network through a print server connected to the network, network-interface printers connect directly to the cabling without requiring an intermediary. These printing devices have built-in network cards.
- **Print server**—The computer where the printer is connected and where the drivers are stored.
- **Printer**—The logical printer as perceived by Windows 2000 Server. As you'll see today, the ratio of printers to printing devices isn't necessarily one-to-one. You can have one printer and one printing device, one printer and multiple printing devices, or multiple printers and one printing device, or some combination of these components. Later in the day, you will see situations in which you might find these arrangements practical.
- **Printing device**—The physical printer itself.
- **Queue**—A group of documents waiting to be printed. In other operating systems, the queue is the primary interface between the application and the printing devices, but in Windows 2000 Server the printer takes its place.

To clarify the preceding points, in Windows 2000 there are two types of printers: physical printers and logical printers. And there are two types of physical printers: server-attached and network-attached. You'll read more about printers later in the day.

Print servers are merely computers configured to collect user print jobs and send them to the printers that are attached to the machine, as needed. Figure 10.1 shows a general idea of how the different components fit together.

FIGURE 10.1

Printing components.

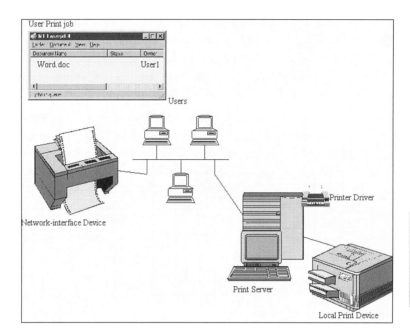

10

Generally, a print queue is a shared area on a file server for storing print jobs in the order in which they are received. Print queues are the method that print servers use to store, or queue, user print jobs. The print queue lines up the print jobs and sends them to the printer in an orderly and efficient manner. In turn, the print server directs the print jobs from the queue to the printer. The printer, which is the actual physical device, receives the job and typically outputs it to paper. When a user sends a print job to a print server, the print server stores the print job in the appropriate print queue until the printer is available to accept the print job. You'll learn more about print queues later in the day.

You can use almost any of the Microsoft line of Windows operating systems as a print server. Most print server PCs share a locally attached printer through one of the following operating systems:

- Windows 2000 Server or Professional
- Windows 95 and Windows 98
- Windows for Workgroups
- Windows 3.1 when running the MS Network Client
- LAN Manager

As you just learned, 2000 also supports direct network-attached printers that use the HP JetDirect card (with built-in service software) or a similar network attachment device.

These direct-attach printers can receive print jobs straight from users. The best way to configure network printers like these, however, is to let a Windows 2000 server act as the print server, collecting print jobs and sending them to the printer when it is available. This way, no user print jobs are delayed or rejected while the printer is printing another job. These printers have a limited buffer to store print jobs.

Fundamentally, the print server spools print jobs in a print queue until the printer is ready. Using print queues and spooling print files is by far the most efficient use of direct network-attached printers. For a Windows 2000 machine to act as a print server for direct network-attached printers, you load the Microsoft DLC protocol in your Windows 2000 server's network setup. Windows 2000 uses the DLC protocol to talk to network-attached printers. This protocol isn't routable however, which limits its use to small networks. For networks using routers or for WANs, you typically use the TCP/IP protocol instead. Other protocols used include AppleTalk and NWLink IPX/SPX. Which protocol you use should be based on the capability of your printer and internal network.

Table 10.1 offers a list of the protocols and some of the reasons for using or avoiding them.

TABLE 10.1 Printer Protocols

Protocol	Advantage	Disadvantage
DLC	Printer-specific protocol	Not routable
TCP/IP	Globally accepted, routable, not OS-specific	Requires more setup
NWLink IPX/SPX	Very easy to set up, routable	Broadcasts more often than TCP/IP
AppleTalk	Directly accessible to Macintosh clients	Not routable, extreme number of broadcasts

Using LAN-transparent applications, the users think they are printing directly to the printer down the hall. This illusion, however, is often difficult for the system administrator to achieve.

This description doesn't explain the whole story, so a more in-depth review of these components is required. Let's start our discussion by looking at printers.

Printers

Printers are the devices your users are most familiar with, except, of course, their workstations. Network printers are shared devices. You can attach them to a file server, a print server, or a local workstation acting as a remote printer.

Today, you also will find intelligent printers with print service and network interface cards built-in that can attach directly to the network and act like workstations with remote printers attached. Apple's printers have worked this way since about 1986.

Printers get print jobs via print servers. It might be useful at this time to refine the definition of a print server. The only thing more critical to the print process than a print user is a printer. As mentioned earlier, there are two types of printers available with Windows 2000 Server and three ways to attach printers to your network. The two types of printers are physical and logical printers. Physical printers are just that: a physical device or printing hardware. It's the thing you touch and scream at when it runs out of paper in the middle of your important print job. Logical printers are a Windows 2000 creation that enables you to set up a single print definition serviceable by multiple physical printers, or multiple print definitions served by the same physical printers. Two ways to attach printers to your network follow:

- **Network-attached (or network printer)**—To attach directly to the network, the printer must have a built-in network interface. For instance, high-end laser printers commonly include built-in Ethernet interfaces.

- **Server-attached (or server printer)**—These use a normal printer cable to connect the printer directly to the back of the Windows 2000 machine.

For example, let's say that you have three identical HP LaserJet 6 printers in your department. You can define a single logical printer on the Windows 2000. This single logical printer then routes print jobs automatically to whichever printer isn't busy.

Note

> When you have multiple physical printers served by one logical printer, the physical printers must be the same: the same model, with the same features installed, and with the same amount of RAM.

Logical printers serve another purpose. Not only can you assign multiple physical printers to one logical printer, but you also can assign multiple logical printers to one or more physical printers. So you can create different share names for the same physical printer, thus enabling you to assign different access rights, access times, and priority levels to different groups.

Let's say that your Customer Service department has two different shifts—first and second. The first shift can use the printer with the share name CSLaser1, whereas the second shift can use the share name CSLaser2 to access the same physical printer. The difference between the two share names is in when you can use each share name. This method might allow you to track printer usage properly and to control who can access the printer during the two shifts.

Print Queues

Now that you understand the difference between logical and physical printers, let's look at where all those print jobs go to wait for printing: the print queue. The print queue is just that—a queue, or line, of jobs waiting to be printed. In W2K, the print queue is transparent to both users and administrators. Therefore, queues are described here mostly for the benefit of those who have used print queues in other network environments, such as you former NetWare administrators—you know who you are.

In W2K, a print queue is an integral part of a logical printer's definition. When a user sends a print job to a printer that is busy printing, Windows 2000 puts the submitted job in a print queue for that logical printer. When the printer becomes available again, Windows 2000 sends the next job in the queue to the printer. Under W2K, you don't use separate definitions or settings for queues.

What if you don't want your print jobs queued? You certainly have that option too. When you install the printer on Windows 2000, you'll see a tab called Scheduling in the Printer Properties dialog box. By choosing this tab you'll see the option to Print Directly to the Printer. If you choose this option, the system passes print jobs directly to the physical printer. There are, of course, some practical reasons for choosing this option. Maybe your print job is confidential and you don't want it available in a queue where some-one might read it. The downside of this setting is that when the physical device is busy, your machine must wait for the physical printer to become available before continuing.

Imagine staring at the Print dialog box in Word for Windows 97 for several minutes while someone's 25MB spreadsheet prints. This illustration points out exactly why print queues make sense. Enable the Print Directly to the Printer option in the Printer Properties dialog box only when you know that's what you want.

 Tip

> Printing directly to a printer makes sense when a printer is available for the person's exclusive use. This is a good idea for clients who deal in confidential information, such as a Human Resources clerk.

Print Servers

A print server is software that takes jobs from the print queue and sends them to the printer. A job inserted into the print queue makes its way to the top of the queue, at which time the print server redirects it to the appropriate network printer. When a printer is out of paper, offline, or jammed, the print server can notify the Administrator or print server operator.

Because the server is software, you should think of it more as a process than a device. The print server can be a dedicated device or a process running on another machine. Print servers don't necessarily have to be your main file server, or even computers with Windows 2000, but there are limitations on who can share a printer with the rest of the network.

Machines running the following operating systems can act as print servers:

- Windows for Workgroups
- Windows 95
- Windows 98
- Windows 2000 Professional
- Windows 2000 Server
- LAN Manager
- MS-DOS and Windows 3.1 (when running the MS Workgroup DOS Add-on)

Regardless of where the service runs, the print server has the responsibility for controlling and redirecting print jobs from workstations to printers.

So do you want a dedicated or a non-dedicated server?—that is the question. Each has advantages and disadvantages. You can retrieve your old PC from its current use as a boat anchor or doorstop if you like because the minimum configuration is an 8088 with a 20MB hard drive and 1MB RAM. On the other hand, using the Windows 2000 as a print server really taxes I/O and memory, two resources used extensively by file service so you should consider using the machine for either print services or file sharing but not both.

Windows 2000 Printer Sharing Features

The unique printer sharing features that Windows 2000 has can make the process of connecting to a networked print device easier than it is with other operating systems. So let's look at some clients.

Windows 2000 Professional Machines Don't Need Printer Drivers

If you're running Windows 2000 Professional (the workstation version of Windows 2000) with your Windows 2000 Server, not needing printer drivers is likely one of your favorite features because it makes the connection process a lot easier. When you're connecting the workstation to a printer on the server, you don't have to specify which kind of printer you want to connect to or tell the system where to find the drivers, as you do when connecting a Windows workstation to a networked printing device. Instead, you need only go to the Printers folder or the Add New Printer Wizard (depending on which version of NT you are running, 3.x or 4.x or 2000), look to see which printers are shared on the network, and double-click on the one you want. After you've done that, you're connected. Windows 2000 Server will find and install the software drivers you need automatically.

Note

> NT's most significant contribution to easy network printing is the concept that a Windows 2000 Professional client isn't required to have a print driver installed locally for the network printer in question. Windows 2000 allows a Windows 2000 Professional workstation client to route print jobs to a network print queue. From there, the Windows 2000 print driver configures the print job and completes the printing process successfully. Imagine not having to install and configure a copy of the printer driver on every company PC. If you keep the print drivers up-to-date on just one machine, Windows 2000, every user's print jobs should print perfectly. Printing is simple: Just select File, Print, and click OK from your Windows application.

Direct Support of Printers with Network Interfaces

To use a network interface print device (one that connects directly to the network instead of requiring parallel or serial connection to a print server), you only need specify it by using a different port. Older HP-JetDirect cards that don't support TCP/IP require the Hewlett-Packard network port that uses the DLC protocol, so for these you need to load the Data Link Control protocol onto the print server. For all newer cards you can use TCP/IP. Each protocol you add affects network performance so don't use the DLC protocol unless you really have to.

Although network interface print devices can connect directly to the network without an intervening print server, those network interface print devices still work best with a connection to a computer acting as a print server because they have only one incoming data path. With only one path, after the printer receives one print job, it cannot queue any other print jobs until the job completes. More paths mean more efficient use of printing time because queuing means that you don't have to keep checking to see whether the printer is done or worry about someone beating you to the printer.

Network interface printers can be useful because, although they can still connect to a print server through the network media, they can also be physically distant from it. This works because network interface printers don't get jobs through the parallel or serial port. The network connection also can speed up the process of downloading documents to the printer because a network connection is faster than a parallel or serial port. The speed difference isn't great, though, because the printer still must access the drivers from the print server.

Setting Up Printing

The Printers window in the Control Panel takes care of all printer maintenance. To connect to, create, fine-tune, or manage a printer, you need only open the Printers window. Basically, you set up printing by carrying out these actions:

* Adding printers to the network
* Customizing printers

Adding a Printer to the Network

Adding a printer to your network is fairly easy. To begin with, you physically hook a printer to your server the same way you'd hook any printer to a computer: by using a printer cable and attaching it to a parallel port on the back of the computer. Then, you must logically attach the printer.

For those of you who fondly remember Print Manager, there is some bad news. With Windows 2000 Server, Print Manager is no longer a part of the program. Now, now, smile; you'll get over it. The functions previously found in Print Manager are now located in the Printer window.

You can find the Printer window by selecting the Control Panel under the Start menu or by going directly to it using Start, Settings, Printers. For those of you familiar with NetWare and NT 3.51, the process of setting up a shared network printer was called "creating" it. Now, you simply go to the Printer window and click the Add Printer icon. The Add Printer Wizard walks you through the process of setting up a printer. You can find the properties for the printer, give permissions for groups to use the computer, and use all other functions and settings for printers from the Printer window—more specifically, in the Properties dialog box in the File menu.

You can add a printer to Windows 2000 Server or Professional; however, the workstation version only offers up to 10 concurrent sessions for file and print services, so if you need more than that you should use Windows 2000 Server. Also, if you want Macintosh and NetWare support, they aren't supported on Windows 2000 professional so again, you need to use the server product. Now let's add a printer.

Task 10.1: Adding a Printer.

Step 1: Description

The first time you're setting up a printer on the network, you need to add it. To do this, you use the Add Printer Wizard and provide the appropriate information, including the type of printer, its share name, and whether it will be shared with the network. With this task, you'll create a printer using the Add Printer Wizard.

Note

You can give one physical printer more than one share name and assign each name to a different group, perhaps with different print privileges. Just repeat the creation process but assign the printer a different name.

Note

Choose Network printer server to connect your machine to a printer managed by another machine in your domain. Choose My Computer to set up a printer for your server to manage.

You need to set up your own printer (as opposed to connecting to one) when you are doing the following:

- Physically installing a printer on a computer
- Physically installing a printer that connects directly to the network
- Defining a printer that prints directly to a file (no hard copy)
- Associating multiple printers with diverse properties for the same printing device

Step 2: Action

1. Double-click the Printers icon in the Control Panel folder.
2. Double-click Add Printer. The Add Printer Wizard appears in Figure 10.2. Click Next.

▼

FIGURE 10.2

The Add Printer Wizard.

3. Choose the type of printer you want to install—one physically attached to this server (Local) or one located across the network somewhere (Remote). For this example, let's select Local. Note that Windows 2000 offers to automatically detect the printer for you. Click Next.

4. Select the port where you will attach this printer, and click Next. If you don't see your port listed, click Add Port to see additional choices. You should see a window like the one shown in Figure 10.3.

FIGURE 10.3

The Add Printer Wizard.

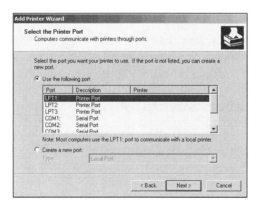

5. After clicking next, you are presented with a list of manufacturers' print drivers. In the left scroll window, select the printer manufacturer (for example, HP). In the right scroll window, select the printer model (for example, HP LaserJet 5). You can find printer drivers for most printers in the list provided. If you don't see your

▼

▼ printer in this screen, click the Have Disk button and follow the onscreen prompts. Be sure to have handy the printer driver from the manufacturer. When the driver you selected is already present, the wizard asks whether you want to replace it. Click Next to proceed.

6. Choose a name for the printer and tell Setup whether you want your Windows-based programs to use this printer as the default printer. The name can be up to 32 characters, including spaces. (You may find some applications that only support 31 characters total including server name and printer name in a UNC.) Click Next.

7. Select whether this printer will be shared. If you decide to share it, you have to give it a share name. So type a share name. The share name doesn't have to be the same as the printer name, but it might be easier to manage the printers when your printer names and share names are the same or at least similar. Make the share name something meaningful, such as HRLaser for the printer in Human Resources, rather than something obscure, such as Printer1. A share name can be up to 12 characters long, including spaces. Some Windows applications, however, can have printer problems if spaces are included, so it might be a good idea to be cautious when using them. Click Next.

Tip   If you want MS-DOS machines to use this printer, you need to make sure that the printer name conforms to DOS's 8+3 naming convention.

8. Next you are asked to enter a comment and location for your printer to help users find it. Add additional data here such as 15th floor corner office or other useful information. You can see an example in Figure 10.4.

FIGURE 10.4

Location and Comment dialog box.

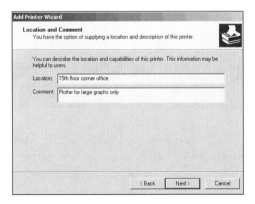

▼

> **Tip**
>
> Windows displays the information stored in the Location and Comment dialog box when a user searches Active Directory for a printer. The information is optional but can help users locate their printer more easily.

9. You are advised to print a test page. Select whether you want to print a test page after the printer is installed. Click on the appropriate check box and then click Next.

10. The Add Printer Wizard shows you the selections you have chosen. You see this in Figure 10.5. If you have made any mistakes, this is the time to go back and fix them by using the Back option. If all is correct, click Finish.

FIGURE 10.5

The Add Printer Wizard Completion dialog box.

11. The Wizard copies the necessary files, completing the addition of your printer. You can now see the printer if you use Start, Settings, Printers option. Once there, select the new printer and right-click on it. Then select Properties to see all that you entered earlier and verify they are correct. You can see this in Figure 10.6.

12. If you want to allow other types of operating systems to access this printer, click on the Sharing tab in the Properties folder. There you see an option called –Drivers for different versions of Windows. Select the Different Drivers option by clicking on it. You are shown a window listing all the other Microsoft Windows versions. Select the ones you want by clicking on the check box beside each name. The OK option will be highlighted once you click on an additional machine. Click OK to continue. Windows will ask for your CD-ROM and, after you provide it, will install the drivers. You have completed your setup of a printer and verified that all the options were set correctly. In a later task we will show you how to allow different operating systems like Macintosh to access the printer.

FIGURE 10.6

The Printer Properties
dialog box.

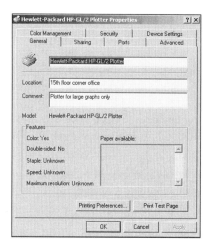

Step 3: Review

As you just saw, adding a printer is simple. To add a printer to your server, double-click
the Add Printer icon in the Printers window. Note that you can also perform this task on
your domain controller by using the Printers option on the Configure Your Server dialog
box that opened when you installed Active Directory. (If this is no longer open, you can
open it by selecting Start, Programs, Administrative Tools, Configure Your Server.)

That is all there is to it—your printer is ready to be used by one and all. Except,
of course, you might not want everyone to use the printer. That is where the user
permissions come in handy (this topic is covered later in this day).

> RISC and x86 machines use different printer drivers, so you need to install
> both kinds on your print server if you have both kinds of machines on your
> network.

The task you just completed adds a logical printer. Remember, you can create multiple
logical printers that point to a single physical printer. Having different people access
the same device from different names allows you to assign different printing priorities
to different users, assign different hours during which the printer is available for printing,
make one printer for network use and another for local use, and so forth. Having two or
more names allows you to fine-tune the network's access to the printer.

The process for adding a second printer to the same print device is the same as that for adding the first one. Select Add Printer from the Printers window and follow the Add Printer Wizard's instructions. Be sure to take the following steps:

1. Select a new name for the printer.

2. Choose the same printer driver for the printer that the other printer on this print device uses, and make sure that all other settings are correct. You don't have to share all printers on the network, even when they're attached to the same printing device.

If you shared the new printer with the network, it is now available for connection.

Printer Pooling

Previously, you read about the situation in which you assign multiple identical physical printers to a single logical printer. Print jobs migrate to the first available printer with that logical designation. Just because you send a print job to a particular print name doesn't mean that your print job has to print at that one particular printer.

NEW TERM To save time for print jobs, you can use the Properties dialog box to pool several identical printers into one logical printer. When you have more than one identical printer, you can share them under the same printer name to facilitate printing. If you do this, the first available printer handles the job when you send it to that printer name. To the network, it looks as though there is only one printer to connect to, but print jobs automatically go to whatever pooled printer is available first. This process is called *printer pooling*. Printer pooling doesn't work unless the pooled printers are physically identical—that is, the same make and model and with the same amount of memory.

Tip

> To set up printer pooling, go to the Ports tab in the Printer Properties dialog box, (you might need to click on the Enable Printer Pooling check box first) and then click on the ports where you've plugged in the other printers. If the ports you need aren't on the list, you can add them by clicking the Add Port button.

To assign multiple physical printers to one logical printer (that is, to employ printer pooling), select Properties from the Printers pull-down menu, and then select Additional Ports. Indicate the ports for each printer you want to pool under this name. Remember, you can pool a physical printer that also is shared under its own share name. In other words, multiple logical printers can point to the same physical printer or printer pool.

10

Customizing a Printer's Setup

After you've done the basic work of adding a printer, you can customize it. You don't have to customize your printer when you first set it up; you can always adjust the settings later with the Properties option on the Printer menu.

Using the Printer Properties Dialog Box

Highlight the printer you want and click the Properties button in the Printers window. From here, you can perform many tasks, including these:

- List the hours that this printer will print. If you restrict the printing hours, jobs still will spool to the printer during the off-times, but they will not print until the hour indicated.

> You might limit the hours that a printer can be used if it is typically used for printing sensitive documents. Normally, you might have a person who watches and removes any documents to ensure they are not seen by unauthorized persons but, when no one is available such as during off-hours, you can prevent anything from printing.

- Choose a separator page file to print before each print job. Separator pages are discussed in detail later in this day.
- Choose the ports you want to print to for printer pooling (more on this topic follows).
- Select the security that you want the machine to use for controlling access (more on this topic later).
- Select the print processor.
- Determine the printer's priority if the printer has more than one name on the network. For example, if you have the same printer shared under the name HP4-Si and HP4, and you assign a higher priority to the printer name HP4-Si, then print jobs sent to that printer name are printed first. The default priority is 1, which is the lowest priority. You can set the priority from 1 to 99.

Setting the Printer Timeout Number

When the printer you are setting up is connected to a parallel port, you can specify the time lapse before the print server decides that the printer isn't responding and notifies the user of an error. Setting the Transmission Retry number higher or lower adjusts the amount of time that the Print Server waits for a printer to prepare itself to accept data.

This setting affects not only the printer you've selected, but also any other local printers that use the same printer driver. To set the number of seconds between the time that you send a print job to the printer and the time that, if the printer doesn't see the job, it informs you of a transmission error, choose the Properties item in the Printer menu. Next, click on the Ports tab, and choose Configure Port in the number of seconds you want for the timeout. To adjust the timeout, just click in the field and type a number.

Separator Pages for Sorting Documents

NEW TERM *Separator pages* are extra pages printed before the main document. You can use them to identify the owner of the print job, record the print time and date, print a message to users of the printer, and record the job number. Separator pages also are useful for keeping documents sent to the printer separate from each other. When several people are using the same networked printer, you probably want to use separator pages to help them keep their documents apart. Several separator-page files are included with Windows 2000, and you also can create your own by using Notepad.

Creating a Separator Page

NEW TERM To make your own separator-page file, begin a new document in Notepad. On the first line, type a single character and then press Enter. This character is now the *escape character,* which tells the system that you're performing a function, not entering text. You should use a character that you don't anticipate needing for anything else, such as a dollar sign ($) or pound sign (#).

Now that you've established your escape code, you can customize your separator page with the variables shown in Table 10.2.

TABLE 10.2 Separator Page Variables

Variable	Description
BS	Prints text in single-width block characters until $U is encountered.
$D	Prints the date the job was printed. The representation of the date is the same as the Date Format in the International section in Control Panel.
$E	Ejects a page from the printer. Use this code to start a new separator page or to end the separator-page file. If you get an extra blank separator page when you print, remove this code from your separator-page file.
$F*pathname*	Prints the contents of the file specified by the path, starting on an empty line. The contents of this file are copied directly to the printer without any processing.

continues

TABLE 10.2 continued

Variable	Description
$Hnn	Sets a printer-specific control sequence, in which *nn* is a hexadecimal ASCII code sent directly to the printer. To determine the specific numbers, see your printer manual.
$I	Prints the job number.
$L*xxxx*	Prints all the characters (*xxxx*) following it until another escape code is encountered.
$N	Prints the username of the person who submitted the job.
$*n*	Skips *n* number of lines (0 through 9). Skipping 0 lines moves printing to the next line.
$T	Prints the time the job was printed. The representation of the time is the same as the Time Format in the International section in Control Panel.
$U	Turns off block character printing.
$W*nn*	Sets the width of the separator page. The default width is 80; the maximum width is 256. Any printable characters beyond this width are truncated.

An example might help at this time. Open Notepad, and enter the following lines:

```
$
$N
$D
$T
$L This is a test separator page
$E
```

When you use this as a separator, your user will get this page:

```
Kelly 18/2/1997 9:15:15 AM This is a test separator page
```

Even though each entry is on a separate line, the output is all on one line because $*n* wasn't used to tell the separator page to skip lines between entries.

Choosing a Separator Page

To specify a particular separator page, choose the General tab in the Properties dialog box, then the Advanced tab and then click the Separator Page button.

When no separator file is listed, you can select one by typing the name of the file you want to use or by browsing for the correct file by clicking the Browse button. After you've selected a separator file, the page with that information in it prints before every print job.

To stop using a separator page, just go to the Separator Page dialog box again and delete the entry in the text box. There is no drop-down list setting like <None> as there is in some menus.

When specifying a separator page, you can type a filename (when you're already in the proper path to find the file) or the filename and path (when you're in another path). You must, however, use a file that is physically located on the computer that controls the printer where you're specifying the separator page. You cannot use any file accessible from the network because the computer controlling the printer stores separator-page information in its registry, so it needs to have that information available locally. If you tell the printer to use a separator file that isn't located on its hard disk or one that isn't in the path you've indicated, you get an error message that says

```
Could not set printer: The specified separator file is invalid.
```

If you followed everything so far in this day, your users could be merrily printing right about now.

Connecting to and Printing from a Shared Printer

How you connect a workstation to a printer connected to a server running Windows 2000 depends on the operating system of the workstation. Windows and Windows for Workgroups machines can connect from the graphical interface, but OS/2 and MS-DOS machines must make connections from the command line. Easiest of all are the Windows 2000 or NT 4.0 machines—they don't even require locally loaded printer drivers.

 Note

To use a Windows 2000 printer from a Macintosh, UNIX, or NetWare client, you need to install special services on the print server first.

Client Machines Running Non-Microsoft Operating Systems

To use a Windows 2000 print server from a workstation that isn't running a version of Windows you need to install additional components on the print server. Table 10.3 lists the requirements for each operating system.

TABLE 10.3. Non-Microsoft Print Services

Access	Description
Macintosh	Services are included with Windows 2000 but aren't installed.
UNIX	UNIX uses a service called TCP/IP Printing (also called Line Printer Daemon or LPD) which is included with Windows 2000 but isn't installed.
NetWare	You need an optional add-on product called File and Print Services for NetWare. It isn't included with Windows 2000.

In the UNIX environment, a program wanting to print something can use a line printer remote (LPR) service to send a document to a print spooler service on another computer. The receiving service is usually called a Line Printer Daemon (LPD).

Microsoft Print Services for UNIX provides both LPR and LPD services. These act independently on a Windows 2000 print server in the following manner:

- LPDSVC on the print server receives documents from native LPR utilities running on client UNIX computers.
- LPRMON on the print server sends print jobs to native LPD processes on UNIX computers to which printers are attached.

To add UNIX Printer Services, you need to add an optional networking component. You do this using the following task.

Task 10.2: Adding Print Services for UNIX or Macintosh.

Step 1: Description

When you need to allow UNIX or Macintosh machines to connect and use one of your printers you must set up the special services that the operating system needs. In this task we specify UNIX service but you can add the Macintosh service by modifying your response in Step 4 to include both operating systems.

Step 2: Action

1. Double-click on Control Panel, Network, and Dial-up Connections.

2. On the Advanced drop-down menu, double-click on Optional Network Components.

3. Select Other Network File and Print Services and click on Details. You see a dialog box like that shown in Figure 10.7.

FIGURE 10.7

*The Add/
Change Windows
Components
dialog box.*

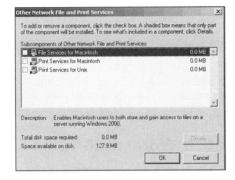

4. Select Print Services for UNIX and click OK. Then click Next.

5. The Wizard will add files from the Windows CD-ROM and set up the service.

Step 3: Review

In this task, you set up your server to allow UNIX machines to use your printers.

With this step complete, you then need to specify the printer your UNIX clients will use and make sure that printer will respond to UNIX requests. You use the following task to do this step.

Task 10.3: Adding an LPD (UNIX) Printer.

Step 1: Description

When you need to allow UNIX machines to connect and use one of your printers, you must set up the special services that this operating system needs. To do this, you used the previous step. Now, however, you need to ensure that the printer is set up to use the Line Printer Daemon service.

Step 2: Action

1. Double-click the Printers icon in the Control Panel folder. (Or use, Select Start, Settings, Printers.)

2. Double-click Add Printer. The Add Printer Wizard appears. Click Next.

3. Click Local printer, and then click Next.

4. Click Other, and then select LPR Port. (LPR is Line Printer Remote and it is a connectivity program that runs on the UNIX machine.) Click Next, and then provide the following information:

   • In **Name or Address of Server Providing LPD**, type the address of the host for the printer you are adding.

▼   • In **Name of Printer or Print Queue on That Server**, type the name of the
          printer as it is identified by the host, which is either the direct-connect printer
          itself or the UNIX computer.

▲   5. Follow the instructions on the screen to finish installing the TCP/IP printer.

Step 3: Review

In this task you set up your printer so that UNIX machines can use it. This allows for a
variety of machines on your network to use your printers.

How Do I Connect a Workstation to a Shared Printer?

The process of connecting a workstation to a networked printer varies with the type
of operating system that the workstation is using. To connect DOS and OS/2 machines,
use the NET USE command from the command prompt. For Windows and Windows for
Workgroups, you can use the Printers folder. For Windows 2000 machines, use the Print
Wizard. Printer drivers for each kind of printer must be manually loaded locally on all
kinds of workstations except Windows 2000 and older versions of NT.

Depending on the type of operating system your network users use, printing on a W2K
network ranges from ridiculously easy to only a little harder than blinking.

Printing from MS-DOS

All DOS workstations, whether they are running Windows or not, require locally
installed printer drivers to share printers on a Windows 2000 network. From a DOS
workstation that isn't running Windows or Windows for Workgroups, you need to install
the MS-DOS printer driver file for the laser printer and make sure that it is accessible to
all your applications. Depending on how your disk is set up, you might have to copy the
file to all your application directories.

To set up a printing port from MS-DOS, go to the command prompt and type **net use**
lpt1:*server**sharename*. For *server* and *sharename*, substitute the name of the print
server and the name by which the printer is known on the network. Substitute another
port name where LPT1 already is in use.

If you want the connection to be made automatically every time you log on to the
network, add the /persistent:yes switch to the end of the command. Just typing
/persistent won't do anything, but if you leave off the persistent switch, it defaults
to whatever you selected the last time you used the NET USE command.

For example, suppose that you have an MS-DOS workstation that doesn't have a locally
attached printer on any of its parallel ports. Because some older DOS programs don't

really give you the chance to select an output port, you want the network printer HP4Si, which is attached to the server Balliol, to intercept any output for LPT1 and print it on HP4Si. Suppose also that you want this network printer attached every time you log on to the network. This would be the command for that:

```
net use lpt1: \\balliol\hp4Si /persistent:yes
```

Tip

> When the print server is using NTFS, workstations might not be able to print from MS-DOS if they have only Read and Execute privileges. The print jobs will spool to the print queue, but never print. To resolve this problem, give all users who print from DOS applications or the command prompt full access to the printer.

DOS workstations, regardless of whether they're running Windows over DOS, use the locally installed printer driver rather than the one stored on the server. Therefore, when you get an updated version of a printer driver, you need to install it at each DOS/Windows workstation individually.

Printing from Windows for Workgroups

Connecting to a Windows 2000 shared printer from Windows for Workgroups is just like connecting to the same printer on a Windows for Workgroups server. To connect, go first to the Control Panel and select the Printers icon. The window shows you the printer connections you currently have. To connect an existing printer to a new port, click the Connect button.

If you want to connect to a new printer, you need to click the Network button in this dialog box. It shows you which printers are available for connection. Click on the printer you want, and when its name appears in the Path box, click OK. You go back to the previous screen, where you can ensure that the printer is connected to the port you want.

That's how you connect to a networked printer when the drivers for that printer are already loaded. When they're not loaded, you need to use the Add button in the first screen to add the printer driver to the system. Click the Add button, and you see a list of printers.

Select the printer you want (for example, the HP LaserJet 4Si), and then click the Install button. You can use the Browse button or type the proper path when the driver is somewhere on the network; otherwise, you need to insert the appropriate disk. After you've installed the correct driver, you're ready to connect to the printer.

Printing from Windows 95 or 98

Connecting to a Windows 2000 shared printer from Windows 95 or 98 is easy. You only need to make a connection to the existing printer and Windows will do the rest. Just browse the network and double-click on a printer or type in the UNC for one if you know it. (The UNC is the actual address and looks like \\server1\printer1.) Your machine automatically downloads the driver it needs from the print server.

If you want to connect to a new printer, you can also use the Add Printers dialog box. This brings up a window asking if you want to connect to a local or a network printer. You would choose the network option to connect to a printer attached to another machine.

Next, the Wizard will ask you to tell it what type of printer it is you are connecting to (ask your network administrator or just walk over and have a look at the actual printer). Choose the correct model and click Next. Now tell your machine what port to use and click Next again. Type in a name so you recognize that printer (HP 5th floor for example) and decide whether you run DOS jobs and need to print from there. Print a test page and click on Finish.

After you complete these steps you are ready to print on that printer whenever you want.

Printing from OS/2

Connecting to a Windows 2000 printer from OS/2 is much like doing it from DOS. To set up a printing port, go to the command prompt (reached from the System folder) and type **net use lpt1:** *server*\ *sharename*. For *server* and *sharename*, substitute the name of the print server and the name by which the printer is known on the network. Substitute another port name if LPT1 is already in use. If you want the connection to be persistent, add the /persistent:yes switch to the end of the command.

When connecting to network printers, OS/2, like DOS and Windows, uses local printer drivers rather than drivers stored on the print server. Thus, you need to load the printer drivers locally for the printer you connect to, and if you update the drivers, you need to install the new ones at each workstation.

Printing From Windows 2000 or Other Versions of NT

When you're using Windows 2000, connecting to a shared printer is easy. Because Windows 2000 Professional workstations can access the printer drivers located on the print server, you don't need to load them locally. This applies to the older versions of NT as well.

Therefore, you don't need to define the proper port, find the drivers, or do anything else; all you need to do is go to the Control Panel, select the Printers icon, and double-click on Add Printer. When you do, you see the first Add Printer Wizard dialog box.

When you've reached the dialog box, choose the Network Printer Server option button, and then click the Next button. The next dialog box shows you the available printers you can connect to.

Double-click on the printer to select it, or click on it once and then click OK. That's it.

NT workstations use the printer drivers stored on the print server, so when you install a newer version of a driver on the print server, the workstations automatically will use it. You don't need to install software on the workstation.

Printer Security

Just because you've networked a printer doesn't necessarily mean that you want everyone on its domain to access it. Maybe it's the color laser printer, which can be costly, or you want to reduce the risk of security breaches by limiting the people who can print company secrets. Either way, you want to control access to the printer just as you would to any other network device.

There are several things you can do:

- Physically protect the printer
- Hide the printer
- Set printer permissions
- Set job priority
- Set printing hours

Physical Security for Confidentiality

The simplest control over printers and print servers is to ensure that they are provided the amount of protection warranted by the type of printing they are doing. For instance, in the Human Resources department, you would want to ensure that you adequately protect the printer and print server. You should physically protect access to a printer with confidential information being printed.

Printers represent a large exposure to most organizations. Employees can wait by any printer and get access to sensitive information they normally would not have. Also, many printers are strategically placed next to the office photocopier. But why would someone take a risk by photocopying a document, when they could probably just walk off with the original? Most users would decide that there must have been a printing problem and would try again. You will need to educate your users about confidentiality!

Hiding a Printer

You can hide the fact that a printer exists but still share it with the network. To do this, attach a dollar sign ($) to the end of the printer share name. This way, the printer name doesn't show up on the list of networked printers, but when the user types the name, the user can connect to the printer.

Setting Printer Permissions

As you'll recall from elsewhere in this book, you secure a Windows 2000 network by setting user rights for what people can do on the network, and setting user permissions for what people can use. Just as you can with other devices on the network, you can restrict printer use by setting permissions on it.

To set or change printer permissions, first go to the Printer window and select the icon for the printer you want. Next, go to the Properties dialog box in the File menu, choose the Security tab, and select Permissions.

The Printer Permissions dialog box lists groups with some kind of printer access set up. Using this dialog box, you can change the access for each group. The access permissions are shown in Table 10.4.

TABLE 10.4 Printer Permissions

Access	Description
No Access	No member of that user group can do anything with the printer, including print.
Print	Members of that user group can print documents.
Manage Documents	Members can control document settings, as well as pause, resume, restart, and delete documents that are lined up for printing.
Full Control	Members can do anything with the printer: print; control document settings; pause, resume, and delete documents and printers; change the printing order of documents; and change printer properties and permissions.

By default, only Administrators and Power Users have full control of the printer. Only those with full control can pause or resume a printer or set its permissions. Those who just have print access can only administer their own documents.

Note

> When a user is a member of more than one group with different printer permissions, the system always grants the highest-level permission. So if user Janet belongs to one group with Print privileges and another one with Full Control privileges, she always has Full Control privileges. The only time print permissions aren't cumulative is when one group that a user belongs to has No Access to the printer. In that case, No Access overrides all higher levels, and the user has no access to the printer.

To change a group's access, highlight the group and then choose the new access type from the Type of Access pull-down menu in the lower-right corner of the dialog box. One group must have Full Control, or you cannot change printer permissions in the future.

To add a user group or user to the printer permissions list, click the Add button. You see an Add Users and Groups dialog box. To add a group to the printer permissions list, highlight the kind of permission you want to give that group, click on the group you want, click Add, and click OK. To add only a particular person to the printer permissions list, you have two options:

- You can select a group that the user belongs to and click on Members. This gives you a list of all the users who belong to the group. Highlight the user you want.

- You can click the Show Users button and scroll down the user groups list until you see the entry for Users. Below this entry is a list of every user on the system. Double-click on the name, just as you would when selecting a user group.

After you've selected the group or user, the name should appear in the Add Names box in the bottom half of the screen. When you're done adding groups or users, click OK.

Removing a group or user from the printer permissions list is simple: Go to the Printer Permissions dialog box, highlight the name of the user or group, and then click Remove.

Setting Print Job Priorities

You can set printer priorities from the Scheduling tab of the Properties dialog box. If you want to share your printer with the network but don't want everyone else's print jobs crowding out your own, you can give the printer two names—a name you use that has a high priority, and a name with a lower priority that is used by everyone else who connects to the printer.

You can give the print jobs of a person or group priority over another person or group. To do this, create another printer for the same print device. Click on the Scheduling tab in the Properties dialog box, and you see an area where you can set printer priorities by sliding the bar along. You can set this number from 1 to 99, with 99 being the highest priority. The default priority is 1.

Setting Printing Hours

To adjust print times, click on the From box and then just click on the up or down arrows of the Available From and To boxes, or type the available times for the printer. When you send a print job to a printer during its "off hours," it doesn't disappear but sits there until the printer is authorized to print again.

Although you can set user logon hours and printer hours, you can't set printing hours for a particular user or group that are different from those of the others who have access to that printer. For example, you can't restrict users to a particular printer between 9 a.m. and 5 p.m. when Administrators can access it at any time, unless you adjust the users' logon times and configure their accounts so that the system kicks them off when their time is up.

Although you can't make a printer accessible to one group for one set of hours and to another group for a different set, you still can customize printer access hours for different sets of users. Simply add more than one printer (remember, printers are logical entities, distinct from the physical printing devices), set the hours for each printer as you require, and then tell each group which printer to use.

Sharing Local Printers

Not all printers on your Windows 2000 network are physically connected. Your only printer may be on an NT or Windows 2000 workstation or some other system, yet you want to allow others to use it. You can make your printer available to anyone on the network by adding a share for it.

Users with printers attached to their machines must create a share for their local printer. From the workstation, right-click on the printer and choose Properties, Sharing. Next, select the Shared option and either accept the name that shows or enter a new description. Finally, you can install extra drivers for all the types of operating systems the other users may use by selecting them in the window that shows. This way, when users want to use your printer, they don't need to have their own version of drivers. They will be able to download the drivers from your machine to use the printer you have installed.

You also can add the shared printer to your server by adding a local port that includes the UNC of the shared device. By adding a new port and filling in the UNC (*server**printersharename*), you add the printer as if it were local to the server.

Given all that to think about, that's it for today.

Summary

So that's printing—Windows 2000 style. Microsoft has made everything as easy as possible by keeping things consistent among all the various Windows versions. By now, you can sit down with any version of Windows and use a server printer to share a local printer with the network world (if the version of Windows allows it).

The purpose of this day was to introduce you to printing. Printing is an important part of your network. Most users will use network printing, and they will be quick to tell you when it doesn't work. It is amazing how fast you'll lose friends when printing is a problem.

In this day, you learned how to add and customize printers and add print servers. Completing these steps makes network printing available to your users.

To help you improve network security, you briefly learned about printer permissions and physical security.

10

Workshop

To wrap up the day, you can review tasks from the day, and see the answers to some commonly asked questions.

Task List

The emphasis of this day has been to set up network printing. As a system administrator, you need to learn how to add printers, define printers, and assign permissions to groups. You learned how to perform several tasks in this day:

- Adding a printer
- Customizing printers
- Pooling printers
- Setting printer permissions
- Setting up UNIX and Macintosh Services

Q&A

Q How do I set up more than one printer with the same name?

A To have more than one printer handle print jobs sent to the same print name, you must set up printer pooling. To do this, go to the Properties item in the File menu, and click the Ports button. Select the ports that correspond to the ports where you've plugged in the other printers.

On a Windows 2000 machine, you need only one copy of the driver for the type of printer you're pooling, unlike Windows for Workgroups, which requires one copy of the driver for each printer.

Q How do I print directly to ports?

A To send print jobs directly to the port where the printer is connected instead of spooling, go to the Properties item in the File menu of the Printers window, and click the Scheduling button.

DAY 11

Understanding Remote Access Services (RRAS) and VPNs

NEW TERM The title of this day is somewhat misleading because it refers to *Remote Access Services* (*RAS*). In NT Server 4, Microsoft attempted to change the name of RAS to *Dial-Up Networking*, or *DUN*, to remain consistent with a term begun in Windows 95. RAS remains widely used, however, and the tools in Windows 2000 refer to the term *RAS*. To avoid any additional confusion, the term *RAS* is used continuously throughout this day. If you are more comfortable with the term *DUN*, mentally translate *RAS* to *DUN* whenever you encounter it.

Note

> The term *RAS* is still used within Windows 2000, although the newer term *Dial-Up Networking* is becoming more familiar in other Windows platforms. Either term works in the general sense of defining remote access—unless you really want to get technical. Windows 2000 Server still refers to *RAS* more than *DUN* in its Help files.

Today, you'll learn all about RAS, what to use it for, how to set it up, and what to look for when implementing it. You'll learn all about

- What RAS is and why you use it.
- The fact that RAS does not install automatically when you first install Windows 2000. You need to specifically install this service and set it up to manage your dial-up connections.
- Administering RAS and setting up the machines that you will call and the protocols that you intend to use.
- The option in W2K's RAS that provides the capability of linking more than one modem together and obtaining a single dial-up connection that is twice as fast; the facility, called *Multilink PPP*, is a facility that you enable on both the server and the client machines.
- What Virtual Private Networking is and how to use it.

What Is RAS?

What is RAS? Consider it an extension of all your local area network functions using a dial-up modem connection. This means that you can read files, update information, print reports, or do almost anything you can do when you connect via your workstation. True, no modem is as fast as a good network connection, but the functionality remains. You get to perform all the functions of your job from a remote location such as your house or the local bar. (Just kidding. We know that you don't work at the local bar; it's far too distracting. This joke, however, highlights some of the difficulty that comes with allowing remote access to an organization's mission-critical local area networks or other machines. Now the Grand Cayman Islands, that's another story. It's ten o'clock. Do you know where your remote users are?)

NEW TERM   You can consider remote access using RAS to be the same as using your serial ports on your laptop as network cards such as Ethernet or Token Ring. Just as you connect at the office to perform your day-to-day work, you connect through a modem to perform the same work at home or in a satellite office. The term *modem* is used here as if it's the only way to connect the machines, but it isn't. RAS also allows connections using the older X.25 packet-switching network, *Integrated Services Digital Network (ISDN)*, null modem cables, and fully digital T1 lines. Windows 2000 expands upon traditional dial-up capabilities by allowing clients to communicate through the Internet and allows them to do this securely by creating a *virtual private network (VPN)*. You'll set up a VPN later today.

NEW TERM In Windows 2000, RAS is found in two places. You find the client side by looking in Accessories, Communications, Network and Dial-up Connections, and you find the server side tools in Administrative Tools, Routing and Remote Access. Remember that *server side* refers to applications that are executed on a server and that receive requests from the workstations, whereas *client side* refers to applications that are executed on a workstation and connect to a server running a companion application—hence the term *client/server*. Obviously, your server can dial-out and act as a client to another system.

Most RAS connections are made using a modem, and that thread is followed throughout today's information. Starting RAS on your machine makes that machine the RAS server, just as you might be using a file server, application server, or database server. This doesn't mean that you need a separate server to run RAS, however; you can set it up to run on your domain controller—as long as the equipment can handle the overall service load.

Note

> You need to review some of the basics concerning network protocols before continuing too far into this lesson, because this information is relevant to the remaining discussion. If you are unfamiliar with networking protocols, you might want to skip ahead to later days on network protocols and review some of the terms that are used before continuing.

11

NEW TERM RAS, therefore, acts as a network to the user, allowing remote access to the familiar desktop. It does this in part by managing to *tunnel,* or hide, certain protocols such as TCP/IP and IPX/SPX within others, such as the Point-to-Point protocol (PPP). This allows NT Server to talk to machines that aren't running RAS or NT.

RAS does allow for the use of the slower and older Serial Line Interface Protocol (SLIP); however, most sites have moved to PPP, and SLIP is slowly fading into the sunset.

Is RAS the same as using packages such as PcAnywhere, Carbon Copy, and Symantec's Remote Control? It is similar in that both types of access permit you to access the network and enable you to perform functions remotely; it differs greatly, however, in what each access does and in its planned intent. PcAnywhere and Carbon Copy enable you to remotely control another PC across a modem. RAS, on the other hand, is just a gateway into a remote network via a modem.

What Is X.25?

NEW TERM   It was mentioned earlier that RAS allows connections between various protocols;
X.25 was also mentioned. What is this protocol and how does it work? *X.25*
enables you to route information through a packet-switching public data network, such as
Tymnet or Datapac. An older technology, it operates at a top speed of 64Kbps, and it was
designed for earlier days when telephone networks were less reliable than they are today.

X.25 is in use today primarily because of its widespread availability throughout the
world. If you are part of a large multinational corporation, you might still use this technology in parts of your network. It is very dependable and can tolerate poor telephone-
line quality, so it offers a reasonable service in countries that use less-reliable telephony.
The error-checking capability that it offers is still attractive even though this capability
slows the connection considerably—better slow data than no data.

NEW TERM   Connecting RAS using an X.25 network requires that you use an *X.25 pad*, or
packet assembler-dissembler. This device takes the data streams from one end of
the connection and converts them so that they can travel over the X.25 network. The pad
at the other end changes the data packets back to their original message format for the
system to use.

Why Use RAS?

What are some of the applications for which you can use RAS? By far, the most common allow users remote access to their W2K network. Using a Windows 95, DOS, Mac,
Windows for Workgroups, or Windows 2000 Professional workstation, the user signs on
to the network from home using her modem. After being connected, the user performs
her daily work duties as if she were at the office.

RAS is also used for remote dial-in to non-NT machines, such as those running the
TCP/IP or IPX/SPX protocols. Additionally, you can use RAS to set up your NT Server
as a gateway or to connect your organization's network to the Internet or to other networks.

NEW TERM   Finally, you can use RAS to set up your server as a Web, Telnet, and FTP server
or even to offer complete *ISP* (*Internet Service Provider*) services. When you
connect to Microsoft's Web page and FTP server, you are talking to a Windows 2000
Server machine.

Requirements for Using RAS

You need not be running Windows 2000 Server to use RAS. As you recall from earlier in the day, RAS is available in the Workstation version of W2K. They work the same, except that in the workstation you are limited to one connection; in Windows 2000 Server you can maintain 256 concurrent sessions.

Apart from a current version of W2K, you also need a minimum of two compatible modems, typically one for the laptop or remote PC and the other for the server that you want to dial. Between these two modems is the telephone line. Note that although you can use a cellular telephone connection and travel across the resulting cellular network, this network isn't as consistent as local telephone landlines. Furthermore, because you travel between cells on the cellular network, the connection might be lost.

You should try to stick to using a standard modem in your network because you'll sometimes encounter difficulties connecting when using different brands of modems on the client and the server. In addition, remember that W2K can be picky and might not work with some brands. This is especially true with higher-speed modems because small differences can affect the operation and each manufacturer can use a different method to achieve the high speed. Sticking to Hayes standard modems and V.32 or V.34 bits standards also helps. Use the Windows 2000 Hardware Compatibility List to determine what modems Microsoft has tested with Windows 2000 Server.

One other method of connecting machines consists of using a serial null modem cable and RAS. A small organization might use this for fast and fairly inexpensive access because null modem cables can be purchased for $10 and up, depending on their length. Using a serial cable connection voids any need for network cards or modems. This method, however, is far slower, and the performance of such a connection isn't stellar. If you plan to try a serial RAS connection, be sure to study the exact null cable specification in Windows 2000 because you cannot use just any cable because of the specific pin connections required by RAS.

NEW TERM A really nice addition to NT 4 available in W2K was the potential for pooling your modems and telephone connections and connecting to an NT Server at a far higher speed than was possible through one modem alone. NT refers to this capability as *Multilink PPP (MPPP)*. (How to do this is detailed later today.)

What are the major components for using RAS? The various pieces include

- Two or more compatible modems
- A telephone or cellular line
- Windows 2000 Server or Professional

11

To use ISDN, the requirements are similar in concept. You must have two ISDN network cards (or the newer external ISDN modems), a digital-grade copper or fiber-optic cable connecting the two cards, and network termination devices to connect the cable to each card. (The network terminators might be built in to your network cards. Most new cards support this method.) This service is becoming very popular now and can be purchased for home use at a reasonable price, which greatly improves your network access speed.

This book focuses on using RAS with modems because this use is more common—and we are limited in the page count available for each subject.

Let's begin by installing a modem for use with RAS.

Installing a New Modem

In the following section, you will install and configure the Remote Access Server software. During the installation, the process asked for information on which modems you are using. The following task shows how to add a new modem and tell Windows 2000 Server all about it.

Task 11.1: Installing a New Modem.

Step 1: Description

In this task, you'll learn to install new modems and tell Windows 2000 Server about them.

Step 2: Action

1. Begin by signing on to your server as Administrator. Next, choose Control Panel and double-click the Add/Remove Hardware icon.

2. The Add/Remove Hardware Wizard starts. Click Next.

3. From the window in Figure 11.1, you have two choices: Add/Troubleshoot a Device or Uninstall/Unplug a Device. Check the former and click Next.

4. From the Choose a Hardware Device window, highlight either the device you want to add or Add a New Device. Click Next.

5. If you selected Add a New Device, you have a choice:

   - Yes, Search for New Hardware
   - No, I Want to Select the Hardware from a List

   Select the latter and click Next. It is recommended that you choose the Don't Search option because usually it is faster and more accurate, although W2K occasionally misses modems and chooses a default setting.

FIGURE 11.1

The Choose a Hardware Task window.

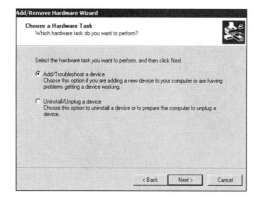

6. From the Hardware Type window shown in Figure 11.2, highlight Network Adapters or PCMCIA Adapters and click Next.

FIGURE 11.2

The Hardware Type window.

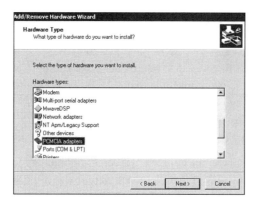

11

7. W2K continues and provides a list of available modems. In the Select a Device Driver left pane, scroll down until you find your card manufacturer and then highlight it. Highlight the Network Adapter in the right pane and click Next.

8. Windows 2000 tells you it is going to install drivers in the Start Hardware Installation panel and asks you to click Next. Click Next.

9. You receive a successful installation message; you need to click the Finish button. You see an example of this message in Figure 11.3. Click the Finish button to complete the task. Remember that you need to restart the system before NT will recognize the new modem.

FIGURE **11.3**

Windows has completed the device setup.

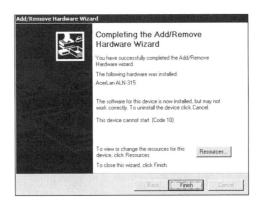

Step 3: Review

This task shows you how to add new modems to Windows 2000 Server. Use this task any time a new modem is installed.

Enabling Multilink PPP Connections

One of the options that you can use in Windows 2000 Server is the capability to allow a connection to occur using more than one modem. For example, you can set up two 56Kbps modems on the client machine to call W2K Server and use the combined speed of both modems as a single connection. Neat! In this example, you end up with a modem speed rivaling 112Kbps. This is only an example, of course; the speed typically doesn't double. It is, however, significantly faster than using only one modem.

In the past, you had to be connecting an NT Workstation client to your server to use this service. It was not offered for other client software. Now you can use this service with Windows 98 and—if you install the DUN 1.2 upgrade—with Windows 95. Of course, you can use this with Windows 2000 Professional. The following task looks at how this service can be set up. Both the server and the client must have multilink enabled.

Task 11.2: Installing Multilink PPP.

Step 1: Description

In this task, you'll learn to install the Remote Access Services facility that enables you to combine a number of modems into one faster connection. You can connect a workstation using two 28.8Kbps modems and obtain a connection with the server at a speed of 57.6Kbps.

▼ Step 2: Action

1. Begin by signing on to your server as Administrator. Next, choose Start, Settings, Control Panel and double-click the Network and Dial-up Connections icon.

2. Right-click the connection where you want to allow multilink, and select Properties.

3. On the Options tab, in the Multiple Devices section, check Dial Devices Only as Needed.

▲ 4. Click OK.

Step 3: Review

This task shows you how to add multilink PPP access and give users the capability to dial in using the combined speed of two separate modems. This is a great way of providing additional bandwidth without paying for higher-cost services such as ISDN or dedicated T1 access.

Installing RAS

RAS does not install automatically when you first set up Windows 2000 Server unless you specify that the new server is participating in an existing network (although you will find a Routing and Remote Access Service snap-in in your Administrative Tools folder). In the book *Windows NT Server Secrets,* Jason Garms, et al, Sams Publishing, 1996, the author states that it is best to wait to install RAS rather than to install it when you first install NT. We suggest this applies to RRAS in Windows 2000 as well. This is because there are a number of things that you need, and the installation and implementation of RAS are a lot easier when these things already exist.

NEW TERM   Before performing the RRAS install, install the necessary network protocols such as TCP/IP or IPX. Don't install protocols that aren't necessary, because each protocol takes memory (TCP/IP is the biggest memory user). Blindly installing everything reduces your system performance.

> **Tip**
>
> If you aren't sure whether you installed TCP/IP correctly, or you don't know how to tell, you might want to jump ahead to tomorrow, "Understanding TCP/IP and DNS."

Ensure that your modems and I/O ports are properly installed and configured as suggested in Day 2, "Installing Windows 2000 and Client Software." For normal RAS dial-in, these are the key components. Should you plan to use RAS for heavier duty, consider installing the *DHCP* (*Dynamic Host Configuration Protocol*) and *WINS* (*Windows Internet Naming Service*) servers as well if they aren't already running somewhere on your network. (See later days for more information on these.) This addition helps minimize your problem solving should something go wrong when you begin to install RAS. Finally, make sure that your modem and I/O ports are correctly configured and working, to minimize the chance of an error further confusing your install of RRAS.

Task 11.3: Installing RRAS.

Step 1: Description

In this task, you'll learn to configure the Routing and Remote Access Services facility.

Step 2: Action

1. Begin by signing on as Administrator.

2. Stop the RRAS server on the server, using the Computer Management snap-in.

3. Select Start, Programs, Administrative Tools, Routing and Remote Access. The Routing and Remote Access snap-in appears, as shown in Figure 11.4.

FIGURE 11.4

The Routing and Remote Access snap-in.

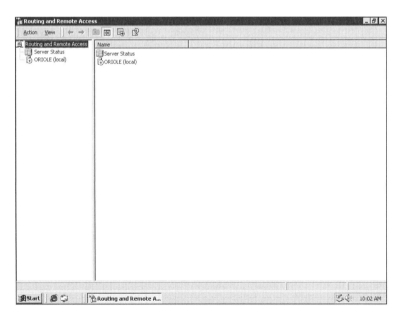

4. Highlight the server where you want to install RRAS. Right-click the server, and select Configure and Enable Routing and Remote Access.

Note

If you skipped step 2 and didn't stop the service, a message box pops up asking you whether you want to stop the RRAS service. Click Yes.

5. You should see the Routing and Remote Access Configuration Wizard (see Figure 11.5). Click Next.

FIGURE 11.5

The Routing and Remote Access Configuration Wizard.

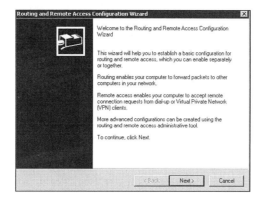

6. The Routing and Remote Access panel shown in Figure 11.6 allows you to

- Enable Server as a Router: Enables the server as a route for Local Routing Only (LAN) or Local and Remote Routing (LAN and WAN)

- Enable Remote Access: Enables the server to accept remote access requests for dial-up or VPN connections

FIGURE 11.6

The Routing and Remote Access panel.

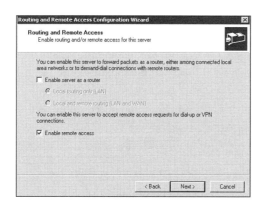

Check Enable Remote Access. Click Next.

11

▼ 7. On the Dial-in or Demand Dial Interfaces panel, you have two choices:

- Enable All Devices for Remote Access (the default)
- Configure Each Device Individually

8. Check Enable All Devices for Remote Access. Click Next. The panel in Figure 11.7 appears. This panel deals with authentication and encryption.

FIGURE 11.7

The Authentication and Encryption panel.

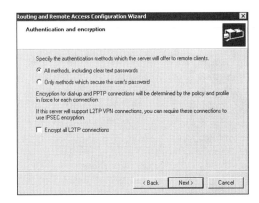

You have two choices for authenticating remote clients:

- All Methods, Including Clear Text Passwords: Specify this option when you have downlevel clients such as Macintosh, Windows 95, or Windows for Workgroups. This is the default.
- Only Methods Which Secure the Password: Specify when you have Windows NT Server, Windows NT Workstation, and Windows 2000 Professional clients that can support encryption.

Select the first option. You now need to decide whether you want to encrypt all L2TP connections. L2TP (Layer 2 Tunneling Protocol) is a multiprotocol tunneling technology developed by Microsoft, Cisco, Ascend, IBM, and 3Com. L2TP supports MPPP, which differs from Microsoft's implementation. Checking this option requires clients to use IPSec encryption. Click Next.

9. The next panel is the Define the Access Rights for Remote Systems. Highlight a protocol such as TCP/IP and check one of the following:

- Access This Server Only
- Access Entire Network

The default is Access Entire Network Only. Click Next.

▼ 10. You should see the panel shown in Figure 11.8.

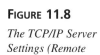

FIGURE 11.8

The TCP/IP Server Settings (Remote Access) panel.

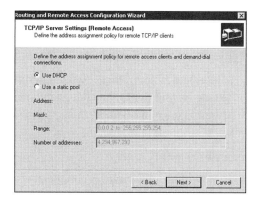

You need to decide whether you want to use a dynamic or static address for incoming clients. If you want dynamic addresses, check Use DHCP. If you want to static addresses, check Use a Static Pool and specify the network address, netmask, and range of addresses to use. If you select this option and set up these options, you should see the number of available addresses.

Check Use DHCP and click Next.

11. Click Finish.

12. A message appears (shown in Figure 11.9) asking whether you want to restart the service. Click Yes to restart the RRAS service.

FIGURE 11.9

The RRAS message.

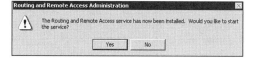

Step 3: Review

You learned about setting up devices such as modems and configuring protocols and other necessary elements. RRAS snap-in installs automatically when you first set up Windows 2000 Server. This task shows you how to add Remote Access Services and give users the capability to dial in and dial out of Windows. The preceding task enables you to use RAS and connect your dial-up machines to the network. RAS cannot be used as a LAN-to-LAN link, however, because it doesn't perform packet broadcasts, sending packets from one LAN segment to another. You now manage the servers using the Routing and Remote Access snap-in.

Administering RAS

You can now permit users to utilize Remote Access Services on your server. It's time to administer access and manage the dial-in process. This is accomplished via the Routing and Remote Access snap-in found in Start, Programs, Administrative Tools.

After starting Routing and Remote Access, you see a dialog box that contains a list of all RAS servers currently running in your domain. Although my domain is very small and uses only one RAS server, yours might have multiple servers set up to run RAS and allow dial-in or dial-out.

Under the server, you see five entries:

- Ports: Lists devices, their type, and the number of them.
- Dial-In Clients: Number of clients and information about them.
- IP Routing: Two parameters for use:

    General: Provides information on event logging, routing preferences, and configured multicast scopes.

    Static Routes: Provides the static routes for your router.

- IPX Routing: You can set up or look at General, NetBIOS Broadcasts, Static Routes, Static NetBIOS Names, RIP for IPX, and SAP for IPX.
- Remote Access Policy: Used to create a policy to apply for your RAS server. In the next task, you will create a Remote Access Policy.

 Note

Should you install AppleTalk instead of IPX or install IPX and AppleTalk, you will see entries reflecting those protocols.

Next, under the Server Status, you see whether a server is active (running) or stopped. The Total Ports section indicates the number of ports configured to provide RAS service, and Ports In Use tells how many of those ports are presently active.

Double-clicking on a server provides additional detail and shows you the actual port addresses that are defined. It also tells you if the addresses are in use, who the user is, and when that dial session began.

Disconnection of a user takes effect immediately and doesn't give the user any warning. On an NT Workstation, the user automatically receives any message sent via the Send Message button. Windows and Windows 95 users must be running NetPopup or other network mail software in order to see a message. To send a message to all the users on this RAS server, use the Send to All button.

Double-click the server on the RAS main screen and you will see several options:

- Install Routing and Remote Access: You just did this in the previous task.
- Start Routing and Remote Access: Enables you to start a RAS server.
- Stop Routing and Remote Access: Enables you to stop a RAS server and automatically disconnect all users.
- Remove Service: Obviously, removes the services.

The Active Directory Users and Computers snap-in contains two additional items. You see these items in Figure 11.10. These are used to allow dial-in or VPN use and to set where a user can call in to the server:

- Remote Access Permissions (Dial-in or VPN): Grants or denies RAS permissions to users. By default, all users are denied access to RAS services.
- Callback Options: Sets up RAS callback options. Enables you to set up RAS to call a user back at a predetermined telephone number. This provides additional security and limits the need for users to dial long distance.

FIGURE 11.10

The user's dial-in properties.

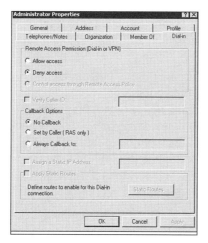

11

The final two menu items are Assign a Static IP Address and Apply Static Routes. The latter defines routes for the dial-in connection.

You can see that various facilities are used in this window to modify RAS according to your needs.

You will need to add Remote Access Services and give users the capability to dial in and dial out of Windows. The following task enables you to use RAS and connect your dial-up machines to the network.

TASK

Task 11.4: Creating a Remote Access Policy.

Step 1: Description

In this task, you'll learn to add or create a remote access policy.

Step 2: Action

1. Begin by signing on as Administrator.
2. Select Start, Programs, Administrative Tools, Routing and Remote Access. Open the RAS server.
3. Right-click the Remote Access Policies icon.
4. Select New Remote Access Policy. This opens the Add/Remote Access Policy dialog box shown in Figure 11.11.

FIGURE 11.11

The Add Remote Access Policy dialog box.

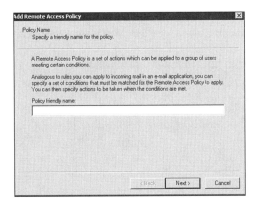

5. Enter a name for the policy in the Policy Friendly Name text box. You can apply this policy to a group of users. Click Next.
6. On the next panel you can specify the conditions to match for dial-in. Click Add. Table 11.1 describes the attributes you can add.

TABLE 11.1 Policy Attributes

Attribute	Description
Called-Station-Id	Specifies the phone number of the dial-up connection used by the user. For example, 555-1234.
Calling-Station-Id	Specifies the phone number of the caller. For example, 555-****.

Attribute	Description
Client-Friendly-Name	Specifies a friendly name for the RADIUS client. For example, RASCL**.
Client-IP-Address	Specifies the IP Address of the RADIUS client. For example, 199.199.199.*.
Client-Vendor	Manufacturer of the network authentication system (NAS). For example, Microsoft RAS, Cisco, or Shiva.
Day-And-Time-Restrictions	Specifies any time-of-day or day/week restrictions on the use of RAS. (see Figure 11.12). Default is that everything is denied.
Framed-Protocol	Specifies the protocol to use. For example, PPP, SLIP, X25, or AppleTalk.
NAS-IP-Address	Specifies the IP address of the NAS. For example, 199.199.199.2.
NAS-Identifier	Specifies a string to identify the NAS originating the request. For example, RADIUS_Server.
NAS-Port-Type	Specifies the physical port used by the NAS originating the request. For example, Async (Modem), Sync (T1 Line), ISDN Sync, and Virtual (VPN).
Service-Type	Type of service user has requested. For example, Administrative-User, Callback-Login, and Shell-User.
Windows-Groups	Specifies the Windows groups where the user belongs. For example, Administrators.

11

FIGURE 11.12

*Time of Day
Constraints
dialog box.*

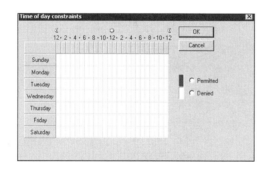

7. Click Next.

8. Use the subsequent panel, shown in Figure 11.13, to set access permissions. You can use this Remote Access Policy to grant access to a group or act as a filter to block group access. Select Grant Remote Access Permission. Click Next.

FIGURE 11.13

*The Permissions
dialog box.*

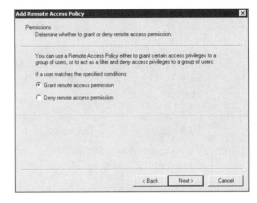

9. Clicking Edit Profile shows Figure 11.14. You set this up when you grant access to users.

FIGURE 11.14

Edit Dial-in Profile.

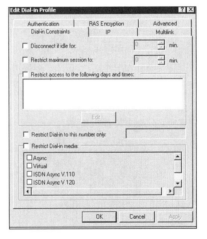

10. Click Finish. You should now see your dial-in policy in the right panel of the RRAS snap-in.

Step 3: Review

You learned about installing RRAS and configuring it. The RRAS snap-in installs auto-matically when you first set up Windows 2000 Server. This task shows you how to add Remote Access Services and give users the capability to dial in and dial out of Windows. The preceding task enables you to use RAS and connect your dial-up machines to the network. RAS cannot be used as a LAN-to-LAN link, however, because it doesn't perform packet broadcasts, sending packets from one LAN segment to another. You now manage the servers using the Routing and Remote Access snap-in.

Disconnecting a User

Now that you have connected users in various ways, how can you forcibly disconnect someone? It isn't difficult. Start a DOS command prompt and type the following command:

```
net session \\computername   /delete
```

Put the name of the computer that you want to disconnect in place of the word *computername* in the preceding command. Although the wording indicates that it will delete something, this is just Microsoft's little joke. It only disconnects, or ends, the connection. Be careful to specify a computer, or W2K disconnects all the currently connected users.

If you prefer, you also can use Windows 2000's GUI interface to disconnect someone. Select Start, Programs, Administrative Tools, Routing and Remote Access.

Open the server where you want to disconnect the user. Double-click Dial-in Clients. In the Details pane on the right, select the user you want to disconnect. Right-click the user and click Disconnect. That user is disconnected from the server. Warn users before disconnecting them; otherwise, they might lose data.

Using Dial-Up Networking

In this section, you'll learn how to use RAS to connect to other services, such as the Internet or another computer.

Task 11.5: Connecting to a Server Using the RAS Client.

Step 1: Description

In this task, you'll learn to use the RAS client software to set up your phone books and make client connections. You must have set up at least one W2K RAS port for dial-out before starting this task. You also need RAS (or Dial-Up Networking) running on both machines for this task to work. Task 11.1 showed you how to add a RAS port (starting at task item number 6).

▼ **Step 2: Action**

1. Begin by selecting Start, Programs, Accessories, Dial-up Networking. The first time you start Dial-Up Networking, W2K tells you that it cannot find a phone book entry and indicates that you need to add one. Click OK, and W2K shows you the New Phonebook Entry Wizard. As mentioned earlier in this book, Windows 2000 offers many of the Windows 95–style wizards to help guide you through various setup routines. The New Phonebook Entry Wizard dialog box is shown in Figure 11.15.

FIGURE 11.15

The New Phonebook Entry Wizard.

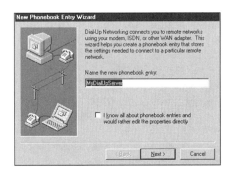

2. Enter a machine name into your phone book, or accept the default name provided by Windows 2000. Click the Next button to continue.

3. If a phone book entry is already in place, W2K shows you the first entry and asks whether this is what you want to dial. Choose to add a New entry if you want, and set up another machine to dial in to. Click the Next button to continue.

4. Check all the options that apply on the screen that shows. Click the Next button to continue.

5. Enter the telephone number of the machine that you want to call, and click Next.

6. Click Finish to end the setup. You now have one or more entries in your Dial-Up Networking telephone book and can choose one of these to call. W2K shows you the main Dial-Up Networking dialog box with the latest telephone number ready for dialing.

7. To perform more detailed operations such as editing an existing entry or setting up preferences, click the More button to see a dialog box similar to the one shown in Figure 11.16.

8. As you see in Figure 11.16, various options are available. The first option, Edit Entry and Modem Properties, enables you to customize your entries. As you see in
▼ Figure 11.17, there are five tabs that permit a detailed degree of customization.

FIGURE 11.16

Additional telephone book options.

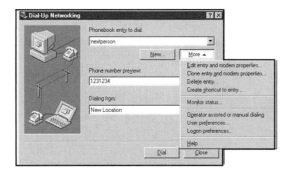

FIGURE 11.17

Customizing telephone book entries.

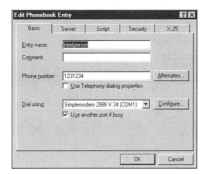

9. Under the Basic tab, you are offered the options of adding a comment, changing the telephone number or name, or modifying the modem. These are all self-explanatory fields. The Server tab offers you a chance to modify the type of protocol that you are using and to set up software compression. The available protocols are PPP, SLIP, and Windows NT 3.1 or Windows for Workgroups 3.11.

10. You set up scripts by choosing the Script tab. Scripts tell RAS how to log in to the host machine. If you are logging in to W2K, Windows, or UNIX machines, it's highly unlikely that you need a script. Typically, the administrator for the machine that you are dialing tells you if there are special requirements. For example, you might use a script to dial in to CompuServe.

11. The Security tab offers you the chance to ensure authentication between you and the server that you are calling. The first option tells W2K not to worry about encryption and allows clear text passwords to be sent. This can be useful if users are having a hard time getting connected via RAS (sometimes the encrypted passwords don't work). This does leave the passwords vulnerable to unauthorized access, however, so only consider this option if it is absolutely necessary. The second option offers an encrypted authentication based on accepted standards, and the

▼

third option offers special Microsoft encryption. Using this option enables you to encrypt all the data that flows between machines—and this option is very secure. The option called Use Current Username and Password offers a degree of single sign on (that is, it limits the number of times you need to enter an account and password to sign on to multiple systems) because RAS uses the account that you signed on to as the RAS authentication.

12. The last tab enables you to set up special X.25 pad connections. By clicking on the question mark and moving your cursor to a field, W2K Help provides specifics about that field.

▲

Step 3: Review

This task shows you how to add and update telephone book entries for the different machines that you might dial up. You use this to set up the specifics about each machine that you want to dial. Using Dial-Up Networking then becomes as simple as choosing the name of the machine you are calling.

You might need to connect to your RAS server using a DOS-based client machine. The next task shows you the steps necessary for connecting.

Task 11.6: Connecting to a Server Using a DOS Client.

Step 1: Description

In this task, you'll learn the tasks necessary for setting up your DOS-based machine to connect to the RAS server. You'll find the drivers mentioned in the \clients\ras directory of your Windows 2000 Server installation CD-ROM. You need to copy them to the DOS machine before starting this task.

Step 2: Action

1. Begin by starting your DOS machine and typing **rasload** to install the necessary RAS drivers.

2. Next, type **rasphone** to open the telephone book. Create and save an entry as needed by filling in the blanks as shown.

3. If a phone book entry is already in place, add entries as necessary, depending on how many machines you intend to dial in to.

4. Press Alt+D or use the menu and choose the Connect option. Fill in your password and other data as requested.

5. A dialog box informs you that the DOS machine is attempting a connection. If you entered the wrong number or want to cancel the call, press the Esc key. When the connection is successful, you can use any resources for which you are authorized as if you were on the network.

▲

Step 3: Review

This task shows you how to set up and use a DOS client for accessing the RAS server. Use this any time you want DOS-based machines to access the server through dial-in.

Finding Out More About Remote Access Server

Microsoft offers an extensive Web site for all its products. The most useful for your purposes is the Knowledge Base, Microsoft's detailed technical support area that is found at `www.microsoft.com/support`. Choose the Support Online option. From here, you can search by category and word for any available articles.

Performing a search for the category `NT Server` or `Windows 2000` and the keyword `RAS` provides a list of topics concerning RAS that can help you correct any problems that occur. Searching for `multilink` provides a couple of articles relating to this service. For example, in Windows NT Server 4, a problem exists with the use of multilink. To use multilink, you need to set the LCP (Link Control Protocol) extensions, or multilink doesn't function.

This search found numerous RAS topics concerning everything from a list of supported modems to logon scripts for Windows for Workgroup clients.

Many of these solutions provide answers to your problems and questions, so this is a good place to look to gather additional problem-solving data.

By using the various Microsoft options on this Web page, you can download new service packs. You can also obtain new drivers or sample files for your applications and equipment.

Under the Feature Articles forum, you can find the latest hardware compatibility list and patches. So if you are having difficulty getting a modem to work, look here and see whether the modem is a Microsoft-certified device.

Finally, a Windows NT Server newsgroup forum provides additional details and user experiences. This is also an excellent way to gather information and query others about a problem. For now, the specific RAS and other communication-issues newsgroup are found at the following address:

`microsoft.public.windowsnt.protocol.ras`

These Microsoft services are an invaluable aid in determining a problem and possibly finding a solution. As in many situations, it's likely that the problem you are having also occurred elsewhere and that other people have repaired the problem and have moved on. They are usually able and willing to share that information with you.

11

Security and RAS

Remote Access Services offer a rich degree of accessibility, but this comes with a price. Installing RAS leaves you somewhat vulnerable to attack from the outside world. So what can you do? Fortunately, there are several things that you can do to enhance the level of security over this important service.

Out of the box, Microsoft supports EAP and the types of password authentication shown in Figure 11.18 when dialing in to the server. Use the Routing and Remote Access administrative tool to see this information. RAS offers the Extensible Authentication Protocol (EAP). This protocol allows software developers to provide authentication mechanisms beyond what W2K supports. EAP currently supports Message Digest 5 (MD5) Challenge Handshake Authentication Protocol (EAP-MD5-CHAP) and Transport Level Security for smartcards or other certificates (EAP-TLS). The next options allow the use of MS-CHAP versions 1 and 2, CHAP, SPAP, and PAP. You choose what algorithm to use. The first two are Microsoft encrypted authentication options, which support more robust encryption of the passwords. SPAP is used by Shiva LAN Rover devices, and CHAP is a challenge-response authentication offering—arguably the best authentication. You can choose standard clear-text passwords or no authentication at all.

FIGURE 11.18

Dial-in server security properties.

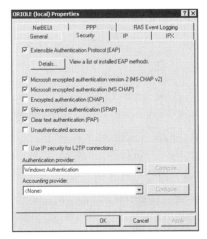

The first two options, Microsoft encrypted authentication, use a special version of CHAP called—strangely enough—MS-CHAP. This version uses an internal algorithm by RSA Data Security Incorporated, offering a very secure level of encryption. Two Windows 2000 machines always use the MS-CHAP authentication when talking to each other. Microsoft offers 128-bit level encryption for North America and those countries and companies that are allowed this high level of encryption.

If you use its option, Microsoft offers additional levels of security by enabling you to fully encrypt the traffic between the machines. This option, although a little slower, provides a strong level of control over outsiders gaining access to data sent over public networks or telephone lines because all the information, not just the password, is encrypted.

The RAS service also offers additional ways to protect your system. After it's installed, RAS enables you to control who can use the dial-up service by providing the capability to control dial-in permissions. By default, no one can dial in to the server. You need to set up access for each user to whom you want to allow RAS access by using the Active Directory snap-in.

NEW TERM Another security mechanism offered by RAS is *callback*. This mechanism enables you to set up specific numbers for each user so that when the user calls in to access RAS, Windows 2000 calls the person back at that predefined telephone number. This technique also offers the organization a way of managing long-distance calls because the RAS server, not the user, initiates the final dial-in call. This is of limited security benefit with today's call forwarding and other telephone options.

After you allow dial-in, you can set up additional controls. Perhaps you want users to perform only certain functions from outside the office and not have the capability to do everything they normally can. By using the network access option, you can restrict users to either the entire network or a particular server. You can find this option in the Routing and Remote Access snap-in.

These options enable you to customize access and ensure a secure dialog between your client machines and the network. Using the fully encrypted mode and restricting access to a single server offer an excellent level of control. However, I would be remiss if I didn't mention that regardless of the level of security added to RAS, if your user community doesn't select hard-to-guess passwords, your security is still weak. Many system penetrations are a result of poor password selection.

Now that you know a little about security protocols and RRAS, you can set up a Virtual Private Network.

Task 11.7: Creating a VPN Service Profile.

Step 1: Description

In this task, you'll learn how to use the Connection Manager Administration Kit to set up a service profile for your VPN.

Step 2: Action

1. Select Start, Run, type **cmak** and click OK to start the Connection Manager Administration Kit (CMAK). You should see the window in Figure 11.19. Click Next.

FIGURE 11.19

The Connection Manager Administration Kit Wizard.

2. Check Create a New Service Profile and click Next.

3. Enter the name of your service in the Service Name box, and add a service profile identifier in the File Name box. Click Next.

4. Click Next.

5. Complete any support information you want to provide, and click Next.

6. Ensure Do Not Add a Realm Name is checked. Click Next.

7. Enter Phone Book Dial-up Networking entries by clicking entries and completing the dialog box. Click OK and then click Next.

8. Click This Service Profile for Use a VPN Connection For. This provides VPN support for your users when using the Internet. Click Next.

9. Select Connect Actions. Click Next.

10. Set Pre-Connect Actions by clicking Add. Click OK and then click Next.

11. Set Post-Connect Actions. Click Next.

12. Set Disconnect Actions. Click Next.

13. Set Auto-Applications, that is, applications you want your users to run while connected, such as an email client. Click Next.

14. Check the bitmap you want to display in the logon dialog box. Click Next.

15. Check the bitmap you want to display in the Phone Book dialog box. Click Next twice.

16. Enter the Name of the phone-book (.pbk) file to be downloaded and the server it is on, and click Next.

17. Select a connection icon and click Next. Click Next again.

▼   18.   Check Use the Default Help File, and click Next.

19.   Check Include the Connection Manager 1.2 Software, and click Next.

20.   Specify a license file, should you have one, and click Next.

21.   Specify additional files and click Next. Click Next again to build the Service Profile. You should see a command prompt window like the one in Figure 11.20.

FIGURE 11.20

The command prompt window.

▲   22.   Click Finish. You now have a service profile.

Step 3: Review

This task shows you how to set up a service profile using the Connection Manager Administration Kit. Use this service profile for your VPN connections.

Understanding the Routing Part of RRAS

RRAS unifies routing with remote access services, allowing one tool to do the job of two. For most organizations, you will probably continue to use RAS, and the information provided earlier in this day will suffice. Some of you, however, might want to use the network capabilities inherent to RRAS.

RRAS offers numerous additional networking components, including support for

- RIP version 1 and 2 for IP
- OSPF
- RIP and SAP for IPX
- Routing APIs

NEW TERM   Routing Information Protocol (RIP) is frequently used in small- to medium-size organizations because it is fairly easy to set up and administer and it provides relatively good performance on a small network. A RIP router maintains a special routing table; also, it sends announcements to inform other routers of the networks that it can reach and to announce when it can no longer reach a particular network. Version 1 uses IP *broadcast* packets for its announcements, whereas version 2 uses the more common *multicast* packets.

NEW TERM *Open Shortest Path First* (*OSPF*) is a standard used to route IP traffic. It is more sophisticated than RIP and offers faster service. The basic premise of this protocol is to provide the shortest path between two points on the network. Each OSPF router maintains a "map" of the network that is updated after any change occurs. It is often called a *link-state network*. This protocol can coexist with RIP and allows for filters and dynamic allocation and deletion of interfaces.

Routing Information Protocol (RIP) and Service Advertising Protocol (SAP) for IPX provide the two components often used in small to medium Novell NetWare IPX networks. This enables interoperability between mixed network environments such as IP and IPX. The SAP service allows services such as file and print servers to announce their presence on the network.

Finally, Routing APIs is a service that enables developers to create new applications and services using Application Programming Interfaces in Windows NT and to add to the overall development of their network.

NEW TERM This new version adds features such as *Remote Authentication Dial-in User Service* (*RADIUS*) authentication servers. These are special dial-up servers that offer additional identification and authentication of dial-up users. Most ISPs use RADIUS servers for authenticating their dial-in users. RRAS supports these servers and offers the use of either internal NT user accounts or RADIUS user accounts for authentication.

When Looking at the RRAS

One advantage of RRAS is its support for server-to-server connections. Whereas before you might have needed to buy and install a router to connect two separate NT networks, you can now use RRAS running on a Windows 2000 machine. In the coming years, expect to see RRAS replace the use of routers in these small- and medium-size organizations. A downside to this, of course, is that if the server goes down, so does the network. Network stability might be a consideration when deciding whether to use Windows 2000 or a hardware router.

With the use of the Point-to-Point Tunneling Protocol (PPTP) or L2TP, you can set up two different networks and allow them to share data using an encrypted network link. Users, of course, can also dial in to your server and establish an encrypted link, thus protecting your important company data from unauthorized people even if you're using the Internet as the dial-in medium.

When you configure RRAS (you install it as you were shown in Task 11.1), you see a slightly different view. This dialog box still enables you to set up the protocols, services, and encryption settings, but now it offers RADIUS or Windows 2000 authentication.

One of the ways to use RRAS is to configure your machine to control which IP packets are allowed inbound or outbound. This helps ensure that your network remains safe— you protect it by controlling the addresses that you don't want to be used.

You can access this aspect of your RRAS server from the main screen using Start, Programs, Administrative Tools, Routing and Remote Access.

Use this snap-in box to configure most of the options mentioned previously. By double-clicking on the IP Routing icon, you are presented with two additional options: Static Routes and General. Selecting the Static Routes icon and then New, Static Route enables the Static Route dialog box, which then enables you to add a new static route address or to view the current routing table.

Getting into further detail is really a network function and, therefore, is best reviewed in depth. You are encouraged to understand that this option exists and that you can use both the extensive Help function in RRAS and external education sources to understand how it might best be used in your environment.

Summary

Today, you learned some of the fundamentals of Windows 2000's Routing and Remote Access Services. This day shows you how to set up and manage a RAS connection and how to set up special options included with RAS, such as encryption and scripts. When you combine this with the information that you'll learn later on regarding other types of connections and networking fundamentals, you'll become quite proficient in managing Remote Access Services with Windows 2000 Server.

Microsoft offers additional technical depth about RAS on its Knowledge Base, and this is a great place to search for additional information. You can find it by going to the Microsoft Web page at www.microsoft.com and by going to the Support forum, where you'll find the Knowledge Base search icon.

Today, you discovered a lot about dialing up other machines. You learned the following points:

- What RAS is and why you use it.
- Why there is some confusion about RAS and Dial-Up Networking and Microsoft's desire to move away from the *RAS* term (perhaps to be consistent with Windows 95 technology).

- That RAS does not install automatically when you first install Windows 2000. You need to specifically install this service and set it up to manage your dial-up connections.

- How to administer RAS and set up the machines you will call and the protocols you intend to use.

- That a really neat option in Windows 2000's RAS is the capability of linking more than one modem together and obtaining a single dial-up connection that is twice as fast using the facility called *multilink PPP*—a facility that you enable on both the server and the client machines.

- How to disconnect a user.

- What Routing Services is and how it differs from RAS.

- How to create a service profile.

Workshop

To wrap up the day, you can review tasks from the day and see the answers to some commonly asked questions.

Task List

The information provided today shows you how to set up and manage the Remote Access Services of Windows 2000 Server. You learned to do the following:

- Install Remote Access Services.

- Create a remote access policy.

- Install a new modem.

- Install multilink PPP services.

- Connect to a RAS server using RAS.

- Connect to a RAS server from a DOS client machine.

- Create a service profile for your VPN.

Q&A

Q Can I connect to the network without using RAS?

A Yes. Remember that RAS enables you to connect only through a dial-up modem, but you can always connect via the network. In fact, if you are connected through the network, you won't use RAS unless you want to call in from home or while traveling. In addition, there are numerous other ways to dial up and connect. Your organization might use special software, such as Citrix, or special dial-up modems that offer additional security features.

Q Can I connect more than one or two modems to the system? I have many people who want to dial up the server and work from home, but I see only two ports available on my computer.

A Yes, you can set up a large number of modems. First, W2K RAS supports up to 256 connections. Next, you need special hardware called *multiport I/O boards* to increase the number of modems you can connect to your system. These boards are designed to use one connection on your system and allow a slew of modems on the other side, which simplifies your problem. Many modem manufacturers offer special rack-mounted modems, so you don't have to have a couple hundred standard-type modems cluttering your computer room. Be sure to check the Hardware Compatibility List, though, because not all multiport boards are certified to run with W2K.

Q I heard that you can connect NT to another machine using two modems and combine their speed somehow to get faster access. How is this possible?

A One of the really great things that Microsoft added to the server technology is a service called *multilink PPP*. Using this service and two NT or 2000 machines, you can set up two modems on one of the NT or 2000 machines and connect to the other through them both. Note that both machines need to be running NT or 2000. Use either 2000 Server, NT Server, 2000 Professional or NT Workstation to do it, however, because they both offer this capability. Windows 2000 or NT recognizes that you have two modems on the machine and that you have set an option telling W2K or NT to use both when calling another machine. W2K or NT then combines the speed of the two modems and connects at the greater speed. The only caveat is this: You must be running only W2K or NT machines, and both machines need to have multilink enabled for this to work. There are a number of people inquiring on the W2K or NT newsgroups why their particular version doesn't work, and it typically is because only one of the machines is running W2K or NT.

Q Why do I want to use RRAS?

A One of the new things Microsoft added was the capability to use your Windows 2000 or NT machines as routers so that you don't have to buy, install, and maintain separate devices. You might do this on a small network to save on equipment costs. Use RRAS to achieve this without a separate physical router.

11

DAY 12

Understanding TCP/IP and DNS

The term *TCP/IP* has become the one to know in the 1990s. From relative obscurity, it is fast becoming the most important protocol in the world through its widespread use. Its very strength lies in its capability to handle network traffic in either the LAN or the WAN arena, a feat that its brethren—NetBEUI, SNA, and X.25—cannot do.

Yesterday, you learned all about using Remote Access Services and dialing in to your server in a secure fashion. Today, you'll learn to use TCP/IP for network services and learn about the way this protocol provides networking services that are robust and efficient. You'll also learn what enables you to use names such as www.microsoft.com to access sites on the Internet instead of using an IP address.

Today you'll learn the following:

- An overview of TCP/IP: what it is, how it functions, and why it has become so popular today
- Details on setting up your Windows 2000 Server to run TCP/IP
- Information on some of the services TCP/IP offers, and how to use those services

- An introduction to a couple of the most common services of TCP/IP: FTP (File Transfer Protocol) and Telnet
- An overview of the Domain Name Service, or DNS, and how to implement it

What Is TCP/IP?

What is *TCP/IP*? It is an acronym for Transmission Control Protocol/Internet Protocol. You can think of it as a collection of tools used originally by the U.S. Department of Defense (DoD) to facilitate communication among the many kinds of computers the DoD had in use.

Now you're probably wondering, what is a protocol? It's simple, really. A *protocol* is the set of rules and formalities used by various computers to pass messages to each other, thereby facilitating a dialog that each can understand. One particular protocol might not be sufficient, so you often find various protocols in use, layered on top of one another. The term *TCP/IP*, as you can see, actually consists of two protocols: the Transmission Control and the Internet Protocol. However, this is misleading because it is actually a suite of protocols and contains many others in addition to the ones identified in the name. For ease of use, it is usually referred to as the *TCP/IP protocol*.

The original goal of TCP/IP consisted of providing solid failure recovery, a capability to handle high error rates, and machine and vendor independence. It was, after all, designed primarily by the military as a defense network.

As discussed earlier, the TCP/IP protocol consists of two separate protocols working in concert to provide communication between disparate computer systems. By looking at how the acronym is created, you can guess that TCP runs on top of the IP protocol, using it for basic networking. Let's look at each protocol in turn and see how each manages its portion of the network. Be warned, however, that the discussion is light and treads only partially into this rather arcane world. For a true understanding of TCP/IP, you need to read and study some of the many books provided on this topic. Here, you'll learn enough to become dangerous and manage the implementation of TCP/IP on your Windows 2000 network.

The Internet Protocol

The Internet Protocol (IP) is the most fundamental part of the Internet network. All data must be packaged in an IP packet to be sent across the network and routed to its destination. In a simple network such as I have in our home office, there is only one segment; therefore, all traffic is sent across the network to all the machines that are connected, and no router is necessary.

NEW TERM   In a larger office network, you might have several separate network segments, each connected by some type of router. In a simple network, all machines hear each other. In the more complex network, machines can hear only those machines that are on their segment; they cannot hear any machine that is on another LAN nearby without some device that takes their message and transports it to the other LAN. This device is typically called a *router*. To perform this routing, the machine needs to know who you are, and this is where your IP address comes into play.

In this hypothetical network, each machine needs to be identified with a particular IP address. Routers then use this address to identify each machine and to transmit data to and from these machines.

The IP address consists of a 32-bit number assigned by the network administrator for each machine in the network. (You'll learn tomorrow that this isn't necessary anymore if you use the service called Dynamic Host Configuration Protocol, or DHCP.) A bit of math tells you this allows for four billion addresses.

Setting up each machine with this 32-bit number, however, is no easy task. Imagine trying not to make a mistake when typing an address such as 11111111 00001000 10101010 00001010 (255 8 170 10). It would be hard to perform without some mistake, and the mistake would be equally hard to find!

To combat this potential problem, the dotted quad or dotted decimal notation was formed. This breaks down the 32 bits into four distinct fields of 8 bits. Each field is then converted to a decimal number that corresponds to the value of the 8 bits it represents. For example, in our earlier example I showed an IP address of 11111111000010001010101000001010. This breaks down into four sections: 11111111 00001000 10101010 00001010. Each of these numbers further breaks down to a decimal value, 255 8 170 10, and this is the number used today to describe an IP address. The technical name used for each of these four 8 bits fields is *octet*, so as you can see, there are four octets in an IP address.

12

Don't worry too much about the need to convert these numbers. Almost no one uses them anymore because you are typically assigned IP addresses using the notation just mentioned. It is helpful, however, to understand how those numbers are generated.

Internally, the IP address contains two parts, the network ID (netid) and the host ID (hostid). Five address classes are available for use: A, B, C, D, and E. Only classes A, B, and C are used for normal company addressing; D and E are reserved for special functions.

The netid portion of the address is what identifies your network as unique. The hostid describes the actual nodes in your network. As you can see in the following list, a class A network has more than 16,777,214 network nodes available to it. Each of the three classes is used to describe a particular type of network. Unfortunately, the developers of this scheme decided to use 8 bits to define each class, severely limiting the real number of addresses available. A class A address uses the first 8 of the 32 bits for its definition. Class B uses the next 8, and class C, the third 8 bits. This leaves the really large networks with huge potential numbers of hosts and leaves class B addresses with up to 65,535 hosts. The lowly class C addresses can have 254 hosts. Here's a rundown of the three classes:

- A: This is used for very large networks. Because only 7 bits are available (one is used to tell how many bits are in the address), there can be only 127 class A networks. Don't bother trying to get one, no matter how large your company. They are all gone. Each network can have 16,777,214 nodes attached.

- B: The class B addresses allow for up to 16,383 networks, each of which allows for 65,534 nodes. This class is used for medium-to-large types of businesses and is quickly running out of available addresses.

- C: This is the most common IP network. There are 2,097,151 networks available, but each can have only 254 network nodes attached. This number is fine for most small companies.

Even with all these huge numbers of networks, the present IP addressing scheme is running out of room. Although several proposals are in place for expanding the numbering scheme for IP, they are subject to great debate, and no solid plan is yet available. The most recent and likely candidate is called *IPV6* and should become available in the next few years. This version of IP immensely expands the range of addresses by using 128 bits instead of the original 32.

> **Note**
>
> You set up a simple router using a computer with two Ethernet (or Token Ring) cards in it. Network staff call this a *multihomed computer*. Each Ethernet card is assigned an IP address. Next, one of the cards is attached to one side of the network, and the other card is attached to the second network segment. The machine must be smart enough to transmit data from one card to the other as necessary, making it the router. It does this by knowing what the addresses of each segment consist of and by applying routing logic to send the packets between machines as needed.

Within each of these networks are a few addresses that are reserved for special functions that cannot be used by one of your machines. Typically, they include the addresses identified in Table 12.1. In the table, the addresses are shown using a convention of A.B.C to represent the first three levels of the address because, of course, these will differ across organizations.

TABLE 12.1   Reserved IP Addresses

Name	IP Address	Description
Loopback	127.0.0.1	This is reserved for loopback testing. To test your computer's response to IP, you can send a message to this address, and it should be returned to you. A class A address, it's a huge waste of an Internet address space.

Name	IP Address	Description
Subnet mask	A.B.C.D	For IP to be routable, it must have a way to establish what part of an address is network specific and what part is host specific. The Subnet Mask allows for this separation to be identified. For example, to split a class C address into two subnets, you use 255.255.255.128 as the subnet mask.
Gateway	A.B.C.1	The first address of your network is typically saved for use as the router address for that subnet. All subnets should have a router address, and by convention this is the address used.
Network number	A.B.C.0	This address is used to tell a router that the entire range of your network is from A.B.C.0 to A.B.C.255.
IP broadcast	A.B.C.255	On a simple C class network, the broadcast address is the last one, or 255.

As the owner of a new class C address, you can add 253 computers because you cannot use some of those addresses. For example, suppose that you have an address of 223.255.100.0. You cannot use that address because it's the one that describes the entire network for you. You cannot use 223.255.100.255 because that is your IP broadcast number. This leaves you with all the rest of the numbers to assign to your machines, a total of 253.

IP addresses identify the particular device on a network. IP's primary job is to provide routing, not error checking. In fact, if an IP packet arrives at its destination with an error saying it was damaged in transit, IP drops the packet and continues to the next one. It doesn't tell anyone, making it not very reliable. So IP doesn't guarantee that a message will arrive when it is sent. Another protocol is needed to help provide that facility, and that is the job of TCP.

The Transmission Control Protocol

The main job of the Transmission Control Protocol (TCP) is to provide the orderly transmission of data from one host to another. Its job is to make sure that the data arrives safely. Whereas IP sends the data and forgets about it, TCP first performs a handshake with the other computer to introduce itself and then sets up the connection between the two machines.

TCP's main job is to provide end-to-end integrity for the messages crossing the Internet on IP. IP packets can arrive in sequence and at any time across the network, leaving TCP to reassemble the packets in order as they reach the receiving host. TCP, then, is in charge of packet sequencing.

12

> An older protocol called *UDP*, or *User Datagram Protocol*, works in a similar manner to TCP except that it doesn't provide the end-to-end integrity that TCP does. Although UDP is still in use for some functions, TCP has overtaken it in popularity and effectiveness with its better data integrity features. A primary difference between the two is that TCP is considered a connection-oriented protocol, whereas UDP is connnectionless. This means that TCP establishes a session using handshaking and acknowledgments and is there-fore slow but reliable. UDP just sends the data with no idea whether it will reach its destination. Because it doesn't perform any initial connection, it is considered faster but less reliable.

TCP also manages flow control, pacing the data being sent so that the receiving host need not worry about sorting each packet. In fact, TCP doesn't send a packet until the receiver is ready for it. Remember that the first task TCP performed is a handshake with the receiving host so that it can coordinate all these functions.

Finally, TCP provides the error detection and correction that IP lacks. TCP manages this task very efficiently, telling the other machine to resend a block if it doesn't hear back quickly enough. Each machine, of course, knows how many blocks it can send and at what speed and knows to expect an acknowledgment when each block is processed. If a block is sent and has an error, the receiver merely drops it and waits for the sender to resend the block after not getting a reply.

Working together, TCP and IP provide a robust error-checking suite of protocols that provides the services for most of the machines using the Internet today.

Understanding Winsock

By now you will know that Windows 2000 and other versions all use and need some-thing called a *socket interface* or, in the case of Windows, a Winsock. Just what is this thing, and why is it crucial to running the network?

As you can already guess, when one machine wants to talk to another, it must know whom to call (the IP address), what type of call to make (TCP or UDP), and which program to talk to at the receiving computer.

TCP uses the IP address to find your machine, but then it needs to know what program to talk to and where to find that program. This is where *port* numbers come into play. The TCP/IP suite assigns each program that uses it a special number known as the *port*. You'll find that these port numbers are fairly consistent for most major programs. The following list shows a few of them:

- 5: Remote Job Entry
- 7: Echo
- 20: FTP (data)
- 21: FTP (control)
- 23: Telnet
- 25: SMTP
- 53: Name server
- 80: Web servers
- 110: Post Office Protocol (POP3)

TCP combines the IP address with a port number to produce the socket address. When my computer calls yours, it asks whether you want to talk on such and such a socket number and mentions that it can accept x amount of data in its buffers. If your computer is waiting, it says, "Okay, start sending me y bytes of data," and the session starts. (The size of the buffer is machine dependent.) It is this exchange that makes TCP so civilized and error free.

After the computers are finished, each machine signs off and hangs up. Your program might then wait for the next connection to begin. The Winsock interface was created some time after various vendors all produced their own versions of a socket program. This led to much confusion because each program needed a particular socket in order to work. The Winsock program helped implement a more consistent approach that all vendors of TCP/IP software could support.

The New IP—Version 6

You learned in an earlier section that each machine needs to be identified with a particular IP address. Routers then use this address to identify each machine and to transmit data to and from these machines.

The IP address consists of a 32-bit number, and this allows for four billion addresses. So you'd think that I have plenty of addresses available for the world to use, right? Unfortunately, the way the addresses have been assigned has sharply reduced that number. You recall that there are essentially three classes of address, A through C. Class A is already fully assigned, and no more addresses are available. The B class is filling fast and will likely be the next to go. There are about 2,097,152 class C addresses, but each of these allows only, at best, about 254 hosts and these, too, are going fast. IPv6 is one answer to this problem. This new version retains most of the features of the current version 4 but adds a slew of new addresses.

Ipv6 moves from the earlier 32-bit range to an address that is 128 bits long! Enough addresses to last forever. (Wait a minute, isn't that what folks said when they created the original IP addressing structure? Well, maybe this one will last a long time at least.)

Instead of using four groups of 16-bit numbers, it uses eight groups. This means the address looks something like this, with each group ranging from 0000 to FFFF:

```
0000.0000.0000.0000.0000.0000.0000.0000
```

How would you like to type an address this size every time you need to talk to another machine? Wow. Thank goodness for DNS. The good news is that several new processes are available to make life a little easier. These include a new Network Discovery Protocol (NDP) process that finds out about the network and nearby systems and a process called *Autoregistration* that adds or updates each computer's hostname and address information to DNS. A third process, called *Autoconfiguration*, acts like a "plug and play" process and automatically assigns Ipv6 addresses to your network card.

Luckily, this new version co-exists with the current version of IP, so there is no need to rush out and throw away your existing network configuration. There is, however, a lot of planning to do when your organization finally moves to this new version of IP to ensure that your network continues to function. Migrating to Ipv6 means changing all your machines to the new protocol, possibly assigning new IP numbers, and making sure that all your machines can still talk to one another as you migrate from one version to the next.

There is a lot of additional information that this new version will bring to a network near you, so you should begin to read up and study this if you plan to be a network administrator.

Installing TCP/IP

So enough about the background already. Let's see what the steps are to install this protocol on a machine. W2K installs TCP/IP automatically as part of the Windows 2000 setup program as long as it finds a network adapter card, so there is no need to install it manually. You only need to do this task if the TCP/IP default selection was overridden during Setup. You can check to see whether it is already installed by right-clicking Network Neighborhood, selecting Properties, then selecting Protocols, and looking for the term *TCP/IP*.

In Task 12.1, I show you how to install TCP/IP.

Task 12.1: Installing TCP/IP.

Step 1: Description

In this task, you'll learn to install the Transmission Control Protocol/Internet Protocol on your Windows 2000 Server. Remember, though, that during the Windows 2000 installation process, it is usually installed automatically.

Step 2: Action

1. Begin by signing on to your server as Administrator. Next, open the Control Panel and double-click the Network & Dial-up Communications icon. The Network dialog box appears, as shown in Figure 12.1.

FIGURE 12.1

The Network and Dial-up Connections dialog box.

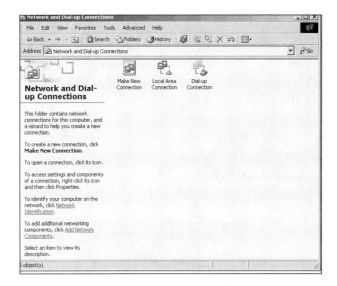

12

2. Click the Local Area Connection icon and then right-click and select Properties. Any protocols you already installed show in the list.

3. Click the Install button and then click on Protocol. Next, Click the Add button to add a new protocol. Windows 2000 builds a list of all the protocols it supports and provides this to you. You see an example in Figure 12.2.

4. Select the TCP/IP protocol from the list, and click the OK button. (You don't see it in Figure 12.2 because the machine I'm using already has it installed.) Windows 2000 asks whether there is a DHCP server on your network and whether you want to use that server to obtain your addresses. For this example, choose No. You'll learn all about using and configuring a DHCP server tomorrow.

FIGURE 12.2

Network protocols available for installation.

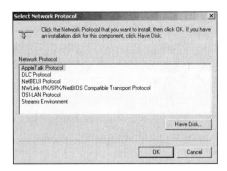

5. You might be asked to provide the address of your installation files. Place the Windows 2000 install CD-ROM in the drive, and enter its path. Click OK when you are ready. Windows 2000 copies a bunch of files to the local system directory. If RAS is installed, the installation asks whether you want RAS configured to use TCP/IP. Choose an appropriate answer to continue.

6. Click the Close button. Windows 2000 goes through *various* binding processes before displaying the Microsoft TCP/IP dialog box.

7. When the install finishes adding TCP/IP to RAS, you should see the TCP/IP protocol configuration by clicking on Local Area Connection, Properties, Internet Protocol, Properties. You can see an example in Figure 12.3.

FIGURE 12.3

TCP/IP protocol properties

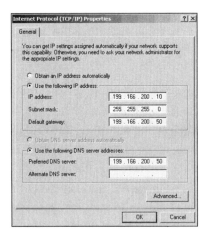

TCP/IP offers various setup options. The first option enables you to specify that IP addresses will come from the DHCP server. Using DHCP allows your network's DHCP server to assign dynamic IP addresses to each client. The next option

▼ enables you to predefine a static IP address, subnet, and default gateway. The first option (DHCP) is best for larger sites because managing addresses becomes difficult as the network grows.

8. Enter the necessary IP addresses for your network or leave the default values; I will discuss those momentarily. Click OK when you are finished. Windows 2000 completes the process and tells you to reboot the server, after which TCP/IP services

▲ are available.

Step 3: Review

This task shows you how to add TCP/IP to your network and enable users to use this dynamic protocol suite. You needed to add some IP addresses to complete the task.

The preceding task enables you to connect your machines by using the TCP/IP over the network. But you don't want to use all these IP addresses all the time. Surely there is another method for finding companies across the Internet. In the next few sections, you'll learn about Automatic Private IP Addressing (APIPA) and using the HOSTS and DNS systems for resolving IP addresses to host names.

Automatic Private IP Addressing

Microsoft provides a simple method for assigning IP addresses on a small network (five servers or less), which you can use instead of defining your own IP addresses. A new feature with Windows 2000, Automatic Private IP Addressing (APIPA) is used to automate Internet Protocol (IP) configuration of network connections.

By default, when Windows 2000 setup runs and a network card is installed in the machine, the computer first attempts to contact a DHCP server on the network and obtain dynamic configuration information. It follows a number of steps:

12

- If a DHCP server is reached and leased configuration is successful, setup finishes TCP/IP configuration using that information.

- If a DHCP server isn't reached or if leased configuration fails, the computer uses APIPA to automatically configure TCP/IP. When using this, Windows 2000 gets an address in a Microsoft-reserved IP addressing range that uses 169.254.0.1 through 169.254.255.254. This address is used until a DHCP server is located. The subnet mask is set to 255.255.0.0.

- Microsoft reserved these addresses with the Internet Assigned Numbers Authority (IANA) so that IP addresses within this range aren't used on the Internet and are available for your network.

You can turn this off if you know you won't need this facility (for example, because your company has its own set of assigned IP addresses). Task 12.2 shows you how to remove APIPA.

Task 12.2: Disabling APIPA.

Step 1: Description

In this task, you'll learn to turn off the Automatic Private Internet Protocol Addressing facility. You'll only do this if you are sure you won't need to use it.

Step 2: Action

1. Begin by signing on to your server as Administrator.

2. Start Registry Editor by clicking Start, Run and typing **regedt32** on the command line. Click OK.

> **Caution**
>
> Remember that editing the Windows 2000 Registry incorrectly can severely damage your system. Make a backup of the Registry before you begin.

3. After you have Registry Editor open, navigate to the following Registry key:
   ```
   HKEY_LOCAL_MACHINE\SYSTEM\CurrentControlSet\Services
   \Tcpip\Parameters\Interfaces\adapter_name
   ```

4. Substitute the name of your network card for the *adapter_name* value. Once there, create the following value entry:
   ```
   IPAutoconfigurationEnabled: REG_DWORD
   ```

5. Then, assign a value of **0** (zero) to disable Automatic Private IP Addressing (APIPA) support for that network adapter card, and close Registry Editor.

> **Note**
>
> If the IPAutoconfigurationEnabled entry isn't present, a default value of 1 is assumed. This indicates that APIPA is being used.
>
> If you have multiple adapter cards installed, you can disable APIPA for all of them by setting the IPAutoconfigurationEnabled entry to 0 (zero) in this key: HKEY_LOCAL_MACHINE\SYSTEM\CurrentControlSet.

Step 3: Review

This task shows you how to remove use of Automatic Private IP Addressing in Windows 2000. You do this because you know that it isn't needed; your company has its own set of assigned IP addresses.

Now you'll learn about using the HOSTS and DNS systems for resolving IP addresses to host names.

The Windows HOSTS Naming System

Microsoft provides a simple method for tracking IP addresses and resolving them to a host name. In this method, a file called HOSTS provides a table of IP addresses and host names. It is a simple ASCII text file you create to store these name resolutions. You store the file in the \winnt\system32\drivers\etc directory in a Windows 2000 system and in the Windows directory on any Windows 98 or Windows client machines. Windows 2000 then looks at this file when trying to resolve a name you specify.

On each line, you type the host computer's IP address followed by at least one space and the computer's host name. That's not too hard, is it? You create this file and maintain it as each computer is added to or removed from your network. The file is read each time the system does a name resolution, so you don't need to reboot to make any changes effective.

Unfortunately, using the HOSTS file isn't quite that easy. You need to create and manage this file on every computer in your network! Every time you make a change, you need to change the file on each workstation manually as well. Aaarghh. There has to be a simpler way to maintain this information. That's where the Domain Name System (DNS) comes into play.

Domain Name System

After managing the overview of IP addressing, you probably wonder why you don't use those numbers when communicating across the Internet. (Some of you might use the IP address, but most folks today use another method.) Most of us today use some form of name when we connect to other domain computers. For example, if you want to connect to Microsoft, you don't use the address 207.68.137.62. You tend to use www.microsoft.com instead. This is the Domain Name System (DNS) at work. Note that I'm not talking about individual machines here; you use DNS to associate domain names and tasks such as mail (MX record) with the IP address necessary to get to that resource.

12

> **Note**
>
> DNS has an identity crisis. It is often referred to as the *Domain Name Service* or the *Domain Name Server*. It can also be called the *Domain Name System*. In fact, it isn't terribly important which of these terms you use because most folks will understand what you mean, regardless. Technically, however, it seems that the proper name is *Domain Name System*. This is the name supplied by the original Request for Comments (RFC) papers numbered 1034 and 1035 that first defined DNS. People often use the *Domain Name Server* term to designate the machine the system runs on.

DNS, then, provides address resolution across the Internet. Instead of trying to remember a bunch of numbers every time you want to connect to another domain, you can use an easier-to-remember name. You learn all about DNS, including how to implement a DNS server on your Windows 2000 machine, at the end of this day. You'll also learn how Microsoft has improved on the DNS concept by adding dynamic updates to it.

TCP/IP Diagnostic and Connectivity Utilities

Windows 2000 provides several utilities that are common to UNIX systems. These are all automatically installed when you install TCP/IP. You'll find these services in the \winnt\system32 directory.

hostname

The hostname command simply shows you the name of the host where the command is run. The name is returned using the computer defined in the DNS tab of your TCP/IP configuration window. There are no options for the command. You see an example in Figure 12.4.

FIGURE 12.4

A sample hostname *command.*

ipconfig

The ipconfig command provides you with a system's TCP/IP configuration data. It is especially useful if you receive your IP addresses using a DHCP Server. You see an example in Figure 12.5.

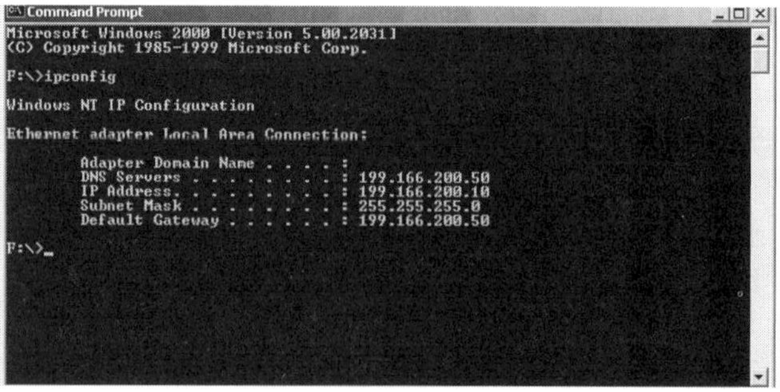

FIGURE 12.5

Using the ipconfig *command.*

Various options are available when you're using this command. As you see in the figure, using the command without any options returns the default IP address, subnet mask, and default gateway address for any network cards bound with TCP/IP.

Following is the syntax for this command:

```
ipconfig /all ¦ /release adapter¦ /renew adapter
```

/all: This switch causes the command to return additional IP information for all network adapters running TCP/IP. This includes the host name, all the DNS servers, the node type, the state of IP routing on your system, the NetBIOS scope ID, information as to whether your system is using DNS for NetBIOS name resolution, and the current state of WINS proxy on your system. You also get the physical address of each adapter using TCP/IP, the IP address of the adapter and its subnet mask, any WINS server it is using, and its default gateway.

/release adapter: When used without a specified optional adapter, this switch releases DHCP bindings for all adapters. You can optionally tell the switch which adapter to release from DHCP. This is useful only when you're using DHCP to obtain IP addresses.

/renew adapter: Useful only when you're using a DHCP server, this switch renews the DHCP lease. When used without a specified optional adapter, it renews DHCP bindings for all adapters. You can optionally tell the switch which adapter to renew.

nbtstat

The nbtstat command displays the status of NetBIOS over TCP/IP. You see an example in Figure 12.6.

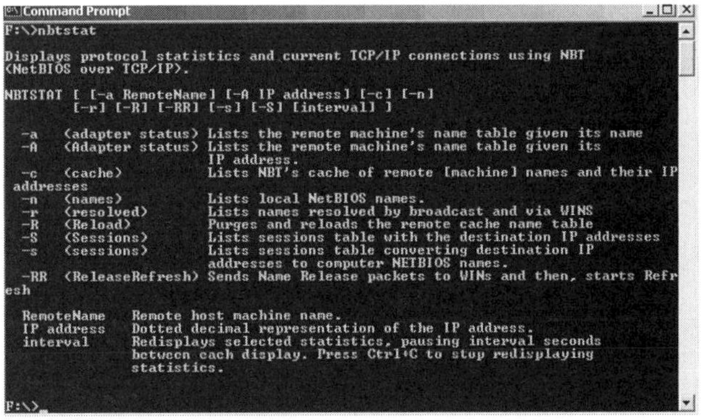

12

FIGURE 12.6

Using the nbtstat *command.*

Various options are available when you're using this command. The syntax consists of

`nbtstat switches`

where `switches` can be any of the following options:

`-a remotename`	Displays the remote computer's NetBIOS name table using the host-name address to find the computer.
`-A IP address`	Displays the remote computer's NetBIOS name table using the IP address to find the computer.
`-c`	Displays the local computer's NetBIOS name cache with the IP address.
`-n`	Displays the local computer's NetBIOS names.
`-r`	Displays names resolved by WINS and broadcast.
`-R`	Purges and reloads a remote computer's cache name table.
`-s`	Displays the sessions table using host names from the HOSTS file.
`-S`	Displays the sessions table with the IP address.
`interval`	Redisplays the selected statistics using the number of seconds indicated by the `interval` parameter as the intervening pause. Ctrl+C stops the display.

netstat

The `netstat` command displays the statistics for all TCP, UDP, and IP connections.

Various options are available when you're using this command. The syntax consists of

`netstat switches`

Here `switches` can be any of the following options:

`-a`	Displays all current connections and listening ports.
`-e`	Displays all Ethernet statistics. Can be combined with the `-s` switch.
`-n`	Displays addresses and port numbers numerically.
`-r`	Displays the contents of the routing table.

`-p` *protocol*	Displays the connections for the protocol specified. The protocol can be TCP, UDP, or IP when used with the `-s` switch.
`-s`	Displays all protocol statistics.
interval	Redisplays the selected statistics using the number of seconds indicated by the *interval* parameter as the intervening pause. Ctrl+C stops the display.

ping

The `ping` command sends small packets to a host to verify whether the host is active. The `ping` command is a very common troubleshooting command for dealing with networks.

Various options are available when you're using this command. The syntax consists of

`ping` *switches*

In this case, *switches* can be any of the following options:

`-a`	Resolves the IP address to the DNS host name.
`-n` *number*	Specifies the number of echo requests to send.
`-1` *size*	Sends the packet length specified. The default is 64 bytes, and the maximum is 8,192 bytes.
`-f`	Sets the `Do Not Fragment` flag.
`-i` *ttl*	Sets the time-to-live field for the packets. Valid values are between 1 and 255.
`-j` *host-list*	Sets the loose source route using the entries in *host-list*.
`-k` *host-list*	Sets the strict source route using the entries in *host-list*.
`-r` *number*	Records the route of the packets in a Record Route field. The maximum is 9.
`-s` *number*	Specifies the time stamp for the *number* of hops specified by number.
`-v` *TOS*	Sets the type of service field to the value specified.
`-t`	Pings the host until interrupted.

12

In Figure 12.7, you see an example of the ping command at work. In our example, I pinged the Microsoft network because it is more readily recognized. I don't suggest that everyone use this, however, in deference to Microsoft. Choose any other Web service to do your test.

FIGURE 12.7

Using the ping *command.*

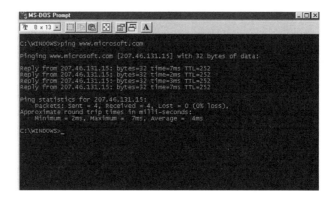

route

The route command is used to manipulate local routing tables for the TCP/IP protocol.

Various options are available when you're using this command. The syntax consists of

route *switches*

In this case, *switches* can be any of the following options:

-f	Empties the routing table of all prior gateway entries. When it's used with another switch, the tables are emptied first, and then the other switch is run.
-command	Can be one of four commands:
	PRINT: Prints a route.
	ADD: Adds a route.
	DELETE: Deletes a route.
	CHANGE: Changes an existing route.
destination	Specifies the host to ping.

gateway	Specifies a gateway.
MASK	Specifies that the next parameter is the netmask.
netmask	Specifies the subnet mask value. The default is 255.255.255.255.
METRIC	Specifies the metric/cost for the destination.
-p	When used with ADD, keeps a route persistent across system boots. Used with PRINT, it displays all persistent routes.

Telnet

The Telnet client utility is used to connect to any service running a standard Telnet server. Many universities offer Telnet services; one, the University of Michigan, offers a weather service. Most people today use the Web rather than Telnet, but if you come from a UNIX background, you'll still find many uses for Telnet. You see an example of the Telnet client window in Figure 12.8.

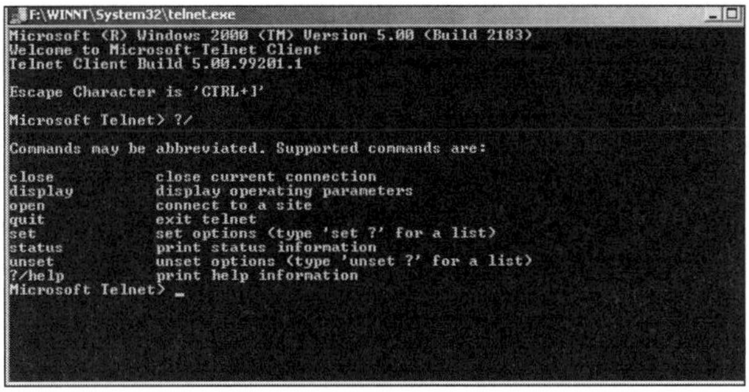

FIGURE 12.8

Using the Telnet utility.

As you see in Figure 12.8, Telnet offers various menu items. Windows 2000 Server now offers a built-in Telnet server. If you want to run a Telnet service on your Windows 2000 system, you can go to Start, Programs, Administrative Tools, Computer Management and then select System Tools, Services, Telnet Server.

You use the Telnet client to connect to other machines running a Telnet Server. You can allow others to connect to your machine by starting and running Telnet Server. This allows the user to use command line applications as if they were sitting in front of your machine. The Telnet Server supports up to 63 clients.

Task 12.3. Running the Telnet Client.

Step 1: Description

In this task, you'll learn to connect to a remote terminal using Telnet. You need to set up your modem and network parameters before starting this task. For further information, refer to Day 11, "Understanding Remote Access Services (RAS) and VPNs."

Step 2: Action

1. Begin by signing on to your server. Next, choose Start, Run and type `Telnet`. Click OK when you are ready.

2. You see a window such as the one shown in Figure 12.8.

3. To connect to a machine, type Open. Telnet provides you with a new command line option.

4. In the area provided, type the address of the computer you are connecting with, and click the Enter button. The address can consist of either an IP address or a host name. Windows 2000 connects you with the specified host. (The default settings work for most Telnet sessions, but it might be necessary to adjust the terminal setting for the desired response.)

5. When you are ready, disconnect by typing Close and pressing Enter, and then type Quit to close Telnet.

Step 3: Review

This task showed you how to use Telnet to connect to a remote host. You use this to connect to any server offering Telnet capability.

If you want to run your own telnet service (a risky business as it allows the user access to your server and a command prompt) you can start the new Telnet Server program.

To start Telnet Server, follow the steps outlined in Task 12.4.

Task 12.4: Starting Telnet Server.

Step 1: Description

In this task, you'll learn to start and run your own Telnet Server program. To allow people to connect to your machine afterwards, you need to set up your modem and network parameters.

Step 2: Action

1. Begin by signing on to your server as an administrator. Next, choose Start, Programs, Administrative Tools, Computer Management, System Tools, Services, Telnet. Right-click and then select Start to begin the program when you are ready.

2. You can see the Services window with Telnet in it in Figure 12.9.

FIGURE 12.9

The Telnet Server service.

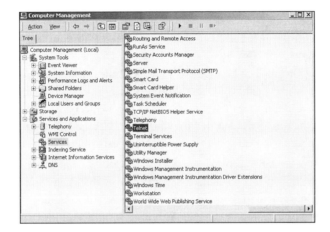

3. When you are ready, you can stop the service by following the same steps and selecting Stop.

4. Telnet lets you create a log of your activity. To start logging, select Terminal, Start Logging. You are asked to provide the name and location of the log file. Enter an appropriate name, and Telnet begins to log all activity. You stop the logging by selecting Terminal, Stop Logging.

Step 3: Review

This task shows you how to start the Telnet Server so that others can connect to your host.

12

You can restrict what access the service has by stopping it and then selecting Properties instead of Start, using the process described in step 1 in Task 12.4. Once on the Properties page, you will see a number of tabs. These are as follows:

- General tab. In the General tab you will find the name that is displayed and a description of the service. In addition, you'll see buttons that let you start, stop, pause, and resume the service, along with the current status. Finally it also shows the start parameter options such as manual, automatic, and disabled. You might change these options to have the service automatically start when Windows first starts up, for example.

- Log On tab. The Log On tab shows you that the service is running using the System account. This means the service has unlimited authority on your system. You can minimize this by creating a special account and only assigning that account the rights needed by your Telnet Server. What rights might be needed depends upon what the service is being used for, of course.

- Recovery tab. Recovery allows you to specify what actions to take if the service should have a problem and become unavailable. You can select a number of options, including taking no action (the default), running a file, restarting the service, or even rebooting your Windows 2000 Server. You choose an appropriate method based upon your needs. When you select an option other than the default, the remaining portions of the panel become available and offer additional options. These include the delay time you want before restarting the service, specific file information, and reboot data. Selecting the reboot server option allows you to further tell Windows how long to take before rebooting and enables you to send a message to your users.

- Dependencies tab. This tab shows a list of other services that the current one depends upon. For example, when you select the tab in Telnet, it shows that Telnet needs (relies upon) a service called Remote Procedure Call (RPC).

You can administer your Telnet Server session using the tool called Telnet Server Admin program. This program allows you to monitor who is logged on and lets you start or stop the Telnet Server. You start the utility by typing **tlntadmn** on the command line. Before you can, however, you must have installed the Admin Tools pack that is offered with Windows 2000 Server. (It is installed automatically in the beta version of Windows 20000).

After it is running, you can configure and manage your Telnet Server using the options provided. You can see an example in Figure 12.10.

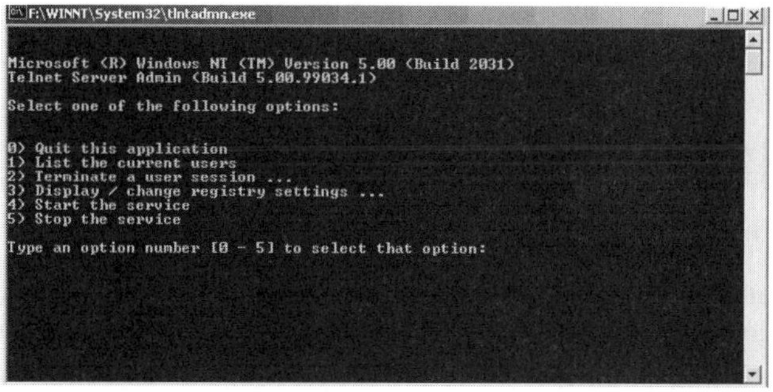

FIGURE **12.10**

*The Telnet Server
Admin utility.*

As you can see, it is a fairly simple application, but at least it offers the options shown in Figure 12.10. As with all options that modify the Registry, be careful if you choose option 3, Display/Change Registry Settings.

FTP

FTP, or File Transfer Protocol, is used to connect to other machines and download or upload files. The FTP protocol is used as a sort of universal way of transporting files over a TCP/IP network. It is common to NT, UNIX, NetWare, Apple Macintosh, VMS, and many more operating systems, so it makes for a very useful weapon to have in your arsenal.

The version that is offered with Windows 2000 provides a fairly extensive Help file, as you see in Figure 12.11.

FIGURE **12.11**

The FTP Help utility.

12

You use the Open command to access a site. Specify the IP address or FTP site address after typing **Open**, and press Enter. The program goes to the site and provides you with the directory list. After you're connected, you use the commands as necessary to perform the work you need. To end the session and close the FTP window, type **BYE** or **QUIT** at the command prompt. If you started the FTP session from the DOS prompt, you need to manually close the FTP window following your BYE or QUIT command.

As you see, FTP isn't designed to be user-friendly or even terribly GUI oriented. This is an old service that provided a sound method for exchanging files long before the Internet became as popular as it is today. You navigate through an FTP site by using methods similar to those under DOS and UNIX (after all, DOS was built based on how UNIX worked at that time). Therefore, if you are familiar with either of these operating systems, the file and directory structure appears normal to you.

You can use the version provided with Windows 2000 because it does work well enough. Several third-party FTP products, however, are far more intuitive and offer a better user interface. One of these is WS_FTP32, by a company called Ipswitch Inc.

Tip

You can reach Ipswitch at info@ipswitch.com or by phone at (781) 676-5700. You can see an example of this shareware program in Figure 12.12.

Figure 12.12

The Session Properties dialog box for the shareware WS_FTP32 program.

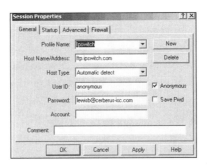

I'm sure you'll agree that using this program is a lot easier than using the more cryptic FTP commands provided with Windows 2000. Finally, if you want to become really fancy and offer your own FTP site for others to access, you can learn to install your own FTP Server in Day 18, "Using BackOffice and Terminal Services."

Finger

Finger is a command-line utility that is used to gather user information from any system running a finger service. Windows 2000 doesn't offer this service. You need to find a third-party program if you want to allow others to access your server using this command.

The syntax for the finger utility consists of

```
finger @hostname
finger username@hostname
```

where *hostname* is the computer from which you want to gather user information. Specifying only the host name provides you with a list of all users presently signed on to that computer. Using a particular username provides the full name, address, or telephone number of the user if present.

Understanding and Implementing DNS

Earlier today, you learned that you use DNS servers all the time when you access Web pages. It is the process that takes the Web site address you use, such as www.microsoft.com, and translates it into the actual IP address where that Web page resides.

DNS is really only a list of IP addresses and an associated name for each address. You might think of it as a table with two entries in the forms of *IP address-name*. For example, you might see an entry such as this:

```
207.68.137.62 - www.microsoft.com
```

So who controls all these names and addresses? The central authority for DNS is the InterNIC Registration Services, the people you go to when you first register a domain name. Makes sense, doesn't it? This organization ensures that your name is unique and that a current IP address is associated with it.

You can do the same thing inside your corporate network by creating and maintaining your own DNS server. But that's for another day.

The Domain Name System uses a hierarchy to establish and manage domain names. Remember the com I mentioned earlier as part of www.microsoft.com? DNS uses the last portion of the name to differentiate between types of domains. In Table 12.2, you see a few of the names used today.

12

TABLE 12.2   DNS Domain Types

Type	Description
com	Commercial
edu	Educational
gov	Government
mil	Military
net	Network providers
org	Organizations
ca	Canada
uk	United Kingdom

Many other names now exist, of course, because more and more countries have been added, but you get the idea.

 Note

> I wrote in the first edition that by the time the book was published, you would be reading of the plan by the International Ad Hoc Committee (IAHC) to add several new top-level names to the Domain Name Service list. The 11-member International Ad Hoc Committee, chaired by Donald M. Heath, president and CEO of the Internet Society, sets the standards for the Internet. This plan increases the number of domains available, and this is good because most of the popular com names are already taken. However, because this is an international committee, all the delays typical with obtaining agreement from such a diverse group continue to plague the process, and we are still waiting for final approval and implementation of these new names, which are
>
> - firm—For businesses or firms
> - store—For those offering goods to purchase
> - web—For those emphasizing activities related to the WWW
> - arts—For those emphasizing cultural and entertainment activities
> - rec—For those emphasizing recreation/entertainment activities
> - info—For those providing information services
> - nom—For individuals or personal nomenclature
>
> In addition, up to 28 new registrars will be established to grant registrations for these new second-level domain names. The new registrars have been selected and are set to offer the same service as InterNIC. We are still waiting for the new names, however.

As you can imagine, the DNS servers must be really busy. InterNIC maintains something like nine of these servers across the world to manage all the requests. To recap, on your own network, you use a local name server, and when you need an address outside your own domain, you begin to use the InterNIC Domain Name Servers.

Let's look at configuring your W2K system to use an existing DNS server.

Task 12.5: Configuring Windows 2000 for Existing DNS Servers.

Step 1: Description

In this task, you'll learn to set the configuration options to let Windows 2000 use an existing Domain Name Server. You perform this task if your organization has set up internal DNS servers.

▼ **Step 2: Action**

1. Begin by signing on to your server as Administrator. Next, select the Control Panel and double-click the Network and Dial-up Connections icon. Choose Local Area Connection and then double-click on it to get a Properties option. Select the Properties tab, and then double-click the TCP/IP protocol. (You can select TCP/IP and then click Properties to get the same effect.)

2. Next, click on the Advanced tab and then select the DNS tab. This tab displays the configuration options, as shown in Figure 12.13.

FIGURE 12.13

The DNS configuration options dialog box.

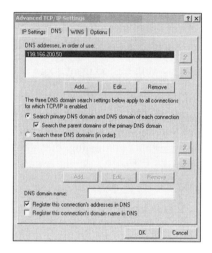

3. Enter the DNS domain name in the DNS Domain Name text box.

4. Click the Add button to add an already existing DNS server. You can specify three servers and change the order in which they are tried by using the up and down arrows. If the first server fails to resolve a name, Windows 2000 tries the next and then the third.

5. Finally, you can assign a search order for default domain suffixes using the box called Search These DNS Domains (In Order).

6. Click OK to finish the setup. Your Windows 2000 machine is now set to use the internal domain names specified.

▲

Step 3: Review

This task shows you how to configure DNS services on your Windows 2000 Server. Use this any time new DNS servers are added to your network.

Microsoft designed the DNS server to integrate with the WINS service to allow the use of WINS on your older clients and programs that require NetBIOS support until such time that you can fully migrate to a Windows 2000 environment. This is the basic difference between the Microsoft version and other third-party versions. In the meantime, because WINS is aware of DHCP, you can use all three together to

- Allow your client machines, using DHCP, to automatically receive dynamic IP addresses and TCP/IP configuration information.
- Have your client machines automatically register their NetBIOS computer name and IP address each time they start up, using WINS.
- Enable, with DNS, your client machines to find any non–WINS type resources through static mappings maintained in the configuration files.

There are numerous other benefits as well, far too many to go into in any real detail in this book.

I will go into enough detail, I hope, to enable you to set up and run your own DNS server on the Windows 2000 machine you are using to study this book. Please note that you need to know whether a DNS server is already running, in which case, use Task 12.5 to enable your machine to use that server.

Setting Up a DNS Server

Microsoft made the DNS server a GUI-based tool, so using it isn't as arcane as it used to be. No command line geek is needed! On the other hand, you must ensure that what you do doesn't impact your existing network, so be careful. First, try this on a standalone network consisting of only a few machines. That way, you can play until you are familiar enough to use it in a production mode. Next, make sure that you assign an IP address for the server that isn't used anywhere else. A duplicate IP address on your network can cause serious problems.

There are three ways to configure your DNS server:

- *Primary Name Server*—This server holds a master copy of the name database and contains records for all hosts in the zone and for all subdomains.
- *Secondary Name Server*—This server contains a copy of the name database. It is updated by the Primary server to ensure that it remains up to date.
- *Caching Name Server*—This server doesn't contain the name database; instead, it is configured with the address of a Primary or Secondary server. When it receives a request, it asks the other server to validate the request and then caches the resulting information so that it can answer directly the second time it is asked.

Larger networks might run numerous DNS servers on different subnets in order to improve network load balancing and fault tolerance. You might also want to have a secondary DNS server to provide redundancy across your network for DNS domain name resolution. A secondary server contains a copy of the information on the primary DNS server. You can see where you'd do this in Task 12.7 by selecting a new zone and then selecting Standard Secondary as indicated in step 4 of the task.

To set up a DNS server in Windows 2000, you must first load the software. If you are unsure whether it is already running on your machine, go to Start, Programs, Administrative Tools, Computer Management, System Tools, Services and look for *DNS Server* in the list of services. If it isn't there, perform the following task.

Task 12.6: Installing a DNS server.

Step 1: Description

In this task, you'll learn to install the software necessary to run your own DNS server. You run this option if you did not choose to install it during the setup of Windows 2000.

Step 2: Action

1. Begin by signing on to your server as Administrator. Next, select Start, Programs, Administrative Tools, Configure Your Server. (You can also use Control Panel, Add/Remove Programs, Windows Components, Networking Services; check DNS and select Apply to accomplish the same thing.)

2. Next, select Networking from the left panel. Now select DNS.

3. Click the Install DNS button and follow the prompts to complete the task.

4. When your system restarts, the DNS Service will be running.

Step 3: Review

This task showed you how to install the DNS server on your Windows 2000 machine. You do this only if you need to run a DNS server and it isn't already installed.

When DNS is running, you have a new tool in the Administrator's toolbox, called *DNS Manager*. You can find it in Computer Management, Server Applications and Management, DNS. (You can also just use the Configure Your Server program.) You use this to set up and configure the server. It is used for all functions except stopping or starting the server. That is done in the Computer Management, System Tools, Services applet. Alternatively, you can use the simple Net commands that follow:

```
Net stop dns
```

```
Net start dns
```

TASK ▼

▲

12

DNS Manager enables you to create zones, place domains and subdomains in that zone, and manage records and hosts in other domains.

Creating a Zone

So now you might be asking, "What's a zone and why do I need one?" A zone is an administrative unit that enables you to distribute administration of different parts of the network. It represents a subtree of DNS, such as `cerberus-isc.com`. Beneath that, I could set up subdomains called `research.cerberus-isc.com` and `on.cerberus-isc.com`. These can all be managed as one part of the company and a separate zone can be created for `us.cerberus-isc.com` and `consult.cerberus-isc.com`, which can then be managed by another part of the firm. This enables us to distribute maintenance of DNS across the company.

 Note   A small firm might only use one zone and not bother with anything further.

When you create a zone, you need to specify whether it contains Forward or Reverse Lookup entries. What does this mean? Most DNS clients perform a forward lookup. That means that they search based on the DNS name of another computer. This type of lookup query expects an IP address as the answer to the query. A forward lookup takes the form of a question, such as "Can you tell me the IP address of the computer that uses the DNS name `www.cerberus-isc.com`?"

A reverse lookup process enables clients to use a known IP address and find a computer's name based on that address. A reverse lookup takes the form of a question, such as "Can you tell me the DNS name of the computer that uses the IP address `192.168.100.25`?"

You use DNS Manager to set up and run these zones. You launch the program through Start, Programs, Administrative Tools, Computer Management, Server Applications and Management, DNS. When you first load it, it will look something like Figure 12.14. It doesn't present much in the way of information when you first install and run it.

You should be aware that you can administer only Windows 2000 DNS servers here. DNS servers running on other platforms, such as UNIX, cannot be configured using DNS Manager. Task 12.7 shows you how to set up a new zone on your DNS server.

FIGURE 12.14

*The Domain Name
Service Manager.*

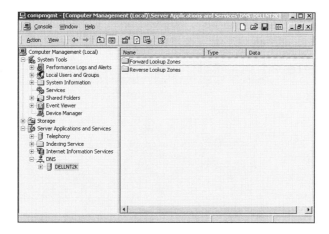

Task 12.7: Creating a Zone.

Step 1: Description

In this task, you'll learn the steps necessary to create a zone on the DNS server you installed earlier.

Step 2: Action

1. Begin by signing on to your server as Administrator. Next, select Start, Programs, Administrative Tools, Computer Management, Server Applications and Services.

2. Next, select DNS from the left panel. Now select the computer that shows and click on that. You see a dialog box with Forward and Reverse Lookup Zones specified.

3. Choose Action, Create a New Zone from the menu. Follow the wizard to complete the task. Click Next.

4. You must tell Windows 2000 what type of zone to create. There are three options:

   • Active Directory Integrated

   • Standard Primary

   • Standard Secondary

   The first option creates a new master copy of the zone and stores it in Active Directory. By selecting the Standard primary option, you create a new master copy in a text file. The third option creates a replica of an existing zone. You can see this in Figure 12.15.

12

FIGURE 12.15

The Create New Zone Wizard.

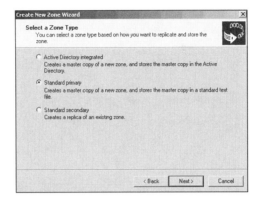

5. Now you must decide whether you are creating a Forward or Reverse Lookup Zone. A Forward Lookup Zone maps names to addresses and provides information about available services. A Reverse Lookup Zone maps IP addresses to domain names. Most DNS lookups are forward based, so let's select that for this example.

6. Type a name for your domain, such as **usa.mycorp.com**, in the Zone Name field. You also need a filename for your domain. By clicking on the Zone File field, DNS Manager will automatically enter a name for you. It adds the .dns suffix to your domain name and stores the file in %systemroot%\system32\dns. You can change the automatically generated name to something else, if you prefer.

7. Click the Next button and then the Finish button. DNS Manager will now show your entry as you see in Figure 12.16.

FIGURE 12.16

DNS Manager shows your new zone.

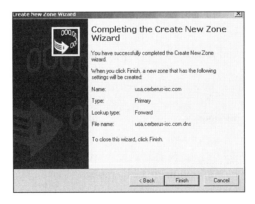

Step 3: Review

This task shows you how to install a new zone on your DNS server. You do this when you want to delegate administration.

By default, two records are created, one called NS and another called SOA. The NS record specifies this machine as the Name Server, whereas the SOA record is the Start of Authority. You can see these by going to Forward Lookup Zone and double-clicking on your new usa.mycorp.com entry. This record describes the best source of authoritative information for the zone, as well as specifying the email address of a possible contact that might be responsible for the domain. You see in Figure 12.17 an example of the information gained by left-clicking on the SOA entry.

FIGURE 12.17

The SOA entry record.

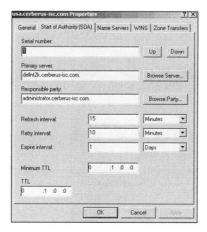

Within this record are the default refresh, retry, expire, and TTL times. For our purposes, you can leave these as the defaults. On larger, more active domains, you would use these to manage traffic patterns more effectively.

Enabling WINS Resolution

Now that you have DNS server running and have created a zone, you might want to ensure that DNS and WINS work together. When the two work together, whenever DNS is asked to resolve a name and it cannot find it anywhere in its database, it passes the leftmost part of the name (the characters before the first period) to the WINS server for resolution. If WINS has a matching NetBIOS name in its database, it returns the IP address to DNS server, which completes the request by forwarding that information back to the originating client.

You enable WINS for a particular zone by following this task.

12

Task 12.8: Enabling WINS Resolution.

Step 1: Description

In this task, you'll learn what to do to get DNS server to ask WINS for an address when it cannot find it in the DNS database. I'll assume that DNS Manager is still open.

Step 2: Action

1. In the Server list, choose the zone you want to enable WINS resolution on and right-click on it.

2. Choose Properties from the menu.

3. Click the WINS Resolution tab. You see a window such as that shown in Figure 12.18.

FIGURE 12.18

The Zone Properties window.

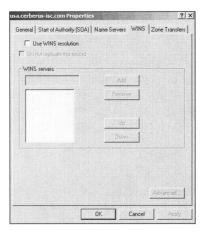

4. Click the Use WINS Resolution box. Then enter the WINS server names in the order you want them to be used by the DNS server.

5. Click the OK button. A WINS record should appear for all the servers you added.

▲   6. Click the OK button to return to the primary DNS Manager window.

Step 3: Review

This task shows you how to tell DNS server to ask a WINS server for an address when it cannot find it in its database.

You can use a task similar to Task 12.5 when you create a new zone, by substituting New Domain for New Zone. Then follow the same prompts, entering the names of subdomains that you want to reside under a particular zone.

DNS server offers a pile of other options, such as adding hosts to your domain and setting up records that specify the servers handling incoming email (an MX record).

You really should study this in more depth than I can go into in this book. This brief introduction enables you to begin using a DNS server in your network.

Summary

Today, you learned about some of the fundamentals of TCP/IP and DNS. The lesson shows you how to set up and manage a TCP/IP connection and how to use some special utilities designed to help you while you're connected to the network.

You learned all about the IP addressing scheme and how TCP uses a program called a *socket* to get the computers to communicate. Finally, you learned that the FTP program that Windows 2000 provides can be replaced by better (in our opinion) shareware versions that you obtain from the Internet.

Today, you discovered a lot about TCP/IP. You learned the following points:

- What the term *TCP/IP* means.
- What the two parts consist of and why they work together to provide error-free networking.
- To talk to another machine, you use a socket program that combines the IP address and the port number to create a socket address. Your computer then uses that socket address to talk to a program on the receiving computer that is associated with that address. For example, on most machines, Telnet is associated with port number 23.
- *DNS* is the acronym for *Domain Name System*, and many other versions of this name are used, *including Domain Name Server and Domain Name Services*.
- How to set up your Windows 2000 system to use a DNS server on the Internet.
- How the IP address is set up and how to convert all those numbers into something more meaningful.
- How to run diagnostic utility programs.
- How to install DNS server.
- What DNS Manager is used for and how to find the program.
- How to set up and manage zones and subdomains and tell DNS server to use WINS when necessary.

12

Workshop

To wrap up the day, you can review tasks from the lesson and see the answers to some commonly asked questions.

Task List

The information provided today shows you how to set up and manage TCP/IP on your Windows 2000 Server. You learned to perform the following tasks:

- Install TCP/IP.
- Run Telnet.
- Install a Telnet Server and client.
- Configure your Windows 2000 system to use existing DNS servers.
- Install DNS server.
- Set up a zone.
- Enable WINS Resolution.

Q&A

Q The TCP/IP protocol suite sounds complicated. Can I learn to use it?

A TCP/IP is a very complex set of protocols, but as you see in this lesson, you can learn enough to use the suite even though you might not clearly understand everything about it. TCP/IP books are plentiful and go into various levels of detail. I provide enough of an overview for you to understand the basics and be able to set up your Windows 2000 Server to use it.

Q I keep hearing that the Internet will soon run out of IP addresses. Is this true?

A As you saw earlier today, around four billion addresses are available under the present IP address scheme. Unfortunately, the way the addresses have been assigned has sharply reduced that number. There are essentially three classes of address, A through C. Class A is already fully assigned, and no more addresses are available. The B class is filling fast and will likely be the next to go. The problem is how the addresses were split to define each class. The IP address is only 32 bits long; the first 8 bits are used to determine a class A address, the second 8 bits determine class B addresses, and the third 8 are class C. This means there are only 127 class A addresses and 16,384 class B addresses, so you can see how they are quickly used up. There can be about 2,097,152 class C addresses, but each of these allows only, at best, about 254 hosts. This is fine for small companies with only a couple hundred machines but is a big problem for anyone using more than that number. A couple of solutions are being looked at, including making the IP address longer and using a newer method for splitting the IP address, called *CIDR*, or *Classless Internet Domain Routing*.

Q Should I create my own DNS server for my network?

A The answer to this question really depends on how large your network is and whether you want to go through the considerable effort needed to implement and manage a Domain Name Server. A small organization might use a HOSTS file and manage its network mostly using manual methods. If you are running a large private network, you are likely going to set up your own DNS server to manage that network. The Internet, of course, uses the InterNIC DNS servers.

12

DAY 13

Understanding DHCP and WINS

Every computer running TCP/IP needs specific information to identify itself uniquely, the network where it is a member, and the location for packets not bound for computers on the local network. This information is referred to as the *IP address*, *subnet mask*, and *default gateway*, respectively. (If you haven't yet completed Day 12, "Understanding TCP/IP and DNS," do so before reading this lesson.)

Windows 2000 supports several methods for determining this information. You must make these protocols recognize one another so that they understand the names you give your computers, users, groups, and network resources. TCP/IP parameters are difficult to manage properly and easy to configure incorrectly, and they require a great deal of administrative overhead.

Microsoft provides W2K facilities such as the Windows Internet Naming Service (WINS), the Domain Name Service (DNS), and the Dynamic Host Configuration Protocol (DHCP) to help.

The Dynamic Host Configuration Protocol, the subject of today, was designed to dynamically configure workstations with IP addresses and related TCP/IP information. This lesson describes how to install DHCP servers and how to use the MMC snap-in to manage these servers. During this day, you'll learn about these topics:

- Naming components and addressing your network properly
- Managing dynamic IP addresses with DHCP
- Implementing DHCP
- Defining DHCP scopes
- Configuring DHCP options
- Administering DHCP clients
- Backing up and restoring DHCP database files
- Configuring WINS Servers
- Starting and stopping the WINS database
- Creating static mappings on a WINS Server
- Backing up and restoring a WINS Server

Before you embark on these tasks, it is important to spend a little time learning about naming and name resolution.

Name Resolution

On a TCP/IP network, computers use IP addresses to find one another. You know from yesterday that IP addresses are the unique identifiers for every computer and device (that is, node) on the Internet. But on the Internet and on a Windows 2000 Server network, users normally rely on computer names because they are easier to remember.

NEW TERM   A computer's Internet address consists of two basic components: a host name and a domain name. A *host name* is the name of a computer (usually the name you gave your computer when you set up Windows 2000 Server). For Internet purposes, a *domain name* is typically an organization name. The domain name is used, along with the host name, to create a Fully Qualified Domain Name (FQDN) for the computer. The FQDN is the host name followed by a period, followed by the domain name. An example is sales01.pdaconsulting.com, where sales01 is the host name and pdaconsulting.com is the domain name. Host names are stored in the Internet Domain Name System in a table that maps names to IP addresses.

Resolving Host Names

On Windows 2000 Server networks, computers typically use WINS and DNS to find the Internet addresses they're looking for.

Using the Windows Internet Name Service

A WINS Server maintains a database that dynamically maps computer names to IP addresses on a Windows 2000 Server network. When you enable the WINS, name resolution takes place automatically. Tables on the WINS Server are created, maintained, and updated automatically by the service. This is a built-in service that ships with Windows 2000 Server; it completely removes the drudgery of manually managing the IP to the host-name mapping table, a formerly tedious IP network-management chore. You'll learn all about this later today.

Using the Domain Name System

DNS is a standard TCP/IP application used to provide domain and host names to IP address translations on the Internet. DNS can handle two-way translations (from name to address and back again). The key task for DNS is to take host names and convert those names to the IP addresses that the Internet requires for transmission. The information DNS needs to do this is maintained on domain name servers that reply to queries for specific name information.

To enable DNS name resolution on a Windows 2000 Server network, all you need do is specify the DNS options in the DNS configuration dialog box that comes up when you install TCP/IP services. In most cases, you'll be furnished with a DNS Server address by your ISP, which you'll use to configure your client IP software and your Windows 2000 Server. For small networks, maintaining your own DNS Server isn't necessary; you should rely on using your ISP's DNS Server. For larger networks, DNS Server is available as standard with Windows 2000 Server.

Configuring TCP/IP

13

If your organization has absolutely no plans to ever connect to the public Internet, you can assign any IP address you choose. If you later want to connect to the Internet, however, you'll be facing a painful reconfiguration process. If your company does plan an Internet connection, you must allocate the IP addresses that have been assigned to your organization by your ISP.

Tip

> If for some reason you already assigned private IP addresses, don't despair for you still can use the Internet. You'll need to install a proxy service such as Microsoft Proxy Server to connect your network to the Internet. You may want to install MPS to hide your internal network through Network Address Translation (NAT). You may want to get a book and explore this issue further.

Whatever plan your business adopts, you have two choices as to how to assign these addresses on your network. As the Windows 2000 Server network administrator, you can assign IP addresses and individually configure each host and device—or you can use the DHCP Server to assign these addresses automatically.

Dynamic Host Configuration Protocol

Using the DHCP service on your Windows 2000 Server network enables you to dynamically assign IP addresses and other configuration parameters from an available address pool to individual computers and devices on the local network or subnet. When installing Windows 2000, you are asked whether you want to install DHCP (and choose at that time). Otherwise, you can install it later from the Control Panel, Add/Remove Programs, Configure Windows, Components panel. You must start by manually configuring a static (unchanging) IP address for the DHCP Server. After you complete this configuration, you set up a pool of available IP addresses into a table on the DHCP Server. Then, when any DHCP client (a machine needing an address—it doesn't have to be a Windows 2000 machine) that is running TCP/IP starts, the DHCP Server automatically configures it from the predefined pool of IP addresses.

Naming Services

You can execute a simple command such as net use f:\\oriole\apps to map drive F: to the apps share on the ORIOLE server. When you're using the TCP/IP protocol, however, it doesn't know how to interpret the name *ORIOLE* as the server. Instead, it understands IP addresses, such as 199.199.199.2.

If you use the TCP/IP protocol on your network, you need a utility to convert IP addresses into computer names, and vice versa. The next sections discuss naming considerations for your network.

NetBIOS Names

A *Network Basic Input/Output System (NetBIOS)* name often is referred to as a *computer name*. When you installed your W2K network, you gave each workstation and server a unique computer name. Then all your related utilities know the machine by its name. Each time you issue a command that requires the computer name, W2K knows what device you're talking about. Previously, you learned about creating good names. The best naming scheme is one that is meaningful and requires the least amount of maintenance.

TCP/IP Names

TCP/IP uses a scheme for names that is different from the NetBIOS/NetBEUI naming scheme. TCP/IP uses 32-bit numbers to construct IP addresses (for example, 199.199.199.2). Each computer, host, or node on a TCP/IP network must have a unique IP address.

IP addresses aren't meaningful to most humans and are therefore difficult to remember. Thus, it's helpful to have a way to convert IP addresses into meaningful names. On an NT network, you use computer names (also known as *NetBIOS names*). The Internet community uses domain names. Translation methods, such as WINS and DNS, maintain databases for converting an IP address to either a computer name (WINS) or a domain name (DNS).

If you've ever used a Web browser on the Internet, you know that you can type a URL (Uniform Resource Locator) such as http://199.199.199.2/default.htm or http://www.pdaconsulting.com/default.htm to obtain access to a particular Web page. That's because the Internet uses DNS to resolve IP addresses to domain names, and vice versa. If you type the IP address, your Web browser goes directly to the location. If you type a domain name, your request is routed to a DNS Server that resolves the name to an IP address, and then your Web browser goes to the location.

The naming scheme you can use when you plan to connect to the Internet is limited. That's because the Internet Network Information Center (InterNIC) is in charge of approving and maintaining the database of Internet domain names. You can request any domain name you want, but when someone else is using it or has a legitimate legal claim to a trade or brand name, you can't use it. For example, you probably cannot use coke.com or honda.com; likewise, when the name pda.com is registered to someone else, you can't get that name for your use.

13

The format of an IP name is *host.domainname*. The domain name is something you can't guarantee, but it typically represents your organization. The host name usually is the name of the computer you attach to when you log on to your network. For example, if your domain name is pdaconsulting.com and your computer name is oriole, your Fully Qualified Domain Name is `oriole.pdaconsulting.com`. To be valid, the FQDN must have a corresponding entry in some DNS Server's database that translates it into a unique IP address; for example, `oriole.pdaconsulting.com` might resolve into `199.199.199.2` (it doesn't).

As long as you're isolated from the Internet, you can assign any names you like on your network. But if you ever connect your network to the Internet, you'll have to go back and change everything. If your network might ever connect to the Internet, obtain and install valid addresses and domain names now. That way, you'll be ready when you go to connect to the Internet. For more information, ask your ISP for details on obtaining a domain name. They will probably need to install it and its corresponding IP address in their DNS Server, so they're the right source for this information.

To learn more about the process of obtaining a domain name in general, visit InterNIC's or your NRA's Web site. You'll find details on name registration services, as well as the directory and database services that support the Internet's distributed collection of DNS Servers.

Protocol Addressing Differences

To summarize, different protocols use different addressing schemes. TCP/IP understands numbers (for example, `199.199.199.2`). NetBIOS understands computer names (for example, \\oriole). When you install W2K on a server, you give it a computer name. If you're using the IP protocol, you also assign an IP address to the server. So now the server has a computer name and an IP address.

Suppose that you're trying to find your server from a workstation. If you're using a utility such as Windows Explorer, you type the server's name rather than its IP address. If you're using a TCP/IP utility such as PING (the Packet Internet Groper), you type the server's IP address.

So how does W2K handle the different addresses? Well, that's the subject for later today, but let's look at it quickly.

Using WINS

WINS is a dynamic database that Microsoft designed to resolve NetBIOS-derived computer names to IP addresses (for example, server name to `199.199.199.2`). You enter a computer name and out pops the IP address. The database is dynamic, which means that as the network changes and names come and go, the database changes automatically. WINS is something like a French-English dictionary that's constantly updated as new words are added. You give it a French word, and out pops the English word or translation.

Note

> Because Windows 2000 no longer relies on NetBIOS for TCP/IP networking, you can get rid of WINS. But before you do, ensure that you don't have any older Microsoft clients that depend upon it. So you'll need to continue to support WINS until you upgrade all your systems to Windows 2000. Luckily, Microsoft still provides a WINS service for backward compatibility. If you are starting from scratch, carefully evaluate whether you need to support the service.

WINS Servers

A WINS Server maintains a database that maps IP addresses to their respective computer names. Instead of sending out broadcasts for address information, which consumes excess network bandwidth, a workstation in need of address information makes a request directly to a nearby WINS Server. This lets workstations take advantage of well-defined local service and obtain address information more quickly and efficiently. Also, when workstations log on to the network, they will provide information about themselves to the WINS Server so that any changes in their names or addresses automatically will cause the server's database to change accordingly.

WINS Clients

When configuring workstations on your network, you'll provide the IP addresses for the WINS Servers on your network. When workstations boot, they provide the WINS Server with their computer names and IP addresses. The server handles everything else. If a workstation needs an IP address that corresponds to a computer name, it asks the WINS Server.

The Automated Method

The best way to implement an address translation service is to automate it and remove the possibility of human error. The WINS Server handles the mapping between computer names and IP addresses, and it maintains a dynamic database that's updated automatically as computer names or IP addresses change. Systems querying the WINS Server to get the translated information are known as *WINS clients*.

The Manual Method

If you've spent any time around LAN Manager networks, you might be familiar with a text file called LMHosts in the \SystemRoot\SYSTEM32\DRIVERS\ETC subdirectory. It, too, can provide a source of information for translating between NetBIOS names and IP addresses.

13

If you want to use LMHosts on your network, you yourself must manually establish and then update the mappings between NetBIOS names (or computer names) to IP addresses. That is, if a computer name or IP address changes on the network, you must update this file by hand. In a large organization, this method is impractical. For small networks of 10 addresses or fewer, it's not unworkable, provided that the names on your network don't change too often.

With the LMHosts approach, an oversight or mistake on your part might introduce an addressing error on your network. A duplicate name or address on your network or a mistake in an address assignment can prevent a user from using the network. Perhaps it's better to let W2K handle this job automatically.

The DHCP Method

Now that you understand why each node on your network needs a unique address, a question arises: How should you assign IP addresses to your entire network? That is, should you assign these addresses manually, which forces them to be assigned permanently (that is, static addresses)? Or should you let the system make the assignments automatically, which means that the addresses are assigned dynamically?

Until the release of Windows NT 4.0, WINS did not make sense for smaller networks. For them, it was easier to assign static IP addresses, but it was a never-ending task. With NT, however, Microsoft included the Dynamic Host Configuration Protocol, which automates the assignment of IP addresses to clients. No more manually managing addresses. With DHCP, your server handles this task. You simply tell the server that it's a DHCP Server. You can do this during installation, or you can add the service later (DHCP runs as an NT service). After DHCP is installed, you configure it to manage a range (also called a *pool*) of IP addresses, and the DHCP service handles the allocation and assignment of these addresses. DHCP even manages variable checkout intervals for individual addresses so that regular users can obtain permanent assignments, and contractors or short-term users can obtain only limited leases on their IP addresses.

You configure your DHCP Server service with a range of IP addresses, any addresses within that range that shouldn't be used, and one or more subnet masks. If you're not sure what a subnet mask is, ask your ISP to explain it to you. You also tell the server how long each assignment should last (that is, the lease period).

For example, let's assume that you assign the DHCP Server the range `199.199.199.60` through `199.199.199.90` with a subnet mask of `255.255.255.224`. Based on that assignment, the server knows that it can assign any unused address within that range (that is, `199.199.199.60`, `199.199.199.61`, `199.199.199.62`, and so on, through

199.199.199.90) to a client that needs an IP address. If you told the DHCP Server to exclude certain addresses, it would not assign those addresses under any circumstance.

When a DHCP-enabled client or workstation boots up with the IP protocol, it sends a message saying, "I need an IP address. Is there a server out there that can give me one?" The DHCP Server responds by sending the workstation an IP address with a lease period. This means that the workstation can use the IP address, but only for a temporary period of time—hence, the term IP lease. You can set the term of an IP lease from DHCP.

The client then knows how long it will have the lease. Even when you reboot or reset your computer, it remembers what lease is active for it and how much longer the lease will be in effect.

Note

> On a Windows 3.x machine, the lease information is kept in DHCP.BIN in the Windows directory.
>
> On a Windows 95/98 machine, it's in HKEY_LOCAL_MACHINE\System\ CurrentControlSet\Services\VxD\DHCP\Dhcp-info*xx*, where *xx* is two digits.
>
> W2K DHCP Clients store their leased IP address in the Registry. Each time the system boots and sends a DHCPDISCOVER message, it requests the IP address that was stored in the Registry.

So if your PC had a five-day lease on some address and you rebooted two days into its lease, the PC wouldn't just blindly ask for an IP address. Instead, it would go back to the DHCP Server that it got its IP address from and request the particular IP address that it had before. If the DHCP Server was still up, it would acknowledge the request, letting the workstation use the IP address. If, on the other hand, the DHCP Server had its lease information wiped out through some disaster, it would do one of two things. It would either give the IP address to the machine (when no one else is using the address) or send a negative acknowledgment (NACK), to the machine, and the DHCP Server would make a note of that NACK in the Event Log. Your workstation would then be smart enough to start searching for a new IP address.

DHCP is an easy service to use and very handy. DHCP remembers which IP addresses go with which machine by matching an IP address with a MAC (Media Access Control, that is, the Ethernet address). If you use the TCP/IP protocol on your network, install DHCP during the NT installation and use it right away. If your workstations already have IP manually installed, you might need to switch over gradually. If you're planning to connect to the Internet, make sure that the addresses you use are valid IP addresses that you can verify with your Internet Service Provider.

13

> **Tip**
>
> If you use DHCP on your network, and you have older clients, also use WINS so that you can see the computer names in the WINS database mapping. By itself, DHCP doesn't tell you anything about NetBIOS computer names.
>
> You'll learn about using WINS later today.

DHCP Overview

DHCP was designed by the Internet Engineering Task Force (IETF) to reduce the amount of configuration required for use of TCP/IP. DHCP is defined in RFCs (Request for Comments) 1533, 1534, 1541, and 1542.

DHCP centralizes TCP/IP configuration and lets you manage the allocation of TCP/IP configuration information by automatically assigning IP addresses to systems configured to use DHCP.

Under W2K, DHCP consists of two services: a DHCP Client service and a DHCP Server service.

Configuring DHCP Servers for a network provides two benefits:

- The administrator can centrally define global and subnet TCP/IP parameters for the entire internetwork and define parameters for reserved clients.
- Client computers don't require manual TCP/IP configuration. When a client computer moves between subnets, it is reconfigured for TCP/IP automatically at system startup time.

How DHCP Works

DHCP was designed as an extension to the Bootstrap Protocol (BOOTP), originally used to boot and configure diskless workstations across the network.

> **Note**
>
> The Bootstrap Protocol was originally defined in RFC 951. The latest BOOTP RFC is RFC 1542, which includes support for DHCP. The major advantage of using the same message format as BOOTP is that an existing router can act as an RFC 1542 (BOOTP) relay agent to relay DHCP messages between subnets. Therefore, with a router acting as an RFC 1542 (BOOTP) relay agent between two subnets, it is possible to have a single DHCP Server providing IP addresses and configuration information for systems on both subnets.

BOOTP's capability to hand out IP addresses from a central location is terrific, but it's not dynamic. The network administrator must know beforehand the MAC addresses of the Ethernet cards on the network. This isn't impossible information to obtain, but it's not fun (usually, typing `ipconfig /all` from a command line yields the data). Furthermore, there's no provision for handing out temporary IP addresses, such as an IP address for a laptop used by a consultant.

DHCP improves on BOOTP because you give it a range of IP addresses that it's allowed to hand out, and it just gives them out—first come, first served to whatever computers request them. If, on the other hand, you want to maintain full BOOTP-like behavior, you can; it's possible with DHCP to pre-assign IP addresses to particular MAC addresses, as with BOOTP.

Generally, with DHCP, you have to permanently assign the IP addresses of only a few machines, such as your BOOTP and DHCP Server and your default gateway.

Leasing an IP Address

A DHCP Client gets an IP address from a DHCP Server in four steps:

1. Initializing State. A DHCPDISCOVER broadcasts a request to all DHCP Servers, requesting an IP address.
2. Selecting State. The servers respond with DHCPOFFER of IP addresses and lease times.
3. Requesting State. The client chooses the offer that sounds most appealing and broadcasts back a DHCPREQUEST to confirm the IP address.
4. Bound State. The server handing out the IP address finishes the procedure by returning with a DHCPACK, an acknowledgment of the request.

Renewing IP Address Leases

DHCP Clients lease their IP address from a DHCP Server. When the lease expires, they can no longer use the IP address. Hence, DHCP Clients must renew their lease on the IP address, preferably before the lease has expired or is about to expire. Once again, during the process of renewing its lease, a DHCP Client passes through states, as listed here:

- Renewing State. By default, a DHCP Client first tries to renew its lease when 50 percent of the lease time has expired. To renew its lease, a DHCP Client sends a directed DHCPREQUEST message to the DHCP Server where it obtained the lease.

  When permitted, the DHCP Server automatically renews the lease by responding with a DHCPACK message. This DHCPACK message contains the new lease, as

13

well as any configuration parameters so that the DHCP Client can update its settings in case the administrator updated any settings on the DHCP Server. After the DHCP Client has renewed its lease, it returns to the bound state.

- Rebinding State. If a DHCP Client attempts to renew its lease on an IP address and for some reason can't contact a DHCP Server, the DHCP Client displays a message similar to this:

```
The DHCP Client could not renew the lease for the IP Address
199.199.199.10. Your lease is valid until Mon March 31 05:55:55 1999.
DHCP will try to renew the lease before it expires. If you want to see DHCP
messages in the future, choose YES. Otherwise, choose NO.
```

When, for some reason, the DHCP Client cannot communicate with the DHCP Server where it obtained its lease, it attempts to contact any available DHCP Server when 87.5 percent of the lease time has expired. The DHCP Client broadcasts DHCPREQUEST messages so that any DHCP Server can renew the lease. Any DHCP Server can respond with a DHCPACK message that renews the lease or a DHCPNACK message that forces the DHCP Client to re-initialize (begin the leasing process anew) and obtain an IP address lease for a new IP address.

Note

When a short lease period is being specified, it's critical that the DHCP Server remains available to accommodate clients seeking to renew leases. Backup servers become particularly important with short lease periods, which can create a great deal of additional traffic on the network.

If the lease expires or the DHCP Client receives a DHCPNACK message, the DHCP Client must immediately stop using the expired IP address. The DHCP Client can, however, return to the initializing stage and attempt to obtain another IP address lease.

Implementing DHCP Servers

Before you actually run DHCP Servers, you should take time to plan the installation carefully. To get ready for DHCP installation, you should

- Have an IP address ready for your DHCP Server; this is one computer on your network that must have a static address.
- Know which IP addresses are available, because you use these available IP addresses to create a scope of IP addresses.

Installing DHCP Servers

You install the DHCP Server during installation, or you add it later by manually adding the service. Before installing a new DHCP Server, check for other DHCP Servers on the network to avoid conflicts.

To install, you must log on as a member of the Administrators group for the computer where you are installing or administering a DHCP Server.

Task 13.1: Installing DHCP Servers.

Step 1: Description

DHCP Servers are the machines that provide IP addresses to machines requesting access to your network. You use the Add/Remove Programs program to install a DHCP Server.

Step 2: Action

1. Double-click the Add/Remove Programs icon in the Control Panel.

2. When the Add/Remove Programs window appears, click Add/Remove Windows Components. The Windows Components Wizard appears. Click Next. You should see the window in Figure 13.1.

FIGURE 13.1

The Windows Components Wizard.

3. Minimize the Add/Remove Programs window.

4. Check and highlight Networking Services, and click Details.

5. You should see the Networking Services box (shown in Figure 13.2).

6. From the Subcomponents of Networking Services list, check Dynamic Host Configuration Protocol (DHCP), and then click OK.

7. Click Next to install the required components.

8. Click Finish to close the Wizard.

       9. Click Close to close the Add/Remove Programs program.

FIGURE 13.2

The Networking Services dialog box.

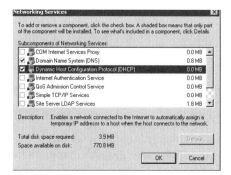

Step 3: Review

With this task, you used the Windows Components Wizard to install a DHCP Server. After you finish, you'll find a new icon in the Administrative Tools group: the DHCP Manager.

> **Caution**
>
> Unless your network is small, you should have two or more available DHCP Servers for the network that can provide a DHCP Client with a valid IP address and configuration information. When there is only one DHCP Server and it fails, the client can no longer use TCP/IP on the network when the DHCP Client's lease on the IP address expires. As a result, the DHCP Clients cannot use TCP/IP to communicate on the network. In addition, new users without a lease cannot use TCP/IP on the network.

After it's installed, the DHCP Server service starts automatically during system startup. You should pause the service while configuring scopes for the first time.

> **Caution**
>
> Remember to register your DHCP Servers with Active Directory. Otherwise, rogue DHCP Servers (that is, providing unauthorized DHCP service) might pop up in your network.

On Day 9, "Managing the File Server," you saw how to use the Computer Management program and the Control Panel to start, stop, and pause services. Use those tools to pause the DHCP service. You also can start, stop, and pause the DHCP service at the command prompt by using the commands `net start dhcpserver`, `net stop dhcpserver`, or `net pause dhcpserver`.

To authorize the server as a DHCP server, right-click the server, and select All Tasks, Authorize.

Understanding DHCP Scopes

For DHCP to give out IP addresses, it must know the range of IP addresses it can give out. How does it find out the addresses? You tell it with a scope. A scope simply is a range of IP addresses or pool of addresses to draw on. You create a scope for each subnet on the network to define parameters for that subnet.

As mentioned, the DHCP Manager icon is added to the Network Administrative Tools group under Programs in the Start menu when you set up a Windows 2000 Server computer to act as a DHCP Server. You use DHCP Manager to perform these tasks:

- Create one or more DHCP scopes to begin providing DHCP services.
- Define properties for the scope, including the lease duration and IP address ranges for distribution to potential DHCP Clients in the scope.
- Define default values for options (such as the default gateway, DNS Server, or WINS Server) to be assigned together with an IP address.
- Add any custom options.

Each scope has the following properties:

- A unique subnet mask used to determine the subnet related to a given IP address
- A scope name assigned by the administrator when the scope is created
- Lease duration values to be assigned to DHCP Clients with dynamic addresses

Creating Scopes

You use DHCP Manager to create, manage, or remove scopes.

Task 13.2: Creating a New DHCP Scope.

Step 1: Description

You'll use the DHCP Manager to create a scope for the DHCP Server.

Step 2: Action

1. Select Start, Programs, Administrative Tools, DHCP Manager.
2. In the DHCP Servers list in the DHCP Manager window, select the server where you want to create a scope.

TASK

13

▼ 3. Right-click the server, point to New, and then select Scope.

4. The Create Scope Wizard will start. Click Next.

5. In the Name box, type a scope name. Although this is optional, it's probably a good idea to name each scope for later reference. Use any name that describes this subnet. The name can include any combination of letters, numbers, and hyphens. Blank spaces and underscore characters are also allowed. You cannot use Unicode characters.

6. Optionally, in the Comment box, type any string to describe this scope, and then click OK. Click Next.

7. The Address Range panel in Figure 13.3 appears. To define the available range of IP addresses for this scope, type the beginning and ending IP addresses for the range in the From and To boxes. The IP address range includes the start and end values. You must supply this information in order for the system to activate this scope.

FIGURE **13.3**

The Address Range panel.

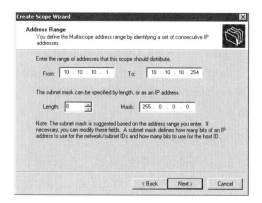

8. In the Subnet Mask box, DHCP Manager proposes a subnet mask based on the IP addresses. Accept the proposed value unless you know that a different value is required. Click Next.

9. The Add Exclusions panel (shown in Figure 13.4) appears.

10. To define excluded addresses within the IP address pool range, use the Exclusion Range controls, as detailed here:

   • Type the first IP address that is part of the excluded range in the Start Address box, and type the last number in the End Address box. Then click the Add button. Continue to define any other excluded ranges in the same way.

   • To exclude a single IP address, type the number in the Start Address box. Leave the End Address box empty, and click the Add button.

▼

- To remove an IP address or range from the excluded range, select it in the Excluded Addresses box, and then click the Remove button.
- The excluded ranges should include all IP addresses you assigned manually to other DHCP Servers, non-DHCP Clients, routers, diskless workstations, and RAS and PPP clients. Click Next.

FIGURE 13.4

The Add Exclusions panel.

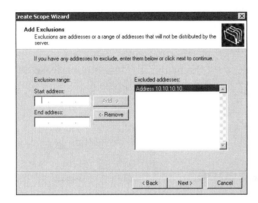

11. To specify the lease duration for IP addresses in this scope, select Limited To. Type values for Day(s), Hour(s), and Minute(s) to specify the length of the address lease. If you don't want IP address leases in this scope to expire, select the Unlimited option (this isn't recommended). Click Next.

12. On the Configure DHCP Options panel, check No. Click Next.

13. Click Finish.

14. In the DHCP window, right-click the scope you created, select All Tasks, and then click Activate.

Step 3: Review

You use the Create Scope Wizard to create a new scope. After you do, you can configure DHCP options. After you have configured the options for this scope, you must activate it so that DHCP Client computers on the related subnet can begin using DHCP for dynamic TCP/IP configuration.

To activate a DHCP scope, right-click the scope, and choose All Tasks, Activate. The menu command name changes to Deactivate when the selected scope is currently active.

Changing Scope Properties

The subnet identifiers and address pool make up the properties of scopes. You can change the properties of an existing scope.

13

Task 13.3: Changing the Properties of a DHCP Scope.

Step 1: Description

Using the DHCP Manager, you can change the properties of an existing scope.

Step 2: Action

1. In the DHCP Servers list in the DHCP Manager window, double-click the scope where you want to change properties.
2. Select Properties.
3. Change any values for the name, IP address pool, lease duration, or comment.
4. Click OK to have the changes take effect.

Step 3: Review

You used the DHCP Manager to change the properties of an existing scope.

Removing a Scope

When you are no longer using a subnet or whenever you want to remove an existing scope, you can use DHCP Manager to remove it. If any IP address in the scope is still leased or in use, you must first deactivate the scope until all client leases expire or all client lease extension requests are denied.

Task 13.4: Removing a Scope.

Step 1: Description

By using the DHCP Manager, you can remove an existing scope.

Step 2: Action

1. In the DHCP Servers list in the DHCP Manager window, select the scope you want to remove.
2. Right-click the scope; select All Tasks, Deactivate. (This command name changes to Activate when the scope isn't active.) The scope must remain deactivated until you are sure that the scope isn't in use.
3. Right-click the scope, and select Delete. (The Delete command isn't available for an active scope.)
4. DHCP asks you to confirm the deletion of the scope.

Step 3: Review

Just as you did to add or change a scope, you use the DHCP Manager to remove a scope.

Configuring DHCP Options

You use DHCP Manager to define the configuration parameters that a DHCP Server assigns to a client as DHCP options. Most options you want to specify are predefined, based on standard parameters defined in RFC 1542.

When you configure a DHCP scope, you can assign DHCP options to govern all configuration parameters. You also can assign, create, edit, or delete DHCP options. These tasks are described in the following sections.

Assigning DHCP Configuration Options

Besides the IP addressing information, you must configure other DHCP configuration options pertaining to DHCP Clients for each scope. You can define options globally for all scopes on the current server, specifically for a selected scope, or for individual DHCP Clients with reserved addresses. Active global options always apply unless overridden by scope options or DHCP Client settings. Active options for a scope apply to all computers in that scope, unless overridden for an individual DHCP Client.

Task 13.5: Assigning DHCP Configuration Options.

Step 1: Description

Using the DHCP Manager, you can assign configuration options to a scope.

Step 2: Action

1. In the DHCP Manager window, select the scope you want to configure.
2. Right-click the Scope Options icon, and then click Configure Options.
3. On the Advanced tab shown in Figure 13.5, you see a number of options. From the Available Options list, select one to configure.

FIGURE 13.5

The Configure DHCP options: Advanced tab.

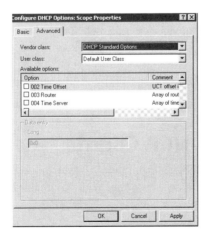

13

▼   4. Complete the appropriate value in the Data entry part of the panel. Table 13.1
         describes the value types (in order of appearance) you can enter.

TABLE 13.1   DHCP Type Values

Value Type	Description
Long	A 32-bit numeric value. For example, `002 Time Offset`.
IP Address	The IP address of a server you added in the Configure DHCP Options, Scope Properties dialog box. For example, `003 Router`.
String value	A character string, that is, an ASCII string containing letters and numbers. For example, `012 Host Name`.
Word	A 16-bit numeric value of specified block sizes. For example, `013 Boot File Size`.
Byte	A numeric value consisting of a single byte. For example, `019 IP Layer Forwarding`.
New value	A decimal or hexadecimal value. For example, `025 Path MTU Plateau Table`.
Binary	A binary value. For example, `043 Vendor Specific Info`.

For example, to specify the DNS name servers for use by DHCP Clients, select
DNS Servers in the Available Options list. Then type a list of IP addresses for DNS
Servers. The list should appear in the order of preference.

 Note

> If you are using DHCP to configure WINS Clients, set options 044
> (WINS/NBNS Servers) and 046 (WINS/NBT Node Type). These options allow
> DHCP-configured computers to find and use the WINS Server automatically.

▲   5. Configure the appropriate value, and then click OK.

Step 3: Review

Besides the IP addressing information, you must configure other DHCP configuration
options pertaining to DHCP Clients for each scope. You use DHCP Manager to do this.

Administrating DHCP Clients

The easiest method for installing and configuring a system to use TCP/IP is to enable
automatic DHCP configuration on the system. With this enabled, the DHCP Client contacts a DHCP Server during system boot for its configuration information: IP address,
subnet mask, and default gateway.

A Windows 2000 Server set up as a DHCP Server can service the following DHCP Clients:

- Windows 2000 Server
- Windows 2000 Professional
- Windows NT Server
- Windows NT Workstation
- Windows 98
- Windows 95
- Windows for Workgroups 3.11 (WFW), with the Microsoft 32-bit TCP/IP VxD installed
- Microsoft Network Client for MS-DOS with real-mode TCP/IP driver (included on the Windows 2000 Server CD)
- LAN Manager 2.2c for MS-DOS (included on the Windows 2000 Server CD)

> **Tip**
>
> You can use the ipconfig utility to troubleshoot the IP configuration on computers that use DHCP. You also can use ipconfig to troubleshoot on TCP/IP-32 clients on Windows for Workgroups 3.11 computers and on computers running Microsoft Network Client version 2.0 for MS-DOS. Windows 95/98 uses a graphical interface called winipcfg.

Managing Client Leases

In DHCP, the lease for the IP address assigned by a DHCP Server has an expiration date, which the client must renew when it is going to continue to use that address. You can view the lease duration and other information for specific DHCP Clients, and you can add options and change settings for reserved DHCP Clients.

You can edit the name, unique identifier, and comment, or click the Options button in the Client Properties dialog box only for clients with reserved IP addresses.

You can cancel the DHCP configuration information for a DHCP Client that is no longer using an IP address or for all clients in the scope. This has the same effect as if the client's lease had expired: The next time that client computer starts, it must enter the rebinding state and obtain new TCP/IP configuration information from a DHCP Server.

Delete only entries for clients that are no longer using the assigned DHCP configuration. Deleting an active client could result in duplicate IP addresses on the network because a DHCP Server might assign deleted addresses to new active clients.

13

You can use `ipconfig /release` at the command prompt to get a DHCP Client computer to delete an active client entry and safely free its IP address for reuse. In Windows 95/98, use the winipcfg utility.

To cancel a client's DHCP configuration, follow these steps:

1. Make sure that the client isn't using the assigned IP address.
2. In the IP Client list of the Active Leases dialog box, select the client you want to cancel, and then click the Delete button.

Managing the DHCP Database Files

Some key files are used by DHCP. These files are stored in the \SystemRoot\ SYSTEM32\DHCP directory that is created when you set up a DHCP Server.

> **Caution**   Don't remove or tamper with the DHCP.MDB and J*.LOG files. If you do, DHCP won't work properly.

Because the DHCP database contains all the DHCP scopes for the server and the configuration parameters, it is a good idea to implement a backup policy. Normally, the system automatically backs up the DHCP database, and this backup is used if the original is corrupted; however, you should not rely on this as your only backup. Instead, back up the database regularly, and copy the files from the \SystemRoot\SYSTEM32\DHCP\ BACKUP\JET directory.

The DHCP database and related Registry entries are backed up automatically at a specific interval (15 minutes by default, according to the Resource Kit), based on the value of Registry parameters. You also can force database backup while working in DHCP Manager.

> **Tip**   You can make DHCP back up the database less or more often with a Registry parameter. In HKEY_LOCAL_MACHINE\System\CurrentControlSet\ Services\DHCPServer\Parameters, look for (or create) a value entry called BackupInterval of type REG_DWORD. Enter the value (in hexadecimal, of course) in minutes. You can enter any value from 5 to 60 minutes. If you select and enter a binary value, the system automatically converts it to hexadecimal for you.

Working with the DHCP Database

Use the Computer Management program to verify that the DHCP services are running. In the Services dialog box for the client computer, Started should appear in the Status column for the DHCP Client service. For the DHCP Server itself, Started should appear in the Status column.

If the necessary service isn't started on either computer, start the service.

In rare circumstances, the DHCP Server might not boot or a STOP error might occur. If the DHCP Server is down, follow these steps to restart it:

1. Turn off the power to the server, and wait one minute.
2. Turn on the power, start Windows 2000 Server, and log on under an account with Administrator rights.
3. At the command prompt, type **net start dhcpserver** and press Enter.

Restoring the DHCP Database

In true NT fault-tolerant fashion, DHCP will check itself for internal problems whenever it starts. If it detects a problem, it automatically restores from the backups.

If, however, you determine that the DHCP services are running on both the client and the server computers, but error conditions persist, the DHCP database isn't available or is corrupt. If a DHCP Server fails for any reason, you can restore the database from the automatic backup files.

To restore a DHCP database, restart the DHCP Server. When the DHCP database becomes corrupted, it is automatically restored from the DHCP backup directory specified in the Registry.

If you have a corrupted primary database file and this isn't detected by the DHCP service, you can force the backup copy to be used by editing the Registry.

To force the restoration of a DHCP database, set the Registry key HKEY_LOCAL_ MACHINE\ SYSTEM\CurrentControlSet\Services\DHCPServer\Parameters\ RestoreFlag to 1. Then restart the DHCP service by entering **net stop dhcpserver** followed by **net start dhcpserver**.

And when all else fails, you can manually restore a DHCP database. When the preceding restore methods don't work, manually copy all DHCP database files from the backup directory to the \DHCP working directory, and then restart the DHCP Server service. Then go into DHCP options and click on Reconcile Database to ensure that the database is internally consistent.

13

Understanding the WINS Service

Maintaining a TCP/IP network can place a huge burden on you, the system administrator. In addition to the normal responsibilities that go along with administrating a Windows 2000 network, TCP/IP introduces another facet of administration: managing computer names and addresses. With LAN Manager and older versions of NT, system administrators manually created and maintained LMHOSTS files to map computer names to IP addresses. But along came DNS (Domain Name Service, or System) and WINS (Windows Internet Name Service) to help administrators. DNS and WINS are distributed databases for registering and querying dynamic computer-name to IP-address mappings.

Note

> As I stated at the dawning of today, you don't need to continue to use WINS unless you have downlevel systems to support. If you are just starting out and have no installed-base, forget WINS and use Dynamic DNS. It will save you a peck of trouble.

Earlier today, you learned about assigning addresses dynamically. For the rest of today, you will learn about WINS operation and how to install and configure WINS Servers.

Let's review name resolution before installing and configuring WINS.

Name Resolution for TCP/IP on Microsoft Windows 2000 Server

NEW TERM   To communicate over a TCP/IP network, your system has to resolve computer names into IP addresses, and vice versa. TCP/IP has no idea how to establish communication with a computer name such as \\sales01, but it does know how to communicate with 199.199.199.2. The process that TCP/IP networks use to discover a computer's IP address from the computer's name is known as *resolution*. Resolving a computer's IP address from its name isn't enough; each node on a TCP/IP network must have a unique name and address. To ensure that each Windows computer on a TCP/IP network has a unique name and address, the computer registers its name and IP address during startup. This process is called *registration*.

How WINS Works

DHCP made IP addressing simpler but ignored the freshly created problem of keeping track of the newly assigned IP numbers and the hosts attached to them (that is, registration). If you sit at a TCP/IP-connected workstation with a host name like, for example, oriole.pdaconsulting.com that got its IP address from a DHCP Server, and if you type **ping oriole.pdaconsulting.com**, you get a timed-out message. Your system wouldn't know its own name because no DNS Server knows what's going on with its dynamic IP address and no one updated a HOSTS file. So your system needs a dynamic name resolver—recall that *name resolution* is the term for determining that `oriole.pda.com` might really be `199.199.199.2`.

This is where Windows Internet Name Service comes in. Whereas DHCP is part of a wider group of BOOTP-related services, WINS is a Microsoft proprietary service that is recognized only by Microsoft client software (2000, NT, 95/98, Windows for Workgroups, DOS, and Windows 3.*x* clients). WINS isn't always DNS-compatible and that's a major problem. You need to use the Microsoft version of DNS because it integrates nicely with WINS. WINS is really good for administering NetBIOS networks.

Basically, this means that the name resolution task can be handled just fine inside your network or internetwork by WINS. Name resolution outside your network—an employee attempting to access a machine on the Internet or someone outside your company trying to resolve a name inside your network—requires a DNS Server.

WINS is, therefore, only half of the answer to the name resolution problem, albeit an important half.

Names in Windows Networking

Consider the two following commands, both issued to the same server, one by using a TCP/IP command to see whether a server is available on the Internet, for example, and the other by using a Microsoft network command:

```
ping sales01.pdaconsulting.com
```

and

```
net use * \\sales01\public
```

In the example that uses the ping command, the server is referred to as `sales01.pdaconsulting.com`. In the example that uses NET USE, that same server is called `sales01`. This difference is important.

Why Two Different Names?

The ping command is clearly a TCP/IP/Internet command. You can't use ping unless you're running TCP/IP. It's a valid command on UNIX, VMS, Macintosh, or MVS machines because those computers have a TCP/IP protocol stack.

In contrast, NET USE is a Microsoft networking command. You can use NET USE on an NT network no matter what protocol you're running, but the command usually isn't valid on a UNIX, VMS, or Macintosh computer.

13

The difference is in the network application program interface (API) that the application is built atop. PING was built on top of the TCP/IP sockets interface, or actually the common PC implementation of TCP/IP sockets, the Winsock interface. Building PING atop sockets was a good idea because then it's simple to create a PING for any operating system, as long as the computer has a socket interface. In fact, people basically use the same source code to create PING for Windows, UNIX, VMS, or MacOS. The sales01.pda.com is a DNS name, so for PING to recognize who sales01.pda.com is, you would need a DNS name resolver—or DNS Server—on your network.

In contrast, NET USE was built atop the NetBIOS API because Microsoft has been selling the software to do NET USE commands since 1985. The \\sales01 name is a NetBIOS name, rather than a DNS name, meaning that to make NET USE work, you would need a NetBIOS name resolver or a NetBIOS name server. That's exactly what WINS is.

If the sales01.pdaconsulting.com and \\sales01 distinction still isn't clear, think of the APIs as communications devices. Telephones and the postal service are communications mediums. PING's job is to communicate with some other PC, and NET USE also wants to communicate with some PC. But PING uses Winsock (the telephone), and NET USE uses NetBIOS (the mail). If you use the telephone to call your friend Barry, the friend's name, as far as the phone is concerned, might be something like (905) 555-2121. As far as the mail is concerned, however, the friend's name might be Barry Lewis, 124 Main Street, Anytown, ON, postal code H0H 0H0. Both are perfectly valid names for Barry, but they're different because different communications systems need different name types.

NetBIOS atop TCP/IP (NBT)

The NetBIOS API is implemented on the NetBEUI, IPX/SPX, and TCP/IP protocols that Microsoft distributes. That makes Microsoft's TCP/IP a bit different from the TCP/IP you find on UNIX, because the UNIX TCP/IP almost certainly won't have a NetBIOS API on it; it'll probably have only the TCP/IP sockets API on it. (Microsoft's TCP/IP also has sockets in the form of the Winsock API.)

NetBIOS on the Microsoft implementation of TCP/IP is essential because if the TCP/IP didn't have a NetBIOS API on it, you couldn't use the NET LOGON, NET START, NET STOP, NET USE, NET VIEW, and other commands to allow your PC-based workstation to talk to an NT Server. Microsoft's NetBIOS on TCP/IP even has a name: NBT.

So the server's name, as far as NetBIOS or NBT is concerned, is sales01, and its name so far as Winsock is concerned is sales01.pdaconsulting.com. (That name type, by the way, is called a *Fully Qualified Domain Name*, or FQDN. In this example, sales01 is the host name.) You can run programs that call on either NBT or Winsock, but you have to be sure to use the correct name.

Name Resolution Issues

After NBT has a NetBIOS name or Winsock has an FQDN, they have the same job: to resolve that name into an IP address. So computers on a Microsoft-based network using TCP/IP need some kind of name resolution.

You could use Domain Name Service. DNS clearly could do the job, so Microsoft could have designed NBT to do its name resolution via DNS. But Microsoft didn't, for a couple of reasons:

- First, DNS isn't dynamic, so you would have to add the new computer's name and IP address to DNS every time you put a new computer on your network. Then you would have to stop the DNS Server and restart it to get DNS to recognize the new name. A dynamic name server obviously would be more desirable.
- Second, Microsoft didn't ship a DNS Server with NT until version 4.0. So DNS was not the answer.

NetBIOS name resolution over TCP/IP isn't simple. Many people realized this fact; hence, there are two Internet RFCs (Requests for Comment) dealing with this topic: RFC 1001 and 1002.

B Nodes, P Nodes, and M Nodes

The RFCs attacked the problem by offering options:

- The first option was simplistic: Just do broadcasts. A computer using broadcasts to resolve NetBIOS names to IP addresses is referred to in the RFCs as a *B node*. To find out who sales01 is, then, a PC running B node software would just shout out, "Is anybody named sales01?"

  Simple, yes, but fatally flawed: Remember what happens to broadcasts when they hit routers. Because routers don't rebroadcast the messages to other subnets, this kind of name resolution would work only on single-subnet networks.

- The second option was to create a name server of some kind and to use it. Then, when a computer needs to resolve the name of another computer, all it needs to do is send a point-to-point message to the computer running the name server software. Because point-to-point messages do get retransmitted over routers, this second approach would work fine even on networks with routers. A computer using a name server to resolve NetBIOS names into addresses is said to be a *P node*.

  Again, a good idea, but it has all the problems of DNS. The name server for NetBIOS name resolution is, by the way, referred to as a NetBIOS Name Server, or NBNS.

13

- The most complex approach to NetBIOS name resolution over TCP/IP is the *M node*, or mixed node. It uses a combination of broadcasts and point-to-point communications to an NBNS. When the people at Microsoft started out with TCP/IP, they implemented a variant of the M node. It was point-to-point in that you could look up addresses in the HOSTS file, or a file called LMHOSTS, and if you had a DNS Server, you could always reference that. Other than those options, Microsoft TCP/IP was mainly a B node, which limited you to single-subnet networks. Clearly, some kind of NBNS was needed, and the simpler it was to work with, the better. Because the RFCs were silent on the particulars of an NBNS, vendors could invent anything they wanted, and they did—and none of them can talk to one another.

That's where WINS comes in. Simply, WINS is Microsoft's proprietary NBNS service. Microsoft client software with WINS actually doesn't implement B, P, or M nodes; rather, Microsoft uses what is called an H, or Hybrid, node.

| Tip | The term *H node* refers to a NetBIOS over TCP/IP mode that defines how NBT identifies and accesses network resources. |

You're probably thinking that M node is a hybrid. Well, M nodes and H nodes use both B node and P node, but the implementation is different:

- With M node, a computer does name resolution by first broadcasting (B node) and, when that fails, communicating directly with the NBNS (P node).
- With H node, a computer tries the NBNS first. If that fails, it tries a broadcast.

So as you can see, the difference merely is in the order of operation.

To resolve the computer name to its IP address, you can use various name resolution methods:

- A static mapping file (HOSTS)
- Broadcast name resolution
- Another static mapping file (LMHOSTS)
- DNS name resolution
- Windows Internet Name Service (WINS)

Broadcasts

Broadcasting on a computer network is similar to taxi dispatch. The dispatcher's voice is put on the air (broadcast) over a channel so that all drivers with radios turned on can hear the message. To contact a particular person, the dispatcher's message customarily includes the name or car number of that person. Every person receiving the broadcast message listens to determine whether it is for him or her, and the person whose name was called in the message responds to the dispatcher.

As with the taxi dispatch system, to make sure that all systems on the network can communicate with one another, all broadcasts are forwarded throughout the network. Depending on the number of name resolutions at any one time, this operation can cause significant network traffic. In addition, every system on the network must examine every broadcast to determine whether the broadcast is meant for that particular system.

By relying on broadcasts to resolve computer names, the network becomes bogged down with additional network traffic. The more computers you have on a given network, the more broadcasts on the network, which can lead to heavy network congestion. Each time a computer tries to make a network connection, it broadcasts one or more times in an effort to resolve the computer name of the system at the other end of the connection to an IP address.

LMHOSTS File

An LMHOSTS file contains a list of computer names mapped to IP addresses. When you use an LMHOSTS file to resolve a computer name to an IP address, you have to maintain that file. As the network administrator, you have to keep track of each workstation's computer name and the IP address used by the workstation. When a workstation changes computer names or IP addresses, you have to update the LMHOSTS file. Because each workstation has its own local copy of the LMHOSTS file, you have to update the file and distribute it to all the other workstations every time a computer name or IP address changes. To decrease this double-duty maintenance, use LMHOSTS files with one of the other two name resolution methods. Typically, administrators are likely to use multiple WINS servers rather than try to maintain LMHOST files.

When the LMHOSTS file is being used for name resolution and the DHCP is being used for IP address assignment, significant overhead is still involved in maintaining the IP-address to host-name mappings. This is because the LMHOSTS file is a static file that must be manually modified each time a DHCP Client receives a new IP address from a DHCP Server. Each DHCP Client requires a copy of the modified LMHOSTS file. For example, workstations that frequently move between subnets receive a new IP address every time they change subnets, which requires you to modify the LMHOSTS file on all workstations.

13

WINS

Microsoft designed the Windows Internet Name Service to eliminate the need for broadcasts and to provide a dynamic database that maintains computer-name to IP-address mappings.

A network typically has one or more WINS Servers that WINS Clients can contact when they need to resolve a computer name to an IP address. You can set up WINS Servers on a given network so that they replicate all computer names to IP address mappings in their WINS databases to one another. In general, you should implement WINS Servers so that you can accomplish the following goals:

- Reduce broadcast traffic on the network—Instead of broadcasting to every computer on a network in an attempt to resolve a computer name to an IP address, the workstation sends a message directly to a WINS Server requesting the IP address for a given computer name. Furthermore, a DHCP Server can provide a DHCP Client with IP addresses for WINS Servers.
- Eliminate the need for the LMHOSTS file—Using WINS eliminates the need for network administrators to maintain the LMHOSTS file. Because administrators don't need to keep track of what computer name maps to what IP address, there is less administrative overhead involved in using TCP/IP.
- Provide dynamic name registration—WINS complements DHCP on a network. When you use DHCP alone, you still have to maintain the LMHOSTS file. Using WINS with DHCP, however, provides dynamic IP addressing and name resolution without broadcasts or static files.
- Prevent duplicate computer names—Every time a WINS Client starts, it registers its computer name with a WINS Server. When the WINS Server already has a registration for the requested computer name, it rejects the WINS Client's registration attempt, thereby preventing duplicate computer names.

How WINS Works

Before WINS, there were two alternatives: Everyone sent a broadcast that could go unanswered, or the administrator had to maintain static files. Now let's look at what happens with WINS.

WINS Needs NT Server

To make WINS work, you must set up an NT or 2000 Server (it won't run on anything else) to act as the WINS Server. The WINS Server then acts as the NBNS Server, keeping track of who's on the network and handing out name resolution information as needed.

WINS collects name information. When a workstation wants to address name resolution questions to a WINS Server, it first must introduce itself to the WINS Server, and in the process, WINS captures the IP address and NetBIOS name of that workstation, augmenting the WINS database further.

WINS Holds Name Registrations

Basically, when a WINS Client first boots, it goes to the WINS Server and introduces itself. (Remember, Microsoft defines a client as "any PC running a Microsoft enterprise TCP/IP network client software designed to use WINS for NBT name resolution.") It knows the IP address of the WINS Server either because you hard-coded it into the TCP/IP settings for the workstation or because the workstation got a WINS address from DHCP when it obtained an IP lease.

That first communication with the WINS Server is called a *name registration request*. In the process of registering its name with a WINS Server, the workstation can ensure that it has a unique name. When the WINS Server sees that another computer has the same name, it tells the workstation it can't use that name. The name registration request and the acknowledgment are both directed IP messages, so they can cross routers. And when a workstation shuts down, it sends a "name release" request to the WINS Server, telling it that the workstation no longer needs the NetBIOS name, enabling the WINS Server to register it with another machine.

During name resolution, the WINS Client follows these steps:

1. Checks to see whether it is the local machine name.
2. Checks its cache of remote names. Any name that is resolved is placed in a cache, where it remains for 10 minutes.
3. Tries to contact the WINS Server.
4. Tries broadcasting.
5. Checks the LMHOSTS file, when configured to use it.
6. Checks the HOSTS file and then a DNS, when so configured.

When a workstation can't find the WINS Server as it boots, the workstation simply stops acting as a hybrid NBT node and reverts to its old ways as a "Microsoft modified B node," meaning that it depends largely on broadcasts but also will consult HOSTS and LMHOSTS when they're present. If the client is an h-node it will return to using the WINS server when that server becomes available again.

WINS Renewal Intervals

Like DHCP, WINS registers names only for a fixed period of time called a *renewal interval*. By default, this period is six days (144 hours). W2K will accept a maximum of 999 hours, and 40 minutes is the least WINS will accept.

13

In much the same way that DHCP Clients attempt to renew their leases early, WINS Clients send "name refresh requests" to the WINS Server before their names expire. According to Microsoft documentation, a Windows 2000 client attempts a name refresh after one-half of the renewal interval, and other clients may refresh at different intervals. The WINS Server usually resets the amount of time left before the name must be renewed again (this time is sometimes called the *time-to-live*, or *TTL*).

Installing WINS

Installing WINS is much like installing all other Windows NT software. The first step is to plan for your installation.

When you're planning how many WINS Servers you need and where to put them, consider that you need not put a WINS Server on every subnet. It is, however, a good idea to have a second machine running as a secondary WINS Server or a backup. Remember that when a workstation comes up and can't find a WINS Server, it reverts to broadcasting, which limits its name resolution capabilities to just its local subnet and adds traffic to the subnet.

Normally, the client would find the server, but occasionally, the WINS Server might be too busy to respond to the client in a timely fashion, causing the client to give up on the server. That's when a secondary WINS Server is useful. If you have a backup domain controller, put a WINS Server on that machine as well. The WINS software actually doesn't use a lot of CPU time, so it probably won't affect your server's performance unless you have thousands of users all hammering on one WINS Server. If that's the case, dedicate a computer solely to WINS.

Task 13.6: Installing a WINS Server.

Step 1: Description

To get a WINS Server set up, use the Add/Remove Programs applet in the Control Panel.

Step 2: Action

Double-click the Add/Remove Programs icon in the Control Panel.

2. When the Add/Remove Programs window appears, click Add/Remove Windows Components. The Windows Components Wizard appears. Click Next.

3. Minimize the Add/Remove Programs window.

4. Check and highlight Networking Services, and click Details.

5. From the Subcomponents of Networking Services list, check Windows Internet Name Service (WINS), and then click OK.

6. Click Next to install the required components.

▼ 7. Click Finish to close the Wizard.

▲ 8. Click Close to close the Add/Remove Programs program.

Step 3: Review

With this task, you used the Windows Components Wizard to install a WINS Server. After you finish, you'll find a new icon in the Administrative Tools group: the DHCP Manager.

After you install WINS, you need to configure its TCP/IP properties so that the computer points to itself. Use My Network Places, Properties, Network and Dial-Up Connections, Local Area Connection, Properties, Internet Protocol (TCP/IP), Properties.

You will find a new icon in the Administrative Tools group: WINS. Start it, and it should look as shown in Figure 13.6.

FIGURE 13.6

The WINS snap-in.

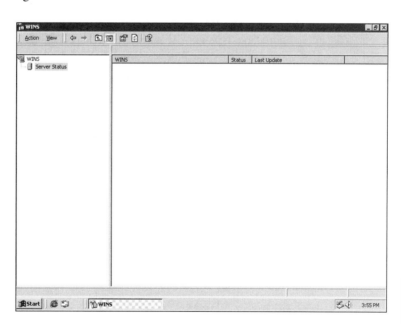

The first thing you should do on your WINS Server is inform it of the machines on your subnet that have hard-coded or static IP addresses. In a WINS environment, you can support non-WINS clients by using static mappings and configuring a WINS proxy agent.

Adding Static Mappings

You can use either of two methods to add static mappings to the WINS database for specific IP addresses:

- Type static mappings in a dialog box.
- Import files that contain static mappings.

Task 13.7: Adding Static Mappings.

Step 1: Description

To add static mappings to the WINS database, use the Static Mappings of the WINS Manager.

Step 2: Action

1. Start the WINS snap-in.

2. In the WINS window, expand the entry for the WINS servers.

3. Right-click Active Registrations, point to New, and then click Static Mapping.

4. From the Create Static Mapping dialog box, type the computer name of the non-WINS client in the Computer Name box. You don't need to type two backslashes because WINS Manager adds them for you.

5. In the Scope box, type an optional scope. A NetBIOS scope is an extension to a computer name that you can use to group computers in a network.

6. Select a Type option to indicate whether this entry is a unique name or a group with a special name, as described in Table 13.2.

TABLE 13.2 Type Options for Static Mappings

Type Option	Description
Unique	Unique name in the database with one address per name.
Group	Normal group, where addresses of individual members aren't stored. The client broadcasts name packets to normal groups.
Internet Group	Groups with NetBIOS names that have 0x20 as the 16th byte. An Internet Group stores a maximum of 25 addresses for members. Members added to this list are considered permanent and remain on the list until removed manually. For registrations after the 25th address, WINS overwrites a replica address, or when none is present, it overwrites the oldest registration.
Multihomed	Unique name that can have more than one address (multihomed computers). The maximum number of addresses is 25. For registrations after the 25th address, WINS overwrites a replica address, or when none is present, it overwrites the oldest registration.
Domain Group	Groups with NetBIOS names that have 0x1C as the 16th byte. An Internet Group stores a maximum of 25 addresses for members. Each member of the group must renew its name individually or be released. For registrations after the 25th address, WINS overwrites a replica address, or when none is present, it overwrites the oldest registration.

▼ 7. In the IP Address box, type the address for the computer. If Domain, Internet Group, or Multihomed is selected as the Type option, the dialog box shows additional controls for adding multiple addresses. Use the down-arrow button to move the address you type into the list of addresses for the group. Use the up-arrow button to change the order of a selected address in the list.

▲ 8. Click OK.

Step 3: Review

Using the WINS snap-in, you can set the Static Mappings. These static mappings are for the machines on your network that have hard-coded IP addresses (aren't WINS enabled).

Importing Static Mappings

You also can import entries for static mappings for unique and special group names from any file that has the same format as the LMHOSTS file. The WINS database ignores scope names and keywords other than #DOM. However, you can add normal group and multihomed names only by typing entries in the Add Static Mappings dialog box.

The specified file or files are read, and a static mapping is created for each computer name and address. If the #DOM keyword is included for any record, an Internet group is created (when it isn't already present), and the address is added to that group.

Configuring WINS Servers

WINS consists of two components: the WINS Server, which responds to name queries and registrations, and the WINS Client, which queries the server for computer name resolution. After you install the WINS Server on a Windows 2000 Server, the WINS Server is ready to receive name registrations and resolve name requests when you restart the computer. Installation is the only step required to get the WINS Server up and running. After the initial installation, however, you might want to configure the WINS Server to improve the performance of the WINS Server and the network.

You use the WINS snap-in from the Administrative Tools group under Programs to configure local and remote WINS Servers. The first step is to select a WINS Server in the WINS snap-in.

Whether a computer name or an IP address is specified in the WINS Manager dialog box determines how WINS Manager establishes the connection to the WINS Server. When a computer name is supplied, WINS Manager establishes the connection to the WINS Server via named pipes. When an IP address is supplied, WINS Manager uses TCP/IP to establish the connection.

13

Configuring WINS Clients

When you install TCP/IP on a workstation, you can configure it to use a WINS Server to resolve computer names to IP addresses by supplying the IP addresses of a primary and secondary WINS Server.

A Windows NT Server version 4.0 operating as a WINS Server can support the following operating systems as WINS Clients:

- Windows 2000 (all versions)
- Windows NT (all versions)
- Windows 98/95
- Windows for Workgroups 3.11 (WFW), with the Microsoft 32-bit TCP/IP VxD installed
- Microsoft Network Client for MS-DOS with real-mode TCP/IP driver, which is one of the clients included on the Windows NT Server version 4.0 CD
- LAN Manager for MS-DOS 2.2c, which is included on the Windows NT Server version 4.0 CD

As you saw yesterday, if you use a DHCP Server to supply an IP address and other configuration information to DHCP Clients, you also can configure the DHCP Server to supply WINS configuration information. To supply the necessary WINS configuration information to DHCP Clients, the DHCP Server must have the following DHCP Options set:

- 044 WINS/NBNS Servers configured with the IP address of one or more WINS Servers
- 046 WINS/NBT Node Type set to 0x1 (B node), 0x2 (P node), 0x4 (M node), or 0x8 (H node)

Using WINS Snap-In

As you saw earlier, when you install a WINS Server, Windows 2000 adds the WINS snap-in to the Administrative Tools group under Programs. You can use WINS manager to view and change parameters for any WINS Server on the internetwork. To administer a WINS Server remotely, run the WINS snap-in on a Windows 2000 Server computer that isn't a WINS Server. You must log on as a member of the Administrators group for a WINS Server to configure that server.

To start WINS Manager, double-click the WINS icon in Programs, Administrative Tools.

Managing the WINS Database

Because your WINS Server uses the same database format as the DHCP Server (a modified Access database), it has the same basic issues. So it is important to manage the various files used by WINS.

The system stores WINS files in the \SystemRoot\SYSTEM32\WINS directory created when you set up a WINS Server. You should back up these files when you back up other files on the WINS Server.

The WINS database contains all the address mappings for your WINS Clients. Like any database, it requires a certain amount of maintenance. The following discussion deals with maintenance issues such as purging entries, compacting the database, and backing up and restoring the database.

As you add and delete records, the database naturally grows larger. Its growth affects the performance of the WINS Server. As with any database, you periodically need to clean up and back up the WINS database of address mappings. As your WINS.MDB database approaches 25MB, you should compact it.

To compact the WINS database, you should carry out the following steps:

1. At the WINS Server, stop the Windows Internet Name Service by using the Control Panel Services option or by typing **net stop wins** at the command prompt.

2. Run JETPACK.EXE (which is found in the \SystemRoot\SYSTEM32 directory) with the following syntax:

   ```
   JETPACK DatabaseName TemporaryDatabaseName
   ```

   DatabaseName is the name of the database to compact (or any fully qualified pathname), and *TemporaryDatabaseName* is a name to use as a temporary database. It, too, can be a fully qualified pathname.

3. Restart the Windows Internet Name Service on the WINS Server.

Caution   Because there is potential for failure caused by the compact utility or by data corruption on your SystemRoot partition, you should back up your WINS databases regularly, and definitely before you compact them. Before you back up or compact the database, you should scavenge (clean) the database to delete old records that are no longer needed.

13

Caution

> The DHCP and WINS MDB databases are in Access format. If you have
> Microsoft Access, resist any temptation to look at these databases. Any acci-
> dental modifications would corrupt the database. If you corrupt it acciden-
> tally, restore from a previous backup.

Scavenging the WINS Database

You should periodically clean up the local WINS database of released entries and old
entries that were registered at another WINS Server but did not get removed from this
WINS database for some reason. This process, called *scavenging*, is done automatically
over intervals based on the renewal and extinction intervals in the Configuration dialog
box. You also can clean the database manually, for example, when you want to verify old
replicas immediately instead of waiting for the specified interval.

The WINS Server automatically performs scavenging in the following manner:

1. If a WINS Client doesn't renew its name registration before the renewal interval
   expires, its registration is marked as "released."

2. After the extinction interval expires for a "released" entry, it is marked as "extinct"
   in the WINS database.

3. Finally, after the extinction timeout has expired, the "extinct" entry is removed
   from the WINS database.

Using the default times for all the intervals and timeouts, a name registration that has not
been removed remains in the WINS database for a few hours. If any of the intervals or
timeouts have been increased, the entry remains in the database even longer. Therefore, it
is possible to use WINS Manager to force the WINS database to be scavenged through
the Initiate Scavenging option under the Mappings menu.

To scavenge the WINS database, right-click the server and choose Scavenge WINS
Database. The WINS snap-in cleans the database and displays its results as shown in
Table 13.3.

TABLE 13.3 Scavenging Results

State Before Scavenging	State After Scavenging
Owned active names in which the Renewal interval has expired	Marked released
Owned released names in which the Extinction interval has expired	Marked extinct

State Before Scavenging	State After Scavenging
Owned extinct names in which the Extinction timeout has expired	Deleted
Replicas of extinct names in which the Extinction timeout has expired	Deleted
Replicas of active names in which the Verify interval has expired	Revalidated
Replicas of extinct or deleted names	Deleted

Backing Up the WINS Database

WINS Manager provides backup tools you can use to back up the WINS database. After you specify a backup directory for the database, WINS performs complete database backups every three hours, using the specified directory. Be sure to perform a full backup by disabling the Perform Incremental Backup option if you plan to use this copy to restore your configuration. You also should periodically back up the Registry entries for the WINS Server.

To back up a WINS database, you take these steps:

1. Right-click the WINS server and choose Backup WINS Database.

2. In the Select Backup Directory dialog box, specify the location for saving the backup files. Windows 2000 proposes a subdirectory of the \WINS directory. You can accept this proposed directory. The most secure location, however, is on another hard disk.

Tip

Don't back up to a network drive because WINS Manager cannot restore from a network source.

13

3. Click OK.

The three files that went into WINS_BAK are essentially all there is to a WINS database. Just put the files back in *SystemRoot*\SYSTEM32\WINS, and the database is restored. But you can't do that while WINS is running, so go to the Computer Management snap-in and stop the Windows Internet Name Service. Then you need only copy the wins.mdb file from the backup location to *SystemRoot*\ SYSTEM32\ WINS and restart the service by going to the same place in the MMC where you stopped the service and start it.

If you modified the settings on the WINS Server, such as modifying the renewal interval or specifying a backup directory, you might want to back those up as well. Your option settings for the WINS Server are stored in the Registry (of course) in the key \HKEY_LOCAL_MACHINE\SYSTEM\CurrentControlSet\Services\WINS. You can save that part of the Registry in this way:

1. Start the Registry Editor, REGEDT32. (Refer to Day 4, "Understanding and Managing the Registry," if you forget how to use the Registry Editor.)

2. Open the HKEY_LOCAL_MACHINE subtree.

3. Click on the SYSTEM\CurrentControlSet\Services\WINS key.

4. Click Registry and Save Key.

5. In the Save Key dialog box, specify the path where you store backup versions of the WINS database files, and click OK. After the key is saved, close RegEdit.

In summary, to rebuild a WINS Server, you should tell the WINS Server where to do backups, and it will do them automatically every day or every few hours. And when you make changes to WINS settings, save the part of the Registry that holds the settings. Most important, run a secondary WINS Server, and then you won't have to worry about backing up your WINS database as much, because you will have two machines working in parallel.

Restoring a WINS Database

If all else fails, you will need to restore your WINS database from backup.

Task 13.8: Restoring Your WINS Database.

Step 1: Description

To restore the settings, use the Registry Editor to restore the WINS key.

Step 2: Action

1. Stop the WINS service by entering **net stop wins** at the command prompt (or use the Computer Management console).

> **Caution**
>
> You have heard it ad nauseum, but make sure that you back up the Registry before making any changes to it.

2. Start the Registry Editor, REGEDT32.

3. Open the HKEY_LOCAL_MACHINE subtree.

▼ 4. Click on the SYSTEM\CurrentControlSet\Services\WINS key.

5. Click Registry and then Restore.

6. Point the dialog box to wherever you stored the backups, and fill in the name of the backup file; then click OK.

7. Click Yes to confirm that you want to overwrite the old key.

8. Exit the Registry Editor.

9. Restart the WINS service. You don't need to reboot your system for these changes
▲   to take effect.

Step 3: Review

Use the Registry Editor to restore the key, and fill in the name of the backup file to overwrite the old key.

WINS Proxy Agents

Using an NBNS (NetBIOS Naming Service) like WINS can cut down on the broadcasts on your network, reduce traffic, and improve throughput. But as you've seen, this method requires that the clients understand WINS. Older network client software just broadcasts as a B node.

WINS can help those older non-WINS Clients with a WINS *proxy agent.* A WINS proxy agent is a network workstation that listens for older B node systems helplessly broadcasting, trying to reach NetBIOS names that (unknown to the B node computers) are on another subnet, and acts on its behalf.

Tip

WINS proxy agents don't store information obtained from a broadcast in the WINS Server's database. This is one reason why you need a proxy agent on each subnet containing older clients—non-WINS. Also, you require a WINS proxy agent on each subnet because routers don't pass broadcast messages. So the proxy agent needs to be on the same subnet as the older clients to receive the broadcast. Make sure, however, that only one WINS proxy agent per subnet exists. Otherwise, two agents will respond, causing unpredictable results.

13

Summary

During this day, you learned about naming conventions and naming resolution.

This day focuses on the Dynamic Host Configuration Protocol (DHCP), used to give out IP addresses dynamically to hosts as they join the LAN. You learned that you can permanently assign IP addresses if you so desire.

DHCP can accomplish the job of giving out unique IP addresses, and that's an important job. But it doesn't handle the big job of relating host names to IP addresses. For that, you need a name service. That service is the Windows Internet Naming Service, or WINS.

You didn't stop there as you learned about name resolution, the HOSTS file, DNS, the LMHOSTS file, and WINS as well. Specifically, you learned about

- Configuring WINS Servers
- Starting and stopping the WINS database
- Creating static mappings on a WINS Server
- Backing up and restoring a WINS Server

Now you know the ins and outs of installing and configuring the Dynamic Host Configuration Protocol and the Windows Internet Name Service.

Workshop

To wrap up the day, you can review tasks from the lesson and see the answers to some commonly asked questions.

Task List

The emphasis of this day has been to introduce you to Windows and Internet naming conventions and tools. As a system administrator, you will need to learn how to implement DHCP and WINS. You completed quite a few key tasks:

- Installing DHCP Servers
- Creating a new DHCP scope
- Changing the properties of a DHCP scope
- Removing a scope
- Assigning DHCP configuration options
- Managing client leases
- Restoring the DHCP database
- Installing a WINS Server
- Adding static mappings

- Importing static mappings
- Editing static mappings
- Filtering the range of mappings
- Configuring WINS Servers
- Configuring WINS Clients
- Starting a WINS Manager
- Connecting to a WINS Server
- Setting WINS Manager preferences
- Compacting, backing up, and restoring the WINS database

Q&A

Q Can I set a lease to Infinite?

A Yes, you can set the leases to Infinite—but don't. This might seem like an easy way to assign fixed IP addresses, but take a look at that. The main problem is that there always is user turnover in an organization. If the DHCP server isn't notified, that address cannot be reused. It is better to use a very long lease duration such as six months. (This is Microsoft's recommendation, in fact). This way, leases will be recovered at some point.

Q How do I get a client to immediately release a lease?

A If you need a DHCP Client to immediately release its IP address on shutdown, the user shutting down the system should first enter `ipconfig /release` from a command prompt, or use the Windows 95/98 winipcfg utility. Otherwise, the DHCP Server maintains the IP address as leased and unavailable for 24 hours after the IP address lease time expires.

Q How do you provide WINS names through DNS service?

A To provide WINS names through the DNS service, follow these steps:

1. Use any text editor to open the PLACE.DOM file.

2. Find or create the Start of Authority (SOA) record for the domain where you want to use WINS names. The SOA record points to the computer that is the best source of information on computer names in the domain. The record can span more than one line when you enclose it in parentheses so that the program reads it as a single line.

3. Create a new line under this line, consisting of the string $WINS. Note that this must be on a line by itself and start in column 1. Don't put the $WINS line in reverse-looking (`IN-ADDR.ARPA.`) domains.

4. Save the file.

13

Q **How can I get my UNIX client to a computer that has a WINS name and a changing IP address (for example, an address acquired through the DHCP service)?**

A Configure the UNIX computer's resolver to use the Windows NT computer running the DNS service, and make sure that the computer running the DNS service has a properly configured WINS Server service. Then decide in what domain the WINS names belong. For example, you might decide that the domain pdaconsulting.com is the space where all WINS computers are named. You then would expect WINS lookup to handle queries for workstation.pdaconsulting.com, looking for the Workstation computer.

DAY 14

Using Advanced Security Services

So far, you have learned a lot about Windows 2000. You have studied how to install it and have learned how the Registry and Active Directory features work. In addition, you have been introduced to some of the security available within Windows 2000 and now know how to set up user accounts, access rules, and manage files and printers.

As a system administrator, you face an enormous challenge in managing hardware, operating systems, and applications. In Windows 2000, security controls allow you to set strong controls over who can access the system and what files or objects each person can access. In this lesson, you'll learn about some additional security components that can be used to add an even greater degree of control over your system.

Today, you learn the following points:

- How the Boot process works
- What options are available when your system won't reboot
- Understanding and using Disk Quotas

- Using the Encrypting File System
- Understanding IPSec and how it works

Let's start with learning how the Boot process works. You can use this to save yourself a lot of wasted time if your system ever has problems starting.

Understanding the Boot Process

 In the old days, we used to call the process of loading an operating system an *IPL* or *Initial Program Load*. Nowadays this is referred to as *booting* up a system.

Many times during a system operator's daily activities you may come across the infamous blue screen. Often, this entails rebooting the machine and repairing or reinstalling the operating system. I believe it would be helpful for you to fully understand how the boot process works. This way, you might find a solution when normal procedures fail.

The boot sequence occurs in five stages:

- Pre-boot sequence
- Boot sequence
- Kernel load
- Kernel initialization
- Logon

In the next few paragraphs, you'll learn about each phase, including what files are used. Because our book emphasizes Intel-based machines, this sequence is directed at those machines. Alpha-based machines have a boot sequence that occurs in two stages: pre-boot sequence and the boot sequence.

Table 14.1 shows the files that are used to boot Windows 2000 on an Intel machine.

TABLE 14.1 Windows 2000 Boot Files

File	Location
Boot.ini	root (C:\)
Ntldr	root (C:\)
Ntdetect.com	root (C:\)
Ntbootdd.sys (optional)	root (C:)
Bootsect.dos (optional)	root (C:)
Ntoskrnl.exe	%systemroot%\system32
Hal.dll	%systemroot%\system32
System	%systemroot%\system32\config
*.sys (device drivers)	%systemroot%\system32\drivers

The Boot Sequence

First, the pre-boot phase begins with the Windows 2000–based computer initializing and then looking for the boot portion of the hard disk. During the pre-boot sequence, four steps occur:

1. The computer runs its power on self-test (POST) routines to determine the amount of physical memory, whether hardware components are present, and so on. If the machine uses a plug-and-play BIOS, enumeration and configuration of hardware devices occur.

2. The BIOS locates the boot device and loads and runs the master boot record (MBR).

3. The master boot record scans the partition table to locate the active partition, loads the boot sector on the active partition into memory, and executes it.

4. The computer loads and initializes the NTLDR file.

 Note   When Windows 2000 is installed, the boot sector is modified so that NTLDR is loaded during system startup.

After the computer loads NTLDR into memory, the boot sequence prepares for the load phases by gathering information about all the hardware and drivers. This sequence uses the following files:

- Ntldr
- Ntdetect.com
- Ntoskrnl
- Boot.ini
- Bootsect.dos (optional)

Within the boot sequence phase, there are four sub-steps. These are the initial boot loader phase, operating system selection, hardware detection, and configuration selection.

During the initial boot loader phase, Ntldr switches the microprocessor from real mode to 32-bit flat memory mode, which is required to carry out any additional functions. Then Ntldr starts the appropriate minifile system drivers. These system drivers are built in to Ntldr so that it can find and load Windows 2000 using either FAT-based or NTFS-based partitions.

Ntldr reads the Boot.ini file, after which the Operating Systems Selection menu appears, listing the operating systems that are specified in Boot.ini. The user selects which

14

operating system to load from the menu. A timer will load the default operating system if no action is taken. If no boot.ini file is present, Ntldr will attempt to load Windows 2000 from the default system root directory. This directory is typically c:\winnt.

After selecting Windows 2000 (or when the timer reaches 0), Ntdetect.com and Ntoskrnl.exe perform hardware detection. If you selected an operating system such as Windows 98, Ntldr loads and executes Bootsect.dos. This file is a copy of the boot sector that was on the system partition when Windows 2000 was installed. Your alternative operating system will then load, using the information in Bootsect.dos. Ntdetect.com collects a list of currently installed hardware components and returns it to Ntfldr, which adds it to the Registry under the HKEY_LOCAL_MACHINE_HARDWARE key. Ntdetect.com will detect the following components:

- Bus/adapter type
- Communication ports
- Floppy disks
- Keyboard
- Mouse
- Floating point co-processor
- Parallel ports
- Video adapters
- Small computer system interface (SCSI) adapters

OS loader now presents you with the option of pressing the spacebar to invoke the hardware profile/configuration recovery menu. This menu contains a list of the hardware profiles that exist on the computer. If there is more than one, you can use the Down arrow key to select a specific profile. You can also invoke the last-known good configuration by pressing L.

Next, the Windows 2000 kernel (Ntoskrnl.exe) loads and initializes while simultaneously loading and initializing the device drivers and services. This is the stage when you see the progress periods (…) appear across the top of the screen. During this phase, Ntldr takes the following steps:

- Loads but doesn't initialize Ntoskrnl.exe.
- Loads the hardware abstraction layer file (Hal.dll).
- Loads the Registry key HKEY_LOCAL_MACHINE_SYSTEM, using the file %systemroot%\system32\config\system.
- Selects the appropriate control set that it will use to initialize the computer. This contains the configuration data used to control the system, such as the device drivers and services that are needed.

- Loads old device drivers with a value of 0x0 for the Start entry. These typically include low-level hardware device drivers such as those needed for the hard disk. The order in which Ntldr loads these device drivers is specified in the Registry key HKEY_LOCAL_MACHINE_SYSTEM\CurrentControlSet\Control\ServiceGroup Order.

After the kernel load phase is complete, the kernel initializes and is passed control by Ntldr. Your system now displays a graphical screen with a status bar indicating the load status. During this stage, four additional tasks are performed:

- The Registry key HKEY_LOCAL_MACHINE_HARDWARE is created using the information collected during hardware detection. As you may recall from Day 4, "Understanding and Managing the Registry," this key contains information about the hardware components and interrupts being used by specific hardware devices.

- The Clone control set is then created by copying the control set referenced in the Current entry of HKEY_LOCAL_MACHINE\SYSTEM\Select. This control set is never modified because it is intended to be an identical copy of the data used to configure the computer and doesn't reflect changes made during the startup process.

- After the clone control set is created, the kernel initializes the low-level device drivers and then scans the HKEY_LOCAL_MACHINE_SYSTEM\ CurrentControlSet\Services subkey of the Registry for additional device drivers.

- If a device driver has an error while loading or initializing, the boot process will proceed based on a value specified in the ErrorControl entry for the driver. The ErrorControl values appear under the subkey—HKEY_LOCAL_MACHINE_ SYSTEM\CurrentControlSet\Services*servicename*\ErrorControl.

Table 14.2 identifies possible values and the resulting boot sequence action.

TABLE 14.2 ErrorControl Values and Resulting Boot Actions

Value	Boot Action
0x0 (Ignore)	The boot sequence ignores the error and proceeds.
0x1 (Normal)	The boot sequence displays an error message and continues.
0x2 (Severe)	The boot sequence fails and restarts using the LastKnownGood control set.
0x3 (Critical)	The boot sequence fails and restarts using LastKnownGood control, unless that control set is causing the error. In that case, the boot sequence stops.

14

Following the device driver load, services are started. The program called Session Manager (Smss.exe) starts subsystems and services. Session Manager executes any instructions located in the BootExecute data item, in Memory Management and in the DOS Devices and Subsystems keys of the Registry.

Commands located in the BootExecute data item are executed before Session Manager loads any services. Paging file information required by the Virtual Memory Manager is contained in the Memory Management key, and Session Manager uses this to create the page file. The DOS devices key is used to create symbolic links that direct certain classes of commands to the correct file system component, and finally, Session Manager uses the Subsystems key to start the Win32 subsystem, which controls all I/O, access to the video screen, and Winlogon.

Following the kernel initialization phase, the logon process begins. Winlogon.exe starts the Local Security Authority (lsass.exe) and displays the logon dialog box. You can logon now, even though Windows 2000 might still be finalizing initialization of network device drivers. Now a program called the Service Controller starts and scans the Services sub-key looking for values containing 0x2 for the Start entry. This value indicates that the associated services are to load automatically. Typical services that start automatically include the Server and Workstation service.

The services that load during the logon phase use values indicated in DependOnGroup or DependOnService entry of the HKEY_LOCAL_MACHINE\SYSTEM\ CurrentControlSet\Services Registry key. The user must log on successfully to the system before Windows 2000 considers startup to be complete. Following a successful logon, the system copies the Clone control set to the LastKnownGood control set, which is then used whenever you invoke the Hardware Profile/Configuration Recovery menu to recover the system.

Your Windows system is now up and running.

Control Sets

So what are these control sets that I identified in the last section? A typical Windows 2000 installation contains a number of control set subkeys. These include Clone, ControlSet001, ControlSet002, and CurrentControlSet. So what do these do?

The CurrentControlSet subkey points to one of the ControlSet00x keys. The Clone control set is a duplicate of the control set used to initialize the computer and is created by the kernel initialization process each time that you start your computer. It isn't available after you log on. Within the Registry subkey HKEY_LOCAL_MACHINE\SYSTEM\ Select are the entries for a number of key control sets. The four key control sets are

- **Current**: This identifies which CurrentControlSet is being used. Whenever you use the Registry editor and update the Registry, you modify the information in CurrentControlSet.

- **Default**: This identifies the control set Windows 2000 will use the next time it starts, unless you select LastKnownGood configuration. Both the default and current control sets typically contain the same control set number.

- **Failed**: This identifies the control set that failed the last time the computer was started using the LastKnownGood control set.

- **LastKnownGood**: This identifies the copy of the control set last used when the computer started successfully. After the user successfully logs on, the clone control set is copied to the LastKnownGood control set in.

In each of these entries, there is a REG_DWORD data type, and the value refers to the specific control set. For example, if the value in Current is set to 0x1, then the CurrentControlSet points to ControlSet001.

Using the LastKnownGood configuration overwrites any changes made since the last successful boot.

This LastKnownGood configuration is what allows you to recover the system when you have problems rebooting. When you make configuration changes, for example, such as adding or removing device drivers, they are saved in the Current control set. After you reboot, the kernel copies this information to the Clone control set during the kernel initialization phase when you successfully log on, and it gets copied to the LastKnownGood control set.

You can learn more about performance monitoring in Day 20, "Windows 2000 Performance Monitoring and Tuning".

If you have problems during Windows 2000 startup, and you think they might relate to configuration changes, shut down the computer without logging on and then reboot. When the OS loader V5.0 prompt appears, press F8 to open the Windows 2000 Advanced Options menu, and select the Last Known Good Configuration option. Alternatively, after you select Windows 2000, you can press the spacebar to open the Hardware Profile/Configuration recovery menu and press L to select Last Known Good

14

Configuration. Now you can reapply configuration changes or, better yet, complete the reboot by logging on and shutting Windows down properly. This way, you reset the default control sets, allowing you to attempt your configuration changes once again and maintaining a path back to a successful logon.

 Note   The LastKnownGood configuration won't help with problems arising from incorrect file permissions or misconfigured user profiles. It also doesn't help with startup failures relating to hardware failures or missing or corrupt files.

Advanced Boot Options

A number of advanced boot options may assist you when you have problems starting Windows 2000. These include

- Safe Mode
- Enable Boot Logging
- VGA Mode
- Last Known Good Configuration
- Directories Services Restore Mode
- Debug Mode

When using these options in Windows 2000, logging is enabled with each option except Last Known Good Configuration. The system writes the log file in the system root folder using the filename ntbtlog.txt.

Safe mode is obtained by pressing F8 during the operating system selection phase. In this mode, Windows 2000 loads and uses only the basic files and drivers needed to operate the system. These include the mouse, VGA monitor, keyboard, and default system services. Using safe mode, your background will be black, and the words Safe Mode will appear in all four corners of the screen. You see an example of this in Figure 14.1.

Selecting Safe Mode with Networking adds the drivers and services necessary to enable networking to function. Safe Mode with Command Prompt is the same as safe mode. When the computer restarts, it displays a command prompt instead of the normal Windows graphical interface.

Using the Enable Boot Logging option logs loading and initialization of all the drivers and services and allows you to troubleshoot boot problems. Everything that happens is logged. All three options of safe mode automatically create this boot log file.

FIGURE 14.1

Using safe mode.

The VGA Mode option merely starts Windows 2000 with a basic VGA driver that is tested by Microsoft. This might help you recover after an error in updating a video driver.

As I mentioned earlier, the Last Known Good Configuration option starts Windows 2000 using Registry information from the last successful start.

The Directory Services Restore Mode option only applies on Windows 2000 server and allows you to restore Active Directory on the Domain Controller.

Finally, Debug Mode turns on the Microsoft debugging option. This option is only for those administrators with a detailed technical background.

Using Disk Quotas

Disk quotas are new to the Windows NT (2000) family. Prior to this release, you had to purchase third-party software solutions in order to manage how much disk space your user community is allowed to use. I anticipate that this will be looked at favorably by all those system administrators out there.

 What are disk quotas? I am so glad you asked. *Disk quotas* enable system administrators to designate an upper limit on the amount of disk space a user is allowed. This can be important because it finally allows a greater degree of disk management and provides a method for ensuring that any one user cannot consume all the disk space on a volume either accidentally or intentionally.

14

NEW TERM   Disk quotas provide a couple of options (which I will discuss later) that vary in
             the degree of control placed on the user. One option, for example, only turns on a
surveillance mode. This warns users if they rise above a certain threshold of space usage
but doesn't prevent them from using it. This can be a useful tool by itself, enabling
administrators to monitor the system without placing actual restrictions on the user.

The other option, of course, enables actual quotas and stops a user from exceeding the
designated space limit. Très cool unless you are that user!

Windows 2000 tracks disk usage on a per-user, per-volume basis using only NTFS
drives, of course. By default, only members of the Administrators group can implement
disk quotas.

Note

Windows 2000 only allows disk quotas to be applied to NTFS volumes,
another good reason to choose NTFS over FAT.

Task 14.1 shows you how to enable disk quotas on your system.

Task 14.1: Enabling Default Disk Quotas.

TASK

Step 1: Description

This task enables the Administrator to start disk quotas on a Windows 2000 machine. All
new users will be affected by this default, although no actual space limitation is imposed.

Step 2: Action

1. Ensure that you are logged on as Administrator.

2. Select a disk drive using Start, Programs, Accessories, Windows Explorer and
   clicking on the drive icon. Be sure you select a drive formatted using Windows
   2000 NTFS. You can also choose to double-click on My Computer and select the
   drive from the resulting dialog box.

3. Right-click on the selected drive and select Properties. You see a screen somewhat
   like the one in Figure 14.2.

4. Click the Quota tab. Now check the box next to the field called Enable Quota
   Management. You see a dialog box like that shown in Figure 14.3.

5. Click OK to set the option. Although you are setting up disk quotas as you can see
   in Figure 14.3, there are no limits being placed on the users. That's another task.

6. You will get a message indicating that Windows 2000 needs to scan the volume to
   set statistics and it might take a few minutes. Click OK again.

FIGURE 14.2

The disk drive proper-ties dialog box.

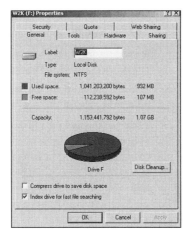

FIGURE 14.3

The quota properties dialog box.

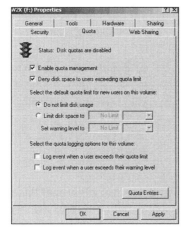

Step 3: Review

In this task, you learned how to set the Initial Disk Quotas option on your machine. Later, you'll learn what additional parameters you can set.

The Quota tab in a disk's properties table contains a number of options, as you see in Figure 14.3. What are these options and how do you use them? In Table 14.3, you will find each option described.

14

TABLE 14.3 Quota Tab Options

Option	Description
Enable Quota Management	This option starts quota management on the drive.
Deny Disk Space to Users Exceeding Quota Limit	When you select this box, users will receive an "out of space" message when they exceed their quota.
Do Not Limit Disk Usage	Use this option when you don't want to limit the amount of space users have available to them.
Limit Disk Space To	Place an amount in the first box and then select whether you want to limit space by kilobytes, megabytes, gigabytes, or even terabytes and larger amounts. What shows in your drop-down box varies with the size of the drive you are using. For drives smaller than 1GB, you only see KB and MB as an option. Larger drives show KB, MB, GB, TB, PB, and EB.
Set Warning Level To	Use this limit to indicate the amount of space before a user is warned he is getting close to his maximum.
Log Event When a User Exceeds His Quota Limit	As indicated, this produces a log record.
Log Event When a User Exceeds His Warning Limit	As indicated, this also produces a log record. You can use this log entry as a tool to prompt you to discuss the ramifications of exceeding the space limit with the user before it happens.
Quota Entries	This option allows you to set up new entries, delete existing ones, or view current usage.

NEW TERM When you enable disk quotas, there are two values that you can set: the disk quota *limit* and the disk quota *warning level*. As you saw in Table 14.3, the quota limit specifies the amount of disk space a user is allowed to use. The quota warning level merely specifies when a user is nearing her quota limit. For example, set a user's disk quota limit to 100MB and her disk quota warning level to 80MB. This allows the user to store no more than 100MB of files on the volume and warn the user when she has reached 80MB of file space.

You can also allow users to exceed their quota limit but warn them when they do reach that limit. This can be useful when you don't want to deny users access to a volume but want to track disk space use on a per-user basis. You can also specify whether to log an event when the user exceeds either his quota warning level or the quota limit.

Enabling quotas causes an increase in server overhead and therefore might slow down your file server performance. You might want to be careful about applying quotas on file servers that are already heavily used. Using file compression doesn't affect quota statistics. For example, if a user is limited to 100MB of disk space, he can only store 100MB worth of files, even if the files are compressed.

W2K disk quotas monitor volume use by individual user, so one user's utilization of disk space doesn't affect the disk quotas for other users. For example, if a user saves 50MB of files on Volume II, that user cannot add any more files to the volume without deleting or moving some of the existing files from it. However, this doesn't prevent other users from saving their assigned maximum (50MB) on that volume.

If a user moves her files from one folder to another on the same volume, her space allocation remains the same (she has moved existing files). However, if users copy their files to a different folder on the same volume, their volume space usage doubles because they are essentially creating additional files.

I discuss folders in this example, but it really has no bearing on disk quotas. The limits apply to the amount of space used, not whether you have one or 10 folders available.

If a single physical disk contains multiple volumes (remember that volumes are similar to the old partitions you used before Windows 2000), and you apply quotas to each of the volumes, each quota applies only to the one specific volume. For example, if you use two volumes, Volume D and Volume E, quotas are tracked independently for the two volumes, even if they exist on the same physical disk.

If you have a volume that spans more than one physical disk, the quota applies to the entire spanned volume. For example, applying a quota limit of 50MB means users cannot save more than 50MB to the volume, regardless of whether that volume resides on one physical disk or spans three physical disks.

In addition to those limits, disk quotas are applied when you become the owner of a file. For example, if User A owns a 5MB file and User B takes over as owner of that file, the quota usage for User A is reduced by 5MB and User B's usage is increased by 5MB.

As with all things in a Windows 2000 system, volume usage information is stored using the security ID (SID) and not the user account name. When you first start Disk Quotas, it must get the current user account names from either the network domain controller or from the local machine and match them to the SIDs for users currently using the volume. This way, the names will appear in the Quota Entries Name field when you open that window. This is done automatically the first time you view quota entries. After the names are obtained, they are saved to a file on the volume so that they are immediately available each time the Quota Entries window is opened. However, because this file may not get updated for several days (it isn't automatic), the usernames in the Quota Entries window may not reflect new user accounts. To update and obtain current usernames, press F5.

14

Windows will then refresh the usernames for each user from the network domain controller or local user manager.

 Note

Quotas don't impact Administrators. Administrators have unlimited volume usage.

So what happens when you convert a FAT or FAT32 volume to NTFS and apply disk quotas? Files on these volumes are owned by the system, so when you convert them, usage is charged to the Administrators who have unlimited access. As users begin to utilize the new volumes, disk quota limits will begin to be applied.

Disk quotas can be enabled on either local or remote volumes. On local computers, they limit the space available to the different users who log on to the local computer. On remote computers, they limit the space used by remote users. Once applied, users will get an "insufficient disk space" message when trying to add files to a volume after they reach their assigned space limit.

You use quotas to ensure that

- Users who log on to the same computer don't interfere with one another's ability to work.
- Users don't use all the disk space via a shared folder on your personal computer.
- One or more users don't monopolize disk space on public servers.

Windows system files are included in the volume usage of the person who installs Windows. When you implement disk quotas on a local volume, you should take into account the disk space used by the Windows files. Depending on the free space available on the volume, you may want to set either a high quota limit or no limit at all for the user who installed Windows. This isn't a problem, of course, if an Administrator installs Windows 2000, because he cannot be denied disk space use even if he surpasses the disk quota limit.

Now that you have a fair idea of all the aspects of disk quota usage, let's adjust the default amount of space for one user. First, you need to continue on from Task 14.1 and impose limits on all users. I show this in Task 14.2. Then in Task 14.3, I will show you how to set a different limit on one user.

Task 14.2: Enforcing a Default Disk Quota for All Users.

TASK

Step 1: Description

This task enables the Administrator to set up an actual default disk quota limit on a Windows 2000 machine and disallow users to exceed their disk space. All users will be impacted by this default.

Step 2: Action

1. Ensure that you are logged on as Administrator.

2. Select a disk drive by using Start, Programs, Accessories, Windows Explorer and clicking on the drive icon. Be sure you select a drive formatted using Windows 2000 NTFS. You can also choose to double-click on My Computer and select the drive from the resulting dialog box.

3. Right-click on the selected drive and select Properties. You see a screen somewhat like the one in Figure 14.2.

4. Select the Quota tab and click on it. Now check the box next to the field called Enable Quota Management. Next, check the box called Limit Disk Space To, input 50 in the first blank, and select MB from the drop-down menu. This will limit users to 50MB on this volume. Next, input 45 in the box next to the field called Set Warning Level To, and then select MB from the drop-down menu. Select both logging options by ticking the appropriate boxes. Your dialog box should look like that shown in Figure 14.4.

FIGURE 14.4

The updated quota properties dialog box.

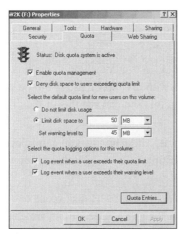

▼

14

▼   5. Click OK to set the option.

    6. You will get a message indicating that Windows 2000 needs to scan the volume to
▲   set statistics and it might take a few minutes. Click OK again to end the task.

Step 3: Review

In this task, you learned how to set the initial disk quotas option on your machine and
enforce disk quotas.

In the next task, you learn how to change the quota limit for one user. As you can see,
this gives you the ability to differentiate between the amount of space a user might have
available, while ensuring that at a minimum, default values are used.

Task 14.3: Establishing Disk Space Limits for One User.

Step 1: Description

This task enables the Administrator to set up a disk quota for one user that is different
from the system default. First, you need to set a global limit and then apply a different
limit for one user.

Step 2: Action

1. Ensure that you are logged on as Administrator.

2. Select a disk drive by using Start, Programs, Accessories, Windows Explorer and
   clicking on the drive icon. Be sure you select a drive formatted using Windows
   2000 NTFS. You can also choose to double-click on My Computer and select the
   drive from the resulting dialog box.

3. Right-click on the selected drive and select Properties. You see a screen somewhat
   like the one in Figure 14.2.

4. Select the Quota tab and click on it. Now click on the box called Quota Entries.
   You are shown all the users with disk space usage on the drive, including those
   users added by an administrator. You can see this in the dialog box shown in
   Figure 14.5.

5. Select a user by clicking on it. Alternatively, you can select Quota, New Quota
   Entry and then select an existing user or a new user. You will see a new dialog box
   like that shown in Figure 14.6.

6. Change the space to limit this user to 5MB disk space and 3MB warning space.
   Then click OK. You see that the user's space limits are changed in the Quota
▼   Entries dialog page in Figure 14.7.

FIGURE 14.5

The quota entries dialog box.

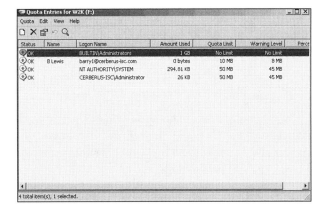

FIGURE 14.6

Setting space limits on one user.

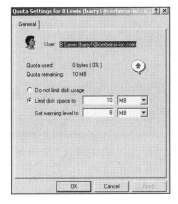

FIGURE 14.7

The Quota Entries dialog box shows new space limits.

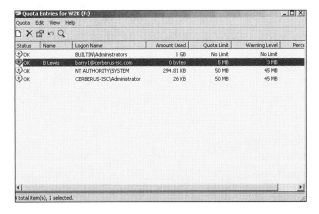

7. Click OK to end.

14

Step 3: Review

In this task, you learned how to set separate disk quotas for one user using different amounts than the default options. You can set higher or lower individual quotas depending upon your needs.

You can only delete disk quota entries for a user after he has removed all his files or if some other user has taken ownership of his files.

Finally, you may need to disable Quota management for some reason. This might be due to the need to reorganize the drive or merely because the administration has become too onerous and poorly documented and your users are having all kinds of space problems. I show you how to do this in Task 14.4.

Task 14.4: Disabling Default Disk Quotas.

Step 1: Description

This task enables the Administrator to disable the disk quota limit on a Windows 2000 machine and allow users to utilize all the disk space they need.

Step 2: Action

1. Ensure that you are logged on as Administrator.
2. Select a disk drive by using Start, Programs, Accessories, Windows Explorer and clicking on the drive icon. Be sure you select a drive formatted using Windows 2000 NTFS. You can also choose to double-click on My Computer and select the drive from the resulting dialog box.
3. Right-click on the selected drive and select Properties.
4. Select the Quota tab and click on it. Now check the box next to the field called Enable Quota Management to disable Quota management. (It should be blank now.) Your dialog box should look like that shown in Figure 14.8.
5. Click OK to set the option.
6. You will get a message indicating that Windows 2000 will need to rescan the volume if you choose to enable them again later. Click OK again to end the task.

FIGURE 14.8

Disabling quotas.

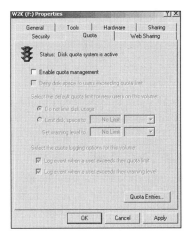

Step 3: Review

In this task, you learned how to turn off the use of disk quotas on your machine.

In this section you learned what disk quotas are used for and how you can set a default quota for all users while allowing individual users to have separate limits. This allows you to let your friends use all the space they need while everyone else has to be careful. Just kidding! I know you wouldn't do that.

Encrypting File System (EFS)

Windows 2000 offers a new and exciting level of security for files that applies encryption, making them virtually invulnerable to attack by unauthorized users. This is especially useful for businessmen and women who travel, because they can use this to help ensure that their important data remains safe, even if the laptop they use is stolen.

What is encryption? You may recall from Day 6, "Introducing Security Services," that it involves a number of things. It is an incredibly complex field populated by mathematical geniuses and is probably understood completely by only a few of them!

NEW TERM In Day 6, I told you that, basically, encryption is the science of protecting data or messages. It uses mathematical algorithms that combine input containing plaintext data and an encryption key to generate encrypted data that is usually referred to as *ciphertext*. In order to decrypt this ciphertext, you need additional data, called a *decryption key*, to perform the transformation back into something understandable.

14

The word *encryption* originates from the Greek words *kryptos* (to hide) and *logos* (word) and is far from new. In fact, the ancient Egyptians used encryption 4,000 years ago. Encryption has really become important in modern society with the advent of the computer.

In traditional secret (or symmetric) key cryptography, the encryption and decryption keys are identical and must be shared by multiple parties. People who want to communicate with secret key cryptography must find a way to securely exchange this key before they can exchange encrypted data. Any person who knows the key can both encrypt and decrypt the message.

Public-key (PK) cryptography, however, uses different encryption and decryption keys and is properly called *asymmetric*. Encryption with a public key is a one-way function; the plaintext turns into ciphertext, but the encryption key is unrelated to the decryption process. In order to decrypt the message, you need the private key that is related, but not identical, to the encryption key. This is where the term *two-key encryption* is derived. So every public key user has a pair of keys consisting of a public key and a private key. By making the public key available to anyone, it is possible to let anyone send you encrypted data that can only be decrypted by using your private key. Think of the secret key as the password that unlocks a message sent to you by another person who uses your public key to encrypt a message. After she encrypts that message with your public key, even she won't be able to see what the message contains. Only you can.

EFS relies on this concept of keys to protect your data. Users work with encrypted files and folders the same way they do with any other files and folders. Encryption is transparent as long as the EFS user is the same person who encrypted the file or folder. The system automatically decrypts the file or folder when the user accesses it later. Because it is integrated with the NTFS file system, it is virtually transparent to the user.

 Note

> Files and folders cannot be encrypted or decrypted on FAT volumes. You must use NTFS. Its primary function is to protect data stored on local computers so that Windows doesn't support sharing encrypted data. You cannot encrypt compressed, read-only, or system files.

EFS doesn't encrypt folders; it encrypts the files that are located within a folder. Likewise, subfolders aren't encrypted; they are marked, however, to indicate that they contain encrypted file data.

The *encryption* process works using the following principles:

- Each file has a unique *file encryption key*, which is also used to decrypt the file's data.
- The file encryption key is also encrypted. It is protected by the user's public key, which corresponds to the user's EFS certificate.
- An authorized recovery agent's public key also protects the file encryption key, allowing the business to recover the data if the user cannot.

Decryption of files uses the following principles:

- In order to decrypt a file, the file encryption key has to be decrypted first. The file encryption key is decrypted when the user has a private key matching the public key.
- A recovery agent can be assigned to allow decryption of the file's encryption key, by using the recovery agent's private key. This ensures that the user isn't the only person who can decrypt the file encryption key.
- After the file encryption key is decrypted, either the user or the recovery agent can use it to decrypt the data in the file.

All the private keys are held in a protective key store, not in the Security Account Manager (SAM) or in a separate directory.

A user can store encrypted files on a remote server; however, this still only allows the user or the recovery agent to decrypt the files. Other users aren't able to read or use these files. Keeping them on a public or private network share allows them to be backed up by that server while ensuring that no one can look at the data within. You should also be aware that the data isn't encrypted as it moves across the network to the file server; it is only encrypted after it resides on a physical disk volume.

While using EFS, users are still able to do all the things they normally do with that data. They can move it, copy it, read it, and delete it.

If an encryption key pair doesn't exist for a user, EFS will automatically generate an encryption key pair. The initial release of EFS uses the expanded Data Encryption Standard (DESX) as the encryption algorithm. This means that it is fairly safe because this is a standard encryption algorithm.

Caution

You can lose data by deleting or playing with these encryption options and making a mistake. Use a test system for this section, and don't turn on the encryption options for folders that contain data you cannot afford to lose, unless you have far more experience than this book offers.

14

NEW TERM So where do you perform encryption? You can use Windows Explorer, or you can elect to encrypt a file or folder using a command-line function called `cipher`. For more information about the `cipher` command, you can type **cipher /?** at a command-line prompt. It is easier to use the GUI in Explorer, but we all know there are command-line weenies amongst us. Task 14.5 shows you how to select encryption at the fold level.

Task 14.5: Viewing Folder-Level Encryption Options.

Step 1: Description

This task enables users to view the encryption settings that are available to them.

Step 2: Action

1. Ensure that you are logged on as either a user or Administrator.

2. Select a disk drive by using Start, Programs, Accessories, Windows Explorer and clicking on the drive icon. Be sure you select a drive formatted using Windows 2000 NTFS. You can also choose to double-click on My Computer and select the drive from the resulting dialog box.

3. Double-click on the selected drive and select a folder.

4. Click the Properties tab and click on it. Look for the field called Advanced and click on that to open the Advanced Attributes dialog box like that shown in Figure 14.9.

FIGURE 14.9

The Advanced Attributes dialog box.

5. Look for the last option, called Encrypt Contents to Secure Data. It should be unselected. Leave it that way for this task. Click Cancel to leave the option without changing anything.

6. Click Cancel once more to close the folder dialog box and complete this simple task.

Step 3: Review

In this task, you learned how to find the encryption option for a folder.

It's really very easy. Users encrypt a file or folder by setting the encryption property just as you do for any other attribute, such as read-only, compressed, or hidden. If a user encrypts a folder, all files and subfolders created in or added to the encrypted folder are automatically encrypted. Microsoft recommends that users encrypt at the folder level.

As a user, you can easily encrypt a file by selecting the Encrypt Contents to Secure Data option on the file or folder. You can also turn off encryption by deselecting this box. Once encrypted, other users cannot see the contents of the folder. If other users try to access the encrypted folder, they receive an Access Denied message.

If an encrypted file is copied to another folder that doesn't have the encryption option set, the file remains encrypted. If an unencrypted file is copied into an encrypted folder, the file is automatically encrypted. Moving or renaming a file doesn't alter its encryption status. If it is encrypted when you move it, it will remain encrypted wherever it ends up.

 Note Files and folders are encrypted by default using 56-bit encryption. North American organizations can enhance this with 128-bit encryption by obtaining the Enhanced CryptoPAK from Microsoft.

After users begin to explore and use encryption, there are several things they might want to consider. These are outlined in Table 14.4.

TABLE 14.4 Recommended User Practices for Encryption

Practice	Description
Encrypt the My Documents folder	This is typically where most user data resides.
Consider encrypting the Temp folder	This protects any temporary files the user creates.
Encrypt at the folder level, not individual files	Folder-level encryption ensures that all files stored in that location are encrypted, including temporary files a user's application might create in that folder.
Ensure that sensitive data automatically saves in your encrypted folder by setting default values in the application.	Word 97, for example, allows you to set the default Save directory by using Tools, Options, File Locations and setting Documents to your encrypted folder.

As you can see, this provides your users with the opportunity to protect their data. Let's take it a step further and test the process so that you truly understand it. I'll do that in Task 14.6.

14

Task 14.6: Setting File Encryption and then Testing It to Ensure that It Works.

Step 1: Description

This task enables a user to set the encryption option on a folder and verify that others cannot see the data. To perform this task, you need two user accounts. Use the information provided in Day 7, "Managing User Accounts," if you have forgotten how to create them. In this task, I will refer to the two accounts as *UserA* and *UserB*.

Step 2: Action

1. Log on to the system as UserA.

2. Select a disk drive by using Start, Programs, Accessories, Windows Explorer and clicking on the drive icon. Be sure you select a drive formatted using Windows 2000 NTFS. You can also choose to double-click on My Computer and select the drive from the resulting dialog box.

3. Double-click on the selected drive and select a folder.

4. Select the Properties tab and click on it. Look for the field called Advanced and click on that to open the Advanced Attributes dialog box.

5. Look for the last option, called Encrypt Contents to Secure Data. It should be unselected. Click on the box to select the option. Click OK to set up encryption. Select the Security tab and make sure that UserB has full rights to the folder.

6. Click OK again to close the folder dialog box and complete this step.

7. Log off as UserA and log on as UserB.

8. Use Explorer to travel to the folder that UserA encrypted, and double-click to select it. Try to read any of the files in the folder. What happens?

9. As you see, unless you are the user who set encryption on a folder (or the authorized Recovery Agent), you cannot view the contents of a file even if you have access to it.

Step 3: Review

In this task, you learned how to set encryption on a folder and then test it to verify that others cannot access it.

So you have users who set encryption on their folders to prevent Administrators and anyone else from seeing what is in the folder. Now you need to access that folder because the user left the firm or because she is on extended leave and management needs the important information that the user is maintaining. So what do you do?

One method, of course, is to apply a new password to the user account and have the manager sign on and access the files. Properly documented and logged, this allows access while retaining the user's accountability, as she will know the account was used when she returns and must be provided with a new password.

However, what if the user loses her private key and cannot access the data? Do you really want your user community with the only keys to the strong box, so to speak? Of course you don't. This is where data recovery comes into play.

Data Recovery

Data recovery is the process of decrypting a file without the private key of the user who encrypted the file. This can occur for the following reasons:

- The user has left the organization.
- Legal reasons, such as suspected fraud.
- The user loses his private key.

EFS provides built-in data recovery support. To protect us from ourselves, Microsoft implemented a Windows 2000 Server security infrastructure that enforces configuration of special data recovery keys. It only allows you to use file encryption if the local computer is configured with one or more of these recovery keys. The user's private key isn't compromised in any way; only the file's unique encryption key is available using the recovery key. This ensures that the person performing a recovery option cannot do anything other than recover a file.

When EFS is used in a standalone or workgroup server environment, it will automatically generate recovery keys and save them in the Registry.

W2K uses the term *recovery policy* to refer to the policy that users must adhere to when recovering encrypted data. A recovery policy is a type of public-key policy. When W2K is installed, a recovery policy is automatically implemented during setup of the first domain controller. Microsoft assigns the domain administrator a self-signed certificate, designating that account as the recovery agent.

This data recovery enforcement is required before users can encrypt files. The recovery policy allows you to designate a person as the recovery agent. By default, when the Administrator logs on to the system for the first time, he or she becomes the recovery agent.

This default recovery policy is configured locally for any standalone machines. For those machines that are part of a network, the recovery policy is configured at the domain, organizational unit (OU), or individual machine level.

14

There are three types of recovery policies that Administrators can define: no-recovery, empty recovery, or a recovery policy with one or more recovery agents.

- **No-recovery**: If an administrator deletes the group recovery policy, a no-recovery policy is implemented. The default local policy on individual computers is then used for any data recovery purposes. This means that local administrators control the recovery of data on their computers.

- **Empty recovery**: If all recovery agents and their public-key certificates are deleted, an empty recovery policy is put into effect. An empty recovery policy means that no one is a recovery agent. User won't be able to encrypt data on any computers within the scope of the recovery policy. In effect, this turns off EFS altogether.

- **Recovery-agent**: Finally, when an administrator adds additional recovery agents, a recovery-agent policy is created. These agents become responsible for recovering encrypted data within their scope of authority. This is the most common type of recovery policy. It makes more sense in most organizations to have more than one person with recovery capabilities.

In Task 14.7, I show you how to change your default recovery policy.

Task 14.7: Changing a Domain's Default Recovery Policy.

Step 1: Description

This task enables an administrator to change the recovery policy. This task assumes that you are still running the domain you created earlier.

Step 2: Action

1. Log on to the first domain controller as Administrator.

2. Select Start, Programs, Administrative Tools, Active Directory Users and Computers.

3. Right-click on the Domain name and select Properties, Group Policy (see Figure 14.10).

4. Click on Edit. This opens up a group policy dialog box. Double-click on Computer Configuration and then double-click on Windows Settings. You should see a dialog box like that shown in Figure 14.11.

5. From this dialog box, you can delete or modify your policies by using the Edit or Delete global policy options. Now double-click on Security Settings and then Public Key Policies. Your screen should look like that shown in Figure 14.12.

▼

FIGURE 14.10

The Group Policy tab.

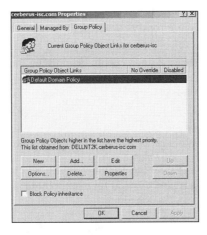

FIGURE 4.11

The Group Policy dialog box showing Security Settings.

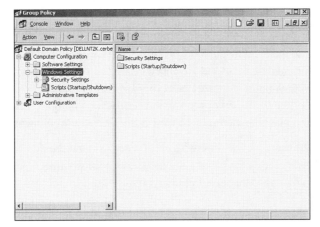

FIGURE 4.12

Public Key Policies.

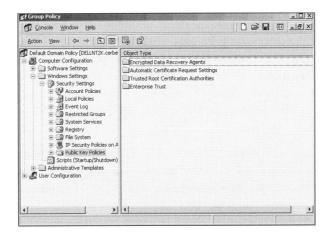

14

▼ 6. Select the Encrypted Data Recovery Agents option and right-click on it. You can now select Add, and a wizard will start that takes you through the remaining steps to add a new Recovery Agent for this domain. (You need to add certificates before doing this.) You can also select Action, Delete Policy to remove the Encrypted Data Recovery Agents Policy. I don't recommend doing this, though. By selecting another agent, you ensure that more than one administrator is available to help
▲   users.

Step 3: Review

In this task, you learned how to delete the policy or add a new Recovery Agent.

Prior to being able to add a new Recovery Agent, however, you need to provide the user with a certificate. So how do you perform that function? There are two primary ways to explicitly request certificates in Windows 2000.

Using the Certificate Request Wizard, you can request certificates from a W2K Enterprise certification authority. This wizard is located in the Certificates snap-in. The wizard takes you through the necessary steps to grant a new certificate.

You can use the Windows 2000 Certificate Services Web pages. There are Web pages for letting users submit basic and advanced certificate requests. These are installed automatically by default and are located at `http://servername/certsrv`, where *servername* is the name of the W2K server hosting the certification authority. If you have a standalone certification machine, you use the Certificate Services Web pages.

Managing, using, and dealing with certificates demand the depth of an entire book all to themselves. I recommend that you pursue this because it becomes more important as industry moves into the world of encryption.

IPSec

IPSec conjures up visions in the minds of most of us, we are sure. What those visions consist of, however, is largely in the eye of the beholder, so to speak. IPSec is the next stage in protection against network and Internet penetration attacks because it works at the IP protocol layer. IPSec consists of a suite of cryptography-based protection services, as well as security protocols. By implementing it at the IP layer, it offers end-to-end security. In other words, the only computers that need to know about it are the sending and receiving machines.

At the moment, most machines using a TCP/IP-based network are vulnerable to any number of network sniffers. These are tools that allow a user to watch and read all the data that crosses their network, whether it is intended for them or not. As long as an unauthorized or disgruntled person can connect to your network, he can listen in and watch. What does this mean? Well, an obvious meaning is that he can look for any passwords that are sent in clear text. After he finds these passwords, he can become a legitimate user, usually with no one the wiser. In addition, of course, he can watch and collect important data such as executive emails or Human Resources data. IPSec promises to make that a thing of the past.

Microsoft defines three general policies for dealing with IPSec. The first, a minimal approach and the default for W2K machines, is no IPSec at all. Next, Microsoft suggests the use of a standard authentication service that tries to balance the need for security with the need for efficiency. Finally, the high security policy requires IP security for all traffic sent or received. Defining this balance for your environment is one of your first tasks when considering implementing IPSec.

As with all W2K tasks, you use an MMC add-in to configure and implement IPSec. You assign IPSec policies to the Group Policy of a computer account, site, domain, or Organizational Unit. If you apply it to the Group Policy for the Active Directory object, it will be applied to all the computer accounts under that Group Policy.

When you are considering using it, you need to think about a number of things. These include

- What machines IPSec should be applied to on your network. There is a system overhead involved, and it is complex to install and manage.

- Applying IPSec to the domain policy overrides any local machine's IPSec policy whenever that machine is connected to the domain.

- You need to remember that Group Policy follows a specific path. If you apply it to the Group Policy for the Active Directory object, it will be applied to all the computer accounts under that Group Policy.

- Assigning policies at the highest possible level is always the easiest to administer and manage without getting bogged down in the details of implementing it on specific domains and machines.

When you implement a new IPSec policy in Active Directory for a computer, the machine must be restarted for the new policy or policy changes to be transferred and updated on the specific machine.

You can find the current IPSec policies in Group Policy, Windows Settings, IP Security Policies on Active Directory. You see an example of these default values in Figure 14.13.

14

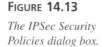

FIGURE **14.13**

The IPSec Security
Policies dialog box.

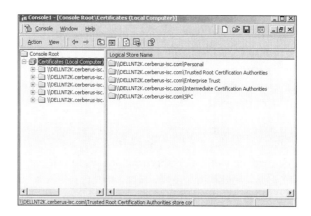

By right-clicking on that policy, you can start an Installation Wizard that guides you
through the implementation process. Be sure you are working on a machine that you can
afford to lose before playing with these options, in case you somehow misconfigure an
option and cannot recover. The wizard will ask you how you want your machine to
respond to requests for security and what authentication methods to use. After you create
a policy, it allows you to edit and further update it.

So how does the IPSec process work once it is implemented? The following list guides
you through an imaginary process between two machines, MachineA and MachineB. It
is a very technical process, simplified here as much as possible.

1. The IPSec driver on MachineA checks the IP Filter List in the active policy for a
   match with the address or traffic type of the outbound packets.

2. The IPSec driver notifies a special service called ISAKMP to begin security negotiations with MachineB.

3. The same service on MachineB receives a request for security negotiations.

4. The two computers perform a key exchange and establish a security association
   and a shared, secret key.

5. The two computers negotiate the level of security for the data transmission, establishing a pair of security associations and keys for securing the IP packets between
   them.

6. The IPSec driver on MachineA signs the packets for integrity and, if confidentiality
   was asked for, encrypts the packets so that no one can see them except the two
   machines.

7. The IPSec driver on MachineA sends the packets to MachineB.

8. MachineB receives the secured packets and transfers them to the IPSec driver.

9. The IPSec driver on MachineB checks the integrity signature and decrypts the packets (if they were also encrypted for confidentiality).

10. The IPSec Driver on MachineB then transfers the decrypted packets to its TCP/IP driver, which transfers them to the waiting application and the user obtains her information.

All of this occurs transparently to the two users on these machines. It makes your data safe from prying eyes if you select to encrypt the data, and it leaves your environment less vulnerable to penetration. There is no need for any of the network components such as routers or switches to even know about the IPSec transaction that is occurring. It is just another network connection. The only caveat is for those routers functioning as a firewall, security gateway, or proxy server. These will require special filtering to enable the secured IP packets to pass through.

As I seem to have to mention numerous times, there is so much information to deal with in Windows 2000 that I am left showing you the extreme basics so that you are at least aware of each new item. I just don't have the pages to go into the detail necessary for you to understand all of the subjects in detail. W2K has increased the complexity of the NT world immensely, and it will take considerable study to understand it all.

Internet Draft References

The W2K version of IPSec isn't exactly the only version that exists. Microsoft has taken information from a number of standards and has combined it and manipulated it to come up with a version it is comfortable with and can implement. The big question will be whether the rest of the industry follows suit and enables a high degree of compatibility. Only if everyone follows a consistent pattern will this level of security truly take off. You can use the following data provided to obtain additional information by searching the Internet for the indicated files.

Microsoft states that the IPSec implementation in W2K adheres to, but doesn't fully implement, the overall recommendations for IPSec designated by the Internet Engineering Task Force (IETF). The IPSec architecture documents it follows are

- draft-ietf-ipsec-doc-roadmap-02.txt

  IP Security Document Roadmap

- draft-ietf-ipsec-arch-sec-07.txt

  Security Architecture for the Internet Protocol

- draft-ietf-ipsec-ipsec-doi-10.txt

  The Internet IP Security Domain of Interpretation for ISAKMP

14

- draft-ietf-ipsec-pki-req-01.txt

  PKI Requirements for IP Security

The Authentication Header protocol is based on the following IETF IPSec drafts:

- draft-ietf-ipsec-ah-MD5-96-03.txt
- draft-ietf-ipsec-ah-SHA1-96-03.txt
- draft-ietf-ipsec-auth-header-06.txt

The Encapsulating Security Payload protocol is based on these IETF IPSec drafts:

- draft-ietf-ipsec-esp-v2-05.txt
- draft-ietf-ipsec-ciph-cbc-02.txt
- draft-ietf-ipsec-ciph-des-expiv-02.txt
- draft-ietf-ipsec-ciph-des3-00.txt
- draft-hoffman-des40-02.txt

As you can see, there is a huge amount of information on IPSec and how it all comes together. Use the preceding documents indicated and the Help information that W2K provides to perform further research.

Summary

There are a number of advanced security features within Windows 2000. These can be complex and take time to clearly understand. Today you learned about the following topics:

- The boot process
- Restarting a failed system in safe mode
- Using disk quotas and understanding how they work
- Using the Encrypting File System
- What IPSec is and how it helps secure your site

Advanced Security Services are important aspects of Windows 2000. The system lets you configure it in many ways. Now, however, let's review what you learned today.

Workshop

To wrap up the day, you can review tasks from the lesson and see the answers to some commonly asked questions.

Task List

With the information provided today, you now can begin your study of Windows 2000 objects. You learned how to carry out the following tasks:

- Enable and enforce disk quotas
- Establish disk space requirements
- Disable disk quotas
- View folder encryption options
- Set folder encryption options
- Change a domain's default EFS recovery policy

Q&A

Q   How do I turn on disk quotas on my machine?

A   You can do this by selecting the Properties of a hard drive and then selecting the Quota tab. Turn on quotas by checking the Enable Quota Management box. You need to decide whether you want enforcement or just monitoring, however, and you do that by checking the appropriate boxes that follow the Enabling dialog.

Q   Is EFS, the Encrypting File System, really worth the effort to use on my machine?

A   This depends. On the one side, if you are using a laptop, the additional protection EFS offers is well worth the effort expended in setting up and using it. On a desktop machine in your secure office, however, it is likely of less benefit unless you don't trust your coworkers or you store sensitive information on your machine.

Q   Should I use IPSec on my machine?

A   Well, this is a tough question. Ideally, you would want to use this enhanced level of network security, but implementing it on your machine is only half the battle. In order for it to be any use, you must apply it to at least two machines. Then those two machines can negotiate and communicate securely.

14

WEEK 3

At a Glance

15

16

17

18

19

20

21

DAY **15**

File Backup and Recovery

Last week, you learned all about files and directories in W2K and how to find, manage, and manipulate them. You also learned that W2K offers the use of more than one type of file system; the older, more accepted FAT system and the newer NTFS (New Technology File System). At this point, you will learn about protecting your files from loss and will learn appropriate methods for backing up and restoring lost files. Today, you'll learn about accepted ways of managing the backup process by using the tools and techniques available to you in a Windows 2000 Server environment.

When you used the Backup program on Day 2, "Installing Windows 2000 and Client Software," you learned a useful backup technique. That command provided a copy of your current Registry that you use to recover your server when a problem arises.

A successful backup program consists of various elements, the most important being the actual backup program and your diligence in performing it regularly. Too many times data loss occurs primarily because the backup did not get done or did not run successfully, and recovery was therefore impossible.

This lesson introduces you to a backup and recovery process that should become one of the key tasks in your day-to-day administration of your Windows 2000 Server system. Tomorrow, you'll look at fault tolerance for W2K, and you'll get your first glimpse of the proper method for setting up and managing a fault-tolerant system, to complement your file backup and recovery. Let's start by quickly looking at backing up your server.

Server Backups

Tomorrow, you'll look at creating fault tolerance and protecting the system from a hardware failure by using special devices. No matter how well you configure the system for fault tolerance, files are accidentally deleted, and even fault-tolerant drives sometimes malfunction, causing data loss.

One of the first tasks is to consider what device to use for providing your backups. Most servers these days have huge data requirements, and therefore some form of tape or optical disk is necessary to manage the amount of data that needs to be backed up.

Next, it might be a good idea to decide the general backup policy you intend to follow. Should you perform daily backups? Should you do a full or incremental backup? What retention cycle should you use, and what about recovering individual files that users might have lost? Finally, how do you verify that the backups are working properly and that you can recover the necessary data if needed? We answer these questions and more in today's session.

Choosing a Tape Drive

In Windows 2000 Server, as always, you must first consider the Hardware Compatibility List (HCL). You remember from previous days that W2K can be very particular about the devices it will use. Limit your problems by using the HCL whenever you add a new device. When considering the purchase of a new device, be sure to use the storage figures offered without using compression, because these are more accurate. Windows 2000 doesn't always allow software compression, so your device might offer only half the storage you expected if you considered only the fully compressed storage figures.

It is a good idea to standardize all of your tape drives within the computer room because this strategy offers greater ease of use and flexibility. It's a lot easier to grab and use a tape from a central storage area than it is to find a particular brand for a particular type of tape drive, mixed up among many types.

You might have a tape drive in each machine or use an autoloader type of device. Using an autoloader becomes useful where you have more than one server to back up or have really extensive amounts of data to back up. Individual tape drives require you to load the tapes needed for each backup cycle. This is fine when all of your data fits on one tape, but it becomes a problem when you need more than one since someone needs to

15

be onsite when the backup job is run. Often backup is done during the night, and your organization might not normally require onsite operations staff during night hours.

An autoloader solves this problem by providing a bay for a number of tapes to fit into, and the autoloader software then uses each tape as necessary. This solution leaves you free to check the backups each morning rather than be onsite.

What types of tapes are available and how do you decide which to use? We see all kinds in use by our clients, indicating that no one type is the be-all or end-all solution. What is right for your environment might be too little or too much for another. The primary types of tape in use consist of 4mm and 8mm formats. These tapes are easily the most available and have been around long enough to be reasonably priced. A standard 4mm tape might hold anywhere from 2GB to 9GB of data, and an 8mm tape holds from 4GB to 25GB of data. Progress moves on for there is now a 4mm tape that can hold 12GB to 24GB worth of data!

When purchasing tapes, you need to be wary of claims about capacity since they usually consist of the maximum amount after compression. If you already use compression, such as NTFS file-level compression, you're unlikely to get any additional compression gain, so the amount of data held on the tape might differ from the suggested specifications. In this case, you might need more tapes than you thought you would.

One of the newer tape formats is called digital linear tape (DLT). It's gaining acceptance as a reliable, fast backup medium for large server backups. DLT uses an extremely fast transfer rate and provides about three times the storage capacity of other tape formats. It uses a unique multipath, serpentine approach for storing data. On each tape are 64 pairs of track; the backup is performed by moving along one track until the end of the tape is reached and then continuing back on the next track to the beginning of the tape. By performing this snakelike back-and-forth movement, DLT stores data in such a manner that access to any particular piece can be very fast because it's not necessary to read through the entire tape.

When purchasing the tape device, be sure to consider the importance of this decision. An inexpensive device might sound like a good deal or a cost-saving measure, but when your backups are lost or the machine readily breaks, is the savings worth it? You need to find a cost/performance balance that you can live with and that protects your important data assets.

Finally, you need to consider the speed of the device and compare it to the amount of data that needs to be backed up. A device that operates too slow means your backups will need hours or even days to finish, and the chance of completing the backups regularly and verifying the data will be diminished by other priorities.

Installing a Tape Backup Device

As you just learned, keeping a backup copy of your data is essential to ensure that the important information on your network is maintained and always accessible. After you decide on a tape drive, you need to add it to your server and tell W2K the device exists.

Physically adding a tape drive might mean removing the cover of your server and installing the device in one of the many drive bays. Or it might mean adding a device to a serial, parallel, or SCSI port on your server. Windows 2000 has greatly improved Plug and Play option, so all you should need to do is add the device and let W2K find it. Should W2K not recognize it, you will need to use the Add/Remove Hardware program. It is under Start, Settings, Control Panel.

Now that your new device is ready for use, you are faced with the task of determining what needs to be backed up and when to perform the backups. You need to develop a strategy that provides you with all the necessary items in case a real disaster occurs and the backup copies become your only source of data.

Creating a Backup Strategy

First, it is important to realize that developing a sound, effective strategy is beyond the scope of this book. We provide you with the necessary fundamentals, but each site has different needs. An effective program is developed using input from many different parts of the organization, such as your audit staff and user community. Why do these people need to provide input to your plan? Because without them, you cannot be certain what files need to be backed up and what type of schedule is most effective for that particular data.

You might decide that all data would be backed up on a cycled basis, regardless of its use to the organization. You need to ask yourself, however, whether this means just the data on your servers or all data, including the client machines. Often, this answer depends on whether your site provides a policy for staff that only company data located on the servers is backed up. Clients might be told they should not keep data on their local drives for this reason.

On the other hand, your site might allow data to be spread out across the network for other reasons, and therefore, your backup policy needs to consider all client machines in addition to the servers.

Note Regardless of the method used to back up—either server only or server and workstation files—it is important to ensure that users are well aware of the strategy. This helps prevent data loss from occurring due to a user storing critical data in a location where it is not backed up regularly. Remember that workstations need to be left on overnight for a backup to work, and this is not always the case—though you can acquire technology to allow you to remotely boot client workstations.

15

It is crucial that the tapes you use be managed well. A rotation cycle needs to be developed that clearly defines the role of each tape in the cycle. For example, a four-week cycle needs four sets of tapes, each labeled according to the week. You might use Week 1, Week 2, Week 3, and Week 4 as your naming convention, or you might use a color scheme with Red, Yellow, Black, and White designating each week.

The cycle needs to include a daily backup and a weekly full backup, using different tapes. If you are concerned about the cost of all these tapes, consider the alternative. How much will it cost to recover your files when they are not backed up? For example, each Saturday you might produce a full backup and produce incremental backups for the rest of the week. This way, you can always recover using the latest weekly full backup and any additional incremental backup tapes you have available.

You might also want to produce a backup tape for each quarter or each month and keep this offsite in the event of a disaster. This way, you can always recover the preceding month's/quarter's data should you lose everything else in a fire or some other disaster.

The most common method for backups is the grandfather/father/son (GFS) rotation. This method is supported by most backup software, is relatively easy to implement and manage, and is fairly efficient. It is primarily used on small- to medium-sized servers. This backup rotation can be implemented using 21 tapes. By increasing the number of daily cycles to protect against excessive tape usage, you can increase the number to 32 or more tapes. In Task 15.1, you'll learn how to set up such a cycle.

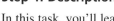

Task 15.1: Setting Up a Grandfather/Father/Son Backup Cycle.

Step 1: Description

In this task, you'll learn to set up and use a GFS tape rotation cycle. You can modify the cycle to suit your particular needs.

Step 2: Action

1. Create four tapes and name them Daily Mon., Daily Tues., Daily Wed., and Daily Thurs. These are your daily backups.

2. Create five weekly cycles and call those tapes Weekly One, Weekly Two, Weekly Three, Weekly Four, and Weekly Five. These become the weekly backups.

3. Now create 12 tapes and label them for each month of the year. These are used as your monthly backups.

4. Use the daily tapes for each week, overwriting the data on each tape on the successive week. For example, the Monday tape is used once per week, on each Monday. For these, you might use an incremental backup.

▼

▼ 5. Follow up each Friday with a weekly tape, and perform a full backup. These tapes are overwritten only once every four or five weeks. (The fifth tape is used for months containing an extra Friday.)

6. Finally, use the monthly tapes on each month end, performing a full backup again and providing a further copy of all files. These, of course, get overwritten only
▲ once per year.

Step 3: Review

This task showed that you could provide a backup program using a straightforward system and only a few tapes. You modify the plan to suit your needs. For example, when archiving is less critical to your organization, substitute the weekly backups with quarterly or semi-annual ones. When it is more important, perform full backups every couple of days or mid-week.

Do not forget to include an offsite rotation for the tapes. Many organizations like to keep the most recent week's backup tapes on hand for quick data recovery of individual files. Users are constantly requiring these, especially, it seems, after they become accustomed to how easily the files are recovered. This retention cycle, however, leaves your site vulnerable to data loss of up to two weeks' worth of information! Carefully consider whether this vulnerability is acceptable, and institute other solutions when you need offsite recovery of less than this time frame. For example, ensure that the full weekly backup is always sent offsite on the following Monday, but retain the incremental tapes for the additional week to allow users to recover files.

One additional method that is very complex is called the Tower of Hanoi method, based on the game of the same name. It is not supported by NTBACKUP and therefore cannot be used without third-party software.

Finally, remember that tapes wear out and that machines sometimes fail in inexplicable ways. Test your backup tapes regularly, such as once per quarter or at least every six months. You do not want to find out the hard way that a tape is no longer any good and the data stored on it is lost.

Your organization's critical data is stored on these tapes, and the tapes are not protected by any form of encryption. If they ever are stolen, everything is accessible and at risk. Lock them up and transport them using only reputable data storage firms. Be sure to institute written procedures to follow for tracking all the tapes during their journeys back and forth between your site and the offsite location to ensure that each is always accounted for and properly tracked.

Various terms are used for backups that you need to understand. Windows 2000 allows you to select the type of backup based on your understanding of these terms:

15

- *The archive bit*: One way for an operating system to track whether a file is backed up is through the use of a bit that gets set each time a file is created or modified. The bit is called the archive bit or *backup marker*. It has been around since the DOS days and has proven to be a reliable method for determining backup status. When you back up the file, this clears or resets this archive attribute.

- *Normal backups*: This backup copies all selected files, regardless of the archive bit setting, and then turns off the archive bit on all those files. This is often referred to as a full backup.

- *Copy backups*: This is identical to a normal backup except the archive bit is never changed. This method is normally used to allow you to take an interim backup without affecting the normal backup cycle you are using. Leaving the archive bit alone allows your regular backup cycle to continue unaffected.

- *Incremental backups*: This type is used to back up all the files that have been modified or created since the last normal or incremental backup. Typically, you run a normal or full backup, and then instead of running another complete backup of all files, you run an incremental backup, copying only the files changed since the normal backup. You continue running incremental backups after that, copying the files that have changed since the last incremental backup. You do this each day of the week, for example, and run a normal on each Saturday. This technique minimizes the work of the backup program yet ensures that all files are properly backed up.

Note Just so you know, incremental backup turns off the archive bit since it is considered a part of your regular backup cycle.

- *Differential backups*: This backup type copies all the selected files with their archive bits set but does not change those archive bits. In this manner, each time you run the backup, the files created or modified since the last full backup are all copied, updating the backup with more and more files each day. Each set contains all the prior sets of files, so it keeps growing. Put another way, a day's worth of differential backups contains all the files up to and including that day. Restoring a damaged disk drive with differential backups means taking the most recent normal backup tape and then the most recent differential tape and using them both to update all the files. Restoring a file is even easier. You look for it on the most recent differential, and if you don't find it, return to the last normal backup because it will not be on any of the other differentials.

- *Daily backups*: This method is used to copy only those files created or modified on a particular day. Again, the option leaves the archive bit unchanged, because it uses the date and does not refer to the archive bit. Using a daily backup means the copy must be run each day or some files do not get backed up. This type of copy also fails to back up modified files where the date stamp is not modified.

These options are used in all backup programs. You might decide to use a normal backup cycle and back up all the files each time. With this option, however, you use a large number of tapes because every file is backed up each time the job runs. In large organizations, this method is far too time-consuming and costly.

You usually end up using a combination of normal, on a weekly basis perhaps, with incremental or differential backups in between the normal jobs. This technique diminishes the number of tapes needed and the time required performing the backup.

Deciding how your disk drives are used plays a role in the type of backup and how often you might run each one. If you use a single server with one drive, it's no issue. Back it up.

In a multiple-server, multiple-disk-drive environment, the issue gets more complicated. Consider setting up the drives to handle the various types of data involved. For example, place user data and other frequently changed data in one area, and segregate it from less-often-changed data such as system files. This way, you can schedule changes to each type of data and minimize how often each needs to be backed up. An occasional normal backup suffices for system files, but an incremental or differential approach is necessary for files that change more often.

The Windows 2000 Backup Program

Windows 2000 Server bundles a backup program. The backup and recovery software provided with Windows 2000 is a vast improvement over previous versions of Windows. The program comes from Seagate Software, which has a history of providing excellent backup software for Windows operating systems. You might need to use other programs should you install an autoloader, because the W2K backup program does not recognize these devices. Follow the directions that program provides to manage your backups.

As you have learned in life: You get what you pay for. So you'll find this free tool rather limiting in its capabilities. Most organizations purchase a higher-end tool that offers improved services such as multiserver capability or the capability to back up multiplatform workstations. In addition, many tools offer the capability to schedule the backups and offer scripting languages for automating your particular backup needs. However, NTBACKUP does provide adequate backup for small sites with modest needs. You'll learn how to set up and run the program in this section.

NTBACKUP handles files residing on either FAT-based or NTFS-based partitions. It also allows you to recover these files onto either system, meaning that a file originally backed up from an NTFS file system can then be restored to a FAT drive, or vice versa.

The files and program icons for NTBACKUP are installed by default when you first install W2K Server. Before using the program, however, you need to set up the tape drive. Following this, the other steps you need to consider before actually beginning your first backup are deciding on the tape rotation cycle, labeling and setting up your tapes, and selecting the files and directories for backup. In the next task, you'll learn to run the tape backup program.

Task 15.2: Backing Up Data.

Step 1: Description

In this task, you'll learn to tell NTBACKUP what files and directories to back up, and you'll complete a backup.

Step 2: Action

1. Log onto the system as an Administrator. You need Administrator or Backup Operator access to ensure that you are authorized to access all the files. Open the program using Start, Programs, Accessories, System Tools, Backup. You see the window shown in Figure 15.1. Alternatively, you can select Start, Run, enter NTBACKUP, and then click OK.

FIGURE 15.1

The opening window for Backup.

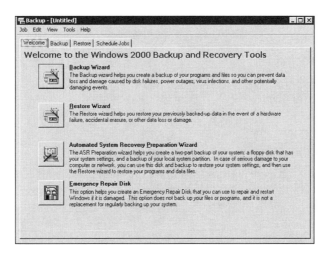

2. Click the Backup Wizard button and you will see the Backup Wizard panel. Click Next.

▼ 3. You have three choices described in Table 15.1. Check the radio button for Back up selected files, drives, or network data. Click Next.

TABLE 15.1 Backup Options

Backup options	Description
Back up everything on my computer	Backs up all files on the computer where you are running Backup, except those files that Backup excludes by default, such as certain-power management files.
Back up selected files, drives, or network data	Backs up selected files and folders. This includes files and folders on the computer where you run Backup and any shared file or folder on the network. When you select this option, the Backup Wizard provides a hierarchical view of the computer and the network (using My Network Places).
Only back up the Systems State data	Backs up System State data along with any other data you select. You only can back up the System State data on the computer where you run Backup.

4. You should see the window in Figure 15.2. On this panel, you have two fields to complete. You can click on the down arrow, you select the target Backup media type, such as Tape of File. You can back up a file to any disk-based medium, including a hard drive, a shared network folder, or a removable disk, such as an Iomega Zip or Jaz drive.

FIGURE 15.2

Where to Store the Backup panel.

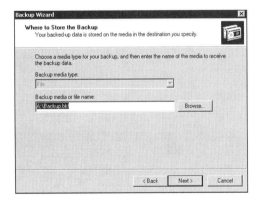

5. You also need to specify the location for the Backup in the Backup media or file name box. For a tape, enter the tape name. For a file, enter the path for the backup file. Should you not know the path or the tape, click Browse to find it. Click Next.

6. You should see a window such as the one in Figure 15.3. This window tells you that you can start the backup by clicking Finish. It also tells you that you can specify additional options by clicking Advanced. Click Advanced.

15

FIGURE 15.3

Completing the Backup Wizard panel.

Note

> When you specify advanced backup settings, you are changing only the default backup settings for the current backup job. These settings cover the media and characteristics of the backup job.

7. From the panel shown in Figure 15.4, select the type of backup from the pull-down box. Your choices are

Normal: All selected components are backed up, and their archive bits are cleared.

Copy: All selected components are backed up, but their archive bits are not cleared.

Incremental: All files and folders with their archive bits set are backed up, and the bits are turned off.

Differential: All files and folders with their archive bits set are backed up, but the bits are not turned off.

Daily: All files and folders modified today are backed up, and their archive bits are ignored.

In addition, check Backup migrated Remote Storage data radio button when you want Windows to back up data that Hierarchical Storage Manager (HSM) moved to remote storage. Click Next.

FIGURE 15.4

Type of Backup panel.

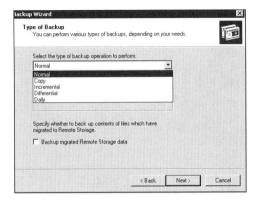

8. On the How to Back Up panel you have two choices: *Verify After Backup* and *Use hardware compression if available.*

   - **Verify After Backup**: This option allows you to decide whether the program is to verify the data it backed up by reading the data again after it is backed up and comparing it to the originals. This verification provides assurance that the backup is successful but nearly doubles the length of time the backup program needs to complete. If you have the time, using this option provides peace of mind and assurance that when you try to recover a file, the file will be there.

   - **Use hardware compression if available**: If your drive doesn't support hardware compression, the box remains grayed and unavailable. Additionally, some tape drives do not support mixing compression (hardware and the backup program's compression), so if the box is grayed out and your device supports hardware compression, that might be why. Replace overwrites existing data.

   Click Next.

9. Looking at Figure 15.5, you can see that you can specify media options.

10. You have to decide what value to check for if the archive media already contains backups. Specify whether to append or replace the existing backup on the backup media. Choose Append to store multiple backup jobs on a storage device. Choose Replace when you do not need to save previous backup jobs and you only want to save the most recent backup data.

11. The next field you can check is the *Allow only the owner and the Administrator access to the backup data and to any backups appended to this media.* This field lets you control who is able to access the data on the tape. When so marked, only the tape's owner, an Administrator, or a Backup Operator can view its contents. This option is available only during a Replace function. Click Next.

15

FIGURE 15.5

Media Options panel.

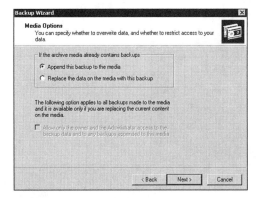

12. The next panel is for the Backup Label. You can specify a name and description for the backup job. The default is Set created DATE at TIME. You can change the name to something more meaningful to your organization.

13. You can specify a name for the backup media. The default is Media created DATE at TIME. You can change the name to something more meaningful to your organization. Click Next.

14. Finally, on the When to Back Up panel, select Now or Later. If you select Later, you can name the job in the Job name box. Backup inserts the current date and time. Click on Set Schedule and you can enter the information required in Figure 15.6. Click Next.

FIGURE 15.6

Schedule Job panel.

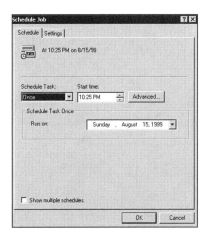

15. You should see a window such as the one in Figure 15.7. This window tells you that you can schedule the backup by clicking Finish. Click Finish.

FIGURE 15.7

The final Completing the Backup Wizard panel.

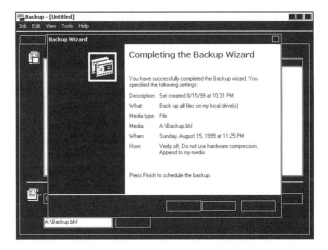

Step 3: Review

This task showed you how to run the backup program that comes with your Windows 2000 system. Running backups should become part of your everyday administration duties.

Windows 2000 has integrated Backup with the Task Scheduler. Scheduling a backup job means that you don't have to be in attendance when the job runs. You can schedule a job to run when your clients are not at work. You also can schedule backup jobs at regular intervals.

Task 15.3: Scheduling Backup Jobs.

Step 1: Description

In this task, you'll learn to use Backup to schedule a job to run at a later time.

Step 2: Action

1. Select Start, Programs, Accessories, System Tools, Backup.
2. Click on the Schedule Jobs tab. You will see the Schedule Jobs panel.
3. Click on the day you want to schedule the job.
4. Double-click the date or click the Add Job button.

> **Note**
>
> When your Task Scheduler service is not running, Windows 2000 will tell you and ask whether you want to start the service. Click Yes.

5. At this point you will walk through Task 15.2 to select the parameters for the backup.

Step 3: Review

This task showed you how to use the Schedule Jobs tab in the Backup program that comes with your Windows 2000 system. Scheduling backups is an important task for an administration.

There is another tab in the Backup program—the Backup tab. You will use this tab to select files for backup. The following task shows you how to select files for backup and then back them up to the hard drive.

Task 15.4: Backing Up Files.

Step 1: Description

In this task, you'll learn to use Backup to back up files to your hard drive.

Step 2: Action

1. Select Start, Programs, Accessories, System Tools, Backup.

2. Click on the Backup tab. You will see the window in Figure 15.8.

FIGURE 15.8

Backup tab.

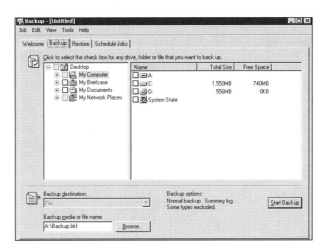

3. Click on + sign beside My Computer. Continue by clicking C: and then select the folder or file you want to back up by ticking it in the small box.

4. Click the Start Backup button.

5. You should see the Backup Job Information box shown in Figure 15.9.

FIGURE 15.9

Backup Job Information dialog box.

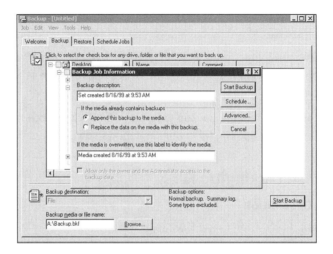

6. You can start the backup immediately by clicking Start Backup. From this dialog box, you can change or select the backup description, whether you want to append/replace the backup, the media label, and the schedule. Click Advanced and you can set the parameters discussed in Task 15.2.

Step 3: Review

This task showed you how to use the Backup tab in the Backup program that comes with your Windows 2000 system. Use this tab to specify the devices, folders, and files you want to back up.

If you scheduled an unattended backup job, then you should check it in the morning. The following task shows you how to view a report from your unattended backup.

Task 15.5: Viewing the Backup Report.

Step 1: Description

In this task, you'll learn to use Backup to view backup reports.

Step 2: Action

1. Select Start, Programs, Accessories, System Tools, Backup.

2. From the Tools menu, select Report.

3. You should see a window similar to the one in Figure 15.10.

▼

FIGURE 15.10

Backup Reports window.

4. From the Backup Reports window, scroll down the reports and select the one you want to view. Note that Backup lists the reports by date, time, and name. Click View.

5. Examine the report (a sample shown in Figure 15.11), and when finished, quit NotePad.

FIGURE 15.11

Backup Report.

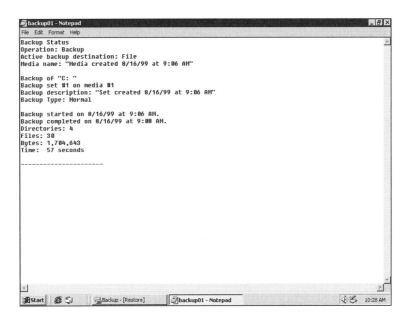

6. You probably should print this report and keep it with the backup. Should you want to print the report, click Print. Otherwise, click Cancel.

▲

Step 3: Review

This task showed you how to use view the Backup report. You also have the option to print the report. Should you or the Backup Operator schedule an unattended backup, you need to review the report as soon as you get to work. Should you schedule a job to run immediately, you can view the report as soon as it finishes. When the Backup Progress dialog box indicates the backup completed, just click Report.

If you like scripting and command-line input, there is a solution for you as well. You can run NTBACKUP from the command line; this method allows you to schedule the operation so that you need not be present when it runs at, say, 2 a.m. each day. On Day 9, "Managing the File Server," you learned to use the AT command and schedule batch jobs. NTBACKUP allows all its options to run from the command line, so you can place the required setup into a batch file and run the program whenever you want. You'll learn how to do this later, in the section called "Running Backups Using the Command Line."

> **Note**
>
> You no longer need to use AT from the command line. You now can use the graphical Task Scheduler. To use it, select Start, Settings, Control Panel, Scheduled Tasks, and then double-click (that is, open) Add Scheduled Task. Just work your way through the Scheduled Task Wizard. Should you forget how to use the Wizard, refresh your memory by looking at Day 9.

Restoring Files Using Backup

Now that your files are safely backed up and you're keeping them on some form of offsite rotation, you need to learn how to recover the files from the backup tapes.

Backup allows you to restore the backup set to the same drive the files were copied from or to a different drive. Doing so is relatively easy, as you'll see in Task 15.6.

Task 15.6: Restoring Files with Backup.

Step 1: Description

After files are safely backed up, you might occasionally need to restore them. Often, users accidentally delete a file and need it recovered, or in rare instances, a drive failure might necessitate a complete recovery. You'll learn how to perform these recoveries in this task.

Step 2: Action

1. Insert the required media. You need to review your backup list to find the necessary media. Remember that each day's backups are created using a definite rotation cycle and numbering scheme.

15

2. Log onto the system as an Administrator or Backup Operator. You need this level of access to restore files. Open the program by using the Start, Programs, Accessories, System Tools, Backup program.

3. Click the Restore button on the Welcome screen (look at Figure 15.1 to see an example of the Welcome).

4. Click Next on the Welcome to the Restore Wizard.

5. The left pane of the What to Restore window shows the name of the inserted tape. Expand the media type containing the data that you want to restore. The media is either tape or file.

6. Expand the appropriate media set until you find the folder or file you want to restore. You have the option to restore a backup set or specific folders and files.

7. Select the data you wish to restore, and you should see the name(s) of the set(s), folder(s), and file(s). Click Next.

   You should see a window that tells you that you can start the restore by clicking Finish. It also tells you that you can specify additional options by clicking Advanced. Click Advanced.

8. From the Where to Restore panel shown, select the destination from the pull down box. Your choices are

   Original location: This option will replace lost or corrupted data.

   Alternate location: Use this option to restore an older version of a file or to practice data restorage.

   Single folder: Takes the files from a tree structure and places them in a single folder.

   When you select the latter two, you will need to specify a path. Click Next.

9. On the How to Restore panel shown in Figure 15.12 you have three choices: *Do not replace the file on my disk (recommended), Replace the file on disk if it is older than the backup copy,* and *Always replace the file on disk.*

   - **Do not replace the file on my disk (recommended)**: This option prevents accidental over-writing of existing data. This is the default.

   - **Replace the file on disk if it is older than the backup copy**: This option verifies that the most recent copy exists on the destination.

   - **Always replace the file on disk**: This dangerous option means Restore will replace the file without providing a warning message when a duplicate is found. Click Next.

FIGURE 15.12

How to Restore panel.

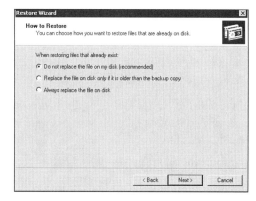

10. The next panel lists the Advanced Restore Options. The message says "Select the special restore options you want to use." Your three choices are

- **Restore Security**: This option applies the original permissions to files restored to a NTFS volume. Security permissions include access permissions, audit entries, and ownership.

- **Restore Removable Storage Management database**: Restores the configuration database for Removable Storage Management (RSM) devices and the media pool settings. You will find the database in \SystemRoot\system32\remotestorage.

- **Restore junction points, not the folders and file data they reference**: This option restores junction points on your hard disk as well as the data where the junction point refers. If you have any mounted drives, and you want to restore the data where the mounted drives point, check this box. If you don't check this box, the junction point will be restored but you may not be able to access the data where your junction point refers.

11. Click Next. You should see a window telling you that you can successfully complete the Restore Wizard by clicking Finish. Verify that it is correct before proceeding. Click Finish.

Step 3: Review

This task showed you how to restore files and folders by using the Backup program that is installed with your Windows 2000 Server system. You are sure to use this information on numerous occasions as users lose files and occasional accidents occur.

Running Backups Using the Command Line

15

You learned how to use the GUI interface of Backup in the earlier parts of this chapter. On occasion, however, you'll need to use the command line to perform these actions. For example, to automate your backups using the AT command, you need to set up a command-line batch file and have the scheduler program execute that batch file.

NTBACKUP provides for this circumstance by allowing you to operate via the command line. Like any other program, it provides a particular syntax and set of parameters for you to follow.

Here is the syntax for running NTBACKUP from a command line:

`NTBACKUP operation path parameters`

Each part of this syntax is explained here:

NTBACKUP: Is the backup program name.

operation: Tells the program whether to run a backup or a restore. Insert the word BACKUP or RESTORE.

path: Tells the program which path or file needs to be backed up or restored. More than one entry is permitted.

parameters: Indicates the specific functions you want the backup program to perform. These are your options:

/a: Tells the program to append data to an existing tape. Not specifying this option tells NTBACKUP to start at the beginning of the tape and replace any existing data. Be careful! It is easy to accidentally replace valuable data by ignoring this field.

/v: Verifies all data after the restore or backup operation. This effectively doubles the amount of time needed yet provides more assurance that your files are safe. Use this option for critical backup and restores.

/r: Enables the restricted access parameter so that only the owner, an Administrator, or a Backup Operator can access the data on the tape.

/d "*text*": Provides a description of the tape using the words specified in the text filed. You might specify words like "Daily Backup of server TOSHIBA_7020, Red Cycle" for a description. You need to use the quotation marks in the command.

/b: Tells the backup to include a copy of the local Registry on the tape.

/hc:on/off: Tells the backup program to use hardware compression. It is viable only if your tape drive performs this function. It cannot be used with the /a function because NTBACKUP automatically uses whatever compression was originally used on that tape when appending data. Specify the command as /hc:on or /hc:off.

/t option: Specifies which type of backup to perform. You specify Normal, Incremental, Differential, Copy, or Daily. Refer to the earlier backup task for explanations of each option.

/l "filename": Allows you to specify a different filename for the log file. By default, the program uses \winnt\backup.log.

/e: The default for logging consists of complete log information, and this can become quite extensive in a large backup operation. The /e option tells the program to log only exceptions.

/tape:x: NT supports up to 10 tape devices. Use this option to tell the program which device to use. By default, it uses device 0.

As you see from the commands provided, you can specify all the options pertaining to performing a backup or restore directly from the command line. We do not recommend that you use this method for everyday activity unless you plan to automate the process.

If you decide that it would be nice to automate your backups, you need to follow the steps given in the following task.

Task 15.7: Using the Command Line for Backups.

Step 1: Description

In this task, you'll learn to tell Windows 2000 Server to automate a backup task by using the command-line function and AT scheduler program.

Step 2: Action

1. Log onto the system as an Administrator. Make sure that the scheduler service is running. Open Start, Programs, Administrative Tools, Computer Management; double-click on System Tools and then Services. View the drop-down list for Task Scheduler and verify that it is started.

2. Review the section on using the AT command on Day 9 to refresh your memory. After all, it has been six days.

3. Create a batch script by using Notepad. In the script, place the specific backup commands you want run. For example, you might want to back up the entire drive C: each Saturday morning.

15

▼ To accomplish this, you might use the following command:

```
ntbackup backup c: /v /d "Full backup of C drive" /b /t Normal /e
```

As you might remember, this command tells backup to perform a backup of drive C:, verify the data it backs up, place a description on the tape, include a copy of the local Registry, perform a normal cycle, and log only exceptions. Use the data gained during Day 9 to devise the particular options you need. Save this file as Weekly.bat.

4. Place the file in a directory of your choice, such as c:\users\backups, so that you know where it is and can inform the scheduler program.

5. Tell W2K when to run the job. To do this, use the following command from your command prompt:

```
at 02:00 /interactive /every:Saturday "c:\users\backups\weekly.bat"
```

6. Windows 2000 now schedules your backup job to run each Saturday at 2 a.m. You
▲ can check the logs on Monday morning to ensure that the job ran successfully.

Step 3: Review

This task showed you how to run backups in an automated fashion by using the features installed with Windows 2000 Server. As you see, it is not a GUI-based task, yet it gets the job done. This is often one reason organizations purchase more robust backup programs that offer automation as part of their services.

You see that it is possible to skip those awful 2 a.m. treks into work by applying some of the features W2K offers. (You can tell we no longer like the late-hour shifts, can't you? Ah, the joys of getting older.)

Use these principles to set up a backup schedule for your organization. If a task is automated, you have far greater assurance that is being accomplished. Leaving tasks to an administrator to remember leaves you prone to error—daily activities and "fire-fighting" make it likely that backups are occasionally not run, and this leaves you vulnerable to data loss.

Summary

Today, you learned about some tools and methods for managing your server's backup and restore process. You should know how to protect your files from loss and how to back up and restore damaged or deleted files. These functions are critical for successful management of your server. What is your answer going to be when your boss asks you to recover a file he or she deleted?

Workshop

Finally, you can review tasks from the lesson, and see the answers to some commonly asked questions.

Task List

The emphasis of this lesson has been to introduce you to file backup and recovery. As a system administrator, you will repeatedly use this process in your daily work. The tasks you should understand from this lesson are listed here:

- Adding a new tape drive
- Setting up a grandfather/father/son backup cycle
- Running Backup
- Scheduling backup
- Backing up files
- Viewing the backup report
- Restoring files using the Backup program
- Using the command line for backups

Q&A

Q How can I schedule backups in Windows 2000 Server?

A You saw that the Backup program has the Schedule Jobs task. Review Task 15.3 to see how to use the wizard.

Windows 2000 Server offers a service called Task Scheduler that, when running, allows use of the AT command. This command enables an administrator to set up any number of tasks and schedule them for any time of day.

The AT command has various options, which you read about on Day 9. Today, you are shown an example of the command used to perform nightly unattended backups. In addition, you can use the Task Scheduler.

Q Should I use Backup or buy some third-party product to perform my backups?

A The answer depends on what your backup needs consist of and whether Backup serves those needs. In a small LAN, the program is likely sufficient for your needs. In a larger LAN, the lack of automation and the incapability to back up multiple workstation operating systems might justify your pursuing alternative tape programs.

15

Q What is this Tower of Hanoi method, and does W2K support its use?

A The Tower of Hanoi method is named after an old game that consisted of three posts and several rings. The object of the game was to relocate the rings, using a minimum number of moves, so that the rings would end up in sequence with the largest ring on the bottom and the smallest on top. By substituting tapes for rings, you can use this same method for backup purposes. The method provides for very even tape wear and a maximum number of saved versions of each file, helping ensure that you can recover from a file loss.

The Tower of Hanoi method is not supported by the present version of Backup or some other third-party programs. It is a complex method for tape backup, and it needs the benefit of software for it to work because it is not easily performed manually.

Q What is the best tape format to use?

A This is again a tough question to answer directly because the answer depends on the amount of data you back up and the frequency of those backups. Many organizations use the DAT tape format because it offers a reasonable degree of speed, and the amount of data that fits on a tape minimizes the need for multiple tapes.

Larger organizations are moving toward the newer, faster, more robust DLT, or Digital Linear Tape, format. This offers tremendous speed and huge amounts of backup data per tape.

The bottom line is that the best tape is the one you use on a regular basis, verify every so often, and retire before it is worn out.

Q How important is a backup strategy? Can't I just use two tapes and rotate them each day?

A A sound backup strategy allows you to recover files when you need to recover them. Using only two tapes minimizes that possibility because very soon you run out of space and need to remove old files. If these files are only one or two weeks old, you might suffer from data loss.

In addition to backing up the files, you need to rotate them offsite to ensure that you can recover in the event of a disaster. This is hard to do with only two tapes.

Proper tape rotation guards against loss by ensuring that files are retained long enough that you are able to recover them if needed. This time frame might be a few weeks or a few months or, in larger organizations, perhaps a year. You need to ask yourself and your users what will happen if a file xx days old becomes unavailable. Typically, the user will respond with anguish at the thought that a file might be unrecoverable. Finding a happy medium is hard to do without a complex risk assessment, so most organizations opt to keep files for daily, weekly, and monthly cycles, obviating any problems.

DAY **16**

Configuring Fault-Tolerance

The data stored on your network is the most valuable part of your network. In fact, it might be the most important asset in your company or department. Its value is much higher than the cost of the equipment that stores it, and its importance is second only to the users who use the information. This information is, however, at risk.

Few of us want to face it. It isn't a question of whether a disaster will strike, but when it will strike. This axiom definitely applies to networks. If you are the system and network administrator, your job is to make sure that information is both available to users and protected from corruption or loss. Attacks on your system by hackers, unauthorized users, or viruses can destroy your weekend plans, leaving you scrambling to recover instead of sitting on the beach at your cottage. Just as harmful is a system failure due to natural causes or overburdened systems. A downed system costs you more than frustration: It might cost your business hundreds or thousands of dollars in lost revenue and create a lot of customer dissatisfaction. It also might cost you your job! Today you'll learn about three topics that directly or indirectly deal with protecting the data on your servers:

- Providing fault-tolerance with disk mirroring and disk striping
- Providing fault-tolerance and data availability by replicating data to other systems
- Addressing and solving power problems

Fault-Tolerance in Windows 2000 Server

Your organization might use its network for an application where access to the data and services is extremely important. Your organization might have moved its critical applications off the mainframe, for example, and put them on the network. As a result, redundancy is needed in your local area network. Redundancy provides protection against downtime because of hardware failure.

Note

> Redundancy can be defined as the state of being superfluous or an unnecessary repetition. It can also be considered a duplication or repetition of elements in electronic equipment to provide alternative functional channels in case of failure.

 Fault-tolerance refers to the protection of systems against potential hardware failures, disasters, and other risks. You protect data by creating redundant copies, usually in real-time, as well as by backing up your data.

Active Directory uses multimaster replication to protect its data. The directory is stored on the initial domain controller but is replicated to each domain controller for recovery purposes. This provides information availability, fault-tolerance, load balancing, and performance benefits.

You can use the following methods to protect your data:

- Mirrored Volumes—In this configuration, two hard disks (or sets of hard disks) are used, and data is simultaneously written to and read from each disk. When one of the disks fails, the other can provide data to users until the mirrored volume is restored.
- Stripe Sets with Parity—In this scheme, data is written evenly over an array of disks rather than to one disk. Parity information also is written to the disks. The parity information is used to rebuild the data if a disk in the set fails.

- Backup Power—Windows 2000 also supports uninterruptible power supplies (UPSs) and includes a program that can detect power failures and provide advance warning before the UPS runs out of backup power.
- Backup with Offsite Archiving—Here data is copied to backup media and carried to safe remote sites for archiving. Backup methods were covered in Day 15, "File Backup and Recovery."

Windows 2000 Server offers several fault-tolerance features that you can use alone or in combination to produce a cohesive strategy to ensure that data is protected from potential media problems. Windows 2000 Server offers fault-tolerance (disk mirroring, disk duplexing, striping with parity, and sector sparing [hot fix]), tape backup, Last Known Good Configuration, Emergency Repair disk, and uninterruptible power supply features to help you protect your data.

Types of Disk Storage

New Term There are now two types of disk storage available for Windows 2000 machines. The standard type used on most systems and that we are all most familiar with is basic storage. Basic storage allows you to divide a hard drive into partitions. A *partition* is a portion of a physical disk drive that acts like it is a completely separate disk drive. It can contain primary partitions, extended partitions, and logical drives. Disks are typically created as basic drives by default in Windows 2000 and they are of course supported by all the Microsoft operating systems.

New Term Windows 2000 now supports a type of storage called *dynamic storage* that creates one single entity that includes the entire disk. Disks created this way are called dynamic disks. One key advantage to this type of drive is that you can size or resize it without restarting Windows 2000. You can then divide the dynamic disk into volumes. Volumes can be created using a part of one physical drive or can be more than one physical drive. This means you can have one volume for your Windows 2000 system, but it could actually be two physical disk drives. Windows 2000 volumes are used to create and manage fault-tolerance.

 Caution | By creating a dynamic disk, other operating systems like DOS, Windows 98, and Windows NT 4 cannot use it.

Regardless of which type you use, it must be formatted to FAT, FAT32, or NTFS for you to use it. Naturally, you should be using NTFS.

Task 16.1: Creating a Dynamic Disk.

Step 1: Description

Before you can use mirroring or other services, you must create Microsoft's new disk type called dynamic disk. In this task, you use Computer Management to set up your disk drives as dynamic. Only do this on a test system and you don't need to let other operating systems access the drive. (You need at least 1MB of free space at the end of the disk for the install process.)

Step 2: Action

1. Log on to the Windows 2000 Server as Administrator.

2. Choose Start, Programs, Administrative Tools, Computer Management, Storage, Disk Management.

3. Click on the disk drive that you want to create as a dynamic disk. Right-click and select the option called Upgrade to Dynamic Disk. You should see a dialog box similar to the one shown in Figure 16.1.

FIGURE 16.1

The Upgrade to Dynamic Disk dialog box.

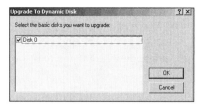

  4. Select OK to continue and follow the instructions to finish the upgrade.

Step 3: Review

In this example, you chose to change your disk type from basic to dynamic. Doing this prevents other operating systems from accessing the drive but offers you the ability to add to or change your disk requirements as needed without rebooting.

If you change your mind later, you can delete any volumes you may have on the drive and use the Revert to Basic Disk command in step 3.

When you upgrade a basic disk to a dynamic disk, existing partitions on your basic disk become simple volumes on the dynamic disk. Any existing mirrored volumes (mirror sets), striped volumes (stripe sets), RAID-5 volumes (stripe sets with parity), or spanned volumes (volume sets) become dynamic mirrored volumes, dynamic striped volumes, dynamic RAID-5 volumes, or dynamic spanned volumes.

Redundant Array of Inexpensive Disks

The fault-tolerance features listed in the preceding section are actually *strategies*. Fault-tolerance strategies are standardized and categorized by the industry in seven levels, 0–6, using the Redundant Array of Inexpensive Disks (RAID) system.

> **Note**
>
> Nowadays, RAID stands for Redundant Array of Independent Disks, a less pejorative term.

16

The levels offer various combinations of performance, reliability, and cost. Windows 2000 Server offers RAID levels 0, 1, and 5, as shown in Table 16.1. (For the sake of completeness, an overview of all the levels is offered rather than just those that are supported by Windows 2000.)

TABLE 16.1 RAID Levels

Level	Description
0	Disk striping
1	Disk mirroring
2	Disk striping with error correction code (ECC)
3	Disk striping with ECC stored as parity
4	Disk striping with large blocks, parity stored on one drive
5	Disk striping with parity distributed across multiple drives

Level 0: Disk Striping

RAID level 0 provides disk striping to multiple disk partitions. With this method, the system spreads a file across several physical drives. This method offers greater speed, particularly when the separate physical drives are on different disk controllers. Because it doesn't provide redundancy, this method cannot be said to be a true fault-tolerant implementation. If any partition in the set fails, you lose all the data. Level 0 requires a minimum of 2—and as many as 32—hard disks. It provides the best performance when used with multiple controllers.

Level 1: Disk Mirroring or Duplexing

RAID level 1 provides disk mirroring or duplexing; that is, the maintenance of multiple identical copies of a physical drive or partition. Disk mirroring takes place at the partition level. You can mirror any partition, including boot or system partitions. Mirroring is the simplest way of protecting a single disk against failure.

Disk mirroring is more expensive than other forms of fault-tolerance because disk space utilization is only 50%. For peer-to-peer and small server-based LANs, however, disk mirroring usually has a lower entry cost because it requires only two disks. RAID strategies higher than level 3 require three or more disks.

Disk duplexing is simply a mirrored pair with an additional disk controller on the second drive. This method reduces channel traffic and potentially improves performance. Duplexing is intended to protect against controller failures as well as media failure.

Level 2: Disk Striping with Error Correction Code

RAID level 2 introduces bit interleaving and check disks. When the system writes a block of data, it breaks up the block and distributes (or interleaves) it across all the data drives. At the same time, the system also writes an error correction code (ECC) for the data block, which is spread across all the check disks. In the event of lost data, the system uses the ECC to reconstruct the lost data via a mathematical algorithm.

ECCs require a larger amount of disk space than do parity-checking methods. Although this method offers marginal improvement in disk utilization, it compares poorly with current technology.

Level 3: Disk Striping with Error Correction Code Stored as Parity

RAID level 3 is similar to level 2 except that the ECC method is replaced with a parity-checking scheme that requires only one disk to store parity data. Disk space utilization is better with this level than it is with RAID level 2.

Level 4: Disk Striping Large Blocks with Parity Stored on One Drive

RAID level 4 moves away from data interleaving by writing complete blocks of data to each disk in the array. This process is known as *disk striping*. A separate check disk is still used to store parity information. Each time a write operation occurs, the associated parity information must be read from the check disk and modified. Because of this overhead, the block-interleaving method works better for large block operations than for transaction-based processing.

Level 5: Disk Striping with Parity Distributed Across Multiple Drives

RAID level 5 is the most common strategy for new fault-tolerance designs. It differs from the other levels in that it writes the parity information across all the disks in the array. The data and parity information are arranged so that the two are always on different disks. If a single drive fails, enough information is spread across the remaining disks to allow the system to reconstruct the data completely.

Stripe sets with parity offer the best performance for read operations. When a disk fails, however, the read performance is degraded by the need to recover the data using the parity information. Also, all normal write operations require three times more memory because of the parity calculation.

Windows 2000 Server supports from 3 to 32 drives in a stripe set with parity. All partitions except the boot and system partitions can form the stripe set. The system uses the parity stripe block to reconstruct data for a failed physical disk. A parity stripe block exists for each stripe (row) across the disk. RAID level 4 stores the parity stripe block on one physical disk, whereas RAID level 5 distributes parity evenly across all disks. The major benefit of RAID level 5 is a performance gain due to distributed I/O for writes.

Windows 2000 still supports the original two methods of protecting your data's integrity: disk mirroring and disk striping, only they must be done on dynamic volumes. Windows 2000 has updated the first to use the term Mirrored Volumes. The following sections take a better look at these two methods.

Mirrored Volumes

Mirrored Volumes is a continuous backup method. The system writes data to two disks at the same time. Because either disk in the set can continue providing data to users when the other fails, you can avoid the downtime and expense of recovering data from backup sets. Disk duplexing is a disk mirroring technique that also duplicates the hardware channel to avoid the downtime that is caused by the need to replace a disk controller.

Keep in mind that mirroring is a hardware backup technique that is used to recover from disk failures. You still need to back up data to protect information from corruption. If information is corrupted, it is stored in that corrupted state on both disks, and you need to restore from backup sets.

Note   A mirrored volume improves disk read performance because data can read from either disk in the set.

Mirroring is one of the most important features of a successful fault-tolerant system. The overall benefit from mirroring is to provide protection against data loss. It provides fault-tolerance to possible hard disk failure by writing the same information to two NTFS-partitioned hard disks. In the event of a hard disk failure, the functioning mirrored disk continues to retrieve and store data. The operating system sends a warning message that disk failure has occurred.

With disk mirroring, the hard disk is duplicated, so you can continue if one hard drive fails. You are still in trouble though if the disk channel goes down.

NEW TERM If you have more than one disk, you can *mirror* a partition on one disk onto free space on another. By doing so, you keep an exact copy of one partition on another disk. After you establish this relationship between the two disk areas, called a *mirrored volume,* every time you write data to disk a duplicate of that data is written to the free space on the other half of the mirror set. Mirrored volumes are the equivalent of RAID level 1.

With mirrored volumes, the system must write data to both drives in the set, but it suffers no performance lag because each disk can do its own writing. In addition, mirrored drives are fast when it comes to reads because data can be pulled from both halves of the mirror set at once.

Mirroring and Duplexing

If you've heard or read anything about disk mirroring, you've also probably heard a term called *disk duplexing.* Disk duplexing is similar to disk mirrors, except that duplexing generally refers to mirroring information on disks that have their own disk controllers so that the data isn't vulnerable to controller failures. In Windows 2000 Server, disk mirroring means both duplexing and mirroring.

You use the Computer Management in the Administrative Tools, Computer Management, Storage group to set up disk mirroring. To create a mirrored disk set, you need to have two disks; each must have a free partition roughly the same size as the other one. Excess space on one of the disks isn't used. You can mirror any existing partition, including the system and boot partitions, onto an available partition of another disk. The disks can use the same or different controllers. The following task shows you how to build a mirrored volume.

Task 16.2: Building a Mirrored Volume.

Step 1: Description

You can mirror a drive's data without affecting that drive's accessibility while you do it. In this task, you use Computer Management to set up a mirror set. (You must be using dynamic disks and have at least two disks available).

Step 2: Action

1. Log on to the Windows 2000 Server as Administrator.

2. Choose Start, Programs, Administrative Tools, Computer Management, Storage, Disk Management. You see a tool like that shown in Figure 16.2.

FIGURE 16.2

The Disk Management window.

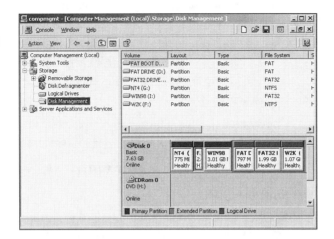

3. Right-click on the free space where you want to create the mirror volume. Click Create Volume.

4. Now choose Next, and then choose Mirrored Volume. Follow the prompts in the wizard to finish the task. You have now established the mirrored volume. The Disk Administrator establishes an equal-sized partition in the free space for the mirror. It also assigns a drive letter to the mirror volume. Now, whenever you save a file to that drive letter, the system actually saves two copies of the file. At this point, your task is complete. The system begins to synchronize the two mirror partitions, and this can cause your system to slow until it completes.

Step 3: Review

In this example, you chose to create a mirrored volume. You can create a mirrored volume on a dynamic disk only.

When something unrecoverable—such as hardware damage—happens to half of the mirrored volume, you need to break the mirrored volume to get to the good data that you've backed up. You'll know when something goes wrong—you'll most likely see a message when you try to write to the mirrored drives when one of the disks isn't working. It probably says something like—Failed Redundancy. You can still use the drive, but the benefits of mirroring are suspended. According to Microsoft, when the primary disk fails, FTDISK.SYS shifts control to the mirrored disk. The program hides all shifting of the primary from the user unless it is the boot or load partition that is mirrored.

If the mirrored volume's status is *Failed Redundancy* the disk's status might be *Offline* or *Missing*. An icon (X) appears in the graphical view of the Missing or Offline disk. You'll need to try to recover the drive as soon as possible. You might be able to reactivate a drive if the mirrored volume's status is *Failed Redundancy* but the disk's status indicates *Online (Errors)*. In this case you'll see an icon like (!) appear in the graphical view of the disk.

Depending upon the severity of the problem, you may be able to resurrect the volume by using Computer Management and then right-clicking the Missing or Offline disk, followed by clicking Reactivate Disk.

If that fails, you may need to replace the defective volume with a new one. You can use Task 16.3 to replace the volume after creating a new volume on some other drive.

Task 16.3: Replace a Failed Mirror with a New Mirror.

Step 1: Description

If an error occurs on one of the disks, you might need to replace it with a new drive. While you're replacing the disk, the other disk can handle requests from users. In this task, you use the Computer Management to replace the drive.

Step 2: Action

1. Log on to the Windows 2000 Server as Administrator.
2. Choose Start, Programs, Administrative Tools, Computer Management, Storage, Disk Management.
3. Right-click the defective volume.
4. Choose Remove Mirror.
5. Click Yes to break the mirror set.
6. Now select your new drive volume and right-click it.
7. Choose Add Mirror and follow the remaining steps in the Wizard to complete the task.

Step 3: Review

In this example, you removed a mirror volume that was defective for some reason and replaced it with a new volume. Breaking a mirror set doesn't affect the information inside it. Still, as always, it is a good idea to back up the drive that holds your data before doing anything with it.

Recovering Data from a Mirrored Volume

After you break a mirror set so that you can get to good data, the good half of the mirror set is assigned the drive letter that previously belonged to the now-defunct mirror set.

The half that crashed is now called an *orphan* and is, in effect, set aside by the fault-tolerance driver so that no one attempts to write to that part of the disk. When you reboot, the crashed disk disappears.

At this point, you can take the good half of the old mirror set and establish a new relationship with another volume, as you did in Task 16.3. When you restart the computer, the system copies the data from the good partition to its new mirror. While the regeneration process is going on, the text on the new half of the mirror set shows in red—but it doesn't take long to regenerate mirrored material. Besides, the process takes place in the background, so you don't have to wait for it to finish if you want to use the computer.

Mirroring Considerations

As you're deciding whether to protect your data by mirroring it, keep these points in mind:

- Mirroring to drives with the same drive controller doesn't protect your data from drive controller failure. If any kind of controller failure occurs, you cannot get to the backup copy of your data unless you mirror (that is, duplex) to a disk with a separate controller.

- For higher disk-read performance and greater fault-tolerance, use a separate disk controller for each half of a mirrored volume.

- Disk mirroring effectively cuts your available disk space in half. Don't forget that figure as you calculate how much drive space you have or need for your server.

- Disk mirroring has a low initial cost because you must purchase only one extra drive to achieve fault-tolerance, but it has a higher long-term cost because of the amount of room that is taken up by your duplicate information.

- Disk mirroring slows down writes because the data must be written in two places every time; however, it speeds up reads because the I/O controller has two places from which to read information.

Disk Striping

NEW TERM *Disk striping* in W2K enables you to spread data over an array of 2 to 32 disks. The disks appear as a single volume to users. Striping divides the data at the byte level and interleaves the bytes over each disk. The system can also write parity information to each disk partition in the volume to give a level of data protection that is equivalent to disk mirroring, but requires less disk space and provides faster read performance. You can manage existing disk stripe sets with Windows 2000 tools, but you cannot create new disk stripe sets unless you are using dynamic disks.

16

Disk striping provides high performance, especially when users read data more than they write it. Writing to striped sets is slower than writing to mirrored sets, but when you use high-performance servers and drives, you won't notice this lack in performance.

Striped volumes offer the best performance of all these Computer Management strategies. However, as with spanned volumes, striped volumes don't provide fault-tolerance. If one disk in a striped volume fails, you lose the data in the entire volume.

Disk striping with parity for Windows 2000 Server requires a minimum of three disks to accommodate the way that parity information is striped across the disk set. Disks need to be roughly the same size. Any extra space on partitions isn't used.

NEW TERM In addition to disk mirroring, Windows 2000 gives you the option of using RAID level 5, also known as *disk striping with parity*. Disk striping with parity differs from regular disk striping in the following ways:

- Although data lost from a stripe set without parity is unrecoverable, data from a parity stripe set can usually be recovered. If more than one disk of the 2–32 hard disk drives fail, you cannot recover your data.

- Regular disk striping improves the speed of data reads and writes compared to using a single drive. Striping with parity slows down writes but improves access speed.

Every time you write data to disk, the system writes the data across all the striped disks in the array, just as it does with regular disk striping (RAID level 0). In addition, parity information for your data is also written to disk, always on a disk that is separate from the one where the data to which it corresponds is written. That way, if anything happens to a disk in the array, the data on that disk can be reconstructed from the parity information on the other disks.

RAID level 5 differs from level 4, which also uses parity information to protect data, because the system distributes parity information in RAID level 5 across all the disks in the array. In level 4, a specific disk is dedicated to parity information. RAID level 5, therefore, is faster than 4 because it can perform more than one write operation at a time.

Updating the Parity Information

The parity information can be updated in two ways. First, because the parity information is the XOR (exclusive OR) of the data, the system can recalculate the XOR each time the data is written to disk. This method requires accessing each disk in the stripe set because the data is distributed across the disks in the array—and that takes time.

NEW TERM What is XOR? Simply, the *XOR*, or exclusive OR arithmetic, is a function that takes two one-bit inputs and produces a single-bit output. The result is 1 if the two inputs are different, or 0 if the two inputs are the same. More specifically

0 XOR 0 = 0

1 XOR 0 = 1

0 XOR 1 = 1

1 XOR 1 = 0

When you use the XOR function on two numbers with more than one bit, just match the bits up and add (XOR) them individually. For example, 1101010 XOR 0101000 equals 1000010. The result that you get from this function is the parity information, which the system uses to recalculate the original data.

A more efficient way of recalculating the parity information, and the way Windows 2000 uses it, is to read the old data to be overwritten and use the XOR function with the new data to determine the differences. This process produces a bit mask that has a 1 in the position of every bit that has been changed. This bit mask can then be added (XORed) with the old parity information to see where its differences lie; from this, the new parity information can be calculated. This process seems convoluted, but this second process requires only two reads and two XOR computations rather than one of each for every drive in the array.

As the administrator, you can create a stripe set with parity.

Task 16.4: Establishing a Stripe Set with Parity (RAID 5 Volume).

Step 1: Description

In this task, you use the Disk Administrator to create a stripe set with parity. It's also called a RAID 5 volume.

Step 2: Action

1. Log on to the Windows 2000 Server as Administrator.
2. Choose Start, Programs, Administrative Tools, Computer Management.
3. Select three or more areas of free space. (This is on 3–32 hard disks. The exact number is determined by your hardware configuration; Windows 2000 can handle up to 32 separate physical disks, but your hardware setup might not be able to.) To select the free space areas, click the free space on the first hard disk, and then Ctrl+click the others, in the same way that you select more than one file using Windows 2000 Explorer.

▼

> **Note**
>
> The free space you select doesn't have to be equal in size because the Computer Management distributes available space evenly and adjusts the size of the stripe set as necessary.

4. Click Create Volume. In the wizard that starts, select Next and then RAID 5 Volume. You see a dialog box that displays the minimum and maximum sizes for the stripe set with parity. Follow the prompts to complete the task.

> **Note**
>
> If you select a size that cannot be divided equally among the number of disks involved in the stripe set, the Disk Administrator rounds down the size to the nearest number that is evenly divisible by the number of disks in the stripe set.

▲

Step 3: Review

To create a stripe set with parity, you opened Computer Management and selected areas of free space on at least three physical disks. Then you chose to create a RAID 5 volume.

The system then initializes the stripe set. As always, you have to format it from the command line or by using disk administrator.

When you restart, rebooting takes a little longer than normal. When you reach the blue screen that tells you what file system the drives on your system are using, the system informs you that the I/O Manager cannot determine the file system type of the stripe set's drive letter—not that the drive is raw, as you've seen before, but that Windows 2000 System Services can't determine the type. Don't be alarmed; the system has to initialize the stripe set. Wait for activity on the stripe set drives to subside, and then format the new partition. If you don't format the drive first, you get an error message. After you format, everything is ready to go.

Retrieving Data from a Failed Stripe Set

When an unrecoverable error to part of a striped set with parity occurs, you can regenerate the information stored there from the parity information stored on the rest of the set. You can even regenerate it when one of the member disks has been low-level formatted.

To recover the data, install a new disk and reboot so that the system can see the new disk. Next, go to the Computer Management tool and select the stripe set that you want to fix, and set free space at least equal in size to the other members of the set. Choose Regenerate, and follow the prompts to complete this task.

To replace a disk in the RAID 5 volume, you must have a spare dynamic disk with unallocated space that is at least as large as the volume you want to repair. If you don't have a dynamic disk with enough unallocated space, the *Repair Volume* command won't be available. (You can verify that you have enough space by right-clicking on the disk, selecting Properties, and then verifying the size in the area called Unallocated Space.)

The fault-tolerance driver collects the information from the stripes on the other member disks and then re-creates it onto the new member of the stripe set. If you open Computer Management while it is performing this job, you see the text on the part being regenerated is displayed in red. Although the regeneration process might take awhile, you still can use the server. You don't need to keep the Disk Administrator open because the restoration process works in the background, and you can access the information in the stripe set. Be aware that server performance suffers until the restoration process finishes.

After the system fixes the stripe set you need to reassign it a new drive letter. The failed portion of the original stripe set, called an *orphan,* is set aside as unusable.

Task 16.5: Repairing a Failed Stripe Set.

Step 1: Description

In this task, you use Computer Management to repair a failed stripe set. You must have a spare volume available that is large enough to replace the broken volume.

Step 2: Action

1. Be sure to back up all the data on the affected stripe set. Then install a new disk and reboot the system.
2. Log on to the Windows 2000 Server as Administrator.
3. Choose Start, Programs, Administrative Tools, Computer Management, Storage, Disk Management.
4. Select the stripe set volume you need to fix.
5. Choose Repair Volume and follow the prompts to finish. The regeneration process takes place in the background.

Step 3: Review

To repair a failed stripe set here, you chose Start, Programs, Administrative Tools, Computer Management, Storage, Disk Management; selected the stripe set that you wanted to fix; and then chose Repair. The regeneration process doesn't affect your ability to use the computer or to access the information that is being regenerated.

Deleting a Stripe Set

To delete a stripe set, select the stripe that you want to delete from the Disk Management tool, and then choose Delete Volume. A message appears advising you that this action will delete all the data and asking you to confirm that you want to take this action. Click Yes to confirm your intention.

Caution | Deleting a striped volume destroys the data in it—even the parity information.

Points to Remember About Disk Striping with Parity

Remember the following points for disk striping with parity:

- Striping with parity has a greater initial cost than disk mirroring does because it requires a minimum of three disks rather than two. Nevertheless, you can get more use out of your disk space.

- Although you can access the information in a stripe set even after one of the members has failed, you need to regenerate the volume as quickly as possible. Windows 2000 Server striping cannot cope with more than one error in the set, so you're in trouble if anything happens to the unregenerated stripe set. Back up the data as soon as a problem is noted, just in case.

- Striping with parity places greater demands on your system than disk mirroring does, so you might get better performance from your system if you add more memory to the system minimum of 64MB.

- When you have fewer than three physical hard disks on your server, you cannot make stripe sets with parity. The option in the menu is grayed out.

Which Is Better: Hardware or Software RAID?

You've seen that you can install several drives on your computer and that you can use them as RAID and mirror sets. From a fault-tolerance standpoint, using them this way is a good idea because the probability that you'll actually lose data is considerably reduced. What do you do when drive damage does occur?

Assume that you have a mission-critical system up and running, and one of the four drives in a stripe set with parity goes bad. You take down the server, replace the bad drive with a new good one, and then add the new drive to the stripe set to recover the data.

In practice, this procedure sounds good. But is it practical? First, you have to take down this mission-critical server for several hours while you swap out the old drive, install a new drive, and put the stripe set back together. This downtime is probably unacceptable for a mission-critical application.

Instead, you can buy a hardware RAID system, a box containing several platters acting as one drive that look to Windows 2000 as one drive. As with Windows 2000 Server's fault-tolerance, researchers have developed disk array systems to prevent loss of data and improve the performance of disk I/O. The most popular disk array, known as RAID, was developed by a team of researchers at the University of California at Berkeley.

An external RAID box costs a bit more, but a hardware-based RAID system can rebuild itself faster than Windows 2000's software can. Best of all, most hardware-based RAID systems enable you to hot-swap the bad drive, that is, to replace the bad drive without taking down the server. So when your application is truly mission critical, think about investing in RAID hardware. This is the best solution if you are concerned about your data. Of course, if you can't afford it, using Windows 2000's software solution isn't bad either.

Fault-Tolerant Replication

NEW TERM *Replication* is a fault-tolerant strategy for duplicating data in real-time from a Windows 2000 Server computer to another computer. Active Directory uses replication to ensure that each controller always has up-to-date information on any changes that occur.

As you may remember from the section on the Distributed File System in Day 8, "Managing Files and Using the Distributed File System," you can have fault-tolerant Dfs roots. In this manner, your main Dfs system is backed up by Active Directory so there is no single point of failure. This is because the Active Directory is replicated across multiple machines, so if one is missing, the others take up the load.

You also recall that replication cannot be configured for standalone Dfs roots because the Dfs topology must be published to Active Directory in order for replication to be enabled and scheduled. Configure your Dfs system for fault-tolerance.

Replication cannot be configured for standalone Dfs roots because the Dfs topology must be published to Active Directory in order for replication to be enabled and scheduled.

Replication also occurs in Active Directory. When administrators make changes to directory information, they don't need to worry about where the change is made because their changes are automatically sent to all the domain controllers. With multi-master replication, administrators are updating a single copy of the Active Directory when they make changes. After they are done, all the other domain controllers are notified of the changes, so their information remains current.

Domain controllers keep track of how many changes have been made to their copy of the directory, and they also keep track of how many changes they have received from all the other domain controllers. If we have domain controllers in Location A and Location B for example, they need to synchronize somehow. If the Location A domain controller finds it doesn't have all the changes from the Location B domain controller, the Location B domain controller will request the new changes (and only the new changes) from the Location A domain controller.

This makes updating a domain controller that has been disconnected from the network simple, as it knows which directory information has changed and therefore needs to be replicated. Changes are tracked by a numerical sequence and not by time so tracking them is easy.

It is possible for two different users to make changes to the exact same object on two different controllers and have both these changes applied using replication. So how does Windows 2000 make sure it doesn't keep making the same change across the network? In this case, both changes are replicated because both appear as originating writes. A domain controller that receives such duplicate changes will examine the timestamp on each and accept the most recent change.

Windows 2000 uses sites and replication change control to optimize its use of replication. It does this by

- Occasionally re-evaluating which connections are used, and using the most efficient network connections
- Using multiple routes to make changes, helping ensure the system is fault-tolerant
- Minimizing the network overhead costs by only sending changed information

Directory information within a site is replicated frequently and automatically every 15 minutes by default. The directory replication topology is automatically created by Active Directory. Active Directory attempts to establish at least two network connections to every domain controller, so if one domain controller becomes unavailable, directory information can still reach the remaining online domain controllers through the other connection.

Active Directory automatically evaluates and adjusts its topology as your network changes. For example, when you add a domain controller to your site, the replication topology is adjusted to add the new machine.

Replication offers a number of methods for helping ensure your system is fault-tolerant.

Automatic System Recovery

Automatic System Recovery (ASR) is another innovation in Windows 2000 that is designed to try and keep you up and running by allowing for fast recovery from a number of problems. If you accidentally change a device driver, for example, and then have problems rebooting, ASR will help. You might try the Last Known Good Configuration or the Repair option, but if that fails and you still cannot reboot, you can usually recover using ASR. Whatta tool!

NEW TERM ASR needs to know that the computer's current configuration and operating system files are saved using Windows Backup. It uses these files along with all the files needed to restore a nonbootable system and creates what it calls a *saveset*. This can then be used later to recover your system.

ASR consists of two components: a login recovery component and a file restore component. The main purpose of login recovery is to bring your machine back to a state where you can log in and start the remaining piece, file restore.

During login recovery, ASR restores the following components:

- Your computer's physical storage configuration, including partition information and the drive's file format
- All the Windows 2000 operating system files, especially those in the %systemroot% directory hierarchy
- The Windows 2000 boot files, Ntldr and Ntdetect.com

To do this, you need to tell ASR to save the relevant information it needs. It does this in a thing called a *saveset*. When you create this saveset, the backup application creates a setup information file (SIF) onto a floppy disk. This file contains

- The physical configuration of the disks that are in the machine
- The attributes of the partition such as its volume label, type, size, and so on
- The name and location of all the device driver files
- The commands needed to invoke the backup and restore applications
- The computer configuration information such as machine name and where Windows originates

The program also creates copies of the autoexec.bat and config.sys files using the %systemroot%repair directory and copies the necessary device driver files onto the floppy. Finally, it copies all the files from the system and the boot partition onto your backup media.

Task 16.6 shows you how to create a saveset file.

Task 16.6: Creating an Automatic System Recovery Saveset.

Step 1: Description

In this task, you use Backup to create an ASR saveset containing all the information needed to restore your system should you have a problem.

Step 2: Action

1. Log on to Windows 2000 as Administrator.
2. Choose Start, Programs, Accessories, Backup. You see a dialog box like that shown in Figure 16.3.

FIGURE 16.3

The Backup program.

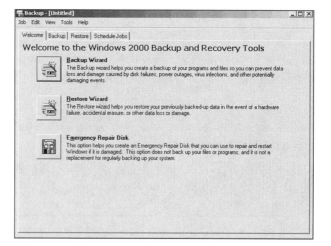

3. Select Tools, Automated System Recovery.
4. Follow the simple prompts to complete the task.

Step 3: Review

This step allows you to save critical data so it can be used later to restore your system after a failure.

You'll want to keep this information up to date by running this task frequently.

When you recover the system, ASR performs two steps as we stated earlier. In the login recovery phase, ASR recovers and reformats the system and boot partitions, and reinstalls the operating system if necessary. First, it repairs any partitions that are missing after comparing the current ones to its files. Next, it recovers the information that was stored on the each partition and copies a new set of Windows 2000 files. Finally it copies

the SIF into your %systemroot%\System32 directory and modifies the Registry so that
the restore applications start when you restart the machine.

When the machine restarts, a graphical mode Setup is launched that restores all the original system files. The system reboots again and your login prompt appears. Now your
restore job starts and you can recover the remaining files, completely rebuilding your
system. Task 16.7 shows how you start the ASR repair.

Task 16.7: Using ASR to Recover Your System.

Step 1: Description

In this task, you use the Repair option to tell ASR to recover your system after a catastrophic failure.

Step 2: Action

1. Log on to the Windows 2000 Server as Administrator. (You can also do this task if
   you are in a Power Users or Server Operators group).

2. Select a directory and right-click and select Properties.

3. Select Sharing and enter a share name or keep the default value.

4. Click on the Caching option. You see a dialog box like Figure 16.4.

FIGURE 16.4

*The Caching Settings
dialog box.*

5. There are three options available. Manual Caching for Documents is the default
   option. The other two are Automatic Caching for Documents and Automatic
   Caching for Programs. The manual method is likely best as the user will need to
   select a file to be downloaded, thus saving network overhead. If necessary, you can
   select automatic caching and all files will be saved on the user's desktop for offline
   use. The Programs option provides read-only access and is useful for allowing programs to be cached without them being modified in any way. Select the option you
   want.

6. Click OK to continue and OK again to complete the task. Your directory is now set
   up for offline use.

TASK

16

Step 3: Review

This step allows you to set up a directory for offline access so users can always have files available even if they disconnect from the network.

Note

> In Windows 2000 Professional, the Allow Caching of Files in This Shared Folder check box is selected by default so all shares are cached. In Windows 2000 Server, it is cleared by default and no caching takes place unless you select it.

Intellimirror

Intellimirror is a set of features aimed at minimizing administration of W2K machines. It is a set of technologies for handling change and configuration management at the desktop. By using the different features in both the server and the client, it enables users' data, applications, and settings to follow them throughout their environment providing a degree of fault-tolerance.

Intellimirror has several different pieces including

- Software installation
- User document management
- User settings management

Using these components together you can set up your environment to centrally install and maintain applications, give your users true roaming abilities, and if needed, enable your mobile users to continue working on files even when they are disconnected.

Software application installation and maintenance works with Group Policy to help you deploy and manage your applications. You can create a Group Policy that defines the applications a user can use regardless of where that user logs in. You can assign or publish the applications. When you assign an application to a user, an icon appears on the user's desktop. When the user clicks on that icon, the application is transparently installed.

When you publish an application, it is listed in the user's Add/Remove Programs area as an optional program. The user can then select it and install it when they so desire. This way, you can publish a bunch of applications for users knowing that most users will only install those they need, when they need it. Finally, an additional option lets you install an application only if the user selects a certain file type such as .PDF or .ZIP. When they click on that type of file, the associated program will be downloaded and installed.

Part of Intellimirror allows you to control the user's desktop configuration as well. This enables administrators to keep track of and manage desktops, ensuring that all user's desktops have a consistent look and feel. By adding roaming profiles, you can ensure that if a user's desktop machine becomes unusable, you can just unplug it and give him a new one! He'll never know.

Finally, the third aspect of Intellimirror implements document management. This allows your user's files to be available even if he isn't connected to the network. It uses caching options that even a user can implement. This is a real update to the old Briefcase icon that Microsoft tried to offer in earlier versions of Windows.

You can see this option at work by clicking on a directory, choosing properties, and enabling sharing. You'll see something like Figure 16.5.

FIGURE 16.5

The Caching option.

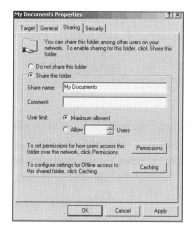

By clicking on Caching you'll see a number of options that enable your users to access this directory while they are offline. In Task 16.8 we show you how to set up caching options.

Task 16.8: Setting Up Offline File Access.

Step 1: Description

In this task, you use the Cache option on a directory and allow the contents to be used while a user isn't connected to the network.

Step 2: Action

1. Start the computer using the Windows 2000 CD-ROM or Setup Disk 1.

  2. Insert the other disks when asked.

▼   3. Press R to select the Repair/Recovery option. Then press R again to select Repair a Damaged Installation.

4. Press F for Fast Repair. If you press M for Manual you are asked to select the following options:

   • Inspect startup environment

   • Verify Windows 2000 System Files

   • Inspect boot sector

   • Continue (perform selected tasks)

   Click on the options you don't want to use and then select Continue and press Enter.

5. When prompted, enter the ASR disk and follow the remaining instructions. Setup displays a message when it is done telling you it has completed the repairs and to
▲   reboot the system.

Step 3: Review

This step allows you to repair your system and recover from a failure. Hopefully you don't have to use it!

An administrator can set up user document management so that it works automatically for the user. If the network connection is lost (or she logs off and takes her laptop home), she can continue to navigate and use her files. Any files she modifies while offline are automatically synchronized when she logs back onto the network.

When these three key parts are combined, user fault-tolerance is definitely enhanced!

Uninterruptible Power Supply

A power outage or interruption can cause considerable damage to your hardware and the data stored on it. Backup power systems provide emergency power in the event of a commercial power outage or interruption. People use the term *UPS* generically to refer to these backup power systems. Most people will tell you that UPS stands for *uninterruptible power supply,* but it really stands for *uninterruptible power system.* Another backup power system is a *standby power system,* or *SPS.* The only difference is that a UPS constantly powers your system, whereas an SPS waits to be called into action. Windows 2000 can work hand-in-hand with intelligent power systems (IPS) to monitor battery time and recharge times. In coordination with Windows 2000, an IPS can orchestrate a *fail-safe* and shut down the whole network.

This matter is fairly complicated, so discuss it with vendors of power supply systems. This topic is also another one to discuss with other administrators because other system administrators who have gone through the purchase of a UPS or IPS will probably be happy to share their experiences.

Using Uninterruptible Power Systems

A basic power and grounding system can be augmented by an uninterruptible power system. A UPS provides electrical power to computers or other devices during a power outage. Your UPS can come in two forms: standby and online. A standby device kicks in only when the power goes down. It therefore must contain special circuitry that can switch to backup power in less than five milliseconds.

An online device constantly provides the source of power to the computer. As a result, it doesn't need to kick in. When the outside source of power dies, the batteries within the unit continue to supply the computer with power. Although online units are the better choice, they are more expensive than standby units. Because online units supply all the power to a computer, however, that power is always clean and smooth.

When you purchase a battery backup system, be aware of the following:

- The amount of time that the UPS battery supplies power
- Whether the UPS provides a warning system to the server when the UPS is operating on standby power
- Whether the UPS includes power-conditioning features that can clip incoming transient noise
- The lifespan of the battery and how it degrades over time
- Whether the device warns you when the batteries can no longer provide backup power
- Whether the batteries are replaceable

Purchase a UPS that the server can monitor to detect drains. A monitoring cable usually attaches to the serial port. Also, make sure that the UPS is compatible with Windows 2000. To determine compatibility, check the Hardware Compatibility List (HCL).

You also need to know the power requirements of the devices that you'll hook to the UPS. For a server installation, they might include the CPU, the monitor, external routers, bridges, hubs, concentrators, and wiring centers. You can determine the power requirements of these devices by looking at the backs of the equipment. Labels on the equipment list the power drawn by the units in watts. Simply add the values of all the devices to come up with the requirements for the UPS. You need not include the wattage for your laser printers as you cannot hook them up to the UPS.

16

Attaching a UPS to the File Server

To install a UPS, just attach the device to your computer according to the manufacturer's instructions. Use a UPS that Windows 2000 can monitor for power loss. When power loss does occur, Windows can perform an orderly shutdown. An interface between the UPS and Windows 2000 sends signals about the state of the UPS so that the server knows to warn users that it might be going down.

After installing the UPS, you need to configure how Windows 2000 is to interact with the UPS. Log on as the Administrator, and double-click Power Options in the Control Panel. Select UPS. The UPS installation dialog box will appear.

Click the top check box to turn on UPS support; then specify the COM port where your server is to communicate with the UPS. Next, fill out the options in the UPS Configuration section based on voltage levels sent by the UPS. Refer to the manual for this information.

In the Execute Command File field, you can specify the name of a program to execute if the power starts to get low. Fill out the lower sections as appropriate for your UPS. You probably need to test the UPS yourself to learn its actual battery life and recharge time instead of relying on the information supplied by your vendor.

Sector Sparing (Hot Fixing)

Redundant data storage is used not only for recovering data after a complete disk failure but also for recovering data from a single physical sector that goes bad. Windows 2000 Server fault-tolerance services add sector-recovery capabilities to the file system during operation.

NEW TERM In a technique called *sector sparing,* the Windows 2000 driver, *FtDisk*, uses its redundant data storage to replace lost data dynamically when a disk sector becomes unreadable. The sector-sparing technique exploits a feature of some hard disks that provide a set of physical sectors reserved as "spares." The file system verifies all sectors when a volume is formatted, and faulty sectors are removed from service. If FtDisk receives a data error from the hard disk, it obtains a spare sector from the disk driver to replace the bad sector that caused the data error. When the system finds bad sectors during disk input and output, the fault-tolerance driver tries to move the data to a good sector and map out the bad sector. When the mapping is successful, the file system isn't alerted of the problem.

FtDisk recovers the data that was on the bad sector (by either reading the data from a disk mirror or recalculating the data from a stripe set with parity) and copies it to the spare sector. FtDisk performs sector sparing dynamically, without intervention from the file system or the user, and sector sparing works with most Windows 2000–supported file systems on SCSI-based hard disks.

Sector sparing isn't supported on the high-performance file system (HPFS) of OS/2. If a bad-sector error occurs, and the hard disk doesn't provide spares, runs out of them, or is a non–SCSI-based disk, FtDisk still can recover the data. It recalculates the unreadable data by accessing a stripe set with parity, or it reads a copy of the data from a disk mirror. FtDisk then passes the data to the file system along with a warning that only one copy of the data remains in a disk mirror, or that one stripe is inaccessible in a stripe set with parity, and that data redundancy is therefore no longer in effect for that sector. The file system must respond to (or ignore) the warning. FtDisk re–recovers the data each time the file system tries to read from the bad sector.

Summary

The purpose of this day was to introduce you to one of the administrator's most important jobs—keeping the network up and running. It is amazing how fast you'll lose users—and maybe your job—when the system is unreliable or unavailable.

To help you improve network availability, you learned about some of the NTS fault-tolerance features.

Workshop

To wrap up the day, you can review tasks from the day, and see the answers to some commonly asked questions.

Task List

The emphasis of this day was to introduce you to fault-tolerance features. As a system administrator, you need to learn how to implement these features. You learned how to perform the following complicated tasks in this day:

- Using Disk Administrator to create and break mirror sets
- Recovering data from a mirror set
- Creating a stripe set with parity
- Regenerating a failed stripe set
- Deleting a stripe set
- Creating an ASR saveset
- Restoring a system using ASR
- Setting up a UPS

Q&A

Q What is the difference between mirroring and duplexing?

A With mirroring, you have two physical drives but one disk controller. With duplexing, you have two physical disk drives and two disk controllers.

Q Does Windows 2000 Professional support disk fault-tolerance?

A No, it does not. However, it does support RAID 0 or disk striping, which, as you learned, is a non–fault-tolerant RAID level.

Q Does Windows 2000 Server provide any other automatic fault-tolerance management facilities?

A Yes, Windows 2000 Server supports symmetrical multiprocessing. The system balances the workload among two or more processors, with the second and subsequent processors providing additional computing power under normal circumstances and full backup in the event of a failure in any processor.

Q Can I do anything else to provide fault-tolerance?

A Yes, you can use redundancy in your network for key components. Just as you saw in the previous question, you can have backup processors, and you can have backups for other components. Windows 2000 Server supports multiple network interface cards in a server, for example, so a network interface card failure doesn't necessarily take down the server.

DAY 17

Security Monitoring and Audit Trails

At the beginning of the week, you learned all about file backup and recovery. You also learned that W2K offers more than one method for performing backups, and you learned how to schedule jobs so that the backups occur overnight with little or no operator intervention. Now you'll learn about ensuring that your critical data files and users are properly monitored, and you'll learn to properly audit W2K. In this lesson, you'll also learn about C2 level security and its relevance to security in most organizations. Finally, you'll learn what features and functions should be monitored to provide you with a reasonable level of assurance that all is well in your server environment.

A successful audit program consists of various elements, the most important being the decision-making over what elements of the system need monitoring and what actions are taken with the logs. Too many organizations are content to record a few details and let it go at that. As you'll find out, a well-designed audit program can be very useful.

This lesson introduces you to the concepts of an audit program, the specific features W2K Server offers, and an approach that provides you with a level of

audit logging and reporting that should become one of the key tasks in the daily administration of your Windows 2000 Server system.

Security and Audit Objectives

An audit program typically is used to define and examine all the necessary elements of a
computing environment. From this examination comes an understanding of the elements
in use, and the auditor is then in a position to assess the level of control over each element. This assessment forms the basis for continuing improvement in the overall system
security and control parameters.

Audit programs have been in existence for many years with the "big iron" mainframes of
the last 25 years as the proving ground. But times are certainly changing as LANs,
WANs, and client/server architectures begin to flourish and grow like weeds across the
corporate landscape.

Your Windows 2000 Server is, in all likelihood, a critical component of your network
and therefore needs a level of control and protection commensurate with that critical
nature. It does not, however, operate in a vacuum; it normally forms a part of the overall-
computing environment. Your computing environment might be small with one server
and a few client workstations, or it might be huge with hundreds of servers and thousands of workstations. The audit program needs to consider all these elements and offer a
reasonable set of objectives.

Finally, no one set of objectives works for every organization. Organizations differ as
greatly as individuals, and their needs and vulnerabilities differ also. We attempt to provide a framework for you to work with in this lesson, but ultimate responsibility for
determining the level of monitoring and audit logging must come from within your own
organization.

Security in today's environment is far more complex than it was a few years ago. Many
organizations were content with their onsite, glass computer room and a well-defined
number of dumb terminals. Life was fairly straightforward, and in most of the environments the risks were fairly well known and understood. That isn't to say they were managed well, but they were most likely always understood and were managed to the degree
each organization felt necessary. If you used this UNIX operating system or that version
of IBM's MVS, the exposures were understood and accepted and were dealt with in the
manner in which the organization felt was appropriate (or could get away with), and all
was well.

Today, however, not only have things changed, but also they are continually changing
and growth appears to be accelerating. In this lesson, you'll learn to manage that change
and help ensure that your Windows 2000 Server is properly audited and controlled.

So what are some of the objectives and principles to keep in mind as you learn to audit your Windows 2000 Server? Some issues and descriptions are provided in Table 17.1. Later, you'll learn how to use the tools within W2K to help monitor and track events to ensure that these issues are properly managed.

TABLE 17.1   Audit Considerations

Principle/Issue	Description
Availability	Ensuring that data, programs, networks, and systems remain accessible for regular use by authorized persons.
Data confidentiality	Using appropriate security controls and mechanisms to help ensure that only authorized persons can see the data.
Data integrity	Seeing that only properly authorized changes occur to data, files, and programs.
Principle of least privilege	Ensuring that users have access only to the data and files they need in order to perform their day-to-day duties. They should not have excessive levels of access (such as write access to a file if they only intend to read the information within the file), and they should not have any file or system access they don't need.
Accountability	Ensuring that users are held accountable for their actions. This process is helped through the use of individual user accounts and passwords and strict policies against password sharing. Sound auditing policies are put in place to track events at the individual account level.
Separation of duty principle	Allocating responsibilities and privileges in such a way that no one person can control key aspects of a process and cause unnecessary loss. For example, controlling the actions of administrators through the use of authorized procedures and regular audit reports.

Types of Controls

As you learn about controls, you'll realize their place within your Windows 2000 Server environment. It is one thing to build and maintain a network using Windows 2000 Server, but it is another thing altogether to manage that network in such a manner that your important assets aren't unnecessarily compromised. Judicious use of controls will help you manage this aspect of your network.

Three major types of controls are involved:

- Preventive
- Detective
- Corrective

NEW TERM   You'll learn to use each type of control in its proper place within W2K and balance each distinctive need to achieve a sound audit program. *Preventive controls* are used to stop an event from happening. They are usually in the forefront of technology, and their needs change constantly. An example of this type of control is user authentication, in which a person needs an account and password to be recognized by the system, preventing unauthorized persons from signing on. You apply these controls by using Active Directory Users and Computers to add and change user accounts and modify access rights.

NEW TERM   *Detective controls* record and report on events after they occur. Does this mean they have no useful purpose? After all, we probably know that a person broke in and stole all our data—what good does a detective control do? Well, you aren't always aware that unauthorized events are occurring in your system until you read about them in a log of some sort, and that is exactly what a detective control does—it lets you know that something bad happened. These controls are very necessary for tracking and correcting problems.

Finally, corrective controls are put in place after an event to help ensure that the event cannot recur. Corrective action typically might consist of a memo to senior management outlining some system deficiency and requesting that they implement a program to correct that deficiency. In addition, corrective controls might notice some activity and take some evasive or corrective action. Just as a skipper on a sailboat periodically recalculates her position using a Global Positioning System (GPS) and takes corrective action, that is, tacks or reaches to get to port, you do the same. For example, should someone try to continually exploit the NBT ports (135-139), you could decide to start logging or even shut down the connection.

Your audit program needs to consider the use of all these types of controls to help find a balance between operating efficiency, system security, and costs/benefits.

You have various other controls to consider within your W2K environment besides these three high-level types of control. A sound security audit program consists of effective management of the three basics—preventive, detective, and corrective—and also considers the more day-to-day control issues presented in the following discussion.

In any audit program, you need to consider how you intend to manage the issues surrounding each of the following controls:

- Management controls
- Logical access controls
- Physical access controls
- Operational controls

- Network controls
- Application controls

This isn't intended to be an exhaustive list; rather it represents the crux of audit issues within your Windows 2000 Server environment. You use management controls each day as you operate your server. How often does the server shut down for maintenance? When will you implement the latest software upgrade, and what steps will you take to protect the present operating system in case things go wrong? Designing and following policies and procedures are all part of management controls.

Logical access controls are very strong within W2K, as you learned last week in the lessons on W2K security and account management. The manner in which users must have unique accounts and regular password changes all form part of the logical access controls present in your system.

Physical security plays a larger role within the client/server world than it does in the older mainframe environments. In those environments, most of your problems involve locking the computer room and managing the network components. Today, you need to ensure the physical security of your Windows 2000 server, regardless of where you might place it. We still find mission-critical servers lying on floors or under people's desks. Their very size makes them more vulnerable because you might treat them like desktop machines rather than the complex operating environments they are today.

Operational controls provide you the flexibility needed to monitor and manage your system, yet protect you from inadvertent error by their procedural nature and straightforward structure. Well-designed operational procedures define when, how, and why a task needs to be done, as well as providing the detailed steps taken in performing that task. For example, clearly defining the backup and recovery process for your Windows 2000 Server and clients helps ensure that the work is accomplished in a consistent manner. This becomes very useful as staff turnover rises and new staff is introduced to manage your servers.

In today's systems, the network has become at least as critical, if not more so, than the operating system it supports. On Days 11 through 14, you learned how to ensure that the proper network controls are used. Today, you'll learn audit techniques available to assist in securing the network.

Finally, all the controls over your operating system and network could be for naught when the user application isn't sufficiently protected and audited. You need to add the appropriate level of control to each application, ensuring that its users can perform only the tasks they are authorized to perform and that adequate audit trails are produced to determine who did what and when, where necessary. You use W2K's extensive rights and permissions to help ensure this level of control.

17

Many organizations still agonize over informal or formal controls. In most cases, the answer is probably a combination of both. Controls need to be formal enough that you understand what controls are needed and what has to be done to ensure compliance, yet they can be informal enough not to require senior management approval or review. The ideal for most organizations, however, likely lies with the formal approach. Only with the involvement of senior management can effective controls sometimes be implemented because administrators are sometimes more concerned with getting the system up and running than with worrying about all those "security" things. Also, by documenting and publishing the controls, staff are aware of what must be done, and by seeing clearly defined policy and procedures, staff need only heed these processes to ensure their compliance with corporate policy. Well-written policy also removes ambiguity because management clearly states the goals and objectives of the security program in black-and-white.

Finally, regardless of what tasks you follow today to audit and secure your system, you need to follow the management control cycle: *Implement the controls, detect any problems, and correct those problems by implementing new controls*. This cycle never ends, so just when you think your Windows 2000 Server is fully secured and well audited, think again. Something will surely have changed.

Windows 2000 Server and C2 Controls

You read a lot on the newsgroups about Windows and C2 security. What is this C2 and why do people seem so concerned? To appreciate the meaning, you need to go back to the U.S. Government and its need for a defined level of security that could be applied to the diverse operating systems of the day in a consistent manner. The National Computer Security Center (NCSC) publishes these guidelines and offers them to the general public should they choose to follow them. Only government departments and agencies must follow the guidelines, but even this compliance is loosely interpreted at present.

What are these guidelines? The Department of Defense published the *Trusted Computer System Evaluation Criteria (TCSEC)*, providing security requirements for Automatic Data Processing (ADP) systems. The book is often called the "orange" book because of its color. You might guess at how long these requirements have been around—the title should give a hint. Anyway, this old tome set the stage for security requirements throughout the government and soon became synonymous with good security practices. The networking version of these standards, called the "red" book, offers the same advice from a networking perspective.

Although you learn about the criteria in this section of the book, realize that unless your server is within a U.S. Government agency or your firm does work for the government, the criteria are merely guidelines. In fact, technically speaking, it is highly unlikely that any organization will meet the criteria because they are very rigid and follow strict conventions on precisely which release of the operating system is used, what can be attached, and which processes can run on the machine. Most organizations violate these restrictions as part of their daily use of the system. However, we digress. The standards at least provide a means for evaluating systems and controls.

The TCSEC criteria consist of four major classes, with class A being the most secure and class D the least. As you can guess, class C fits somewhere in between these two extremes. Within each class are several levels, designated by a simple number scheme. The different levels and classes are listed in Table 17.2.

TABLE 17.2 NCSEC Evaluation Criteria

Class	Description
D	The minimal level assigned. Provided to any system that fails to achieve a higher class.
C1	Also termed discretionary protection, this level used to be popular in the early 1980s as system security began to become an issue. User-level controls are expected. Users need a unique identity and password.
C2	A popular level today, most systems use this as the minimum basis for their controls. Access to files must be granted or restricted on a user-by-user basis. Users can be held accountable, and audit tracking is performed on a user basis.
B1	The standard that most mainframe software currently achieves. It requires that data be labeled, and the labels must transfer with the data. A user cannot override a given label despite having individual privileges.
B2	Even tighter controls. Requires a formal, structured policy with tighter user authentication. All output needs to be labeled with an appropriate sensitivity description. Requires a guaranteed trusted path for initial login.
B3	Scrutinized and tested security system containing no code not relating to security. Highly resistant to penetration and generally considered tamper-proof.
A1	Security that is the same level as B1 but formally verified and tested.

As you see, there are several levels; explaining each is probably counter-productive because the topic gets very technical and difficult to assess. For your purposes, it is enough to know that software cannot be assigned one of these levels without approval from the Department of Defense. The fact that Windows NT Server was assigned a C2 level is enough; getting into long-winded arguments about whether the "red" book version or the "orange" book version is applied is only really beneficial to academics or theoreticians. In fact, Microsoft suggests that Windows 2000 Server is so secure that certain processes such as identification and authentication, and the capability to separate a user from their functions, meets B2 security requirements. As you can see, the debate can easily rage on, ad infinitum.

Microsoft has offered the C2 level of control for Windows NT 3.5.1 with Service Pack 3. Windows 2000 Server comes C2-equipped out of the box. Does that mean it is C2 compliant when it is installed? No. It merely means it is designed to be a C2 system. How you implement and use it determines whether it can be classified as C2. For example, not requiring your users to enter a password before being signed on invalidates C2 (and any other reasonable expectation of security). We have seen many Z1 implementations of C2 systems!

Note   The C2 rating serves as a guide for certain government agencies. You use it in other industries only to provide a guide as to whether a particular system meets this minimal level of security and control. It is far more important how you manage the system than whether it is C2-compliant.

Auditing Windows 2000 Server

Here, we introduce the concepts and show you some tasks designed to allow you to assess or control the level of audit and control within your W2K system. Later today, we show you how to change and manage the specific audit logs and events to set up a secure environment.

By default, W2K doesn't initiate any audit logging. This is primarily due to the fact that auditing takes processing time and disk storage and needs to be carefully considered.

As an administrator, you need to consider what you want to record and log, and what you will do with those logs after they are created. Following are some of the things you might be interested in knowing:

- Is anyone attempting unauthorized access by trying to sign on to one account many times or to different accounts in some form of pattern?
- Are all uses of privileges authorized?
- Who is logging on after hours?
- Are certain sensitive files being accessed too often, or are unauthorized persons trying to access them?
- When is the server shut down and started?
- How many user accounts remain unused in the system?

Answers to these and other questions provide you with important information about your system and its safety. Only through an effective audit program can you provide these answers and understand their impact.

Windows 2000 Server provides a unified view of auditing through its Event Viewer, enabling you to find out data about the operating system events or application or security events from a single source. You customize the auditing of events to a greater degree than previously possible and do so in an intuitive, GUI-based manner. W2K's audit logs are kept secure from casual browsing and snooping, helping ensure that a cracker doesn't wipe out all trace of his activity.

How much activity you need to audit depends to some degree on your organization's data and services on the machine. Is the server considered mission critical? Are sensitive files or databases stored within its file system? Does it merely perform as a router service or gateway? It is a safe bet that whatever your needs, the installed level of audit function is insufficient and you need to do something. You begin by reviewing what can be audited, and then you have a benchmark to work with in deciding how much of that you need.

W2K provides a wide range of events that can be audited and logged. Using them all might have a serious impact on the throughput of your system. You need to test what sort of impact the number of audit features you want to use will have on your server. Try turning on all auditing for a few days and see what the impact is and whether throughput is affected for your users. Note that this is likely to be an issue only on extremely high-use systems, because W2K's auditing normally offers little effect on the system except for the log size, and you set this by using the event log.

The Audit Event Logs

To facilitate the audit function, W2K uses three separate types of logs to store events. Each log maintains events that are relevant, enabling you to manage the space require-ments of each log on an as-needed basis. For example, your system log might be larger than the security log file should you choose to limit the logging of security events.

To start logging, you must activate auditing through the use of various tools. Security auditing is turned on through Group Policy. You set file and directory auditing on NTFS volumes by using Windows Explorer, right-clicking on a file or directory and selecting Properties, selecting the Security tab, clicking the Advanced button, and then clicking the Auditing tab.

You turn on printer auditing by choosing Settings, Printers from the Start menu, high-lighting the printer and selecting Properties. From Print Server properties, you select the Security tab, click the Advanced button, click the Auditing tab, click the Add button, and select the events to be logged for users.

These three logs consist of

- The System log
- The Applications log
- The Security log

The events stored in each log are viewed with the Event Viewer, as shown in Figure 17.1. As you see, you open each log by using the Log drop-down menu and selecting the required log file by name.

FIGURE **17.1**

The Event Viewer.

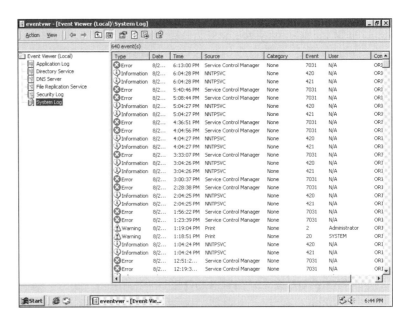

Each log contains events relevant to the type of log. For example, the System log contains a record of events logged by the system components, such as the failure of a driver to start or shut down and startup of the system.

The Security log contains events such as changes to the security system, logon and logoff, user privilege use and security policy changes, and file and directory access events.

The Application log maintains those events logged by your applications. You find database errors and other application-related problems recorded in this file.

TASK
▼

Task 17.1: Using the Event Logs.

Step 1: Description

▼ In this task, you'll learn how to use the event logs to review the present status of your system.

Step 2: Action

1. Log in as system administrator to the server.

2. Open Event Viewer by using Start, Programs, Administrative, Event Viewer. You see an example of the Event Viewer.

3. As you see, in the console window, there are several items to choose from when you're using the Event Viewer.

4. You choose a log by clicking on it. Right-click the log in the console, select New, Log View and you can open an old log file to view, rather than the current ones. Also from this menu, you can select All Tasks, Save Log File As, which takes the current log you are viewing and saves it elsewhere as a different name.

   Be careful using the option All Tasks, Clear all Events because this option performs precisely what it says, wiping out your log file. The option does ask whether you want to save the log before clearing it. You should always select Yes and save it to another file.

   Select View, Filter, and click the General tab. The log option provides you with the chance to change how large your log files are and how events are managed within those logs.

   You can view the log files on another machine by selecting the Connect to Another Computer option. You must have the necessary privileges on that machine before you can view the logs.

5. Next, select the View menu. This menu provides options for managing the current logs. The default option provides a list of all events. Choose to filter events by using the Filter menu option. As you see in Figure 17.2, the Filter tab offers various options for choosing how to see the data presented.

   As you see in the figure, W2K allows you to filter events by date and time or by all events. The viewer also allows you to set the filter for the types of events, limiting the amount of data you need to look at when you are searching for a particular type of event. For example, you can set the viewer to show only the Error events. Finally, each type of event can be further restricted via the Source and Category fields. You could use the Event Viewer to filter for a source of Security and a

▼ Category of Logon/Logoff.

17

FIGURE 17.2

*The Event Viewer
Filter tab.*

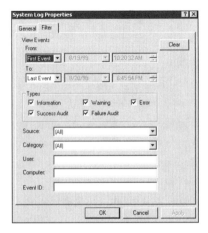

6. Next, you can sort the events using either Newest First or Oldest First, by clicking on the required option under the View menu. Select the Oldest First option to see how the list of events changes. You use these two options to select the events according to your needs.

7. The Event Viewer also offers an extensive Find option. Select it by choosing View, Find. As your logs grow, these options become increasingly useful to you. The options are, for the most part, self-explanatory and similar to those already discussed in the Filter option. You see an example in Figure 17.3.

FIGURE 17.3

*The Event Viewer
Find dialog box.*

8. Finally, you can refresh the options selected by clicking on Refresh. Click Refresh to see how the options are refreshed for you.

9. When you are finished viewing the logs, click on the small X in the upper-right corner.

Step 3: Review

In this task, you used the Event Viewer to view all your system logs. You learned to perform filtering and perform extensive find operations. Finally, you learned that the log viewer offers a wide diversity and allows you to manage the logs according to your needs.

In the next task, you're shown how to modify the size of each event log to maximize the use of your disk space and ensure that each log is large enough for your event logging activities.

Task 17.2: Changing the Size of the Event Logs.

Step 1: Description

In this task, you'll decide on the required size for each log and then set each log to operate with that size limit.

Step 2: Action

1. Log in as system administrator to the server.
2. Decide the size for each log file. You can select the default size or choose a larger or smaller size, depending on your needs.
3. Open Event Viewer by using Start, Programs, Administrative Tools, Event Viewer.
4. Select the Log, right-click it and select the General tab. You see a dialog box similar to the one shown in Figure 17.4. You can change to another log by typing its name in the Display Name box.

FIGURE 17.4

The System Log Properties dialog box.

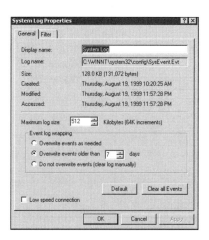

5. You change the maximum log size by typing the required number in the scroll box or by scrolling until the size you want shows.

▼ 6. Next, choose how you want the log file to act in the Event Log Wrapping section. You have three options to consider:

- Overwrite Events as Needed

- Overwrite Events Older than x Days

- Don't Override Events (Clear Log Manually)

Each option has its pros and cons. You might consider using the default setting and putting a procedure in place that automatically copies the log file each week to an archive for safekeeping. Regardless, be sure that events aren't overwritten and lost forever.

▲ 7. Implement the changes by clicking OK when you are finished setting all three log sizes.

Step 3: Review

In this task, you used the Event Viewer to set up the size of your log files and help ensure that events aren't lost due to inadequate log size. You performed this action after deciding which events are to be logged in your server and how long you want to maintain those events.

So what functions can you record, and just how detailed do these recordings get? W2K offers many kinds of log events for you to choose from as you design your audit system. The handy reference table shown as Table 17.3 details the events available for logging within the various parts of W2K. Use the table as a guide. We designed the table as a handy reference so that you can check each event and track whether to audit it.

TABLE 17.3 W2K Audit Events

Description	Y - Audit N - No audit	S - Success F - Failure
Logon and logoff		
File and object access		
Use of user rights		
User and group management		
Security policy changes		
Restart, shutdown, and system		
Process tracking		

Description	Y - Audit N - No audit	S - Success F - Failure
Printer Access by Group or User		
Print		
Full control		
Delete		
Change permissions		
Take ownership		
File and Directory by Group or User		
Read		
Write		
Delete		
Execute		
Change permissions		
Take ownership		

Each of these events, when selected, records in the associated log file an entry for each occurrence of the event. Log files can become unwieldy and data can be lost, depending on the size and settings chosen. Be sure to back up each log file regularly. The log files are found in the following directory:

```
\winnt\system32\config\*.evt
```

You'll see how to select and update W2K to use each of these entries later today.

Performing a Windows 2000 Audit

Next, you need to learn the steps necessary to perform an audit of your W2K server. As you review this section, you can keep one step ahead of your internal auditors and perform regular audits to ensure effective server security and control.

This section offers a sample audit list that provides you with the necessary detail to determine whether your basic W2K options are set and managed appropriately. As you can imagine, each organization has particular needs, and therefore an audit program is ideally customized for each company. What you'll learn here, however, are the baselines necessary to effect sound security practices. You choose the specific settings depending on your industry needs.

Sample Audit List

- Define the current platform
- Identify all servers, and categorize as server or domain controller
- Identify all workstations, and categorize as 2000, NT, Windows, UNIX, and so on
- Identify all backup media devices
- Define the software in use
- Identify version, release of W2K
- Identify current status of service packs
- Identify all major applications, databases
- Define the network in use

  Ethernet, Token ring, FDDI, or other

  Network protocols

  RAS usage

- External networks

  Internet

  Other organizations

- Control points

  Routers

  Bridges

  Gateways

- Organization

  Is administration setup centralized or decentralized?

  How many administrators?

  Is there supervisor review of changes?

  Is there a corporate policy statement?

  Are there security standards and guidelines?

  Do administrators follow written procedures?

- Physical access control

  Are servers in a locked room?

  Is access to the room appropriately restricted?

  Are cable rooms locked and properly managed?

Is the room adequately protected against fire?

Are fire extinguishers available?

Are papers stored in the server room kept to a minimum?

Is the room clear of clutter?

Are the systems protected with an adequate UPS system? Backup generator?

- Operations

    Are operators adequately trained?

    Are there procedures for backup and maintenance?

    Are changes to the system scheduled?

    Is capacity planning performed?

    Is a backup and restore policy in place, and is it followed?

    Has a contingency/disaster recovery plan been implemented?

    Is fault tolerance in use and adequate for the needs of the server?

    Is a virus-protection program in effect, and is it followed?

- Security Administration

    Are procedures documented?

    Do users follow a formal change request program to initiate changes?

    Who controls the administrator account?

    Has the administrator account been renamed?

    Is the guest account disabled?

    Who is in the Admin group, and is the list reasonable?

    Who is in the Backup Operators group, and is the list reasonable?

    Who is in the Server Operators group, and is the list reasonable?

    Are access permissions granted to the Everyone group reasonable?

    Are other groups set up in a reasonable manner (both privileged groups such as Print operators, account operators, and so forth, as well as user groups)?

    Are user account policies reasonable?

    Are passwords changed at least every 30 to 90 days?

    Are passwords a minimum of six characters? Are weak passwords blocked?

    Are users forced to change their passwords at next logon?

    Are all users assigned a password?

    Are old, unused accounts deleted?

17

Are logs reviewed regularly, and are they adequately protected?

Is the log review done by someone other than an administrator?

- File and directory protection

    Is NTFS the only file system in use?

    Are controls adequate over any FAT-based files?

    Are file and directory permissions appropriately set up? (Select a sample of files and directories to verify.)

    Is sharing in use?

    Are sharing controls adequate?

    Are there clear procedures for assigning users access to files and directories?

    Is a review of access permissions performed on occasion?

    When a new directory is created, W2K automatically assigns Full Control to Everyone. Are procedures in place telling administrators to remove this right?

- Application development and change control

    Do users create new applications?

    Are all applications properly documented?

    Is an application development life cycle followed?

    Are revisions tested before being implemented into production?

    Is there adequate separation of duty between developers and operations staff?

    Are user accounts named consistently, such as last name and initial?

    Are formal approvals required for adding new users and assigning privileges?

- Audit logging

    Is logging being performed?

    Are the security logging options adequate?

    Are the log files being copied for safekeeping on a regular basis?

    Have procedures been developed to manage the storage of the logs to ensure that they remain available for a set period?

    Have any programs been developed to ease the process of reading the logs and to provide management summary reports?

This brief summary of functions should help you understand the items you need to review when performing an audit of W2K. You can find a more extensive Windows NT Server audit program at `http://www.pdaconsulting.com/winnts.htm`. You should take this list or the one on that page and begin to develop a personalized Windows 2000 version with the specific settings your organization chooses to use.

Using the Windows 2000 Server Audit System

As discussed, auditing is critical to maintaining the security of your servers and networks.

A network system should collect and maintain information that can be analyzed to detect potential and actual violations of a system security policy. So, Microsoft developed an auditing system for W2K.

The W2K auditing system lets you track events that occur on individual servers related to security policies, system events, and application events. The auditing system produces logs you can view with the Event Viewer. With this system, you can track activities performed by authorized users as well as users who have gained unauthorized access through another user's account.

For auditing to be meaningful, your organization should have system security policies and procedures in place. These guidelines should set the baseline for auditing the client/server environment. A security violation can then be defined as any change to the security of the system and any attempted or actual violation of the systems access control.

Types of Monitoring

Monitoring involves the regular review of system-level attributes which, when not properly controlled, could introduce integrity exposures. Reporting and follow-up in the event of attempted violations is another aspect of monitoring. Auditing verifies compliance with these monitoring procedures as well as the effectiveness of follow-up actions.

Status and event monitoring are two types of security monitoring. Status monitoring looks at the current state of the system or process. The security administrator usually performs status monitoring; line staff also should do it. The hands-on technical person is familiar with the system and can recognize any general deviance from normal operations. The security administrator should monitor all security-related events on an ongoing basis.

17

Event monitoring is based on audit trails. Unlike status monitoring, event monitoring occurs after the fact. You should review security audit trails, provided by either the operating system or the application, or both, on a timely and regular basis. Any violations in security should be reported and followed up on immediately.

Security Auditing

Security auditing refers to two different activities: day-to-day security monitoring tasks and periodic security audits. The day-to-day monitoring should be part of the administrator's responsibility. Administrators probably will perform these tasks every day, whereas part-time administrators might monitor less frequently.

Periodic reviews and audits can be performed by internal or external auditors annually or less frequently, depending on the size and security needs of an organization.

Built-in audit reporting utilities, such as those provided in Windows 2000 Server, help the administrator monitor the status of system security in addition to providing audit trails.

Events to audit should include the following events:

- User identification and authentication
- Assignment and use of privileges and rights
- File and object access
- Account and group authorization
- Changes in audit status
- Critical file/utility auditing
- Changes in trust relationships
- Changes in system configuration
- System initialization
- Program installation
- Account modification
- Transfer of information into or out of the system

Windows 2000 Server provides facilities to audit all these events.

Auditing Features

Windows 2000 Server auditing features record events to show this information:

- Which users access which object
- The type of access attempted
- Whether or not the access attempt was successful

For domains, the system writes all auditable events to the Security log on the domain controller and refers to events that occur on the controller and all servers in the domain. For standalone W2K workstations, all auditable events are written to the workstation's Security log.

Note	By default, only the administrator has the Manage Auditing and Security Log right.

Managing Security Policies

Active Directory Users and Computers is part of a quartet of programs that provides network security options in Windows 2000 Server. Whereas the Windows Explorer/My Computer tandem and the Printer Folder control specific access to files, directories, and printers, Active Directory Users and Computers gives the administrator the capability to assign systemwide rights and to determine the auditing policies of the network.

In Active Directory Users and Computers, an administrator can manage the following security policies:

- Account, which controls the characteristics of passwords for all user accounts
- User Rights, which determines what system rights are assigned to a user or group
- Audit, which defines the kinds of security events for logging

Password Characteristics

Earlier you learned about the Group Policy where you can set and adjust the password characteristics for all user accounts in the domain. You learned in detail about this topic on Day 7, "Managing User Accounts." To see these rules, choose Security Templates from the MMC window. Then double-click C:\SystemRoot\Security\Templates, and double-click basicdc. You can set policies for passwords, account lockout, and security policies. Select Account Policies and then Password Policy, as shown in Figure 17.5.

You can set the following options:

- Maximum Password Age—This option sets the maximum time period for a password before the system requires the user to pick a new one.
- Minimum Password Age—This value is the time that a password has to be used before the user is allowed to change it again. If you allow changes to the password to be made immediately (not a very secure option), be sure to choose Do Not Keep Password History in the Password Uniqueness box.

17

- Minimum Password Length—This option defines the fewest number of characters that a user's password can contain.

- Enforce Password Uniqueness By Remembering—Here you can specify the number of new passwords that must be used before a user can repeat an old password. If you choose a value here, you must specify a password age value under Minimum Password Age.

FIGURE 17.5

The Password Policy attributes.

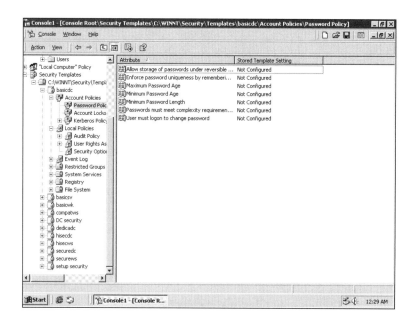

Remember that you also could set account lockout options. Select Account Policies and then Account Lockout Policy, as shown in Figure 17.6.

- Account Lockout—This option prevents anyone from logging onto the account after a certain number of failed attempts.

- Account Lockout Count—This value defines how many times a user can attempt to log on.

- Reset Account Lockout After—This setting defines the time in which the count of bad logon attempts starts over. For example, suppose you have a reset count of two minutes and three logon attempts. If you mistype twice, by waiting two minutes after the second attempt, you'll have three tries again.

- Lockout Account For—This setting determines whether the administrator must unlock the account manually or can let the user try again after a certain period.

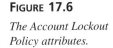

FIGURE 17.6

*The Account Lockout
Policy attributes.*

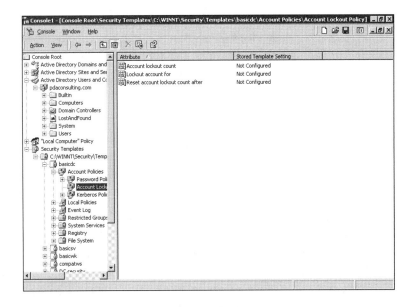

User Rights and Object Permissions

User access to network resources—files, directories, devices—in Windows 2000 Server
is controlled in two ways. The first way is by assigning rights to a user that grant or deny
access to certain objects (for example, the capability to log on to a server). The second
way is by assigning permissions to objects that specify who is allowed to use objects and
under what conditions (for example, granting read access for a directory to a particular
user).

What does this mean? Well, consider the groups Users and Administrators.
Administrators can log on right at the server; users can't. Administrators can create users
and back up files; users can't. So, administrators have rights that users don't have.
Remember that what separates one group in W2K from another mostly has to do with the
rights the groups have. You control who gets what rights via the User Manager for
Domains.

Rights generally authorize a user to perform certain system tasks. For example, the ordinary user can't just sit down at a Windows 2000 Server and log on. This is a right
assigned to an administrator. Also, backing up and restoring data or modifying printer
options on a shared printer are user rights. You can assign user rights separately to a single user, but for reasons of security organization, it is better to put the user into a group
and define the rights granted to the group. You manage user rights in Active Directory
Users and Computers.

Permissions, on the other hand, apply to specific objects such as files, directories, and printers. For example, changing files in a directory on a server is an example of a permission. The creator or owner of an object sets permissions. Permissions regulate which users have access to the object and in what fashion.

> **Tip**
>
> You can set permissions only on particular files on an NTFS volume. Directory and file permissions are administered in My Computer and the Windows Explorer, or from the command line; printer permissions are regulated in the Printers folder.

As a rule, user rights take precedence over object permissions. For example, let's look at a user who is a member of the built-in Backup Operators group. By virtue of membership in that group, the user has the right to back up the servers in the user's domain. This requires the ability to see and read all directories and files on the servers, including those whose creators and owners have specifically denied read permission to members of the Backup Operators group; thus the right to perform backups overrides the permissions set on the files and directories.

There are two types of user rights: regular user rights and advanced user rights. Windows 2000 Server's built-in groups have certain rights already assigned to them; you also can create new groups and assign a custom set of user rights to those groups. As we've said before, security management is much easier when all user rights are assigned through groups instead of being granted to individual users.

To look at or change the rights granted to a user or group, select the domain where the particular user or group resides (when it isn't in the local domain), and then choose Policies, User Rights.

Click the down arrow next to the currently displayed user right to see the entire list of regular user rights. By clicking on one of the rights, you can see the groups and users who currently have been granted that particular right. In the figure, you can see that the right Access This Computer from Network has been granted to the Administrators and Everyone group.

Following are the regular rights used in Windows 2000 Server:

- Access this Computer from Network—Allows a user to connect over the network to this server.
- Add Workstations to Domain—Allows you to add a workstation to a domain.
- Back Up Files and Directories— Allows a user to back up files and directories. As mentioned earlier, this right supersedes file and directory permissions.

- Change the System Time—Grants a user the right to set the time for the internal clock of a computer.
- Force Shutdown from a Remote System—Note that, although presented as an option, this right isn't currently implemented by Windows 2000 Server.
- Load and Unload Device Drivers—Lets a user add or remove drivers from the system.
- Log On Locally—Allows a user to log on locally at the server computer itself.
- Manage Auditing and Security Log—Gives a user the right to specify the types of events and resource access to audit. Also allows viewing and clearing the Security log.
- Restore Files and Directories—Allows a user to restore files and directories. This right supersedes file and directory permissions.
- Shut Down the System—Grants a user the right to shut down Windows 2000.
- Take Ownership of Files or Other Object—Lets a user take ownership of files, directories, and other objects that are owned by other users.

The advanced rights in Windows 2000 Server are summarized in Table 17.4. These rights are added to the rights list when you click the Show Advanced User Rights option located at the bottom of the User Rights Policy dialog box.

TABLE 17.4 Advanced User Rights

Advanced User Right	Allows Users To
Act as Part of the Operating System	Act as a trusted part of the operating system. Some subsystems have this privilege granted to them.
Bypass Traverse Checking	Traverse a directory tree even when the user has no other rights to access that directory; denies access to users in POSIX applications.
Create a Pagefile	Just as it says: Create a pagefile.
Create a Token Object	Create access tokens. Only the Local Security Authority can have this privilege.
Create Permanent Shared Objects	Create special permanent objects used in W2K.
Debug Programs	Debug applications.
Generate Security Audits	Generate audit-log entries.
Increase Quotas	Increase object quotas. (Each object has a quota assigned to it.)

continues

TABLE 17.4 continued

Advanced User Right	Allows Users To
Increase Scheduling Priority	Boost the scheduling priority of a process.
Load and Unload Device Drivers	Load and unload drivers for devices on the network.
Lock Pages in Memory	Lock pages in memory to prevent them from being paged out into backing store (such as `PAGEFILE.SYS`).
Log On as a Batch Job	Log on to the system as a batch queue facility.
Log On as a Service	Perform security services (the user that performs replication logs on as a service).
Modify Firmware Environment Values	Modify system environment variables (but not user environment variables).
Profile Single Process	Use W2K profiling capabilities to observe a process.
Profile System Performance	Use W2K profiling capabilities to observe the system.
Receive Unsolicited Device Input	Read unsolicited data from a terminal device.
Replace a Process Level Token	Modify a process' access token.

Most of the advanced rights are useful only to programmers who are writing applications to run on W2K, and most aren't granted to a group or user. However, two of the advanced rights—Bypass Traverse Checking and Log On as a Service—might be useful to some domain administrators. Bypass traverse checking is granted by default to the Everyone group in Windows 2000 Server.

Auditing Events

W2K provides auditing at the system-event level and at the object level. Any user holding the Manage Auditing and Security Log right can set auditing at the system-event level by using the Group Policy. Auditing at the object level for access to files and directories can be defined in File Manager. W2K can record auditing changes to the Registry and to printer auditing.

System Event Auditing

To turn on auditing, in Group Policy, choose Computer Configuration, Windows Settings, Security Settings, Local Policies, Audit Policy, and select the Audit These Events attribute. If the No Auditing option is shown, all Windows 2000 Server auditing is completely turned off.

 Note | By default, auditing is off. This is not, however, recommended under any circumstance.

When you select No Auditing, system-level auditing and file and directory auditing are turned off. When you select Change Local Policy To, individual events can be selected for auditing. For each event, you can specify whether to audit failed events, successful events, or both.

Windows 2000 Server maintains three event logs where entries are added in the background: the System log, the Applications log, and the Security log. You can set up security auditing for a number of events on Windows 2000 Server. Use the Group Policy Editor snap-in to help track user access to various parts of the system. To enable security auditing, select Audit Policy. You then see the window in the right panel as shown in Figure 17.7.

FIGURE 17.7

The Audit Policy window.

As you can see, the Audit Policy window gives you the option to activate auditing and shows a list of the types of security events you can audit. The default setting is off for auditing. If you choose to activate auditing, the information about that event is stored as an entry in the computer's Security log. This log, along with the System and Application logs, can then be viewed with the Event Viewer. Table 17.5 describes the auditing options you can select.

TABLE 17.5 The Security Auditing Options

Auditable Events	Description
Account Logon Events	Tracks a request to authenticate a user.
Account Management	Tracks changes in user accounts or groups (creations, changes, deletions), such as User Created or Group Membership Change; notes when user accounts are renamed, disabled, or enabled; tracks setting or changing passwords.
Directory Service Access	Tracks access to an Active Directory object. To use this logging feature, you must configure specific Active Directory objects for auditing.
Logon Events	Tracks user logons and logoffs, as well as the creating and breaking of connections to servers. Provides information on the type of logon and whether it was successful. To minimize unnecessary entries, monitor only failed logon and logoff attempts rather than both successful and failed attempts.
Object Access	Tracks access to a directory or file that has been selected for auditing under Explorer; tracks print jobs sent to printers that have been set for auditing under the Printers folder. To minimize unnecessary log entries, as a rule monitor only failed access attempts. Object access audits a user's access to files, folders, and printers.
Policy Change	Tracks changes made to the User Rights and Audit policies, such as granting or revoking user rights to users and groups or establishing and breaking trust relationships with other domains.
Privilege Use	Notes when users make use of a user right (except those associated with logons and logoffs). To minimize unnecessary log entries, monitor only failed attempts of Use of User Rights.
Process Tracking	Records detailed tracking information for program activation, some types of handle duplication, indirect object accesses, and process exit. Unless necessary, don't enable process tracking because this can generate high numbers of log entries and cause unnecessary system overhead.
System Events	Tracks when the computer is shut down or restarted; tracks the filling up of the audit log and the discarding of audit entries when the audit log already is full. Also, tracks events affecting W2K security.

Because auditing is turned off by default (see column 3 in the right half of Figure 17.7), you need to turn on each necessary audit explicitly. To set a policy, right-click on the policy, select Security from the menu, and set the audit policy. Although it's possible to log each and every user action, event, and process, this activity can generate a tremendous amount of relatively trivial log entries and make it difficult to locate the important entries—those attempts that were unsuccessful. Although the system can record both successes and failures to provide complete audit information, it is important to balance the need to monitor every event against the resources required to do so.

It's important to keep in mind that all the event logs are limited in size. The default size for each of the logs is 512KB, and the default overwrite settings allow events older than seven days to be discarded from the logs as needed. When managing the auditing policy in User Manager for Domains, choose your events to audit carefully. You might find that you get what you ask for, sometimes in great abundance. For example, auditing successful File and Object Accesses can generate a tremendous number of Security log entries. A reasonably simple process, such as opening an application, opening a single file within that application, editing and saving that file, and exiting the application, can produce more than 60 log events. A couple of users on a system can generate 200 log entries in less than two minutes. Auditing of successful Process Tracking events can produce similar results.

Should your network require you to monitor events that closely, be sure to choose the appropriate log size and overwrite settings. You can change these settings for the Security log (and for the other two logs, for that matter) in the Event Viewer. (See the section "Enabling Event Auditing" later in this lesson.)

File and Directory Auditing

In any network, the administrator sometimes needs to monitor user activity, not just to assess network performance, but for security reasons. Windows 2000 Server provides administrators the opportunity to audit events that occur on the network.

To record, retrieve, and store log entries of events, the administrator must activate auditing on the server. Not surprisingly, file and directory auditing on NTFS volumes is activated within the Security tab in the Windows Explorer. Right-click on the volume, and select Properties to see the tab.

Auditing for File and Object Access

With Windows 2000 Server, an administrator can specify which groups or users, as well as which actions, should be audited for any particular directory or file. The system collects and stores this information in the Security log, which you can view with the Event Viewer.

For folders and files to be audited, you must first set the security audit policy in Group Policy to allow the auditing of file and object access.

An available auditing option in the list is File and Object Access; be sure to select it. As you can see from the dialog box, you can audit both successful and failed accesses.

After activating file and object access auditing, you have to choose which files and/or folders, as well as which groups or users who might use the files and folders, you specifically want audited. To do this, right-click the desired folder or file in the Windows Explorer window. Then, select Properties, Security, Advanced, Auditing. Click the Add button and select the users for whom you want to audit file and folder access, and then click OK.

You can choose a specific set of events to audit for each different group or user in the Name list. Table 17.6 shows the meaning of the file and folder access options.

In the Audit Entry dialog box (shown in Figure 17.8), select the Successful or the Failed check box for the events that you want to audit.

FIGURE 17.8

The Auditing Entry for Capture dialog box.

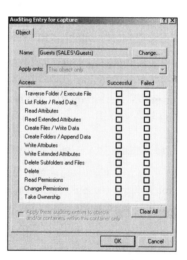

TABLE 17.6 File and Folder Audit Options

File Access	Directory Access
Displaying the file's data	Displaying names of files in the folder
Displaying file attributes	Displaying folder attributes
Displaying the file's owner and permissions	Changing folder attributes
Changing the file	Creating subdirectories and files
Changing file attributes	Going to the folder's subdirectories
Running the file	Displaying the folder's owner and permissions

File Access	Directory Access
Deleting the file	Deleting the folder
Changing the file's permissions	Changing folder permissions
Changing the file's ownership	Changing directory ownership

Table 17.7 describes when to audit these events.

TABLE 17.7 User Events and Triggers

Event	User Activity that Triggers the Event
Traverse Folder/Execute File	Running a program or gaining access to a folder to change directories
List Folder/Read Data	Displaying the contents of a file or a folder
Read Attributes and Read Extended Attributes	Displaying the attributes of a file or folder
Create Files/Write Data	Changing the contents of a file or creating new files in a folder
Write Attributes and Write Extended Attributes	Changing attributes of a file or folder
Delete Subfolders and Files	Displaying the folder's owner and permissions
	Deleting a file or subfolder in a folder
Delete	Deleting a file or folder
Read Permissions	Viewing permissions or the file owner for a file or folder

By default, auditing settings apply only to the selected folder and its files. To audit all subdirectories, select Allow Inheritable Auditing Entries from Parent to propagate this object. If inheritance is selected, auditing changes apply to files in subdirectories as well. In general, they both should be selected, unless you have a particular reason to not audit subdirectories.

 Note To audit files and folders, the File and Object Access option must be selected in the Audit Policy dialog box in Group Policy.

17

To add users and groups to those whose access to the file is being audited, click the Add button and specify the new users and groups in the resulting dialog box. Remove a user or group by selecting it in the Current Name list and clicking Remove.

As with file auditing, you can set auditing for each group or user in the list by selecting the name of a group or user in the Name list and specifying which events will be audited for that group or user.

To remove file auditing for a group or user, select that group or user and click Remove. To add groups or users to the audit, use the Add option. When you are satisfied with the auditing options, click OK. The results appear in the Event Viewer. The Viewer isn't the clearest thing in the world, but it gives you the rough information you need in order to track a security violation—provided that you enable auditing. On the other hand, auditing is costly in terms of CPU time and disk space; when you turn on all file audits, you will fill up your event log in no time.

Registry Auditing

The Windows 2000 Server Registry contains information relevant to security and auditing. You learned all about the Registry on Day 4, "Understanding and Managing the Registry." As you saw, it contains the default configuration for the event log files, the maximum sizes of those files, and the retention period for data in each file. Registry auditing is set up via the Registry Editor utility. In Registry Editor, you can specify the groups and users whose activities you want to audit for selected Registry keys, and then choose the Auditing command. Registry-related audited events can be viewed in the Security log in Event Viewer.

Task 17.3: Setting Up Registry Auditing.

Step 1: Description

This task explains how to set auditing for the Registry by using the Registry Editor.

Step 2: Action

1. Select Start, Run.
2. Type `C:\\SystemRoot\SYSTEM32\REGEDT32.EXE` and click OK.
3. In the Registry Editor, highlight a key you want to audit.
4. Select Security, Permissions.
5. Click the Advanced button, and then select the Auditing tab. Click Add.
6. From the Select User, Computers, or Group window, highlight a user and click OK. You should see a window like that shown in Figure 17.9.

FIGURE **17.9**

*The Registry Key
Auditing dialog box.*

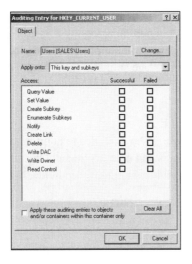

17

7. When you have added all the keys for auditing, click OK. Table 17.8 explains the
Registry audit options.

TABLE **17.8** The Registry Audit Options

Audit Option	Events Audited
Query Value	Events that attempt to open a key with Query Value access
Set Value	Events that attempt to open a key with Set Value access
Create Subkey	Events that attempt to open a key with Create Value access
Enumerate Subkeys	Events that attempt to open a key with Enumerate Subkeys access (that is, events that try to find the subkeys of a key)
Notify	Events that attempt to open a key with Notify access
Create Link	Events that attempt to open a key with Create Link access
Delete	Events that attempt to delete the key
Write DAC	Events that attempt to determine who has access to the key
Read Control	Events that attempt to find the owner of a key

Step 3: Review

Registry auditing is turned off by default. To turn on Registry auditing, first turn on File
and Object Access auditing in Group Policy. In Registry Editor, select a key and choose
Security, Permissions, Advanced, Auditing, and then add users and attributes to audit. All

keys and subkeys can be audited individually. You should set up Registry auditing on a case-by-case basis, as warranted.

When you want to audit changes to a particular key by a user or an application, you can turn on auditing for that key. Most installations audit only those events that fail. Auditing successful events might produce so many entries that your Security log will quickly fill up.

Printer Auditing

To keep an eye on a printer's usage, it's a good idea to audit it. To set up auditing, first go to the User Manager for Domains and enable File and Object Access auditing. After you've done that, you can set up printer auditing for individuals and groups.

Task 17.4: Setting Printer Auditing.

Step 1: Description

To configure printer auditing, go to the Printer Properties dialog box and select the Auditing option in the Security tab.

Step 2: Action

1. Click the Printers icon in the Control Panel under Start, Settings.
2. Right-click on the printer you want to audit from the icons in the Printers window.
3. Select Properties from the menu that pops up.
4. Click the Security tab, and then click Add.
5. Before you can audit printer activity, you have to select a group or user to audit. To do this, select the appropriate users or groups for whom you want to audit printer access, click Add, and then OK.
6. In the Apply Onto box, select where the auditing setting applies.
7. For each group or user you've chosen to audit, you can select different items to keep track of by checking the appropriate check boxes. The printer audit options are described in Table 17.9.

TABLE 17.9　The Printer Audit Options

Audit Option	Events Audited
Print	When someone prints a document
Full Control	When someone changes job settings for a document; pauses, restarts, moves, and deletes a document; shares a printer; or changes the printer's priorities

Audit Option	Events Audited
Delete	When someone deletes a printer
Change Permissions	When someone changes printer permissions
Take Ownership	When someone takes ownership of a printer

Under Events to Audit, select the Successful box or the Failed check box for the events that you want to audit.

8. Click OK in the appropriate dialog boxes to exit.

Step 3: Review

To turn on printer auditing, select Properties for the printer under Start, Settings, Printers.

When you highlight a group in the Name box here, you see the auditing items you selected for that particular user or group. No defaults are attached to auditing a particular group, so you have to set them all by hand. To view the audit information, use the Event Viewer in the Administrative Tools program group.

If you want to remove printer auditing for a group or user, follow these steps:

1. In the Auditing dialog box, select the name of the group or user from the list.
2. Click Remove.
3. Click OK.

Active Directory Object Auditing

Auditing Active Directory object access is similar to auditing file and folder access. You audit AD objects to track access to the objects, such as changing properties on a user account.

Task 17.5: Setting Active Directory Auditing.

Step 1: Description

To enable Active Directory auditing, set the audit policy to track directory service access.

Step 2: Action

1. Select Start, Programs, Administrative Tools, Active Directory Users and Computers.
2. From the View menu, select Advanced Features.
3. Right-click the object you want to audit, select Properties from the menu, select the Security tab from the window that appears, and then click the Advanced button.

▼   4. Select the Auditing tab.

5. Before you can audit AD activity, you have to select a group or user to audit. To do this, select the appropriate users or groups for whom you want to audit, click Add, and then OK. Should you add Everyone from the window, you should see Figure 17.10.

FIGURE **17.10**

The Active Directory Auditing dialog box.

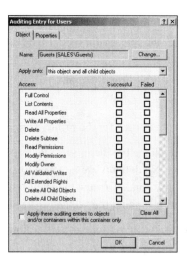

6. For each group or user you've chosen to audit, you can select different items to keep track of by checking the appropriate check boxes. The audit options are described in Table 17.10.

TABLE **17.10** The Active Directory Audit Options

Audit Option	Events Audited
Full Control	When any type of access is made to the directory object
List Contents	When someone views the objects within the audited object
List Object	When someone views the audited object
Read All Properties	When someone views any attribute of the audited object
Write All Properties	When someone writes or changes any attribute of the audited object
Create All Child Objects	When someone creates any object within the audited object
Delete All Child Objects	When someone deletes any object within the audited object
Read Permissions	When someone views the permissions for the audited object

▼

▼

Audit Option	Events Audited
Modify Permissions	When someone changes permissions for the audited object
Modify Owner	When someone takes ownership of the audited object

Under Events to Audit, select the Successful box or the Failed check box for the events that you want to audit.

▲   7. Click OK in the appropriate dialog boxes to exit.

Step 3: Review

To turn on AD auditing, use the Active Directory Users and Computers, select Properties for the object by right-clicking it. Select the Security tab, click Advanced and the Auditing tab, and the click Add.

When you highlight a group in the Name box here, you see the auditing items you selected for that particular user or group. No defaults are attached to auditing a particular group, so you have to set them all by hand. To view the audit information, use the Event Viewer in the Administrative Tools program group.

If you want to remove AD auditing for a group or user, follow these steps:

1. In the Auditing dialog box, select the name of the group or user from the list.

2. Click Remove.

3. Click OK.

Dial-Up Networking Auditing

You don't have to rely on intuition and your problem-solving ability when it comes to troubleshooting dial-up networking (DUN). You can either monitor connection attempts as they occur by using the DUN Administrator or check the record of all auditing and error messages stored in the Event Viewer.

Examining Logged Information

If you're having trouble with the connection, note that connection information about each DUN session is saved in a file called DEVICE.LOG in the \SystemRoot\SYSTEM32\RAS directory. DEVICE.LOG contains the strings that are sent to and received from the serial device (that is, the modem or X.25 PAD) that transmits the information between client and server. When looking at this file, be sure to use a text editor that can handle both regular characters and hexadecimal output. You can track the entire progress of a session with this file. It contains the command string sent to the serial device, the echo of the command, the device's response, and, for modems, the rate of transmittal.

17

Before you can use DEVICE.LOG, you must create it. The process is explained in the following steps:

1. Hang up any remote connections currently in place, and exit DUN.

2. Open the Registry by running REGEDIT32. You can also access the Registry from inside WINMSD. Remember Day 4 where we covered editing the Registry. Be very careful when editing the Registry. Be smart and make a backup before starting.

3. Go to HKEY_LOCAL_MACHINE and access the following key:

   SYSTEM\CurrentControlSet\Services\RasMan\Parameters

4. Change the value of the logging parameter to 1 so that it looks like this:

   Logging:REG_DWORD:0x1

Logging begins whenever you click the Dial-Up Networking icon or restart the service. You don't need to shut down the system or log off and on first. To view the log, open it in WordPad or another text editor. Be sure to use an editor that can handle hexadecimal information, or part of the log ends up unreadable. Also, when looking at this file, you can disregard the hOD and hOA characters at the end of each line, which are, respectively, carriage-return and line-feed bytes. They have no other significance.

 Caution | As always, before editing the Registry, you should make a backup copy of it. Making a mistake with the Registry can affect your system badly so that you need to re-install the operating system. See Day 4 for information on Registry backup and restore.

DEVICE.LOG records information about only dial-up connections. If you're having trouble with a direct connection, this file cannot help you.

Enabling Event Auditing

As you just saw in this lesson, if you want to determine who might be using shared network resources or abusing their privileges on the network, you need to enable the auditing features provided in Windows 2000 Server. Auditing is divided into several categories and isn't enabled in a single application. To audit system events related to account usage or modification and the programs running on the server, choose Policies Audit in the Server Manager for Domains dialog box.

When you select an event for auditing, it is entered in the Security log, which can be viewed with the Event Viewer. You can select to audit the successful use of a privilege, the failure to obtain access (which indicates a security violation attempt), or both. As you have seen, the following events can be audited:

- Logon and Logoff—Use this option to determine who has logged on or off the network. You could enable this option for success and failure to determine who might be using the network.

- File and Object Access—This option works in conjunction with other applications that have been used to specify auditing. For example, you can use File Manager to enable auditing of a directory and then enable auditing of the success or failure events for the File and Object Access to record access to the audited directory.

- Use of User Rights—This selection allows you to audit any use of a user right, other than logon and logoff, such as the capability to log on as a service.

- User and Group Management—This option allows you to track any user account or group. For example, it records when a new user is added, an existing user password is enabled, or a new user is added to a group. If you have continuous problems with a particular user account or group being modified, and you cannot determine who is making these changes, you can enable this option for both success and failure. This step can help you determine who might be making the changes. For example, you might find problems caused by personnel who have administrative privileges but have not been adequately trained. By using this option, you can determine who needs additional training or who should have their administrative privileges revoked.

- Security Policy Changes—Use this option to help you determine who might be making changes to system audit policies, user right policies, or trust relationships. You could enable this option both for success and failure to determine who might be modifying network policies—particularly when you have several administrators and find that things have been changing without anyone admitting responsibility.

- Restart, Shutdown, and System—This option enables you to determine who might be shutting down servers or creating any event that affects system security or the Security log.

- Process Tracking—Use this option to determine which applications are executing on your system. Auditing the success events for Process Tracking can fill up the Security log in a matter of minutes. Enable the previous event for success only when absolutely necessary.

Using the Event Viewer to Monitor Problems

To monitor past problems, you can check the Event Viewer and see what it has to say about a situation. Make sure that auditing is enabled. Three kinds of events are recorded in the Event Viewer:

17

- Information—A normal event recorded for administrative reasons. A normal connection would be recorded as an audit. You can choose to audit only successful events, failed events, or both.
- Warning—An irregular event that doesn't affect how the system functions.
- Error—A failed event or network error.

Security Event Logs

Every Windows 2000 Server system has three logs that record system-, security-, and application-related events:

- The System log records errors, warnings, or information generated by the Windows 2000 Server system.
- The Security log records valid and invalid logon attempts and events related to the use of resources such as creating, opening, or deleting files or other objects. In other words, anything you decide to audit.
- The Application log records errors, warnings, and information generated by application software, such as an electronic mail or database program.

All three logs are kept in the same subdirectory:

`\SystemRoot\SYSTEM32\CONFIG`

Anyone can view the System and Application logs. But only system administrators or users with the Manage Auditing and Security Log right can view the Security log. To view the events in the Security log, open Event Viewer and choose Security Log.

The Security log is protected by an ACL that restricts access to all but the administrator. The Security log must be secured using NTFS so that the ACL can be used. This is the pathname of the Security log:

`\SystemRoot\SYSTEM32\CONFIG\SECEVENT.EVT`

The Security log contains a header and version number that is placed at the beginning of each log file. This header can be used to ensure that the file being read or written to is a valid log file. The event log service will validate an existing file before writing events to it. It uses the Alert service to inform the administrator when the file isn't a valid event log file. When a log file is full, that is, the next record to be overwritten is within the retention period, an alert is sent to the administrator, and the record isn't written to the log.

 Tip

You should take care to protect the APPEVENT.EVT, SECEVENT.EVT, and SYSEVENT.EVT audit log files stored in the `\SystemRoot\SYSTEM32\CONFIG` directory. You should then assign access to these files only to the person or persons responsible for auditing in your organization.

Note

You can use the NET START EVENTLOG command to start the event log, which audits selected events on the network, such as file access, user logons and logoffs, and the starting of programs. You can select which events you want to log, and also whether you want the log to consist of both successful and failed attempts, just failures, or just successes (although recording only successes doesn't sound terribly useful if you're trying to monitor the system). If you're not sure how the NET commands work, review Appendix B, "Windows 2000 Command Reference."

After you've selected the log to display in Event Viewer, the viewer can sort, filter, and search for specific details about events based on fields in the header portion of the Event Detail. When you're viewing the Security log in Event Viewer, double-clicking an event displays a more detailed breakdown of that event for analysis (see Figure 17.11).

FIGURE 17.11

The Event Detail window.

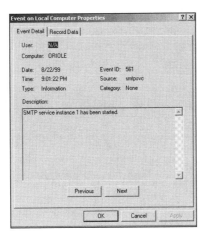

Table 17.11 explains the header information in the Event Detail.

TABLE 17.11 Detailed Event Information

Header Item	Description
User	The account name translation of the SID of the subject that generated the event. This username is the impersonation ID of the client when the subject is impersonating a client, or it is the user name of the primary ID when not impersonating.
Computer	The computer name for the computer where the event was generated.

continues

TABLE 17.11   continued

Header Item	Description
Date	The date the event was generated.
Time	The time the event was generated.
Event ID	A unique module-specific ID of the specific event.
Source	The name of the system that submitted the event. For security audits this will always be Security.
Type	Successful or unsuccessful audited security access attempt, depending on whether auditing was set up to audit successful and/or failed events.
Category	A classification of the event by the event source. For example, security categories include Logon and Logoff Policy Change, Privilege Use, System Event, Object Access, Detailed Tracking, and Account Management.
Description	Details of the security-related event.

Table 17.12 shows the various categories of events in the Security log and what they mean.

TABLE 17.12   Security Categories

Category	Description
Account Management (User and Group Management)	These events describe high-level changes to the user accounts database, such as User Created or Group Membership Change. Potentially, a more detailed, object-level audit is also performed (see Object Access events).
Detailed Tracking (Process Tracking)	These events provide detailed subject-tracking information. This includes information such as program activation, handle duplication, and indirect object access.
Logon/Logoff (Logon and Logoff)	These events describe a single logon or logoff attempt, whether successful or unsuccessful. Included in each logon description is an indication of what type of logon was requested or performed (interactive, network, or service).
Object Access (File and Object Access)	These events describe both successful and unsuccessful accesses to protected objects.
Policy Change (Security Policy Changes)	These events describe high-level changes to the security policy database, such as assignment of privileges or logon capabilities. Potentially, a more detailed, object-level audit is also performed (see Object Access).

Category	Description
Privilege Use (Use of User Rights)	These events describe both successful and unsuccessful attempts to use privileges. The log also includes information about when some special privileges are assigned. These special privileges are audited only at assignment time, not at time of use.
System Event (Security Policy Changes)	These events indicate that something affecting the security of the entire system or audit log occurred.

Using the Log Filter

If you have a busy system, you will have many log records. To make review of the log easier, you might want to filter the log records. You can use the filter to define the date range, type of events, and category of events displayed.

By right-clicking the log and choosing View, Filter and the Filter tab, you can specify certain event log parameters for filtering. Figure 17.12 shows the Filter tab.

FIGURE 17.12

The Filter tab.

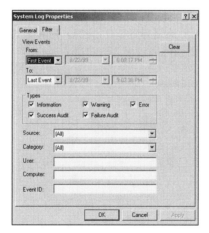

Table 17.13 lists the log filter options.

TABLE 17.13   The Log Filter Options

Option	Description
View From	Select either the beginning of the log (First Event) or a particular start date and time. The default is First Event.
View Through	Select either the end of the log (Last Event) or a particular end date and time. The default is Last Event.

continues

TABLE 17.13 continued

Option	Description
Types	Filter according to whether the audited security access attempt was successful or unsuccessful, depending on whether auditing was set up to audit successful and/or failed events. Or filter according to the type of event: information, warning, or error. The default is all types.
Source	Select the name of the system that submitted the event. For security audits, this will always be Security. The default is All.
Category	Select whether you want to include Logon and Logoff Policy Change, Privilege Use, System Event, Object Access, Detailed Tracking, and Account Management records. The default is All.
User	Enter the account name for the SID you want to view.
Computer	Enter the computer name for the computer you want to view.
Event ID	Enter the unique module-specific ID of the event.

Using Event Log Settings

By right-clicking the log and choosing View, Filter and the General tab, you can specify certain event log parameters for size and event logging. Figure 17.13 shows the General tab of the System Log Properties dialog box.

FIGURE 17.13

The System Log Properties dialog box.

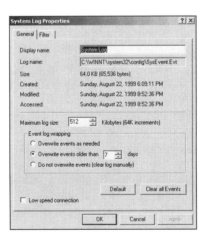

Event logging begins at boot time. When all options in the Audit Policy dialog box (in User Manager), including Process Tracking, are enabled, W2K can log a significant amount of activity to the security event log, thereby filling up the log. If the Security log becomes full, the system will halt. W2K provides a wrapping facility to ensure that the event log does not become full and cause the system to halt. By default, the maximum size of the log file is 512KB per log. The log capacity can be increased to accommodate system auditing. This number can be set in accordance with disk and memory capacities. An administrator cannot set the log for a smaller size than the current size of the log; the log must be cleared first.

Each organization should outline standard policies for archiving the event log. Archiving, when used in conjunction with one of the three available options for event-log wrapping, can help ensure that all system events are logged and that the log does not become full and halt the system.

Table 17.14 shows the event-log wrapping options available in the Event Log Setting dialog box. You can access the options via the Log Settings menu option in Event Viewer.

TABLE 17.14 The Event Log Options

Option	Description
Overwrite Events As Needed	When this option is selected, each new event replaces the oldest event when the event log is full. This is the default setting.
Overwrite Events Older Than x Days	This is the best choice to use in conjunction with a regular archive policy. The default is 7 days.
Do Not Overwrite Events (Clear Log Manually)	This ensures a complete audit log. When it's selected, you must clear the log yourself. Another good choice depending on your archive policy.

You should monitor your system to determine the optimal maximum log size. This is a balance between storage constraints, the amount of auditing being done, and archiving strategies. The Do Not Overwrite Events (Clear Log Manually) option should be selected so that events aren't lost.

> **Caution**
>
> To avoid bringing down the system when the log is full or when there isn't enough memory to allocate a buffer for the next audit record, set the following Registry flag:
>
> `\Registry\Machine\System\CurrentControlSet\Control\Lsa\CrashOnAuditFail`
>
> When this flag is set and the system cannot for any reason log an audit record (for example, the security event log is full or there is no memory to allocate a buffer for the audit record), the system is brought down. When this flag isn't set and the audit log is full, an alert message is displayed to the system administrator.

Summary

In this day, you learned all about auditing your Windows 2000 Server environment. First, you learned how to set security and audit objectives for your system. Next, you learned a little about the ubiquitous C2 rating for Windows 2000 Server and what that means to most organizations. In addition, you learned the tasks necessary to perform an audit of your server.

Logging and monitoring are key administrative duties. W2K provides several facilities to perform monitoring and logging. On Day 20, "Windows 2000 Performance Monitoring and Tuning," you'll learn about the Performance Monitor and how it helps fine-tune and troubleshoot your server and network.

You found in this lesson that you can set the following security policies:

- Account, which controls the characteristics of passwords for all user accounts
- User Rights, which determines which user or group is assigned particular system rights
- Audit, in which the kinds of security events to be logged are defined
- Trust Relationships, which establishes how other domains on the network interact with the local domain

This lesson also showed you how to set up the following items:

- System event auditing
- File and directory auditing
- Registry auditing
- Printer auditing
- Active Directory object auditing
- Dial-up networking (DUN) auditing
- Event Viewer to monitor problems

Well, that's it for today. Tomorrow, you'll learn about aW2K facility that needs monitoring and auditing: BackOffice.

Workshop

To wrap up the day, you can review tasks from the lesson, and see the answers to some commonly asked questions.

Task List

The emphasis of this day has been to introduce you to audit and security of W2K. You learned all about the things you need to do to ensure a reasonable level of control. As a system administrator, you need to learn how to use the System, Application, and Security logs. Several tasks were introduced in this lesson:

- Using the Event Viewer
- Changing the size of the event log
- Setting user rights
- Setting up file and directory auditing
- Setting printer auditing
- Setting up Registry auditing
- Setting up Active Directory auditing
- Setting up DUN auditing
- Using the log filter
- Changing event log settings

Q&A

Q How do I know what an effective audit program consists of?

A Normally, a successful audit program consists of various elements, the most important being the decision-making over which elements of the system need monitoring and what actions are taken with the logs. Too many organizations are content to record a few details and let it go at that. A well-defined audit program not only logs the correct information but also follows up and uses those reports to watch over system activity and take appropriate actions when needed.

Q I don't like to reinvent the wheel. Isn't there a standard audit program that will work for me?

A Unfortunately, no one set of objectives works for every firm. Organizations differ as greatly as individuals, and the needs and vulnerabilities of each organization and industry segment differ also. We attempt to provide a framework for you to work with in this lesson, but ultimate responsibility for determining the detailed level of monitoring and audit logging must come from within your own organization. For a head start, check out `http://www.pdaconsulting.com/winnts.htm`. Of course, you'll need to update it for Windows 2000 or wait for the update.

17

Q   We keep hearing about this C2 certification. Is it important for us, and do we need to do anything to get it?

A   Windows NT Server 3.51 comes certified at the C2 level based on the DoD Orange book criteria. Unless you deal with the federal government in your business or are a government agency, this certification has little if any impact. If you are impacted, the certification criteria sets out specific requirements that must be in place for your site to be properly certified. Contact a specialist in government certification for details.

Q   How long should we retain our audit logs?

A   This answer depends on various factors. The industry you are in might have legal restrictions on the length of time logs need to be kept, and you'll need to follow these criteria. Apart from legality, you want to ensure that logs are available to help you should an issue arise some time after the event. It's probably a good idea to keep logs at least six months, and one year is even better. This way, you can review actions taken at any time within that period and determine when an event occurred. For example, you might want to track when a terminated employee last logged in and prove that she had not used the account since that time.

Q   Where are the audit logs so that I can back them up and copy them to archive files?

A   The log files are found in the following directory:

```
\winnt\system32\config\*.evt
```

From here, you should copy them on a regular basis to an archive area and keep track of the logs in some consistent fashion so they are always available for viewing. For example, you might copy them to file names based on the system they are from and the date and time they were originally produced.

Q   How do I set up event auditing for a printer?

A   To keep track of printer events, go to the Auditing tab in the Printer Properties Security tab. By default, no groups are selected for auditing, so you must select a group. Click the Add button, and a list of possible groups to audit appears. Select a group, click the Add button so that the group name appears in the lower box, and then click OK. After you've selected a group for auditing, you can choose the events you want to audit from the list. For each group you audit, you can set up a special auditing schedule.

DAY 18

Using BackOffice and Terminal Services

So far, you have learned about many of Windows 2000 Server's different aspects, including file management, auditing, and communication gateways. It has been a busy time for you.

In this session, you'll learn how Microsoft's BackOffice products offer *database* management, electronic mail, and a host of other services. By now, you might be asking the following questions: What is BackOffice? How does it relate, if at all, to Microsoft Office? You'll find the answer to these during this day.

> **Note**
>
> Perhaps you have heard of BackOrifice. No, this isn't a new product from Microsoft. BackOrifice is a Trojan backdoor from the Cult of the Dead Cow. It provides an easy method for intruders to install a backdoor on a compromised machine. A Windows 2000 version is in use today. It is not a nice product and should not be confused in any way with BackOffice.

Microsoft BackOffice is best described as a series of products offering a degree of inter-action similar to that of the client software called Microsoft Office. The BackOffice suite contains Exchange Server, which is the electronic mail system; SQL Server, the database product; System Management Server (SMS), a software management and distribution tool; and SNA Server, a mainframe connectivity tool. Various other products are also part of the package. Those are discussed near the end of this day in the section called "Additional Products." This is primarily because these products are more specialized and are less likely to be utilized by most Windows 2000 customers.

You might think of Microsoft BackOffice as the equivalent product of Microsoft Office—the Word, Excel, and Access suite. Just as these client tools are integrated and use a common interface, BackOffice strives to manage the same feat for the server.

The use of suites of tools, all combining to enable a user to quickly and easily integrate data among products (and even using a consistent interface), is becoming ever more popular. Microsoft sees how well the Office suite sells and realizes that a server suite of tools might easily gain the same prominence.

This day delves into the use of these tools on a Windows 2000 machine, where most of them must be run. It discusses how to install and manage each product and offers additional information about using them.

At the time of this writing, many of these products remain NT versions. That is to say, they don't offer complete integration with Active Directory. Microsoft states that this integration will occur, and we expect to see new versions in the coming months that fully integrate into Windows 2000.

BackOffice Overview

First, here's a review of the basics of this product called BackOffice so that you can see how it helps in the management of a server. At one point early in the creation of client/server systems, the server was a place that ran business applications—and little more. As servers quickly gained acceptance, they grew to include many additional fea-tures designed to help improve their capability to serve the end user and enhance the business cycle.

As we write this book, we are using Windows 2000 beta software. It remains to be seen how much, if anything, will change when Microsoft begins to actively sell Windows 2000. As far as I am aware, these products will remain the same with no significant changes other than normal product development.

Today's servers use many kinds of tools, including, as you have seen in previous days, Remote Access Services (RAS), network printing and file sharing, screen savers, sound players, and even telephony support. The Windows 2000 system is more powerful than ever, and it offers organizations the tools and services that they need in a fast-paced world.

Microsoft charges for these additional services, however, so you don't find them installed everywhere. Although Microsoft probably thinks that everyone needs these tools and products, to add them to the base price of the server drives that already expensive option even higher. (All right, all right. Perhaps it's not that expensive.) With tight integration and excellent services, the BackOffice product becomes a formidable addition to your business system arsenal.

BackOffice offers various products that have already been alluded to. The following brief review provides you with some idea of what those products are:

- Exchange Server—This product enables an organization to manage electronic mail across the network. Efficient and effective storage and management of mail mean more effective communications and increased ease of data transfer.

- Proxy Server—This product enables you to deliver Internet access to all the desktop machines in your organization in an easy, secure, and cost-effective manner.

- Site Server—A newer product for enhancing, deploying, and managing intranet sites on Windows 2000 Server and Internet Information Server.

- SNA Server—Many client/server networks still depend on the mainframe for legacy information and storage of large files and databases. Although TCP/IP is growing in popularity, the main connectivity option is using the IBM network topology called SNA (System Network Architecture).

- SQL Server—SQL Server is Microsoft's answer to the Oracle database product. The ease of use of large database systems provides an unparalleled opportunity to quickly gain access to important data. No longer must a user wait for some large "flat" file to sequence completely through its length before providing the answer to a *query*.

- Systems Management Server (SMS)—The Systems Management Server provides the capability to monitor, manipulate servers, and distribute client software. It is no longer necessary to sign on to every workstation to upgrade software or add a new application.

- Seagate Software Crystal Info—A reporting and analysis system that enables you to access, analyze, and distribute information from every BackOffice data source. Seagate Crystal Info offers the capability to perform ad hoc queries, to perform reporting and scheduling, and to analyze and schedule reports from a Web browser.

18

- Integrated, Single-Server Setup—Customize your server installation by selecting the setup that most closely matches your needs.
- Web-based Administration Tools—You can use most Web browsers to access management tasks on your BackOffice server, including common BackOffice services (user and group management, services management, and event logs), Windows 2000 services, and IIS services.
- Intranet Starter Site—A ready-to-use intranet site with sample Web-based applications.

Together, these tools provide the basis for the BackOffice family of tools. Working together, Windows 2000 Option Pack and BackOffice provide a more or less seamless interface for the user—one that is getting better each year.

Installing BackOffice

Microsoft recommends the following system requirements for BackOffice:

- Intel and compatible systems—Pentium 166 or higher
- 128MB of RAM
- 2GB of available hard-disk space
- CD-ROM drive
- Network adapter card
- VGA, Super VGA, or video graphics adapter compatible with Windows 2000 Server
- Microsoft Mouse or compatible pointing device

Be careful about using Microsoft's recommendations. They are just recommendations. Your needs depend greatly upon what you use your machine for and how busy it is. On Day 20, " Windows 2000 Performance Monitoring and Tuning," and Day 21, "Fine-Tuning and Troubleshooting Your Network," you will learn about performance tuning and how to find out the optimum settings for your environment.

Here's a look at how well these two products, Windows 2000 and BackOffice, integrate. Windows 2000 Server manages the overall network needs of the clients, offering network *protocol* support such as TCP/IP and NetBEUI or IPX. It provides the file and directory management for all the services that run, and it enables the clients to print their reports and share access to their files and databases.

Because the BackOffice products are integrated with Windows 2000 Server, they share Windows 2000's security and access control features and are managed through the Microsoft Management Console. This setup allows for less overhead and administration because user authentication and access control are performed in one place. Finally, most BackOffice products use similar tools for viewing events, managing users, and providing disk services. This consistency makes the learning curve for administrators a lot easier.

In the later sections of this day, you'll review some of the more common products and learn how to use them. In Task 18.1, you'll learn how to install the products.

Task 18.1: Installing BackOffice Products.

Step 1: Description

This task shows you how to install the various components of the BackOffice family. It describes a basic installation methodology for all the products instead of reiterating each installation. All the products install in a similar manner.

Step 2: Action

1. Log on to your system using an administrator account.
2. Insert your BackOffice CD-ROM.
3. Double-click the setup.exe file to start. (Setup might begin automatically if your CD-ROM has an autorun icon.)
4. Follow the instructions as they are presented. For each product, you are provided with choices pertaining to where the product is to reside, how much disk space is needed (SQL Server needs around 65MB–180MB, depending on which options you choose), and what name to register under.
5. Setup takes awhile, especially when you are installing all the products. Choose Reboot when you're finished because the products aren't available until after the system boots.

Step 3: Review

Setup of most Windows 2000 products is driven by simple installation steps with options that only you can answer. You can decide whether to install additional items, such as documentation or support for certain protocols, depending on your particular installation needs.

Using and Understanding MS Exchange Server

MS Exchange Server is a reincarnation of the old Microsoft Mail product. MS Mail, designed in earlier days, doesn't support the large number of users common in today's client/server environments. The new Exchange is designed to handle a large number of users and to use 32-bit processing more effectively.

MS Exchange provides various features for its users, including the following:

- Electronic mail between users
- File attachments
- The capability to talk to other mail packages
- The capability to set up special public folders for sharing information among all your users and also to set up Exchange as a Chat server.

Microsoft Exchange integrates well with Windows 2000 as long as you are running Active Directory. Exchange doesn't run with workgroups, so you may need to reinstall Windows 2000 if you aren't using a domain structure.

MS Exchange offers a robust and scalable electronic mail system. It does, however, utilize an impressive number of resources, and you need to be sure that the system you choose to run it on isn't already busy. Because the mail system is similar to the standard Microsoft Office products, a certain degree of familiarity is already designed into the system. This is helpful in diminishing your learning curve.

MS Exchange enables you to manage your mail by using a preprocessor called the *Inbox Assistant*. This assistant, which enables you to write certain rules for handling your mail, is a major benefit of the package. By assigning a rules-based scenario to your messages, you can delete, forward, move, and copy (among other things) any of the incoming messages that you receive. If you get loads of mail each day, using this tool enables you to get rid of the junk and manage the rest.

MS Exchange also integrates its security with Windows 2000. You manage your users for Windows 2000 and Mail all from one place, eliminating overhead and redundancy.

Implementing Exchange takes planning and organization; you can best handle the task by reviewing all the material before you start. You can find numerous white papers concerning this topic in the support section of Microsoft's Web page at `http://www.microsoft.com/exchange/default2.htm`.

You also can find various planning documents and tools in the Migrate directory of your CD-ROM. If you are using a test version of Windows 2000 Server throughout this book, read the documents before starting, and then do the implementation. You needn't be overly concerned because you will delete it all anyway. If you don't have this luxury, be careful because after the site, organization, and server names are designated, they cannot be changed without a reinstallation of the product.

You'll use the Microsoft Exchange Administrator to handle most of your tasks when dealing with Exchange. Although various other tools are also on the menu, these mostly deal with optimization and speed issues. Administrator performs the day-to-day tasks.

As was mentioned earlier, the install adds some items to your server menu under the name *Microsoft Exchange*. You can see that these additions are mostly concerned with managing the performance of the system. Does this mean it is a big issue and you need to be concerned? Perhaps. You certainly need to know that Exchange requires significant memory, depending on how large your user base is and how much it is used. These tools consist of the following items:

- MS Exchange Administrator
- MS Exchange Migration Wizard
- MS Exchange Optimizer
- MS Exchange Server Health
- MS Exchange Server History
- MS Exchange Server IMC Queues
- MS Exchange Server IMC Statistic
- MS Exchange Server IMC Traffic
- MS Exchange Server Load
- MS Exchange Server Queues
- MS Exchange Server Users
- MS Exchange Setup Editor

18

Exchange offers these tools to help you monitor and address the various components of the system, enabling you to customize how your system reacts. The documentation provided in the Books Online section that you can optionally install with the product offers a comprehensive overview of the product. It is important to consider the disk configuration of your Exchange Server machine. Also, be sure that adequate hardware is present before installing Exchange Server or any of the BackOffice products. You'll learn most of what you need to know by using these books.

After installing MS Exchange, you are offered the chance to run a program called the *Optimizer utility*. Running it right away offers the best chance of making sure that your system manages user access in the most efficient fashion. This program determines the best locations for its files and configures memory usage to best advantage, considering other programs and services that might be running alongside the mail program. Run the program every time your user accounts increase significantly or when you change your system configuration.

Task 18.2: Running MS Exchange Optimizer.

Step 1: Description

This task shows you how to use the Optimizer program included with MS Exchange. Run the program whenever changes are made to the system.

Step 2: Action

1. Log on to your system using an administrator account.

2. Start the program using Start, Microsoft Exchange, Microsoft Exchange Optimizer. (If you are still installing Exchange, run the program by selecting Run Optimizer on the Setup box that is shown.)

3. Specify the number of users, the type of server, and the expected total number of persons in your organization by using the boxes shown. Use the Limit Memory Usage box when other services are in use, and specify the RAM to be used by Exchange. You need 64MB for Exchange to run effectively, but once again, more is better! If you don't limit the memory usage, Exchange uses it all, degrading other services that might be running. Click Next to continue.

4. The program suggests the best locations for its files and enables you to modify those locations in the panel that appears next. Unless you need to move the files, leave them where they are installed.

5. If Optimizer recommends moving files, consider the action and be sure that the files are backed up before allowing any movement to occur. Click Finish to complete the job and restart Exchange.

Step 3: Review

Because MS Exchange consumes resources, it is prudent to run this Optimizer program regularly to maximize the way that it manages the system resources. Running Optimizer each time your system resources change is an effective method of ensuring that MS Exchange runs efficiently.

After your server program is running, you need to update the client workstations to enable them to use Exchange. Installation is necessary regardless of whether your clients are running Messaging or other client mail *packages*. Installation of the client updates drivers and access to the public folders in Exchange and sets up the machine to use the new features of Exchange Server. You can find the software for this on the Exchange Clients CD-ROM.

After your installation of MS Exchange is completed, you'll find that Active Directory Users and Computers provides you with a new choice called *Exchange* when you're adding users. This is integration at its best.

Finally, use the Administrator utility to add new mailboxes and set the properties of all the Exchange Objects. This utility provides for distribution list management and user management. You'll find that it becomes an important aspect of your daily administration of Exchange.

In this brief section, you learned a small piece of the Exchange story. Entire books are available on this topic. Although there is limited space here, we hope that you've learned enough to install and begin to learn the product and that you'll continue your learning through experience and more product-specific books.

Using SQL Server

New Term SQL Server provides you with a comprehensive relational database management system server. Along with Oracle and DB2, SQL Server adds to the already popular use of relational databases. The acronym *SQL* comes from *Structured Query Language*, a programming language used for maintaining and managing database information.

A relational database consists of tables containing your information. One of the main roles of a relational database is to enable you to manipulate these tables to provide you with access control and a link between each table so that data can be compared and updated.

New Term The SQL Server product adheres to industry standards, using *American National Standards Institute* (*ANSI*) SQL support, while adding to these standards with such things as declarative referential integrity and server cursor support.

To run SQL Server, you need an Alpha AXP processor, an Intel x86 or Pentium, or a MIPS machine. As with all Windows 2000 products, it is best to refer to the Hardware Compatibility List to be certain that your machine is supported. Microsoft recommends a minimum of 64MB of memory. You might need more, depending on the use of the system. As with most Windows 2000 software, more is better.

Like Microsoft Exchange, Microsoft recommends that you don't run this product on a controller due to the overhead of these services.

When SQL Server is installed, you are provided with various programs. Each of the services provides an aspect of your database management system. In the following list, you see a brief overview of each service and learn a little about which ones you'll use the most:

- ISQL_w—Interactive Structured Query Language for Windows. A graphical utility for querying the SQL database, analyzing plan executions, and viewing statistics.

18

- Microsoft ODBC (Open Data Base Connectivity) SQL Server Driver—A Help file for providing information on SQL Server.

- Readme.txt—A standard readme file providing additional information about installing or upgrading the SQL Server.

- SQL Client Configuration Utility—A utility that enables you to modify the settings pertaining to SQL Server Client; it provides settings for a default network, and several advanced options.

- SQL Distributed Management Objects—A Help file providing detailed information on what these objects are and providing data such as the properties of each object and how to use them.

- SQL Enterprise Manager—One of the major administrative tools for managing SQL Server. It enables you to manage job scheduling, logons, and database management services.

- SQL Performance Monitor—A tool that enables you to monitor server activity and performance, including the number of connections, page writes, and command batches executed.

- SQL Security Manager—The tool for integrating server security with Windows 2000. You choose whether a user must have separate accounts and passwords or if he can use his Windows 2000 account and password—or some mix of the two. It also manages all the grants and recalls that provide database security.

- SQL Server Books Online—A comprehensive library of information on running and managing the product.

- SQL Service Manager—A utility that enables you to start and stop the services associated with running a relational database.

- SQL Setup—The program install routine. Enables you to modify or add selected options.

- SQL Transfer Manager—A utility that enables you to transfer objects and data from one database server to another.

One of the most helpful aspects of SQL Server is the Books Online documentation. If you are unsure of how to use and manage a database, this is a good place to start. During the database setup, you are offered an opportunity to place this documentation on your hard drive or use the CD-ROM. If space is at a premium, you can run directly from the CD-ROM.

Books Online is quite extensive in its offerings and provides a great place to start if you are at all unsure.

> **Caution** SQL Server isn't an easy tool to set up and configure. Anyone setting it up needs to thoroughly read all documentation concerning setup and configuration *before* attempting the install; otherwise, it won't run correctly, if it runs at all.

Starting SQL Server on your system requires you to begin with the SQL Service Manager icon. Start the service by selecting the one you need in the dialog box (the default is MSSQLServer) and double-clicking on the Start/Continue option. This first option starts the databases themselves, allowing interaction to begin. The other option, SQLExecutive, enables you to schedule server tasks. Start it by selecting it and double-clicking on the Start/Continue option as before.

Close the dialog box when you're finished, or leave it minimized on your desktop. You can select the particular server you want if you have more than one SQL Server running. The database services are now available for you.

Next, you might want to control the database configuration, and for this you need SQL Server Enterprise Manager. After starting the service, you need to register your server.

A dialog box appears for you to perform this task. Type the name of the server to which you are connecting, and add your user account and password, making sure that you are authorized for access. By configuring the option in Security Manager, you can set up the database to allow trusted communications so that you don't need to sign in each time.

Type the default user account name of **sa** where you see Login ID, and click Register. SQL Server automatically supplies this default account for you with no password. At some point, you need to supply a password to protect your database. After processing stops, click the Close button to continue.

Open each branch as you open any Windows object, by clicking on the small plus sign next to the object. By double-clicking on the object, you obtain an editing dialog box that enables you to modify the selected object.

In the dialog box, you see three tabs: Options, Database, and Permissions. Each of these offers specific fields that you can modify. In the example, you can see the current permissions that apply. A small icon representing a stoplight indicates the selected server. On your server, you see a green color when the server is running. Red and yellow colors indicate a stopped or paused server, respectively.

The expandable menu provides a simple method for managing the server, and as you play with it, you see that it is easy to work with and offers all the flexibility that you need.

18

As mentioned earlier, you can change the password for access to the server. You can do so through this window or through the Security Manager. Double-click on the user account you want, and a menu that enables you to modify the account is provided.

You'll learn how to add a new user to SQL Server in Task 18.3.

Task 18.3: Adding a New User to a SQL Server Database.

Step 1: Description

This task shows you how to add users to specific databases using the SQL Enterprise Manager utility.

Step 2: Action

1. Be sure that SQL Server is running by starting the database services using SQL Service Manager.

2. Start SQL Server Enterprise Manager.

3. Sign on to the server using the sa account or an administrator account that you have already created.

4. Select Manage, Logins.

5. Type an account name and password. You can change the language by selecting the Default Language menu. When you add an account name, the Add button lights up.

6. Select the database objects that the user is allowed to access by clicking on the Permit field next to the ones you want. In the earlier example, a few default testing databases were selected.

7. Click the Add button when you are ready. You are asked to confirm the password, and the user is added. The Add button becomes the Modify button, enabling you to change the new user if you want. The dialog box doesn't go away, however, because it thinks you have more accounts to add.

8. Note that you can also select a particular database from the object branch and then select the Manage and Users options. This provides access to only that database because no others are selected. Adding a user here does the same as adding one with the Logins option and specifying the database. For purposes of this task, Logins was chosen because of its greater flexibility. Click the Close box to finish.

Step 3: Review

This simple task shows you how easy it is to set up new users and access permissions on your database server.

Using the Security Manager, you can decide whether access is controlled through Windows 2000 sign on or through a separate user account within SQL Server. By default, all Windows 2000 administrators are provided with the system administrator privilege in SQL Server.

One other tool that you use consists of the utility that actually enables you to change and work with the data in your database. When you open the ISQL_w dialog box, you are shown four major tabs:

- Query
- Results
- Statistics I/O
- Showplan

Using this utility, you run queries against your database and view the results. Those of you who are familiar with SQL queries can use this utility. It enables you to create and run scripts on-the-fly.

Many organizations use additional products to manage queries, such as the Microsoft Query GUI-based tool. By playing with the options, you can learn how to form simple queries and obtain information. To perform a query, simply type the commands in the Query window, and then click the green forward arrow, or select Query, Execute.

Your results are automatically shown in the Results window. Use the extensive Help menu to get more information or to buy one of the many books on the SQL Query language.

Finally, you might need to manage your system's performance when running SQL Server. To do so, it is necessary to know how the system is performing; this is where Performance Monitor is helpful. You can see an example of the program in Figure 18.1.

18

FIGURE 18.1

Using Performance Monitor.

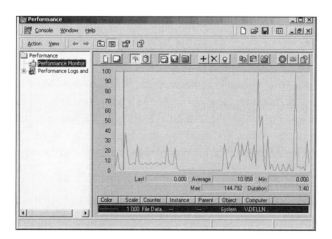

Using this tool is similar to using the Windows 2000 Performance Monitor that is described on Day 21. You can read about the details when you reach that day.

Using a complex database such as SQL Server is beyond the scope of this book. You have learned some of the simple aspects, but you might need to attend database training classes or read some of the books available to really get a handle on the power of this product. One good book to consider is *Microsoft BackOffice Administrator's Survival Guide*, from Sams Publishing.

Systems Management Server

The Systems Management Server product is probably destined to become far more popular than it currently is because it addresses a common administration nightmare: software maintenance across a large network.

In the networks of today, managing all the resources becomes difficult. Whereas once we made do with huge machines and dumb terminals, we now have many smaller (and often just as large) servers with thousands of not-so-dumb machines. User access formerly came through terminals with no software concerns, but now terminals are usually thought of as workstations—and they carry all the overhead of a small mainframe.

The SMS program provides various aids to help us manage these increasingly complex networks:

- The capability to distribute software over the network, helping ease the problem of updating hundreds or thousands of computers
- The capability to gather a hardware and software inventory, enabling you to better manage your resources
- A Help Desk to gain control of an end-user machine for support and troubleshooting
- The capability to control application license usage to ensure that you stay within your license agreements

Like all the other products in BackOffice, SMS provides tools and utilities for the purpose of performing all these tasks. The key here is centralized management of your far-flung computing resources. Using the tools in SMS, you gain a new level of control over these resources. When you open the main menu, called System Management Support, you see a list of items. The list contains the following utilities:

- SMS Administrator—The primary administration tool.
- SMS Books Online—The Help file option that provides you with an extensive amount of detail on using SMS. Nowadays, you get this file rather than printed documentation.

- SMS Frequently Asked Questions—A list of common questions. These are popular in Internet newsgroups, and they enable beginners to make sure that a question they have has not already been answered.
- SMS Help—The more normal Help Facility.
- SMS MIF Form Generator—A Management Information Format forms generator to help design reports.
- SMS Release Notes—The latest information about the product that is usually not reflected in the manuals and other documentation.
- SMS Security Manager—The utility for providing access control and user account management.
- SMS Service Manager—The utility that enables you to start and stop the various services run by SMS.
- SMS Setup—The setup program that enables you to modify your existing setup decisions.

You probably already see a similarity between these offerings and those outlined earlier, in the section on SQL Server. This is all part of the BackOffice concept. After you know one product, you can more easily learn the others. It appears that most of the Microsoft product line is heading in this direction of shared GUI interfaces and utilities.

To run SMS on your server requires a minimum of 28MB of RAM, and that is before you run any other services. As usual, consider increasing memory to better take advantage of this—and all other—Windows 2000 applications. Do you ever wonder whether Microsoft owns part of Intel or other machine manufacturers? It sometimes appears that way when you see the need for memory increasing all the time, but that's just the price you pay for today's applications.

In addition to the memory that you need, you must run a SQL database for SMS to use as its repository. Installing SMS requires about 100MB of disk space, which must reside on an NTFS partition. SMS doesn't install on a FAT-based partition.

> **Caution**
>
> Microsoft recommends that you don't store SMS on a compressed drive because performance suffers. SMS also must be installed on an NTFS partition.

 To install SMS, you must first design a site hierarchy to establish how SMS sees your network. Next, you build and configure sites. A *site* is a logical collection of domains that are built in to an administrative unit and use a central site server for management. Using SMS requires a Site Server, the SQL Server, and the Site Domain Server.

A well-designed topology is essential for managing SMS properly and effectively. SMS uses the site concept to distinguish different geographical areas, such as Toronto or New York. Create a Primary site by establishing an SMS Server in that location. This server is then responsible for maintaining all the information from that site. Any site that doesn't have a SQL Server is a secondary site and is managed by one of the primary sites on the network. Finally, create one of the SMS servers as the Central Site for managing all the others.

Designing all this with proper consideration of bandwidth and server capacities is essential. After SMS has been established, it provides for the central collection of all the data from each site, enabling you to quickly gather and report on your inventory information.

SMS servers use a service called a *sender* to communicate with one another. You can use a LAN, RAS, or SNA sender, depending on your network needs. As indicated by their names, you use the LAN Sender if your servers are on either Ethernet or Token Ring LANs; use SNA when you connect to an IBM mainframe. The RAS Sender allows for connectivity through a modem, X.25, or ISDN connection. Due to its popularity, many sites use the X.25 connection for international connectivity.

Setting up the SMS Server isn't as easy as setting up Exchange or SQL Server. It requires up-front thought and planning. It is strongly suggested that you read the Online Books thoroughly before attempting the initial setup.

The main tool in this package is the SMS Administrator utility. Like most other Office products, it provides a GUI-based view of the maintenance functions that are available.

Task 18.4: Logging on to the SMS Administrator.

Step 1: Description

This task shows you how to log on to the Administrator tool and to use the features it offers.

Step 2: Action

1. Start by selecting Start, Programs, System Management Server, SMS Administrator.

2. SMS displays the Administration Login box. Choose the server and the SQL database if necessary, and type the SQL Server administrator account name to sign in. Click OK to continue.

3. You see an Open SMS Administrator dialog box. This might not have appeared if you previously selected and cleared the Show This Dialog Box option.

▼ 4. Select the window Type that you want to use. You see a brief description of each window you select. Take a few moments and review this information to familiarize yourself with the function of each. Click OK when you are ready to continue. Following is a list of each window that is shown:

Sites	Displays all the sites in your SMS environment
Jobs	Enables you to create and administer jobs
Packages	Manages all the software that SMS inventories or installs
Alerts	Manages the alerts that you enable to inform you of system events
Machine Groups	Provides the capability to put servers and workstations into groups for easier administration
Site Groups	Provides for groups of sites
Program Groups	Allows for control of shared SMS programs
Events	Allows for system monitoring of your server

   5. After choosing a window, follow the specific needs of that window.

▲ 6. Click the Close button when you finish with SMS Administrator.

Step 3: Review

This simple task shows you how easy it is to use the SMS Administrator tool and manage your various SMS sites.

In each of the previously outlined windows, double-clicking on a selected item brings you choices that are particular to the window that you choose. In sites, you see the properties of the selected site and gain detailed information about it. The Packages window shows you the elements necessary for software distribution. You create packages containing the files, configuration information, and identification data that you need for the job, and then install them where needed.

Three packages are available. The Workstation package provides support for your workstations. Sharing packages enable you to set up data on a network file server for distribution, and Inventory packages define the rules that SMS uses to identify and inventory workstations. After you create a package, use the Jobs window to set it up to be delivered and run.

SMS includes a version of Crystal Reports, which produces professional reports using the SMS data that it collects about your systems. You can find it on the CD-ROM in the

Reports directory. Included are several preformatted reports that you use as a template. Support is provided by the Crystal Reports technical staff.

In Remote Control, you are furnished with various useful tools. These include support for Windows 95 or 98 clients and remote chat. This product allows your Help Desk to communicate with a remote user via typed text messages that are displayed at the recipient's machine. This method can sometimes be easier to use than other communication methods. For example, when the Help Desk operator is telling a client what to type, he can show the command instead of relying on voice communication.

SMS also supports the use of the `ping` command. The administrator can `ping` the client machine to determine whether it can talk on the network.

The SMS package holds great promise for managing the resources of large corporations and for helping to reduce the cost of this management. Organizations spend considerable time and effort upgrading and maintaining desktop computing resources. Budget restrictions and staff reductions pose new challenges for this aspect of system management and control.

Using the Remote Troubleshooting help desk functions of SMS provides an opportunity for increasing assistance to users while minimizing the associated costs.

The hardware and software inventory controls offer unprecedented opportunities for cost control, compliance checking to corporate standards, and, most importantly, reduction of the overhead involved in performing all these tasks.

Another cost-saving aspect involves using SMS for software distribution. Some of our clients recently performed complete desktop refreshes to install new, consistent software on all their workstations. The task took more than one year to perform and involved on-site visits across the organization.

Using SMS solves many issues of cost control, inventory management, and staff reductions; therefore, it offers organizations a fairly solid level of Enterprise Management. Look for more and more firms to begin using this and similar products. Like most of the BackOffice tools, this one offers incredible complexity, and we recommend that you purchase a book directly related to only SMS and learn from there.

Microsoft Proxy Server

Proxy Server helps prevent unauthorized Internet users from connecting to your organization's private network by integrating tightly with your Windows 2000 Server user authentication. This enables your system administrator to control who uses the Internet and which services they use. By implementing this product, you are installing a firewall between your network and the Internet.

You can deliver high-performance Internet access to the desktop by using Proxy Server. By sharing a single, secure gateway, the product eliminates the need to share one dedicated machine for the Internet among multiple users or to run multiple Internet lines into the organization to provide each desktop with a separate connection. This technique helps keep costs down and simplifies Internet administration.

Microsoft Proxy Server acts as a gateway and provides security between your Local Area Network (LAN) and the Internet. It can also be used with Windows 2000's Routing and Remote Access Service to provide secure Virtual Private Networks (VPN).

Proxy Server provides the following features:

- Dynamic packet filtering—Inbound and outbound filtering
- Multi-layered services—Application and circuit layer security
- Packet event alerting and logging—Email and EventLog alerts
- Shielding of internal network addresses—Network Address Translation (NAT) of IP and IPX addresses
- Reverse proxy, server proxying, and virtual hosting—Shielding of Internet server applications
- Active, passive, and distributed caching—Web performance enhancement

Proxy Server dynamically determines which packets it will allow through to your network's circuit and application-layer proxy services. It doesn't require manually predefined and permanently opened application ports because it will open ports automatically only as needed and then close the port when communication ends.

The WinSock proxy and the newer SOCKS proxy services provide application-transparent circuit gateways. This allows access to Telnet, RealAudio, NetShow server, and other Internet services if desired. Proxy Server uses Network Address Translation to act on behalf of your client PC and interact with the Internet resource. In this way, your network topology and IP or IPX addresses are never revealed to the outside network.

Alerting thresholds and other variables provide real-time monitoring by ensuring that messages are sent to your administrators whenever something critical happens.

By using the Reverse proxy feature, you can place your Web server behind Proxy Server. This lets you provide a Web site without compromising the security of the Web server or its data. Proxy Server will "impersonate" your real Web server to the outside world. Reverse hosting allows several Web servers to sit behind Proxy Server and publish to the Internet, providing flexibility, as well as security. These additional Web servers can publish independently or appear as directories in a single, large virtual Web server.

18

With Server proxying, Proxy Server can listen for inbound packets that are destined to a server that is connected behind the Proxy Server computer. It will then forward the incoming requests to that machine. This can allow incoming mail to be directed to your Microsoft Exchange Server computer, for example.

No service is complete without logging and Proxy Server logs to specific log files or to ODBC databases. Logging is fairly extensive and includes alert information and login and access control activity.

Proxy Server also permits SSL tunneling, which provides an encrypted path between the client and remote server. This feature is useful for secure Internet transactions and other applications. You have undoubtedly used this as you browse the Internet or buy stuff from the various vendors out there in cyber-land. (Good grief, did I really use that term?)

To use Proxy Server 2.0, you must install Windows 2000 Server and Microsoft Internet Information Server. You need an update to Proxy Server 2.0 in order to run it on W2K.

To install Microsoft Proxy Server 2.0 on your W2K system, do the following:

- Close any Microsoft Management Consoles that may be running.
- Download the Microsoft Proxy Server 2.0 Update Wizard for Microsoft Windows 2000. You can either save the file to disk or choose to run it immediately. If you are using a x86 platform, obtain the download from `http://download.microsoft.com/download/proxy20/SP/1/NT5/EN-US/msp2wizi.exe`.
- Run the Installation Wizard and follow the instructions provided. You'll need the Proxy Server CD-ROM to complete the install.

During the install process, you see a screen like that shown in Figure 18.2.

You can leave the default values in place. The next screen asks whether you want to enable the security options. Leave these options set as you see in Figure 18.3.

After you have installed Proxy Server, it appears in your menu under Start, Programs, Microsoft Proxy Server.

When Proxy Server is running, you can use a myriad of techniques to lock down access to your internal network. When you start up Proxy Server and then double-click on Internet Information Services, you'll see a screen similar to that shown in Figure 18.4.

FIGURE 18.2

Installing Proxy Server.

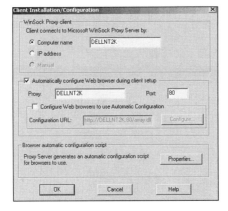

FIGURE 18.3

Enabling security options in Proxy Server.

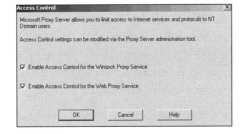

18

FIGURE 18.4

MMC with Proxy Server.

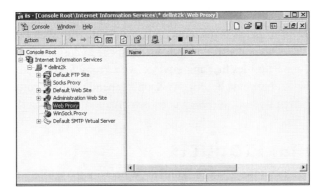

By selecting Socks, Web, or Winsock Proxy and right-clicking, you'll be presented with a dialog box that allows you to set up and manage the security options available in the product. You can see an example of the Socks Proxy in Figure 18.5.

FIGURE 18.5

The properties dialog box.

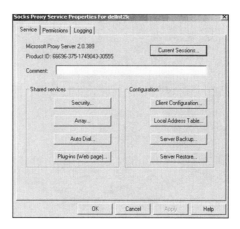

Under the Service Tab, the Current Services option shows you who is currently connected to your machine. Under Shared Services, the Security option lets you choose who can access the machine, using packet and domain name filtering. It also lets you set up your logs and alerts. The Configuration options let you set up your internal network addresses, server backups and restores, and client configuration options.

The Permissions Tab is where you can specify the addresses that are permitted or denied access. Finally, the Logging tab shows all the options you have for storing your log files and taking action when the log files are full.

Each of the proxies has its own dialog box options, with Web Proxy having the most tabs to review. This book doesn't provide us the space to completely review this product, but if you use the help files that are provided with Proxy Server and take your time, you can set it up without too much difficulty. Don't depend on it to protect your production network, however, without spending considerably more time than this section offers.

Additional Products

You learned about the basic BackOffice products in the earlier sections. Here you'll learn a little about some of the more commercially oriented products that have been added to BackOffice. For more detailed information on these highly specialized tools, it is recommended that you visit the Microsoft Web site at `http://www.microsoft.com/backoffice` or `http://backoffice.microsoft.com`.

Site Server

This product enables small organizations to build stores and sell products over the Internet. It offers templates of store designs and order-acceptance tools that you can adapt to your own business needs. There is built-in order management that handles inventory, tax, shipping and payment processing, and so forth. It includes a security component that helps ensure that processing orders and getting customer credit information are handled safely and reliably. It uses a secure payment support method called *Verifone vPOS*, an Internet-based, payment-processing software solution.

To run Site Server, you need

- Pentium 100 or larger (166 recommended)
- 64MB of RAM (128MB recommended)
- 1GB hard drive space
- Internet Explorer 4.01
- CD-ROM, VGA or better video, Network Adapter card, and mouse

Vendors might purchase and use this product to begin an Internet-based store and offer goods and services online.

Site Server Commerce Edition

This product is the more enhanced version for commercial users. It includes a comprehensive set of features, sample sites, and tools that enable you to transact business online. Some of the features include

- Site Builder Wizard and Sample Sites that remove the complexity of building your site. The simple, step-by-step approach of the Site Builder Wizard easily reduces the development time and lets you get your site up and running quickly and easily. The product provides a number of sample sites for business-to-consumer and business-to-business applications.

- The Dynamic merchandising feature allows for simple, real-time administration of your products and price promotions from any remote Web browser. An additional feature called *Intelligent CrossSell* uses previous shopper trends to automatically make recommendations for the consumer.

- The Order Processing Pipeline handles product tax, shipping and handling charges, payment authorizations, and inventory checks according to rules that you specify when you set it up. You can integrate it with your existing business systems.

- You can use Dynamic catalog generation to create custom Web catalog pages that change according to the perceived needs of your customers as they visit your site.

- Microsoft Wallet support provides a way for customers to supply credit card information by inputting the information when in their browser's Wallet and then using that information when they want to pay for something while online at your site.

- Naturally, you should use the Industry-standard security that allows for HTTP Authentication and Windows Challenge Response, SSL, and Secure Electronic Transaction (SET).

To run Site Server Commerce, you need

- Pentium 100 or larger (166 recommended)
- 64MB of RAM (128MB recommended)
- 1GB hard drive space
- Internet Explorer 4.01
- CD-ROM, VGA or better video, Network Adapter card, and mouse

Vendors might purchase and use this product to begin an Internet-based store and offer goods and services online.

SNA Server

To understand the acronym *SNA*, you either have a need to connect to IBM big iron or to be one of those lucky souls who have to manage a network containing both mainframes and client/server machines.

On the other hand, you might be one of those older folks like me who actually lived through the golden age of mainframes, before the golden age of client/servers.

NEW TERM   *SNA*, or *System Network Architecture*, is IBM's protocol for connecting networks. It is definitely an older architecture, but it is still the de facto protocol for all the "big iron" in use today—although this is beginning to change, with TCP/IP services becoming more widely used on mainframes. So you might need to live with and learn to understand this architecture if an IBM mainframe is in your organization and you are going to connect to it.

Microsoft's SNA Server is one answer to the problem of connecting these disparate networks. It seeks to provide a simple (as simple as mainframe connectivity can be, that is) solution for allowing you to talk to both your NT machines and your mainframes.

Connecting to SNA networks involves attaching to the particular wiring scheme and managing access in products, such as VTAM and Netview, that support this complex network.

Using SNA Server and its components allows an organization to fully integrate applications regardless of whether they are mainframe or client/server based. For instance, the Shared Folders Gateway feature allows users to access AS/400 shared folders and their associated files as if they were on a local drive of your Windows 2000 Server. This allows you to apply the same Windows NT security permissions and access rights to these shared folders as with any other file.

The new ODBC Driver for DB2 allows your users to access DB2 data on a mainframe. You can develop new business applications that use live DB2 data and bring that data directly to the end users desktops.

The VSAM File Transfer facility allows copying of legacy mainframe files to Windows 2000 Server. This utility allows users to transfer VSAM files to their Windows 2000 Server using a simple command-line interface. As you can see from this brief description, the SNA Server product allows a broad range of services that integrate your Windows 2000 machines with all those mainframes in a fairly painless way.

One other solution is to connect each machine by using terminal emulation cards and the software to run the cards. Each machine then uses both a LAN access and a terminal emulation card and cable for mainframe access. This method provides for duplication of the components; it isn't always the most cost-effective method.

Finally, IBM provides support for TCP/IP within its large mainframes, so this is likely the route to go. Newer versions of IBM's operating system even offer complete UNIX compatibility (OpenEdition, for instance). IBM's and Microsoft's initiatives serve only to enhance the prospect of easier connectivity between IBM's mainframes and Windows 2000 Server.

Using an SNA network involves various critical network functions and is beyond the scope of this book. Here you learned that connectivity is possible and that, with the assistance of your mainframe experts, you can connect your Windows 2000 Server to the mainframe by using SNA Server.

The last word on BackOffice is that it comes in two additional flavors. One, the Back-Office Small Business Server, provides businesses with the essential tools to share information and connect with business partners and customers. This product is designed for business with 50 or fewer PCs. The other, the BackOffice Server, provides a commercial-grade server. Both these products are anticipated to include Windows 2000 instead of NT 4.0 as their base operating system shortly after Microsoft releases Windows 2000 for general use.

Summary

You learned the products that compose BackOffice and how to use them on your server. In addition, you learned how to install the products and manage their use. Finally, you became familiar with the different products and realized their particular benefits.

In this day you discovered the following points:

- What BackOffice is and what the various components are
- How to install the different components of BackOffice
- How SQL Server provides database management
- Whether SMS needs an NTFS partition or can use a FAT-based system
- What SMS Server does and why it is useful
- The memory requirements of Microsoft Exchange and the benefits of Microsoft Exchange
- How to use SNA Server to connect to IBM mainframe computers and their specific network topology
- That there are several additional BackOffice products designed to enhance your ability to do business over the Internet

Workshop

To wrap up the day, you can review tasks from the day and see the answers to some commonly asked questions.

Task List

The information provided in this day shows you how to manage the files and folders within a Windows 2000 server. You learned to perform the following tasks:

- Install BackOffice products.
- Run the Microsoft Exchange Optimizer program.
- Add a new user to a SQL Server database.
- Log in to the SMS Administrator.

Q&A

Q Do the BackOffice products come as part of the Windows 2000 Server software?

A No. Although the Internet Information Server and FrontPage program are being combined with Windows 2000 Server 4, Microsoft sells the BackOffice products as a separate entity. This is becoming a lucrative market for Microsoft as interest in using the new electronic mail Exchange Server and the SMS distribution components grows. You can expect Microsoft to update BackOffice to Windows 2000 from NT 4.0 soon after the Windows 2000 becomes generally available.

Q What products come with BackOffice, and can I buy them separately?

A BackOffice has four major components. They consist of Microsoft Exchange, an electronic mail server; SQL Server, a relational database management system; System Management Server, or SMS, which provides for both distribution of software from a central site and inventory management; and finally, SNA Server, which allows your network to talk with IBM mainframes on their System Network Architecture network. Microsoft doesn't offer these products for sale individually. They wouldn't be a suite then, right? Note that Windows 2000 is currently included in the BackOffice bundle, so technically you can say it is part of BackOffice. But the intent is to show the additional components, not Windows 2000 Server, in this day. You will also find that several other components have been added to the original BackOffice offering. These include Microsoft Merchant Server, Microsoft Site Server Commerce, Microsoft Proxy, and Microsoft Transaction Server. The BackOffice suite is changing rapidly with new products being added regularly. Visit the Microsoft Web page to get the most recent information.

Q My organization uses mainframes and IBM AS/400 machines. Can I connect my network to these machines?

A Microsoft provides a tool called the *SNA Server* for connecting SNA-based networks with your local area or wide area network. Doing so, however, is an arduous task that must be considered carefully because, typically, mainframes are still the primary mission-critical systems and they cannot afford network problems. Be sure to talk with your mainframe folks before attempting to set up and run this service.

18

WEEK 3

DAY 19

Understanding and Using the Microsoft Option Pack

With Windows NT, Microsoft introduced a set of tools called the *Option Pack*. The Option Pack delivers a set of new Web and application services that enable you to develop a complex and interesting Web site. To date, Microsoft has offered these programs free, and you can add them using the Windows Components Wizard. Because Microsoft will offer these as options in the future, we will refer to these components collectively as the *Option Pack*. Today, you will learn all about

- Where you can find the Options Pack
- Setting up and running IIS version 4
- Using the various components found in the Option Pack

These tools change on a regular—and frequent—basis, so this day provides an overview of each service rather than explicit details. This serves as an introduction and sampling of what is available to you.

What Is the Option Pack?

Microsoft bundled a series of tools that is offered for free if you want to download it from Microsoft's Web site. Alternatively, you can order the software on CD for a small fee if it didn't ship with your copy of Windows 2000.

The Option Pack is designed to provide everyone from a small business to a large company workgroup or an Internet service provider (ISP) with the tools that are needed to provide Web-based business solutions. The stated intent is to enable you to set up and deliver content faster and easier than with prior solutions and to reduce your costs as you do so. Whether this is fact or reality, of course, is for you to decide.

The primary components in the Option Pack consist of

- Certificate Services
- Internet Information Services
- Management and Monitoring Tools
- Message Queuing Services
- Microsoft Indexing Service
- Script Debugger
- Networking Services
- Other Network File and Print Services
- Remote Installation Services
- Remote Storage
- Terminal Services
- Terminal Services Licensing

Table 19.1 describes the optional components. Today, you will review these various components in a variety of detail.

As with most software these days, you can install different pieces of the Option Pack, configuring your machine as you see fit.

You must evaluate your hardware requirements. Your hardware needs do depend on what you are using the different options for and whether you are running more than one of the options on a single server. Your needs also depend on how extensively options are to be used. As with any application, a bigger, faster machine is always better for any serious work.

TABLE 19.1 Windows Optional Components

Component	Description
Certificate Services	This component installs a certification authority (CA). With CS, you can create or request X.509 certificates for authentication. As you learned previously, certificates provide a method for the verification of users' identities over non-secure networks, such as the Internet. In addition, the service provides a method for securing communications.
Internet Information Services (IIS)	This component includes WWW, FTP, NNTP, FrontPage, transaction, and ASP support. It also includes Internet Security Manager for managing IIS components.
Management and Monitoring Tools	This component includes tools for network monitoring and Simple Network Management Protocol (SNMP).
Message Queuing Services	This component includes Microsoft Message Queuing (MSMQ) Routing Server or Client. MSMQ provides developers with an asynchronous programming model and built-in support for Microsoft Transaction Server (MTS) transactions.
Microsoft Indexing Service	This component enables full-text searches of data stored on a computer or the network.
Microsoft Script Debugger	This component installs a tool for client and server-side debugging of ActiveX engines, such as VBScript and Jscript.
Networking Services	This component includes the Domain Name System (DNS), Dynamic Host Configuration Protocol (DHCP), simple TCP/IP services, Site Server LDAP Services, Windows Internet Name Service (WINS), and other networking services.
Other Network File and Print Services	This component shares files with Macintosh clients and shares printers with Macintosh and UNIX clients.
Remote Installation Services	This component provides you with the capability to remotely install the client Windows 2000 Professional.
Remote Storage	This component provides a set of services and tools to help you store data from infrequently used files on magnetic tape.
Terminal Services	This component includes services and tools that allow you to host Windows-based terminals and Microsoft Windows NT Server Terminal Server Edition client computers.
Terminal Services Licensing	This component provides a licensing server for Terminal Services.

19

Consider whether you want to run these services on the same machine. Generally, you would not run the WINS service on the same system that you run IIS or Terminal Services.

Because most of the people who will read this book probably use Microsoft's Internet Information Server, a considerable amount of this day is spent discussing that component. There are many other good aspects of the Option Pack; an entire book can be written on the subject. This is a Windows 2000 book, however, so we need to restrict the information that is provided here. It is recommended that you research other Sams books for any additional details that you might desire.

Some Pre-installation Tasks for IIS

Internet Information Server 4 requires at least Windows NT Server 4. You need to be sure that you properly configured the TCP/IP installation on your Windows 2000 Server for the Internet services. One way to check whether you configured TCP/IP correctly is to PING yourself at 127.0.0.1.

You can run multiple Internet servers on your Windows 2000 Server (such as www.pdaconsulting.com and www.sales.pdaconsulting.com). The sites can share two of their three main characteristics: domain or host header name, IP address, and port. One of these must be set differently to differentiate the site.

Note   In general, a single IIS installation can support up to five virtual servers. Using more than five, however, requires you to jump through hoops and delve into the depths of your IIS documentation.

Before installing the Internet Information Server software, you need to already have the following items:

- Software—Microsoft Internet Information Server 4 software.
- Network Connection—To allow your organization to access the server through a Web browser, both the server and the client machines need to install TCP/IP.

During the installation, you need to enter the Internet information from the following list, so you need to obtain this information in advance from your Internet service provider (ISP):

- The numeric IP address for your Windows NT Server. (If you don't have an Internet connection, obtain this address from your ISP.)

- The computer name (the name chosen by whoever performed your installation) of your Windows NT Server (also called the *Web server* in this day).
- The email address of the Web server administrator (used to support the users who access information on the server).
- The numeric IP address for your DNS server (also available from your ISP).

If you're setting up Internet Information Server for internal publishing (on your intranet), you might want to install the Microsoft Windows Internet Name Service (WINS). This step is optional, especially for a smaller system, but this way, users can employ friendly names instead of IP addresses when connecting to your server from your internal network. Of course, you can also accomplish this using Microsoft DNS Server. Unless you have downlevel systems, you should use DNS for address resolution.

Installing Windows Components

After you determine what services you want to install, you are ready to add them.

Task 19.1: Installing Windows Components Using the Wizard.

Step 1: Description

To install Windows Components, such as WINS, DHCP and IIS, perform the following task.

Step 2: Action

1. Make sure that you are logged on to your server as Administrator.
2. To install these programs, select Start, Settings, Control Panel, and then open Add/Remove Programs. From the panel, click on Add/Remove Windows Components. You should then see Figure 19.1. Click Next.

19

FIGURE 19.1

The Windows Components Wizard.

▼

▼ 3. From the Windows Components panel shown in Figure 19.2, check the components you want to install on this computer.

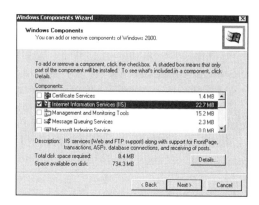

4. Highlight IIS after you check it, and click Details. You should see the window in Figure 19.3.

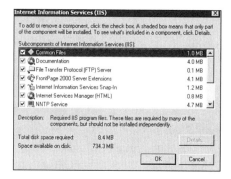

5. Check all the subcomponents you want to install. Click OK.

6. Click Next.

7. You may install components that require more information, such as Certificate Services.

▲ 8. Click Finish.

Step 3: Review

With the Windows Components Wizard, you can install services such as WINS, DHCP, and IIS. Just work your way through the wizard's panels.

Installing the Microsoft Internet Information Server

When you ran the Windows Components Wizard, IIS installed itself as one of the components that you selected. By selecting default values, there is little you need to do to enable IIS on your system.

Tip

> As far as security goes, it's best if you install IIS on a Windows 2000 server that's using the NTFS file system. Then you need to enable auditing.

Note

> You can find the documentation for installing the Microsoft Internet Information Server by pointing your Web browser at http://localhost/iisHelp/iis/misc/default.asp.

You can set up the Microsoft Internet Information Server in a matter of minutes. It loads as a service and runs in the background after it's installed. In fact, after running the setup wizard, you can start a browser on your own network and access the sample Web documents immediately.

Most of your involvement with the server lies in planning the connections to your intranet or to the Internet, deciding on the structure and content of the Web server, and planning security, which includes figuring out who can access the server and what level of access the users are to have. Some tools and techniques for managing the server are covered in the following sections.

Adding Microsoft Internet Information Server is as simple as starting the Windows Components Wizard. If you already have the necessary Internet or intranet connection, you can accept all the default settings during setup. For many organizations, the default setup configurations are suitable without any further modifications.

Internet Information Server installs with some helpful sample home pages that you can use as a starting point to create your own home pages. After you write your own page, you can replace the sample content and have your own personalized Web server.

If you didn't add all services at installation, it isn't too late. On prior versions of IIS, after the installation you saw a new group called Microsoft Internet Server (Common) under the Start menu. With Windows 2000, select Start, Progams, Administrative Tools, Internet Services Manager. The IIS MMC snap-in will open. Figure 19.4 shows you the ISM snap-in.

19

Figure 19.4

The ISM snap-in for administering IIS.

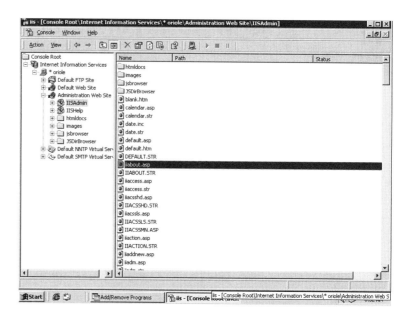

Click on the + sign associated with your Web site. You then should find the collection of services that you selected earlier along with Microsoft Internet Information Server. Perhaps you have decided it is time to install a new service (for example, you might not have installed FTP originally, but your users are clamoring for the service). To install a new service, right-click the site—Oriole, in the window in Figure 19.4. From the menu, you can select New, FTP Site. You are presented with the FTP Site Creation Wizard.

Task 19.2: Adding a New Service to IIS Using a Wizard.

Step 1: Description

When you install IIS, you can install FTP, Web, NNTP, and SMTP services. This task shows you what to do should you want to add a new site after installation.

Step 2: Action

1. Make sure that you are logged on to your server as Administrator.

2. To install these programs, select Start, Programs, Administrative Tools, Internet Security Manager.

3. Right-click the computer name where you want to add the service. From the menu, select New, FTP Site. You should see the FTP Site Creation Wizard in Figure 19.5. Click Next.

FIGURE 19.5

The FTP Site Creation Wizard.

4. The next panel is the FTP Site Description panel. Enter a description of the site in the Description box. Click Next.

5. From the IP Address and Port Settings panel shown in Figure 19.6, select the IP address and TCP port. Unless you have a good reason not to, go with the defaults. Click Next.

FIGURE 19.6

The IP Address and Port Settings panel of the wizard.

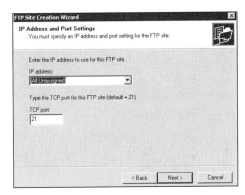

6. On the next panel, enter the path to your FTP home directory. Click Next.

7. Next you see the FTP Site Access Permissions panel. Check Read or Write. This sets the permissions for the home directory. The default is Read. Click Next.

8. Click Finish.

9. You'll need to start the service. Right-click the site you just created and select Start.

19

Step 3: Review

With the FTP Site Creation Wizard, you can install your first or an additional FTP site. Using the wizard is simple when you understand TCP/IP services.

To remove a service is quite easy. Ensure that no one is using the service—pause it for a while to make sure. Right-click the FTP or Web site you want to delete. From the menu, select Delete. Internet Services Manager requires you to confirm the delete. Click Yes and the site is gone.

The Remove All button does exactly as advertised: It deletes all hints of Internet Information Server and all other Option Pack software from your server, although the content files created for Internet use remain.

Some of the other new functions within IIS include the Microsoft NNTP and SMTP Virtual Servers. NNTP lets you run a newsgroup server. With SMTP, you can run your own mail server.

Web Protocols and Standards

NEW TERM By now, you are probably somewhat familiar with the terms presented here. The *World Wide Web* Server is an HTTP server that facilitates transactions between a Web browser and a Web server. *File Transfer Protocol*, or *FTP*, oversees file transfers between Internet software and an FTP server. ODBC drivers are used to connect with ODBC-compliant databases using SQL statements. *Network News Transfer Protocol* is a transmission protocol for the transfer of Usenet news. *Simple Mail Transfer Protocol* facilitates the transfer of mail from a message transfer agent on a sending host to a message transfer agent on a receiving host.

Testing Your Microsoft Internet Information Server Installation

After installation, any services that you specified for installation are up and running. You can have an instant Internet or intranet site by copying content files in the home directories to which you agreed earlier in the installation process. You can copy the World Wide Web pages, for example, to the \wwwroot directory.

Testing the Internet Server

IIS places a home page called default.htm in the \inetpub\wwwroot directory. You can check whether the installation succeeded by opening a connection to the Internet with a Web browser (such as Internet Explorer or Netscape Navigator) and viewing the files in your home directory.

Task 19.3: Testing a Server Connected to the Internet.

Step 1: Description

In this task, you test your installation by using Internet Explorer or Netscape Navigator to view the files in your home directory.

Step 2: Action

1. Start Internet Explorer (or another Web browser) on a computer that has an active connection to the Internet. This computer can be the server you're testing, although using a different computer is recommended.

2. Type the Uniform Resource Locator (URL) for the home directory of your new server. The URL is `http://` followed by the name of your server, followed by the path of the file that you want to view. (Note the forward slashes.) If your server is registered in DNS as `www.pdaconsulting.com`, for example, and you want to view the file default.htm in the root of the home directory, in the Location box you type the following:

   `http://www.pdaconsulting.com/default.htm`

   Then press Enter. The home page appears on the screen.

Step 3: Review

In this task, you tested the installed IIS on a machine named pdaconsulting.com and viewed the default.htm file, using the following URL: `http://www.pdaconsulting.com/default.htm`. The default home page then appeared on the screen.

Error Messages

You might receive a few error messages. The most common one appears when your service provider hasn't yet installed your DNS entry and your Web browser can't find your Internet location. This error message ends when your service provider finalizes your Internet installation.

The other common error message occurs when the Web browser successfully finds your Web site but can't find the file. This situation usually occurs when you've misnamed a file (such as default.html rather than default.htm).

Testing the Intranet Server

You use some slightly different procedures to test your intranet server; these changes are mostly due to the different naming conventions used in an intranet.

19

After making sure that the DNS or WINS service is running, you can fire up your Web browser to connect to the server. Instead of specifying an Internet URL such as `www.pdaconsulting.com`, you specify the Windows machine name (such as oriole), followed by the directory (if needed) and the name of the file that you want to view. To view the HTML page named default.htm on the Windows machine named oriole, use the following address:

```
http://oriole/default.htm
```

The default home page appears on the screen.

You might think that a few things are odd about this system (and when compared to the Internet and Windows conventions at large, they are). Even though you're running on a Windows 2000 system, you still use forward slashes (/) to specify paths (not the backward slashes used in the DOS/Windows world). Because you're going right to a file, you don't need to tell the Web browser what sort of file (HTML, FTP) you're grabbing.

Task 19.4: Testing a Server on Your Intranet.

Step 1: Description

In this task, you test a server on your intranet by using Internet Explorer, Netscape Navigator, or another Web browser to view your home page.

Step 2: Action

1. Ensure that your computer has an active network connection. Use `ping IP address` to ensure that you can see another machine on the network.

2. Start Internet Explorer or your Web browser.

3. Type the address for the home directory of your new server. The address is `http://` followed by your Windows 2000 Server name, followed by the path of the file you want to view. (Note the forward slash marks.) When your server is registered with the WINS Server as Oriole, for example, and you want to view the file homepage.htm in the root of the home directory, type the following in the Location box:

   `http://oriole/default.htm`

   Then press Enter. The home page appears on the screen. (Alternatively, you can just use an IP address to connect, such as `http://199.199.199.2/default.htm`, where the IP address is your machine. Figure 19.7 shows you the default IIS Web page.

FIGURE 19.7

IIS default Web page.

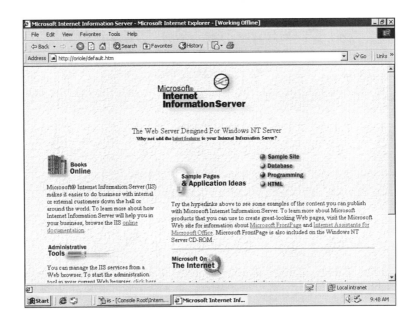

Step 3: Review

In this task, you used Internet Explorer (or your favorite Web browser) to view default.htm on your intranet.

Configuring IIS with the Internet Service Manager

19

Internet Information Service uses the Internet Service Manager to oversee the World Wide Web server and any other Internet services (such as FTP, SMTP, or NNTP) that you have running. The Internet Server Manager is a Windows-based graphical management tool that is used to configure the server and its security options. In reality, it is a Microsoft Management Console (MMC) snap-in. You use it to manage Web services, FTP services, SMTP services, and NNTP services. It is installed automatically on the Web server itself, but you can copy the files to any Windows 2000 system and manage Internet Information Servers on the network. You already saw an example in Figure 19.4.

To start the Server Manager, choose Start, Programs, Administrative Tools, Internet Service Manager. Double-click the server that you want to manage. What you see first are the services you chose to install, such as the Default FTP Site and Default Web Site. Choose a service such as the Default Web Site, right-click on it, and choose Properties.

You should see the window in Figure 19.8. The options on these property sheets are discussed next.

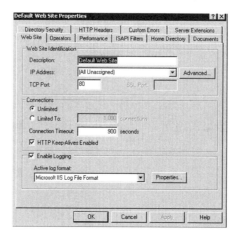

With property sheets, you can manage the following tasks:

- Establish Web site identification, connection, and logging options.
- Configure administration permissions.
- Set performance options.
- Specify home directories and other virtual directories.
- Enable specific default documents.
- Set access and security options and view current sessions.
- Enable or disable server access for specific IP addresses.
- Set custom error messages.

Working with Properties

From the Internet Service Manager window, you can change properties by right-clicking on a service and choosing Properties. Because the WWW service is popular now, the following sections deal with changing the properties of that service.

The WWW Service Properties are governed by their own dialog box. As shown in Figure 19.8, it has 10 property sheets: Web Site, Operators, Performance, ISAPI Filters, Home Directory, Documents, Directory Security, HTTP Headers, Custom Errors, and Server Extensions.

The Web Site Property Sheet

The most important aspects of the configuration options of the Web Site property sheet govern who can access the WWW service and under what conditions. Each of these aspects is covered here.

Web Site Identification

You set this area to describe your Web site using the Description field. By default, the IP Address field allows IIS to respond to all addresses assigned to the computer and makes it the default Web site. Web-based activity usually uses the following default: TCP Port 80. The Advanced button allows the setup of multiple Web sites on this machine, so you might have www.pdaconsulting.com and sales.pdaconsulting.com.

Connections

The Connections section contains three options: Unlimited, Limited To, and Connection Timeout. By default, IIS uses the Unlimited option to specify that there can be any number of connections to this Web site. You might change this to Limited To and specify a number based on how fast your server responds to requests.

The Connection Timeout setting specifies how long (in seconds) before a connection between the server and an inactive user is severed. The default is 15 minutes (900 seconds). Closing inactive connections is important for a busy Web site; you don't want inactive users to keep valuable connections alive. In addition, the HTTP protocol can contain small errors that do not change a connection when the user has specified one.

Enable Logging

The Enable Logging option tells IIS what to log and when. Logging is an important tool when evaluating your Web server and supported traffic. The Enable Logging check box determines whether logging is turned on. You'll want to enable logging.

Basically, logging tells you who logged on to your Web server (well, it tells you the IP addresses of those logging on, anyway), when they logged on, and under what circumstances. This information is valuable as you analyze your server loads and where the hits are coming from. In addition, this information can be passed along to Web analysis tools that perform detailed analyses of your Web traffic. Finally, the same information can be used to track down hackers and other unauthorized access attempts.

19

> **Tip**
>
> By default, IIS uses its own log text format, called W3C Extended Log File Format. If you want to convert the log files to European Microsoft Windows Academic Center (EMWAC) or CERN common log format, you need to use the convlog.exe DOS command. For a discussion on how to use this utility, refer to the section "Converting Log Files."

Note

> The logging mechanism you choose here applies only to the specified service, not to the server as a whole. The default is to log everything to the same file. However, you can log NNTP and FTP requests to one log and your server requests to another.

Properties

Clicking the Properties button presents you with further logging options.

General Properties

The New Log Time Period check box tells IIS when to open a new log, as opposed to keeping one huge log. Smaller log files are easier to analyze and manage. The default is to start a new log file daily, although most sites get along fine by starting new logs weekly. If your Web site isn't really busy, you can probably get by with starting new logs monthly. You also have the option of opening a new log file when the log file reaches a certain size, or you can allow an unlimited file size, which is a handy option for busy sites. Be aware that choosing the Unlimited option might cause your server to crash if you run out of space on your hard drive.

If you choose to open a log on a daily, weekly, or monthly basis, the system closes existing log files when a new log record is entered after midnight of the last day of the existing log file. If you look at the new log file, you'll see that it includes the first day on which activity took place.

Note

> IIS also enforces other log limits. For example, the maximum size of a log-file line is 1,200 bytes, with 150 bytes maximum per field in a log text file and 200 bytes maximum per field in an ODBC log file.

The Log File Directory field specifies the directory in which log files are stored. The default is SystemRoot\System32\LogFiles. Each log file is stored with a similar filename. If you choose a new log file to be opened at a specific time, such as daily, the log file begins with EX, followed by the year, month, and date, with a suffix of log. Weekly files use a year, month, and week extension, and Monthly files use year and month. A monthly log file opened on January 1, 1999, therefore, is named EX9901.log, with an absolute pathname (assuming default install options) of `C:\WINNT\System32\LogFiles\EX9901.log`.

If you select the size of the file to determine when a new log is opened, using either the Unlimited or the When File Size Reaches options, the filename format is extend#.log (where # is a number that is increased each time a new log file is opened).

ODBC Logging

The ODBC Logging option logs information to a text file rather than to an ODBC database. Unless you have some analysis tools that require SQL/ODBC input, you probably log information to a text file. Because most third-party analysis tools use CERN or EMWAC common log files as input, you need to begin with text-format files to get these files out of IIS.

The Operators Property Sheet

This property sheet controls who is allowed to have operator privileges on your Web site. By default, only those accounts in the Administrators group are allowed access. You can add and remove users and groups as needed. You cannot delete the default Administrator group.

The Performance Property Sheet

You can tune IIS to suit your particular business needs using these options. Change the first option to set how many "hits" you anticipate receiving.

Bandwidth throttling enables you to override any current network settings and limit the amount of bandwidth used by the Web site. This is a term, of course, generally used to indicate load (as in kilobytes per second).

The ISAPI Filters Property Sheet

ISAPI filters are programs that respond to events during the processing of an HTTP request. They are loaded into memory. This option shows which filters are present and indicates their status.

The Home Directory Property Sheet

The Home Directory property sheet governs which directories and files the Web will use.

The first options consist of where the directories exist—on the local server, on a network share, or on some other machine as directed by a particular URL. By default, the directories exist on the local machine. The path is shown in the Local Path field.

You can specify four types of access for directory permissions. If you are using NTFS (which you should be), those settings must match the following, or else the most restrictive of the four is used by IIS:

- Script source access—With this setting, users can view the source of scripts on the site when either Read or Write set. Source code includes Active Server Pages.

19

- Read—With the Read setting, users can view the files in the directory but cannot change the files or add files of their own. This option is the most secure. You enable the Read option on publishing directories and disable it on directories that contain programs, so clients can't download your programs.

- Write—With the Write setting, users can upload or change information on the Web site. You must use the HTTP 1.1 protocol to support the PUT command for this to work.

- Directory browsing—If the Directory Browsing box is selected, users can browse through directory listings sent back by the Web server. If you have a completely secure system and don't mind making all the files visible to a Web browser user, you can select this button. If you're storing files on a server and want to make sure that a user knows exactly what he or she wants when connecting to your Web server, leave this box unchecked. You can have Microsoft's Indexing Server include this directory in a full-text index of your Web site by checking the Index this directory option.

Note

Do not enable the Write permission on directories that hold executable scripts. Intruders or hackers can use the directory to upload and run programs that damage your system.

Review other settings as part of the installation, such as application settings and execute permissions.

When you install the Microsoft Internet Information Server, a directory called \SCRIPTS is created. This directory has the Execute permission (not the Read permission) and branches from the root directory of the installation drive. Store all your Internet Server API (ISAPI) applications and Common Gateway (CGI) scripts in this directory, or create another directory with the same Execute permission for storing scripts.

The Documents Property Sheet

The Enable Default Document setting specifies a default document that users always see when they log on to your Web server without listing a specific file. This document is usually called default.htm or index.htm. You'll also see default Active Server Pages—default.asp and iisstart.asp.

The Directory Security Property Sheet

This setting contains numerous security options. The following subsections outline the individual options.

Anonymous Access and Authentication Control

Use the Edit option to see the individual settings that are available. When you install the Microsoft Internet Information Server, a special anonymous Guest account is created with the name IUSR_*computername,* where *computername* is the name of the server (or the *anonymous user account*). This account can log on locally, so when someone accesses the Web server without providing any sort of logon credentials, that person is granted access to the server as if he or she were logging on locally (at the console). The account is a member of the Guests local group and the Domain Users group.

Caution

> You don't want to leave this anonymous account online for too long. Intruders know that this account exists and will try to use it to gain access to your system. Change it as soon as possible.

The anonymous user account does not require users to enter usernames or passwords, which makes it easy for users to access your server.

After you create a directory and add it to the Directories property sheet, anonymous users can access a designated directory under one of three conditions:

- The Everyone group has at least Read or Execute rights in the directory.
- The IUSR_*computername* account has been specifically granted at least Read or Execute rights in the directory.
- The Guests group (of which IUSR_*computername* is a member) has been specifically granted at least Read or Execute rights in the directory.

19

If you create a directory and want only anonymous users to access the directory, remove the Everyone and Guests groups from the permissions list and add only the IUSR_*computername* account.

If Everyone or the IUSR_*computername* account does not have permission to access a directory, anonymous users cannot access the directory. By removing these two groups, you restrict a directory to anonymous Web users and require logon access, as described next.

Using Password Authentication

If you want to restrict access to a directory to only users who have accounts on the server and require those users to log on when they access the Web server, follow these steps:

1. Restrict anonymous user access to directories by removing Everyone, Guests, and IUSR_*computername* accounts from the permission list for the directory.
2. Add the specific user or group you want to access the directory, and assign the appropriate access rights by making a selection in the Type of Access field.

3. In the Internet Service Manager, add the directory to the Directories property sheet if it is not a subdirectory of a directory that is already specified.

4. Enable Basic or Challenge/Response in the Service dialog box. These options are discussed later in this day.

Following are essentially two levels of access for the Web server:

Anonymous access—This anonymous user option enables Web users to log on to the IUSR_*computername* account. When this option is enabled (as it is by default), users can access directories where Everyone, the Guests group, or the IUSR_*computername* accounts have access. If Allow Anonymous is checked and the Basic and Windows 2000 Challenge/Response check boxes are both cleared, only anonymous users can log on. If you disable this option, you must enable Basic or Windows 2000 Challenge/Response (and then all users must log on by providing usernames and passwords, and those users must have appropriate user accounts on the Web server before any users can log on).

Authenticated access—All users are authenticated when using the server. There are three ways of authenticating users: Basic, Digest, and Integrated Windows.

- Basic Authentication (Password is sent in Clear Text)—The Basic option requires users to enter usernames and passwords to access a secure folder. This feature is useful when you want to set up a "subscription" service that requires users to log on with a password after they have been "registered" with the service. This option sends passwords in scrambled clear text, a code that's easy for any hacker to break. The password can be compromised, and if it is the same password that users use to log on to more secure accounts, a hacker who captures the password can gain unauthorized access to those accounts. Use this option with care. If you require logon for users who access nonsensitive information, however, perhaps you require passwords as a formality and encryption is not essential.

- Digest authentication for Windows domain servers—This option assumes that users are using certificates. The server and the client exchange the authentication information using a Transaction Layer Security (TLS) protocol such as Secure Sockets Layer (SSL). When the Web server receives a client request that contains credentials, the anonymous logon user account is bypassed, and the credentials are used by the service to log the user on.

- Integrated Windows 2000 Authentication—This option assumes that users have already been authenticated by some other Windows 2000 (or compatible) computer. When this option is set, the header information in the user's HTTP requests, which contains the user's credentials (username and password), is used to log the user on to the restricted directory. This option is mostly used in cases in which the Web server is connected to an internal intranet and users on the network have already been logged on, although you can also use it over the Internet. The Windows 2000 Challenge/Response protocol uses an encryption technique that prevents passwords from being transmitted across the network in the clear.

IP Address and Domain Name Restrictions

In this area, you specify who can access your Web server based on IP addresses. Use the Edit button to see these options. The IP Access Control section of the property sheet controls who can access your Web server. The default is to allow everyone access (as indicated by the Granted Access radio button). You can narrow down this access by specifying IP addresses that are not allowed access. List IP addresses and subnet masks to be denied access under the Except Those Listed Below section. You can choose the Add button to specify a particular IP address or a range of IP addresses. You might want to block the IP address of a competitor, for example, to prevent people in that company from accessing your server, or you might want to block the IP address of someone who is overrunning your server with requests in a denial-of-service attack.

The two models for specifying IP addresses are Granted Access and Denied Access:

- Granted Access—Allows all hosts access to the Web server, except for the IP addresses that are added to the Lower Exception list box.

- Denied Access—Denies all hosts access to the Web server, except for the IP addresses added to the Lower Exception list box. You can choose the Add button to specify an IP address or a range of IP addresses. For example, you might choose to limit access to all computers except those that use IP addresses controlled by your organization. To do so, select the Denied Access radio button and add your organization's IP addresses.

You must specify one of the models and then add IP addresses to the Exception list box:

- Add button—Click this button to add IP addresses to the exception list. The Add button brings up a dialog box that enables you to specify whether the restriction applies to a specific computer, a group of computers, or a particular Domain Name or IP address. Set it according to your needs.

Restricting access by IP address is not a foolproof security measure. A hacker or intruder can simply move to a computer with a different IP address or change the IP address. It is, however, an effective way to block known users on your own internal network or users who are flooding your network with unnecessary or intrusive requests.

19

Secure Communications

You can tell your IIS server to allow secure communications between users and your Web site. This is commonly used when your site collects sensitive information such as credit card data. This option enables you to set up the initial certificate for your server and manage the SSL Keypairs. Consider obtaining more detail than can be found in this book before moving into this area.

The HTTP Headers Property Sheet

This area is used to set content expiration options and to present custom HTTP headers. It also enables you to create and set Content Ratings for your Web site so that third-party software knows that the site is suitable for a particular group of people. Finally, you can configure additional MIME types that the Web Service sends to browsers.

The Custom Errors Property Sheet

Use these properties to set up specific error messages for the users of your Web site. You can add new messages or just edit the existing ones by using the Edit Properties button. It's a good way to make your Web site users a little more aware by providing easier-to-understand error messages.

The Server Extensions Property Sheet

The Server Extensions sheet allows you to add server-side functionality to your Web site. You can allow JavaScript and VBScript authoring. You can set whether you want security settings to be inherited or not.

You also can set a mail address for contacting the Web administrator.

Managing and Analyzing Log Files

Earlier , you learned how to set up the logging capabilities of the Internet Information Server. In the following sections, you'll delve deeper into the topic.

When someone logs on to your Internet server, that person leaves a trail of what he or she did and when he or she did it. This information is stored in the IIS log files. You learned about log files earlier in this day when you followed the steps to set them up.

A log file has 20 fields:

- Date—The date the system created the log.
- Time—The time the system created the log.
- Client's IP Address—Lists the Internet Protocol address of the client that is logging on to the server.

- User Name—Refers to the name of the client when you've chosen mechanisms for which users need to log on.
- Service Name—Refers to the Internet service requests. *W3SVC* refers to the World Wide Web service, *MSFTPSVC* refers to the Microsoft FTP service, *MSNNTPSVC* refers to the NNTP service, and *MSSMTPSVC* refers to the SMTP service.
- Server Name—Refers to the computer name of the server.
- Server IP—Refers to the IP address of the server.
- Server Port—Refers to the port number to which the client is connected on the server.
- Method—Tells what the client asked of the server. For Web servers, the most common operations are GET, HEAD, or POST, whereas other services use their list of operations (for example, the FTP server typically uses file to indicate a file request).
- URI Stem—The resource accessed, such as the HTML page or CGI program.
- URI Query—The query, if any, that the user was trying to perform.
- HTTP Status—Refers to a special number that indicates what action was taken.
- Win32 Status—The status of the action in Windows 2000 terms.
- Bytes Sent—Specifies the bytes sent from the server to the client.
- Bytes Received—Specifies the number of bytes sent from the client to the server, usually in the form of HTTP requests.
- Time Taken—Specifies the length of time the action took.
- Protocol Version—Which protocol (FTP, HTTP, and so on) is used by the client.
- User Agent—Refers to the browser used on the client.
- Cookie—The content of a cookie sent or received, if any.
- Referrer—The site on which the user clicked to bring them to your site.

19

 Note These fields are separated by commas in the log file. Where no information exists for a field, a hyphen (·) is used.

Converting Log Files

The Microsoft IIS uses its own log file format. Microsoft, however, has included a utility called convlog.exe to convert IIS logs to two formats widely used in the Internet world: the EMWAC log file format or the Common Log Format.

To run `convlog.exe` and see a list of options, open a command prompt and enter the following command lines:

```
C:\> cd \winnt\system32\inetsrv
C:\winnt\system32\convlog
```

The syntax for `convlog.exe` is

```
convlog options LogFile
```

In this example, *options* refer to command-line options and *LogFile* refers to the log file that is being converted.

Table 19.2 lists several useful command-line options.

TABLE 19.2 `convlog` Options

Option	Description
`-d`	Converts IP addresses to DNS.
`-f`	Specifies the temporary file used by `convlog` to convert the files. The default is to use the default temporary file as specified in the tmp system variable (usually `C:\TEMP`).
`-i[i, n, e]`	Specifies the input logfile type. Use `I` for MS Internet and `n` for NCSA or W3C standard log formats.
`-l[0, 1, 2]`	Specifies date locale format for MS Internet Standard. Use `0` for MM/DD/YY, `1` for YY/MM/DD, or `2` for DD.MM.YY formats.
`-n[m[cachesize], i]`	Converts IP addresses to computer or domain names. The default is not to do so. If you do decide to perform this conversion, use the `m` command-line option; you use the accompanying *cachesize* to designate how large a cache to use in this operation (the default is 5,000 bytes).
`-o`	Specifies the directory for the output. The default is to use the current directory.
`-s[f, w]`	Specifies the services to convert. The default is to convert log entries for all services (you don't need to use `-s` if this is what you want), but you can specify an individual service (`f` for FTP and `w` for World Wide Web).
`-t[ncsa[:GMTOffset], none]`	Specifies the format of the new log file. The default is to use the EMWAC format.
`-x`	Saves the non-WWW entries to a .dmp file.

Other Tools and Techniques

The Windows 2000 Server and the Microsoft Internet Information Server include some additional features:

- You can write server programs using the Common Gateway Interface (CGI) or Microsoft's Internet Server API (ISAPI). Of the two, ISAPI is your best bet because it compiles programs into libraries that get loaded into the Internet server's memory and stay there, thus improving performance. Another advantage of ISAPI is achieved by "pluggable" filters, which allow preprocessing of requests and post-processing of responses. This feature permits site-specific handling of HTTP requests and responses. There was some security breaches using CGI in the first version of the Internet Information Server.

- You can limit the amount of information that can be sent from the server at any one time so that other requests can be serviced with a fair share of time through bandwidth throttling.

- You can set up several Internet Information Servers on their own network, isolated from your internal network but connected to the Internet. You can then manage these servers with the Internet Service Manager, running from a Windows 2000 workstation.

- The server creates logs that contain information about user activity. You can view logs to see what has been accessed and when. Server logs must initially be configured.

- The Windows 2000 Performance Monitor utility can perform real-time measurements of your Web server and provide statistical information that you can use to troubleshoot the system, track usage, or justify the need to upgrade equipment.

- You can use SSL, PCT, or TLS. Microsoft Web clients and servers support the Secure Sockets Layer (SSL) and the Private Communication Technology (PCT) protocols for securing a communication channel. SSL is an older standard, whereas PCT is a more efficient and secure upgrade to the SSL protocol. The Microsoft Internet Security Framework supports SSL versions 2.0 and 3.0 and PCT version 1.0, as well as a new security protocol called Transport Layer Security (TLS). TLS incorporates both SSL and PCT into a single standard that supports both certificates and password-based authentication.

19

Getting the Word Out That You're Up and Running!

Setting up a Web site on a Windows 2000 Server can be fun, easy, and rewarding—especially when you're using Microsoft Internet Information Server. After you've set up your site, don't forget to spread the word. You can send a message to the Usenet newsgroup `comp.infosystems.www.announce` and register your Web site with the "What's New" sections of major search engines such as Excite, Lycos, and Yahoo! to tell the world that you're online.

You can inform the search engines and lists in several ways. You can submit information to each search engine in turn; not many major search engines are available yet, so submitting information won't take much of your time. You can also go through one of the new announcement Web resources that take your information and submit it to a wide range of search engines and lists. Using these announcement services is simple. You give them information about your Web site (such as the main URL and the content), and they send that information to search engines and lists. Although some commercial announcement services are available, don't spend money to do something that these announcement services (such as the ones listed here) do for free.

Following is a short listing of search engines and lists:

- AltaVista (`http://altavista.digital.com`)
- BizWiz (`http://www.bizwiz.com/bizwiz/`)
- Comfind Business Search (`http://www.comfind.com/`)
- Excite (`http://www.excite.com`)
- Galaxy (`http://galaxy.einet.net/`)
- HotBot (`http://www.hotbot.com`)
- InfoSeek (`http://guide.infoseek.com/`)
- Lycos (`http://lycos.cs.cmu.edu`)
- Magellan (`http://www.mckinley.com`)
- Open Text (`http://www.opentext.com`)
- Point (`http://www.pointcom.com`)
- Starting Point (`http://www.stpt.com/`)
- WebCrawler (`http://webcrawler.com`)
- Yahoo! (`http://www.yahoo.com`)

Following is a short list of noncommercial announcement services:

- Add It! (http://www.liquidimaging.com/submit/)
- Add Me! (http://www.addme.com)
- GetNet-Wide (http://www.gonetwide.com/gopublic.html)
- Submit It! (http://www.submit-it.com/)

For the remainder of the day, you'll learn about the other major Windows Components.

Certificate Server

The Internet opens up a whole new area for most businesses these days, allowing electronic commerce to begin to flourish. As a result, there is a greater need for secure communication. This is often established using public key cryptography, digital certificates, and such technologies as Secure Sockets Layer (SSL) and Secure Electronic Transactions (SET). Certificates are used to provide assurance of a server's identity. A user connecting to a Web site that has a certificate signed by a trusted authority can be reasonably sure that the site is actually run by the company identified by the certificate.

In a similar vein, users can utilize certificates to establish their identity with others at the moment that you obtain certificates from trusted organizations (such as VeriSign) and pay for that service. Companies who want to use and establish certificates for use throughout their own company might use Microsoft's Certificate Server.

Certificate Server enables organizations to easily manage issuance, renewal, and revocation of certificates without having to rely on these external certificate authorities. With Certificate Server, an organization has full control over how it issues, manages, and revokes certificates, as well as the format and contents of the certificates themselves. Certificate Server also logs all transactions, which enables the administrator to track, audit, and manage the various certificate requests. The product allows authentication of a user, based on that user's Windows 2000 logon, and enables an administrator to directly approve or deny a certificate request.

19

You can find the product listed along with the other Option Pack programs you installed. You use Start, Programs, Administrative Tools to find it.

When you install the product, you must define the CA information that it is to use (Domain name, Common Name, key storage, and so on) and then set up distributed CA hierarchies. Next, you generate a CA certification request and, finally, distribute the CA root certificate to your users.

The topic of setting up and managing certificates is not something that can be quickly perused. You can find more detailed information on Microsoft's Web site a `http://www.microsoft.com/workshop/security/client/certsvr.asp`

You can be sure that this topic will become more popular and well worth any effort you might put into learning about it. Using encryption is the only way to fully secure your data and authenticate yourself.

Finally, Certificate Server is built upon industry standards and open technologies and supports X.509 version 3 certificates, RSA and PKCS, and both hardware and software signing methods.

Message Queuing Server

The Microsoft Queuing Server (MSMQ) provides loosely coupled and reliable network communications services based on a messaging queue model. It is a communications technology that enables applications on different systems to communicate with each other if systems and networks occasionally fail. It provides message delivery, cost-based message routing, and full support for transactions. When a particular network fails, MSMQ automatically uses the next lowest cost route to deliver the messages, based on input from the MSMQ administrator. It runs on either TCP/IP or IPX network protocols.

The package integrates easily with both Internet Information Server and Microsoft Transaction Server. The product enables developers to assure that messages are delivered exactly one time and in the order in which they were sent. This is important for many custom and off-the-shelf applications.

MSMQ enables applications to send messages to—and receive messages from—other applications using asynchronous communications. While messages are in transit between the applications, MSMQ keeps copies in holding areas called *queues*, hence its name. A message can consist of data in any format that is understood by the applications.

Microsoft Indexing Server

Microsoft's Indexing Server works with Windows 2000 and IIS 4.0 to provide access to all your organization's documents that are stored on your intranet or the Internet. It enables you to perform full-text searches and retrieve all types of information from any Web browser with the click of a button.

It has a number of features, including the following:

- Indexing of all documents—This enables the end user to query indexes and entire documents stored on Windows 2000 Server with IIS.

- Customize query forms—The Webmaster can create custom queries enabling users to just fill in the blanks.

- Customize the results page—The Webmaster can also create custom results pages, such as setting the number of hits per page and highlighting the words used in the search.

- Administrative tools—Indexing Server provides a number of built-in tools for administering and managing the product. It also supports multiple languages so that users can query in any one of seven languages including Dutch, English, French, German, Italian, Spanish, and Swedish.

Organizations use Indexing Server to facilitate document management techniques within the company. Index Server is a great tool that enables you to deploy a graphical search engine similar to those found on the Internet. You set it up to create an index of items such as documents and spreadsheets on your servers' hard drives. Then, when a user is looking for a particular Word document on the network but can't remember where he saved it, he can open his Web browser, enter a few keywords, and presto, Index Server presents him with a list of possible matches!

Networking Services

You can install several services available with Networking Services:

- COM Internet Services Proxy—This enables the Distributed Component Object Model to travel over HTTP using IIS.

- Domain Name System(DNS)—On Day 12, "Understanding TCP/IP and DNS," you learned that the DNS server answers query and update requests for names.

- Dynamic Host Configuration Protocol (DHCP)—On Day 13, "Understanding DHCP and WINS," you learned that DHCP assigns a temporary IP address to a host.

- Internet Authentication Services (IAS)—IAS offers authentication services using RADIUS servers. These third-party tools provide additional user account and password controls for dial-up users, enhancing the level of security and control. It also reduces administration for companies already employing RADIUS servers by telling Windows 2000 to use them when needed.

19

- QoS Admission Control Service—This service allows you to specify the Quality of Service of the network connection for each subnet. A QoS standard allows administrators to control which users and groups can reserve bandwidth on a network. QoS is critical for supporting streaming media on the Internet or an intranet.
- Simple TCP/IP Services—This option supports small UDP and TCP services: CHARGEN, DAYTIME, DISCARD, ECHO, and Quote of the Day.
- Site Server LDAP Services—This service scans TCP/IP stacks and updates directories with the most current user information.
- Windows Internet Name Service (WINS)—On Day 13, you learned that WINS provides a NetBIOS name service for registering and resolving NetBIOS names.

System requirements include Windows 2000 and at least 4MB of free disk space.

Remote Installation Services

Remote Installation Service (RIS) gives administrators the ability to power on and boot remote desktop systems without an installed operating system. If the computers have a PXE (Pre-Boot eXecution) boot ROM, RIS can boot the remote systems.

Remote Installation Services requires DHCP, DNS, ADS, and RIS servers. The RIS servers actually store the information about the operating system required for the client to boot.

RIS uses the functionality of IntelliMirror, which you learned about on Day 16, "Configuring Fault-Tolerance." There is a wizard that allows you to set the server up to remotely install Windows 2000 Professional on remote-enabled computers.

Remote Storage

Remote Storage Service (RSS) provides a Hierarchical Storage Management (HSM) functionality to Windows 2000. RSS monitors the amount of available space on your local hard drive and launches into action when the free space on your primary hard drive slips below a predefined level.

Terminal Services and Licensing

Windows 2000 is the first operating system from Microsoft to ship with Terminal Services (TS) and its supporting services. With TS, clients can run interactive applications on a remote server. The client system accepts input from and output to the client. There is no local processing; all the processing is done on the server.

NEW TERM This new technology allows the use of thin clients and helps reduce the Total Cost of Ownership of the network. A *thin client* is a desktop system with minimal hardware and software. In fact, the client need not have a hard drive or a floppy drive. The Terminal Services does all the work. The thin client merely forwards requests to the server.

Terminal Services allows you to continue to use your Windows for Workgroups and Windows 95 clients without upgrading. You can run 32-bit applications and extend the life of the hardware and software. In addition, TS supports Windows NT 4.0, Windows 98, and Windows 2000 Professional clients.

Should you decide to use this technology, you'll need to evaluate your server hardware. Because the server is taking more of the processing load, you will most likely need more powerful servers. But you'll probably find that the additional cost of the server is offset by the reduced client costs. Obviously, there are administration advantages as well. With Terminal Services, you have less software and hardware to update. You also have more control over applications because they are stored entirely on the server. Change it once and everybody has access to the new application.

Looking at this lesson, you can see that you have a lot of flexibility when installing Windows 2000 and its components. Enough for today, let's review what we did.

Summary

Today, you learned about Internet Information Servers and the other products offered within the Microsoft Option Pack (Windows Components). Organizations are using Windows 2000 more and more as their platform of choice for Internet services for two primary reasons: improved TCP/IP support and the bundled Internet/intranet services.

As you learned on Day 12, Microsoft continues to make TCP/IP more central to its networking capabilities. With Windows 2000, Microsoft has made enhancements to the default network installation and numerous improvements to 2000's IP capabilities.

In addition, the Option Pack includes Microsoft's Internet Information Server, a fully functional Web server. Organizations can, therefore, set up and run Web servers right out of the box. The Option Pack also includes a number of significant services that enable you to fully install and run a commercial Web site that can offer your clients significant benefits.

This day also introduces you to the Web server, focusing on the Microsoft Internet Information Server bundled with Windows 2000. Basically, the process of installing and configuring a Web server isn't complicated; servers practically install themselves, and

19

because Web servers don't really do a whole lot (basically, they respond to HTTP requests), you don't have to configure much.

We focused only on IIS today. You can, of course, go into an amazing amount of depth configuring and using all the services available with Windows Components—far more detail than there is room for in this book.

The Windows Components and Windows 2000's combination of features and functions makes it hard to beat for organizations that are setting up Internet services. Whether you elect to publish internally or publicly over the Internet, this is a platform that can address your information publishing needs.

Workshop

To wrap up the day, you can review tasks from the day and see the answers to some commonly asked questions.

Task List

The emphasis of this day is to teach you to install and configure the Internet Information Server. As a system administrator, you might decide to publish documents over the Internet or for your intranet. You learned the following tasks in this day:

- Installing Windows Components
- Testing an IIS server connected to the Internet
- Testing IIS on your intranet
- Configuring an FTP server

Q&A

Q How do I connect to the Internet?

A In most cases, you connect your Web server to the Internet as a standalone system. Your primary concern is then to prevent Internet hackers from attacking the server itself and accessing unauthorized information or corrupting the system.

In some cases, you might have the Web server connected to an internal network outside a firewall, or you might even have a small LAN connected to the Web server for attaching other servers or for attaching the workstations of content developers.

Q Should I use the Guest account for Internet users?

A Disable the Guest account on any Internet connected systems (use only the
IUSR_*computername* account for anonymous logon) and make sure that the
Everyone group does not have excess permissions in sensitive directories. Also
keep in mind that, by default, the Everyone group gets automatic access to any
new directories you create, so you need to check permissions after creating new
directories.

19

DAY 20

Windows 2000 Performance Monitoring and Tuning

In the past two weeks, you learned about installing and exploring Windows 2000. You learned about the Registry settings and how to manage security and audit the server. By now, you should be comfortable using and manipulating the different components of Windows 2000 Server.

In today's session, you'll learn how to fine-tune the server to obtain maximum performance using the tools and techniques provided by Microsoft. You'll learn how to use the Performance Monitor and Network Monitor, two of the critical tools that are part of the server software.

Using a systematic approach, you'll find out how to discern any network failures, monitor your network for proficiency, and troubleshoot any problems you might encounter. Because so much depends on the type of server you use, the number of users you connect, and the type of work being performed, it is difficult to provide figures that might give you some idea of how well your particular environment is running. For the most part, Windows 2000 Server does a fine job of performing with maximum speed and efficiency; in fact, Microsoft offers a few ways for you to manipulate the manner in which it manages this function.

In this day you'll discover the following points:

- How to start and use the Performance Monitor
- Which tasks Windows 2000 allows you to modify to improve overall system performance
- The different tools available to tune Windows 2000 Server
- How to control the vast amounts of data offered by Performance Monitor
- How to export data from Performance Monitor logs into your spreadsheets or word processors
- How to set up and manage disk-drive capacity using the tools available with Windows 2000 Server

We start the day by reviewing some fundamentals, and then look at the main tools—the Performance Monitor and Network Monitor.

What Windows 2000 Can and Cannot Do for Performance

For the most part, Windows 2000 does a good job of managing performance. If you are at all unsure about its performance, you are better off allowing the server to manage this aspect of your operation.

There are, however, several things that affect performance and Windows 2000 can do nothing about them; you need to know about these and decide what path you will follow to provide maximum performance. Performance management might be a sound goal for you to achieve, but it is also extremely challenging. You must decide whether the challenge is worth the additional work.

Naturally, performance is excellent when you purchase the largest machine available, have a huge amount of disk space and memory, and provide services for only a hundred or so people who aren't demanding in their needs. What? Your company doesn't do this? We can hear you laughing already. So what can be done for real-world users?

Purchasing a high-end computer is an obvious—although sometimes neglected— aspect of performance. Whether you use an Intel Pentium Pro or a Symmetrical Multi-Processing system has an effect that is hard to mitigate any other way. In addition, using 128MB rather than 64MB is a limitation that you can easily resolve by adding memory. Windows 2000 does neither of these things for you. Memory is so inexpensive these days that adding more memory is often a quick solution for speeding up a system.

Does your machine use older IDE technology as opposed to newer Ultra-Wide SCSI-3 drives? Are you using the latest PCI technology or an older EISA bus type? These factors all affect the performance of your server. The PCI format offers 32-bit data transfer rather than 16-bit, effectively doubling the speed at which data moves across the bus.

Configuring your data and disk drives offers methods for increasing (or decreasing) performance. By using a file server with only one drive for all your data, instead of spreading it across a number of drives, you reduce the server's performance.

Moving applications around can buy you significant processor time. When you are running two heavily used applications on the same server, you can increase the server speed by spreading the applications across multiple servers. Using Microsoft's SMS and SQL Server in addition to IIS can bring your server to its knees when they are all heavily used. Spreading the load across other servers is more efficient and effective.

The type of network cards you use and their respective speeds also conspire to add or detract from system performance. If you think that because your network is an Ethernet 10 or 100Mbps it isn't critical to worry about the particular cards you use, think again. Just as some manufacturers offer faster video cards through more effective design, so do many network card manufacturers. The use of a card primarily designed for a client machine rather than a server can significantly affect service.

In addition, you can slow down your system by loading too many protocols. This is a common mistake we see in many organizations. Adding unnecessary protocols affects your server's memory and CPU time. Each protocol requires a separate browser list, and these browser lists take services from the master browser—which is often your server.

In addition to all the factors already mentioned, you'll find that as you add *controllers* to the network, they can affect your server—especially when they are tuned to update too often. By default, Windows 2000 uses a 15-minute cycle to maintain synchronization between its controllers; this might be too often for your network. Raising the limit somewhat can help overall system performance. How often do you perform these updates? It really depends on several factors: The number of users, how busy the system is, how widespread it is, and how critical it is to have instant recovery all play a part in setting this value.

Finally, the applications that you run can become your largest bottleneck. A poorly designed application offers little opportunity for performance improvement, and you

20

have to live with that. It is important that your developers understand the need for well-designed, fast processes, and that they don't rely on the machine, instead of improved application design, for processing power.

All these things affect performance, and offer Windows 2000 Server no effective way of improving that performance. You need to manage these items—in addition to the things that Windows 2000 allows you to manage—in order to coax the best out of your server.

Tuning Windows 2000 Server boils down to managing how Windows 2000 uses its memory and whether the virtual memory usage is well defined for maximum speed. By far, the single most important change you make to improve performance is to add more memory. If you use a machine with 64MB, adding another 64MB or even another 128MB will perform wonders. This is often the fastest and, relatively speaking, least expensive method for speed improvement in Windows 2000 Server.

Managing Server Memory

This is one area where you have a reasonable level of control when tuning your server. Besides the obvious addition of physical memory, you can use various methods to improve memory management over the memory that is presently installed.

NEW TERM   Here's a review of the basics of how Windows 2000 manages memory. First you need to know a couple of terms. Later today, you'll learn to use the Performance Monitor and configure it to provide you with log data for later use. One of the terms used with this tool is *available bytes*. This term applies to how much actual memory Windows 2000 can acquire at any given time. You need to be aware that when this figure from Performance Monitor falls below about 4MB or 5MB, most of the memory is in use, and your system begins to clog up.

NEW TERM   Another term used is *commit bytes*. This term refers to the actual amount of memory that all the applications need at any given moment. As applications start up, they reserve memory but don't actually begin to use it without committing it first. If all the applications running commit to more memory than your server provides, Windows 2000 begins to thrash the hard drive to page out the applications and continue processing. The more that Windows 2000 pages data to and from the hard drive, the slower your system becomes.

NEW TERM   Windows 2000 manages disk *paging* a little differently from Windows; it needs some *virtual memory*—disk space used as memory—regardless of how much physical memory it has available. Windows 2000 enables you to manage some aspects of this memory usage.

Task 20.1: Managing Virtual Memory Usage.

Step 1: Description

This task enables you to decide how Windows 2000 uses memory and to set out whether system performance or memory usage is more important to your server.

Step 2: Action

1. Log on to your system using an administrator account.

2. Open the MMC for Computer Management by clicking Start, Programs, Administrative Tools, Computer Management. You see a screen similar to the one shown in Figure 20.1.

FIGURE 20.1

The Local Computer Management window.

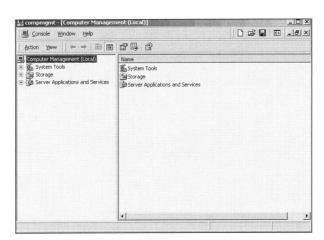

3. Right-click on Computer Management (Local) in the left pane and select Properties. You'll see a dialog box containing three tabs—General, Network Identification, and Advanced. Select the Advanced tab. You should see a screen similar to that in Figure 20.2.

4. Click on Performance Options to see two areas, Application Response and Virtual Memory. By default, the system uses the figure that you supply for disk space as the amount of memory. In the Application Performance area, you can modify how Windows 2000 Server responds to applications running on the server. If you set this bar to Background Services (the default), Windows 2000 doesn't provide any special priority to the applications running in the foreground.

20

FIGURE 20.2

The Advanced properties tab.

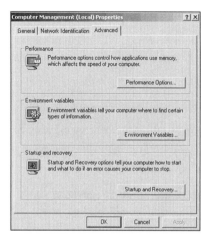

Note

Generally, you don't want to change Application Performance. It is the server's job to give priority to requests from clients and background applications such as SQL Server.

5. Next, click the Change button in the Virtual Memory field. You get a dialog box similar to the one shown in Figure 20.3.

FIGURE 20.3

The Virtual Memory dialog box.

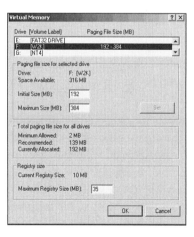

6. Choose the various settings according to your needs. For this task, change them to see what happens. As you can see, various options are available. For the most part,

▼

the Windows 2000 settings are probably fine. If you have trouble, modify them to provide relief. The paging file can grow to 384MB on my machine, although it is currently restricted by the amount of hard disk space available that shows as 316MB, as you can see in Figure 20.3. The administrator has to examine what needs to run on the server to determine the size of the page file needed.

Use the Performance Monitor to benchmark your system, and then make adjustments and evaluate the effects of the change. This is a trial and error process. Microsoft recommends that you set the size of the paging file equivalent to the amount of RAM plus 12MB.

You might see that the Set tab is grayed out in the picture. It doesn't offer the option until you change one of the values in the Initial or Maximum Size fields. It is most effective if you set the value to the recommended amount and use this on all your drives. You don't see a paging file in the picture on some drives as I am currently triple-booting this machine. This means I have drives on the laptop for Windows 98, Windows NT 4.0, and Windows 2000. I don't want Windows 2000 using space on the other boot drives.

7. Exit by clicking the OK button three times to close all the windows. If you decrease one of the paging file sizes, you will need to reboot the machine. Increases can be done with no reboot.

Caution	You can delete a page file by setting the two paging options to zero. You should not do this without a clear understanding of the ramifications, as it will severely affect your computer's performance.

▲

Step 3: Review

By specifying different settings, you can provide some measure of performance management. By using the Performance Monitor, discussed later, you can monitor the amount of committed bytes over a specific time frame and note the maximum value reported. This provides you with a guide as to how much memory is needed, and you can set the paging file size accordingly, with a small additional overhead for future growth.

Of course, you can perform this action on any other Windows 2000 computer you have administration rights for on your network. You do this by selecting Action, Connect to Another Computer and entering the name of the machine you want to connect to and manage. Naturally, this assumes that you can access the other computer across your network and that you have the necessary administrative authority.

Before you tune anything, however, you need to know if there is a problem—you find this out by using the monitoring tools offered by Windows 2000.

20

So what are some of the things that Windows 2000 allows you to monitor? In the following list are some of the tasks and counters available:

- Cache
- Memory
- NetBEUI
- Objects
- Physical disk
- Processes
- RAS
- Server
- System
- TCP

Now that you understand some of the tasks that Windows 2000 performs, and some of the tasks that you need to perform to improve performance, you need to know what the current performance is before deciding whether anything needs to be done. That's the job of the Performance Monitor.

Understanding and Using the Performance Monitor

Windows 2000 provides new graphical tools for monitoring the system. These are, in our opinion, an improvement over the older designs because, as Confucius once said, "a picture is worth a thousand words."

Graphs and charts, however, are only a part of the picture. You need to ensure that you understand the reference in order to make sense of the numbers. For example, providing a component load figure without providing a frame of reference is useless. Did the load occur over one second or over a month? Figures provided by Windows 2000 tools usually give you that frame of reference so that you can use them in the proper context.

Finally, using data with little or no long-term frame of reference might not be the most effective method. You need to gather data and try to relate that data to a useful trend. For example, you need to review performance over a week or month to see the long-term aspects, yet you also need to review one day compared to another and one part of a day compared to another part to ensure that short-term bottlenecks aren't bringing users to their knees. Part of performance monitoring lies in combining these aspects to provide a comprehensive short- and long-term strategy.

The Performance Monitor provides you with several options. In Task 20.2, you'll learn how to open the Performance Monitor.

Task 20.2: Starting and Running the Performance Monitor.

Step 1: Description

This task shows you how to start the Performance Monitor tools and begin collecting valuable data.

Step 2: Action

1. Log on to your system using an administrator account.

2. Go to Start, Programs, Administrative Tools and find the tool called Performance. Click on this option to start the monitor. You see a screen similar to the one shown in Figure 20.4.

FIGURE 20.4

Using Performance Monitor.

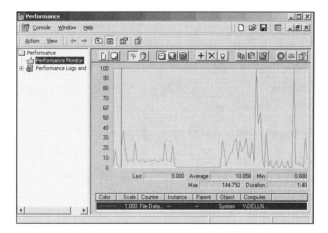

3. By default, the monitor starts in Chart mode. You can change the mode to another option such as Histogram or Report.

4. Right-click on the Details pane and select Properties. You should see a picture something like that shown in Figure 20.5.

5. As you see in the Type field, Performance Monitor uses three types of modes. These include the Default Graph, a Histogram Mode, and a Report Mode.

6. Choose the various modes and experiment with changing them.

7. Exit Performance Monitor by selecting Console, Exit.

20

FIGURE 20.5

Performance Monitor Properties.

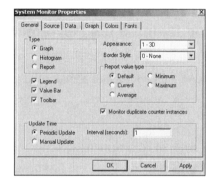

Step 3: Review

By using Performance Monitor, you see how your system is managing its resources, and you collect valuable information. In this task you see how to start the program and show information using various methods such as charts and reports. This is a significant tool in your performance-management arsenal.

In the following section, you'll learn how to manipulate and use the various parts of Performance Monitor.

Using Performance Monitor

Now that you know how to start Performance Monitor, you need to learn about the various logging and reporting aspects of the tool. Notice that the monitor isn't actually doing anything yet. Microsoft doesn't want to presume that it knows what events you want to use when starting the monitor, so you need to tell it to perform a function. (You'll learn to do that a little later in this section.) Following is a basic introduction to the components of this tool.

The main menu across the top of the screen shows the typical MMC options of Console, Window, and Help. Beneath those are the Action and View menus that allow you to add a new window or view the tool in a different manner such as with or without the console tree or status bar.

The icons presented just below offer a quick jump to managing properties. From left to right, the standard icons consist of the following:

- Set a new counter
- Clear the current display
- View current activity

- View log file data

- Chart, histogram, and report displays

- Adding or deleting counters

- Highlighting the display

- Copy, paste, and display properties

- Freeze the display

- Update the data

- Help

These icons represent a fast method for performing certain tasks—because they are useful, it is recommended that you learn them.

Begin using the Performance Monitor by adding a counter. Click on the plus sign or right-click on the Details panel and select Add Counters. You see a dialog box similar to the one shown in Figure 20.6.

FIGURE 20.6

Adding counters to Performance Monitor.

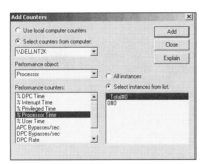

Using this dialog box, you set the options you want. Each option represents a different function, explained as follows:

- **Use Local Computer Counters**—You use this box to select the local machine that you are going to monitor (the one you are currently using).

- **Select Counters from This Computer**—You use this box to select the computer that you are going to monitor. You can monitor any machine on the network, provided that you have the necessary privileges. Naturally, this applies only to Windows 2000 Servers and Workstations. As you see in Figure 20.6, you can select the computer by typing the computer name preceded by a double-backslash or selecting it from the drop-down list.

20

- **Performance Object**—This is a drop-down list that enables you to select the object that you want to monitor. You can monitor almost two dozen different objects, as shown in the following list:

  ACS/RSVP Service

  Active Server pages

  Browser

  Cache

  Distributed Transaction Coordinator

  DNS

  FileReplicaconn

  FileReplicaset

  FTP Service

  ICMP

  IP

  Job Object

  Job Object Details

  LogicalDisk

  Memory

  NBT Connection

  NetBEUI

  NetBEUI Resource

  NWLink IPX

  NWLink NetBIOS

  NWLink SPX

  Objects

  Paging File

  PhysicalDisk

  Process

  Processor

  RAS Port

  RAS Total

  Redirector

Server

Server Work Queues

System

Telephony

Thread

> What you see in the drop-down box depends on what is installed on your system.

- **All Instances**—Most of the objects that you monitor have multiple instances, and this option enables you to set up all those instances for monitoring. An instance relates to the number of items; for example, if you have more than one RAS port, this information shows in the Instance window. You only see this option highlighted if the object you specify uses it.

- **Select Instances from List**—Because most objects have multiple instances, this option enables you to select one of them for monitoring. You only see this option highlighted if the object you specify uses it.

- **Performance Counters**—This scrollable list permits you to select the object's associated counters that you want to monitor.

- **Add**—This button enables you to add the selected counter to the list for monitoring.

- **Close**—Click this button to close the option and go back to the main dialog box.

- **Explain**—You can obtain a more detailed explanation of any counter that you select by clicking this button. As you see in Figure 20.7, you are shown additional information in the Counter Definition box that appears.

The Performance Monitor enables you to monitor more than one machine at a time by selecting the processor objects you want. (You can select multiple objects by holding the Shift key while scrolling down the list and then clicking the Add option.) Using the chart option is fine, but as you see in Figure 20.8, you'll have a problem if you use too many objects. Although the program colors each line differently, you'll find that the lines are difficult to follow.

20

Tip
> Press Ctrl+H to highlight the line in the graph that corresponds to the counter that you selected from the list at the bottom of the screen. This helps you when you are monitoring multiple counters in the view graph.

FIGURE 20.7

FIGURE 20.7

Obtaining additional information in the Add Counters dialog box.

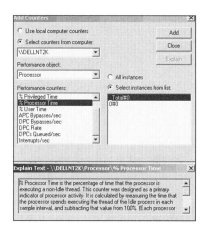

FIGURE 20.8

Lines can become complex if you try to chart too many objects in the Performance Monitor.

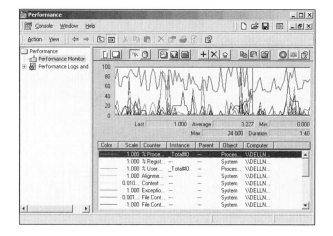

By changing the chart options, you can present the data in a different fashion that is a little easier to read. Do this by right-clicking on the Details pane and selecting Properties. The program shows you a dialog box similar to the one shown in Figure 20.9. This dialog box offers a multitude of settings and enables you to control the way that data is presented. By playing with the various controls, you can find a comfortable view for your server.

Performance options typically start by showing you the General tab. If you click on the Histogram option, the chart changes to show a chart similar to the one shown in Figure 20.10. As you see in the picture, the data appears in a chart style using vertical bars instead of lines for each option that is selected.

FIGURE **20.9**

Changing chart options.

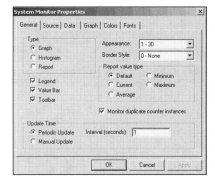

FIGURE **20.10**

Using options to modify the chart.

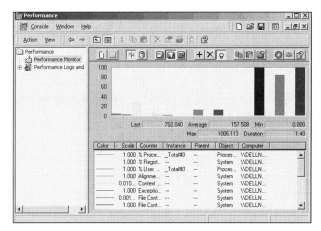

As you can see in Figure 20.9, the Legend, Value, and Toolbar options are on. By turning them off you get a totally different look to your monitor. You can see this in Figure 20.11.

The Legend option shows you the values associated with each chart or line to enable you to tell what each object on your chart represents. Unless your chart is simple, it is recommended that you leave this option selected.

The Value Bar option provides several counters, including Last, Average, Minimum and Maximum, and Graph Time. Specify whether these are to be displayed by clicking on the Value Bar box.

20

FIGURE 20.11

Turning off Legend, Value, and Toolbar.

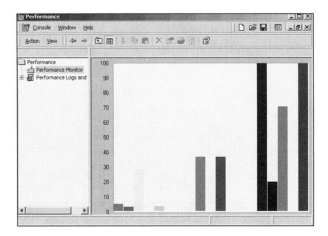

Tip

You might find yourself with a display that doesn't contain the Toolbar. This can be disconcerting when you did not actively choose to hide it. You can choose to show this menu bar by right-clicking on the details of the dialog box and selecting Properties. Then click on the Toolbar option and click Close. By using these options, you can set up the display to use a minimal amount of your desktop space.

As you saw in Figure 20.9 there are many options for displaying the performance information on the machine you are monitoring. You can change the Appearance by selecting the default 1-3D or by selecting 0-Flat from the drop-down menu on the right side of the dialog box. You can also change the Border style. In the Report Value area, there are a number of options. You can set the tool to show the averages for your selected fields, or show just the minimum or maximum.

Note

Using report value types other than Default or Current when you are monitoring data in real-time incurs a lot of overhead because of the need to make the necessary calculations across all the samples for each value you want displayed.

The field called Monitor Duplicate Counter Instances is selected by default. It shows counters that support multiple instances with an index number. You turn off this feature by clearing the check box. This changes the data you see in the Select Instances from List box when you use the Add option. Finally, the Update Time dialog allows you to select how quickly Performance Monitor updates its data. By selecting Manual, the tool waits until you tell it to update its data, reducing system overhead as the tool sits idle until you perform the update. After setting this option, you need to click the Update icon (next to the Help icon) whenever you want to see updated information.

The Properties dialog has a number of other tabs, however. These include Source, Data, Graph, Colors, and Font. You use these to manipulate additional aspects of the tool. Under the Source tab you can select Saved Log File and then select only the Time Range you want displayed. This is useful when you are reviewing data from your log files and want to review only a particular time frame.

The Data option shows the currently selected data fields and allows you to add or delete fields and change the color, width, and style associated with each field as well as selecting the scale you want to show. You can see these in Figure 20.12.

FIGURE 20.12

Changing the Data Display Options.

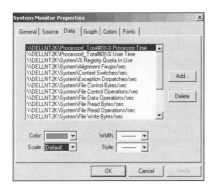

The Graph display allows you to set up your graph with a title and label to make it easier to view. You can also turn on horizontal or vertical grids and decide what scale you want to show. In the following task, you set up Performance Monitor to show grid lines and display a title.

Task 20.3: Setting Up Performance Monitor Graph Options.

20

Step 1: Description

This task focuses on showing you how to set up Performance Monitor to show your graphs with titles and labels.

Step 2: Action

1. Log on to your system using an administrator account.

2. Go to Start, Programs, Administrative Tools, Performance.

▼ 3. Right-click on the Details pane and select Properties. Choose the Graph tab.

▼ 4. In the area called Graph Title type the following: `Cool Stuff Displayed`.

5. Now select the Y-Axis Label field and type `Other info`.

6. Click on both the Horizontal and Vertical Grid options. You can leave the scale options with their default values. Your options should look like Figure 20.13.

FIGURE 20.13

Setting Up Graph Options.

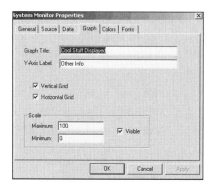

7. After you have completed steps 1–6, select OK to finish. You should see your Performance Monitor details change to reflect these new options. It should look like Figure 20.14.

FIGURE 20.14

Performance Monitor with Title and Y-Axis set.

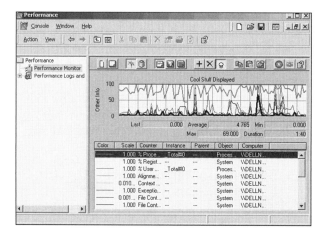

▲

Step 3: Review

By using the Graphing Options you can change the look of your graph by adding titles or grid lines.

Note

For the best results when monitoring, you might want to do the following before starting:

- Stop screen-saver programs.
- Turn off any services that are non-essential or not relevant to monitoring.
- Increase the paging file to physical memory size plus 100 MB.

The Performance Logs and Alerts view in Performance Monitor is used to manage your logs and to set up special options that tell Performance Monitor to alert someone when a particular event occurs. The two log types are Counter logs and Trace logs. Counter logs provide information about those counters you set earlier (refer to Figure 20.6). Trace logs are used to monitor and trace specific information.

Any existing logs appear when you double-click on the Log field in the Details pane. A green icon indicates that a log is running; a red icon indicates that a log has been stopped. Windows 2000 provides you with a default System view log that you can use as a starting point. By default, log files are created in the PerfLogs folder on your root directory, and a sequence number is appended to the file name you entered. The file type is defined as binary (with the .blg extension).

Trace logging of file I/O and page faults can generate a very large amount of data. Microsoft recommends that you limit your trace logging of file I/O and page fault options to a maximum of two hours.

Alerts are useful for keeping an eye on several conditions within your server in order to detect problems as they occur. Using this view enables you to set various parameters and tell the monitor program to log the events. This way, you can run the monitor over a selected time frame and quickly see only the data that you requested.

Normally, the data that is collected in a Performance Monitor log file is of little use to you, or is only selectively useful. Wading through all that data to find out the condition of your server is inefficient. Use the Alert view to select only those critical values that interest you.

For example, you might log the object called Server and select Logons Per Second and Logons Total to see how quickly your system grows. These values provide a reasonable indicator of the speed at which your system expands. If the numbers change quickly, your system might be growing quickly, and you need to take care that bottlenecks aren't developing.

20

In Task 20.4, you'll learn to set up the Performance Monitor to perform in Alert mode and collect only the data that interests you.

Task 20.4: Setting Up Performance Monitor to Issue Alerts.

Step 1: Description

This task focuses on showing you how to set up Performance Monitor to issue alerts concerning the conditions that you select.

Step 2: Action

1. Log on to your system using an administrator account.

2. Go to Start, Programs, Administrative Tools, Performance.

3. Select the Alert view by clicking the area called Performance Logs and Alerts. Existing alerts will show in the Details pane. In the right Details pane, right-click and select New. You see the New Alert Log screen shown in Figure 20.15.

FIGURE 20.15

Showing the New Alerts options.

4. Select the Create New Alerts options. You are shown a dialog box asking for a name. Type **My Alerts** and click OK. You see a dialog box like that shown in Figure 20.16.

FIGURE 20.16

The Create New Alerts options.

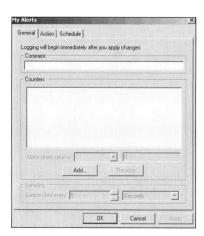

5. You can add text to the Comment field if you'd like to further describe your alerts. Select the items about which you want to be alerted by using the Add button to tell the monitor program which ones you want to use.

▼
6. After you choose an alert, the Alert When Value Is field is made available for you to enter the out-of-range value indicating when you want a record written.

7. Select whether the record is written only when a certain value is Over or Under the value that you specify.

For example, you might select the PhysicalDisk object and the % Disk Time counter, using an Alert When Value is Over 60 to indicate that a record is written every time the disk drive spends more than 60 percent of its time servicing read and writes. You see this in Figure 20.17.

FIGURE 20.17

A sample Alert log.

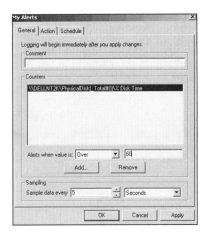

8. You can choose any number of Alert events using all the data available to you in the options dialogs. When you are finished, select Console, Exit to finish.

▲

Step 3: Review

By using the Alert view, you can select the data you want to see and not be inundated with information. Use this view to detect problems or select parameters on your server.

In the next task, we show you how to monitor the system and have it alert you when there are problems with disk free space.

Task 20.5: Setting Up Performance Monitor to Alert You About Free Space.

Step 1: Description

This task shows you how to set up Performance Monitor to issue alerts concerning the amount of free space left on your drives.

20

▼ **Step 2: Action**

1. Log on to your system using an administrator account.

2. Go to Start, Programs, Administrative Tools, Performance.

3. Select the Alert view by clicking on Performance Logs and Alerts menu item.

4. Click on the Alerts item. You will see the alert you just created in Task 20.4 called My Alerts. Select My Alerts, Properties. You see a dialog box similar to the one shown in Figure 20.16.

5. Select Add and then select the Object called LogicalDisk.

6. Select the Counter called Free Megabytes and click Add and then Close.

7. Decide on the amount of free space about which you want to be informed. Choose whether the figure is to be used as the low or high number by selecting Over or Under. For example, you might select 50 and Under if you want to be informed when the drive has only 50MB of space left on it.

8. Click the Add button to activate the logging. Click Done to complete the action. The Performance Monitor begins logging; it tells you when the drive has fewer than 50MB of free space available.

9. Allow the monitor program to run as long as you need. When you are finished, you
▲   can select Console, Exit.

Step 3: Review

By using the Alert view, you can select specific data about which to be alerted and use this to manage your server effectively.

You learned to use the Performance Monitor to your advantage in this section. Setting up and managing the various log activities isn't onerous; however, you do need to remember that the act of using this tool might affect some of the figures that you log. Like any application, the program uses resources, and if you attempt to log too many objects and counters the overall system performance is affected.

Figuring Out Which Counters to Use

A difficult aspect of monitoring is determining exactly what to monitor and how to set the limits and counters associated with the objects being monitored. Why is this task so difficult? The difficulty arises because each site has different needs and operational requirements. Additionally, you often have to perform this task along with all your other jobs, and this leaves little time for sifting through all the potential data that is available.

Many of the available counters are extremely specialized and too complex for this book to discuss. Most sites, when they perform monitoring at all, do only what is necessary—and that is what is being done in this section.

By providing a small amount of guidance, we hope to ensure that you are aware of what items you might consider monitoring and how to set the particular counters for each object. Use the suggestions that follow, and consider increasing the settings as needed when a problem occurs.

The best path for you to follow might be to use the available tools and begin monitoring your network to obtain a baseline that fits your needs. In this way, you ensure that any figures used are relevant and reflect both how your server is used and its idiosyncrasies. If you have the luxury of time and resources, you might consider performing stress tests and loads on the system to see how it handles the excess.

Following are some of the counters that you might use:

- **Server:Bytes/second**—This counter tells you how busy your server is at any given time. It tells you how many bytes are transmitted across the network cards per second, enabling you to gauge the activity levels and compare them to your acceptable network load levels.

- **Server:Logons total**—This counter tells you how many users are signing on to the server and provides some idea of when the machine is its busiest. It also provides an indication of how big your server is becoming (if tracked over time).

- **PhysicalDisk:Percent Disk Time**—This counter helps you recognize and perhaps mitigate a disk bottleneck. Look for figures that show that the disk is being utilized 80 or 90 percent of the time, and consider ways to reduce the load on the drive.

- **PhysicalDisk:Disk Queue Length**—This counter also helps you recognize and perhaps mitigate a disk bottleneck. If the queue is greater than two or three too often, look for ways to reduce the load.

- **Processor:Processor Time**—If your machine is constantly running near the top of its capacity (80 percent or more), look for ways to reduce the processor load. You might move applications or services to other machines, or add additional processors to the existing machine.

- **Interrupts:Second**—Use this to determine whether too many interrupts are occurring, for example more than about 3000 to 3500 on a Pentium machine. Perhaps the video-board driver is poorly designed—or faulty.

- **Memory:pages/second**—The pages-per-second counter is used to help determine whether the server has a reasonable balance between physical memory and disk space usage. Some paging is normal, but when too much occurs, the system slows.

20

A number is difficult to determine because it differs by machine. Watch the counter carefully for a while, and develop a threshold that works for your site. Look for numbers somewhere between 5 (or fewer) and (no more than 20).

Sending Alerts

You have other options available to you besides logging the events. You can also tell Performance Monitor to send a message to a user when the event occurs. Select the Properties dialog box again and click on the Action tab. You see a dialog box that enables you to modify how the program manages data. If you select the Send a Network Message field and specify a user, Performance Monitor sends that user a message when the event occurs. Naturally, it is important to ensure that the number of messages you send isn't excessive, or the user will be inundated with them. You see an example of a message to a user who is running WinPopUp in Figure 20.18.

FIGURE 20.18

Sending an alert to a user.

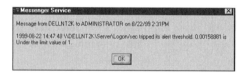

In addition to sending the user a message, the dialog box enables you to log the events in the Application Log and set whether the service updates automatically on a periodic basis or manually.

Finally, collecting the data you need often results in a large amount of information, and the Windows 2000 Server Tools are poorly equipped to manipulate this data. It is likely that you will export the data to a spreadsheet or other program for manipulation. Task 20.6 shows you how to export this data to another application.

Task 20.6: Exporting Data by Using Performance Monitor.

Step 1: Description

This task shows you how to export the data collected using Performance Monitor, and how to send it to another application for manipulation.

Step 2: Action

1. Log on to your system using an administrator account.
2. Go to Start, Programs, Administrative Tools, Performance.
3. You need to be logging the data first. Follow the instructions in Task 20.5 and select whatever logging options you need.

▼   4. To export a log choose one. For this exercise choose the Alerts item and then click
        on Action, Export List. You are shown a dialog box that asks for the location of the
        export file and its name, as well as the type of file you are creating. Select the file
        type and name, and click the Save button to produce your export file. The resulting
▲   file is ready to export into your application for manipulation.

Step 3: Review

The Performance Monitor enables you to create export files consisting of selected information, ready to be used in your external programs. This provides an effective means for
manipulating the data from large files and for providing more detailed and graphical
business reports.

Deciding How Often You Should Monitor

You need to consider how often and under what circumstances you will perform monitoring of your system. Microsoft suggests some general guidelines. For routine monitoring,
start by logging activity over 15-minute intervals and see how that affects your environment. If you are monitoring to manage a specific problem, vary the interval to try to capture a good snapshot of what's happening. To monitor a specific process at a specific
time, set up a frequent update interval, unless you are monitoring a problem that mani-
fests slowly, such as a memory leak. For lingering problems like that you will want to
use a longer interval.

You also need to consider the overall length of time you want to monitor. Updating data
every 30 seconds is reasonable if you aren't monitoring very long, such as a couple of
hours. But if you'll be monitoring a system for eight hours or more, you shouldn't use an
interval shorter than 300 seconds (5 minutes). Using too frequent a setting can cause the
system to generate a large amount of data, which can be difficult to work with as well as
can increase system overhead.

Finally, if you want to monitor a large number of objects and counters, this can generate
large amounts of data and consume disk space. You should try to strike a balance
between the number of objects you plan to monitor and the sampling frequency to keep
your log file size manageable.

20

Load Balancing

One of the things you use all these tools for is to ensure that your servers are using
resources in an optimal fashion. By balancing the load across your servers you can
maximize throughput and better serve your clients.

Before you start trying to tune your system you should consider the following:

- Only make one change at a time. This way you can easily rectify any impact and notice if your change fixes the problem. Making multiple changes often makes it difficult to assess the impact of each individual change.

- Monitor the system after every change. This can help you understand the effect of the change and determine whether additional changes are required. Make one change at a time and test the effects on performance.

- Review the event logs. Some performance problems generate output that can be read using Event Viewer.

- Compare performance. Consider comparing the performance of programs that run over the network with locally run programs. This can let you see whether the network is part of the problem.

To balance the load on your network servers, you need to know how busy the machine's disk drives are. Check the Physical Disk\% Disk Time counter, as this indicates what percentage of time the drive is active. If % Disk Time is high (more than 90 percent), check the Physical Disk\Current Disk Queue Length counter to see how many system requests are waiting for disk access to determine if this is the problem. The number of waiting I/O requests should be kept to no more than 1.5 to 2 times the number of spindles making up the physical disk. Most drives only have one spindle so this isn't too hard to figure out. You might have more if you are using RAID drives.

You can use the values in the Current Disk Queue Length and % Disk Time counters to detect bottlenecks with your disk subsystem. If the values are consistently high, you might need to consider upgrading the disk drive or moving some of the files to an additional disk or server.

You can also distribute programs among your servers, reducing the load on any one machine. This is especially important for heavily used programs. You can also use Dfs as we discussed on Day 8, "Managing Files and Using the Distributed File System."

Finally, disk-usage data can help you monitor the workload on your network servers. You can use two types of disk counters: physical disk counters and logical disk counters. *Physical counters* are typically used for capacity planning and for troubleshooting while *logical counters* provide statistics on free space and can help find the source of activity on a physical volume.

When you set up logging for disk performance you should put the log data on another disk or computer so that it doesn't interfere with the disk you are testing.

At a minimum, Microsoft recommends that you monitor the following counters:

- Physical Disk\Disk Reads/sec and Disk Writes/sec
- Physical Disk\Current Disk Queue Length
- Physical Disk\% Disk Time
- Logical Disk\% Free Space

There are many other things to do when trying to balance the load across your servers; this section shows you a few of the more common methods.

Using Event Viewer to Monitor Your Network

On Day 17, "Security Monitoring and Audit Trails," you learned how to use the Event Viewer to review and manipulate the log files. You also use this service to monitor events that might affect your system.

This tool records events that have been defined for later use and analysis. These events include server failure, startup and shutdown, and other activities.

Use this tool when Performance Monitor isn't running. This doesn't mean that there is no data, although it is certainly not as prolific as when you select data using the monitor program. Nonetheless, there is still useful information for you to peruse.

As you recall from Day 17, you start the Event Viewer by selecting Start, Programs, Administrative Tools, Event Viewer. The data it collects is always waiting for you to review, and sometimes you'll find it useful in solving a performance problem.

Looking at the collected data, you can see when staff log on or off the system and view such activities as privilege use and system events. For example, when a user cannot sign on, you can use the event data to see whether a service failed (such as RAS), or whether the user has the necessary access rights and privileges.

By double-clicking on a particular event, you get a description of what occurred. Figure 20.19 shows the event detail for an application log, indicating that the number of logons is low.

As shown in this example, regardless of whether you run Performance Monitor, some data is available for troubleshooting if you have set up the Event Viewer as shown on Day 17.

20

FIGURE 20.19

An event log showing logon warnings.

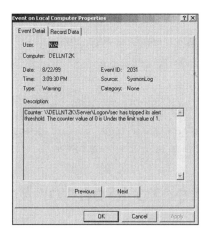

Using Other Windows 2000 Tools

As you learned in the preceding sections, Performance Monitor provides a vast amount of data for use in detecting and solving performance problems. This, however, isn't the only tool available. Windows 2000 offers some other tools that, individually, provide you with information.

Using these tools in addition to the main tool offers you an opportunity to gather information quickly and possibly solve a problem.

Using the Services Applet

The Services applet offers you a quick method for determining what services are running at a given moment. One of your first tasks during a performance crisis might be to see whether any services are running unnecessarily and to shut them down. Use this applet to perform that task.

Start the program by opening Start, Programs, Administrative Tools, Computer Management (Local), System Tools and double-clicking the Services icon. You can see an example in Figure 20.20.

From this dialog box you can see what is running on your machine and decide whether that is appropriate.

Using Dr. Watson

Dr. Watson comes to the rescue by providing a program error-detection utility. Although this isn't really a performance tool, I'm stretching the point a bit because this utility does provide critical information concerning your applications when they fail, and this failure often affects the system. If a program is crashing consistently and taking your server response with it, this tool might be useful in helping determine the problem.

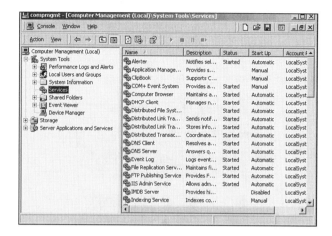

The program starts automatically whenever a program crashes. To start the program manually, select Start and type **DRWTSN32** in the Run command line, or open a DOS command prompt and type the word there. You see an example in Figure 20.21.

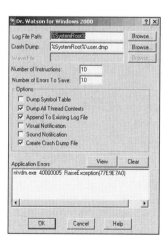

Within this program are options that enable you to set up a log file and maintain a crash dump file for later perusal.

20

Using the Task Manager

Finally, the Windows 2000 Task Manager provides Performance data. To access the Task Manager, press the Ctrl+Alt+Delete keys at the same time. Yes, this is the same key sequence that you use to log on. A dialog box titled Windows 2000 Security pops up. From this box, you can Lock Workstation, Log Off, Shut Down, Change Password, and access the Task Manager. Click on Task Manager, and select the Performance Tab. You see a window similar to the one shown in Figure 20.22.

FIGURE 20.22

The Task Manager's Performance information.

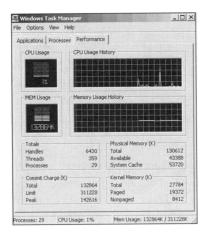

From this tab, you get a quick snapshot of critical performance counters. You can see current CPU and memory usage, as well as some historical information regarding CPU and memory usage.

You can select the Applications, Processes, or Performance window to see different data on what is running. The Processors window is often useful as it tells you how much CPU Time each process is currently consuming.

Summary

Today, you learned how to monitor and manage performance on your Windows 2000 system. Using several tools, you learned that manipulating and logging performance details is fairly easy.

This day offers a challenge to both the writer and reader in finding the optimal balance between too little and too much information. We certainly have not provided too much information because you can buy entire books concerning Windows 2000 tuning, and we have but a few pages to offer. We have, however, provided enough data to whet your appetite and offer some direction concerning the tasks available to you as you begin to use Windows 2000 Server. If your server is part of an extensive network, you might consider the multitude of more detailed tuning books available to help increase your knowledge and capability to set up your server in the manner that best serves your interests. In addition, consult the Performance Analysis and Optimization of MS Windows 2000 Server, Part 1 & 2, for more performance information.

Workshop

To wrap up the day, you can review tasks from the day, and see the answers to some commonly asked questions.

Task List

The information provided today showed you how to manage the files and folders within a Windows 2000 server. You learned to carry out the following tasks:

- Manage virtual memory usage
- Set up and run the Performance Monitor tool
- Set up Performance Manager to use different graph options
- Set up Performance Monitor to issue alerts
- Set up Performance Monitor to alert you about free space
- Export data using Performance Monitor

Q&A

Q Is there a lot I can do to improve the overall performance of my server?

A Windows 2000 provides a reasonably well-managed level of performance, but at times you might need to act to improve the performance of your machine. You can do many things to improve performance, such as purchase faster hard drives or increase system memory. The single fastest way to speed up the system is to provide additional physical memory. In most instances, adding another 64MB or 128MB to a machine speeds things up considerably.

Q Are there ways to monitor what Windows 2000 is doing at any given time so that I can see where bottlenecks occur?

A Yes, you run Performance Monitor to see what is happening in the system. This tool provides you with a wealth of information. You need to be careful when using it, however. The addition of the monitoring can affect your system results because the very act of monitoring activity takes resources. Judicious use of this tool provides the administrator with an excellent overview of system bottlenecks.

20

Q What types of activity can I monitor in Windows 2000?

A Many objects, counters, and instances are available for monitoring. Using Performance Monitor, you monitor events such as processor times, logical and physical disk activities, paging usage, server work queues, and RAS port activity. Be careful not to monitor too much, however, or you will quickly fill disk space and affect system performance.

WEEK 3

DAY 21

Fine-Tuning and Troubleshooting Your Network

Microsoft designed Windows 2000 to run smoothly and to connect to just about anything right out of the box. As you saw way back on Day 2, "Installing Windows 2000 and Client Software," Windows 2000 provides connectivity to various operating systems and hardware platforms through its native support for NetBEUI, TCP/IP, and NWLink (IPX/SPX) transport drivers.

Moreover, Windows 2000 is a general-purpose operating system. Different organizations use W2K for different purposes. So after you install W2K, you'll need to fine-tune the operating system.

As the system administrator, you often are caught up in the pursuit of increased performance and greater reliability. You must balance user demands for more resources against your organization's budgetary restraints. So you need to get as much as possible from your investment in computer technology.

Yesterday, you learned to use the Performance program to view some of the elements controlling how Windows 2000 Server operates. Fine-tuning your server is important, as is fine-tuning your network. You can employ this tool and others to tune and troubleshoot your network. In the remainder of this day, you'll consider where to start tuning your system.

Tuning is important to maximize your existing resources, but it is not as important as keeping your network up and running. In the network management hierarchy, the corner-stone is reliability. If your network experiences sporadic problems or is not up most of the time, people will find alternatives to your network. So troubleshooting and monitoring your network is a key system administrator responsibility. This day discusses client connectivity and the problems you might experience, along with some solutions. Just as with fine-tuning, the first place to check is the "Troubleshooting" section in the Windows 2000 Help facility. It appears as a topic in the Topics list (which you get to by clicking the Contents tab in the Help main window).

Specifically, in this lesson you will learn about network bottlenecks and how to over-come them. You will learn about optimizing network parameters. You also will learn about troubleshooting protocols and the tools to use.

When fine-tuning or troubleshooting your network, approach with care. A minor change can quickly leave your system unusable. If you're not sure, don't be shy about asking questions in a user forum or asking someone with more experience.

Having said that, let's get started with the fine-tuning suggestions that provide the biggest benefit to your network—software.

Optimizing Software for Network Bottlenecks

Fine-tuning software, especially application software, provides the biggest bang for the buck. If you have access to the application's source code, you can try to optimize the application itself; otherwise, try optimizing the network parameters as described in the following sections.

Optimizing Windows 2000 Network Parameters

Optimizing network parameters is a simple procedure that provides great benefits. Setting Registry keys for NetBEUI and TCP/IP is easy and effective.

Caution

> On Day 4, "Understanding and Managing the Registry," you learned about the consequences of altering the Registry. Be careful when editing the Registry. It always is a good policy to back up the Registry before making any changes.

The NetBEUI parameters are found in the following path:

`HKEY_LOCAL_MACHINE\SYSTEM\CurrentControlSet\Services\LanmanServer\Parameters`

Figure 21.1 shows the key and its parameters. Table 21.1 describes the parameters you won't find, but you might want to add to optimize network software.

FIGURE 21.1

Registry Editor showing the contents of the LanmanServer parameters.

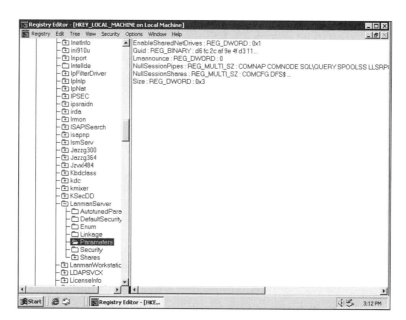

TABLE 21.1   The NetBEUI Parameters

Parameter	Description
EnableOplocks	Specifies whether the server allows clients to use oplocks on files. Oplocks are a significant performance enhancement but have the potential to cause lost cached data on some networks, particularly wide area networks.
MaxWorkItems	Specifies the maximum number of receive buffers, or work items, the server can allocate. If this limit is reached, the transport must initiate flow control at a significant performance cost.
RawWorkItems	Specifies the number of special work items for raw I/O that the server uses. A larger value can increase performance but costs more memory.

21

The corresponding TCP/IP parameter is found in this path (see Figure 21.2):

```
HKEY_LOCAL_MACHINE\SYSTEM\CurrentControlSet\Services\Tcpip\Parameters
```

FIGURE 21.2

*Registry Editor show-
ing the contents of the
TCP/IP parameters.*

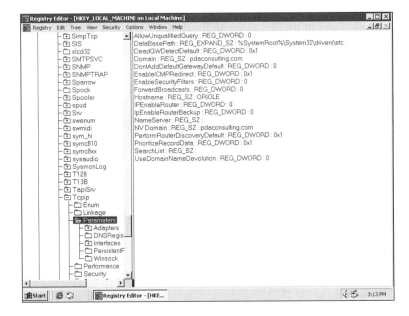

Optimizing Network Traffic

Another way to improve the performance of your network is to increase network
throughput. You can increase network throughput in two ways:

- Provide regular network traffic by submitting loads on the network in a periodic
  pattern; try to avoid output queues. This decreases the number of collisions on the
  wire and therefore increases the overall network throughput.
- Submit a few large files rather than many small ones. The optimum is a file size
  just lower than the expected network media capacity (1.25MB for Ethernet).

Network Performance Issues

Network bottlenecks show up in various ways. Usually, the culprit is the physical LAN
infrastructure, the workstation, or software application demands.

There are three types of network performance problems, each causing the network
protocol to transmit each block of data many times (or to time-out):

- A server overload. The server is asked to do more than it can, possibly because of another inadequate resource such as memory.

- A network overload. The amount of data that needs to be transferred is greater than the capacity of the physical medium.

- A data integrity loss. The network is faulty and intermittently transfers data incorrectly.

For optimal network performance, pay attention to the components you select for your network. This means knowing both hardware and software components: the network medium (for example, 10Base2, 10BaseT, 10BaseF, and 100BaseT), the adapter (NIC) type, the NIC driver, the topology (for example, Ethernet, Token Ring, and star), the frame type, and the network speed. For example, selecting Category 5 cabling provides the best results. Careful selection of hardware and software can make a network operate both more quickly and more reliably. Remember that it is a good idea to select hardware from the Hardware Compatibility List (HCL).

You should take the following basic steps before changing performance parameters:

- Install a high-performance network adapter card in the server. Network adapters can provide widely varying levels of performance. An adapter's bus type, bus width, and amount of onboard memory affect performance the most. Bus types include ISA, EISA, MCA, and PCI bus architectures. Currently, PCI bus slots on the system board provide the best performance. Bus width translates into the number of pins that connect from the adapter to the bus of the computer where it is installed. When the bus width of the adapter matches (or closely matches) the bus width of the computer, performance tends to be better. Always try to use adapters that match the bus width.

- Disable protocols and network cards that you do not use in your environment.

- Use multiple network adapter cards, where appropriate. A characteristic of Windows 2000 Server is its capability to support multiple adapters in the server computer. In the server computer, multiple adapters can be used to connect the server to multiple network segments. This, in effect, increases the total network bandwidth available for accessing the server, because traffic from a given segment does not have to share the network media with traffic from another segment. Also, multiple adapters can be used to connect different network topologies (Ethernet and Token Ring, for example).

- Segment the LAN, where appropriate. Think of your city or town. Every time someone builds a new subdivision next to the main thoroughfare (say, Interstate 95), the traffic increases. The more traffic, the higher the likelihood that an accident will occur. The more accidents, the higher the likelihood that the politicians

21

will approve a new highway (say, I-295 and I-495). Then some of the traffic will use the new routes, decreasing the likelihood of an accident on the original highway.

How to Determine a Network Bottleneck

Yesterday, you saw how to use the Performance program. You can use the Performance program to find bottlenecks. To use Performance to find a network bottleneck, look for situations that indicate that the demand on network resources is larger than the demand on any other resource in your network.

Network Counters

The Network Interface object type includes those counters that describe the rates at which bytes and packets are sent and received over a network TCP/IP connection. It also describes various error counts for the same connection. Table 21.2 lists the Network object counters.

TABLE 21.2 The Network Object Counters

Counter	Description
Bytes Received/sec	The rate at which bytes are received on the interface, including framing characters.
Bytes Sent/sec	The rate at which bytes are sent on the interface, including framing characters.
Bytes Total/sec	The rate at which bytes are sent and received on the interface, including framing characters.
Current Bandwidth	An estimate of the interface's current bandwidth in bits per second (bps). For interfaces that do not vary in bandwidth or for those for which no accurate estimate can be made, this value is the nominal bandwidth.
Output Queue Length	The length of the output packet queue (in packets). If this is longer than two, delays are being experienced, and the bottleneck should be found and eliminated where possible. Because the requests are queued by NDIS in this implementation of Windows 2000, this value will always be 0.
Packets Outbound Discarded	The number of outbound packets that were discarded—even though no errors had been detected—to prevent their being transmitted. One possible reason for discarding such a packet could be to free up buffer space.
Packets Outbound Errors	The number of outbound packets that could not be transmitted because of errors.

Counter	Description
Packets Received Discarded	The number of inbound packets that were discarded—even though no errors had been detected—to prevent their being delivered to a higher-layer protocol. One possible reason for discarding such a packet could be to free up buffer space.
Packets Received Errors	The number of inbound packets that contained errors, preventing them from being delivered to a higher-layer protocol.
Packets Received Non-Unicast/sec	The rate at which non-unicast (that is, subnet broadcast or subnet multicast) packets are delivered to a higher-layer protocol.
Packets Received Unicast/sec	The rate at which (subnet) unicast packets are delivered to a higher-layer protocol.
Packets Received Unknown	The number of packets received via the interface that were discarded because of an unknown or unsupported protocol.
Packets Received/sec	The rate at which packets are received on the network interface.
Packets Sent/sec	The rate at which packets are sent on the network interface.
Packets Sent Non-Unicast/sec	The rate at which packets are requested to be transmitted non-to-non-unicast (that is, subnet broadcast or subnet multicast) addresses by higher layer protocols. The rate includes the packets that were discarded or not sent.
Packets Sent Unicast/sec	The rate at which packets are requested to be transmitted to (subnet) unicast addresses by higher-layer protocols. The rate includes the packets that were discarded or not sent.
Packets/sec	The rate at which packets are sent and received on the network interface.

Counters to Watch

Because a network utilization counter is not available, use some of the preceding counters to determine network utilization; that is, compare the total bytes sent and received with the network bandwidth. Find out whether data is waiting on the output queue to the network from the client to the server and from the server to the client.

Compare also the expected network capacity (for Ethernet, 1.25Mbps) with the actual (Bytes Total/sec) and W2K's estimate of bandwidth. You most likely will find that Windows 2000's estimate of the bandwidth is considerably lower than the expected network capacity. This is due to collisions on the wire that cause the adapter to retry the transmission after a random delay. Urban myth has it that Ethernet networks start to have significant collision at about 67% utilization, or 833,375 bytes per second under random load. To obtain higher network throughput, provide a regular traffic pattern on the net-

21

work where possible. Also, we said previously, you can install faster network interface cards, such as Fast Ethernet, to improve throughput.

Use the following counters with the counters just mentioned to determine whether the network, and not the processor, disk, or something else, really is the bottleneck:

- Processor Time% (Total Processor Time% if more than one processor)
- Page File: %Usage
- Memory: Available Bytes
- Memory: Cached Bytes
- Disk: Bytes Total
- Interrupt rate

Microsoft has some suggestions as to what is acceptable. Processor Time% more than 85% processor usage indicates the processor has become a system bottleneck. Where your system has multiple processors, monitor the counter "System: % Total Processor Time." Also, for systems with multiple processors, System Processor queue length should be two or fewer. Page File usage also should be less than 99%.

Available memory bytes should be a minimum 4MB. In addition, committed bytes should be less than physical RAM.

For Disk Bytes, the higher the average, the more efficient the system is running.

Table 21.3 describes other counters to watch.

TABLE 21.3 Object Counters

Resource	Object: Counter	Suggested Threshold
Disk	Logical Disk: % Free Space	15%
Disk	Logical Disk: % Disk Time	90%
Disk	Physical Disk: Current Disk Queue Length	Number of spindles plus 2
Memory	Memory: Pages/sec	20
Server	Server: Bytes Total/sec	Maximum transfer rate of the network
Server	Server: Work Item Shortages	3
Server	Server: Pool Paged Peak	Amount of physical RAM
Server	Server Work Queues: Queue Length	4

If Performance consistently reports these values, you need to tune or upgrade the affected resource as it is likely a bottleneck.

Configuring Operating System Settings

Windows 2000 includes the capability to configure system settings. You use the Control Panel to configure the system settings.

For information on setting operating system settings, refer to the Release Notes documents—Relnotes.doc—in the root directory of the Windows 2000 Server CD-ROM.

Task 21.1: Configuring the Operating System Settings.

Step 1: Description

You can configure the System settings using the System icon in the Control Panel.

Step 2: Action

1. From the Control Panel, double-click on the System icon.
2. Click the Performance Options button on the Advanced tab. You should see a dialog box like the one in Figure 21.3.

FIGURE 21.3

Performance Options dialog box.

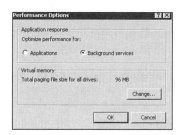

3. Select either Applications or Background services for Application response. Windows 2000 uses the Application Response settings to distribute microprocessor resources among running programs. (Should you select Applications, Windows 2000 will allocate more resources to the foreground application, which is the active program responding to user input). Selecting Background Services allocates an equal amount of resources to all programs.

4. In the next section, you see the total paging file size that Windows 2000 uses for virtual memory. W2K uses *demand paging* to exchange data between random access memory (RAM) and paging files. When you installed Windows, Setup created a virtual memory paging file—Pagefile.sys—on the partition where you installed Windows 2000. Click Change.

21

▼ 5. From the Virtual Memory dialog box shown in Figure 21.4, select the drive. This
      dialog shows the drives where paging files reside and allows you to change the
      paging file size for the selected drive and the Registry size.

FIGURE 21.4

*Virtual Memory
dialog box.*

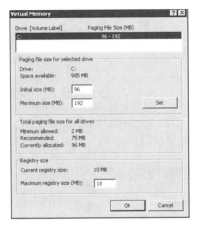

Paging files never decrease below the Initial Size shown that Setup set during
installation. You can enhance your system's performance by setting the initial size
of the paging file to the value in the Maximum Size box. This eliminates the time
required to enlarge the file from the initial size to the maximum size.

Tip

> You can enhance performance by moving the paging file off the drive con-
> taining the SystemRoot folder, for example, \winnt. Moving the paging file
> avoids contention between various reading and writing requests.
>
> Should you place a paging file on the system partition for the recovery fea-
> ture (My Computer, Properties, Advanced Tab, Startup, and Recovery), create
> multiple paging files. Because the Virtual Memory Manager (VMM) alter-
> nates write operations between the paging files, Windows 2000 will access
> the paging file on the boot partition less frequently.
>
> You also can improve performance by creating a paging file for each disk
> when you have multiple disk drives. Distributing information across multiple
> paging files improves performance since the disk drive controller can read
> from and write to multiple drives concurrently. The VMM will attempt to
> write to the paging file on the drive that is available or the least busy.
> Click Set.

   6. Click OK to close the Virtual Memory dialog box.
   7. Click OK to close the Performance Options dialog box.
▲ 8. Click OK to close the System Properties dialog box.

Step 3: Review

Setting system settings enhances the performance of your system. In this task, you saw that you could configure performance options and paging file settings. Use these settings to improve the performance of your system. Again, check out the release notes and Microsoft's site to gain more information about improving the performance of your system.

> **Caution**
>
> The Control Panel programs you use to configure the operating system settings affect the operating environment regardless of the client using the system.

General Tips for Configuring Application Software

Whenever you install application software on your Windows 2000 network, you should think carefully about the implications of the various installation options. Pay particular attention to network traffic, network response time, and resource usage.

When you install network-aware application software, you typically are asked to decide where to store the application's executable data files. You usually have three options:

- Place a single, read-only version of the executable files on a share area on the server (where all client users can share them).

- Place individual copies of all the executable files on the client's local hard disk.

- Use some combination of the first two options (some executables on the server and some on the client's hard disk).

The primary difference in these approaches involves the amount of network traffic each configuration generates, the response time, and the reliability/error recovery implications.

The first option generates the most network traffic. When you store all executables on the server, the system must copy the entire executable over the network to load into client memory. A problem often arises with this option when all the clients load some application programs as part of the boot process. This action can result in large spikes of network activity in the morning when all the PCs are being booted up at the same time. This is the morning traffic jam. In such situations, with very large networks, demand might exceed network bandwidth. This causes performance to suffer. Therefore, it makes better sense to use the third option (a combination of executables stored locally and on the server) when possible.

21

Another application program issue to consider is the use of overlays. Certain application programs (word processors, in particular) make extensive use of overlays. The system calls these overlays into memory when needed and then returns them to disk when not needed. In a network configuration, these overlays might reside on the server (by default); when they are called, they are loaded over the network. This can cause heavy, unanticipated network traffic, which, when not planned for, can affect overall network performance. It is worthwhile to determine whether any of your applications operate in this manner and, if so, to evaluate how to configure the application to minimize this type of traffic.

Network Response Time

Response time over a network configuration clearly is variable—it can be affected by any number of factors. In general, your goal should be to achieve response times that approximate local resource response times (meaning, for example, that you can load a program over the network in about the same time it takes to load from your local disk). This is how your clients will evaluate response time.

If you experience response time problems, check to see whether they are related to throughput. A simple way to check this is to use the Windows 2000 Performance Monitor tool. This tool provides the throughput (Kbps read and write) for network drives.

Network Resources

Your application software configuration should make efficient use of network resources. A good rule of thumb is to use only the network resources necessary for the task currently at hand. Often, clients are configured to create multiple links to multiple servers at boot time when, in reality, only two or three of the links are active at any given time. A good solution to such a situation is to use an application launcher product. You can configure these launchers to create the links for an application package when that package is invoked.

Transport Protocol Software

Windows 2000 supports multiple transport protocols:

- NetBEUI (NetBIOS Extended User Interface), which is a small, efficient, and fast protocol tuned for small LANs.
- TCP/IP (Transmission Control Protocol/Internet Protocol), which provides communication across wide area networks (WANs) and routers.
- NWLink (NetWare Link), which provides a protocol compatible with the Novell NetWare IPX/SPX protocol so that Windows 2000 computers can interoperate with Novell NetWare servers.

- DLC (Data Link Control), which provides connectivity between an IBM mainframe and an MS-DOS–based PC. DLC is a transport protocol defined by IBM. Chiefly, it is used to communicate with IBM mainframes and minicomputers, typically model 3270 or AS/400 machines. In addition, Windows 2000 also uses DLC to communicate with network printers, such as the Hewlett-Packard (HP) LaserJet 4Si. Such printers have a network interface card (NIC) that contains a MAC and a DLC protocol stack.

Tuning TCP/IP Server Transport Protocol

The Windows 2000 Server uses Microsoft's TCP/IP software regardless of the type of TCP/IP software used on the client workstations (Microsoft's, NetManage's Chameleon software, FTP's TCP/IP software, or Wollongong Pathway Access's TCP/IP software).

The TCP/IP parameter that most affects network performance is window size. The TcpWindowSize parameter determines the maximum amount of data (in bytes) that can be sent or received by the system. By default, it uses 32KB (32,768 bytes) as its window size. Because the default is set for the maximum, increasing your client's window size can often improve the performance of large data transfers. If your typical network client/server operations involve the transfer of large, contiguous files, increasing the default window size on the client to 16KB might improve file transfers. In general, larger receive windows will improve performance over high bandwidth networks. For highest efficiency, the window should be an even multiple of the TCP Maximum Segment Size (MSS).

Troubleshooting Network Problems

Network problems can be the toughest to troubleshoot because there are many different components, and the path causing the problem might not be active when you begin troubleshooting.

When troubleshooting network problems, start by verifying the network's operating status before and during the error condition. To evaluate the network problem, check these factors:

- Loose adapter cable. The first rule of troubleshooting network problems is to make sure that the network is plugged into the network interface card. It sounds silly, but it is always worth checking.
- Network adapter failure. Check the event log for system errors related to the network adapter, the workstation, and the server components. Use PING to determine whether the machine is getting out on the wire and how far. When PING cannot talk to its closest neighbor, you might want to enlist the help of a LAN protocol

21

analyzer to determine whether packets are getting onto the network. If not, work forward from the network control card to isolate the faulty component. When the machine is getting to the wire but not its nearest neighbor, use the analyzer to look for congestion, jitter (Token Ring), and broadcast storms.

- IRQ conflict with new adapter. Use W2K Diagnostics to determine a free IRQ, and then set the IRQ of the adapter to a free IRQ. If you suspect an IRQ conflict, disable the mouse in the Registry by setting the start value to Ox4. You also might want to disable the serial ports. A little later, you'll see how to use WINMSD to check out the assigned IRQs.

- Protocol mismatch. When two machines are active on the same network but still cannot communicate, it might be because they are using different protocols. To communicate successfully, both machines must use the same protocol. If machine A is speaking only NetBEUI, and machine B is speaking only TCP/IP, the two machines cannot establish a successful connection. Use the Network applet in the Control Panel to determine supported protocols.

- External network problems. If the hardware on the local machine checks out, there might be an external network error. Use PING to isolate the problem. Attempt to ping the closest neighbor (moving out) until a problem is seen. Also, use a LAN protocol analyzer to help locate jitter (Token Ring only), congestion, and broadcast storms.

Isolating Hardware Problems

Isolating configuration errors from hardware errors is often the easiest way to pinpoint the source of a problem. Hardware problems might originate from a defective network adapter or an incompatible network adapter driver. This is why you always should install Microsoft's Loopback adapter when you install Windows 2000 Server. This way, you can log on to the system even when the network adapter completely fails.

On a Windows 2000 Professional or a Windows 2000 Server operating in server mode, you always can log on using the local account database. You log on locally by selecting the computer name rather than the domain name in the logon dialog box's From field. You then can use the Administrator account you created when you installed Windows 2000 Professional—that is, if you remember the Administrator password. If you do not know the password and you have no cached authentication information to use, the only recourse is to solve the problem in a blind fashion, as detailed here:

1. Replace the network card with one of the same type configured the same.
2. Try the repair process assuming you haven't updated the Rescue Disk.

3. Copy the system event log to a disk where the file system is a FAT partition.

4. Read the log using another Windows 2000 computer to try to discover the cause of the failure.

If this process does not work, you have to delete and reinstall Windows 2000.

Standalone Card Tests

It's a good idea to test the card and the LAN cable before going any further. The four kinds of tests you do on most networks include these:

- On-board diagnostic
- Local loopback test
- "Network live" loopback test
- Sender/responder test

The first three tests usually come on a diagnostics disk that you get with the LAN board. The first test is a simple test of the circuitry on the board. Many boards have a "reset and check out" feature, so this program just wakes up that feature. If the chips check out okay, this step is successfully completed.

The first test can be a useful check of whether you've set the IRQ to a conflicting level, or perhaps placed any on-board RAM overlapping other RAM.

The second test is one wherein you put a loopback connector (exactly what a loopback connector is varies with LAN variety) on your network board. The loopback connector causes any outgoing transmissions from the LAN board to be "looped back" to the LAN board. The loopback test then sends some data out from the LAN card and listens for the same data to be received by the LAN card. If that data isn't received by the LAN card, something is wrong with the transmitter or the receiver logic of the network card.

Notice that for the first two tests, you haven't even connected your system to the network yet. In the third test, you do the loopback test again, but this time while connected to the network. The board should pass again.

The final test, sender/responder test, involves two computers, a sender and a responder. The responder's job is to echo back anything it receives. For example, if Barry's machine is the responder and Peter's is the sender, any messages that Peter's machine sends to Barry's machine should cause Barry's machine to send the same message back to Peter's machine.

To make a computer a responder (and any computer can be a responder; you don't have to use a server), you have to run a program that turns it into a responder. But that's where the

21

problem arises. The responder software is packaged on the same disk as the diagnostic software that comes with the network board, and, unfortunately, the responder software usually runs only on network boards made by the company that wrote the diagnostic software. So, for example, if you have an Ethernet network that is a mixture of 3Com, Intel, and SMC boards, and you want to test a computer with a new 3Com Ethernet board, you have to search for another computer that has a 3Com board so that you can run the responder software on that computer.

 Caution   Sometimes running a NIC diagnostic will disconnect the computer from the network. Don't do this on a production server until you have ensured that all files are closed and it is safe to do so.

Isolating Resource Conflicts

Resource conflicts generally fall into four categories: an interrupt conflict, an I/O (input/output) port conflict, a DMA (Direct Memory Access) conflict, or a memory conflict. Following are some ways to isolate the conflict.

Interrupt conflicts are the most common problems, particularly because there are only 16 interrupts and not all of them are available for use. If the network adapter is using one of the reserved interrupts or one that is rarely available, that might be the problem. If this is not the case, you might have an I/O conflict, which is generally more difficult to diagnose. If your Windows 2000 computer is still working, you can try to use WINMSD.EXE (access the Windows 2000 Diagnostics by selecting Start, Run and typing WINMSD) to help you solve the problem.

Starting WINMSD starts the System Information snap-in. Click Hardware Resources and open the Conflicts/Sharing folder. A window similar to the one shown in Figure 21.5 should appear.

WINMSD does not, however, list every interrupt (check the IRQs folder) or I/O port (check the I/O folder) used by the system—only those in use by installed device drivers. Just keep in mind that most manufacturers' I/O port summaries include only a starting I/O address; they rarely include the complete I/O range. It is possible to have I/O overlap, in which one I/O port range starts inside an existing I/O range.

FIGURE 21.5

The Windows 2000 System Information snap-in.

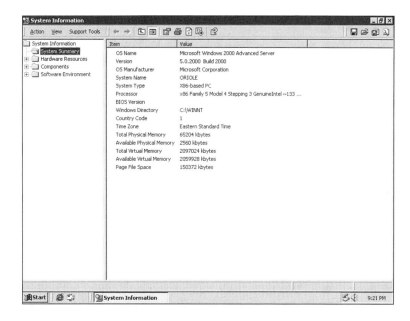

Tip

If you have a Plug and Play BIOS, such as those commonly used in computers on a PCI expansion bus, take a look at the BIOS settings. Some PCI components can have their interrupt assigned by the BIOS. This can override the Plug and Play capability to assign an interrupt dynamically. It also can cause problems with Windows 2000's capability to detect or change an interrupt assignment for a network adapter.

As you can see the System Information snap-in provides the following information:

- System Summary—Provides OS name, version, and manufacturer; system name and type; processor; BIOS; system root; country code and time zone; physical, available physical, virtual, and total virtual memory; and page file space.
- Hardware Resources—Provides information about conflicts/sharing; forced hardware; I/O ports; IRQs; and memory.
- Components—Provides information about multimedia; display; infrared; input; modem; network (see Figure 21.6); ports; storage; printing; problem devices; and USB.
- Software Resources—Provides information about drivers; environment variables; jobs; network connections; running tasks; loaded modules; services; program groups; startup programs; and OLE registration.

You can save any of the information from the System Information snap-in by double-clicking the folder and selecting Save as System Information File or Save as Text File. Keep these files and compare with other information.

21

FIGURE 21.6

Network Protocol system information.

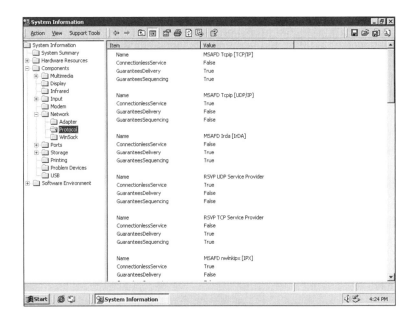

Supporting Windows 2000 Clients

Connecting a Windows 2000 workstation to another computer running Windows 2000 Server or Windows 2000 Workstation is the easiest connection you can make. Most of the problems you might experience with Windows 2000 clients have to do with authentication, provided that the hardware is functioning properly.

Troubleshooting Authentication Problems

You can attribute many network troubles to a failing or improperly configured network card or incorrect network transport drivers. The symptoms caused by a bad network card or an incorrect driver show up in one of two ways:

- Authentication problem. The client workstation cannot find the domain controller and, therefore, cannot gain access to the network.

- Connectivity problem. Users on a client workstation cannot access a particular shared resource.

The first indication that you have a hardware-related network problem is a message stating that the initial authentication process failed and that Windows 2000 has used cached information for authentication and to log you onto the system.

Note You can log on using cached information only when you have previously logged on successfully.

If Windows 2000 cannot complete authentication, you cannot log on to the system to solve the problem. On a Windows 2000 Server domain controller, the incapability to be authenticated is a serious problem. If you encounter an authentication problem just after system installation during the initial logon, it's difficult to correct the problem.

Authentication problems fall into two basic groups. The domain controller might fail to authenticate you during the logon sequence or while attempting to access a shared resource on the domain.

Authentication failures that are not caused by a failed network adapter, as discussed in the preceding section, are often caused by one of the following problems:

- No computer account. If a Windows 2000 client is a member of the domain but has no computer account on the domain controller, there is no trusted connection between the Windows 2000 client and the domain controller. This means that the domain controller cannot authenticate you or log you on to the system.

  A similar problem can occur when a Windows 2000 client changes from a domain to a workgroup and then attempts to rejoin the domain. Even though a computer account still exists on the domain controller, the client cannot reuse the account. Instead, you must create a new computer account, although it can have the same name. This is because computer accounts are like user or group accounts in that they have an assigned security identifier (SID). The system stores the SID in the computer account on the domain controller and in the Registry of the Windows 2000 client. When a user changes from a domain to a workgroup or from one domain to another, however, the system reassigns the SID based on the new configuration.

- No user account. Generally, this problem occurs when the user attempting to log on does not have a user account on the domain controller or the user mistypes the user account name or password. You can experience similar problems when you have set up the user account so that the user must enter a new password at the next logon, or when the account has been locked out due to repeated attempts to log onto the system with an invalid password.

Authentication problems related to accessing shared resources usually have to do with a user's specific permissions or rights. The same problem can occur for printer access or

21

named pipe access. To solve these authentication problems, check the client permissions in the following order:

- Group membership. Make sure that the user account is a member of the group that has permission to access the shared resource.

- Share permissions. Check the shared resource to ensure that the group has the appropriate permission to access the sharepoint. Also, make sure that the user is not a member of any group for which you have assigned the No Access permission. As you saw earlier, the No Access permission assignment overrides any other group permission level for the user. For example, if you have a printer called HP_Laser and you assign a user to the LaserPrinter group that has Print permission for that printer, and you also assign the user to the ColorPrinter group that has the No Access permission assigned for the printer, the user cannot print to the HP_Laser print queue.

- Directory and file permissions. If the user can access the sharepoint but cannot access directories and files, the user account probably is not a member of the appropriate group. The user also can be a member of a group that has the No Access permission assigned.

- Cached account information. Windows 2000 also caches group account information when accessing a shared resource. If you add a logged-on user to a group that has the appropriate permissions to access the shared resource, the user still cannot access the shared resource. The user must log off and then log back on again to flush the cache. When the user attempts to access the resource again, the system permits access.

| **Note** | To flush an internal cache, sometimes you have to shut down and restart the computer instead of just logging off and then back on again. |

Solving Physical Network Problems

The most effective way of monitoring the status of your physical network is by the ongoing use of intelligent network hardware, which might support, for instance, the Simple Network Management Protocol (SNMP). These devices collect and store status information that you can use to evaluate the health of your physical network.

If your network does not use such devices, use a network protocol analyzer (such as the Network Monitor tool) to assess the health of your network. You can use these analyzers to capture samples of network traffic and then analyze the captured data for any of the indicators of physical network problems.

If you have the opportunity to analyze network traffic, it usually is worthwhile to identify the longest (in terms of bit delay, not necessarily in terms of physical distance) client-to-server path through the network. Then, you should use that path to generate network traffic for your data capture (for example, copy large files to and from the server over this path).

TCP/IP Troubleshooting Tools and Strategies

Your approach to troubleshooting TCP/IP should be no different from troubleshooting any other computer problem. Ask yourself the following questions:

- What works? What doesn't work? When did it last work?
- Is there any relationship between the things that do and don't work?
- Did the component or service ever work on this computer or network?
- If yes, what has changed since it last worked?
- Have any errors been generated on any log?

With those questions answered, you're ready to proceed with the troubleshooting process. As you work on and solve network problems, you should develop a troubleshooting flowchart. In addition, you should document all problems and their resolutions. This documentation serves two purposes. One, it provides a series of steps for less-experienced staff to follow. Two, it minimizes the amount of time you spend on problem-solving in the future. You can learn from your mistakes.

The following section describes the tools you'll use to troubleshoot TCP/IP problems.

TCP/IP Commands: Network Utilities

If you do not have access to network analyzers or intelligent hubs, you can use some software-only network statistics programs provided with Windows 2000 to gauge the relative health of the network. You can use these tools to monitor, troubleshoot, and maintain TCP/IP networks.

In most cases, the following tools are designed for internal networks, but you can use some of them over the Internet:

- ARP (Address Resolution Protocol): Lets you view and manage the mapping between IP addresses and physical network addresses.
- IPCONFIG: Displays diagnostic information about TCP/IP networks and current TCP/IP network configuration values.

21

- NBTSTAT: Reports information about NetBIOS over TCP/IP connections.
- NETSTAT: Displays current TCP/IP connections and protocol statistics.
- PING: Tests connections on TCP/IP networks.
- ROUTE: Displays or modifies the route table.
- TRACERT: Traces how packets hop around your network or the Internet.

Using ARP

The ARP command is useful for viewing the ARP cache. When two hosts on the same subnet cannot PING each other successfully, try running the ARP -a command on each computer to see whether they have the correct MAC (hardware) addresses listed for each other. You can determine a host's MAC address using IPCONFIG. When another host with a duplicate IP address exists on the network, the ARP cache might have had the MAC address for the other computer placed in it. You can use ARP -d to delete an entry that might be incorrect. And you can add an entry by using ARP -s.

Using IPCONFIG

IPCONFIG is a command-line utility that prints out the TCP/IP-related configuration of a host. When used with the /ALL switch, it produces a detailed configuration report for all interfaces, including any configured serial ports (for example, RAS). This is especially useful when you're using RAS and connecting to the Internet. Sometimes RAS is assigned one IP number that's no good, and you can track it down this way. IPCONFIG provides information such as the IP address for each interface device and subnet masks.

Output from this report can be redirected to a file and pasted into other documents.

Using NBTSTAT

The NBTSTAT command displays information and statistics about the current TCP/IP connections using NetBIOS over TCP/IP (that is, NBT). It provides network statistics for active and pending NetBIOS connections. This diagnostic command displays protocol statistics and current TCP/IP connections using NetBIOS over TCP/IP.

You can type the remote name or IP address of another system on a network to get information about it, such as local usernames. Use the following syntax:

```
NBTSTAT [-a remotename] [-A Ipaddress] [-c] [-n] [-R] [-r] [-S] [-s] [interval]
➥[-?]
```

Table 21.4 describes the parameters used in the preceding syntax.

TABLE 21.4 NBTSTAT Parameters

Parameter	Description
-a *remotename*	Lists the remote computer's name table using the computer's name.
-A *Ipaddress*	Lists the remote computer's name table using the computer's IP address.
-c	Lists the contents of the NetBIOS name cache, giving the IP address for each name.
-n	Lists local NetBIOS names.
-R	Reloads the LMHOSTS file after purging all names from the NetBIOS name cache.
-r	Lists name resolution statistics for Windows networking. On a Windows 2000 computer configured to use WINS, this option returns the number of names resolved and registered via broadcast or via WINS.
-S	Displays both workstation and server sessions, listing the remote hosts by IP address only.
-s	Displays both workstation and server sessions. This option attempts to convert the remote host IP address to a name using the HOSTS file.
interval	Redisplays selected statistics, pausing interval seconds between each display. Press Ctrl+C to stop redisplaying statistics. When you omit this parameter, NBTSTAT prints the current configuration information once.
-?	Displays help information.

Caution

Microsoft recommends that you change the name of the administrator when you install. This is a good policy; however, using the command NBTSTAT -A *Ipaddress* provides the administrator's name.

The column headings that are generated by the NBTSTAT utility are described in Table 21.5.

TABLE 21.5 NBTSTAT Output

Heading	Description
Input	The bytes received.
Output	The bytes sent.
In/Out	Whether the connection is from the computer (outbound) or from another system to the local computer (inbound).

continues

21

TABLE 21.5 continued

Heading	Description
Life	The remaining time that a name table cache entry will live before it is purged.
Local Name	The local NetBIOS name associated with the connection.
Remote Host	The name or IP address associated with the remote host.
Type	The type of name. A name can be either a unique name or a group name.
<03>	Each NetBIOS name is 16 characters long. The last byte often has special significance, because the same name can be present several times on a computer. This notation is simply the last byte converted to hexadecimal. For example, <20> is a space in ASCII.
State	The state of NetBIOS connections. The possible states are shown in Table 21.6.

TABLE 21.6 Possible States for NetBIOS Connections

State	Description
Accepting	An inbound session is currently being accepted and will be connected shortly.
Associated	A connection endpoint has been created and associated with an IP address.
Connected	The session has been established.
Connecting	The session is in the connecting phase where the name-to-IP address mapping of the destination is being resolved.
Disconnected	The local computer has issued a disconnect, and it is waiting for confirmation from the remote system.
Disconnecting	A session is in the process of disconnecting.
Idle	This endpoint has been opened but cannot receive connections.
Inbound	An inbound session is in the connecting phase.
Listening	This endpoint is available for an inbound connection.
Outbound	A session is in the connecting phase where the TCP connection is currently being created.
Reconnecting	A session is trying to reconnect if it failed to connect on the first attempt.

So NBTSTAT is a useful tool for troubleshooting NetBIOS name resolution problems. NBTSTAT -n displays the names that were registered locally on the system by applications, such as the server and redirector. NBTSTAT -c shows the NetBIOS name cache with its name-to-address mappings for other computers. NBTSTAT -r purges the name cache and reloads it from the LMHOSTS file. `NBTSTAT -a <remotename>` performs a NetBIOS adapter status command against the computer specified by *remotename*. The adapter status command returns the local NetBIOS name table for that computer plus the MAC address of the adapter card. The command `NBTSTAT -s` lists the current NetBIOS sessions and their statuses, including statistics.

Using NETSTAT

The `NETSTAT` tool gathers statistics from the network adapter of the local computer or a specified remote computer, as well as some transport layer protocol driver data. You can use the statistics to determine the relative health of that machine's network connection based on the incidence of errors recorded.

The `NETSTAT` utility provides statistics in the TCP/IP world. If you're running a TCP/IP application on another host, it gives you statistics on the IP address and port number of local and remote computers. Typing **NETSTAT host** produces the statistics information.

Table 21.7 lists the statistics provided by the NETSTAT utility.

TABLE 21.7   NETSTAT Statistics

Statistic	Description
Foreign Address	The IP address and port number of the remote computer where the socket is connected. The name corresponding to the IP address is shown rather than the number when the HOSTS file contains an entry for the IP address. When the port is not yet established, the port number is shown as an asterisk (*).
Local Address	The IP address of the local computer, as well as the port number that the connection is using. The name corresponding to the IP address is shown rather than the number when the HOSTS file contains an entry for the IP address. When the port is not yet established, the port number is shown as an asterisk (*).
Proto	The name of the protocol used by the connection.
(state)	The state of TCP connections only.

To use `NETSTAT` to display protocol statistics and current TCP/IP network connections, use the following syntax:

```
NETSTAT [-a] [-e][n][s] [-p protocol] [-r] [interval]
```

Table 21.8 describes the parameters used in the preceding syntax.

21

TABLE 21.8 NETSTAT Parameters

Parameter	Description
-a	Displays all connections and listening ports; server connections usually are not shown.
-e	Displays Ethernet statistics. This can be combined with the -s option.
-n	Displays addresses and port numbers in dotted decimal format (instead of attempting name lookups).
-p protocol	Displays connections for the protocol specified by protocol; protocol can be TCP or UDP. If used with the -s option to display per-protocol statistics, protocol can be TCP, UDP, or IP.
-r	Displays the contents of the routing table.
-s	Displays per-protocol statistics. By default, statistics are shown for TCP, UDP, and IP. The -p option can be used to specify a subset of the default.
interval	Redisplays selected statistics, pausing interval seconds between each display. Press Ctrl+C to stop redisplaying statistics. When this parameter is omitted, NETSTAT prints the current configuration information once.

NETSTAT displays protocol statistics and current TCP/IP connections. NETSTAT -a displays all connections, and NETSTAT -r displays the route table, plus active connections. The -n switch tells NETSTAT not to convert addresses and port numbers to names.

Using PING

PING, or Packet Internet Groper, is a TCP/IP utility. The utility sends a message and looks for a reply. If you get a reply, you know that the system is there, and you can talk with it. If you don't get a response, you know there's a problem, and you won't be able to communicate.

PING uses Windows socket-style name resolution to resolve the name to an address, so if pinging by address succeeds but pinging by name fails, the problem lies in address resolution, not network connectivity.

From your workstation, you can ping another host and wait for a response. The syntax is PING Ipaddress or PING host (for example, PING 199.199.199.2 or PING microsoft.com). Type **PING -?** to see which command-line options are available. For example, PING allows you to specify the size of packets to use, how many to send, whether to record the route used, what TTL value to use, and whether to set the don't fragment flag.

PING is a tool that helps verify IP connectivity. When troubleshooting, you use the PING command to send an ICMP echo request to a target name or IP address. First try pinging the IP address of the target host to see whether it responds, because this is the simplest case. If that succeeds, try pinging the name.

Using ROUTE

Use ROUTE to view or modify the route table. ROUTE PRINT displays a list of current routes known by IP for the host. Use ROUTE ADD to add routes to the table, and use ROUTE DELETE to delete routes from the table. Note that routes added to the table are not made permanent unless you specify the -p switch. Nonpersistent routes last only until someone reboots the computer.

For two hosts to exchange IP datagrams, they must both have a route to each other or use default gateways that know of a route. Normally, routers exchange information with each other by using a protocol such as the Routing Information Protocol (RIP) or the Open Shortest Path First (OSPF). Windows 2000 did not include support for either of these routing protocols; therefore, when these computers are used as routers, it is often necessary to add routes manually. Microsoft is working on RIP and OSPF support for Windows 2000.

Using TRACERT

If you're experiencing problems connecting machine A to machine B on the Internet, you can use TRACERT to trace the routes a packet takes as it traverses the wires. You'll see a screen dump of all the routers the packet travels through, the routers' names, and the time it takes to reach those routers.

TRACERT is a route-tracing utility that uses the IP TTL field and ICMP error messages to determine the route from one host to another through a network.

Sometimes TRACERT is useful when you're selecting an ISP, because you can trace the route between the ISP's router and another point to see how many hops are in between and how long it takes to send a transmission between the two. If the ISP routes your packets all over the world before reaching its destination, you'll want to avoid that ISP. Accessing this utility is as simple as typing TRACERT host (for example, TRACERT pdaconsulting.com) or TRACERT 199.199.199.2 from the command prompt.

You've now seen how the ARP, IPCONFIG, NETSTAT, NBTSTAT, PING, ROUTE, and TRACERT utilities can provide useful information when you are trying to determine the cause of TCP/IP networking problems. Windows 2000 provides other troubleshooting tools such as the Performance Monitor and the Network Monitor.

Start with the simple stuff first. Can you PING the site? Can you see a route using TRACERT? Try out these utilities until you feel comfortable with them. Get yourself a good book on troubleshooting NetBIOS and TCP/IP networking.

21

Monitoring Activities with the Performance Snap-in

The Performance snap-in is a graphical charting and statistics-gathering tool you can use to display performance information about your servers and network. You can have it alert you when certain events occur. Alerts are based on preset values that exceed or fall below a critical limit. You can use the monitoring, charting, and logging features of the Performance Monitor to help with initial performance troubleshooting and capacity planning for the local server or for other servers on the network.

You can start the Performance snap-in by selecting it from the Administrative Tools group. You can choose what to track and then store the collected information in files for later analysis. Here is a partial list of what you can do with Performance:

- Set alerts to warn you about intruder activities or attempted unauthorized access to files.
- View information about multiple computers at the same time. You can open multiple copies of the Performance Monitor and track multiple events on each copy.
- Collect information in the form of charts, logs, alert logs, and reports.
- View the charts and dynamically change settings to fit your needs.
- Export the information you collect to spreadsheet or database programs for further analysis and printing.
- Set up alerts to track and compare counter values against preset thresholds.
- Create long-term archives by appending information to log files. Save current settings and values for future charting sessions.

Yesterday, you learned about the use of the Performance snap-in. Like most network management systems, the Performance monitor tracks *objects*, or processes and services running in Windows 2000 Server computers. Every object has counters that keep track of specific events or activities. Here's a partial list of the objects you can monitor:

- Browser
- Cache
- FTP (File Transfer Protocol) service
- Gopher service
- HTTP service
- Memory
- NetBEUI and NetBEUI resource

- Network interface and segment
- NWLink IPX, NWLink NetBIOS, and NWLink SPX
- Physical disk
- Processor
- Remote Access Services
- Server
- System
- TCP/IP

The counters for objects are tracked and charted in the Performance window. You can view a complete list of objects to track and get a description of what they are by clicking the Explain button. The explanation window then opens at the bottom of the dialog box.

Using the Network Monitor

NEW TERM   NETMON, for *Network Monitor*, is a network diagnostic tool that monitors local area networks and provides a graphical display of network statistics. Network administrators can use these statistics to perform routine troubleshooting tasks, such as locating a server that is down or that is receiving a disproportionate number of work requests. NETMON is available as a part of Microsoft's Systems Management Server product.

NEW TERM   Microsoft shipped the Network Monitor, a *sniffer* application, as part of the Systems Management Server (SMS) for the past few years. But SMS is expensive and it really should have been part of W2K Server from the start. In Windows 2000 Server, Microsoft provides a slightly crippled version of the Network Monitor.

The version of Network Monitor shipping with W2K Server records only network frames that either originate with or are destined for the particular server where it is running. So if you want to use Network Monitor to examine traffic from your server to machine A, and from machine A to your server, you can use the version that ships with W2K Server. On the other hand, if you want to use Network Monitor to examine traffic moving between machine A and machine B, you can't do that from your server (assuming that your server is neither machine A nor B). You can when you use the Network Monitor that comes with SMS.

21

Note

]The Network Monitor with SMS runs in *promiscuous mode*. The Network Monitor agent collects statistics from the computer's network adapter card by putting it in promiscuous mode. The version included with W2K Server runs in *non-promiscuous mode*.

A NIC is *promiscuous* when it copies all data into memory rather than only the data intended for the node. You can view the statistics by using Performance Monitor.

Network Monitor captures packets as they travel across the wire. You then can analyze those packets to troubleshoot hardware and software problems (such as tracking down a faulty NIC). If you can't figure out the problem, you can send a captured trace someplace where it can be read.

The Network Monitor is a diagnostic tool for monitoring local area networks, locating a downed server, or locating bottlenecks on the network. It provides a graphical display of network statistics.

Installing the Network Monitor Agent

You can use Network Monitor Agent services on other Windows 2000 computers to capture statistics on those computers and have them sent to your Network Monitor computer.

 ### Task 21.2: Installing the Network Monitor Agent.

Step 1: Description

You can install the Network Monitor Agent by opening the Add/Remove Programs utility in the Control Panel and selecting the Services tab. This task will show you how to install the Network Monitor Agent on a Windows 2000 computer.

Step 2: Action

1. From the Control Panel, double-click on the Add/Remove Programs icon.
2. Double-click Add/Remove Windows Components.
3. When the Windows Components Wizard starts, click Next.
4. From the Windows Components window, highlight Management and Monitoring Tools, and click Details.
5. Check Network Monitor Tools, and then click OK.
6. Click Next.
 7. Click Finish.

Step 3: Review

You can install the Network Monitor agent by using the Windows Components Wizard in the Control Panel and selecting the Add/Remove Programs icon.

Task 21.3: Adding Network Monitor Performance Counters.

Step 1: Description

To use the Network Monitor under Administrative Tools, you need to start the agent.

Step 2: Action

1. Under Start, Programs, Administrative Tools, select the Network Monitor agent. You should see a window like that in Figure 21.7.

FIGURE 21.7

Network Monitor agent.

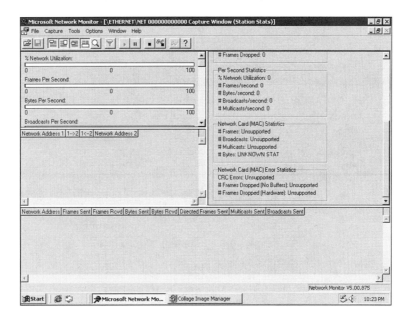

2. From the taskbar, select Capture, Networks.
3. From the Select a network window, select the network segment you want to start monitoring.
4. Click OK.
5. From the Capture menu, select Start.

Step 3: Review

After you have installed the Network Monitor Agent by using the Network icon in the Control Panel, you must start the Network Monitor Agent.

21

> **Note** The Network Segment object and associated counters are available only when you install the Network Monitor Agent.

The Network Monitor's Help system provides more information on setting up and using its information-gathering tools. With proper use, you can monitor the traffic of users.

The layout of the Network Monitor might look confusing, but notice that it contains four separate windows, each holding information:

- Information about the host that sent a frame onto the network
- Information about the host that received the frame
- The protocols used to send the frame
- The data, or a portion of the message, being sent

The address is a unique hexadecimal (or base-16) number that identifies a computer on the network; it's the hardware address assigned to every network interface card. To discover the hexadecimal address of a system, type one of the commands shown next, replacing *Ipaddress* with the IP address of the computer in question, or *computername* with the NetBIOS name of the computer.

```
NBTSTAT -A Ipaddress
NBTSTAT -a computername
```

The Network Monitor uses a "capture" process to gather information about the network for a certain time period. During this period, information about all the frames transmitted over the network is recorded and made available in the Network Monitor display. You can view information in the graphical display as it occurs, and you can save the captured information to files for later viewing.

When capturing information, you can set filters to view only the information that is essential for detecting intrusions or other problems. For example, you can filter by protocol to view frames related to a particular command that a user might be using. You also can filter by network address to capture frames from specific computers on your network. That lets you track the activities of a particular client. Up to four specific address pairs can be monitored. An address pair includes the addresses of two computers communicating with one another. You also can filter by data patterns, which lets you capture only frames that have a specific pattern of ASCII or hexadecimal data. You also can specify how many bytes of data into the frame the pattern must occur.

NEW TERM You also can set *triggers*, or conditions that must be met before an action occurs. For example, you can set a trigger that starts capturing when a pattern (such as a code or sequence used by a client) is found, or you can set a trigger to stop the capture of data.

Note that display filters also are available. You can use them to view information that has already been captured.

Because the Network Monitor captures a large amount of information you might not need, you can create filters that prevent it from capturing specific types of frames. You also can set triggers that start a predesignated action when an event occurs on the network, such as when the buffer space is close to being full or when frames might be corrupted.

The Network Monitor requires a network adapter that supports what is usually called promiscuous mode. In this mode, a network adapter passes all the frames it detects on the network to the network software, regardless of the frame's destination address.

Securing the Network Monitor

As you just read, the Windows 2000 Network Monitor captures only frames sent to or from the computer where you are running the utility. It also displays statistics for the network segment that the computer is attached to, such as broadcast frames, network utilization, and total bytes received.

To protect a network from unauthorized use of Network Monitor installation, the Network Monitor provides password protections and the capability to detect other copies of Network Monitor on the local segment of the network. The passwords can prevent someone at a Windows 2000 Server computer that is running System Management Server from connecting with the computer and running the Network Monitor on that computer.

You use the Monitoring Agent icon in the Control Panel to change the passwords for the Network Monitor or Network Monitor Agent.

If other users run a copy of Network Monitor on their computers, they could use it to watch packets on the network and capture valuable information. Network Monitor detects other Network Monitor installations and displays the information about them, such as the name of the computer, the user, and the adapter address, and whether the utility is running, capturing, or transmitting information.

Note Unfortunately, Network Monitor can only detect the existence of another version of Network Monitor. It cannot detect third-party monitoring software and hardware.

21

Configuring Alerts

NEW TERM   When NETMON starts monitoring unusual activity, you might want the system to send someone a warning message, that is, an *alert*. Alerts are used to notify a domain administrator of a serious problem that has occurred on a Windows 2000 computer. You can send an alert to a particular domain user or a specific computer that is monitored by several administrators or support personnel. You can determine which users and computers are notified when administrative alerts occur at a selected computer.

The system generates administrative alerts relating to server and resource use. They warn about security and access problems, user session problems, server shutdown because of power loss when the UPS service is available, and printer problems.

If you want to guarantee that the alerts are sent, you should also modify the client workstation to start the Alert and Messenger services at system startup. This makes sure that the services are functioning and available to send administrative alerts. If the services are left in their default startup setting of manual, the services attempt to send the alert but might fail due to unforeseen circumstances. If the services fail, the alert cannot be sent. Also, to receive an administrative alert, the Messenger service must be running.

In the last lesson, "Windows 2000 Performance Monitoring and Tuning," you learned how to set up an alert. You should refresh your memory by reviewing Task 20.4, "Setting up Performance Monitor to issue alerts."

Looking for More Help?

The information in this lesson is somewhat limited. You can purchase other books that focus on fine-tuning or troubleshooting your network. So this section provides some online resources for administering your server and network.

First, you can check out the online users forum on CompuServe. Type `GO WINNT` to find the W2K forum.

If you want to find more fixes, check out `http://www.microsoft.com/NTServer/all/downloads.asp`. If you want to look for help troubleshooting try `http://support.microsoft.com/support/c.asp`. The Internet obviously provides a wealth of information for the Windows 2000 administrator. For instance, you can find mailing list servers at `http://www.ntpro.org/listserv.html`. You also might want to check the `comp.os.ms-windows.nt.admin.misc`, the `comp.os.ms-windows.nt.admin.networking` or the `comp.os.ms-windows.pre-release` Usenet newsgroups. For the time being, this is where the Windows 2000 discussions will take place.

Furthermore, there is a database of well-known errors out there. You can find a list of possible causes and corrections on the Microsoft Web site (http://www.microsoft.com) or on the WINNT forum on CompuServe. Check these areas for hints or try contacting Microsoft support at 206-637-7098. Another good source is Microsoft's TechNet CD, a useful compendium of W2K-related information. The subscription costs $299 USD per annum (see http://www.microsoft.com/technet/subscription/how.htm).

Summary

The goal in tuning Windows 2000 is to determine which hardware resource is experiencing the greatest demand (bottleneck) and then adjust the operation to relieve that demand and maximize total throughput. A system should be structured so that its resources are used efficiently and distributed fairly among the users. The concepts presented in this lesson should be used as guidelines and not as absolutes. Each Windows 2000 Server environment is unique and requires experimentation and tuning appropriate to its conditions and requirements.

This day also looked at some networking tools available with Windows 2000 that you can use to problem-solve.

Well, you made it through 21 tough, grueling days. We wish you success in administering your server and network. Maybe someday we'll be surfing the Net and we'll visit your site. Good luck.

Workshop

To wrap up the day, you can review tasks from the lesson, and see the answers to some commonly asked questions.

Task List

The emphasis of this day has been to introduce you to network fine-tuning and troubleshooting. As a system administrator, you will need to learn how to tune your scarce resources. Moreover, you will need to fix problems occasionally. You learned three simple tasks in this lesson:

- Configuring system settings
- Installing the Network Monitor Agent
- Adding Network Monitor Agent performance counters

21

Q&A

Q **Is there another way to configure and start the Alerter service?**

A Yes, you can use the command NET START ALERTER at the command prompt. The Alerter service sends messages about the network to users. You select what events you want to trigger alerts in the Performance Monitor. For these alerts to be sent, both the Alerter and the Messenger services must be running on the computer originating the alerts, and the Messenger service must be running on the computer receiving them.

Q **How can you determine whether TCP/IP is installed correctly on a Windows 2000 system?**

A Try using ping on the local system by typing the IP loopback address (127.0.0.1) from the command line, like so: `PING 127.0.0.1`. The system should respond immediately. If ping is not found or the command fails, check the event log with Event Viewer and look for problems reported by Setup or the TCP/IP service. You also should attempt to ping the IP addresses of your local interface(s) to determine whether you configured IP properly. Successful use of ping indicates that the IP layer on the target system is probably functional.

Also try IPCONFIG to examine the current TCP/IP settings.

Q **I cannot get a W2K machine to connect to the network. Other machines on the network work fine. What can I do?**

A Well, in typical Microsoft troubleshooting fashion, you should start over. Often you change so many parameters that it just isn't easy to get things set up.

So make sure that there isn't a cabling problem by substituting a working W2K machine in place of the one having the problem. Also, confirm that the network adapter is working by trying it in a different machine. Then go into the problem machine, open the Network applet in the Control Panel, and remove everything, including the device drivers for the network adapter. Then reboot the machine. Now, when you go back into the Network applet, it asks whether you want to install the network drivers. Do so, but install only the NetBEUI protocol. This is the simplest protocol, so it has the highest chance of a successful implementation. See whether that protocol can see the rest of the network by trying to connect to something using the Explorer (assuming that another machine is running NetBEUI). That almost will certainly work unless there are hardware problems. Now add in the other pieces incrementally, and you are set.

APPENDIXES

At a Glance

A

B

C

APPENDIX **A**

Microsoft Windows 2000 Certification Programs

In the previous weeks, you learned about installing, exploring, and managing your Windows 2000 Server. Now you can learn how to become a certified user of Windows 2000. Because Microsoft changes these details from time to time, it is always best to refer to its Web site (www.microsoft.com/mcp/mktg/cert.htm) for the latest information.

As we write this book, Microsoft has not yet released Windows 2000–specific training courses. We don't anticipate that the overall Certification Program will change as a result of this new system except for the addition of Windows 2000–specific courses. We provide this appendix, therefore, with as much information as we know and we have included a few notes where the certification might be expected to differ as Windows 2000 is officially introduced.

Throughout this appendix, we state the current needs and specify those places where we believe Windows 2000 will be incorporated. Microsoft regularly "expires" exams based on newer product releases being available and NT will be no exception. It remains to be seen how fast Microsoft will drop the current

NT 4.0 exams and replace them with Windows 2000 as we can expect the NT 4.0 version to be around for some time while companies consider, plan, and finally migrate, to Windows 2000. Our best information would suggest that you will see both products remaining in the training program for at least the next year as Windows 2000 becomes established.

Microsoft (MS) offers certification programs designed around its product lines. These include

- Microsoft Certified System Engineer (MCSE)
- Microsoft Certified System Engineer + Internet (MCSE+Internet)
- Microsoft Certified Professional (MCP)
- Microsoft Certified Professional + Internet (MCP+Internet)
- Microsoft Certified Professional + Site Building (MCP+Site Building)
- Microsoft Certified Database Administrator (MCDBA)
- Microsoft Certified Solution Developer (MCSD)
- Microsoft Certified Trainer (MCT)

MCSE graduates are those who achieved the ability to plan, develop, implement, and maintain a wide range of computing platforms and information systems using Microsoft Windows 2000, NT Server, and the Microsoft BackOffice family of products. Each of the products with the +Internet portion is for those who learn additional knowledge about managing and administering Web sites. The +Site Building is for those persons who are qualified to plan, build, maintain, and manage Web sites using Microsoft technologies and products. The credential is appropriate for people who manage sophisticated, interactive Web sites that include database connectivity, multimedia, and searchable content.

Those with the MCP designation demonstrated their expertise in particular MS products. To obtain the designation, you must have an in-depth knowledge of at least one MS operating system, such as Windows 2000 Server, Windows 95, or Windows 98. You can take any certification exam that is current and earn the credential of Microsoft Certified Professional. You should be aware that Microsoft updates its Web site with notice of those exams that have expired, so visit the site before you do any studying. The one exception to this is Exam 70-058: Networking Essentials, it doesn't qualify you by itself. You will see an example like the one shown in Figure A.1.

FIGURE A.1

A Microsoft expired exam.

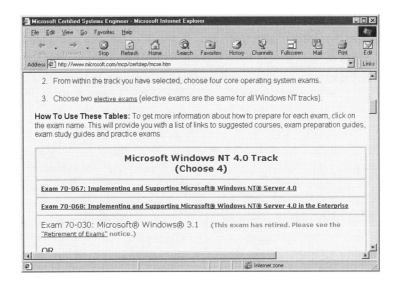

Obtaining an MCSD requires that you are qualified to design, develop, and create business applications by using MS tools and platforms such as BackOffice and Windows 2000 or Windows NT.

The MCDBA certification is for professionals who plan to implement and administer Microsoft SQL Server databases. Those who determine physical database designs, create physical databases, manage and maintain databases, and install and configure Microsoft SQL Server typically attain this designation.

Finally, an MCT has passed the qualifications and testing necessary to instruct others on official MS curriculum for the various Microsoft Authorized Technical Education Centers.

Why is certification offered, and how does it benefit you? As with any field of endeavor in the computing field, it is often hard to ascertain a person's credentials without some form of assistance. Certification helps fill that gap by providing a base level of expected competence and the assurance that those who are certified pass reasonable examinations and have the anticipated level of knowledge.

Training and certification through this process is time-consuming and expensive. Obtaining the certification for MCSE by taking the needed courses and the exams costs several thousands of dollars. You need to decide whether the cost in time and money is worth the gain. If you plan to work in this field for any length of time, these certification programs might give you the prestige necessary to get that new job or prove to management your dedication and qualifications. Naturally, you can self-study and just take the exams to qualify.

Finally, you should recognize that no certification can take the place of experience. There are thousands of Microsoft certified persons, each with varying levels of skill and experience. Don't expect that the world will fall all over you if you decide to pursue this goal. We don't mean to be negative here, but over the years we have seen too many people work hard and spend a fair amount of money to become certified, and then be disappointed because their expectations are set too high. Pursue your education, but recognize that the school of hard knocks plays a significant part as well.

Certification is obtained through hard work, hands-on study, and test-taking. There is little substitute for these tasks. If you believe that you can obtain certification easily, you are either very smart, or know something we don't. To obtain a particular designation, you don't have to take any courses at all, although we'll discuss them in detail in the remainder of this appendix. What you must do however, is take and pass the necessary exams. Perhaps you are already fully qualified through years of experience and need only take the exam, or you are just starting out and think taking the courses would be a good idea. We cannot decide this for you of course, but offer this caveat. Be sure you know the subject extremely well before venturing out to take an exam. They are comprehensive and you need to fully understand the subject in order to pass.

In the remaining section, we discuss each qualification according to Microsoft criteria, and you'll learn more about what you need to become certified.

Why Obtain Certification?

You might want to become certified for many reasons. Company leaders realize that they must invest in qualified computer professionals who have clearly demonstrated knowledge of how to design, develop, and support the wide variety of mission-critical solutions that are often utilizing the latest technologies and platforms.

Company leaders also realize that they must upgrade the skills of their existing workforce to remain competitive in an ever-changing marketplace. Certification becomes a cost-effective and useful tool for providing objective methods of measuring competence and ensuring the qualifications of technical professionals, thus helping companies in their quest for excellence.

Finally, information systems are shifting to smaller and smaller groups, and knowledgeable staff are becoming more important. Companies need technical professionals who can implement and maintain the enterprise systems, develop new solutions, and provide technical support and they need to be sure that the staff they have are able to perform these functions well. Certification helps provide those assurances.

Microsoft offers detailed information concerning the benefits of certification, including several studies that show the improvements in customer satisfaction and cost reduction through the use of certified individuals. Visit Microsoft's Web site for additional information. Look for the document called Mcpback.doc, which clearly outlines these advantages, especially if you are trying to sell the benefit to your boss.

You can also obtain a Microsoft Windows–based application that allows you to quickly create a personal training and certification plan. This application, called the Microsoft Roadmap to Education and Certification, is available electronically from the following locations:

Internet: `ftp://ftp.microsoft.com/Services/MSEdCert/E&CMAP.ZIP`

MSN: Go To `MOLI`, Advising Building, E&C Roadmap

CompuServe: `GO MECFORUM`, Library #2, E&CMAP.ZIP

Microsoft TechNet: Search for `Roadmap`

Certification remains a viable and effective method for individuals and corporations to ensure a useful measurement of skills and competence.

Obtaining Certification

You have several steps to take to obtain your certification. First, you need to decide which program best serves your background and interests. Study the four programs and determine which one is best for you.

After deciding on a particular program, consider studying the exam Preparation and Study Guides that Microsoft offers to find out a bit about the exam you will take and what is expected. This effort will give you an idea of how the exam is created, what types of questions are asked, and how the questions are scored. In addition, you can find information about preparing for the exam and topics that you might be tested on.

Now you need to decide whether your qualifications are sufficient to pass the exam or whether you need additional preparation and training. Our book provides you with a sound base for dealing with the MCSE or MCP designations, but you must decide for yourself whether you have learned enough to pass these exams. Our book isn't designed to be the only studying you perform, and you should consider additional training or help before becoming certified.

Microsoft offers instructor-led seminars, as well as self-paced training. The self-paced option offers you ample opportunity to take a course even if your job requires travel or time is hard for you to schedule. Using a self-paced method is fine as long as you are disciplined enough to continue the course with nobody pressuring you. (You might decide to use the self-paced training and have your spouse provide support. Of course, this could introduce too much stress, depending on your personal habits.)

Before taking any of the courses, finish this book and gain additional experience with the product so that you are completely familiar with each function. Then you will be ready to take a self-assessment exam to see how you might fare. You can find these exams on the Microsoft Web site mentioned later, in the section called "Where Can I Find Out More?" This exercise provides you with a good idea of whether your present skill level is adequate or whether you need additional work before taking the official exam. Note that passing an assessment exam doesn't necessarily mean that you'll pass the official exam. Make sure that you're comfortable with your proficiency before spending the time and money on certification.

Finally, Microsoft has an arrangement with a company called Sylvan Prometric for exam sessions. This company has offices across North America and offers exams on a regular schedule. Contact Microsoft for details, or call Sylvan Prometric at 1-800-755-EXAM to register in Canada and the United States, or use their Web site at www.2test.com. If you are at all in doubt, or if you are in another country, Microsoft suggests that you call the local Microsoft office for details.

The Microsoft Certified System Engineer

Obtaining the MCSE certification shows that you are proficient in the planning, implementation, and maintenance of Microsoft Windows 2000 or NT and Microsoft BackOffice. It provides you with industry recognition and offers a chance to be one step ahead of an uncertified person, providing that all other things are equal. The I.T. world is fast becoming dependent on such qualifications, much like a university degree, to try to gain an edge in managing the differing levels of expertise available.

Many companies offer incentives to obtain the MCSE. For example, we know of companies that pay staff a bonus for each certification and then provide an increase in salary when they obtain the MCSE designation. Often, performance plans are tied to each employee's ability to improve himself and it is worth considering the potential compensation you might gain from obtaining an MCSE in your company.

Although we believe that this certification is a valuable tool in your business arsenal, we don't believe that it is the be-all and end-all. You still need all other quantifiable aspects of business, including experience. Getting a designation at the expense of obtaining bona fide experience in the industry is never a sound decision.

Microsoft offers you various benefits if you obtain the MCSE. The organization provides access to technical information through a subscription to one of its magazines, *Microsoft TechNet*. It also offers discounts on product support.

You also become a member of Microsoft's beta program, allowing you to participate in future product development and see the new products before their release. Another magazine, *Microsoft Certified Professional*, is developed especially for certified folks, and you also get this for some time, along with an update letter that keeps you informed of what is happening in the certification program.

Finally, Microsoft provides you with a forum on its MSN network to communicate with other certified professionals and with Microsoft. The site is now offered as a secured area of the MCP Web site and as such isn't available to non-certified persons.

So what is necessary for you to become a certified system engineer? We provide an answer but strongly suggest contacting Microsoft for details because these programs change without notice, and this material can quickly become dated.

An MCSE needs to pass four operating-system exams and two elective exams to qualify for the designation. The operating-system component includes exams concerning NT 3.51 or 4.0, Windows 98, or Windows 95. The electives are chosen from such areas as Microsoft SQL Server, SMS, and Microsoft Exchange.

To add the +Internet to your designation you must take seven operating system exams and two elective exams. These include the standard MCSE exams plus others such as Internet Information Server, Networking Essentials, or Internet Explorer 4.0.

Is certification for you? That's a question you'll have to answer. In our opinion, it is one additional qualification, and that is rarely a bad thing in these competitive days.

Microsoft Certified Professional

The MCP designation is for persons demonstrating competence with a particular Microsoft product. So what is necessary for you to become a certified product specialist? We provide an answer but again strongly suggest contacting Microsoft for details because these programs change without notice and this material can quickly become dated.

You need knowledge of at least one operating system, and you can take additional exams to further qualify your skills with such products as BackOffice and Windows 95.

For our purposes, you are on your way to qualifying for this particular designation after you complete this book. You would take the Microsoft Windows 2000 Server exam.

To add the +Internet you must pass three exams including

- Internetworking Microsoft TCP/IP on Windows 2000 or NT 4.0
- Implementing and Supporting Windows 2000 or NT Server 4.0

and one of either

- Implementing and Supporting Microsoft Internet Information Server 4.0 and Microsoft Index Server
- Implementing and Supporting Microsoft Internet Information Server 4.0

To obtain a +Site Building certification you must take two additional exams concerned with building Web sites using FrontPage 98, designing Web sites using Microsoft Site Server 3.0, Commerce Version, or developing Web solutions using Microsoft Visual Interdev 6.0.

Microsoft offers you various benefits if you obtain the MCP. You're given access to technical information through a free copy of *Microsoft TechNet CD* and a 50% discount on the TechNet Information Network service, which provides information through the issuance of monthly CDs.

You also get another magazine developed especially for certified folks, *Microsoft Certified Professional*, for one year. And you get an Update newsletter that keeps you informed of what is happening in the certification program.

Finally, Microsoft gives you a forum on its MSN network and the secure Web site to communicate with other certified professionals and with Microsoft.

Microsoft Certified Database Administrator

The MCDBA offers something for persons who plan to manage and design database systems. It is a new offering by Microsoft and the exams were recently made available in the first quarter of 1999. You are required to pass four core exams and one elective dealing with NT Server and SQL Server 7.0. You may want to partake in this if your long-term goal is directed more towards database systems, rather than networks or Windows NT.

Microsoft Certified Solution Developer

The MCSD credential is for those who design and develop custom business solutions with Microsoft development tools, technologies, and platforms. It contains a new track that includes certification exams that test users' abilities to build Web-based, distributed, and commerce applications using SQL Server, Visual Studio, and Microsoft Component Services.

Microsoft Certified Solution Developers are required to pass three core exams and one elective exam from a selection of more than a dozen disciplines. The core technology exams require proven competency in solution architecture, desktop applications development, and distributed applications development.

Microsoft Certified Trainer

This final program, MCT, offers something for persons who plan to provide training on Microsoft products. It shows that you are qualified and certified to teach Microsoft's official curriculum. It is available only to trainers who will deliver courses at Microsoft Authorized Technical Education Centers and so is somewhat limited in its use.

To qualify, you go through various steps that Microsoft suggests. First, you need to complete Microsoft's special application form and present your qualifications to Microsoft. Next, you need to prepare and be ready to present the particular course you are being certified to lead. You need to pass the relevant exams for the product you are teaching. And, finally, you must attend one of the courses you plan to teach so that you can see how it is managed and understand any labs that might be involved. For some courses, you might be able to attend a special trainer prep course instead; although you don't receive any normal course credit for attending the special class. After these steps are completed to Microsoft's satisfaction, you are licensed to be an MCT. This allows you to sell your services as a certified trainer.

Obtaining Files and Sample Tests

Microsoft offers additional information for you and provides various files and test samples that you download from Microsoft's Web page. Included in this download page are exam preparation guides and assessment exams that test your current knowledge, allowing you to determine whether you are ready to take the exam and obtain certification.

You also can obtain additional certification guides and updates providing the latest information and changes to these programs. A particularly interesting paper is one called "The Value of Certification for Solution Developers White Paper." This authoritative paper from Southern Illinois University at Carbondale provides an immensely detailed discussion on the value of obtaining this certification. If you are looking at the MCSD designation and need additional data to convince your boss of its value, we strongly suggest downloading this file and using the material to help your cause.

The paper describes in detail the needs and responsibilities of a developer and uses extensive analysis and survey techniques to provide you with a solid answer to the program's effectiveness. We don't intend to give away the answer here, but we again recommend that you find and read the paper for yourself if you have any expectation of obtaining the MCSD designation.

In addition to this guide, you can obtain assessment tests to provide you with some degree of comfort about your present skill levels, and several certification updates.

Finally, there is a Windows NT 4.0 self-administered assessment file (around 585KB in size) that offers you some assessment of your knowledge. We'd expect a similar file to become available for Windows 2000 some time soon to give you an idea how you are doing now that you are finished with this book. By taking this assessment, you can discover which areas you might need to review and know for certain where your strength lies.

You can find all of these materials by using the following address:

```
http://www.microsoft.com/Train_Cert/download/downld.htm
```

Where Can I Find Out More?

If you have finished reading the information in this appendix, you are ready to obtain more detailed information on when and where testing takes place and how to sign up for the courses.

Microsoft offers detailed information on all aspects of training on its Web page, and that is a good place to start. There is also a Web page for the certification programs. You can find these pages at

```
http://www.microsoft.com/train_cert/default.htm
```

or at

```
http://www.microsoft.com/mcp/mktg/choices.htm
```

We also suggest visiting the Sylvan Web site at `www.2test.com` to see what they offer and determine if that is appropriate for you. Finally, seminars are also available at many universities and these can prove to be less expensive than commercial offerings. It might benefit you to call your local university and inquire about their curriculum.

Microsoft used to offer you a way to download the entire site and view it offline. Although this is a good idea, you need an extensive network connection and about 4MB of hard drive space to take advantage of the option. With the advent of faster Internet connections, it appears that this has gone the way of the dodo bird; it's no longer available. Of course, you could find third-party software that will go out and grab the pages of the Web site for you but that's up to you.

If you are a dial-up user, however, this method might save you time because the Microsoft site is fairly extensive. Traveling through it, and stopping to take in all the information, takes a fair amount of time especially if you choose to study each section in any detail.

APPENDIX **B**

Windows 2000 Command Reference

Because you might occasionally need to use the command prompt, this appendix serves as a useful reference of Windows 2000 NET commands. You can do just about anything from the command prompt that you can do in a normal session, but typing a command correctly is a bit more awkward than pointing and clicking.

An advantage to using the command prompt over the graphical interface is that you don't have to remember where anything is. When you remember the command name, you can do everything from the same place. Another advantage is that you can run these commands in a batch file or login script. For instance, you can create a batch file to set your account policies and then use it on each machine you set up. In this manner you won't have to remember all the parameters you need to set—just run the batch file.

In general, the people who need to use the command prompt to connect are the network's OS/2 and DOS clients. If you're administering the server, you probably don't have many occasions to use the command prompt, except when making adjustments to DOS and OS/2 workstations.

The information for each command can include some or all of the following elements:

- The name of the command
- A description of the command
- The command syntax
- Command parameters (if necessary)
- The procedure for using the command
- Notes about the usage of the command, if appropriate

NET ACCOUNTS

To make individual adjustments to user accounts, you use the NET USER command (discussed later in this appendix). To make adjustments concerning such things as forcible logoff and password age to the entire user account database, you use the NET ACCOUNTS command. When used without switches, NET ACCOUNTS displays the current account information.

Syntax

```
net accounts [/option] [/domain]
```

Parameters

Option	Description
/FORCELOGOFF: {number | NO}	Sets the number of minutes a user has between the time that his account expires or logon period ends and the time that the server forcibly disconnects the user. The default is Never.
/MINPWLEN:{number}	Specifies the minimum number of characters that a user's password account must have, from 0 to 14. The default is 6.
/MAXPWAGE: {number | UNLIMITED}	Specifies the maximum number of days that must pass before the user modifies her password. The possible range for /maxpwage is 0 to 49,710 days (a little more than 136 years, which makes you wonder how Microsoft decided on that maximum value), with a default value of 90 days. According to Help, the range is 1 to 999 days. You also can set the value to UNLIMITED if you want the password to never expire.

Option	Description
/MINPWAGE:{number}	Specifies the minimum number of days that must pass before the user modifies his password. You can set the /minpwage from 0 to 49,710 days, but its default value is 0 days, meaning that the user can change the password whenever desired, even more than once a day. Again, according to Help, the range is 1 to 999 days.
/SYNC	Updates the user accounts database.
/UNIQUEPW:{number}	Determines the number of unique passwords a user must cycle through before repeating one. The highest value you can assign to this variable is 24.
/DOMAIN	Specifies that the command should be performed on the primary domain controller rather than the local SAM when the command is executed on a Windows 2000 Server operating in server mode or from a Windows 2000 Professional.

Procedure

1. Select Start, Programs, Accessories, Command Prompt.
2. Type the command at the C:\ prompt.

Usage

When you're performing this operation on a workstation that doesn't have W2K Server loaded, add the domain/switch to the end of the command to make the command apply to the domain controller of the domain you're in. If the machine has W2K Server on board, the information automatically passes to the domain controller.

NET COMPUTER

The NET COMPUTER command adds or deletes computers (not users) from a domain.

Syntax

```
net computer \\computername\ {/add ¦ /del}
```

Procedure

1. Select Start, Programs, Accessories, Accessories, Command Prompt.
2. Type the command at the C:\ prompt.

Usage

The computername is the name of the computer to be added to or deleted from the local domain. This command works only on computers running W2K Server.

Note, by the way, that NET COMPUTER applies to computers, not to users. Users aren't members of domains, only computers are.

NET CONFIG

You can use the NET CONFIG command to see how a machine is configured to behave on the network and, to a limited extent, change that configuration.

Syntax

```
net config {server ¦ workstation}
```

Parameters

SERVER displays configuration information for the Server service.

WORKSTATION displays configuration information for the Workstation service.

Procedure

1. Select Start, Programs, Accessories, Command Prompt.
2. Type the command at the C:\ prompt.

Usage

NET CONFIG names the configurable services (namely, the server and the workstation). If you include one of the configurable services in the command, for example, when you type NET CONFIG SERVER, you will see the following items of information:

- The name of the computer
- The software version
- The network card's name and address
- That the server is visible to the network
- The limit to the number of users who can log on

- The maximum number of files that can be open per session with another computer
- The idle session time

The NET CONFIG WORKSTATION command displays information about the configuration of the workstation service.

NET CONTINUE

To restart a paused service, you use the NET CONTINUE command.

Syntax

```
net continue service
```

Procedure

Type the command at the C:\ prompt.

Usage

The NET CONTINUE command affects the following default services:

- FILE SERVER FOR MACINTOSH
- LPDSVC
- NET LOGON
- NETWORK DDE
- NETWORK DDE DSDM
- NT LM SECURITY SUPPORT PROVIDER
- REMOTE ACCESS SERVER
- SCHEDULE
- SERVER
- SIMPLE TCP/IP SERVICES
- WORKSTATION

NET FILE

You can use NET FILE to find out what files are open and who is using them.

Syntax

```
net file [file ID] [/close]
```

Procedure

1. Select Start, Programs, Accessories, Command Prompt.

2. Type net start workstation.

3. Type the command at the C:\ prompt.

Usage

Without switches, you can use the NET FILE command to display the open files. The output lets you know what's open and who (users, not computers) is using it. When you add the switches, you can identify that file to the server and shut it down, removing all file locks.

NET GROUP

The NET GROUP command provides you with information on global groups on a server and enables you to modify this information.

Syntax

```
net group [groupname] [/comment:"text"] [/domain]
net group groupname {/add [/comment:"text"] ¦ /delete} [/domain]
net group groupname username [...] {/add ¦ /delete} [/domain]
```

Parameters

Option	Description
/ADD	Adds a new global group to the domain.
/COMMENT:{"text"}	Adds a descriptive comment to a new or an existing group.
/DELETE	Deletes a new global group from the domain.
/DOMAIN	Specifies that the command should be performed on the primary domain controller rather than the local computer. This command only applies to Windows 2000 Professional.

Procedure

1. Select Start, Programs, Accessories, Command Prompt.

2. Type the command at the C:\ prompt.

Usage

Typed without parameters, NET GROUP just lists the global groups on your server, but you can use the options to modify the membership of global groups, check on their membership, add comments to the group names, or add or delete global groups on the server.

Use the username option when you want to add or delete a user from the group.

When you are executing the NET GROUP command from a workstation where Windows 2000 Server isn't installed, add the /domain switch to the end of the statement to make the command apply to the domain controller. Otherwise, you perform the requested action only at the workstation you are working from. When you're working on a server with Windows 2000 Server installed, the /domain switch isn't necessary.

NET HELP

You can use the NET HELP command to get information attached to a command. The command's Help file is displayed.

Syntax

```
net help [command] ¦ more
```

Procedure

1. Select Start, Programs, Accessories, Command Prompt.
2. Type the command at the C:\ prompt.

Usage

The ¦ more switch is necessary for commands with more than one screen of information.

Optionally, you can get the same information by typing this:

```
net print /help or net print /?
```

Typing net print /? doesn't net you much information under W2K Server, it merely gives you the proper syntax for the command. To view an explanation of all the command syntax symbols, just type this:

```
net help syntax
```

NET HELPMSG

NET HELPMSG works as a decoder for the Windows 2000 error, warning, and alert messages. When you see an error message with a number attached, use this command to see the Help file attached to that error message.

Syntax

```
net helpmsg number
```

Procedure

1. Select Start, Programs, Accessories, Command Prompt.

2. Type the command at the C:\ prompt.

Usage

The number is the four-digit error message number.

NET LOCALGROUP

The NET LOCALGROUP refers to local user groups, and NET GROUP refers to global, or domainwide, ones. Unlike NET GROUP, this command can be used on Windows 2000 workstations as well as servers.

Syntax

```
net localgroup [groupname] [/comment:"text"] [/domain]
net localgroup groupname {/add [/comment:"text"] ¦ /delete} [/domain]
net localgroup groupname username [...] {/add ¦ /delete} [/domain]
```

Parameters

Option	Description
/ADD	Adds a new local group to the domain.
/COMMENT:{"text"}	Adds a descriptive comment to a new or an existing group.
/DELETE	Deletes a new local group from the domain.
/DOMAIN	Specifies that the command should be performed on the primary domain controller rather than the local computer. This parameter only applies to a Windows 2000 Professional.

Procedure

1. Select Start, Programs, Accessories, Command Prompt.
2. Type the command at the C:\ prompt.

Usage

Typed without parameters, NET LOCALGROUP just lists the local groups on your server, but you can use the options to modify the membership of local groups, check on their membership, add comments to the group names, or add or delete global groups on the server.

NET NAME

You're not dependent on email to send messages across the network. From the command prompt, you can send messages and arrange to have your own forwarded so that they catch up with you wherever you are. As long as your computer and the computer where you direct the messages are running the message service, you can reach anywhere on the network.

Syntax

```
net name username [/ADD ¦ /DELETE]
```

Parameters

Option	Description
username	The name of the user to receive messages. The name can be up to 15 characters.
/ADD	Adds a new name to the computer.
/DELETE	Deletes a name from the computer.

Procedure

1. Select Start, Programs, Accessories, Command Prompt.
2. Type the command at the C:\ prompt.

Usage

The NET NAME command adds or deletes a messaging name (also known as an alias) at a workstation. The messaging name is the name that receives messages at that station; any messages sent over the network go to where the messaging name is. Although this command comes with two switches, /add and /delete, the /add switch isn't necessary to add a messaging name to a workstation; instead, you would need only type NET NAME username.

NET PAUSE

If you need to halt a service temporarily, you can use the NET PAUSE command to do it.

Syntax

```
net pause service
```

Procedure

1. Select Start, Programs, Accessories, Command Prompt.
2. Type the command at the C:\ prompt.

Usage

The NET PAUSE command affects the following default services:

- FILE SERVER FOR MACINTOSH
- LPDSVC
- NET LOGON
- NETWORK DDE
- NETWORK DDE DSDM
- NT LM SECURITY SUPPORT PROVIDER
- REMOTE ACCESS SERVER
- SCHEDULE
- SERVER
- SIMPLE TCP/IP SERVICES
- WORKSTATION

NET PRINT

With the NET PRINT command, you can control print jobs, just as you can with the Print Manager.

Syntax

```
net print \\computername\sharename
net print [\\computername] job# [/delete ¦ /release ¦ /hold]
```

Procedure

1. Select Start, Programs, Accessories, Command Prompt.

2. Type the command at the C:\ prompt.

Usage

You can get a list of all the jobs currently printing or waiting on that printer by specifying sharename, or the name of the printer as it is shared on the network.

You can delete a print job by referring to that number and using the /delete switch. If you want to hold a print job (keep it in the print queue but let other jobs print ahead of it) or release it (free a held job to print), substitute the /hold or /release switch for /delete.

NET SESSION

Used on servers, this command displays information about sessions between the server and other computers on the network.

Syntax

```
net session [\\computername\] [/delete]
```

Procedure

1. Select Start, Programs, Accessories, Command Prompt.

2. Type the command at the C:\ prompt.

Usage

When you type the command without switches, you get a screen showing all the computers that are logged on to that server. When you include NET SESSION switches, you can get more detailed information about a session with a particular computer, or delete a session (that is, disconnect a computer from the server).

 Caution   Be careful when using the /delete switch. If you neglect to include the computer name in the command, you end all current sessions, and everyone has to reconnect to the server.

B

NET SHARE

The NET SHARE command applies to resources that the server is sharing with the network. The command provides you with information about that particular shared resource.

Syntax

```
net share sharename
net share sharename=drive:path [/users:number ¦ /unlimited] [/remark:"comment"]
net share [/users:number ¦ /unlimited] [/remark:"comment"]
net share {sharename ¦ devicename ¦ drive:path} [/delete]
```

Parameters

Option	Description
sharename	Name of the shared resource. Using just this parameter displays information about that share.
drive:path	Absolute path of the shared directory.
/USERS:number	Sets the maximum number of users who can simultaneously access the shared resource.
/UNLIMITED	Specifies an unlimited number of users who can simultaneously access the shared resource.
/REMARK:"comment"	Adds a descriptive comment for the shared resource.
drivename	Specifies one or more resources shared by sharename.
/DELETE	Stops sharing the resource.

Procedure

1. Select Start, Programs, Accessories, Command Prompt.
2. Type net start workstation.
3. Type the command at the C:\ prompt.

Usage

Used alone, this command lists all resources currently being shared with the network. With its switches, you can create and delete shared resources.

NET SHARE is a useful command not only for viewing the setup of existing shared devices, but also for creating new ones and configuring existing shares. You must be using an account with administrative rights to use this command; ordinary user accounts can't use it.

To stop sharing a device, type **NET SHARE**, the share name, device name, or drive and path, and then add the /delete switch.

Note

> When using the NET SHARE command, keep in mind that when you enable the guest account, any devices you share with the network are automatically available to the entire network; you can't set individual or group permissions with this command. Should you want to restrict access to devices or drives, you must set the permissions on the pertinent device or drive from the File Manager or Print Manager. You also can use the CACLS program to set permissions.

B

NET START

The NET START command comprises a long list of network services that can be started. The command cannot start all the services available from the Services icon in the Control Panel, but only the network-related ones. On its own, it doesn't do anything except list the services that have already been started. The list you see when you type **NET START** isn't a complete list of all the network services available.

Syntax

```
net start [servicename]
```

Parameters

The default services in Windows 2000 are shown here.

Service	Description
ALERTER	Sends messages about the network to users. You select what events you want to trigger alerts in the Performance Monitor. For these alerts to be sent, both the Alerter and Messenger services must be running on the computer originating the alerts, and the Messenger service must be running on the computer receiving them.

Service	Description
CLIPBOOK SERVER	Allows you to start a temporary or permanent storage place for text or graphics that you want to cut and paste between applications. You see a message that the service has started, or if you've already started it from W2K Server, you see a message that the service was already started.
COMPUTER BROWSER	Allows your computer to browse and be browsed on the network. When you start it from the command prompt, however, you get no further information than the fact that the service has started.
DHCP CLIENT	Start a DHCP client.
DIRECTORY REPLICATOR	Allows you to dynamically update files between servers. You must have replication rights to use this command, which means you have to set up a user account with replication rights before you start this service.
EVENTLOG	Begins the event log, which audits selected events on the network, such as file access, user logons and logoffs, and the starting of programs. You can select what events you want to log, and also whether you want the log to consist of both successful and failed attempts, just failures, or just successes (although just recording successes doesn't sound terribly useful when you're trying to monitor the system).
LPDSVC	Starts the lpdsvc when TCP/IP has been installed.
MESSENGER	Starts the messenger service, which must be running on both the machine sending the message and the receiving one(s) for NET SEND and the Alerter service.
NET LOGON	Starts the net logon service, which verifies logon requests and controls replication of the user accounts database.

Service	Description
NETWORK DDE	Provides a network transport for dynamic data exchange (DDE) conversations and provides security for them.
NETWORK DDE DSDM	Used by the DDE service described earlier, the DDE share database manager (DSDM) manages the DDE conversations.
NETWORK MONITORING AGENT	Starts the Network Monitoring Agent.
NT LM SECURITY SUPPORT MANAGER	Provides Windows 2000 security to SUPPORT PROVIDER RPC applications that use transports other than LAN Manager named pipes.
PLUG AND PLAY	Starts Plug and Play.
REMOTE ACCESS CONNECTION MANAGER	Starts the Remote Access Connection Manager service. Requires the installation of Remote Access Service.
REMOTE ACCESS ISNSAP SERVICE	Starts the Remote Access ISNSAP Service. Requires the installation of Remote Access Service.
REMOTE ACCESS SERVER	Starts the Remote Access Server.
REMOTE PROCEDURE CALL (RPC) LOCATOR	Allows distributed applications to use CALL (RPC) LOCATOR, the RPC-provided pointer by directing the applications to those pointers. This service manages the RPC NSI database.
REMOTE PROCEDURE CALL (RPC) SERVICE	Enables programmers to develop CALL (RPC) SERVICE distributed applications more easily by providing pointers to direct the applications. The default name service is the Windows 2000 Locator.
SCHEDULE	Starts the scheduling service, which must be running to use the AT command. The AT command can be used to schedule commands and programs (like the backup program, for instance) to run on a certain computer at a specific time and date.

B

Service	Description
SERVER	Controls access to network resources from the command line. This service must be running before you can perform named pipe, directory and printer sharing, and RPC access.
SERVER	Starts the Server service to enable a computer to share resources on the network.
SIMPLE TCP/IP SERVICES	Starts Simple TCP/IP Services service.
SNMP	Starts the SNMP service and allows a server to report its current status to a SNMP manager on a TCP/IP network. Requires SNMP and TCP/IP installation.
SPOOLER	Provides print spooler capabilities.
TASK SCHEDULER	Starts the Task Scheduler.
TCPIP NETBIOS HELPER	Enables the NetBIOS Helper over TCP service.
UPS	Starts the uninterruptible power system.
WORKSTATION	Enables workstations to connect to and use shared network resources. After you start this service, you can see what's on the network and connect to it.

Procedure

1. Select Start, Programs, Accessories, Command Prompt.
2. Type the command at the C:\ prompt.

Usage

All two-word commands, such as "clipbook server" and "computer browser" must be enclosed within quotation marks for the NET START commands to work.

In addition to the default Windows 2000 Server services, you can start the following special services:

- Client Server for NetWare
- DHCP Client
- File Server for Macintosh

- FTP Server
- Gateway Service for NetWare
- LPDSVC
- Microsoft DHCP Server
- Network Monitoring Agent
- OLE
- Print Server for Macintosh
- Remote Access Connection Manager
- Remote Access ISNSAP Service
- Remote Access Server
- Remoteboot
- Simple TCP/IP Services
- SNMP
- TCP/IP NETBIOS Helper
- Windows Internet Name Service

B

NET STATISTICS

The NET STATISTICS command gives you a report on the computer where you run it.

Syntax

```
net statistics [server ¦ workstation]
```

Procedure

1. Select Start, Programs, Accessories, Command Prompt.
2. Type the command at the C:\ prompt.

Usage

If you use STATISTICS without a switch, you get a list of the services where statistics are available (server and/or workstation, depending on whether you use the command on a Windows 2000 Professional or Server machine).

You can use either NET STATISTICS SERVER or NET STATISTICS WORKSTATION from any Windows 2000 Professional or Server machine, but the command can give you information only about the machine where you run it.

NET STOP

NET STOP works in the same way that NET START does. On its own, it can't do anything, but when you add the name of a service that you want to stop, this command stops it. See the "NET START" section, earlier in the appendix, for details on what each of the services does.

 Caution Be careful when stopping a service! Some services are dependent on others (such as NET START, NET LOGON, and NET START WORKSTATION), so when you shut down one, you might shut down another without meaning to. If you just need to stop a service temporarily, use NET PAUSE instead. Fortunately, you need administrative rights to stop a service.

Syntax

```
net stop servicename
```

Procedure

1. Select Start, Programs, Accessories, Command Prompt.
2. Type the command at the C:\ prompt.

NET TIME

Some services, such as directory replication, depend on the server's and the workstations' clocks being set to the same time. To automate this process, you can use the NET TIME command.

Syntax

```
net time [\\computername ¦ /domain:[domainname] ¦ /rtsdomain:[domainname]]
➡[/set]

net time [\\computername] /querysntp

net time [\\computername] /setsntp[:ntp server list]
```

Parameters

The default services in Windows 2000 are shown following.

Service	Description
computername	Name of the computer you want to check or synchronize with.
/DOMAIN[:domainname]	Specifies to synchronize with the PDC.
/RTSDOMAIN[:domainname]	Specifies to synchronize with a Reliable Time Server.
/SET	Sets the time with the specified computer or server.
/QUERYSNTP	Displays the currently configured Network Time Protocol (NTP) server.
/SETSNTP[:ntp server list]	Sets the NTP servers for this computer.

B

Procedure

1. Select Start, Programs, Accessories, Command Prompt.

2. Type the command at the C:\ prompt.

Usage

The NET TIME command works differently when you execute it from a server than when you execute it from a workstation. When you run it from a server, it displays the current time; when you run it from a workstation, you can synchronize your computer's clock with that of the time server, even selecting a server from another domain where there is a trusted relationship between your domain and the other one. Ordinary users cannot set the server time from a workstation; only members of the Administrators or Server Manager groups, logged onto the server (logically, if not physically), can set the system time. Use this command in a login script to synchronize the time across your domain.

NET USE

After you've browsed the network with NET VIEW, you can connect to all the available goodies (or disconnect from those you don't want) with the NET USE command. Use this command to connect to drives D through Z and printer ports LPT1 through LPT9.

Syntax

```
net use [devicename ¦ *] [\\computername\sharename[\volume] [password ¦ *]
[/user:[domainname\]username]
net use [devicename ¦ *] [password ¦ *]] [/home]
net use [/persistent:{YES ¦ NO}]
```

Parameters

Option	Description
/HOME	To connect to your home directory (the directory on the server that has been assigned to you, assuming that there is one).
/PERSISTENT:{YES | NO}	No matter what kind of connection you make, you can make it persistent (that is, remake it every time you connect to the network) by adding the switch /persistent:YES to the end of the line. If you don't want it to be persistent, type /persistent:NO instead. The default is whatever you chose last.
/DELETE	Use this to disconnect from a resource.

Procedure

1. Select Start, Programs, Accessories, Command Prompt.

2. Type **net start workstation**.

3. Type the command at the C:\ prompt.

Usage

To get information about the workstation's current connections, use the command without options. To actually make connections, use the command's switches.

Also, you use this command to connect to a shared resource such as a printer. You get to specify the port name or drive letter that you want to connect a resource to, but you're restricted to drive letters D through Z and ports LPT1 through LPT9. Also, when the computer that you're getting the resource from has a blank character in its name (that is, has two words in it), you must put the name in quotation marks.

When a password is attached to the resource that you're trying to connect to, you need to include that password in your connection command. Or if you want the computer to prompt you for the password so that it isn't displayed on-screen, append an asterisk. Passwords go before the user's name in the statement.

Note If you get help on this command, you'll notice that it claims that you can use only printer ports LPT1 through LPT3. Technically, this isn't true, but the Help file probably puts it this way because some MS-DOS applications aren't able to access printer ports with numbers higher than 3.

B

NET USER

You can use the NET USER command from the server to control user accounts—to add them, delete them, and change them. When you type this command without parameters, you get a list of the user accounts for that server. You can use switches and parameters to manipulate accounts.

Syntax

```
net user [username [password ¦ *] [/options]] [/domain]
net user username {password ¦ *} /add [options] [/domain]
net user username [/delete] [/domain]
```

Parameters

Option	Description
asterisk (*)	Placing an asterisk after the user's name prompts you to enter and confirm a new password for the user account.
/ACTIVE:{YES ¦ NO}	This option determines whether the account is active or inactive. If it's inactive, the user cannot log on to this account. Deactivating an account isn't the same thing as deleting it: A deactivated account can be reinstated if it's simply reactivated, but a deleted account is dead. A deleted account's parameters are lost, and even when you create a new account with the same name and password, you need to rebuild the user rights and other account information. The default is YES.
/COMMENT:"text"	Enclose the comment text (no more than 48 characters, including spaces) in quotation marks. You don't have to put a comment on an account.

Option	Description
/COUNTRYCODE:nnn	This option selects the operating system's country code so that the operating system knows what language to use for help and error messages. The default for this option is 0.
/EXPIRES:	If you enter a date after the {date	NEVER} colon, the account will expire on that date; NEVER sets no time limit on the account. Depending on the country code, type the expiration date as mm,dd,yy or dd,mm,yy (the format in the U.S. is mm,dd,yy). You can enter the year with either four characters or two, and months as a number, spelled out, or abbreviated to two letters. Use commas or front slashes (/), not spaces, to separate the parts of the date.
/FULLNAME:"name"	This is the user's full name, as opposed to the username. Enclose the name in quotation marks.
/HOMEDIR:pathname	If you've set up a home directory for the user, this is where you include the pointers to that directory. You have to set up the home directory before you set up this part of the account.
/HOMEDIRREQ:{YES	NO}	If the user is required to use a home directory, select YES. You must have already created the directory and used the /HOMEDIR switch to specify where the directory is.
/PASSWORDCHG:	This option specifies {YES	NO} whether the user can change the password. The default is YES.
/PASSWORDREQ:	This option specifies {YES	NO} whether a password is required on the user account. The default is YES.
/PROFILEPATH:path	This option specifies a path for the user's logon profile, when there is one for the account.
/SCRIPTPATH:pathname	This option specifies where the user's logon script is located.

Option	Description
/TIMES:{times | ALL}	This option specifies the user's logon hours. Unless you specify ALL, you must spell out the permitted logon times for every day of the week. Days can be spelled out or abbreviated to three letters; hours can be indicated with either 12- or 24-hour notation. Separate day and time entries with a comma, and days with a semicolon. Don't leave this option blank; if you do, the user will never be able to log on.
/USERCOMMENT:"text"	With this option, you can add or change the user comment for the account.
/WORKSTATIONS:	This option lists up to eight {computername{,...| *} computers where a user can log onto the network. If no list exists or the list is *, the user can log on from any computer.

B

Procedure

1. Select Start, Programs, Accessories, Command Prompt.
2. Type the command at the C:\ prompt.

Usage

When you're performing this operation on a workstation that doesn't have W2K Server loaded, add the domain/switch to the end of the command to make the command apply to the domain controller of the domain you're in.

NET VIEW

You can use this command to see what's available on the network, how to connect to it, and who's using it. You can't change anything with the NET VIEW command; you only can use it to see the resources being shared on the servers and domains on the network.

Syntax

```
net view [\\computername ¦ ¦domain[:domainname]]
net view /network:nw [\\computername]
```

Procedure

1. Select Start, Programs, Accessories, Command Prompt.
2. Type the command at the C:\ prompt.

Usage

When you type the command on its own, you get a list of the local servers on the domain. When you want to see a list of the resources that the server is sharing with the network, you can append the name of the server that you want to look at to the command. For example, if the server is named Balliol, you would type this:

```
net view \\balliol
```

If you omit the domain name from the command, you see a list of all domains on the network.

APPENDIX C

Migrating to Windows 2000

In the previous three weeks, you learned about installing, exploring, and managing your Windows 2000 Server. You might be reading this appendix with trepidation because you've been assigned the odious duty of moving all your original NT users onto Windows 2000, and now you are wishing you had never heard of Windows 2000 Server.

Over the next few years, I predict that this section of the book will gain popularity as more and more organizations convert to this new and far more exciting version of Windows. Am I biased? Perhaps. After all, in writing this book on Windows 2000, I have seen how far the product has advanced and it is now reaching a stage where many of the shortcomings in NT 4.0 are resolved while many new features have been added.

If you are reading this appendix, you are likely in the position of needing to move users from NT to Windows 2000, and that is what I concentrate on for the remainder of the section.

You can find additional information on Microsoft's Web site where you will find a slew of documents to help you. You might begin by looking for the document titled "Planning and Migrating to Active Directory."

Migrating or Integrating

First you need to decide whether your interest lies in actually moving all your present NT users over to Windows 2000 and, in the process, removing the old version, or whether you are interested in being able to let users access both an NT and a Windows 2000 server. This section relates primarily to moving users from their NT system and placing them entirely onto a Windows 2000 Server. First, however, some discussion about mixing the two environments might be appropriate.

NT workstations are able to connect to either an NT 4.0 or a Windows 2000 server of course, allowing user to access both systems as their needs dictate. This is probably the more common initial scenario, the sharing of both NT and Windows 2000 on the same network.

There are many advantages to migrating all your machines to Windows 2000, yet how fast you do this likely depends upon how large an environment you have. Those with a small number of servers might migrate all the machines to Windows 2000 fairly quickly while those with a large number of machines are more likely to integrate Windows 2000 into the existing environment, taking a slower path.

You learned the advantages of using Windows 2000 as you progressed through the 21 days and perhaps one or more of these advantages will help you decide how quickly you want to move to implement Windows 2000 across your organization.

The following list recaps a few of these advantages:

- Active Directory offers a far better method for connecting machines, reducing the cumbersome use of Domains and Trusts of the earlier versions.
- Security is far more granular, providing a vastly improved capability for decentralizing your administration, while ensuring that only the necessary authority is granted.
- There are no more limitations to the size of your domains. The SAM is replaced by Active Directory and this can be 17 terabytes in size and contain around a million objects.
- Logon security is improved with Kerberos and Smart Card support built in.

There are many, many more advantages, many of which you should know by now if you finished reading this book. I merely reiterate a few here to remind you.

Larger sites are more likely to integrate their present Windows NT 4.0 machines with the newer Windows 2000, allowing both to coexist. This is the most likely scenario dealing with large numbers of machines.

There is no reason to attempt a complete conversion of all systems overnight. With foresight and planning, your implementation of Windows 2000 can take place at a pace you are comfortable with as both systems coexist. Users connecting from downlevel clients (Windows 95 and so on) will think they are connecting to an NT 4.0 machine, as Windows 2000 allows for backward compatibility. It will appear as a Windows 2000 server to those users with Windows 2000 Professional workstations.

This appendix will cover a large number of items for you to consider as you integrate or migrate to Windows 2000. Implementing Windows 2000 across your environment can be an onerous task. Hopefully I will make that task a little easier by providing you a number of steps to follow that I believe will help ensure that your implementation goes as smoothly as possible.

Regardless of whether you choose to integrate Windows 2000 into your existing environment or migrate fully to a Windows 2000 site, there are a number of key steps you should understand and follow.

 Caution Be sure to complete the 21 days in this book before beginning. You will want to understand Windows 2000 fully before you implement across your environment.

Inventorying Your Current Status

Your first step should be to ensure that you know exactly what you're dealing with. This typically means ensuring that you have a complete inventory of your current servers and workstations along with the applications they are running. Although you may think you have this committed to memory, in our experience it's highly unlikely, as organizations change far too frequently and what once was true is quickly outdated. Users may have installed software, non-standard equipment, or applications of which you know nothing.

To inventory your environment, it would be best to use one or more tools designed to automate the process. Although using these tools helps facilitate the task, there will be areas where you will need to perform the inventory manually. The tools include:

- One useful tool for inventorying and finding computers is NetCensus by Tally Systems. This product takes a complete hardware inventory and recognizes most of the software programs in use today. You may need to update its database so that it can recognize customized software that you may be using.

- Smaller sites might want to use a relatively inexpensive program called Visio. This program has a version that will automatically seek out and list all the machines on your network. It doesn't, however, research all the software that may be running on each machine.

- One tool you may want to seriously consider using if you are a large site is Microsoft's own Systems Management Server (SMS). The latest version provides a complete hardware and software inventory for all of its clients. This includes the services and devices your Windows NT clients are running. Reports can be generated using Microsoft Access, Visual Basic, or other third-party reporting tools. Although SMS is an expensive tool, your organization may already be using it. If this is the case it may be the perfect tool for you as your organization already has it, probably already has people who are experienced using it, and it is essentially free as far as your project is concerned.

Finally, regardless of the tools you may use there is likely to be a certain amount of manual work. It might be necessary to actually visit a server and determine exactly what is on it or to interview technical staff to ensure that you're not missing anything. Sometimes a machine may be offline, the network connection might be broken, or a software glitch may prevent the tool from working. Taking precautions now may serve you well as you begin to implement Windows 2000 across your environment.

After you've completed your inventory you should have a comprehensive view of your computing systems. Combined into a database this can be used to provide a baseline for your Windows 2000 environment, helping ensure that machines meet the physical requirements of Windows 2000, and that applications and software are Windows 2000–compatible.

Note   In addition, of course, this is a good time to ensure that your licensing is up-to-date and accurate. This will be of great benefit should you receive a visit from the Software Publishers Association (SPA), as you will be able to prove you are compliant with all licensing needs.

Develop and Implement Standards

After you have a good idea of your current environment, you need to begin deciding what your new environment will look like. This short appendix will give you a number of ideas and tasks, but you should understand that depending on the size of your organization this can be a sizable task.

As with any major project, this is a good time to implement a number of standards. These standards include such things as the type of hardware you plan to use, the applications and services, naming schemes and security. By taking the time to agree on these things before you begin to implement Windows 2000, you'll reduce the total cost of ownership, simplify your environment, and establish sound practices.

Total cost of ownership can be reduced through effective systems management and standardization. Saving just a few dollars per computer often results in significant cost reductions when you apply that savings across your environment.

Some of the items you'll want to include in your standards consist of

- Hardware
- Applications
- Naming conventions
- Server and workstation security

Hardware is often one of the more difficult areas to apply standards to because hardware quickly becomes out of date. This is why it is generally a good idea to establish minimum requirements, rather than precise configurations. For example, Microsoft recommends that Windows 2000 Server use 64MB of RAM and a Pentium 166. They also provide a list of recommended vendors through the hardware compatibility list (HCL). Your organization may use particular vendors and specific machines as a simple way of standardizing the equipment necessary for each server and each workstation.

The applications in use vary widely across organizations and therefore it is difficult for us to suggest any particular standard. However, as part of your Windows 2000 implementation, this is a necessary step for you to take. Standardizing software can often be painful in an organization that has never performed this before. Users become accustomed to using specific applications and are often reluctant to change. Factors that help include the informal standards typically in use such as a company-wide email program and standard desktop tools, such as Microsoft Office.

Additionally, it is important to ensure that your applications will run under this new environment.

Tip

Although most NT 4.0 applications should not experience any problems when moved on to a Windows 2000 machine, it is a good idea to test each one prior to your conversion just to be sure.

C

If you have created special NT Services, you should definitely ensure that these will still work as this is one area that is significantly different, primarily due to the new Active Directory structure.

Some of the naming conventions you need to consider include domain names, computer names, and usernames. Domain names are more important for larger organizations spanning more than one domain than for those organizations using only one domain. Ideally, make your domain names descriptive allowing for easier administration. Domains such as Sales and Accounting are far easier to understand than names like D01 and Gen10. As you no doubt recall from earlier chapters in the book, you should restrict these names to DNS legal characters.

You should also strive to make your computer names DNS-compatible. Although it might be cool to have computers with names like Snoopy or SkyWalker, it is best to use names that help ease day-to-day administration. For example, use separate naming standards for your servers and your workstations. Although many books suggest naming machines by their location, this can prove to be costly as your organization grows and you need to move machines. You should also resist the temptation to name computers based on their primary user's account name as turnover is inevitable and after a while many machines won't match the current user. Using a serial number or similar descriptive helps minimize the need to change the name at a later date.

Deciding on a consistent method for creating your user accounts can be the most difficult task. Typically organizations already use one or more naming conventions and deciding to change that convention at this stage may prove onerous. You will need to decide whether this is a task to undertake at this juncture. The most typical account name consists of first initial and last name. Using this convention allows for easy recognition of staff and minimizes the risk of confusion when administering the system. If you already use a similar scheme, you are all set. If not, you have a fairly onerous additional chore to add to the project.

Finally, design a sound and effective set of security standards. The standard should be used to implement a baseline for all your machines and users to follow. The best time to implement these standards is during your Windows 2000 implementation. You are setting up each machine anyway, so you may as well do it right in the first place. It's one way to actually complete that security chore you've always considered but never gotten around to completing.

Standards should clearly identify User Rights and permissions for servers and for workstations. By this, of course, I don't mean that each and every file or privilege should be identified, but that the global settings should be clear. These global settings would include such things as Windows 2000 Policies, Registry settings, and audit requirements.

The standards would clearly identify such things as password length and expiration time, whether users would have administrative rights on their workstations, and all the other aspects you learned in the chapters on security.

Plan Your Domain Structure

After you have some basic standards in place, you need to decide what type of Domain Structure you will use in your new Windows 2000 environment. The design process for Windows 2000 domains is very different from what you used in your Windows NT 4.0 domain. Prior to this new version of Windows, your domains were primarily driven by the size and type of your organization. These limitations no longer exist.

With Windows 2000 it is best to try and use as few domains as possible. With NT 4.0 you might have created numerous domains, because of the size of your organization. Also, many companies created resource domains so that they might delegate administrative authority. With Windows 2000, there are few restrictions on how large your domains can be and authority can be delegated at almost any granularity so you are able to make your decision based upon your needs and not on the technical restrictions that the older version forced upon you.

To create the Windows 2000 domains you might take the following actions:

- Determine your current business environment and set up domains.
- Organize the domains into Trees or Forests.
- Develop the Organizational Units (OU) that you need.
- Set up sites to manage replication traffic.

This is a good opportunity to reassess your current business environment and ensure that your new domain is established using your organization's particular characteristics. For example, how is your company physically organized? Does it operate locally, regionally, or internationally? An international company is more likely to run its network based upon its physical geography. For example, the European portion might operate separately from the North American side of the firm. Therefore each country may want to set up their own domains so each country has control over their particular resources. W2K domains are not the same as NT 4.0 since there is little need for the Master Resource solutions that were enforced in NT 4.0 to manage users and resources. W2K domains can be any size and can be administered in either a centralized or decentralized fashion using standard W2K functions.

You also need to consider the technical requirements of your network. The speed of each network link and how they are organized across the company has an impact on Active

Directory replication. As you learned in Day 5, Active Directory replication can be managed using multiple domains. You need to know the type of network links and the speed at which they can communicate to determine the impact replication will have on any given part of the network.

Other considerations for creating your domains include supporting different policies for different parts of the business, addressing international differences, and complying with internal political pressures. As they used to say in the TV series *Mission: Impossible*, "Your task, Mr. Phelps, should you accept this mission, is to consider and finalize all these items before beginning the conversion."

Next, you need to decide whether a single Tree or a Forest of Trees is necessary. Both Trees and Forests form a structure in which all domains share the same configuration, global catalog, and schema. As you add domains to this hierarchy, a two-way transitive trust relationship is created. Ensure that you take as much time as necessary to whether you need a Tree or a Forest. Typically, companies that operate as a single entity will use a single Tree whereas companies that operate as partnerships or conglomerates might use a Forest to separate the various businesses. Because Windows 2000 uses the location services of dynamic DNS, creating a suitable name for your internal root domain is critical. Likewise, naming your company's subdomains should follow a few general guidelines. Using names that may quickly become obsolete or names that are hard to understand will only cause you trouble down the road. For example, asia.mycompany.com and cdn.mycompany.com might be good examples whereas y2k.mycompany.com and ab-d2.mycompany.com are less useful. Try to set up a structure that is meaningful yet simple to understand and use.

Next, you need to consider how to arrange your organizational units. You use OUs to organize resources in a meaningful hierarchy. As you recall, an OU is a simple container object. They contain other objects such as users and groups. As such, they can help to delegate administrative tasks. Your primary goal, therefore, is to make this structure fit the way you want to manage security and resources. As you may recall, you can set these to reflect your business or your company's physical locations, depending upon your particular needs. It is best not to let the hierarchy get too deep however; Microsoft recommends using no more than about five levels.

You might also consider the role of sites. In your NT 4.0 network, the logical structure usually mirrored the physical structure. In Windows 2000, the structures don't have to match. You use site objects to define areas of good network connectivity. When you configure a site object in Active Directory, you associate it with one or more TCP/IP subnets. This allows you to control replication traffic, isolate workstation logons, and identify resources by proximity.

Migrate to Windows 2000

The actual implementation of Windows 2000 isn't complex. Just make sure that you have completed your planning, coordination, and decision-making before you actually begin to install the product.

Upgrading your servers to Windows 2000 is fairly straightforward. Like most Windows installations, it is Wizard-driven and pretty well hands-free. There are a number of steps you might take to migrate from your present implementation to W2K. These include

- Ensure that you have a full backup of each machine prior to upgrading.
- Create a plan to allow you to restore the original domain should it be necessary.
- Start by migrating the PDC to W2K and then migrate a BDC to provide a recovery path.
- Test each migrated machine to ensure it is connected to the network.
- Decide whether to switch from a mixed domain that allows you to use NT 4.0 machines to a dedicated Windows 2000 network.

C

Like any major change, it is important to ensure that you have a full backup of each machine prior to upgrading. You should also have a plan for restoring the original domain itself should it be necessary. This will allow you to restore the user accounts and policy information in your original database if the upgrade to Windows 2000 should fail for some reason.

Your backup plan should contain the steps necessary to recover your original configuration. It might also contain one or two precautions. These precautions include moving a Backup Domain Controller offline or turning it off before you upgrade the primary Domain Controller. Or, move the primary Domain Controller onto an isolated environment and then upgrade it. Either of these options reduces your risk. You may even want to do both. Naturally, I cannot stress enough that having a complete up-to-date backup stored in a safe place would be prudent.

Start your installation by upgrading your existing PDC. After you have Windows 2000 fully installed and Active Directory started, install it on one of your BDC's to provide for immediate recovery. Now, continue to upgrade all your domain controllers except for the one you placed offline for recovery purposes. You want to leave the Backup Domain Controller that you placed offline until the end to ensure that the Windows 2000 installation is fully functional before that final machine is upgraded. By leaving it offline you ensure that no replication takes place and it remains unchanged. After you are certain you have finished your implementation and everything is working, you can convert this final machine.

After you complete the upgrade on each machine, you should verify it with a series of simple tests. These can help ensure that your servers are in good working order. First, run a few basic connectivity tests to confirm that your server can communicate on the network. Next, verify your installation of Active Directory. You might want to check that the database is created in the location you specified. The default is usually %systemroot%\ntds\ntds.dit.

Next, launch the directory management tool and ensure that you can navigate through the hierarchy. Finally, verify that users, groups, and computers are present in Active Directory and check to see that the system volume was created in the location you specified. The default is typically %systemroot%\sysvol.

Now test to see whether dynamic DNS is functioning. Verify that you can resolve a hostname to an IP address and launch the DNS MMC snap-in to ensure that it's working.

After all your domain controllers are running Windows 2000 and Active Directory, you can choose to switch the domain from a mixed domain to a pure Active Directory domain. You need to be very sure before you take this step because after you commit to it, you can no longer add NT 4.0 controllers. Several things happen during the switch:

1. The entire domain begins using the new Active Directory replication protocol.

2. It is no longer possible to add the old NT 4.0 domain controllers to the domain.

3. The server that was your PDC prior to migration is no longer the master of the domain; all domain controllers begin acting as peers. There is no single point of failure.

4. Clients can access resources anywhere in the domain tree based upon the level of security granted to them.

This switch isn't performed automatically by Active Directory; you must initiate it.

 Caution   Be sure that you won't need NT 4.0 domain controllers ever again before making the switch to a pure Active Directory domain. It is a good idea to ask senior management about plans to acquire other companies prior to doing this as a merger could create headaches for you if the other company uses NT 4.0.

Other than the enhanced domain tree access, client workstations won't be aware of any changes following this switch.

Naturally, there is an intense amount of detail that I don't have room for in this book. Migrating to Windows 2000 takes effort, dedication, planning, and attention to detail. The checklist that follows should provide you with an adequate start.

Tip

> The following link offers additional information concerning a broad range of Windows 2000 topics. http://www.microsoft.com/windows/server/default.asp. Search on the keyword "migration" to obtain more specific topics.
>
> You can also use Technet and perform a search using "migrating to Windows 2000". It will point you to some good articles including an installable self-paced training course (Course No. 1555). This training course is a wealth of information that covers all the bases.

Migration Checklist

Our primary goal in this appendix is to provide you some indication of the steps you need to take when considering your migration to Windows 2000. How well you carry out the task depends upon your preparation and dedication. This checklist isn't a replacement for a full understanding and familiarity with both your existing environment and the one you propose to implement.

Use this list as a basic template for creating your own more detailed checklist as part of your conversion project.

Task	Your Data
Determine current environment	Domain structure
	Administrative strategy
	Business locations
	Number and type of machines
	Operating systems
	Applications
	Network protocols
	Current standards
Assess critical applications	Identify the applications
	Test and verify problems
	Determine upgrades
	Schedule purchase of replacement applications
Determine strategy	Migrate
	Integrate
	Decide the conversion order for each domain

C

Task	Your Data
Create standards	Machines
	Security
	Network protocols
	Naming conventions
	Software
	Naming conventions
Design recovery plans	Number and location of backups
	Place PDC/BDC offline
	Prepare fallback plan
Plan Domain structure	Examine current operational needs
	Consider business plans
	Identify administrative needs
	Plan administrative delegation
	Decide number of domains
	Organize Trees and Forests
Plan OU hierarchy	Determine needs
	Determine what each level represents
	Build the hierarchy
Consider site creation	Examine physical locations
	Determine replication needs
Create DDNS structure	Plan the DDNS namespace
	Implement naming standards
	Form replication strategy
	Consider current DNS needs
Design rollout plans	
Obtain management approvals	
Implement	

GLOSSARY

access   The ability and the means necessary to approach, to store in or retrieve data from, to communicate with, and to make use of any resource of a computer system.

access category   One of the classes to which a user, a program, or a process in a system can be assigned because of the resources or groups of resources that each user, program, or process is authorized to use.

access control entry (ACE)   An entry in an access control list (ACL). The entry contains a security ID (SID) and a set of access rights. A process with a matching security ID is allowed access rights, denied rights, or allowed rights with auditing.

access control list (ACL)   The part of a security descriptor that enumerates the protection (that is, permission) given to an object.

access control mechanisms   Hardware or software features, operating procedures, management procedures, and various combinations of these designed to detect and prevent unauthorized access and to permit authorized access to a system.

access guidelines   Used here in the sense of guidelines for the modification of specific access rights. A general framework drawn up by the owner or custodian to instruct the data set security administrator on the degree of latitude that exists for the modification of rights of access to a file without the specific authority of the owner or custodian.

access list   A catalog of users, programs, or processes and the specifications of access categories to which each is assigned.

access period   A segment of time, generally expressed daily or weekly, when access rights prevail.

access right   A permission granted to a process to manipulate a particular object in a particular manner (for example, calling a service). Different object types support different access rights, which are stored in the object's access control list (ACL).

access token   An object uniquely identifying a user who has logged on. An access token is attached to all the user's processes and contains the user's security ID (SID), the names of any groups to which the user belongs, any privileges the user owns, the default owner of any objects the user's processes create, and the default access control list (ACL) to be applied to any objects the user's processes create.

access type   An access right to a particular device, program, or file, for example, read, write, execute, append, allocate, modify, delete, create.

access validation   Checking a user's account information to determine when the subject should be granted the right to perform the requested operation.

accessibility   The ease with which information can be obtained.

accountability   The quality or state that enables violations or attempted violations of a security system to be traced to individuals who can then be held responsible.

Active Directory   A Windows 2000 structure that lets you track or locate any object on a network. Active Directory is the directory service used in Windows 2000 Server and the foundation of Windows 2000 distributed networks. It provides administrators with a hierarchical view and a single point of administration.

address   A number or group of numbers uniquely identifying a network node within its network (or internetwork).

administrator   The administrator is the person responsible for the operation of the network. The administrator maintains the network, reconfiguring and updating it as the need arises. With Windows NT Server, it also is the default user account created during setup.

alert   (1) An audible or visual alarm that signals an error or serves as a warning of some sort. (2) An asynchronous notification that one thread sends to another.

algorithm   A step-by-step procedure, usually mathematical, for doing a specific function, for example, a PIN verification algorithm or an encryption algorithm.

American Wire Gauge (AWG)   The adopted standard wire sizes, such as No. 12 wire and No. 14 wire. The larger the gauge number of the wire, the smaller the wire; therefore, a No. 14 wire is smaller than a No. 12 wire.

analog   A system based on a continuous ratio, such as voltage or current values.

analog transmission   A communications scheme using a continuous signal, varied by amplification or frequency. Broadband networks use analog transmissions.

analytical attack   An attempt to break a code or cipher key by discovering flaws in its encryption algorithm.

ANSI   The acronym for American National Standards Institute, which sets standards for many technical fields.

AppleTalk   Macintosh native protocol.

application   The user's communication with the installation. A software program or program package enabling a user to perform a specific job, such as word processing or electronic mail.

application program/software   A program written for or by a user that applies to the user's work.

application programming interface (API)   A set of routines that an application program uses to request and carry out lower-level services performed by the operating system.

application system   A collection of programs and documentation used for an application.

architecture   The general design of hardware or software, including how they fit together.

ARCnet (Attached Resource Computer Network)   A token-passing local area network scheme developed by Datapoint. It uses a bus topology and is rated 2.5Mbps.

ASCII   The acronym for *American Standard Code for Information Interchange.* Pronounced "ASK-ee." It is an 8-bit code for character representation, that is, 7 bits with parity.

assembler   A language translator that converts a program written in assembly language into an equivalent program in machine language. The opposite of a disassembler.

assembly language   A low-level programming language in which individual machine-language instructions are written in a symbolic form that is easier to understand than machine language itself.

asynchronous   A method of data communications in which transmissions are not synchronized with a signal. Local area networks transmit asynchronously.

attach   To log a workstation into a server. Also, to log a workstation into another file server while the workstation remains logged in to the first.

attacks   The method used to commit security violations, such as masquerading and modification.

attenuation   The difference in amplitude between a signal at transmission and at reception. The signal weakens as it propagates across the network.

audit policy   Defines the type of security events logged for a domain or for an individual computer; determines what NT will do when the security log becomes full.

audit trail   A chronological record of system activities sufficient to enable the reconstruction, review, and examination of the sequence of environments and activities surrounding or leading to each event in the path of a transaction from its inception to the output of results.

auditability   The physical or mental power to perform an examination or verification of financial records or accounts.

auditing   The ability to detect and record security-related events, particularly any attempt to create, access, or delete objects. Windows 2000 uses security IDs (SIDs) to record what processes performed the action.

authenticate   (1) To confirm that the object is what it purports to be. To verify the identity of a person (or other agent external to the protection system) making a request. (2) To identify or verify the eligibility of a station, an originator, or an individual to access specific categories of information.

authentication   The act of identifying or verifying the eligibility of a station, originator, or individual to access specific categories of information.

authorization   The process that grants the necessary and sufficient permissions for the intended purpose.

authorize   To grant the necessary and sufficient permissions for the intended purpose.

automated security monitoring   The use of automated procedures to ensure that the security controls implemented within a system are not circumvented.

back up   To make a spare copy of a disk, a directory, or a file to another storage device such as a disk or tape drive.

backbone   A central network cable system that connects other networks.

background   A background task or program runs while the user is doing something else. The most common example is a print spooler program. Used in contrast to *foreground*.

backup   A copy of a disk or of a file on a disk.

backup domain controller   For Windows NT Server domains, refers to a computer that receives a copy of the domain's security policy and domain database and authenticates network logons.

backup procedures   The provisions made for the recovery of data files and program libraries and for restart or replacement of equipment after the occurrence of a system failure or disaster.

bandwidth   The range of frequencies available for signaling; the difference expressed in Hertz between the lowest and highest frequencies of a band; or simplistically, the rate that a network can transfer data. Standard Ethernet operates at 10Mbps, whereas Fast Ethernet operates at 100Mbps.

BASIC (Beginner's All-Purpose Symbolic Instruction Code)   A high-level programming language that is easy to use. It is used mainly for microcomputers.

batch   The processing of a group of related transactions or other items at planned intervals.

baud   A unit of signaling speed. The speed in baud is the number of discrete conditions or events per second.

bit   A contraction of the words *binary digit*. The smallest unit of information a computer can hold. The value of a bit (1 or 0) represents a simple two-way choice, such as yes or no, on or off, positive or negative, something or nothing.

board   Chiefly, a term used for the flat circuit board that holds chip sets and other electronic components and printed conductive paths between the components.

boot   (v) To start by loading the operating system into the computer. Starting is often accomplished by first loading a small program, which then reads a larger program into memory. The program is said to "pull itself up by its own bootstraps"—hence, the term *bootstrapping*, or *booting*. It also means to start a computer or initial program load. (n) The process of starting or resetting a computer.

Boot Protocol (BOOTP)   A protocol used for remotely booting systems on the network.

bps (bits per second) A unit of data transmission rate.

breach A break in the system security that results in admittance of a person or program to an object.

bridge A device used to connect LANs by forwarding packets addressed to other similar networks across connections at the Media Access Control data link level. Routers, which operate at the protocol level, are also called *bridges*.

broadband A transmission system in which signals are encoded and modulated into different frequencies and then transmitted simultaneously with other signals. Simplistically, signals are multiplexed so that more than one host can transmit on the same media.

broadcast A LAN data transmission scheme in which data packets are heard by all stations on the network.

brute-force attack A computerized trial-and-error attempt to decode a cipher or password by trying every possible combination. Also known as an *exhaustive attack*.

buffer A temporary holding area of the computer's memory where information can be stored by one program or device and then read at a different rate by another, for example, a print buffer. Also, the printer's random access memory (RAM), measured in kilobytes. Because computer chips can transfer data much faster than mechanical printer mechanisms can reproduce it, small buffers are generally inserted between the two, to keep the data flow in check.

bug An error in a program that prevents its working as intended. The expression reportedly comes from the early days of computing when an itinerant moth shorted a connection and caused a breakdown in a room-size computer.

bulletin board system (BBS) An electronic system that supports communication via modem among computers. Typically, a bulletin board system supports public and private electronic mail, uploading and downloading of public-domain files, and access to online databases. Large, commercial bulletin board systems, such as AOL, CompuServe, and Prodigy, can support many users simultaneously; smaller, local boards permit only one caller at a time.

bus A common connection. Networks that broadcast signals to all stations, such as Ethernet and ARCnet, are considered bus networks.

byte A unit of information having 8 bits.

cabling system The wiring used to connect networked computers.

CACLS   A Windows 2000 command-line program that allows you to modify user permissions by using the DOS command prompt or by placing them within a file and running that file. A handy utility to manage large numbers of changes, such as user and group administration.

card   Another name for *board*.

catalog   A list of files stored on a disk or tape. Sometimes called a *directory* or *folder*.

CDFS   CD-ROM file system.

central processing unit (CPU)   The "brain" of the computer; the microprocessor performing the actual computations in machine language.

certification   The technical evaluation, made as part of and in support of the accreditation process, establishing the extent that a particular computer system or network design and implementation meet a specified set of security requirements.

channel   An information transfer path within a system. Can also refer to the mechanism by which the path is effected.

character   Letter, numerical, punctuation, or any other symbol contained in a message.

chip   Slang for a silicon wafer imprinted with integrated circuits.

choose   As used in this book, to select or pick an item that begins an action in Windows NT. For example, you often choose a command on a menu to perform a task.

CISC   Complex Instruction Set Computer.

classified   Subject to prescribed asset protection controls, including controls associated with classifications.

classify   To assign a level of sensitivity and priority and, hence, security control to data.

clear text   Information that is in its readable state (before encryption and after decryption).

client   A computer that accesses shared network resources provided by another computer (a server). In a client/server database system, this is the computer (usually a workstation) that makes service requests.

client/server   A network system design in which a processor or computer designated as a server (file server, database server, and so on) provides services to other client processors or computers.

coax   Also known as *coaxial*, this is a cable that consists of two wires running inside a plastic sheath, insulated from each other.

collision   A garbled transmission resulting from simultaneous transmissions by two or more workstations on the same network cable.

command prompt   The window in NT that provides DOS-like capabilities, letting you enter commands that execute within that window.

commit bytes   The actual amount of memory and hard disk space for paging that all the applications need at any given moment.

communication link   An electrical and logical connection between two devices. On a local area network, a communication link is the point-to-point path between sender and recipient.

communication program   A program that enables the computer to transmit data to and receive data from distant computers through the telephone system or some other communication system.

compartmentalization   The breaking down of sensitive data into small, isolated blocks for reducing the risk to the data.

compiler   A language translator that converts a program written in a high-level programming language (source code) into an equivalent program in some lower-level language, such as machine language (object code) for later execution.

compromise   The loss, misuse, or unauthorized disclosure of a data asset.

computer name   For Windows 2000 purposes, a unique name of up to 15 uppercase characters identifying a computer to the network. The name cannot be the same as any other computer or domain name in the network, and it cannot contain spaces.

confidential   A protection classification. Loss, misuse, or unauthorized disclosure of data with this protection classification could, at most, have a major negative impact. Such an incident would be harmful to the organization.

confidentiality   A parameter showing the privacy of the information (used particularly in costing functions involving information that has a security classification or is considered proprietary or sensitive).

configuration   (1) The total combination of hardware components—central processing unit, video display device, keyboard, and peripheral devices—forming a computer system. (2) The software settings allowing various hardware components of a computer system to communicate with each other.

connect time The amount of time a user connects to the file server.

connection-oriented A reliable communications method that creates a virtual circuit to establish an actual session. There are three distinct steps: 1) a handshake to establish the line of communication, 2) the actual data transfer, and 3) a formal end to the session. TCP is a connection-oriented communication protocol.

connectionless An unreliable communications method where there is not a virtual circuit and the only step in the process is data transfer. UDP is a connectionless communication protocol.

console In Windows 2000, a text-based window managed by the Win32 subsystem. Environment subsystems direct the output of character-mode applications to consoles. Alternatively, it is data termination equipment (DTE) where commands are entered.

control codes Nonprinting computer instructions such as carriage return and line feed.

control program A program designed to schedule and supervise the performance of data processing work by a computing system.

control set A complete set of parameters for devices and services in the HKEY_LOCAL_ MACHINE\SYSTEM key in the NT Registry.

controlled sharing The scope or domain where authorization can be reduced to an arbitrarily small set or sphere of activity.

counter As used with the Performance Monitor, the measurement of activity for a particular object, such as bytes read per second.

crash (n) A malfunction caused by hardware failure or an error in the program. (v) To fail suddenly.

critical Data with this preservation classification is essential to the organization's continued existence. The loss of such data would cause a serious disruption of the organization's operation.

criticality A parameter indicating dependence of the organization on the information.

crosstalk The unwanted transmission of a signal on a channel that interfaces with another adjacent channel. Signal interference created by emissions passing from one cable element to another.

cryptoanalysis The steps and operations performed in converting messages (cipher) into plain text (clear) without initial knowledge of the key employed in the encryption algorithm.

cryptographic system   The documents, devices, equipment, and associated techniques that are used as a unit to provide a single means of encryption (enciphering or encoding).

cryptography   The transformation of plain text into coded form (encryption) or from coded form into plain text (decryption). Simply, it is the science of keeping data confidential.

cryptology   The field that includes both cryptoanalysis and cryptography.

customer related   Identifying or relating specifically to a customer of the organization.

data   Processable information with the associated documentation. The input that a program and its instructions perform on and that determines the results of processing.

data contamination   A deliberate or accidental process or act that results in a change in the integrity of the original data.

data-dependent protection   Protection of data at a level commensurate with the sensitivity level of the individual data elements, rather than with the sensitivity of the entire file that includes the data elements.

data diddling   Unauthorized alteration of data as it is entered or stored in a computer.

data integrity   Verified correspondence between the computer representation of information and the real-world events that the information represents. The condition of being whole, complete, accurate, and timely.

data leakage   The theft of data or software.

Data Link Control (DLC)   A printer and host access protocol primarily used by PCs to communicate with IBM minicomputers and mainframes.

data   protection measures to safeguard data from undesired occurrences that intentionally or unintentionally lead to modification, destruction, or disclosure of data.

data security   The result achieved through implementing measures to protect data against unauthorized events leading to unintentional or intentional modification, destruction, or disclosure of data.

data storage   The preservation of data in various data media for direct use by the system, for example, hard disk, tape drive, and CD-ROM.

database   A collection of information organized in a form that can be readily manipulated and sorted by a computer user.

database management system   A software system for organizing, storing, retrieving, analyzing, and modifying information in a database, for example, SQL Server and Oracle.

database server The "back end" processor that manages the database and fulfills database requests in a client/server database system.

debug A colloquial term that means to find and correct an error or the cause of a problem or malfunction in a computer program. Usually synonymous with *troubleshoot*.

debugger A utility program that allows a programmer to see what is happening in the microprocessor and in memory while another program is running.

decipher To convert, by use of the appropriate key, cipher text (encoded, encrypted) into its equivalent plain text (clear).

dedicated file server A file server that is not used as a user's workstation. The machine is devoted to file service.

device A generic term for a computer subsystem, such as a printer, serial port, or disk drive. A device frequently requires its own controlling software, called a *device driver*.

device driver A software component that enables a computer system to communicate with a device. For example, a printer driver is a device driver that translates computer data into a form understood by the intended printer. In most cases, the driver also manipulates the hardware to transmit the data to the device.

DHCP (Dynamic Host Configuration Protocol) A tool that allows dynamic IP address allocation, simplifying machine configuration in your network.

digital A system based on discrete states, typically the binary conditions of on or off.

digital transmission A communications system that passes information encoded as pulses. Baseband networks use digital transmissions, as do microcomputers.

directory Pictorial, alphabetical, or chronological representation of the contents of persistent storage or a network. Used to organize or group files on a disk. A directory is sometimes called a *catalog* or *folder*. The operating system uses it to keep track of the contents of the disk.

disclosure The act or instance of revelation or exposure. A disclosure can be obvious, such as the removal of a tape from a library, or it can be concealed, such as the retrieval of a discarded report by an outsider or a disgruntled employee.

discretionary access control (DAC) The protection that the owner of an object applies to the object by assigning various access rights to various users or groups of users.

disk A data storage device on which data is recorded on concentric circular tracks on a magnetic medium.

disk drive   An electromechanical device that reads from and writes to disks. Two types of disk drives are in common use: floppy disk drives and hard disk drives.

disk mirroring   Thel procedure of duplicating a disk partition on two or more disks, preferably on disks attached to separate disk controllers so that data remains accessible when either a disk or a disk controller fails. Disk mirroring provides a measure of fault tolerance.

disk partition   A logical compartment on a physical disk drive. A single disk might have two or more logical disk partitions, each of which would be referenced with a different disk drive name.

disk striping   The procedure of combining a set of same-sized disk partitions residing on separate disks into a single volume, forming a virtual "stripe" across the disks. This fault-tolerance technique enables multiple I/O operations in the same volume to proceed concurrently, thereby increasing performance.

documentation   A complete and accurate description and authorization of a transaction and each operation a transaction passes through. The written (can be automated) description of a system or program and how it operates.

domain   A collection of computers that share a common domain database and security policy. Each domain has a unique name.

domain controller   The server that authenticates domain logons and maintains the security policy and the master database for a domain.

domain name   A name assigned to a domain.

domain name system (DNS)   A distributed database system that allows TCP/IP applications to resolve a host name into a correct IP address.

download   To transfer a file from a large computer or BBS to a personal computer. To upload is to perform the opposite operation.

DUN   The acronym for *Dial-Up Networking*. Easy to confuse with RAS because it is the newer version of RAS and it performs the same function. We think it was renamed to provide some consistency with Windows 95 terms.

duplexing   The concept of using two disk drives and two disk controllers to store data, one serving as primary and the other for backup purposes.

Dynamic Host Configuration Protocol (DHCP)   The protocol used by a server to dynamically allocate IP addresses on a network. Designed to allow networked hosts to access configuration information across the network, instead of having to be configured by hand directly.

eavesdropping   Unauthorized interception of data transmissions.

EISA   Enhanced Industry Standard Architecture. An older system data transfer bus architecture that was designed to manage 8-, 16-, and 32-bit data transfers. Widely used, most expansion cards support this architecture.

emulation   The imitation of a computer system, performed by a combination of hardware and software, that allows programs to run between incompatible systems.

encipher   To convert plain text (clear) into unintelligible form by a cipher system.

enterprise network   A network bringing all sites together through a communications medium.

error log   An audit trail of system warning messages displayed for the file server.

Ethernet   A local area network protocol developed by Xerox in 1973 and formalized in 1980. It is the most widely used network protocol.

event   Any significant occurrence in the system or in an application that requires users to be notified, or an entry to be added to a log.

event log service   A service that records events in the system, security, and application logs.

expected lifetime   A parameter indicating the length of time the information is operative or has value to its owners.

exposure   A quantitative rating (in dollars per year) expressing the organization's vulnerability to a given risk.

extended partition   Free space on a hard disk that is used to allow the disk to be further partitioned into logical partitions or drives.

fail safe   The automatic termination and protection of programs or other processing operations when a hardware or software failure is detected in a system.

fail soft   The selective termination of affected non-essential processing when a hardware or software failure is detected in a system.

fault tolerance   A computer and operating system's capability to respond gracefully to catastrophic events, such as a power outage or hardware failure. Usually, fault tolerance implies the capability either to continue the system's operation without loss of data or to shut down the system and restart it, recovering all processing in progress when the fault occurred.

fiber-optic cable   A cable constructed using a thin glass core that conducts light rather than electrical signals.

field   A particular type or category of information in a database management program, for example, a variable. A location in a record where a particular type of data is stored. In other words, a field is a single unit of data such as a name or address.

file   A single, named collection of related information stored on a magnetic medium.

file allocation table (FAT)   A table or list maintained by some operating systems, such as MS-DOS, to keep track of the status of various segments of disk space used for file storage.

file attribute   A restrictive label attached to a file that describes and regulates its use, for example, archive, hidden, read-only, and system.

file server   A computer that shares files with other computers. Also, a computer that provides network stations with controlled access to shareable resources.

file size   The length of a file, typically given in bytes.

file system   In an operating system, the overall structure by which files are named, stored, and organized.

Forest   A structure created by domains in two or more Trees sharing the same configuration, schema, and global catalog but not sharing the same DNS namespace.

format   The process of setting up a drive space to allow an operating system to use the space. Each operating system, such as MAC, DOS, and NT, uses distinct file system formats, and a drive must be formatted in order for the system to be able to use it.

FTP   File Transfer Protocol. A program that enables clients to transfer files between computers.

fully qualified domain name (FQDN)   The complete host name and domain name of a network host.

gateway   A device that provides routing and protocol conversion among physically dissimilar networks and computers, for example, LAN to host, LAN to LAN, X.25, and SNA gateways. That is, a multihomed host used to route network traffic from one network to another. Also used to pass network traffic from one protocol to another.

grant   To authorize.

GUI   Graphical user interface.

hacker   A computer enthusiast; also, one who seeks to gain unauthorized access to computer systems.

handshaking   A dialog between a user and a computer, a computer and another computer, and a program and another program, for identifying a user and authenticating his identity through a sequence of questions and answers based on information either previously stored in the computer or supplied to the computer by the initiator of the dialog. Also, when used in context, it refers to the controlled movement of bits between a computer and a printer.

hardware   In computer terminology, the machinery that forms a computer system.

hardware abstraction layer (HAL)   A dynamic link library that encapsulates platform-dependent code. Think of it as a layer of software provided by the hardware manufacturer that hides, or abstracts, hardware differences from higher layers of the Windows NT operating system. Different hardware looks alike to the operating system, thus removing the need to tailor the operating system to each and every hardware type.

HCL   Microsoft's Hardware Compatibility List. This is a list of all hardware that is certified to run with NT. You can find the list on the Internet at the following address:

`http://www.microsoft.com/isapi/hwtest/hcl.idc`

hertz (Hz)   A measure of frequency or bandwidth. The same as cycles per second.

hierarchical database   A database organized in a treelike structure.

High Performance File System (HPFS)   The file system designed for OS/2 Version 1.2.

host computer   The computer that receives information from and sends data to terminals over telecommunication lines. It is also the computer that is in control in a data communication network. The host computer can be a mainframe computer, minicomputer, or microcomputer.

host name resolution   The process of determining a network address when presented with a network host name and domain name, usually by consulting the domain name system.

HPFS   The acronym for *High Performance File System*, provided by OS/2 operating systems. Files in this format can be read by NT.

hub   (1) A device used on certain network topologies that modifies transmission signals, allowing the network to be lengthened or expanded with additional workstations. The hub is the central device in a star topology. (2) A computer that receives messages from other computers, stores them, and routes them to other computer destinations.

I/O device (input/output device)   A device that transfers information into or out of a computer.

icon   In graphical environments, a small graphics image displayed onscreen to represent an object that can be manipulated by the user; for example, a recycle bin can represent a command for deleting unwanted text or files.

IDE   The acronym for *Integrated Drive Electronics*, the older disk drive architecture that usually integrates directly with the disk drive instead of using a separate card.

identification The process that enables, generally using unique machine-readable names, recognition of users or resources as identical with those previously described to a system.

IEEE (Institute of Electrical and Electronic Engineers) One of several groups whose members are drawn from industry and who attempt to establish industry standards. The IEEE 802 committee has published numerous definitive documents on local area network standards.

IETF (Internet Engineering Task Force) Groups set up to work on developing open standards for use with the Internet.

information Includes input, output, software, data, and all related documentation. Its combination is comprehensible and usually provides value.

information pool Consists of data designated as accessible by authorized individuals.

initialize (1) To set to an initial state or value in preparation for some computation. (2) To prepare a blank disk to receive information by organizing its surface into tracks and sectors; same as *format*.

input/output (I/O) The process by which information is transferred between the computer's memory and its keyboard or peripheral devices.

instance An NT term relating to particular tasks in each object. Objects often have more than one instance, such as the Processor and its %Interrupt Time or %User Time or %Processor Time.

integrity Freedom from errors.

interface A device or program that allows two systems or devices to communicate with each other. An interface provides a common boundary between the two systems, devices, or programs. Also, the cables, connectors, and electrical circuits allowing communication between computers and printers.

interrupt request lines (IRQ) Hardware lines over which devices can send signals to get the attention of the processor when the device is ready to accept or send information. Typically, each device connected to the computer uses a separate IRQ.

intruder A user or another agent attempting to gain unauthorized access to the file server.

IP address A 32-bit network address that uniquely locates a host or network within its internetwork.

ISDN (Integrated Services Digital Network) A digital phone line that allows faster transmission speeds (128Kbps) than analog phone lines (56Kbps).

ISP (internet service provider)   A firm that offers connections to the Internet for a fee.

jitter   Instability of a signal for a brief period.

job   A combined run of one or more application programs that are automatically processed in sequence in the computer.

kernel   The core of an operating system. The portion of the system that manages memory, files, and peripheral devices, maintains the time and date, launches applications, and allocates system resources.

key   In the Registry, one of five subtrees. Each key can contain value entries and additional subkeys. A key is analogous to a directory, and a value entry is analogous to a file. In cryptography, a sequence of symbols that controls the operations of encryption and decryption.

LDAP (Lightweight Directory Access Protocol)   A lightweight version of the X.500 directory access protocol. In Windows 2000, it is used to read, write, and search the Active Directory.

least privilege   A principle that users should be assigned only the access needed to perform their business functions.

local area network (LAN)   A communications system using directly connected computers, printers, and hard disks, allowing shared access to all resources on the network.

Local Security Authority (LSA)   An integral subsystem of the Windows NT security system. The LSA manages the local security policy and provides interactive user authentication services. It also controls the generation of audit messages and enters audit messages into the audit log file. Creates a security access token for each user accessing the system.

logic bomb   Malicious action, initiated by software, that inhibits the normal system functions; a logic bomb takes effect only when specified conditions occur.

logical access   Access to the information content of a record or field.

logical file   The data that a file contains.

logical partition   A subpartition of an extended partition on a drive, commonly called a *logical drive*. See *extended partition*.

login   The process of accessing a file server or computer after physical connection has been established.

logon   The process of identifying oneself to a computer after connecting to it over a communications line. During a logon procedure, the computer usually requests the user's name and a password. Also called *login*.

mainframe   The term used for very large computers that support thousands of users and huge databases.

map   (1) To assign a workstation drive letter to a server directory. (2) To translate a virtual address into a physical address.

Media Access Control (MAC)   Part of the physical layer of a network that identifies the actual physical link between two nodes.

menu   A list of options from which users select.

menu option   An option on a menu that performs some action, prompts the user for additional information, or leads to another menu.

microcomputer   A general term referring to a small computer having a microprocessor.

mirroring   A method of ensuring data replication using two hard drives that are connected to the same disk controller. Less robust than duplexing because of the shared controller. Otherwise, duplexing and mirroring can be considered to be essentially the same thing.

modem   A modulator-demodulator. A device that lets computers communicate over telephone lines by converting digital signals into the phone system's analog signals, and vice versa.

modification   The partial alteration of an asset such that the form or quality of it has been changed somewhat. A file can appear intact and can be perfectly usable, but it can contain erroneous information.

monitoring   The use of automated procedures to ensure that the controls implemented within a system are not circumvented. Monitoring also is a process of observing a system or network to detect security holes and performance bottlenecks.

multihomed   A computer that has more than one network card, either physically or logically. Often used as a router for connecting two networks.

need-to-know   The necessity for access to, knowledge of, or possession of sensitive information to fulfill official duties. Responsibility for determining whether a person's duties require that he have access to certain information, and whether he is authorized to receive it, rests on the owner of the information involved and not on the prospective recipient.

NetBIOS Extended User Interface (NetBEUI) A small, fast protocol that requires little memory but is not routable.

network A collection of interconnected, individually controlled computers, printers, and hard disks, with the hardware and software used to connect them.

network adapter A circuit board that plugs into a slot in a PC and has one or more sockets to which you attach cables. Provides the physical link between the PC and the network cable. Also called *network adapter card*, *network card*, and *network interface card (NIC)*.

network address A unique identifier of an entity on a network, usually represented as a number or series of numbers.

Network Basic Input/Output Operating System (NetBIOS) A network file-sharing application designed for use with PC DOS personal computers, usually implemented under TCP/IP at the application layer.

network drive An online storage device available to network users.

network interface card See *network adapter*.

network operating system An operating system installed on a server in a local area network that coordinates the activities of providing services to the computers and other devices attached to the network.

network station Any PC or other device connected to a network by means of a network interface board and some communications medium. A network station can be a workstation, bridge, or server.

node A point of interconnection to a network. Normally, a point at which a number of terminals are located.

nonce A 16-byte challenge issued by the authentication service.

NTFS An NT file system acronym for *New Technology File System*. The particular way data is stored on an NT system when chosen over the FAT file system. NTFS supports file system security and recovery and extremely large storage media.

object (1) A single runtime instance of a Windows NT defined object type containing data that can be manipulated only by use of a set of services provided for objects of its type. (2) Any piece of information, created by a Windows-based application with object linking and embedding capabilities, that can be linked or embedded into another document. (3) A passive entity that contains or receives data. Access to an object potentially implies access to the information it contains.

object handle   Includes access control information and a pointer to the object itself. Before a process can manipulate a Windows NT object, it first must acquire a handle to the object through the Object Manager.

object linking and embedding (OLE)   A way to transfer and share information between applications.

offline   The state in which the printer or some other device is not ready to receive data.

operating system   Software that controls the internal operations (housekeeping chores) of a computer system. Operating systems are specific to the type of computer used.

Organizational Unit   A container object in Active Directory used to separate resources such as users, groups, and printers into one or more logical units.

owner   An employee or agent of the client who is assigned responsibility for making and communicating certain judgments and decisions regarding business control and selective protection of assets and for monitoring compliance with specified controls.

package   A generic term referring to any group of detailed computer programs necessary to achieve a general objective. For example, an accounts receivable package would include all programs necessary to record transactions in customer accounts, produce customer statements, and so forth.

packet   A group of bits transmitted as a whole on a network.

pad   The short term the for packet assembler-dissembler used in X.25 technologies.

paging   The act of moving data to disk when physical memory is full. A component of *virtual memory*.

parallel interface   A device interface that handles data in parallel fashion, 8 bits (1 byte) at a time.

parity bit   A way of marking the eighth bit in a data byte so that 7-bit ASCII characters between 0 and 127 are sent and received correctly. There are three kinds of parity: odd, even, and none.

partition   A portion of a physical disk that functions as though it were a separate unit.

password   Privileged information given to, or created by, the user and entered into a system for authentication purposes. A protected word or secret character string used to authenticate the claimed identity of an individual, a resource, or an access type.

PCI   A 32-bit data transfer bus used in newer machines and generally faster than the older EISA bus. Most Intel-based machines built today support this standard.

penetration   A successful unauthorized access to a system.

peripheral   Any device used for input/output operations with the computer's central processing unit (CPU). Peripheral devices are typically connected to the microcomputer with special cabling and include such devices as modems and printers.

permission   (1) A particular form of allowed access, for example, permission to read, as contrasted with permission to write. (2) A rule associated with an object (usually a directory, file, or printer) to regulate which users can access the object and in what manner.

physical drive   The actual hardware that is set in the computer and used to store information. Often called the *hard drive*, *C drive*, or *D drive* after the letter assigned to it by the system.

physical security   Physical protection of assets achieved through implementing security measures.

PING   A network application that uses ICMP to verify reachability of another host on any internetwork.

plain text   Intelligible text or signals that have meaning and that can be read or acted on without the application of any decryption.

polling   A means of controlling or monitoring devices on a line.

port   (1) A connection or socket used to connect a device to a computer, such as a printer, monitor, or modem. Information is sent from the computer to the device through a cable. (2) A communications channel through which a client process communicates with a protected subsystem. Ports are implemented as Windows NT objects.

principal   The entity in a computer system to which authorizations are granted; thus, the unit of accountability in a computer system.

print queue   A shared storage area on the file server where the system sends every print job before sending to the print server or print device.

print server   Software that takes jobs from the print queue and sends them to the printer.

privileges   A means of protecting the use of certain system functions that can affect system resources and integrity. System managers grant privileges according to the user's needs and deny them to restrict the user's access to the system. See *need-to-know*.

processing   A systematic sequence of operations performed on data.

protocol   A set of characters at the beginning and end of a message that enables two computers to communicate with each other. In networking, procedures or rules that control the way information is sent or received over the network.

queue   A first-in/first-out data structure, used for managing requests to process data; for example, files to be printed.

RAS (Remote Access Services)   This is the NT 3.x version of Dial-Up Networking; it is used to connect machines together via telephone or other means.

read   A fundamental operation that results only in the flow of information from an object to a subject.

read access   Permission to read data.

read-only   A term used to describe information stored in such a way that it can be played back (read) but not changed (written).

record   A collection of related information (fields) that is treated as one unit within a file.

redirector   Networking software that accepts I/O requests for remote files, named pipes, or mail slots and then sends (redirects) them to a network server on another machine. Redirectors are implemented as file system drivers in Windows NT.

Registry   As used here, the database repository for information about the computer's configuration, including the hardware, installed software, environment settings, and other information.

Registry Editor   An application provided with Windows NT that allows users to view and edit entries in the Registry.

remote administration   Administration of one computer by an administrator located at another computer and connected to the first computer across the network.

repeater   A device that extends the range of a network cable segment. A hub is really just a multiport repeater. See attenuation.

Request for Comments (RFC)   The official designation of the Internet standards documents.

resource   In a system, any function, device, or data collection that can be allocated to users or programs.

resource sharing   The concurrent use of a resource by more than one user, job, or program.

revoke   To take away previously authorized access from some principal.

rights   User capabilities given for accessing files and directories on a file server.

ring   A network topology that connects each workstation in a circular fashion and sends the network signal in a unidirectional manner through the circle.

RISC   Reduced Instruction Set Computer.

risk   The potential that a given threat has of occurring within a specific period. The potential for realization of unwanted, negative consequences of an event.

risk analysis   An analysis of system assets and vulnerabilities to establish an expected loss from certain events, based on estimated probabilities of the occurrence of those events.

router   A Layer 3 device that connects two or more networks together. A router reads packets sent along the network and determines its correct destination.

scavenging   Randomly searching for valuable data in a computer's memory or in discarded or incompletely erased magnetic media.

SCSI   The acronym for *Small Computer System Interface*. Originally designed for the UNIX world, it is designed to handle high speeds and multiple devices, such as disk and tape drives.

security   Protection of all those resources that the client uses to complete its mission.

Security Account Manager (SAM)   A Windows NT protected subsystem that maintains the SAM database and provides an application programming interface (API) for accessing the database.

security descriptor   A data structure attached to an object that protects the object from unauthorized access. It contains an access control list (ACL) and controls auditing on the object.

Security ID (SID)   A unique name that identifies a logged-on user to the security system. Security IDs can identify one user or a group of users.

security policy   The set of laws, rules, and practices that regulate how an organization manages, protects, and distributes sensitive information. For Windows NT, the security policies consist of the Account, User Rights, and Audit Policies, and they are managed using User Manager for Domains.

Security Reference Manager (SRM)   A Windows NT Server security subsystem that authenticates user logons and protects system resources.

sensitive   A data classification category. Loss, misuse, or unauthorized disclosure of data with this protection classification would have a serious negative impact. Such an incident would be very harmful to the organization.

sensitive program   An application program whose misuse through unauthorized activity could lead to serious misappropriation or loss of assets.

serial interface   An interface that handles data in serial fashion, one bit at a time.

server   A computer that shares its resources, such as files and printers, with other computers on a network.

Server Manager   An application used to view and administer domains, workgroups, and computers.

share name   The name of a shared resource.

shared directory   A directory where network users can connect.

shielding   Protective covering that eliminates electromagnetic and radio frequency interference.

sneaker   A computer professional who seeks to test security by attempting to gain unauthorized access to computer systems.

software   Programs and routines to be loaded temporarily into a computer system, for example, compilers, utilities, and operating system and application programs.

stack   As used in this book, a synonym for *protocol*.

star   A topology in which each node is connected to a central hub.

subject   The combination of the user's access token and the program acting on the user's behalf. Windows NT uses subjects to track and manage permissions for the programs each user runs.

submenu   A menu below the main menu.

subnet   A physical or logical subdivision of a TCP/IP network; usually a separate physical segment that uses a division of the site's IP network address to route traffic within the organizational internetwork.

TCP/IP (Transmission Control Protocol/Internet Protocol)   This is the protocol suite that drives the Internet. Very basically, TCP handles the message details and IP manages the addressing. It is probably the most widely used network protocol in the world today.

TCSEC   The Trusted Computer System Evaluation Criteria. The standard is used to evaluate a system and specify the trust you can place on it.

telecommunication   The electronic transfer of information via telephone lines from computer to computer. See *bulletin board system*, *modem*.

telnet   A program that allows terminal emulation for communicating between machines via TCP/IP.

TFTP   A simpler version of the FTP program that operates using UDP/IP services.

threat   One or more events that can lead to either intentional or unintentional modification, destruction, or disclosure of data. If this eventuality were to occur, it would lead to an undesirable effect on the environment.

Token Ring   A network topology regulated by the passing of a token that governs the right to transmit.

topology   The physical layout of the network cabling.

transaction   A set of operations that completes a unified task.

transient   An abrupt change in voltage, of short duration.

transmission-on/transmission-off (X-ON/X-OFF)   A type of software handshaking.

trapdoor   A set of special instructions, originally created for testing and troubleshooting, that bypasses security procedures and allows direct access to a computer's operating system or to other software.

Tree   A hierarchy of domains sharing a contiguous namespace, configuration, schema, and global catalog.

Trojan Horse   A program, purporting to do useful work, that conceals instructions to breach security whenever the software is invoked.

trust relationship   Links between domains that enable passthrough authentication, in which a user only has one user account in one domain yet can access the entire network. A trusting domain honors the logon authentications of a trusted domain.

twisted pair   A common type of wiring that uses wires twisted together yet insulated from each other. Can be purchased shielded or unshielded.

UDP   The User Datagram Protocol, an older protocol that does not offer good error detection or recovery. It is used by SNMP and TFTP, as well as the Network File System (NFS).

unbounded media   Media that use radio frequencies, microwaves, or other media to transmit data.

Unicode   A fixed-width, 16-bit character encoding standard that is capable of representing all the world's scripts.

user   Used imprecisely to refer to the individual who is accountable for some identifiable set of activities in a computer system.

user group   A computer club in which computer users exchange tips and information, publish a newsletter, support a local BBS, and listen to sales pitches from vendors at meetings. A meeting of like-minded individuals who practice information sharing, for example, GUIDE, SHARE, DECUS, SANS, ISSA, and ISACA.

User Manager   A Windows NT Workstation tool used to manage the security for a computer. Administers user accounts, groups, and security policies.

User Manager for Domains   A Windows NT Server tool used to manage the security for a domain or an individual computer. Administers user accounts, groups, and security policies.

User Rights policy   Manages the assignment of rights to groups and user accounts.

utilities   Useful programs with which you can rename, copy, format, delete, and otherwise manipulate files and volumes.

verification   Confirmation that the object is what it purports to be. Also, confirmation of the identity of a person (or other agent external to the protection system) making a request.

virtual memory   Combines the physical RAM available in the machine with disk space to simulate an environment in which you have more memory than you physically have in RAM. NT tries to assess what parts of memory are least likely to be used and pages this information out to the disk area until it is needed.

virus   A program, usually a Trojan Horse, that copies itself into new databases and computers whenever the infected parent program is invoked.

volume   A storage device, such as a disk pack, mass storage system cartridge, or magnetic tape. For our purposes, diskettes, cassettes, mag cards, and the like are treated as volumes.

volume set   A collection of partitions, possibly spread over several disk drives, that has been formatted for use as if it were a single drive.

vulnerability   The cost that an organization would incur should an event happen.

wideband   A communications channel that has greater bandwidth than voice-grade lines.

Windows Internet Naming Service (WINS)   A service that translates Windows computer names (or NetBIOS names) to IP addresses.

wiretapping   Monitoring or recording data as it moves across a communications link; also known as *traffic analysis*.

workstation   In general, a powerful computer having considerable calculating and graphics capability. For Windows NT, computers running the Windows NT Workstation operating system are called *workstations*, as distinguished from computers running Windows NT Server, which are called *servers*.

worm   A program that deletes data from a computer's memory.

WOW   Windows on Win32.

write   A fundamental operation that results only in the flow of data from a subject to an object.

write access   Permission to write an object.

X.25   A protocol that allows you to route information through a packet-switching public data network, such as Datapac. An older technology, it operates at a top speed of 64Kbps, and it was designed for earlier days when telephone networks were less reliable than today.

Index

Symbols

0x0 ErrorControl value, **563**
0x1 ErrorControl value, **563**
0x2 ErrorControl value, **563**
0x3 ErrorControl value, **563**
**/1 option (ping command),
493**
**/? option (NBTSTAT com-
mand), 813**

A

/a option
    nbtstat command, 492,
    813
    netstat command, 492, 816
    NTBACKUP command,
    615
    ping command, 493

**Accepting state (NetBIOS),
814**
access categories, 875
**access control, 310-311,
318.** *See also* **user accounts**
    access periods, 876
    ACEs (access control
    entries), 875
    ACLs (Access Control
    Lists), 158, 193-195,
    261-262,
    DAC (discretionary access
    control), 876, 885
    dial-in restrictions,
    323-324
    discretionary access con-
    trols, 258-261
    guidelines, 875
    mechanisms, 875
    permissable logon hours,
    318-322

    Registry
        rights, 193-195
        user profiles, 193
    restricted logon worksta-
        tions, 322-323
    rights, 876
    tokens, 246, 261, 876
**access control entries
    (ACEs), 240, 262, 875**
**Access Control Lists
    (ACLs), 158, 261-262,
    193-195**
**Access This Computer
    From Network right, 672**
access validation, 876
accessibility, 876
**Account lockout option
    (Account Policy dialog
    box), 670**
**Account Operators group,
    303**
accountability, 876

bytes, 880
    available bytes, 762
    commit bytes, 762
    definition of, 882
Bytes Received/sec counter,
    796
Bytes Sent/sec counter, 796
Bytes Total/sec counter, 796

C

/C option (CACLS com-
    mand), 376
/c option (nbtstat com-
    mand), 492, 813
C$ D$ share, 359
C1 class security, 655
C2 class security, 654-656
cabling (networks), 13
    BNCs, 14
    coaxial, 14-15, 882
    definition of, 880
    fiber-optic, 16, 887
    twisted-pair, 15-16, 899
cache
    automatic caching, 356
    manual caching, 355
CACLS command, 375-377,
    881
calculating permissions,
    363-364
callback (RAS), 469
callback options (dial-up
    networking), 324
Called-Station-Id attribute
    (remote access policies),
    460
Calling-Station-Id attribute
    (remote access policies),
    460

Carrier Sense Multiple
    Access (CSMA), 29
Carrier Sense Multiple
    Access with Collision
    Detection (CSMA/CD), 29
CAs (Certificate
    Authorities), 255
catalogs
    definition of, 881
    GC (global catalog),
        205-206
Category option (log filters),
    692
CD-ROM drives, 42
CD-ROMs
    automatic startup, bypass-
        ing, 353
    installation from, 72
central processing units
    (CPUs), 881
Certificate Authorities
    (CAs), 255
Certificate Server, 751-752
Certificate Services, 727
certificates, digital, 254-255
certification programs,
    829-834, 881
    benefits of, 832-833
    guides/assessment tests,
        837-838
    MCDBA (Microsoft
        Certified Database
        Administrator), 836
    MCP (Microsoft Certified
        Professional), 835-836
    MCSD (Microsoft
        Certified Solution
        Developer), 836
    MCSE (Microsoft
        Certified System
        Engineer), 834-835

MCT (Microsoft Certified
    Trainer), 837
    online resources, 838
CFG option (secedit com-
    mand), 281
CGI scripts, 749
Change Permissions (print-
    er auditing option), 685
Change the System Time
    right, 673
changing
    ACLs (Access Control
        Rights), 193-195
    file ownership, 366-367
    passwords, 313
    permissions
        as Administrator, 373
        command-line process-
            ing, 375-377
        as user, 374
channels, 881
characters, 881
charts (Performance
    Monitor), 772-775
child nodes, adding to root
    directory, 381-383
chips, 881
choosing passwords,
    312-313
cipher command, 365, 580
ciphertext, 253, 577
Class A addresses, 480
Class B addresses, 480
Class C addresses, 480
classification, 881
clear text, 881
Client for Microsoft
    Networks Properties
    dialog box, 97
Client-Friendly-Name
    attribute (remote access
    policies), 461

logons, 244-245
  home domain, 249
  multiple domains,
   251-252
modes, changing, 226-227
names, 516
organizing, 212-213
planning, 869-870
primary domain con-
  trollers, 68
security, 54-55
types of, 501-502
viewing, 225-226
zones
  creating, 507-509
  definition of, 506

DOS
commands, rasload, 466
dial-up networking,
 466-467
logging off, 131
print services, 436-437
dotted decimal notation, 479
**downlevel domain names,
294**
downloading files, 886
**DPA (Distributed Password
Authentication), 241**
Dr. Watson tool, 786-787
drag-and-drop
files, 143
scraps, 144
drivers, 885
dual-booting, 83-84, 340
DUN. *See* **Dial-up
Networking**
**duplexing disks, 342, 628,
886**
Dword editor, 181
dynamic disks, 624
**Dynamic Host
Configuration Protocol.
See DHCP**

E

**/E option (CACLS com-
mand), 376**
/e option
NETSTAT command, 492,
 816
NTBACKUP command),
 616
**e-commerce. Site Server,
718**
Commerce Edition,
 719-720
system requirements, 719
eavesdropping, 886
**ECC (error correction
code), 626**
**Edit menu, Add Key com-
mand, 181**
editing
disk quotas, 574, 576
Registry, 157, 180-181
 cautions, 179
 example, 171-174
 REGINI scripts, 180
 remote edits, 179,
  186-189
editors
Policy Editor, 195
Registry Editor, 157, 160,
 174-175
 adding keys, 181
 compacting Registry
  data, 183-184
 definition of, 896
 editing keys, 180-181
 pathname, 174
 read-only mode, 161
 restoring Registry data,
  182-183
 running, 175-176
 saving Registry data,
  181-182

searches, 177-179
View/Find key, 177
**EFS (Encrypting File
System), 364-365, 577-579**
data recovery
 configuring, 584-586
 definition of, 583
 Empty recovery policy,
  584
 No-recovery policy,
  584
 Recovery-agent policy,
  584
folder-level encryption
 options
 setting, 582-583
 testing, 582-583
 viewing, 580-581
recommended practices,
 581
**EISA (Enhanced Insdustry
Standard Architecture,
887**
**email, Exchange Server,
701-703**
documentation, 702
Inbox Assistant, 702
Optimizer, 704-705
**Embedded (Windows 2000),
31**
**emergency repair disks,
77-79**
emulation, 887
**Enable Logging property
(IIS), 739**
**EnableOplocks parameter
(NetBEUI), 793**
enabling
disk quotas, 568-569
event auditing, 686-687
logging, 739

Server:Bytes/second,
781
Server:Logons total,
781
graphs, 775-777
menu icons, 768-769
reporting data, 782-783
scheduling, 783
starting, 767-768
**Performance property sheet
(IIS), 741**
**Performance snap-in,
818-819**
**performance tuning,
759-762, 791-792**
authentication, 808-810
Dr. Watson tool, 786-787
Event Viewer, 785
Exchange Server, 704-705
load balancing, 783-785
memory
available bytes, 762
commit bytes, 762
virtual, 762-766
NETMON (Network
Monitor), 819-820
alerts, 824
capturing information,
822
installing, 820-821
performance counters,
821
security, 823
triggers, 823
windows, 822
networks
bottlenecks, 796-799
data integrity loss, 795
hardware issues,
795-796
network overload, 795
network throughput,
794

physical network prob-
lems, 810-811
server overloads, 795
Windows 2000 net-
work parameters,
792-794
operating system settings,
799-801
Performance Monitor,
766-767
alerts, 778-780, 782
charts, 772-775
counters, 769, 771,
780-782
graphs, 775-777
menu icons, 768-769
reporting data, 782-783
scheduling, 783
starting, 767-768
Performance snap-in,
818-819
resource conflicts,
806-807
Services applet, 786
software, 801-802
network resources, 802
network response time,
802
transport protocol soft-
ware, 802-803
standalone card tests,
805-806
Task Manager, 788
peripherals, 895
**permissable logon hours,
318-322**
**permissions, 362-363,
367-368**
assigning
as Administrator, 373
as a user, 374
calculating, 363-364

command-line processing,
375-377
compared to rights, 672
defaults, 372
definition of, 895
EFS (Encrypting File
System), 364-365
file ownership, 365-367
Group Policy setting,
124-125
printers, 440-441
Registry keys, 194-195
shares, 359-360
types, 369-371
**Permissions command
(Security menu), 194**
**Permissions dialog box,
367**
**/PERSISTENT option (NET
USE command), 858**
**physical access controls,
653**
**Physical Disk:Disk Queue
Length counter, 781**
**Physical Disk:Percent Disk
Time counter, 781**
physical drives. *See* **hard
drives**
**physical network problems,
810-811**
physical topologies, 25-26
**ping, 493-494, 812, 816-817,
895**
plain text, 895
planning domains, 869-870
**Plug and Play (PnP), 36,
807**
**/PLUG AND PLAY option
(NET START command),
853**

SAMS
Teach Yourself
in 21 Days

Sams Teach Yourself in 21 Days teaches you all the skills you need to master the basics and then moves on to the more advanced features and concepts. This series is designed for the way you learn. Go chapter by chapter through the step-by-step lessons or just choose those lessons that interest you the most.

Sams Teach Yourself Microsoft Windows 2000 Server in 24 Hours

Barrie Sosinsky
& Jeremy A.
Moskowitz
ISBN: 0672317044
US $19.99/CAN $29.95

Other Sams Teach Yourself Titles

Microsoft Windows 2000 Server Unleashed
Rob Scrimger & Chris Miller
ISBN: 0672317397
US $49.99/ CAN $74.95

Programming Microsoft Windows 2000 Unleashed
Mickey Williams
ISBN: 067231486X
US $49.99/ CAN $74.95

Sams Teach Yourself Windows Networking in 24 Hours
Peter Kuo
ISBN: 0672314754
US $19.99/CAN $29.95

Sams Teach Yourself TCP/IP in 24 Hours
Joe Casad &
Bob Willsey
ISBN: 0672312484
US $19.99/CAN $28.95

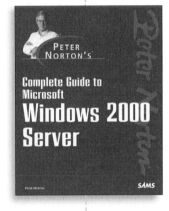

Peter Norton's Complete Guide to Microsoft Windows 2000 Server

Peter Norton & John Mueller
ISBN: 067231777X
US $29.99/CAN $59.95

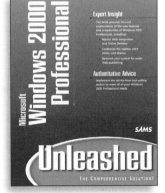

Microsoft Windows 2000 Professional Unleashed

Paul Cassel
ISBN: 0672317427
US$49.99/CAN $74.95

SAMS
www.*samspublishing*.com

All prices are subject to change.